Developing Critical Reading Skills

There is no darkness but ignorance.

—William Shakespeare

Developing Critical Reading Skills

Ninth Edition

Deanne Spears
City College of San Francisco

The McGraw-Hill Companies

Mc Graw Hill

Connect
Learn
Succeed™

DEVELOPING CRITICAL READING SKILLS, NINTH EDITION

5 6 7 8 9 10 LCR 21 20 19 18

ISBN 978-0-07-340732-6
MHID 0-07-340732-1

Vice President & Editor-in-Chief: *Michael Ryan*
Vice President of Specialized Publishing: *Janice M. Roerig-Blong*
Publisher: *David Patterson*
Senior Sponsoring Editor: *Debra B. Hash*
Marketing Coordinator: *Jaclyn Elkins*
Project Manager: *Jolynn Kilburg*
Design Coordinator: *Brenda A. Rolwes*
Cover Designer: *Studio Montage, St. Louis, Missouri*
Cover Image: *© Getty Images*
Buyer: *Laura Fuller*
Media Project Manager: *Sridevi Palani*
Compositor: *MPS Limited*
Typeface: *10/12 ITC Stone Serif Medium*
Printer: *LSC Communications*

Library of Congress Cataloging-in-Publication Data

Milan Spears, Deanne.
  Developing critical reading skills / Deanne Spears.—9th ed.
    p. cm.—(Developing critical reading skills)
  ISBN 978-0-07-340732-6 (acid-free paper)—ISBN 0-07-340732-1 (acid-free paper)
  1. Reading (Higher education) 2. Reading comprehension. I. Title.
  LB2395.3.M55 2012
  428.4071'1—dc23
                                                                    2012014169

www.mhhe.com

ABOUT THE AUTHOR

Deanne Spears is originally from Portland, Oregon. She now considers herself a native Californian, having moved to Los Angeles when freeways and smog were relatively new concepts. During her childhood and adolescence, she spent carefree summers in a small farming community in northwest Iowa. After receiving a B.A. and an M.A. in comparative literature from the University of Southern California, she began teaching composition and reading at City College of San Francisco. She continues to tutor students in reading and composition and to conduct teacher-preparation workshops for the college. In addition to her primary interests—reading and studying Italian—she and her husband David enjoy cooking, watching movies (there are over 100 titles in their Netflix queue), kayaking in Princeton Harbor, camping (especially in the Gold Lakes Basin area of Northern California), and searching out inexpensive ethnic restaurants. Deanne is the author of *Improving Reading Skills* (7th edition, 2013) and, with David Spears, *In Tandem: College Reading and Writing* (2007), also published by McGraw-Hill.

CHAPTER 3

Reading between the Lines: Making Accurate Inferences 80

PART 2
Discovering Meaning: The Importance of Form 119

CHAPTER 4

Methods of Paragraph Development 120

CHAPTER 5

Patterns of Paragraph Organization 161

PART 3

Discovering Meaning: The Importance of Language   189

CHAPTER 6

Language and Its Effects on the Reader   190

CHAPTER 7

Tone, Point of View, and Allusions   245

CHAPTER 10

Practical Applications in Evaluating Arguments   407

PART 5

Reading Essays and Articles   443

PREFACE

I am gratified that *Developing Critical Reading Skills* is now going into its ninth edition. The text has evolved over its many editions, in response to instructors' concerns, to our students' needs, and to the changing world. The consequences resulting from the 2001 terrorist attacks, the wars in Iraq and Afghanistan, and the enormous political and cultural shifts now going on in the United States, helped along by social networking (Web 2.0), have made it imperative for us to be an educated populace, able to read with accuracy and skilled in identifying claims and in detecting manipulation, emotional appeals, bias, and propaganda. More than ever, students of all ages need to develop a worldview and a rational means of evaluating arguments.

Finally, recent events and our military involvement in the Middle East have also made it more important than ever to acquire knowledge about other cultures, particularly about those cultures that have different worldviews and whose members, thus, behave in seemingly incomprehensible ways. Perhaps this book can do a small part to help students—indeed, all of us—to be better thinkers and better citizens, able to participate fully in the democratic process.

Although the world has changed a lot since the first edition, the underlying premise of *Developing Critical Reading Skills* has not. The premise of the text is that good reading and clear thinking go hand in hand. For this reason, it emphasizes practice in sustained, analytical reading. Because learning to read analytically requires concentration and an intense engagement with the text, the text emphasizes the importance of reading with a pencil in one's hand and deliberately omits practice in speed techniques. Students first work with high-quality short passages before moving on to more substantive pieces of greater complexity. The readings explore diverse subjects: anthropology, sports, human behavior, politics, social policy, education, ethics, autobiography, personal reminiscence, the minority and immigrant experience, humor, satire, and so forth. The passages also reflect diverse writing styles, thereby giving students the experience of reading high-level prose by its best practitioners.

This book succeeds if students become more self-assured about their reading and if they recognize that reading well—with confidence, fluency, and enjoyment—is a significant part of their emotional and academic lives. My hope is that students will feel genuine excitement when they encounter a writer who shows them a new way of looking at their lives and at the world. It is this feeling—or inspiration, perhaps, for lack of a better word—that I hope to impart.

■ CHANGES TO THE NINTH EDITION

I am grateful for the many thoughtful and practical suggestions review-ers and colleagues have given me, which almost without exception I have incorporated. I hope that these new features will make the ninth edition attractive and pedagogically useful.

Perhaps the most noticeable change in the ninth edition is greater focus on subjects that I hope will appeal to our current generation of readers—readings on the deleterious effects of Facebook on friendships and college GPAs, the observation that our reliance on Google might actually be making us stupid, and the value of a college education, to cite just three examples.

Here is a brief overview of the major changes in the ninth edition:

- A new section titled "Some Thoughts on E-Readers."
- Continued emphasis on vocabulary acquisition, including more variety in vocabulary exercise material.
- Annotating, paraphrasing, and summarizing exercises appear in greater numbers. One of these three follows almost every long selection.
- An increased number of Critical Thinking Exercises and material for online research called Online Learning Centers.
- Exercises to give students practice in distinguishing between fact and opinion and in determining how arguments could be strengthened or weakened with added information.
- An expanded discussion of making inferences in literature (Chapter 3) and of tone (Chapter 7). Poetry has been added.
- Chapter 8 begins with a new discussion of worldview, asking students to examine the differences between Middle Eastern culture and our own.
- The critical reading chapters—Chapters 8, 9, and 10—have been completely revised and slightly expanded. They reflect the spectrum of political opinion and offer current examples of manipulative and fallacious thinking from both politics and the real world.
- Expanded coverage of critical reading and evaluation of visual material, including political cartoons, graphs, advertisements, and public service announcements.
- Two paired editorials in the argument section: The first one consists of arguments for and against the proposal to make national service compulsory for 18-year-old Americans. The second topic is the proposal to return to a system of corporal punishment (flogging) for criminals, but in this case, both writers argue the same point of view. The student's task is to determine which one does the better job of persuasion.
- By popular request, I have brought back Steven Jay Gould's little gem of an essay, "Preposterous: What Has Happened to the Rhinoceros Is as Hard to Fathom as the Beast Itself," which is the basis for further instruction in annotating, paraphrasing, and summarizing at the beginning of Part 5.

New Readings
- Just about half of the longer readings throughout the text are new, and all but one of the editorials are new. In addition to Barack Obama's stump speech on the campaign trail and an analysis of his rhetorical and persuasive devices, reprinted in the ninth edition is Martin Luther King's "I Have a Dream" speech from 1963.
- Here are some of the new writers represented in the ninth edition: Sherry Turkle, Gregory David Roberts, Mark Spragg, Paul Theroux, Alexandra Teague, Alvaro Huerta, Ruben Navarrette, Jr., Naomi Schaefer Riley, Paul Krugman, Kathleen Parker, Nicholas Carr, and Mary Roach. There are four new short stories: Paul Theroux, "Eulogies for Mr. Concannon" and J. Robert Lennon, "The Cement Mailbox" (both examples of flash fiction), Ernest Hemingway, "Hills Like White Elephants," and Katherine Mansfield, "Miss Brill."

Other Helpful Features
- As in the eighth edition, each chapter begins with an explanation of the chapter objectives and a list of topics covered in the chapter. Important information and Key terms throughout the text are boxed for convenient reference.
- In Chapters 1–9, short practice exercises interspersed throughout the text allow students to reinforce the particular skills under discussion. As before, each chapter in Parts 1–3 ends with three short exercises and a longer essay to analyze.
- Each of the book's longer essays and articles ends with suggestions for further exploration: Features called "In the Bookstore" or "On DVD" point the students to relevant books and films thematically connected to the reading. "On the Web" points students to websites thematically connected to the reading, also giving them an opportunity to do simple research tasks related to the reading.
- Suggestions for using the text and answers to the exercises are available as Microsoft Word files in the instructor portion of the book's website.

ANCILLARY MATERIALS

Supplements for Instructors
- **Online Learning Center** <www.mhhe.com/spears>. Instructors can find a variety of tests to accompany the text on a password-protected area of the text's website. Class-tested sets of exams are available for Chapters 2–3; Chapters 2–5 (midterm); Chapters 6–7; Chapters 8–9; and final examinations. (Click on the book's cover to reach the site.)

Supplements for Students
- **Online Learning Center** (www.mhhe.com/spears) Students will find an extensive array of practice exercises accompanying Chapters 2–9 of the text. Click on the book's cover to reach the site.

ACKNOWLEDGMENTS

No textbook can be created without the assistance of many people. First, I am grateful to the many teachers across the country who read the manuscript for this edition carefully and made many judicious recommendations:

Amy Freese, Santiago Canyon College

Darnell Kemp, Fullerton College

Carol Fregly, City College of San Francisco

Melissa Grahek, Normandale Community College

Melanie Haeri, Irvine Valley College

Melissa Dalton, Lanier Tech College

I am grateful to my colleagues at City College of San Francisco for their kind words and sensible recommendations, specifically Jessica Brown, Joan Wilson, Eleanor Brown, Carol Fregly, Pamela Gentile, Amy Miles, and Susan Zimmerman. Special thanks to these faculty members at American River College for their comments and suggestions for the eighth edition: Pauline Fountain, Nancy Bertoglio, Leah Arambel, Shannon Pries.

The following people are sources for exciting new writers to explore: My daughter, Charlotte Milan, and my brother, Geoffrey Koziol, both of San Francisco; the FMI group—Julia Hansen, Carole Levine, Marlene Mann, Naomi Mann, all of San Francisco; Robin McKnight, of El Granada, California; Geri McCauley, of Sebastopol, California; my old high school friends, great readers all—Julie Green, of Divide, Colorado; Cathy Griffin of Rancho Mirage, California, Janet Allen-Shaw of La Jolla, California, Mary Brent Wehrli, of Palm Springs, California, and Kareen Sturgeon of McMinnville, Oregon. And finally special thanks to my oldest reading friend, Jennifer Ruddy, of Rockport, Maine.

Warmest thanks to Janice Wiggins-Clarke for her attention to endless details and efficient handling and disposition of a complicated revision process, and to Deb Hash and Jolynn Kilburg for their patience and efficiency during the production process. Finally, special thanks to my husband, David, for his kind and steady heart.

Instructors who have comments, suggestions, or questions are invited to contact me via e-mail at *dkspears@gmail.com*. I will do my best to answer within a day or two of receiving messages.

Deanne Spears
City College of San Francisco
San Francisco, California

TO THE STUDENT

Several years ago I was shopping with the man who is now my husband and his daughter in downtown San Francisco. A street musician, whom my husband was acquainted with from his own musician days, was playing the tenor saxophone on a street corner. His name is Clifford, and he had attracted a crowd with his wonderful performance. After he finished, my husband introduced him to me and to Sarah, his daughter. Clifford asked Sarah if she played an instrument, and when she replied that she was taking trumpet lessons and played in her junior high school band, he said, "That's fine, little lady. Learn your instrument well and you can play anything."

Somehow these simple and wise words struck me as fitting not only for an aspiring trumpet player but also for a reader. When you learn to read well, you can read anything you want—not just the daily newspapers and blog and Facebook posts, but more difficult reading, such as philosophy, anthropology, film criticism, particle physics, military history—whatever interests you. Your choice of reading would not be limited in any way. Assuming you had the vocabulary—or at least a good dictionary at your side—you could pick up a book or article, concentrate on it, and make sense of the writer's words.

Reading well requires a sort of internal translation. You take in the writer's words, not only to understand their surface meaning but also to understand what they suggest beyond that. Rather than reading passively, sitting back and letting the writer do all the work, in this course you will learn to interact with the text. You will learn to read with a pencil in your hand. When you read, you enter into a peculiar relationship with the writer, a two-way process of communication. Although the writer is physically absent, the words on the page are nonetheless there to be analyzed, interpreted, questioned, perhaps even challenged. In this way, the active reader engages in a kind of silent dialogue with the writer.

Reading instruction in American schools often ends at elementary school, and students may have difficulty as they progress to higher grades. The reading material becomes harder, yet they still must tackle their assignments armed with elementary school reading skills. The result, too often, is frustration and loss of confidence. And the assigned reading in your college courses will be even more demanding than the readings were in high school—both in complexity of content and style and in the amount of reading assigned. *Developing Critical Reading Skills* is designed to accomplish several tasks: to teach you the skills that will enable you to read with greater comprehension and retention, to help you undertake reading assignments with confidence, and to show you how to become an active, fluent reader.

This is the ninth edition of the text. With each edition and with each class, I have learned a great deal. You will be the recipient of the many excellent suggestions, which, along with various reviewers' and colleagues' remarks, I have incorporated. Take some time to look through the table of contents to become familiar with the book's layout and scope. You will begin with basic comprehension skills and gradually move toward the more difficult skills associated with critical reading. In this edition, the readings now more closely duplicate the breadth of reading you do in every part of your daily life, including material from textbooks, newspaper articles and editorials, magazine articles and essays, online material, and of course, whole works of both fiction and nonfiction.

As you glance through Parts 1, 2, and 3, you will see that these seven chapters treat the paragraph extensively, including explanations, illustrative passages, and exercises. At first it may seem odd—and perhaps artificial—to devote so much time to short passages, which after all, are seldom read in isolation.

Yet my students have found that concentrating on short passages early in the course promotes careful reading. The paragraph is the basic unit of writing and, in fact, is often referred to as the primary building block of the essay. Studying paragraph structure closely and examining short passages for placement of main idea, methods of development, patterns of organization, inferences, language (especially connotation and figurative language), and tone will teach you how to analyze effectively on a small scale. Certainly it is less intimidating to practice with a hundred-word paragraph than with a five-page essay. Once you are proficient with short material you will then know how to apply the same analytical skills to longer works.

The text also includes visual elements—charts, graphs, cartoons (both humorous and political) and magazine advertisements—along with a discussion of how to "read" visual elements and, more important, how to evaluate them critically. Finally, Chapters 8, 9, and 10 offer you the opportunity to look at several issues—the Facebook and Google phenomenon and their effects, whether or not national service should be compulsory for 18-year-olds, the value of a college education in today's economy, and so on—from a variety of perspectives by means of several opinion pieces.

Much emphasis has been placed on increasing reading speed, on skimming and scanning, on zipping through material simply to get the gist of what the writer is saying. These techniques have their place: A football fan skims through the sports pages to find out if the Green Bay Packers beat their archrival team, an employee scans the help wanted columns to look for a new job, and a student zips through the electronic card catalog for likely research sources. But skimming is inappropriate for the major part of the reading you will have to do in college. For this reason, *Developing Critical Reading Skills* does not include instruction in speed-reading techniques.

During the course, as you sharpen your skills, your work should have two results. The first will be an improvement in your own writing. Good reading skills and good writing skills are most certainly interrelated. When you understand how professional writers organize, develop, and support their ideas, you will become more aware of how to deal with your own writing assignments. But more important, you will learn to be a better thinker as well. These skills will serve you well for the rest of your life.

On the website accompanying this text, you will find many ancillary exercises where you can get extra practice with the skills taken up in Chapters 1–10. Answers are also provided. The address is www .mhhe.com/spears. Click on the book's cover and then click on Student Resources. If you have comments, suggestions, or questions about the text, you can contact me either on the website or by e-mail at *dkspears@ gmail.com.* I will do my best to answer within a day or two of receiving messages.

Deanne Spears
Half Moon Bay, California

Introduction

This introductory section includes the following information:

- An overview of the text
- The reading process defined
- College reading assignments
- How to read this textbook (and other textbooks)

■ AN OVERVIEW OF THE TEXT

Becoming a good reader, rather than merely a competent one, is crucial if you are to do well in your college courses. In my teaching experience, students often find their first college academic experience bewildering: They may not know what their instructors expect of them, nor are they sure how to proceed with reading assignments or what to look for when they read. They find their assignments more burdensome than those they encountered in high school.

Each semester I begin the course by asking students to evaluate their past experiences with reading. We try to determine what makes some readers really good and others merely adequate—decoders of print but not much else. The session helps them focus on what they need to do in the course (as well as over the course of their lives) to become the very best readers they can. Students often write or e-mail me after they have transferred to a four-year university like San Jose State University or UC Davis, typically saying that they are stunned by the amount of reading they are expected to do in their upper-division courses. They report that some courses require them to read as many as 8 or 10 books over a semester. Clearly, unless you are exceptional, the skills that got you through high school won't be up to this task.

Developing Critical Reading Skills will help you with all of these matters. You will learn how to look critically and analytically at essays and articles, and how to discern the substance, the parts, the level of language, and the strengths and weaknesses of the writer's arguments. As you work through this text, you will find your ability to comprehend difficult prose, your confidence, and, most important, your enjoyment in the experience of reading improving. Although these are admittedly ambitious goals, the text takes up these elements one at a time in a logical sequence.

Sequence of Skills

- Techniques for improving vocabulary (Chapter 1).
- Learning to annotate, paraphrase, and summarize (Chapter 1).
- Identifying the main idea, the focus or controlling idea, and the writer's purpose (Chapter 2).
- Discerning the relative importance of supporting ideas (major and minor support) as they relate to the main idea (Chapter 2).
- Making accurate inferences; reading between the lines, and identifying what the writer does not explicitly say but surely suggests (Chapter 3).
- Identifying the methods of development, the logical connections between the parts of an essay, and the arrangement of ideas the writer imposes on the subject (Chapters 4 and 5).
- Understanding the denotative and connotative values of words and identifying deliberate misuse of language (Chapter 6).
- Learning to identify and to analyze figurative language (Chapter 6).
- Identifying the writer's point of view and tone, or emotional feeling (Chapter 7).
- Recognizing strategies—both fair and unfair ones—in argumentative and persuasive writing; learning not to believe everything you read just because someone published it or put up a website; learning to evaluate arguments in opinion pieces, cartoons, political speeches, advertisements, and websites (Chapters 8, 9, and 10).

Reading is much more than merely decoding words. The real meaning of a text lies in the relationship the words have with each other. Reading well requires us to recognize these relationships and to put together the meaning of the text. When you think about everything that goes on simultaneously in the human mind as one reads, the process not only defies easy explanation but also takes on almost magical qualities. Isolating the steps makes the process seem mechanical or reducible to a formula. But nothing about reading is mechanical or formulaic. And as your reading assignments become more sophisticated and demanding, your problems as a reader multiply.

The Characteristics of Good Readers

College reading instructors might identify these habits as characteristic of good readers:

Good Readers

- Preview the assignment to get an overview of its content (not just to count the pages or the pictures).
- Start reading assignments early enough to complete them thoroughly and carefully (not at 10 p.m. the night before or on the morning bus ride to campus).
- Underline or circle vocabulary words to look up and then do so.
- Become actively involved with the text; they read with a pencil in their hands, annotating main points and writing question marks next to puzzling material.
- Identify relationships between ideas and examine how the parts of an essay fit together.
- Question the writer and look beneath the surface for implications.
- Anticipate questions for quizzes, discussion, or in-class writing assignments.
- Maintain focus and block out distractions as much as is humanly possible.
- Consider each reading assignment as a challenge and as a way to learn, even if the subject matter is not particularly interesting, and not as an unpleasant task to be put off until the very last minute.

If you have not yet developed these habits or if they sound too daunting, keep in mind that you will not have to learn everything at once. You will undertake each element singly, with lots of opportunities for practice. Take advantage of your instructor's office hours and of your campus's tutoring center to help you through the rough patches. In the meantime, get as much practice as you can outside of class. Go to your campus reading laboratory, if your college has one. Most reading teachers recommend that students try to fit in at least an hour of reading every day on their own—not required assignments for your classes but reading for pleasure.

A long-term study by the National Endowment for the Arts reached one inescapable conclusion: Americans are reading less. In the Online Learning Center box at the left is the URL for an Associated Press article summarizing the NEA findings. Two examples: "In 2002, only 52 percent of Americans ages 18 to 24, the college years, read a book voluntarily, down from 59 percent in 1992. . . . The number of adults with bachelor's degrees and 'proficient in reading prose' dropped from 40 percent in 1992 to 31 percent in 2003."

Online Learning Centers

These Online Learning Center boxes appear occasionally throughout the text and give you an opportunity to read further about a subject mentioned in the text. However, I cannot guarantee that the websites or URLs quoted here or throughout the text will remain available for the life of this edition. If you can't find a site mentioned here, perform a search with your favorite search engine.

> **Online Learning Centers**
>
> You can access the Associated Press article at this address: www.newsvine.com/_... /1107039-government-study. Or type in "Hillel Italie, Americans Reading Less, Associated Press" in the search box of your favorite search engine.

Becoming a First-Rate Reader

The reading process is very different from watching television, where the images wash over us as we sit like passive automatons. The good reader is engaged with the text and participates fully in the world the writer re-creates on the page. However—and this is the magical part— the good reader is unaware of these elements as she reads. They occur involuntarily and effortlessly, the sweep and flow of the words transporting her along and down the page. Let us now turn to some specific suggestions for improving your concentration. When your English instructor assigns an essay in your reading or composition class, a careful reading requires more than a single, cursory reading. Divide your reading time into three stages:

1. *Preparing to Read.* This preparatory step gives you an overview of the material. Read any chapter objectives or preview questions, turn through the pages, noting the graphic design of the material, the primary and secondary headings (these will be explained later in this introduction), and any discussion, review, or study questions at the end.

2. *The First Reading.* Read through the assignment without stopping. Be sure to keep a pencil in your hand and quickly underline any unfamiliar words (these you will look up later). Put a question mark next to any sentence or passage that is unclear.

3. *The Second Reading.* In this reading, you will be reading the material again, but this time more carefully. Now that you have an overview of the whole text, you will look for connections between the various parts, question the writer and look for larger implications, and anticipate discussion questions or essay topics that your instructor might assign.

■ COLLEGE READING ASSIGNMENTS

If you are just beginning your college career, you may be unaccustomed to the many types of texts and reading assignments college classes require. Typically, college students aren't assigned only a single textbook, which serves as a sort of academic bible for the term. While you will undoubtedly be asked to study from a standard textbook in many of your courses, you may also be asked to read material in a course reader, a collection of pertinent readings your instructor has compiled that complement the course material. Or you may be asked to read articles in magazines or periodicals that the instructor has put on reserve in the library or on assigned websites.

In your English and humanities classes, you will surely be asked to read fiction, both novels and short stories, and perhaps poetry and plays. In your introductory composition courses, you will be assigned nonfiction prose—articles and essays by writers who are generally considered masters, whether for their observations and perceptions of the human condition or world affairs, the clarity of their expression, or their use of various rhetorical devices. For all of these types of reading assignments, *Developing Critical Reading Skills* will help you develop the skills you need to navigate them. Working through this text and faithfully completing the exercises will teach you the skills you need to read your other texts.

How to Read This Textbook (and Other Textbooks)

Like all textbooks, *Developing Critical Reading Skills* reflects features common to the genre. As you should with any other textbook, take a few minutes to become familiar with the features and structure of this book. Unlike essays and articles, which typically consist only of straight, unembellished text, textbooks (like this one) provide considerable help for students. A textbook chapter typically includes chapter objectives to give you something to guide your reading; various types of headings to indicate the relative importance of the various types of material; tables, boxes, charts, and graphs to present data succinctly; often photographs or drawings to reinforce ideas or to provide visual examples; self-quizzes and study or review questions to aid in review and mastery—all in addition to the text. The headings, for example, indicate the relative importance of the various types of material.

For example, if you look at the headings on the previous and following pages, you will see that their relative importance is shown

However, now that I have read several books on the iPad, the concentration problem seems to have resolved itself, and the new medium no longer interferes with my comprehension. But these are only one person's experiences. I still prefer printed matter, but it is also wonderful to have another way to access reading material.

Getting the Most out of This Text

To gain maximum benefit from this text, look over each chapter before beginning to read it and study the chapter objectives. *Most important*, while you are reading each chapter, be sure to study the explanatory section in relation to each illustrative passage. If you are unsure about the connection between the explanation and the illustrative passage, ask your instructor for clarification.

1

Reading for Understanding: Practice in Basic Comprehension Skills

1

Building a Foundation: Vocabulary, Annotating, Paraphrasing, and Summarizing

---

CHAPTER OBJECTIVES

This first chapter will help you improve your reading comprehension by reviewing some essential skills and concepts associated with the reading process:

- Suggestions for improving your vocabulary

- Annotating—reading with a pencil in your hand

- Writing paraphrases

- Writing summaries

■ IMPROVING YOUR VOCABULARY

A good vocabulary is probably the single most important skill associated with good reading. Every other skill—comprehension, retaining information, making inferences, drawing appropriate conclusions, evaluating—depends on whether you know what the words on the page mean in relation to each other and in their context. After all, if you don't know what the words on the page mean, you cannot fully know what you are reading. Sometimes it is possible to wing it, getting the general idea without having a complete understanding. Most often, however, and especially with the analytical reading you will do in this course, your understanding of a passage will certainly hinge solely on the meaning of a single word, a situation where guessing is hazardous.

E. D. Hirsch, a professor of education and humanities at the University of Virginia, offers these remarks on vocabulary and its relationship to reading comprehension:

> Vocabulary experts agree that adequate reading comprehension depends on a person already knowing between 90 and 95 percent of the words in a text. Knowing that percentage of words allows the reader to get the main thrust of what is being said and therefore to guess correctly what the unfamiliar words probably mean. (This inferential process is of course how we pick up oral language in early childhood and it sustains our vocabulary growth throughout our lives.)[1]

One of my colleagues characterizes the problem of not looking up important words as the "swiss-cheese" approach to reading—as if the text has holes scattered through it, like a slice of swiss cheese. Ignoring new words in your reading assignments, hoping that they don't really matter or assuming you know what a word means when you really don't, may impair your comprehension. An incident that occurred recently in one of my classes illustrates these risks. While doing a context clue exercise, the students came across this sentence:

> Sue Grafton is a remarkably *prolific* writer. Nearly every year she publishes a new mystery in her alphabet series. The latest book in the series is *U Is for Undertow*.

The answer choices were (a) productive; (b) suspenseful; (c) popular; (d) rich.

Online Learning Center

Read what happened when athletic shoe maker Reebok failed to consult a dictionary before it released a new line of women's running shoe called "Incubus." Using the search box of your favorite search engine, type "Nike product name, Incubus."

Two or three students chose "popular" for the answer because they had always assumed that a prolific writer was a popular one. In fact, *prolific* has nothing to do with popularity; it means "productive." The context clues in

[1]Quoted in "Reading Comprehension Requires Knowledge," *American Educator*, Spring 2003.

the second and third sentences reinforce this definition: A writer who publishes a new book nearly every year is certainly productive. Because "U" is the 21st letter of the alphabet, we can infer that Grafton has published 21 mysteries in her series.

Vocabulary in Perspective

The process of acquiring vocabulary is a lifelong pursuit, and it is both naive and unrealistic to think that a single course in reading or in English can remedy your vocabulary weaknesses. At first, learning dozens of new words may seem like a discouraging, perhaps an even overwhelming, prospect, but it is possible. Everyone has to start somewhere, and even the best reader comes across words in his or her daily reading that require looking up. (The fifth edition of *The American Heritage Dictionary* lists over 420,000 words, 10,000 of them new.)

The sheer number of words in the language partly explains why acquiring a good vocabulary takes so long. Because college reading assignments are so much more difficult than high school assignments, an extensive vocabulary is an essential requirement for good understanding. Many studies point to American students' diminished vocabulary, demonstrating the importance of getting your level up to par at the beginning of your college career.[2]

Daily Reading and Vocabulary Improvement—A Personal Sidenote

An exhaustive treatment of vocabulary acquisition is not within the scope of this book. However, resist the temptation to memorize long lists of words or spend money on vocabulary self-help books; you simply won't remember many of them. The very best way to learn new words is to read as much as you have time for. Certainly, the reading you will do in this book will expose you to dozens of college-level vocabulary words. Since most of the words you recognize in your reading you know because of prior exposure, it seems obvious that words are best learned—and retained—when you encounter them in your reading. Reading for pleasure an hour a day, or at least a half hour a day, will pay big dividends.

I can attest to the benefits of daily reading as an aid to building vocabulary. For the past seven years, I have been taking intensive Italian courses. Someone once observed that learning a new language as an adult is as simple as picking up a truck—an apt comparison. Yet I have found that reading Italian short stories, online newspaper articles, and novels—for an hour a day, or at least a half an hour a day—has started to pay off. In Italian, there is a phrase, *piano piano*, meaning "slowly, slowly." Vocabulary acquisition occurs this way—little by little. You can't rush the process, and though the gains one makes in a single day may not seem like much, over a period of weeks or months, these incremental gains eventually add up to something substantial.

[2]From *Harper's* Index for August 2000: "Average number of words in the written vocabulary of a 6- to 14-year-old American child in 1945: 25,000. Average number today: 10,000." These figures reflect research done by Gary Ingersoll of Indiana University.

The experience of learning a foreign language as an adult has given me a renewed appreciation for the difficulties students, and especially English-language learners, have in getting the meanings of new words to stick. It's discouraging to read a text with a lot of new words: You have to jump back and forth from the page to the dictionary. If there are too many unfamiliar words, it's tedious. Fortunately, my hour a day self-imposed regimen means that now I don't need to look up as many new words as I did two years ago. For me, writing meanings of words on index cards was a waste of time. For several weeks, I wrote seemingly hundreds of words on colored cards, but when I reviewed them, I remembered very few because they were too far removed from the pages where I had encountered them. Writing the definitions in the margins didn't work, either. There were too many words, making the page messy, and it was too easy to cheat and consult the definition instead of using the context to trigger my memory.

So, after a few months of experimenting, I found a system that works for me, and perhaps it will be useful to you as well. As I read, I write down important new words and their meanings, but instead of writing the definitions in the margin or writing them on index cards, I write them in a binder, along with the page number where they occur in the text. I focus on words that are essential to understanding the story or on words that I have seen before but can't readily define or remember. A sample: here are four illustrations of my method from the book my class is reading now:

p. 93   *sventatamento*—in a scatterbrained manner
p. 95   *ciondolare*—to hang around
        il ceffone—a slap, smack
p. 96   *premuroso*—thoughtful, attentive, considerate

Now here's the important part: Just writing them down isn't enough. *Rereading the text immediately after* the first reading has resulted in my retaining a much higher percentage of words, which means that when I encounter them again in different contexts, I might not have to look so many up again. And while I am rereading the text, if I can't remember a word, I simply refer to the appropriate page in my notebook.

I have gone on at some length about this matter because most beginning college students know that their vocabulary needs work, and they often hope for a magic formula to help them. There is no magic formula, of course, but a daily dose of reading, looking up words, writing down meanings of key words, and then rereading the material has made me a more confident and fluent reader. It takes discipline to be sure, but the rewards are huge. Ultimately, though, you have to find your own way, and I encourage you to try several methods to find the one that works best for you.

Further Suggestions for Vocabulary Improvement

Besides the notebook method described above, here are some other suggestions to help your vocabulary level:

- *Invest in a new hardback dictionary.* If you do not have an unabridged dictionary published recently, buy one. It will be money well spent. A new dictionary will last well beyond your college years. Some appropriate unabridged dictionaries are listed in the next section.

- *Develop an interest in words and their origins.* When you look up a new word in an unabridged dictionary, look at its **etymology,** or history; many English words have unusual origins. The etymology of a word is usually printed in brackets following the definitions; it explains and traces the derivation of the word and gives the original meaning in the language or languages the word is derived from. For example, one dictionary traces the history of the word *sinister* meaning "causing evil" or "presaging trouble" like this:

  [Middle English *sinister*, unfavorable, from Old French, from Latin *sinister*, on the left, unlucky]

  It may be this negative linguistic association that accounts for the historical prejudice against left-handed people. Not too long ago in the United States, children who wrote left-handed were often forced by their well-meaning teachers to switch hands.
      Here is another example:

  The word *curfew* comes from medieval French. Because most houses in France during the medieval period were made of wood and had thatched roofs, the danger of fire was always great, particularly at night. Every evening residents had to put out their candles when a bell was rung and the order *couvrefeu* (meaning "cover fire") was given. The Norman French conquerors brought the word to England, where it evolved into our word *curfew*.

Practice Exercise 1— Etymology Exercise

Using an unabridged dictionary, locate the etymology (language of origin) of these words and their current meanings:

fan	intifada	shampoo	stigma	curfew
succotash	tsunami	fatwa	fjord	vilify

Online Learning Center

For a comprehensive list of Latin and Greek prefixes and roots, click on the "Student Edition" button on the website accompanying the text. In the white box labeled "Choose One," pull down to "Word Parts."

- *Learn the most common prefixes and roots.* Approximately 60 percent of the words in English come from Latin and around 15 percent come from Greek. Therefore, learning Latin and Greek prefixes and roots can add to your vocabulary stock. For example, consider the word *benediction* ("blessing"), which you will encounter later in the chapter. The Latin prefix *bene-* always means "good," and you can see this meaning in the words *benefit, beneficiary, benefactor,* and *beneficence.*

- Learn to see words as members of related groups. For example, the Latin root *spirare,* meaning "to breathe," for example, gives us the English words *inspire, respiration, perspiration, conspiracy* (literally, to "breathe with"), *aspire,* and *expire.* A question on the quiz show *Jeopardy!* recently went something like this: "*Spiracles* are openings on butterflies that allow them to do this." The answer: "What is to breathe?" Even if you know nothing about the anatomy of a butterfly, knowing the Latin root gets you the right answer.

- Play word board games like Balderdash, Perquackey, and Scrabble. An online website for playing a game similar to Scrabble either in real time or via e-mail is available at www.lexulous.com. If you have an iPod, iPhone, or iPad, Words with Friends is an app for a similar Scrabble-like game. A variety of word games are available at www.yourdictionary.com. One final vocabulary game website is www.freerice.com, which has the added benefit of helping to solve the problem of world hunger. For every correct answer, 10 grains of rice are donated to the sponsor, the World Food Programme.

- *Try the three-dot method.* When you look up a new word in the dictionary, place a small dot with a pencil next to it. The next time you look it up, add a second dot. The third time, add a third dot and learn the meaning of the word. The idea is that any word that crops up three times in a short period of time is probably worth knowing.

- *Subscribe to one or more Word-of-the-Day websites.* These sites offer a painless, entertaining way to learn new words. You can either visit a site every day or, more conveniently, subscribe to their service, which sends the word of the day to your e-mail address. Most offer interesting, relatively challenging words; most include—besides the definitions and pronunciation—the etymology and some illustrative sentences using the word. Some include hyperlinks taking you to other sites of interest relevant to the word of the day. All are free, though most do have banner ads. You can evaluate a few of these sites in the accompanying critical reading exercise.

Critical Reading Exercise

Here are four popular word-of-the-day websites. Spend a few minutes examining each one. Which site would be most helpful to you as a way of improving your reading vocabulary? Some things to consider are ease of use, appropriate level of vocabulary words offered, and the quality of information provided for each word. The italicized word following each site shows you four representative entries.

dictionary.com: Click on Word of the Day
abscond, imbroglio, risible, verdant

Merriam-Webster www.merriam-webster.com/word-of-the-day
lucid, ragtag, proselytize, torpedo
Yahoo Word of the Day education.yahoo.com/reference
adversity, perfunctory, *solace, diverge*

Using the Dictionary

Traditional (Print) Dictionaries

No electronic device, no matter how flashy, can surpass the convenience and the abundance of information in a good print dictionary. You should have two: an abridged (or shortened) paperback edition for class or perhaps a dictionary app on your smart phone if you have such a device, and an unabridged (complete) edition to use at home. Both print versions should be up-to-date. (Using your father's tattered dictionary from the 1970s or a cheap garage-sale edition is a foolish economy; an old dictionary cannot reflect the wealth of new words that have entered the language even during the past decade.) Ask your instructor to recommend one, or choose one from this list. All are available in less expensive college editions.

Online Learning Center

www.mhhe.com/spears
For an exercise to help you become familiar with your dictionary, scroll down to Chapter 1. The exercise is under "More Resources."

- *The American Heritage Dictionary of the English Language*
- *The Random House Webster's College Dictionary*
- *Webster's New World Dictionary*
- *Webster's Collegiate Dictionary*

See how many of these words and phrases you know. Check your print dictionary, and your online dictionary (or dictionary app) if you use either one, to see how many are included.

pescatarian	infinity pool	dirty bomb	netbook
netroots	netizen	malware	air quotes
edamame	hugfest	mental health day	pretexting
drama queen	fatwa	microgreens	brewski
wiki	air kiss	combover	hashtag
soul patch	regift	telenovelas	sexting
locavore	netiquette	fashionista	cyberwar

> ### Critical Thinking Exercise
>
> Study the list of new words above. Categorize them according to the particular fields they derive from. What do these words suggest about contemporary American culture?
>
> A second question: Each year the *New Oxford American Dictionary* chooses a Word of the Year. In 2009 the word was *unfriend*. Why do you suppose the editors chose this word?
>
> A final assignment: Using your favorite search engine, locate the Words of the Year that the editors of the *New Oxford American Dictionary* chose in years subsequent to 2009. What significant changes do these choices reveal about the ways in which our society is changing?

Online Dictionaries

The computer revolution has extended to the world of dictionaries. As I am updating this list in the spring of 2011, these are the best known currently available online.

Merriam-Webster Online Dictionary	www.merriam-webster.com
The American Heritage Dictionary of the English Language	www.ahdictionary.com
Webster's New World College Dictionary	www.yourdictionary.com
The Free Dictionary	www.freedictionary.com

Each site works a little differently, and it is worth spending time with each one to see which best suits your needs.

Electronic Dictionaries

Many students rely on electronic dictionaries because they are portable and efficient. However, they do have their limitations, and I recommend a good paperback dictionary as a much less expensive and equally portable source for looking up new words. A student I tutored recently was struggling with Jonathan Rauch's rather difficult essay, "In Defense of Prejudice: Why Incendiary Speech Must Be Protected." The student's electronic dictionary indicated that *incendiary,* obviously a key word since it occurs in the title, means "passionate." In fact, referring to hate speech, *incendiary* means "inflammatory," "arousing strife," or "inciting hostility." Its connotation, or emotional value, is highly negative, whereas "passionate" is positive. No wonder the student was confused!

Synonyms

The most frequently used context clue is a **synonym**, a word or phrase similar in meaning to the unfamiliar word. Although the synonym may not have the exact meaning, it may be close enough to give you an approximate definition.

> When the class bully gets sent to the principal's office, when another corporate executive is found guilty of committing fraud and is sent to jail, when a fellow student whom we don't like is caught cheating—we may experience *schadenfreude*, the feeling of taking guilty pleasure in another's misfortunes.

In this case, the writer defines *schadenfreude* for you, making the sentence easy to read. Consider this example:

> Steve Wozniak and Steve Jobs put together the *prototype* for the original Apple computer in a Cupertino, California, garage.

Prototype most likely means
- (a) the first working model.
- (b) a knock-off or cheap imitation.
- (c) the final product.

The word *original* helps you determine the meaning of *prototype*.

Antonyms

When a sentence suggests a contrast or a contradiction, the context clue may be in the form of an antonym, a word or phrase that means the opposite of the word in question. If you know the antonym, then you may be able to figure out the unfamiliar word. For example:

> The demonstration turned ugly late in the day, with protestors throwing rocks and bottles at the police, but the *mayhem* finally died down and order was restored by nightfall.

Since it is obviously being contrasted with "*order,*" a word with which you are probably familiar, *mayhem* means the opposite, "a state of violent disorder." Here is another example:

> When a highly reputable chef went to work for Burger King to help the company revise its menu selections, fine dining restaurant chefs were horrified. According to them, a Whopper at the local Burger King outlet is the *antithesis* of fine dining, and the famous chef was accused of selling out.

Antithesis most likely means

    (a) highest point

    (b) the exact opposite

    (c) a compromise

Given the situation described—the obvious contrast between fast food and fine dining establishments—the best answer is (b).

Examples and Illustrations

The meaning of an unfamiliar word may be suggested by nearby examples and illustrations. In this case, no single word or phrase implies the definition, but taken together, the examples help us infer the meaning. Try this sentence:

> Joseph Smith, Jr., the religious leader and founder of the Church of Jesus Christ of Latter Day Saints, received little formal schooling. But he read a lot on his own, and like most *autodidacts*, he was concerned with the big questions that his reading awakened in his mind.

From the passage as a whole, you can probably determine that an *autodidact* is a person who is self-taught. Also the prefix *auto-* always means "self." Now try this one:

> Maria is a teenager who has been having a difficult time with her family. Her brother has been in and out of a school for troubled teens, her father is out of work, and the family is behind on their mortgage payments, with foreclosure likely. Lately, Maria has been arguing constantly with her mother. After one particularly *acrimonious* exchange, Maria decided to go live with her grandmother.

The situation described, when coupled with the constant arguing, suggests that *acrimonious* means "hostile" or "harsh."

Opinion and Tone

This last kind of context clue is less direct and consequently more difficult to rely on. The writer's **tone**—that is, his or her attitude toward the subject or the **opinions** the writer expresses—may give you a clue for an unfamiliar word. Study this example:

> Some critics of mass media blame daytime television talk shows for their *insidious* influence on the viewing public. These programs parade their guests' bizarre and deviant behaviors and create an unhealthy fascination for ever more grotesque revelations.

**Practice
Exercise 3**

Few places on earth have seen their *indigenous* cultures more shattered than the Amazon. The jungle is eroding before road builders, loggers, cattle ranchers, and slash-and-burn farmers. Their numbers drastically shrunken, thousands of remaining Amazon Indians are migrating to towns and cities in search of work, on the poverty-stricken margins of the machine-based civilization that has largely destroyed their own. But the news from the Amazon is not entirely *bleak*. In one unheralded corner of the rain forest, there is a small but startling migration in reverse. Indians are pulling their children out of mission schools, are leaving the frontier towns, and are rebuilding their traditional dwellings deep in the forest. And all this is happening, amazingly, in the *benighted* country of Colombia.

When we picture Colombia, we think of guerrilla warfare, paramilitary death squads, cocaine cartels. And that picture is true. *Paradoxically,* however, of the nine countries that share the Amazon watershed, Colombia has done by far the most to preserve the endangered rain forest and its people. Colombia has set aside in *perpetuity* more than one quarter of the nation's entire land surface as protected areas for the Indians. And, most remarkable of all, the country's new constitution says that Indians living in these areas may choose, if they wish, to live completely outside the normal framework of government.

Adam Hochschild, *Finding the Trapdoor*

For each italicized word, in the first space write your definition according to the context. Then check the meaning in your dictionary and in the second space write the appropriate definition. Compare the two to see how close you came to the correct meaning.

1. *indigenous*
   Your definition _____

   Dictionary definition _____
2. *bleak*
   Your definition _____

   Dictionary definition _____
3. *benighted*
   Your definition _____

   Dictionary definition _____
4. *paradoxically*
   Your definition _____

   Dictionary definition _____
5. *perpetuity*
   Your definition _____

   Dictionary definition _____

Practice Exercise 4

Read this paragraph. Then using only context clues, not your dictionary, write your definitions for the two italicized words in the passage.

> In the drug wars that rack Mexico—the death toll over the past four years is approaching thirty thousand—Tijuana is an *anomaly*. It is a place where public security has actually improved. In 2007 and 2008, the city was a killing field. During the last three months of 2008, nearly five hundred people were murdered here, many in *gruesome* public displays: decapitations, dismemberments, corpses left hanging from bridges, piles of bodies with their tongues cut out. There were daylight shoot-outs between gangs using automatic weapons and rocket-propelled grenade launchers in downtown streets and shopping malls. Kidnapping for ransom got so bad that many wealthy and middle-class families fled to the United States.
>
> William Finnegan, "In the Name of the Law," *The New Yorker*

anomaly   _____

gruesome   _____

Improving Your Reading Vocabulary

- Read the assignment one time through. While you are reading, underline or circle unfamiliar words.
- Read the assignment a second time. This time, working with one or two paragraphs at a time, try to determine the meanings of the unfamiliar words—by using context clues and by breaking the word down into its component parts (prefix, root, suffix).
- Look up any words that are necessary to understand the meaning. Write the word in a notebook, based on the context, including the page number and its definition.
- When you are finished, review: Reread the selection, and try to recall the meanings of the words. If you can't remember a definition, refer to your notebook.
- Review again the next day, reading through the list of words in your notebook from the previous session to see how many you remember.

■ ANNOTATING—READING WITH A PENCIL IN YOUR HAND

Let us illustrate a crucial skill—annotating. To **annotate** means to write brief notations in the margins, specifically, writing questions to raise in class, noting important points, and circling unfamiliar words. If you have trouble concentrating or if you are easily distracted as you read by the passing world around you, reading with a pencil in your hand will do wonders to help you comprehend better, maintain focus, and stay on track.

Reasons for Annotating

Improving Comprehension

- To help you maintain focus and concentration while you are reading.
- To help you untangle particularly knotty passages with difficult concepts and vocabulary, especially on subjects that you are unfamiliar with.

Completing Writing Assignments

- To prepare for writing a summary of the selection.
- To prepare for writing an analytical or synthesis essay on one or more readings.

Fostering Enjoyment

- To give you an opportunity to record your reactions to what you are reading.
- To comment on passages you might want to reconsider or share with another person.

Reprinted here are the first two paragraphs from an essay by surgeon-writer Richard Selzer, "An Absence of Windows." The passage is rather difficult, so do not be discouraged if you don't completely understand it after the first reading. That's what the annotations are for—to help you make sense of it. Think about these questions first:

- What do you envision when you think of a hospital operating room?
- What is the likely source of that image?
- Have you ever seen the inside of an actual operating room?
- What is your general impression of surgeons? Where does it come from?

Now read the passage. Then read it again, this time paying attention to the marginal annotations and to the circled words, which might not be familiar.

What's the benefit of windows in operating rooms?

What's a benediction? Why does he mention thunder?

Why would windows deflate a surgeon's ego?

What have surgeons lost now that windows in operating rooms can no longer open to the outside world?

Why would watching cattle graze help surgeons?

Not long ago, operating rooms had windows. It was a boon and a blessing in spite of the occasional fly that managed to strain through the screens and threaten our very sterility. For the adventurous insect drawn to such a ravishing spectacle, a quick swat and, Presto! The door to the next world sprang open. But for us who battled on, there was the benediction of the sky, the applause and reproach of thunder. A Divine consultation crackled in on the lightning! And at night, in Emergency, there was the pomp, the longevity of the stars to deflate a surgeon's ego. It did no patient a disservice to have Heaven looking over his doctor's shoulder. I very much fear that, having bricked up our windows, we have lost more than the breeze; we have severed a celestial connection.

Part of my surgical training was spent in a rural hospital in eastern Connecticut. The building was situated on the slope of a modest hill. Behind it, cows grazed in a pasture. The operating theater occupied the fourth, the ultimate floor, wherefrom huge windows looked down upon the scene. To glance up from our work and see the lovely cattle about theirs, calmed the frenzy of the most temperamental of prima donnas. Intuition tells me that our patients had fewer wound infections and made speedier recoveries than those operated upon in the airless sealed boxes where now we strive. Certainly the surgeons were of a gentler stripe.

What did you understand clearly? What didn't you understand? To what extent is your lack of understanding a matter of unfamiliar vocabulary? To what extent is it because of Selzer's style? Write two or three questions that occurred to you while you were reading the passage.

_____

_____

_____

_____

Next, let's define the circled words, which might cause readers some difficulty.

Paragraph 1

boon	a benefit
benediction	a blessing
reproach	an expression of disapproval, blame
pomp	a dignified or magnificent display
	("Pomp and Circumstance" is the hymn played at graduations.)
celestial	pertaining to the sky and the heavens

Paragraph 2

temperamental	describing one who is moody, irritable, or unpredictable
prima donnas	a temperamental, conceited person (from Italian, the female lead in an opera)

Read the passage a third time, this time connecting the definitions above to the circled words. Now that you have laid the foundation, answer these critical thinking questions.

1. What seems to be Selzer's general opinion of surgeons? How can you tell? _____

    _____

    _____

2. Is Selzer being literal or imaginative in this phrase—"the benediction of the sky, the applause and reproach of thunder"? _____

    _____

    _____

3. What does Selzer mean in paragraph 1 when he refers to the "longevity of the stars"? _____

    _____

4. Who benefited when operating rooms had windows? _____

    _____

    _____

5. What evidence does Selzer offer to support the idea that patients had "fewer wound infections and made speedier recoveries" when surgeons could look out and see the world? _____

    _____

6. When Selzer describes operating rooms as "airless sealed boxes," what is his ultimate concern? _____

    _____

    _____

    _____

_____

_____

Finally, write a sentence or two in your own words stating Selzer's main point. _____

_____

_____

_____

_____

This exercise illustrates the analytical method employed in this text-book. Throughout the course, you will be asked to read and annotate passages—longer ones than this—using these techniques. As you can see from this exercise, critical analysis and a thorough comprehension on this level are possible only by reading carefully, by annotating, and by looking up unfamiliar words. For many of you, this process may involve a whole new way of reading. Yet it should prove that skimming through reading material may allow you to get the drift but not the full meaning.

■ WRITING PARAPHRASES

To *paraphrase* means to restate a writer's ideas in your own words. Paraphrase also lies at the heart of summarizing, which is taken up in the next section. I cannot stress how crucial these two skills are. Although paraphrasing and summarizing are writing skills, they are closely wedded to reading and must be mastered. The ability to read a passage and to say what it is about in your own words and to condense the central meaning into a few words will serve you well in your academic and work life.

Your reading instructor may ask you to write paraphrases of short passages. In your English composition classes, you will be assigned papers to write, often based on your careful reading and analysis of one or more readings—essays, short stories, articles, abstracts, even entire books. In your other college classes, you will be asked to write research papers, requiring you to incorporate ideas of other writers in support of your thesis. This means, of course, that you both must understand the ideas accurately and be able to explain them in your own words, using proper citation.[3] Whatever the assignment, writing a paraphrase is an excellent way to check the accuracy of your comprehension.

[3]To copy the material and pass it off as your own is plagiarism, a serious offense that can warrant an F in the course. Even when you paraphrase a writer's ideas in a research paper, you still have to document it—meaning that you must cite the author, the source, and all other relevant information.

Here are five suggestions for writing paraphrases, each of which is illustrated below.

Techniques for Paraphrasing

1. Use synonyms for key words without changing the meaning.
2. Change the order of ideas within the original sentence.
3. Omit unimportant details or excess verbiage.
4. Combine ideas and sentences.
5. Maintain the same tone and style as the original passage.

To demonstrate paraphrasing, first read this excerpt from Peter Bernstein's book *The Power of Gold: The History of an Obsession*:

> Over the centuries, gold has stirred the passions for power and glory, for beauty, for security, and even for immortality. Gold has been an icon for greed, a vehicle for vanity, and a potent constraint as a monetary standard. No other object has commanded so much veneration over so long a period of time. (54 words)

Now study this sample paraphrase that a student wrote. Notice that it is somewhat longer than the original passage, which is perfectly acceptable.

> The desire for glory, power, beauty, financial protection, even the desire to live forever—gold has fueled the human passion for all of these throughout history. We use gold as the traditional representation of greed, gold feeds our sense of self-worth and pride, and it has been used as a way to measure the value of money. There isn't another substance that has been as revered as much as gold has. (71 words)

A couple of remarks: First, the paraphrase preserves the meaning and flavor of the original, it does not introduce new information or the student's opinion, nor has anything important been omitted. Finally, the student did not go to silly extremes in finding synonyms. For example, she called "*gold*" gold rather than using a wordy phrase like "a soft precious yellow metal."

Practice Exercise 5

Here is an excerpt from an article called "Verbicide" (another excerpt from this article appears in an exercise at the end of Chapter 2). The writer, David Orr, argues that English is experiencing a decline in what he calls "working vocabulary." In this excerpt Orr offers one reason to explain this decline. Write your paraphrase in the spaces following the passage.

> Language reflects the range and depth of our experience; and our experience of the world is being impoverished to the extent that it is rendered artificial

and prepackaged. Most of us no longer have the experience of skilled physical work on farms or in forests. Consequently, as our reality becomes increasingly artificial, words and metaphor based on intimate knowledge of soils, plants, trees, animals, landscapes, rivers, and oceans have declined. . . . We've become a nation of television watchers and Internet browsers, and it shows in the way we talk and what we talk about. More and more we speak as if we are spectators of life, not active participants, moral agents, or engaged citizens. (117 words)

_____

_____

_____

_____

_____

_____

_____

Instruction in writing summaries follows the Practice Essay at the end of the chapter exercises, which will give you additional practice in the skills discussed thus far—vocabulary and context clues, annotating, and paraphrasing.

■ CHAPTER EXERCISES

Selection 1

Each year children see forty thousand television commercials, most of which are for unhealthy foods. But that's only the tip of the iceberg. Susan Linn, author of *Consuming Kids,* starkly describes how technological advances—such as the Internet and cell phones—are exploited to bypass parents and target children directly. Product placement (Coca-Cola merchandise on *American Idol*), cross promotions and movie tie-ins (*Star Wars* toy promotions at Burger King), brand licensing (Pop-Tarts boxes adorned with cartoon hero SpongeBob SquarePants), and marketing in schools all make television commercials seem tame by comparison.

Michele Simon, *Appetite for Profit*

A. *Vocabulary*

Using a dictionary, write the part of speech for each of these italicized vocabulary words from the passage. Then write the definition that best fits the context.

1. exploited to *bypass* parents?

_____

2. *target* children directly?

_____

3. boxes *adorned* with cartoon hero Spongebob?

_____

4. make television commercials look *tame*

_____

B. Annotating

To annotate Simon's paragraph, what one idea would you pull out as being the most important? _____

C. Paraphrasing

(Note: The original passage is 93 words long.)
Write a paraphrase of the paragraph. _____

_____

_____

_____

_____

_____

_____

Answers for Selection 1

A. Vocabulary

1. *bypass:*   verb; ignore, be heedless of, get around their influence
2. *target:*   verb; aim for, direct their attentions toward
3. *adorned:* adjective; decorated, enhanced
4. *tame:*   adjective; toned down, softened

B. Annotating

The huge number of TV commercials targeted to children each year

C. Paraphrasing

(Note: The original passage is 93 words long.)

One suggested paraphrase: The huge number of TV commercials children see every year, especially for foods that aren't nutritious, is only part of the problem. According to the book *Consuming Kids* by Susan Linn, cell phone and Internet ads are now aimed directly at children, far removed from parents' influence. Even more exploitive than TV commercials are product placements on TV programs, movie tie-ins, promotions at fast food restaurants like Burger King for toys associated with movies like *Star Wars,* and brand licensing. (80 words)

Selection 2

Cancer is "the modern disease" not just because we understand it in radically new ways but also because there's a lot more cancer about. For some cancers, the rise in incidence is clearly connected with things that get into our bodies that once did not—the causal link between smoking and lung cancer being the most spectacular example. But the rise in cancer mortality is, in its way, very good news: as we live longer, and as many infectious and epidemic diseases have ceased to be major causes of death, so we become prone to maladies that express themselves at ages once rarely attained. At the beginning of the twentieth century, life expectancy at birth in America was 47.3 years, and in the middle of the nineteenth century it was less than forty. The median age at diagnosis for breast cancer in the United States is now sixty-one; for prostate cancer it is sixty-seven; for colorectal cancer it's seventy. "Cancer has become the price of modern life," an epidemiologist recently wrote: in the U.S., about half of all men and about a third of women will contract cancer in their lifetime; cancer now ranks just below heart disease as a cause of death in the U.S. But in low-income countries with shorter life expectancies it doesn't even make the top ten.

Steven Shapin, "Cancer World," *The New Yorker*

A. Vocabulary—Dictionary Definitions

Each of these vocabulary words from the selection is followed by two or more dictionary definitions. Choose the best definition for the way the word is used in the context.

1. *radically* new ways—describing ways that
   (a) go to the root source
   (b) are extreme
   (c) are complete
   (d) are fundamentally different

2. the most *spectacular* example
   (a) lavish, fantastic
   (b) of unusual length
   (c) impressive
   (d) elaborate

3. we have become *prone* to
   (a) having a tendency to
   (b) lying face downward

4. at ages once rarely *attained*
   (a) accomplished, achieved
   (b) reached, arrived at
   (c) conquered

A. Vocabulary—Using Context Clues

For each italicized word, in the first space write your definition according to the context. Then check the meaning in your dictionary and in the second space write the appropriate definition.

Compare the two to see how close you came to the correct meaning.

1. *tethered* to their phones; a fully-*tethered* life
   Your definition _____
   Dictionary definition _____

2. *simulation* to be second best
   Your definition _____
   Dictionary definition _____

3. sometimes *endured*
   Your definition _____
   Dictionary definition _____

4. the *compulsions* of the networked life
   Your definition _____
   Dictionary definition _____

B. Annotating

Assume that you are writing an essay on contemporary attitudes toward being networked. Annotate the passage in the left margin, identifying only the most important points.

C. Paraphrasing

Paraphrase the following excerpts from the passage.

1. Today's young people have grown up with robot pets and on the network in a fully tethered life. In their views of robots, they are the pioneers, the first generation that does not necessarily take simulation to be second best.

   _____

   _____

2. . . . they view it [online life] as one might the weather: to be taken for granted, enjoyed, and sometimes endured. They've gotten used to the weather but there are signs of weather fatigue.

   _____

   _____

D. Critical Thinking

What is Turkle's opinion of young people's being constantly tethered to their cell phones? How do you know? What evidence is there in the passage?

Note: A summarizing exercise based on this passage can be found at the end of the chapter.

PRACTICE ESSAY

From *Seabiscuit: An American Legend* "How Jockeys Controlled Their Weight"
Laura Hillenbrand

In the developed world, eating disorders—specifically anorexia and bulimia—have become a major health problem, especially for young women. It's a complicated issue, with no simple causes or solutions. Although an eating disorder is usually an individual health problem, athletes (particularly female gymnasts and figure skaters) and ballet dancers are often pressured by their coaches and trainers to keep their weight abnormally low. Another culprit is the obsession in the United States with thinness evident in both the mass media and advertising.

But jockeys must also watch their weight. This excerpt, which explains the often absurd lengths to which jockeys went to keep their weight in check, is from Laura Hillenbrand's best-selling 2001 book Seabiscuit: An American Legend, *about the legendary racehorse. The book introduces the reader to the world of Thoroughbred horse racing and examines the social and cultural forces at work during the 1930s and the dark years of the Depression when America needed a diversion from its economic woes.*

Seabiscuit, an ungainly and not particularly attractive horse, represented one such diversion. He won race after race and astonished the nation with his incredible speeds. Since 1989 Laura Hillenbrand has been writing about Thoroughbred racing for Equus *magazine. Her most recent book is* Unbroken: A World War II Story of Survival, Resilience, and Redemption *(2010).*

Preview Questions

1. What do you know about horse racing? Have you ever attended a horse race or watched one of the nation's premier horse races on television (i.e., the Kentucky Derby, the Preakness, the Belmont Stakes)? What are some reasons that horse racing has been a popular pastime for Americans?

2.   Why must racing jockeys be small? What is a handicap, and how is it determined?

The first paragraph has been annotated for you. Continue annotating in the left margin as you read the essay.

1   They called the scale "the Oracle," and they lived in slavery to it. In the 1920s and 1930s, the imposts, or weights horses were assigned to carry in races, generally ranged from 83 pounds to 130 or more, depending on the rank of the horse and the importance of the race. A rider could be no more than 5 pounds over the assigned weight or he would be taken off the horse. Some trainers trimmed that leeway down to just a half pound. To make weight in anything but high-class stakes races, jockeys had to keep their weight to no more than 114 pounds. Riders competing in ordinary weekday events needed to whittle themselves down another 5 pounds or so, while those in the lowest echelons of the sport couldn't weigh much more than 100. The lighter a rider was, the greater the number of horses he could ride. "Some riders," wrote Eddie Arcaro,[4] "will all but saw their legs off to get within the limit."

[margin annotations: jockeys were slaves to the scale / couldn't be more than 5 lbs. over wt. assigned / the lighter the wt. the more horses jockeys could ride]

2   A few riders were naturally tiny enough to make weight without difficulty, and they earned the burning envy of every other jockey. Most of them were young teenagers whose growth spurts lay ahead of them. To ensure that they didn't waste time and money training and supporting boys who would eventually grow out of their trade, contract trainers checked the foot size of every potential bug boy,[5] since a large foot is a fairly good sign of a coming growth spurt. Many also inspected the height and weight of a potential bug boy's siblings. Trainer Woody Stephens, who began his racing career as a bug boy in the late 1920s, always felt he got lucky in this respect. In vetting him for the job, his trainer neglected to look at his sister, a local basketball phenom.

3   Virtually every adult rider, and most of the kids, naturally tended to weigh too much. Cheating, if you did it right, could help a little. One pudgy 140-pound rider earned a place in reinsman legend by fooling a profoundly myopic clerk of scales by skewing the readout to register him at 110. No one is exactly sure how he did it, but it is believed that either he positioned his feet on a nonregistering part of the scale or his valet stuck his whip under his seat and lifted up. He made it through an entire season before someone caught him.

4   Most jockeys took a more straightforward approach: the radical diet, consisting of six hundred calories a day. Red Pollard[6] went as long as a year

---

[4] Eddie Arcaro was a famous American jockey who won the Kentucky Derby five times and the Triple Crown twice during his long career.

[5] A bug boy is an apprentice jockey who gets a weight allowance to compensate for his inexperience.

[6] Red Pollard and George Woolf (mentioned later, in paragraph 5) both rode Seabiscuit. Sunny Jim Fitzsimmons was another well-known jockey in the late 1930s.

eating nothing but eggs. Sunny Jim Fitzsimmons confessed that during his riding days a typical dinner consisted of a leaf or two of lettuce, and he would eat them only after placing them on a windowsill to dry the water out of them. Water, because of its weight, was the prime enemy, and jockeys went to absurd lengths to keep it out of their systems. Most drank virtually nothing. A common practice was to have jockey's room valets open soda cans by puncturing the top with an ice pick, making it impossible to drink more than a few drops at a time. The sight and sound of water became a torment; Fitzsimmons habitually avoided areas of the barn where horses were being washed because the spectacle of flowing water was agonizing.

5   But the weight maximums were so low that near fasting and water deprivation weren't enough. Even what little water and calories the body had taken in had to be eliminated. Many riders were "heavers," poking their fingers down their throats to vomit up their meals. Others chewed gum to trigger salivation; Tommy Luther could spit off as much as half a pound in a few hours. Then there were the sweating rituals, topped by "road work." This practice, used by both Red Pollard and George Woolf, involved donning heavy underwear, zipping into a rubber suit, swaddling in hooded winter gear and woolen horse blankets, then running around and around the track, preferably under a blistering summer sun. Stephens remembered seeing jockeys in full road-work attire gathering at a bowling alley, so lathered that sweat spouted from their shoes with each step. After road work, there were Turkish baths, where jockeys congregated for mornings of communal sweating. The desiccation practices of jockeys were lampooned by turf writer Joe H. Palmer in a column written on jockey Abelardo DeLara: "DeLara has to sweat off about two pounds a day to make weight. Last year, by his own estimate, he lost 600 pounds this way. Since he weighs about 110, it is a mere matter of arithmetic that he would be a bit more than 700 pounds if he hadn't reduced so regularly."

A. Comprehension

Choose the answer that best completes each statement. Do not refer to the selection while doing this exercise.

1. In the 1920s and 1930s, jockeys had to maintain a weight of no more than
   (a) 95 pounds.
   (b) 100 pounds.
   (c) 114 pounds.
   (d) 145 pounds.
2. Jockeys called the scales they had to weigh themselves on
   (a) "the Oracle."
   (b) "the Career Breaker."
   (c) "the Monster."
   (d) "the Master."

3. Horse trainers did not want to waste their time training bug boys (young apprentice jockeys) if eventually they would
   (a) grow bored with racing and drop out.
   (b) prove not to be winners.
   (c) grow to be too big to ride.
   (d) leave and sign on with another trainer.
4. Because it added weight to their bodies, most jockeys did everything they could to avoid
   (a) eating vegetables.
   (b) drinking alcohol.
   (c) eating bread or other carbohydrates.
   (d) drinking water.
5. To ensure that they would meet weight restrictions, many jockeys
   (a) performed exhausting workouts in the gym.
   (b) underwent various types of sweating rituals.
   (c) became anorexic.
   (d) lied about their weight or cheated.

B. Vocabulary

Look through the paragraphs listed below and find a word that matches each definition. Refer to a dictionary if necessary.

1. reduce gradually [paragraph 1]

   _____

2. ranks, levels [1]

   _____

3. slang for a remarkable or outstanding person [2]

   _____

4. subjecting to a complete examination or evaluation [2]

   _____

5. near-sighted [3]

   _____

6. putting on an article of clothing [5]

   _____

7. made fun of [5]

   _____

8. removing moisture [5]

   _____

C. Structure and Meaning

Complete the following questions.

1. Why do you think that jockeys referred to the weight scale as "the Oracle"? _____

   _____

2. Why does Hillenbrand emphasize that jockeys ideally weigh no more than 100 pounds? _____

3. What is the most important point that should be annotated in paragraph 5? _____

   _____

4. Read the end of paragraph 5 again, where the turf writer Joe H. Palmer commented on the weight lost by the jockey Abelardo DeLara. What point was Palmer trying to make? _____

   _____

D. Questions for Discussion and Analysis

1. What might be the reason that racehorses carry imposts, or weights? What do these imposts have to do with the subject of this essay, jockeys' attempts to keep their weights at certain prescribed levels?
2. Why might teenage boys coming of age during the Depression have been attracted to horse racing?

Critical Thinking Exercise

The headnote accompanying this selection alludes to the problem many athletes face: the necessity to control their weight. How serious is the problem of anorexia and bulimia in the sports world? Type "eating disorders" and "athletes" in the search box of your favorite search engine. Why might eating disorders be so common in the sports world? Which sports are most likely implicated?

■ WRITING SUMMARIES

A colleague describes a summary as a distillation of ideas. As she put it, "We can reduce a large number of grapes into a very small but potent glass of wine. The grapes are still there, but in a different, more condensed and powerful form." A summary is a condensed version of an essay, article, or book; it presents the writer's thesis, the supporting ideas, and the conclusion—in other words, only the important information.

Writing summaries provides many intellectual benefits: A summary is a good measure of your reading and writing skills. Like a paraphrase, it requires that you understand a passage accurately. But summarizing goes beyond a paraphrase because the process forces you to weigh the relative worth of ideas, deciding what is essential and what is nonessential, what to retain and what to omit. It forces you to discern the arrangement of ideas and requires you to restate the ideas concisely, accurately, and fairly, without intruding your own opinion or judgment or distorting the thinking. Finally, it helps avoid plagiarism (copying). Your ability to restate the main ideas of a passage in your own words is a true indicator of how well you understand it.

How long should a summary be? Unless your instructor requires you to conform to a particular length, use this formula as a guide: A summary should be roughly between 5 and 15 percent of the original. Some instructors ask that a summary be no more than a single typed page, double-spaced, or roughly 200 to 250 words. The Hillenbrand essay at the end of this chapter is relatively short, about 825 words, so your summary should be between 50 and 125 words. One hundred words would be the perfect length.

How to Write a Summary

Follow these suggestions to write an effective summary:

- Read through the passage at least twice so that you have a good understanding of the content. Circle any unfamiliar words and look them up.
- Annotate it, noting main ideas and key supporting statements. Determine where the piece breaks into sections.
- Transfer your annotations to a separate sheet of paper. Write the main point of each section (or of each paragraph, if the piece is short). Leave plenty of space between each point to make changes or to add material.
- Maintain the balance between main ideas and supporting details in the original. Include only the supporting details that best support the main points.
- Paraphrase the writer's ideas as much as possible, but do not change key terms. For example, in writing a summary of "How Jockeys Controlled Their Weight," it would not be plagiarizing to use words or phrases from the essay like "jockeys" or "assigned weights." Don't strain to find synonyms for words that form the basis of the essay.
- Insert transitional words or phrases as necessary to show the relationship between ideas. (See Chapter 5 for a list of common transitions and their functions.)
- Prepare a final draft by rewriting your sentences. Check to see that your summary is accurate and free of your own ideas and opinions. (Note, however, that many instructors assign a summary-response paper, in which you would be asked both to summarize an essay and then to evaluate it by explaining your objections, criticisms, or other observations. In this case, your instructor is asking for your point of view. If you are unsure about an assignment, ask for clarification.)

Online Learning Center

Purdue University's website has one of the oldest and best Online Writing Laboratories in the nation. Its OWL offers students dozens of handouts on all the elements of writing an essay, including how to write a summary and how to avoid plagiarism. The address is http://owl.english.purdue.edu/ Further information on the difference between quoting, paraphrasing, and summarizing is available at http://owl.english.purdue.edu/handouts/research/r_quotprsum.html

- Your summary's first sentence should include the author's name and the essay title as well as its main idea. Use the present verb tense throughout. If you use quotations, do so sparingly.
- Do a word count, making sure that your summary is the appropriate length. If it is too long, cut unnecessary verbiage or supporting examples.

Sample Summary— The First Draft

Laura Hillenbrand's essay, "How Jockeys Controlled Their Weight," describes the often absurd lengths that jockeys in the 1920s and 1930s went to keep their weight within required limits. Jockeys were not allowed to weigh more than 5 pounds over the assigned weight; further, jockeys in high-stakes races could not weigh more than 114 pounds, while in less important races they couldn't weigh more than 100 pounds. Naturally, a jockey who was light was able to ride more horses than a heavier one, which favored teenage jockeys who hadn't reached their adult weight yet. Jockeys controlled their weight by eating very little (one jockey even dried the water on his lettuce leaves) and by severely limiting their water intake. Some jockeys vomited after eating, while others engaged in bizarre sweating rituals or congregated in Turkish baths, all with the purpose of keeping their riding weight within prescribed limits. (147 words)

Comment

Because my first draft was almost 50 words over my self-imposed limit of 100 words, some cutting was in order. After studying my draft, I decided that the second sentence could easily be condensed. I also tightened up the language (for example, "eating very little" became "fasting") and omitted a couple of little details. Even though I wanted to save the idea that one jockey went so far as to dry lettuce leaves on a windowsill, it had to go. The final draft is just over 100 words.

Sample Summary— The Final Draft

Laura Hillenbrand's essay, "How Jockeys Controlled Their Weight," describes the often absurd lengths that jockeys in the 1920s and 1930s went to control their weight. Depending on the type of race, jockeys had to restrict their weight to between 100 and 114 pounds. Naturally, a jockey who was light could ride more horses than a heavier one, so teenage boys were especially envied because they had not yet reached their adult weight. Jockeys lost weight by fasting and by avoiding water. Some jockeys vomited after eating, while others engaged in elaborate sweating rituals and congregated at Turkish baths for "communal sweating." (101 words)

The One-Sentence Summary

Writing a one-sentence summary of an essay, article, or other sustained piece of writing is an especially good way to check your comprehension of the writer's main point. Distilling a lengthy discussion to a single sentence is useful outside of college in the real world of meetings, proposals, and strategy sessions. Here is a one-sentence summary of Hillenbrand's essay:

> During the 1920s and 1930s jockeys often went to extreme lengths to keep their weight within prescribed limits—by fasting, avoiding water, and engaging in sweating rituals.

Practice Exercise 6

Return to the passage by Steven Shapin on pages 32–33 and write a one-sentence summary of it.

_____

_____

Practice Exercise 7

Return to the passage by Sherry Turkle on pages 34–35 and write a summary, trying to use no more than 50 words.

_____

_____

_____

_____

Reading for the Main Idea
and Author's Purpose

CHAPTER OBJECTIVES

This chapter will help you improve your comprehension by showing you how to identify the:

- Main idea in paragraphs

- Placement of the main idea

- Implied main ideas

- Levels of support—major and minor supporting details

- Author's purpose and modes of discourse

■ MAIN IDEA IN PARAGRAPHS

In the first five chapters of this book, the focus of our study is on the individual paragraph. It might seem odd to devote so much time to paragraphs. After all, the texts of essays, articles, and textbook chapters consist of long strings of paragraphs, and we seldom read paragraphs in isolation. Yet focusing on shorter passages, at least initially, promotes careful reading and analysis. To practice comprehending nonfiction prose, it is less intimidating to analyze a 100-word paragraph than a 10-page essay.

Nonfiction refers to prose that deals with real subjects, as opposed to fiction, which is imaginative. In nonfiction prose, the paragraph is the fundamental unit of written thought. Simply put, a paragraph is a group of related sentences that develop and support one idea. It may be any length as long as it keeps to that one idea. The main idea of a paragraph is a general statement telling the reader what it is about. The main idea may be explicitly stated in a sentence that *often* appears at or near the beginning of the paragraph. As you will see, however, many writers of adult prose do not adhere to this pattern.

Main Idea and Controlling Idea

In elementary school, you were probably taught that the first sentence of a paragraph is the topic sentence. This rule is convenient but misleading; to assume that the first sentence is the main point may result in inaccurate comprehension, since professional writers frequently violate this principle. For this reason, I prefer the term **main idea.** If a main-idea sentence is present, it consists of two parts: the **topic** and the **controlling idea.** The topic is the general subject the paragraph is about (though not necessarily the grammatical subject). The controlling idea—often a descriptive word or phrase—limits, qualifies, or narrows the topic to make the larger subject manageable. Diagrammed, then, a typical main-idea sentence might look like this:

> Topic + Controlling Idea = Main Idea

Consider this sentence:

Global warming is the most serious environmental problem the world faces today.

In this example, the topic—"global warming"—is underlined once, and the controlling idea—"the most serious environmental problem the world faces today"—is underlined twice. Notice that if the writer shifts the order, beginning with the controlling idea and ending with the topic, the relationship between topic and controlling idea does not change:

The most serious environmental problem the world faces today is global warming.

As you can see, the controlling idea restricts the writer and helps him or her select pertinent supporting details. This means that in a well-constructed paragraph all the other sentences support the phrase "the most serious environmental problem." If the writer were to shift direction and discuss another aspect of global warming, the main idea sentence might look something like this:

> As the heaviest users of fossil fuels, <u>the United States, China, and India</u> <u>must share the largest burden of fighting the problem of global warming</u>.

A third example with another controlling idea shows still another direction for the paragraph:

> Although the results of global warming may not be evident yet in our towns and cities, <u>the melting of the polar ice cap</u>, a direct result of global warming and the burning of fossil fuels, <u>is already having a significant impact on the polar bear population in the Arctic</u>.

Note that you do not need to label everything, as the third example suggests. The first part of the sentence (beginning with "Although") will probably not be discussed because the writer is not interested in global warming on a local scale. In this example, the topic, "the melting of the polar ice cap," already focuses on one aspect of global warming, and the controlling idea—"the impact on polar bears"—will serve as a sort of umbrella for the remainder of the paragraph. Discerning these two crucial elements of main-idea sentences helps you keep on track as you read.

Occasionally, a writer may ease into the main idea, as these two sentences from Robert Coles's book, *The Moral Intelligence of Children*, illustrate. Which sentence represents the main idea—the first or the second? Underline the topic and controlling idea in the sentence.

> "Moral intelligence" isn't acquired only by memorization of rules and regulations, by dint of abstract classroom discussion or kitchen compliance. We grow morally as a consequence of learning how to be with others, how to behave in this world, a learning prompted by taking to heart what we have seen and heard.

Practice Exercise 1

Label these main-idea sentences by underlining the topic once and the controlling idea twice. Start with these easier examples.

1. The bathroom is the most dangerous room in the house.
2. The most dangerous room in the house is the bathroom.
3. Despite their exotic appearance and reputation for being difficult to cultivate, orchids are actually nearly foolproof plants that require only minimal care.
4. The World Wide Web has revolutionized the way we obtain and retrieve information.
5. According to MIT researcher Sherry Turkle, the concept of separation is being reinvented as adolescents remain tethered to their parents via cell phones.

6. Powell's City of Books, which occupies an entire city block in Portland, Oregon, and which is so large that patrons need a map to find their way around, is widely regarded as the most comprehensive bookstore in the country.

7. The turmoil in the Middle East, with massive protests and the toppling of long-time autocrats, has had a significant impact on the international scene.

8. As Greg Critser explains in his recent book *Fat Land*, the reasons that Americans are the most obese people in the world are varied and complex and go beyond the usual culprits, the fast-food industry with its super-sized meals.

Now try these more difficult main-idea sentences taken from published material, some of which you will encounter later in this book.

9. Coral reefs are under threat for a host of reasons: bottom trawling, dynamite fishing, coastal erosion, agricultural runoff, and, nowadays, global warming. (Elizabeth Kolbert)

10. Skating [skateboarding] is a narcotic that offers release and a negation of self that defies analysis. (Jocko Weyland)

11. The text-driven world of rapid response does not make self-reflection impossible but does little to cultivate it. (Sherry Turkle)

12. Montana in general, and the Bitterroot Valley in its southwest, are a land of paradoxes. (Jared Diamond)

13. Generally speaking, our calendar is a flexible affair, full of inconsistencies. (Witold Rybczynski)

14. Such a simple invention, or discovery, the compass. (Jonathan Raban)

15. Much of the wildlife is nocturnal and it creeps through the nights, poisonous and alien. (Luis Alberto Urrea)

16. Cancer is "the modern disease" not just because we understand it in radically new ways but also because there's a lot more cancer about. (Steven Shapin)

Critical Thinking Exercise

Does the first item in Practice Exercise 1 represent a fact or an opinion? Defend your answer. How would you prove the assertion that the bathroom is, in fact, the most dangerous room in the house?

■ PLACEMENT OF THE MAIN IDEA

In your academic textbooks, the main ideas are generally fairly easy to spot. Contemporary textbook publishers often use graphic elements such as boldface or italic type to make the main ideas conspicuous.

For example, consider this paragraph from a standard psychology text:

circadian rhythm
(sur-kã´ dē-un)
Internally
generated cycles
lasting about
24 hours a day that
regulate sleepiness
and wakefulness,
body temperature,
and the secretion
of some hormones.

When is it time to go to sleep? For some of us, drowsiness takes over not long after sundown. Others are night owls who find that they are wide awake until the wee hours of the morning. But all of us—even those who do not sleep well—are on a biological cycle of approximately 24 hours that regulates our pattern of sleep, called the **circadian rhythm** (*circa* = about; *dia* = day). Much remains to be learned about the biological basis of circadian rhythms. One part of the hypothalamus has been implicated as a part of the body's internal "clock." Its activity increases and decreases in a regular pattern that lasts about 24 hours. In addition, variations in the hormone *melatonin* that fluctuate on a 24-hour pattern appear to be a key factor in regulating sleepiness (Gilbertini, Graham, & Cook, 1999).

Benjamin B. Lahey, *Psychology: An Introduction*

Although the term *circadian rhythm* is not stated at the beginning of the paragraph, it is printed in boldface and further defined in the left-hand margin. What is the etymology of *circadian*?

As a college reader, you must learn to cope with diverse writing styles and techniques, requiring you to rewrite some of the rules you may have been taught in the past. Adult nonfiction (nontextbook) prose is not so neatly formulaic as students would like it to be, and the careful reader has to be alert for variations. The main idea may be delayed, it may be buried in the middle of the paragraph, it may be at the end; it may occur in bits and pieces throughout the paragraph, or it may only be implied, not stated explicitly. Let us examine a few paragraphs to see the location of the main idea, beginning with a passage from Laura Hillenbrand's book about the famous racehorse, Seabiscuit. Study my annotations:

main idea

dominant idea
throughout—a
thoroughbred
racehorse runs at
impressive speeds &
is born to run

A Throughbred racehorse is one of God's <u>most impressive engines</u>. Tipping the scales at up to 1,450 pounds, he can sustain *speeds* of forty miles per hour. Equipped with reflexes much faster than those of the most quick-wired man, he <u>swoops</u> over as much as twenty-eight feet of earth in a single stride, and corners on a dime. His body is a paradox of mass and lightness, crafted <u>to slip through air with the ease of an arrow</u>. His mind is impressed with a single command: <u>run</u>. He pursues <u>speed</u> with superlative courage, pushing beyond defeat, beyond exhaustion, sometimes beyond the structural limits of bone and sinew. In flight, he is nature's ultimate wedding of form and purpose.

Laura Hillenbrand, *Seabiscuit: An American Legend*

The underlined words and phrases all reinforce the controlling idea ("most impressive machines"). Rather than repeating the word *speeds*, Hillenbrand uses several synonyms. Everything works together to create "a network of interlocking ideas," as Richard Marius has described the paragraph. Reading in this way makes it easier to follow the chain of ideas.

human hand and towards the robot, a transition as significant in the context of airline logistics as that from the washboard to the washing machine had once been in the domestic sphere. However, few users seemed capable of producing the precise line-up of cards and codes demanded by the computers, which responded to the slightest infraction with sudden and intemperate error messages—making one long for a return of the surliest of humans, from whom there always remains at least a theoretical possibility of understanding and forgiveness.

Alan de Botton, A Week at the Airport

Which of the following statements best expresses the implied main idea?

1. Computers are too difficult for most people to use.
2. Airline passengers prefer dealing with a clerk, no matter how rude, rather than with a check-in computer.
3. The robot check-in service at airports is a radical change that saves time and money.
4. The computer check-in service at airports is too complicated for most people to use.

Either number 2 or number 4 accurately expresses de Botton's main point.

Now as a check on your comprehension, paraphrase the second sentence:

_____

_____

_____

Practice Exercise 2

Read these paragraphs and then complete the exercises as directed.

A.

BLUE. We live under blue skies, surrounded by blue seas. Yet, try to catch the blueness in your hand, and it is gone. The bulk of our planet is made up of browns, grays, yellows, reds, and greens. Perhaps because it is so evanescent, popular lore has long endowed the color blue with magic qualities. Blue stands for truth, chastity, divinity. Druidic priests wore blue. So did the Jewish high priest. And so did Odin, the one-eyed Nordic god of war and wisdom. The Virgin Mary (the "Blue Lady") is clothed in heavenly blue. How to get blue onto a paint brush was long a problem . . . Marco Polo (c. 1254–1324), on his way east, detoured to see the legendary mines in the snowbound headlands of the Kokcha River in Afghanistan, which then possessed a world monopoly of lapis lazuli ("azure stone") production. Soon, chunks of the "blue gold" were carried west along the ancient Silk Route by camel caravan, and shipped from Middle-Eastern ports to Venice. There, specially skilled craftsmen crushed the stone, nuclear planners. The local area has three hundred Evangelical churches. Friday-night high school football is a religion. The Panhandle is conservative, and in 1964 it voted against Lyndon Johnson, a fellow Texan, and for right-wing Republican Barry Goldwater. Amarillo lacks the cosmopolitan culture of Dallas, Houston, and other posturban pods; nor does it have an intellectual community like the university towns of Austin and College Station, with their computer software firms. This is still unadulterated, barren Texas, with state flags everywhere and a corrugated look to everything, especially when the wind blows the gritty dust against the road signs.

Robert D. Kaplan, An Empire Wilderness: Travels into America's Future

Write a complete sentence in your own words that states the main idea of the paragraph.

_____

■ LEVELS OF SUPPORT—MAJOR AND MINOR SUPPORTING DETAILS

Now we can turn our attention to the paragraph's supporting sentences and the importance of being able to distinguish between **major supporting statements** and **minor supporting statements.** Although good readers probably don't consciously label sentences as will be demonstrated in this section, learning to separate major and minor support is an important thinking skill. Briefly, **major** statements directly relate to and develop the main idea, whereas **minor** ones further explain, illustrate, or otherwise develop the major ones. Analysis of levels of support trains you to think logically because you must weigh the relative importance of ideas in relation to the main idea. In an ideally constructed paragraph, a diagram of the supporting sentences might look like this:

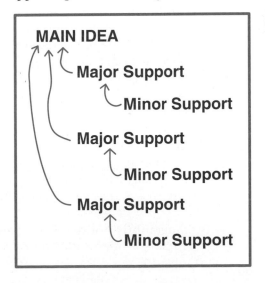

The following paragraph by Mortimer Adler, who was a prominent American educator and thinker, exemplifies this ideal construction. The paragraph's six sentences reinforce the main idea, stated in the first sentence. Notice that the major supporting sentences identify each of the three types of book owner, and the minor supporting sentences comment on each type, using parentheses. (In Chapter 4, you will learn that this paragraph is developed by a method called classification.)

[1]There are three kinds of book owners. [2]The first has all the standard sets and best-sellers—unread, untouched. [3](This deluded individual owns wood-pulp and ink, not books.) [4]The second has a great many books—a few of them read through, most of them dipped into, but all of them as clean and shiny as the day they were bought. [5](This person would probably like to make books his own, but is restrained by a false respect for their physical appearance.) [6]The third has a few books or many—every one of them dog-eared and dilapidated, shaken and loosened by continual use, marked and scribbled in front to back. [7](This man owns books.)

Mortimer Adler, "How to Mark a Book," *Saturday Review*

The following paragraph varies this pattern. It is by Alexander Petrunkevitch, who was one of this country's foremost arachnologists (an expert in spiders). Notice that the first two sentences consist of introductory descriptive details; they are minor descriptive details.

[1]The entire body of a tarantula, especially its legs, is thickly clothed with hair. [2]Some of it is short and woolly, some long and stiff. [3]Touching this body hair produces one of two distinct reactions. [4]When the spider is hungry, it responds with an immediate and swift attack. [5]At the touch of a cricket's antennae the tarantula seizes the insect so swiftly that a motion picture taken at the rate of 64 frames per second shows only the result and not the process of capture. [6]But when the spider is not hungry, the stimulation of its hairs merely causes it to shake the touched limb. [7]An insect can walk under its hairy belly unharmed.

Alexander Petrunkevitch, "The Spider and the Wasp," *Scientific American*

This paragraph is printed again here, this time in graphic form showing the relative importance of the supporting details in relation to the main idea:

Main idea:
Touching this body hair produces one of two distinct reactions. [sent. 3]

Major support:
When the spider is hungry, it responds with an immediate and swift attack. [sent. 4]

Minor support:
At the touch of a cricket's antennae the tarantula seizes the insect so swiftly that a motion picture taken at the rate of 64 frames per second shows only the result and not the process of capture. [sent. 5]

Major Support:
But when the spider is not hungry, the stimulation of its hairs merely causes it to shake the touched limb. [sent. 6]

Minor support:
An insect can walk under its hairy belly unharmed. [sent. 7]

Just because we label minor details "minor" does not mean they are of no importance. Without them, we would not know how fast the spider's rate of capture is when hungry nor the spider's indifference to the presence of prey when not hungry. As you can see, supporting sentences operate on two different levels—some general, some more specific—suggesting two considerations: Supporting sentences have relative significance, and they are not all equally important. Unfortunately, not every paragraph is balanced as this one is, nor does every paragraph follow this alternating pattern. Still, the ability to distinguish between the two helps you see the *texture* (for want of a better word) good writers try hard to achieve; good readers unconsciously sort out these details as they read. In summary, the most important part of the paragraph is the main idea, and two types of supporting details are there to buttress and reinforce this main idea.

> *Mapping Exercise*
>
> Using the first example from Practice Exercise 1, map out your own paragraph using major and minor support to provide evidence for this sentence: The bathroom is the most dangerous room in the house.
>   You don't need to write a paragraph, just indicate the ideas and label them *major* and *minor*.

**Practice
Exercise 3**

Try your hand at distinguishing between the two kinds of support in this paragraph. The subject is the care and feeding of the various animals the writer—a naturalist and zookeeper—kept in his nature preserve on an island off the coast of England. In the space before each sentence, indicate whether the sentence represents the main idea (MAIN), major support (MA), or minor support (MI). Finally, for the main idea, underline the topic once and the controlling idea twice.

_____ Feeding, of course, is one of your main problems. _____ Not only do you have to have a fairly extensive knowledge of what each species you are liable to encounter eats in the wild state, but you have to work out a suitable substitute if the natural food is unavailable, and then teach your specimen to eat it. _____ Also, you have to cater for their individual likes and dislikes, which vary enormously. _____ I have known a rodent which, refusing all normal rodent food—such as fruit, bread, vegetables—lived for three days on an exclusive diet of spaghetti. _____ I have had a group of five monkeys, of the same age and species, who displayed the most weird idiosyncrasies. _____ Two of the five had a passion for hard-boiled eggs, while the other three were frightened of the strange white shapes and refused to touch them, actually screaming in fear if you introduced such a fearsome object as a hard-boiled egg into their cage. _____ These five monkeys all adored oranges but, whereas four would carefully peel their fruit and throw away the skin, the fifth would peel his orange equally carefully and then throw away the orange and eat the peel. _____ When you have a collection of several hundred creatures, all displaying such curious characteristics, you are sometimes nearly driven mad in your efforts to satisfy their desires and so keep them healthy and happy.

Gerald Durrell, *A Zoo in My Luggage*

■ THE AUTHOR'S PURPOSE AND MODES OF DISCOURSE

The last skill we will take up in this chapter is identifying the **mode of discourse,** which refers to the kind of writing in nonfiction prose. These modes are closely related to the **author's purpose**—why the writer is writing and what he or she wants to accomplish. There are four modes: (1) **narration,** to tell a story; (2) **description,** to show what something looks or feels like; (3) **exposition,** to inform, explain, or set forth; and (4) **persuasion,** to convince the reader to adopt the writer's point of view. The following box shows the relationship between mode of discourse and author's purpose.

Author's Purpose ⟶	*Mode of Discourse*
• To tell a story ⟶	Narration
• To show what something looks like or feels like ⟶	Description
• To inform, to set forth, to explain, to discuss ⟶	Exposition
• To convince the reader to adopt the writer's point of view ⟶	Persuasion

Narration

Narration, which is the most easily recognized mode of discourse, means simply to tell a story. In narration the writer relates real events in chronological order; his or her purpose is not to entertain, but to provide evidence for some larger truth, as Lewis Thomas does in this passage:

> We may be about to rediscover that dying is not such a bad thing to do after all. Sir William Osler took this view: he disapproved of people who spoke of the agony of death, maintaining there was no such thing.
>
> In a nineteenth-century memoir on an expedition in Africa, there is a story by David Livingston about his own experience of near-death. He was caught by a lion, crushed across the chest in the animal's great jaws, and saved in the instant by a lucky shot from a friend. Later, he remembered the episode in clear detail. He was so amazed by the extraordinary sense of peace, calm, and total painlessness associated with being killed that he constructed a theory that all creatures are provided with a protective physiologic mechanism, switched on at the verge of death, carrying them through in a haze of tranquillity.
>
> Lewis Thomas, "The Long Habit," *Lives of a Cell*

State the main idea that this little narrative supports.

_____

_____

Description

The mode of discourse called **description** shows what someone or something looks like or what something feels like. In description the writer shows a visual picture of a *particular* scene, not a generalized one based on a composite of many such scenes. Descriptive writing typically relies on details that appeal to the five senses. It may also use figures of speech (imaginative comparisons such as metaphors and similes, which are covered in Chapter 6). Although a descriptive passage by itself usually does not have a sentence stating the main idea, there usually is a **dominant impression**, revealed little by little as the details accumulate.

Read this descriptive passage from Jeanette Walls's fictionalized memoir about her family:

> We had a homestead on Salt Draw, which flowed into the Pecos River, in the rolling gritty grassland of west Texas. The sky was high and pale, the land low and washed out, gray and every color of sand. Sometimes the wind blew for days on end, but sometimes it was so still you could hear the dog barking on the Dingler ranch two miles upriver, and when a wagon came down the road, the dust it trailed hung in the air for a long time before drifting back to the ground.

When you looked out across the land, most everything you could see—the horizon, the river, the fence lines, the gullies, the scrub cedar—was spread out and flat, and the people, cattle, horses, lizards, and water all moved slowly, conserving themselves.

It was hard country. The ground was like rock—save for when a flood turned everything to mud—the animals were bony and tough, and even the plants were prickly and sparse, though from time to time the thunderstorms brought out startling bursts of wildflowers. Dad said High Lonesome, as the area was known, wasn't a place for the soft of head or the weak of heart, and he said that was why he and I made out just fine there, because we were both tough nuts.

Jeanette Walls, *Half Broke Horses*

Which of the five senses (taste, touch, sight, hearing, or smell) does the writer appeal to in the passage? _____

_____

What is the dominant impression of the homestead? _____

_____

The following descriptive passage is by Jason Elliott, a British writer who traveled extensively in Afghanistan in the late 1990s. In it, he describes Afghan buses. The wealth of detail suggests that they are very different from their North American counterparts. Underline the key details as you read it.

Afghan buses are full of character, and are fastidiously maintained by the men who risk their lives daily by driving them. They run until they disintegrate, after which they are frequently reborn in mutated incarnations, their various parts salvaged from scrapyards and lovingly reassembled. Loose bodywork is reinforced with riveted sheet metal. There was one bus with its engine housing built entirely from timber, and the frame of was another patched with strips of Russian field runway. I once saw a bus in a Kabul street that had been run over by a tank. 'We'll have it back on the road in a few days,' joked the undaunted owner.

Floral ironwork, with more whorls than a Provençale bell-tower, decorates rear windows, or is welded to roofs to serve as an anchor for mountains of luggage. Sometimes chains and metal pendants, which jangle musically with a rocking chassis—the modern vestiges, perhaps, of the caravan's camel bells—are draped on their sides in the manner of a necklace. Fertility symbols—a pair of fishes is the most common motif—are stitched into the leather of radiator-grille covers. Buses as well as trucks are often lovingly painted. I saw several idyllic alpine scenes, complete with Swiss chalets and cotton-wool clouds; others bore images of budgerigars, leaping lions and moonlit water-gardens, and above their windscreens in big multicoloured letters:

'Hero Bus', 'Welcome to Bus', 'Modern Bus', 'King of the Road', 'Good Your Journey', or 'We Trust In God'. Always the driver's cockpit is festooned with tassels, tinsel, extra mirrors and plastic flowers, stickers of eyes, the slender hand of a woman, cars and animals. Each has a talismanic and protective significance, as does the traditional religious paraphernalia of dangling pendants carved in the name of God, the Prophet, and his Caliphs, and stick-on verses of the Qur'ān[1] or pictures of the Ka'bah at Mecca.

Sometimes the destinations are painted on the sides of the buses; more often you listen for the voice of a driver shouting out the name of the place you are going. There is no schedule; the bus leaves when the driver decides it is full enough. Even as it pulls away the driver's teenage accomplice hangs from the wing mirror yelling the destination in the hope of sweeping up a few extra passengers.

Jason Elliott, An Unexpected Light: Travels in Afghanistan

In your own words, write a sentence summarizing the dominant impression that the details in the passage suggest. _____

_____

_____

Exposition

Exposition, or expository writing, is the most common kind of reading you will encounter in your college courses. Expository readings very likely make up the bulk of the reading in your freshman English anthology and in your textbooks. Exposition is essentially objective writing with a straightforward purpose: to inform, to explain, to make clear, to discuss, to set forth. Expository writing is usually *factual*, consistent with its purpose to provide information. By its very nature then, exposition presents subject matter without trying to influence our opinions or emotions or to criticize or argue. In this first example, Elizabeth Kolbert, a science writer who specializes in writing about marine biology and the health of the oceans, presents the reader with a variety of facts about coral reefs.

Coral reefs grow in a great swath that stretches like a belt around the belly of the earth, from thirty degrees north to thirty degrees south latitude. The world's largest reef is the Great Barrier, off the coast of northeastern Australia, and the second largest is off the coast of Belize. There are extensive coral reefs in the tropical Pacific, in the Indian Ocean, and in the Red Sea, and many smaller ones in the Caribbean. These reefs, home to an estimated twenty-five per cent of all marine fish species, represent some of the most diverse ecosystems on the planet.

Elizabeth Kolbert, "The Darkening Sea," *The New Yorker*

[1]A variant spelling of the Koran.

Textbook writers employ exposition in academic discourse to explain difficult concepts, to trace historical events, and to provide information. Examine this passage from an introductory anthropology textbook, in which the writer examines the roots of ethnic conflict. Notice that, despite the controversial nature of the subject, the author presents the information objectively, without intruding personal opinion or judgment.

> Ethnicity, based on perceived cultural similarities and differences in a society or nation, can be expressed in peaceful multiculturalism or in discrimination or violent interethnic confrontation. Culture can be both adaptive and maladaptive. The perception of cultural differences can have disastrous effects on social interaction.
>
> The roots of ethnic differentiation—and therefore, potentially, of ethnic conflict—can be political, economic, religious, linguistic, cultural, or "racial." Why do ethnic differences often lead to conflict and violence? The causes include a sense of injustice because of resource distribution, economic and/or political competition, and reaction to discrimination, prejudice, and other expressions of threatened or devalued identity.
>
> Conrad Phillip Kottak, *Anthropology: The Exploration of Human Diversity*

Persuasion

The terms *persuasion* and *argumentation* are often used interchangeably, though technically there is a difference. **Argumentation** refers to writing supported by logical evidence. In contrast, **persuasion** is an attempt to change another person's feelings or opinions by using emotional or ethical appeals. A writer persuades when he or she wants to *convince* the reader.

Unlike exposition, persuasion deals with controversial issues. In addition, persuasive writing may use facts, but these facts are used to support an opinion. While the distinction between argument and persuasion is not important now, the distinction between fact and opinion is crucial. Facts are provable statements, whereas opinions are subjective, meaning that they exist in the mind, influenced by experience and opinion—rather than in external objective reality. You will study argumentative techniques in much greater detail in Chapters 8 through 10. This passage by Sam Harris, who has studied both philosophy and neuroscience, is from his best-selling book *The End of Faith*, in which he argues that even moderate religious faith is antithetical to civilized values based on reason.

> It is time we admitted, from kings and presidents on down, that there is no evidence that any of our books was authored by the Creator of the universe. The Bible, it seems certain, was the work of sand-strewn men and women who thought the earth was flat and for whom a wheelbarrow would have been a breathtaking example of emerging technology. To rely on such a document as the basis for our worldview—however heroic the efforts of

redactors—is to repudiate two thousand years of civilizing insights that the human mind has only just begun to inscribe upon itself through secular politics and scientific culture. We will see that the greatest problem confronting civilization is not merely religious extremism: rather, it is the larger set of cultural and intellectual accommodations we have made to faith itself. Religious moderates are, in large part, responsible for the religious conflict in our world, because their beliefs provide the context in which scriptural literalism and religious violence can never be adequately opposed.

Sam Harris, *The End of Faith*

According to Harris, what are the two aspects of religious faith that he finds most troubling?

_____

_____

Harris's discussion, though intended to be persuasive—that is, to make us think about religious conflict in a new way—is rational and measured. In contrast, consider the persuasive intent of this opening paragraph from a short magazine article. Notice the word choice and the way this anonymous writer uses language almost as a weapon.

Hey, all you guilt-stricken liberals. Let the water run. Throw those recyclable milk jugs in the trash. And drive that 15-year-old gas-guzzling truck all over town. Heck, flip off a bicyclist while you're at it. Not interested? Fine. Go ahead and eschew these eco-heretical lifestyle choices; just don't go feeling high and mighty about it. That's the takeaway from a biting essay in **Orion** (July-Aug. 2009), written by the always provocative Derrick Jensen. Railing against "simple living as a political act," the radical environmentalist argues that focusing on our personal choices as a salve for eco-destruction is not only misguided, but also ineffective. "Would any sane person think Dumpster diving would have stopped Hitler, or that composting would have ended slavery or brought about the eight-hour workday . . . or that dancing naked around a fire would have helped put in place the voting rights act of 1957 or the Civil Rights Act of 1964? Then why now, with all the world at stake, do so many people retreat into these entirely personal 'solutions'?"

"Simple Living Is for Suckers." *Utne*

Critical Thinking Exercise

Can you detect any flaw in this argument—that individuals who practice "simple living" will not stop "eco-destruction"? Comment on the relevance and quality of the examples the writer attributes to Derrick Jensen.

Mixed Modes of Discourse

Thus far, each passage you have read in this section represents one dominant mode. But in nonfiction prose like an essay or article, writers often combine two or more modes. In this excerpt from an article on Afghanistan before the overthrow of the Taliban regime, Jon Lee Anderson shifts back and forth between two predominant modes of discourse.

> One afternoon in Dasht-e-Qala, two women, one in a deep-violet burkha and the other wearing emerald green, floated past, briefly enlivening the backdrop of beat-up olive-green military vehicles, brown desert, and dusty shop fronts. The sight of women, or at least discernibly human creatures in feminine clothes, is about the only thing that relieves the harshness of the landscape. The visible part of Afghan society is unremittingly male, as is the land, which is drab and muscular. There is nothing soft about anything here, none of the creature comforts a Westerner takes for granted. Dust clogs your throat and coats hair and skin, and the people, who cover their faces with scarves and turbans, have learned to live with it in much the same way the British have grown used to rain. Much of northern Afghanistan today is a pre-industrial society, without electricity, running water, or telephones. There are not even toys for the children. Water is pumped by hand from wells that have been dug with shovels, and roads are made by crews who break rocks and produce gravel with sledgehammers. Barefoot boys walk back and forth through beds of harvested rice, turning the grains with their toes to dry them in the sun. In the bazaars, porters carry poles with reed baskets on the ends, filled with everything from water to rock salt, which is sold in pinkish-gray chunks before being ground down to powder. Lambs are tethered next to men with long knives who slaughter them and hang the carcasses from hooks, hacking them into a steadily diminishing mess of blood and meat and bone and fat by day's end. Grain and vegetables are weighed in tin scales that are balanced with stones. On market days, people walk from distant village—some even cross Taliban lines—to buy livestock (donkeys, camels, cattle, and horses) and then they herd the animals back home. The flat horizon is dotted with robed men riding donkeys, others on camel back, and the odd motorbike spitting up clouds of dust.
>
> Jon Lee Anderson, "The Warlord," *The New Yorker*

Which two modes of discourse predominate in this passage?

_____

In your own words, state the two main points about northern Afghanistan Anderson emphasizes.

_____

_____

_____

Practice Exercise 4

For the first three passages, first identify the dominant mode of discourse and then write a complete sentence stating the main idea in your own words. (For descriptive passages, write the dominant impression.) For the last two passages, identify two modes of discourse.

A.

The **fossil record** represents the history of life on Earth recorded in the remains or traces of organisms that lived in the past. In order to be a fossil, the remains or traces have to be at least 10,000 years old. There are many types of fossilization. Fossil mammoths have been found embedded in ice from Siberia, and a variety of organisms have been encased in fossil tree sap known as amber. Skeletal parts and even wood have undergone petrification, where the living material has been replaced by minerals. Many fern fossils are found as impressions in shale. For the past two centuries, paleontologists have studied fossils from the Earth's strata (layers) in all places of the world and have pieced together the story of life.

The fossil record is rich in information. One of its most striking patterns is a succession of life-forms from the simple to the more complex. Catastrophists offered an explanation for the extinction and subsequent replacement of one group of organisms by another group, but they never could explain successive changes that link groups of organisms historically. Particularly interesting are the fossils that serve as transitional links between groups. For example, famous fossils of *Archaeopteryx* are intermediate between reptiles and birds. The dinosaur-like skeleton of these fossils has reptilian features, including jaws with teeth and a long, jointed tail, but *Archaeopteryx* also had feathers and wings. Other transitional links among fossil vertebrates include the amphibious fish *Eustheopteron*, the reptile-like amphibian *Seymouria*, and the mammal-like reptiles, or therapsids. These fossils allow paleontologists to deduce the order in which vertebrates (animals with backbones) evolved from fishes to amphibians to reptiles to mammals and birds.

Sylvia S. Mader, *Biology*

Mode of discourse _____

Main idea or dominant expression _____

_____

_____

B.

What alarms so many life historians is not that extinctions are occurring but that they appear to be occurring at a greater rate than they have at all but a few times in the past, raising the specter of the sort of wholesale die-offs that ended the reign of the dinosaurs. Do we want, they ask, to exile most of our neighbors to posterity? Exactly how much of our planet's resources do

Two modes of discourse   _____

Main idea or dominant impression   _____

_____

_____

■ CHAPTER EXERCISES

Selection 1

¹Over the last three decades, fast food has infiltrated every nook and cranny of American society. ²An industry that began with a handful of modest hot dog and hamburger stands in southern California has spread to every corner of the nation, selling a broad range of foods wherever paying customers may be found.

³Fast food is now served at restaurants and drive-throughs, at stadiums, airports, zoos, high schools, elementary schools, and universities, on cruise ships, trains, and airplanes, at K-Marts, Wal-Marts, gas stations, and even at hospital cafeterias. ⁴In 1970, Americans spent about $6 billion on fast food; in 2000, they spent more than $110 billion. ⁵Americans now spend more money on fast food than on higher education, personal computers, computer software, or new cars. ⁶They spend more on fast food than on movies, books, magazines, newspapers, videos, and recorded music—combined.

⁷Pull open the glass door, feel the rush of cool air, walk in, get in line, study the backlit color photographs above the counter, place your order, hand over a few dollars, watch teenagers in uniforms pushing various buttons, and moments later take hold of a plastic tray full of food wrapped in colored paper and cardboard. ⁸The whole experience of buying fast food has become so routine, so thoroughly unexceptional and mundane, that it is now taken for granted, like brushing your teeth or stopping for a red light. ⁹It has become a social custom as American as a small, rectangular, hand-held, frozen, and reheated apple pie.

Eric Schlosser, *Fast Food Nation: The Dark Side of the All-American Meal*

A. Vocabulary

For each italicized word from the selection, choose the best definition according to the context in which it appears.

1. fast food has *infiltrated* [sentence 1]:
   (a) gradually penetrated.
   (b) transformed.
   (c) removed the harmful elements from.
   (d) caused a revolution in.

2. every *nook and cranny* [1]:
   (a) economic and social class.
   (b) every area, even the smallest.
   (c) aspect, position.
   (d) trend, custom.

3. so thoroughly *mundane* [8]:
   (a) routine, commonplace.
   (b) monotonous, boring.
   (c) inexpensive, economical.
   (d) efficient, time-saving.

B. Content and Structure

Complete the following questions.

1. Which *two* modes of discourse are represented in the passage?

   _____

2. Which is the best title for the paragraph?
   (a) "$6 Billion for Fast Food Every Year?"
   (b) "Why Americans Eat So Much Fast Food."
   (c) "The Pervasiveness of Fast Food Restaurants."
   (d) "A McDonald's or a Burger King on Every Block."

3. Taken together, what idea do sentences 3 through 6 support? _____

   _____

4. Look again at the details in sentence 7. Which of these ideas do they support?
   (a) Teenagers are exploited in the fast food industry.
   (b) Fast food restaurants are clean and sanitary.
   (c) Fast food restaurants are uniform, and they all operate alike.
   (d) Fast food restaurants offer inexpensive food served quickly.

5. Label the following sentences from paragraph 1 as follows: MAIN (main idea); MA (major support); or MI (minor support).

   sentence 1 _____   sentence 2 _____   sentence 3 _____

   sentence 4 _____   sentence 5 _____   sentence 6 _____

Online Learning Center

This information appears in the paperback edition of *Blood River* by British journalist Tim Butcher:

Ever since Stanley first charted its mighty river in the 1870s, the Congo has epitomized the dark and turbulent history of a failed continent. However, its troubles only served to increase the interest of Daily Telegraph correspondent Tim Butcher, who was sent to cover Africa in 2000. Before long he became obsessed with the idea of recreating Stanley's original expedition—but travelling alone.

Despite warnings, Butcher spent years poring over colonial-era maps and wooing rebel leaders before making his will and venturing to the Congo's eastern border. He passed through once thriving cities of this country and saw the marks left behind by years of abuse and misrule. Almost, 2,500 harrowing miles later, he reached the Atlantic Ocean, a thinner and a wiser man.

More information about this engrossing book, including maps, reviews, and Butcher's blog, is online at www.bloodriver.co.uk/.

Selection 3

This excerpt from *Blood River* describes a typical village in the Congo, the adjective form of which is *Congolese*.

_____ There is something primordial about Congolese villages. _____ The villagers themselves wear modern clothes, often in tatters, but modern nevertheless in that they are factory-made and delivered by the occasional trader who ventures along the river. _____ But the houses are at the base level of simplicity. _____ There is not a single pane of glass, metal hinge, cement plinth or fitting that connects this place with the modern era. _____ There is no litter, no plastic bags, empty cans or cigarette butts. _____ Without any painted signs, it is a place of browns, greens and duns, a settlement built in the jungle and out of the jungle, utterly separate from the modern world.

The doors are made of split cane, held together by a rope of woven vines and kept in place by wooden sticks. The walls are mud thrown against a cane trellis, baked hard by the sun and fissured with a crazy paving of cracks so intricate it looks almost man-made. And the roofs consist of layers of wide, dry banana leaves held down by lengths of split bamboo.

This region is one of the rare places in the world that fails what I called the Coca-Cola test. The test is simple: can you buy a Coke? I have been to many remote places where Coke is an expensive and rare luxury, but it is still almost always possible to find a trader who, for a price, can procure me a Coke. Out here on the upper Congo River, where a hundred years ago a Belgian hunter could buy ferry tickets, I could no more buy a Coke in 2004 than fly to the moon.

Tim Butcher, *Blood River: A Journey to Africa's Broken Heart*

A. Vocabulary

Each of these italicized vocabulary words from the passage is followed by two or more dictionary definitions. Choose the definition appropriate for the context.

1. something *primordial*
   (a) happening first in sequence of time; original.
   (b) primary or fundamental.
   (c) characteristic of the earliest stage of development.
2. *ventures* along the river
   (a) takes a risk, dares.
   (b) proceeds despite possible dangers or risks.
3. cement *plinth*
   (a) block or slab upon which a pedestal or statue is placed.
   (b) a continuous line of stones supporting a wall.
   (c) a square base, usually for a vase.
4. What is somewhat unusual about the word *fissured* in the second paragraph? What does it mean? _____

    _____

B. Content and Structure

1. The first sentence of the passage states the main idea. Underline the topic once and the controlling idea twice. "There is something primordial about Congolese villages."
2. In relation to the main idea stated above, label the remaining sentences in the first paragraph according to whether they represent major support (MA) or minor support (MI).
3. Look again at the details Butcher provides in the second paragraph in which he describes the features of Congolese houses. What is the implied idea behind them?

    _____

4. Explain in your own words the Coca-Cola test.

    _____

    What point about the Congo is Butcher making by citing its failure to pass this test?

    _____

PRACTICE ESSAY

From *Among the Thugs*
Bill Buford

In Great Britain the word football *refers to the game Americans and Canadians call* soccer. *European soccer matches are notoriously rowdy, and British football fans have perhaps the worst reputations of all Europeans in this regard.*

Many British football club members follow their local teams as they compete all over Europe, drinking, picking fights, and engaging in public drunkenness, violence, and lawlessness. In his 2001 book Among the Thugs, *from which this selection comes, Bill Buford writes a personal account describing the phenomenon of crowd violence and British hooliganism. Buford spent several months in England traveling around with two or three footfall clubs, observing their fans' behavior and the crowd mentality that marks it. He notes that these fans tend to be working-class people who engage in these activities for weekend entertainment.*

Bill Buford is now a staff writer for The New Yorker, *where he was fiction editor for eight years. He was also the founding editor of* Granta *magazine and publisher of* Granta Books.*

Preview Questions

1. How, generally, do American crowds behave at athletic events? Have you ever witnessed a crowd's becoming out of control? If so, how did the crowd's members behave?
2. What are some other instances, besides soccer matches, where crowd mentality takes over?

1   It is not uncommon, in any sport, to see spectators behaving in a way that would be uncharacteristic of them in any other context: embracing, shouting, swearing, kissing, dancing in jubilation. It is the thrill of the sport, and expressing the thrill is as important as witnessing it. But there is no sport in which the act of being a spectator is as *constantly* physical as watching a game of English football on the terraces. The physicalness is insistent; any observer not familiar with the game would say that it is outright brutal. In fact, those who do not find it brutal are those so familiar with the traditions of attending an English football match, so certain in the knowledge of what is expected of them, that they are incapable of seeing how deviant their behavior is—even in the most ordinary things. The first time I attended White Hart Lane on my own, everyone made for the exit within seconds of the match ending: I looked at the thing and couldn't imagine an exit more dangerous—an impossibly narrow passageway with very steep stairs on the other side. There was no waiting; there was also no choice, and this peculiar mad rush of people actually lifted me up off my feet and carried me forward. I had no control over where I was going. Stampede was the word that came to mind. I was forced up against the barrier, danger looming on the other side, was crushed against it, wriggled sideways to keep from bruising my ribs, and then, just as suddenly, was popped out, stumbling, as the others around me

stumbled, to keep from falling down the remaining stairs. I looked up behind me: everyone was grimacing and swearing; someone, having been elbowed in the face, was threatening to throw a punch. What was this all about? This was not an important moment in the game: it was the act of leaving it. This, I thought, is the way animals behave, but the thought was not a metaphoric one. This was genuinely the way animals behave—herd animals. Sheep behave this way—cattle, horses.

2   At the heart of any discussion about crowds is the moment when many, many different people cease being many, many different people and become only one thing—a crowd. There is the phrase, becoming "one with the crowd." In part, it is a matter of language: when the actions of diverse individuals are similar and coherent enough that you must describe them as the actions of one body, with a singular subject and a singular verb. They are . . . It is . . . The many people are . . . The crowd is . . . The English football game expects the spectator to become *one* with the crowd; in a good football game, a game with "atmosphere," the spectator assumes it: it is one of the things he has paid for. But, even here, it is more than an ordinary crowd experience.

3   It is an experience of constant physical contact and one that the terraces are designed to concentrate. The terraces look like animal pens and, like animal pens, provide only the most elementary accommodation: a gate that is locked shut after the spectators are admitted; a fence to keep them from leaving the area or spilling on to the pitch; a place for essential refreshment—to deal with elementary thirst and hunger; a place to pee and shit. I recall attending the Den at Millwall, the single toilet facility overflowing, and my feet slapping around in the urine that came pouring down the concrete steps of the terrace, the crush so great that I had to clinch my toes to keep my shoes from being pulled off, horrified by the prospect of my woollen socks soaking up this cascading pungent liquid still warm and steaming in the cold air. The conditions are appalling but essential: it is understood that anything more civilized would diffuse the experience. It seems fitting that, in some grounds, once all the supporters have left in their herdlike stampede, the terraces are cleaned by being hosed down: again, not just the images but the essential details are those of an animal pen. That is what the terraces offer, not just the crowd experience but the herd experience, with more intensity than any other sport, with more intensity than any other moment in a person's life—week after week.

4   Here, in Cambridge, on a Tuesday night, me a stranger among strangers: the physicalness was constant; it was inescapable—unless you literally escaped by leaving. You could feel, and you had no choice but to feel, every important moment of play—through the crowd. A shot on goal was a felt experience. With each effort, the crowd audibly drew in its breath, and then, after another athletic save, exhaled with equal

exaggeration. And each time the people around me expanded, their rib cages noticeably inflating, and we were pressed more closely together. They had tensed up—their arm muscles flexed slightly and their bodies stiffened, or they might stretch their necks forward, trying to determine in the strange, shadowless electronic night-light if this shot was the shot that would result in a goal. You could feel the anticipation of the crowd on all sides of your body as a series of sensations.

5   Physical contact to this extent is unusual in any culture. In England, where touch is not a social custom and where even a handshake can be regarded as intrusive, contact of this kind is exceptional—unless you become a member of the crowd.

6   When I arrived at this match, coming straight from a day of working in an office, my head busy with office thoughts and concerns that were distinctly my own, I was not, and could not imagine becoming "one" with any crowd. It was windy and cold and that biting easterly weather was felt by *me* personally—in *my* bones. I was, in what I was sensing and thinking, completely intact as an individual. And it was *me,* an individual, who was then crushed on all sides by strangers, noticing their features, their peculiarities, their smells—*except* that, once the match began, something changed.

7   As the match progressed, I found that I was developing a craving for a goal. As its promises and failures continued to be expressed through the bodies of the people pressed against me, I had a feeling akin to an appetite, increasingly more intense, of anticipation, waiting for, hoping for, wanting one of those shots to get past the Millwall goalkeeper. The business of watching the match had started to exclude other thoughts. It was involving so many aspects of my person—what I saw, smelled, said, sang, moaned, what I was feeling up and down my body—that I was becoming a different person from the one who had entered the ground: I was ceasing to be me. There wasn't one moment when I stopped noticing myself; there was only a realization that for a period of time I hadn't been. The match had succeeded in dominating my senses and had raised me, who had never given a serious thought to the fate of Cambridge United, to a state of very heightened feeling.

8   And then the game—having succeeded in apprehending me so—played with me as it played with everyone else. It teased and manipulated and encouraged and frustrated. It had engendered this heightened feeling and, equally, the expectation that it would be satisfied: that there would be gratification—or not. That the team would score—or be scored against. That there would be victory—or defeat. Climax—or disappointment. Release: But what happens when all that energy, concentrated so deep into the heart of the heart of the crowd, is not let go?

9   At ninety minutes, there was the whistle. There was no score. There would be extra time.

5. Look again at the two sentences that comprise paragraph 5. With respect to the main idea of the essay, label them as major support (MA) or minor support (MI).

(a) _____ Physical contact to this extent is unusual in any culture.

(b) _____ In England, where touch is not a social custom and where even a handshake can be regarded as intrusive, contact of this kind is exceptional—unless you become a member of the crowd.

6. Why does Buford end the essay as he does? What feeling in the reader is he trying to appeal to? _____

D. *Questions for Discussion and Analysis*

1. Is Buford's description of English football matches primarily favorable or unfavorable? What evidence can you locate to support your assessment?

2. As Buford has described it, how does a crowd behave? What are its characteristics?

3. Soccer is not a popular sport in the United States, at least not the way it is in Latin America, Europe, Africa, and elsewhere. What factors do you think account for this relative indifference to soccer?

ON THE WEB

- Violence among sports fans is not limited to British football enthusiasts. American sports, in particular football and baseball, have seen their share of thuggish behavior among fans, often fueled by alcohol. Do some research on this subject. Begin by typing in "sports fans violence" in the search box of Google or your favorite search engine. The late sociologist Irving Goldaber, director of the Center for the Study of Crowd and Spectator Behavior in Miami, Florida, also did a great deal of research in this area.

- After the Canucks lost in Game 7 to the Boston Bruins in the 2011 Stanley Cup finals, residents of Vancouver, Canada, went on a rampage. An account of the riot by Canucks' fans and an analysis of how a crowd can become a mob in an instant was published in the *Los Angeles Times* (June 17, 2011). In the search box of your favorite search engine, type in "Sam Farmer, Sports Can Be an Excuse to Riot, Los Angeles Times."

ON DVD

- *Green Street Hooligans* (2005) stars Elijah Wood as a former Harvard student who was kicked out on phony drug charges, which he is unable to fight. He flees to England to stay with his sister, who is married to an Englishman. There he becomes enamored with the Green Street Elite, a thuggish and very violent bunch of football fans who change his life.

Reading between the Lines: Making Accurate Inferences

CHAPTER OBJECTIVES

Chapter 3 is a crucial chapter as you move beyond basic comprehension and learn to see beneath the literal and to see implications in your reading. You will practice making inferences with material of varying levels of difficulty in this chapter, which includes the following topics:

- Facts and inferences
- Inferences defined
- Inferences in the real world
- Problems with inferences
- Using evidence to make inferences
- Making open-ended inferences
- Making inferences in literature
- Making inferences with visual material

■ FACTS AND INFERENCES

We must first distinguish between inferences and facts. A fact is a verifiable piece of information; that is, it can be duplicated, measured, confirmed in other sources, demonstrated, or proved. If I say that our living room is 20 feet long, the matter can easily be proved or disproved with a tape measure. Here are three more facts:

- Eucalyptus trees are native to Australia.
- The gestation period for an elephant is 18 months.
- Pomegranates contain more antioxidants than bananas.

Inferences are *derived* from facts. From the above facts, we might infer the following:

- Eucalyptus trees probably grow well in Australia.
- The size of an animal determines the length of gestation. (For this inference, we draw on common knowledge: The human gestation period is nine months; an elephant's is 18.)
- We should eat more pomegranates to maintain good health.

■ DEFINITION OF INFERENCES

William Lutz has defined an inference as "a statement about the unknown based on the known."[1] We make inferences by reading between the lines, by connecting facts to make sense of them when no explanation is offered, or by drawing a conclusion about a future course of action. In the real world we infer all the time. Consider this example.

Rumors about the doping scandal in the world of professional cycling began to emerge. Lance Armstrong, seven-time winner of the prestigious Tour de France, had been accused of taking performance-enhancing drugs, which the International Cycling Union specifically bans. Two banned practices are wearing testosterone patches and receiving red-blood transfusions, which boost a rider's red-blood-cell count, giving him more strength during grueling mountain rides. Recently, Floyd Landis, formerly a professional cyclist, went public to expose not only his own use of performance-enhancing drugs but that of Lance Armstrong and other cyclists, as well.

In a *Wall Street Journal* article, "Blood Brothers" (July 3–4, 2010), published just before the 2010 Tour de France began, sports writers

[1]William Lutz was a linguist and professor of English at Rutgers University. This definition comes from his essay "Abstracting Our Way into Doublespeak," from *The New Doublespeak* (1996).

A mystery, a romance novel, an adventure novel, a science fiction work, a horror novel

_____

_____

E. Each December, researchers at Google pore through the millions and millions of search terms that people used over the course of the year to get a sense of the Zeitgeist, German for "spirit of the times." In December 2010, Google released this list of the fastest rising search terms. If you are not familiar with one or more of these items, do your own search to identify it. Then, considering all ten items taken together, draw a conclusion about the direction American culture is headed in based on this information.

chatroulette	ipad	justin bieber	nicki minaj	friv
myxer	katy perry	twitter	gamezer	facebook

Next, using Google's search box, enter this string: "top search terms, _____." In the blank space, insert the current year. Study the list. Has the trend observed in 2010 changed or not? If so, how?

From these examples, you can see that inferences are part of the way we form judgments and draw conclusions in the real world. They each depend on facts, but they are not facts themselves.

Practice Exercise 2

Carefully read the following report and the observations based on it. On the basis of the information presented, indicate whether you think the observations are true, false, or doubtful. Circle "T" if the observation is definitely true, circle "F" if the observation is definitely false, and circle "?" if the observation may be either true or false. Judge each observation in order.[3]

A well-liked college teacher had just completed making up the final examinations and had turned off the lights in the office. Just then a tall, broad figure with dark glasses appeared and demanded the examination. The professor opened the drawer. Everything in the drawer was picked up and the individual ran down the corridor. The dean was notified immediately.

1. The thief was tall, broad, and wore dark glasses.   **T   F   ?**
2. The professor turned off the lights.   **T   F   ?**
3. A tall, broad figure demanded the examination.   **T   F   ?**

[3]This exercise is adapted from Joseph A. DeVito, _General Semantics: Guide and Workbook_. The test is based on one developed by William Honey, _Communication and Organizational Behavior_, 3rd ed. (Irwin, 1973).

4. The examination was picked up by someone.   **T**   **F**   **?**
5. The examination was picked up by the professor. **T**   **F**   **?**
6. A tall, broad figure appeared after the professor
    turned off the lights in the office.   **T**   **F**   **?**
7. The man who opened the drawer was the professor. **T**   **F**   **?**
8. The professor ran down the corridor.   **T**   **F**   **?**
9. The drawer was never actually opened.   **T**   **F**   **?**
10. In this report three persons are referred to.   **T**   **F**   **?**

Answers

1. **?** There is no evidence that there was a thief.
2. **?** Are the college teacher and the professor the same person?
3. **T** There is an exact statement in the story that proves this to be true.
4. **?** There is no mention of the examination being or not being picked up by someone.
5. **?** We don't know if anyone picked up the examination.
6. **?** We don't know who turned off the lights.
7. **?** We don't know if the professor was a man or a woman.
8. **?** We don't know who ran down the corridor.
9. **F** The drawer was opened.
10. **?** There could have been three or four people: We don't know if the professor and the college teacher were the same person.

■ PROBLEMS WITH INFERENCES

The foregoing little exercise reveals at least three difficulties with inferences:

- We may make assumptions that get in the way of making accurate inferences.
- We may not read carefully enough or pay close enough attention to new vocabulary.
- We may indulge in stereotyping. This problem is particularly evident in question 7, if we incorrectly infer that a professor is more likely to be a man than a woman.

In the real world, the same holds true: The more we get carried away with our assumptions and make inferences based on facts we do not have, on an isolated fact, or on facts we choose to ignore, the less probable it is that our inferences are correct.

■ USING EVIDENCE TO MAKE INFERENCES

The crucial element in learning to make accurate inferences is to consider carefully the writer's words—what he or she surely intends to suggest but does not say directly. This constitutes the **evidence**—the justification for the inference. As you saw from the foregoing exercise, we should not read into the writer's words beyond what they suggest or imply. Relying on our necessarily limited experience may lead us astray from the writer's real intentions, with the result that we misread or misinterpret. Thus, in this textbook, it is safer to restrict your answers only to what the writer suggests, and not base them on something you have read or experienced outside the text. In other words, an inference must be tied to the evidence.

Initially in the inference exercises, you will label inference questions in three ways.

- **Probably accurate (PA).** This kind of inference follows from the facts the writer presents or it is strongly implied by the author's words. We have enough information to say that the inference is most likely accurate.
- **Probably inaccurate (PI).** An inaccurate inference misstates or distorts the writer's words and observations.
- **Not in the passage (NP).** These are inferences that you can't reasonably make because they're not implied in the passage. Either there is insufficient evidence or there is no information in the passage to determine whether the inference is accurate or not.

Of course, when you read on your own, you would not label a writer's ideas in this way. You are asked to do so here as an intellectual exercise to distinguish between appropriate and inappropriate inferences. To begin, read these two short passages and label the inference statements as directed. Then study the answers and explanations that follow. The first is a short excerpt from Tobias Wolff's engaging autobiography, *This Boy's Life*. In it Wolff describes the grades he received while attending the public high school in Concrete, a town in eastern Washington State.

> I brought home good grades at first. They were a fraud—I copied other kids' homework on the bus down from Chinook and studied for tests in the hallways as I walked from class to class. After the first marking period I didn't bother to do that much. I stopped studying altogether. Then I was given C's instead of A's, yet no one at home ever knew that my grades had fallen. The report cards were made out, incredibly enough, in pencil, and I owned some pencils myself.

Tobias Wolff, *This Boy's Life*

On the basis of the evidence in the paragraph, mark these statements as follows: PA (probably accurate), PI (probably inaccurate), or NP (not in the passage).

1. _____ Students at the high school in Concrete had to work hard to receive A's.

2. _____ Wolff wanted to get good grades so that he could go to college.

3. _____ The narrator continued to receive good grades only because he erased the teacher's marks and changed them to higher ones.

4. _____ The teachers were naive to record students' grades in pencil.

Let's look at these inferences and their answers one by one while at the same time considering the evidence in the paragraph. Inference 1 is most likely inaccurate based on Wolff's description of the amount of studying he did to get good grades (not to mention his cheating). Surely even the easiest test would require more studying than one would do in a few minutes walking from class to class. Since there is no information in the paragraph about hopes for college, Inference 2 should be marked NP. Inference 3 is probably accurate, since, as Wolff so succinctly puts it, "I owned some pencils myself." This reference to pencils suggests, without his stating it directly, that he erased the low grades and wrote in higher ones. Thus, Inference 4 is also accurate. In this case, it is imperative to know that "naive" means lacking worldly experience and understanding, which certainly describes teachers who think that grades written in pencil couldn't be tampered with! Often knowing the meaning of an unfamiliar word is crucial in making correct inferences. Here is a second passage. This one represents a parable, a little story written to illustrate a moral truth.

A customs officer observes a truck pulling up at the border. Suspicious, he orders the driver out and searches the vehicle. He pulls off panels, bumpers, and wheel cases but finds not a single scrap of contraband, whereupon, still suspicious but at a loss to know where else to search, he waves the driver through. The next week, the same driver arrives. Again the official searches, and again finds nothing illicit. Over the years, the official tries full-body searches, X rays, and sonar, anything he can think of, and each week the same man drives up, but no mysterious cargo ever appears, and each time, reluctantly, the customs man waves the driver on.

Finally, after many years, the officer is about to retire. The driver pulls up.

"I know you're a smuggler," the customs officer says. "Don't bother denying it. But damned if I can figure out what you've been smuggling all these years. I'm leaving now. I swear to you I can do you no harm. Won't you please tell me what you've been smuggling?"

"Trucks," the driver says.

Todd Gitlin, "Trucks,"
Media Unlimited: How the Torrent of Images and Sounds Overwhelms Our Lives

On the basis of the evidence in the parable, label these inferences as follows: PA (probably accurate), PI (probably inaccurate), or NP (not in the passage).

1. _____ The customs officer made a lifetime career out of trying to catch the truck driver smuggling illegal goods.

2. _____ The first time the customs officer encountered the truck driver, he had good reason to be suspicious.

3. _____ The truck driver had been smuggling illicit goods for many years, but they were so cleverly hidden that the customs officer never found them.

4. _____ Sometimes in their fixation on observing small details, people miss the obvious.

Again, let us examine each inference in light of the evidence in the passage. Inference 1 should be marked PA. The phrases "over the years" and "after many years" strongly suggest that the customs officer indeed made a "lifetime career" out of trying to catch the truck driver. This type of inference is called a *local inference* because it is directly tied to the evidence. Inference 2 should be marked NP. Gitlin does not offer any particular reason for the customs officer's suspicion. Perhaps customs officers are just naturally suspicious; after all, their job is to identify smugglers. Inference 3 should be marked PI. After all those years of careful searches, the officer surely would have discovered contraband concealed in the truck. The last inference should be marked PA, because this is the lesson that the parable is meant to illustrate. We call this a *global inference*—a logical conclusion derived from a reading as a whole.

As you can see in the two preceding examples, making accurate inferences requires you to connect details, to infer explanations when the writer offers none, and to draw logical conclusions. In sum, the inference must be tied to some evidence. In the following practice exercise, complete these inference questions. Be sure to locate the evidence that leads to the inference and be prepared to defend your choice.

Practice Exercise 3

A. This excerpt describes the poet Gary Soto's early experiences in elementary school.

For four years I attended St. John's Catholic School where short nuns threw chalk at me, chased me with books cocked over their heads, squeezed me into cloak closets and, on slow days, asked me to pop erasers and to wipe the blackboard clean. Finally, in the fifth grade, my mother sent me to Jefferson Elementary. The Principal, Mr. Buckalew, kindly ushered me to the fifth grade teachers, Mr. Stendhal and Mrs. Sloan. We stood in the hallway with the principal's hand on my shoulder. Mr. Stendhal asked what book I had read in the fourth grade, to which, after a dark and squinting deliberation, I answered: *The Story of the United States Marines*.

Mr. Stendhal and Mrs. Sloan looked at one another with a "you take him" look. Mr. Buckalew lifted his hand from my shoulder and walked slowly away.

Gary Soto, *Living Up the Street*

1. Which of the following can you infer about the author?
   (a) He was a model student.
   (b) He had a reputation among teachers for being a troublemaker.
   (c) He had been asked to leave Catholic school.
   (d) He enjoyed public school more than Catholic school.

2. What inference can you make about the book Soto says he read in fourth grade, *The Story of the United States Marines*?
   (a) It was assigned reading at his former school.
   (b) He probably hadn't read it.
   (c) He probably had read it.
   (d) There is no way to tell whether he had read it or not.

3. What inference can you make about his new teachers, Mr. Stendhal and Mrs. Sloan?
   (a) They were impressed with Soto's answer.
   (b) Soto ended up in Mrs. Sloan's class.
   (c) Soto ended up in Mr. Stendhal's class.
   (d) They both thought Soto was something of a wise guy.

   B. The following concerns the criminal justice system in Saudi Arabia. The information was compiled by Human Rights Watch, a nonprofit group dedicated to fostering human rights throughout the world in a report titled "Adults Before Their Time: Children in Saudi Arabia's Criminal Justice System." What follows is a summary of this report.

Suffer, Little Children

In Saudi Arabia, breaking the law can lead to the chopping block for a public beheading—even for minors, according to a new report. The first fact-finding visit by a human-rights group allowed by the Saudi government turned up disturbing evidence about the country's justice system: children under 18 are routinely tried as adults, with potential sentences of flogging, amputation, or death; legal counsel is often unavailable for youth offenders; and juvenile-detention facilities are so overcrowded and poorly supervised that minors sometimes end up in the some cells as hardened criminals. Many of the tens of thousands of children trafficked into the country—for use as beggars or for sexual exploitation—end up on the streets, where they're treated as criminals and risk deportation. Youths can be detained for exchanging phone numbers with the opposite sex, and girls can face prosecution for "seclusion," or being alone with a male who's not a relative. The authors report that at least 12 children have been sentenced to death in recent years, and that at least three were executed in 2007.

"Suffer, Little Children," *The Atlantic*

On the basis on the evidence in the passage, mark these statements as follows: PA (probably accurate), PI (probably inaccurate), or NP (not in the passage).

1. _____ Capital punishment in Saudi Arabia is administered by beheading.
2. _____ Saudi Arabia has permitted other human-rights groups to investigate abuses in the past.
3. _____ Trafficking for begging and sexual exploitation affects children more than adults in Saudi Arabia.
4. _____ Relations between the sexes are strictly monitored in Saudi Arabia.
5. _____ The term "seclusion" refers to the type of confinement criminals, including children, are subjected to in prison.

C.

By the end of the 1860s, when they were all the rage, bicycles were called velocipedes. They were nicknamed bone-shakers. Cartoonists made fun of people falling off bicycles all the time, of bicyclists getting stuck in packs behind horses and carriages, of bicyclists crowding onto the very few paved roads. Most bicyclists lived in cities; they toured into the countryside on the weekends. As a group, they petitioned for better roads around the city and into the country, establishing, by the 1880s and 1890s, what became known as the Good Roads Movement.

Robert Sullivan, *Cross Country*

Mark these statements as you did before.

1. _____ Bicycles, or velocipedes, were called bone-shakers because they were poorly designed.
2. _____ There is a strong connection between the Good Roads Movement and the increased popularity of bicycles at the end of the nineteenth century.
3. _____ The writer is a bicycle enthusiast.

D.

Sometime during the late 1980s—no one can pinpoint the exact date—Ron Magruder, the president of the thriving Olive Garden chain of Italian restaurants, received a telephone call from a dissatisfied customer. The call had been patched all the way up to Magruder because it was so . . . different. The caller, named Larry, wasn't complaining about the food or the service or the prices. Instead, Larry was upset that he could no longer fit into any of the chairs in his local Olive Garden.

"I had to wait more than an hour and half to get a table," Larry told Magruder. "But then I found that there wasn't a single booth or chair where I could sit comfortably."

Magruder, a heavyset man easily moved to enthusiasm, was sympathetic to Larry's plaint. And as president, he could do something about it. He had his staff contact the company that manufactured the chairs for the chain and order a thousand large-size chairs. He then had these distributed, three each, to every Olive Garden restaurant in the nation. It was, as Magruder later told the eminent restaurant business journalist Charles Bernstein, a perfect example of his management philosophy: . . .

Greg Critser, *Fat Land: How Americans Became the Fattest People in the World*

The passage ends with a quotation from Ron Magruder, which has been deleted. Which of the following quotations is most likely what Magruder told Charles Bernstein?

(a) "These customers are a pain in the neck. As president of Olive Garden, I'm not going to cater to their every little demand. Why doesn't he just lose some weight?"

(b) "We are going to go the extra mile for any customer, no matter what the situation is."

(c) "If every restaurant provided special chairs for its customers, we'd all soon be broke."

What specific evidence in the passage leads you to this conclusion? _____

_____

_____

■ MAKING OPEN-ENDED INFERENCES

Making *open-ended inferences* asks you to draw your own inferences and state them in your own words, which is a more realistic way that we make inferences in our everyday reading. Study this first example, in which the writer John Hildebrand describes a horse named Blue.

Not much bigger than a pony, Blue stood fourteen hands high and weighed 950 pounds. His mother was a bucking horse bought from a rodeo, mean and ornery as they come, her history written in overlapping brands that covered her flanks.

John Hildebrand, *Mapping the Farm*

Why did Blue's mother have so many brands? _____

_____

_____

(Making the correct inference here depends on your knowing the meaning of the word *brand* as it pertains to livestock. If you are unsure, check the dictionary.)

**Practice
Exercise 4**

A. In this first passage, David Lamb describes a cross-country bicycle trip he made from Virginia to California.

Here he contrasts the typical overweight American's concern with dieting and his own nutritional intake while on the road.

> Between 1980 and 1991—when the diet business was in full bloom—the average adult American put on eight pounds. That, says the National Center for Health Statistics, is the equivalent of an extra one million tons of fat on the waistline of a nation where one in three persons is certifiably overweight. Ironically, the more we spend trying to get thin—$15 billion a year on diet soft drinks alone, another $4 billion on stuff like Lean Cuisine and pseudo-food appetite suppressants—the plumper we become. Something is clearly out of whack. These contradictions were of no concern to me, however, because I had learned the secret of gluttony without guilt. Day after day I started the morning with French toast or pancakes, enjoyed apple pie with double scoops of ice cream during pre-noon coffee breaks, drank milk shakes, Hawaiian Punch and chocolate milk by the bucketful, snacked on three or four candy bars in the afternoon and often had room for a hot dog or two before I started thinking about dinner. Unlike the rest of America, the more I ate, the less I weighed. I could eat two pieces of coconut custard pie at 11 A.M. and within an hour on the road burn off the 450 calories and then some. By the time I reached western Arkansas, the love handles on my waist had disappeared and I had to tighten my belt an extra notch to keep my pants up.

David Lamb, *Over the Hills*

According to Lamb's experiences (and aside from overeating), why are so many Americans overweight? _____

B. California's Golden Gate Bridge, which connects San Francisco and Marin County, has been the site of over 1,000 suicides since it opened in 1937. In a lengthy *New Yorker* article about the bridge, Tad Friend ends with this anecdote.

The bridge comes into the lives of all Bay Area residents sooner or later, and it often stays. Dr. Jerome Motto, who has been part of two failed suicide-barrier coalitions, is now retired and living in San Mateo. When I visited him there, we spent three hours talking about the bridge. Motto had a patient who committed suicide from the Golden Gate in 1963, but the jump that affected him most occurred in the seventies. "I went to this guy's apartment afterward with the assistant medical examiner," he told me. "The guy was in this thirties, lived alone, pretty bare apartment. He'd written a note and left it on his bureau. It said, 'I'm going to walk to the bridge. If one person smiles at me on the way, I will not jump.'"

Motto sat back in his chair. "That was it," he said. "It's so needless, the number of people who are lost."

Tad Friend, "Jumpers," *The New Yorker*

What can you infer about the reason Dr. Motto's patient committed suicide?

_____

_____

Why do you think the author ends his article with this anecdote? _____

_____

_____

C. John McWhorter is a linguist at UC Berkeley.

Rebracketing: The Story of Gladly, the Cross-Eyed Bear

My mother used to recall how, when her church choir would sing the hymn "Gladly the Cross I'd Bear" when she was a little girl, she thought they were singing about a little storybook bear named Gladly, who was afflicted with an ocular misalignment. The problem here was my mother misassigning functions to the words: the adjective *cross-eyed* instead of *cross I'd* and the animal *bear* instead of the verb *bear*. Language change is driven in large part by misassignments of a similar nature, although on a less fantastical scale.

It starts with little stuff. Did you ever wonder what the *nick* in *nickname* was? What's "nick" about the name? As it happens, the word began as *ekename*; in earlier English, *eke* meant "also." Now that made sense—your "also" name. Through time, however, because the word was used so often after *an—an ekename*—people began to interpret the *n* in *an* as the first letter of the following word. Hence *a nickname*.

What had occurred is a "rebracketing": what began as [an] [ekename] became [a] [nickname]. *Apron* began as *napron*, borrowed from the French word *naperron* for "napkin." Through the same process that created *nickname, a napron* became *an apron.*

John McWhorter, *The Power of Babel*

1. When my brother was around 7 years old, he asked me what the word "donzerly" meant. When I asked him where he had heard that word, he said, "You know, the 'donzerly' light." (He meant "the dawn's early light" from the national anthem.) Which of the two concepts that McWhorter discusses in the above passage—misassignment or rebracketing—is "donzerly" an example of?_____

2. Explain the linguistic concept of rebracketing, using the change in the word "napron" to "apron." _____

_____

_____

_____

D. Probably all of us have heard the truism that no two snowflakes are identical. Cullen Murphy explains where this idea originated and comments on its accuracy.

For all the scientific awareness of the symmetrical character of snow crystals, the ubiquity of their popular image—the one we see in children's paper cutouts and on bags of ice and signs for motels that have air-conditioning—is a relatively recent phenomenon. What snowflakes actually looked like was not widely known until the middle of the nineteenth century, when the book *Cloud Crystals,* with sketches by "A Lady," was published in the United States. The lady had caught snowflakes on a black surface and then observed them with a magnifying glass. In 1885 Wilson Alwyn ("Snowflake") Bentley, of Jericho, Vermont, began taking photographs of snowflakes through a microscope. Thousands of Bentley's photomicrographs were eventually collected in his book *Snow Crystals* (1931). The fact that not one of the snowflakes photographed by Bentley was identical to another is probably the basis for the idea that no two snowflakes are ever exactly the same—an idea that is in fact unverifiable.

Cullen Murphy, "In Praise of Snow," *The Atlantic Monthly*

The writer ends by saying "the idea that no two snowflakes are ever exactly the same" is "in fact unverifiable." Why is this statement likely to be true?

_____

_____

■ MAKING INFERENCES IN TEXTBOOK MATERIAL

The straightforward presentation of material in textbooks would suggest that there is little left to the imagination. Textbooks are the perfect example of expository writing whose purpose is to inform and to present information. Still, even textbook material requires one to make accurate inferences.

Practice Exercise 5

The following from an introductory broadcasting textbook represents part of a chapter on the effects of electronic media. Read the passage and then answer the questions that follow.

Issues: How Much Is Too Much?

The newspaper headlines were certainly alarming: "Violence linked to one hour of TV"; "Hour a day the safe limit"; "More than one hour of TV a day turns teens to violence"; "Too much TV for young breeds violent adults." These headlines were typical of the news coverage that greeted the March 2002 publication of a survey in the journal *Science* that examined the link between television viewing and aggression in young people.

The study examined 700 people. It started in 1975, when most were about 14, and ended in 1993. The researchers interviewed the subjects four times during that 18-year period, grouping them into those who watched less than an hour of TV a day, 1-to-3-hour watchers, and 3-hour-plus watchers. Aggression was measured by asking the respondents and their mothers to report specific acts of violent behavior. The researchers also checked state and federal records to see whether respondents had been arrested for some violent crime.

The results noted that among those young people who watched less than an hour of TV per day when they were 14, only about 6 percent had committed aggressive acts by the ages of 16 to 22. On the other hand, among those who watched 1 to 3 hours of TV daily, the corresponding figure was nearly 23 percent. For those who watched more than 3 hours daily, the figure jumped to 29 percent.

This longitudinal panel study is impressive because it covers such a long period of time. In addition, the researchers controlled for other factors that might be related to aggression: low income, family neglect, prior history of violence, low parental education, and neighborhood violence. The link between TV watching and aggression persisted even after these factors were removed. The survey also provides evidence that the impact of viewing might extend well beyond adolescence into young adulthood.

The study's conclusions, however, should be taken with some skepticism. In the first place, the researchers measured overall TV viewing. They did not measure how many violent programs these young people watched. There's no reason to think that viewing 2 hours of situation comedy or 2 hours of the Discovery Channel should be linked to violence. The study would have been much stronger had the researchers established a link between aggression and specific programs that contained violence. Second, there were relatively few people (about 12 percent of the sample) who watched an hour or less of TV per day. This lack of viewing might be due to the fact that this group might be spending more time with their parents or who have parents who closely supervise their behavior. Those who watch a lot of TV might be spending their time away from their parents and parental supervision. In short, some other factor, not measured by the researchers, might be causing the relationship. This survey once again highlights how difficult it is to establish a causal link between TV viewing and violent behavior.

Joseph R. Dominick, Fritz Messere, and Barry L. Sherman,
Broadcasting, Cable, the Internet, and Beyond: An Introduction to Modern Electronic Media

Label these inferences PA, PI, or NP, as you did in the preceding exercises.

1. _____ The newspaper headlines announcing the results of the *Science* study were sensationalized and to some degree misrepresented its results.

2. _____ The 700 young people studied for the television-viewing habits were evenly divided between boys and girls.

3. _____ The purpose of the study was to investigate a possible link between the amount of violence the young people viewed on television and aggressive behavior.

4. _____ The link between the amount of television violence young viewers are exposed to and aggression is neither overwhelming nor completely convincing.

5. _____ The term "longitudinal," as the writers use it, most likely refers to a study conducted over many years.

6. _____ The textbook's authors are uncritically accepting of the study's results.

7. Which one of the following suggestions would have weakened the study's conclusions and the link between aggression and TV viewing if the researchers had included it in their interviews?

   (a) Having teens in the study fill out a TV-viewing log to record the programs they routinely watched.

   (b) Interviewing these adolescents' teachers to inquire about any violent tendencies they might have observed.

   (c) Interviewing more than 700 teenagers.

   (d) Asking the teen subjects how many hours a day they played violent video games.

   Defend your answer. _____

■ MAKING INFERENCES IN LITERATURE

When reading fiction—novels and short stories—delving into the characters' minds and into the significance of their actions inevitably involves making inferences. Trying to discern a character's essence, what makes a character "tick," involves reading carefully between the lines, looking at the specific details the writer has chosen, and assessing the relationship between the character and his or her surroundings and those he comes into contact with. In the next exercise, you will have an opportunity to practice making inferences from some literary excerpts.

A. This little excerpt is from Tom Rachman's recent best-selling novel, *The Imperfectionists* (2010). This short paragraph describes Kathleen Solson, editor-in-chief of an English-language daily newspaper in Rome. As you read it, consider what the narrator is implying about her character and about her values. (Note: Nigel is Kathleen's husband.)

> When she realizes that Nigel is having an affair, her first sentiment is satisfaction that she figured it out. Her second is that, despite all the palaver about betrayal, it doesn't feel so terrible. This is pleasing—it demonstrates a certain sophistication. She wonders if his fling might even serve her. In principle, she could leave him without compunction now, though she doesn't wish to. It also frees her from guilt about any infidelities she might wish to engage in. All in all, his affair might prove useful.
>
> Tom Rachman, *The Imperfectionists*

Kathleen's response to this news seems quite different from the way most wives would react if they discovered that their husbands were having an affair. From this brief description, we can infer that she is self-centered (the fact that she is impressed with having figured it out). Her admission that a certain betrayal has resulted is muted by the knowledge that his affair may actually be liberating to her. She can do as she pleases with impunity. Thus, we can infer that Kathleen lacks a moral compass, that she turns adversity to her advantage for selfish reasons. She is not a likable person.

Practice Exercise 6

A. In this excerpt from a novel, Trond, the 15-year-old narrator, his father, and Franz, a neighbor, are going logging in the rural area of Norway where they live. He describes this scene:

> . . . from among the tools I picked up a pike pole and hung a coil of rope over my shoulder, and my father took a pike pole too and two axes and a sheath knife, and Franz took a crowbar and a freshly sharpened saw, and all this we kept in the shed and more too: saws and hammers and two scythes and clamps and two planes and chisels of different sizes, and various files hung from nails in rows along the wall, and there were angle-irons and a good many tools whose use I did not know, for it was a well-equipped workshop my father had in that shed, and he loved those tools and sharpened them and polished them and soaked them with different oils so they would smell good and keep for a long time, and each and every thing had its appointed place where it hung or stood and was always ready for use.
>
> Per Petterson, *Out Stealing Horses*

What can you infer about the father from the description of the way he keeps the tools in his workshop?

The nearby town is still baffled by her strange behavior. As for the actress, she has said nothing about her experience in our area, except that she was unaccustomed to town life and was glad to be back where she belonged.

Based on your careful reading of the passage, answer these questions in your own words.

1. Why did the actress leave Hollywood? What was she trying to escape?

_____

_____

2. Why did the townspeople leave the actress alone, respect her privacy, and treat her as they would treat anyone else?

_____

_____

3. What is a little strange about the townspeople's decision to treat her as they would treat anyone else, according to the way the story is narrated?

_____

_____

4. Why did the actress erupt in the diner during a meal? Why did she characterize the townspeople as the "unfriendliest bunch of bastards she'd ever encountered?" What essential quality does this incident reveal about the actress's true character?

_____

_____

5. How would you characterize the actress's level of introspection? What conclusion does the narrative imply about celebrity status?

_____

_____

6. Why were the townspeople "baffled" by the actress's decision to move back to California? What were they apparently not aware of?

_____

_____

■ MAKING INFERENCES WITH VISUAL MATERIAL

Cartoons   Cartoons, especially political cartoons, often require one to make inferences.[5] A cartoon strips a situation down to its essential elements, and the careful reader must piece these elements together to make connections, especially if the cartoon doesn't include a caption. Cartoons on the editorial page of major metropolitan newspapers are especially effective at molding public opinion and commenting on the news of the day or on social trends in a humorous or ironic way. Study this *New Yorker* cartoon and then answer the question that follows it.

"That's what you're wearing?"

© Robert Leighton/The New Yorker Collection/www.cartoonbank.com

What does the pronoun "it" refer to in the phrase "It Starts"? _____

_____

[5]For further instruction in interpreting cartoons, see Chapter 10.

Gone?" *The Wall Street Journal*, February 19–20, 2011.) Study this graph and the comments that follow:

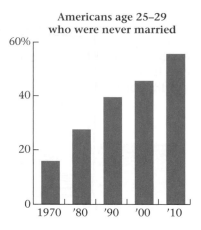

**Americans age 25–29
who were never married**

The title of the graph along the top horizontally is the subject. On the left are percentages ranging from 0 to 60, and the five bars represent percentages from 1970 to 2010, or 40 years. The graph leads us to this inference: The percentage of both men and women who have never married in their mid to late 20s has dramatically increased, from about 18 percent in 1970 to nearly 60 percent in 2010. However, and this is an important point, the graph does not allow us to infer why this is so. It presents only data. We can speculate, of course, but such speculation lies outside the graph's function.

Graphs and charts present data in a succinct and readable format. These visual elements accompany articles in magazines and newspapers or appear in textbooks to reinforce and clarify complex material. Since long lists of numbers and percentages are difficult to apprehend when printed as text, the chart or graph format allows the reader to see relationships and trends over a period of months or years, depending on the underlying idea of the article.[6]

**Practice
Exercise 8**

The following bar graph, which compiles research done by the Kaiser Family Foundation,[7] accompanied an Associated Press article, which summarizes the findings of the American Academy of Pediatrics concerning television viewing for young children. These physicians recommend that children under the age of 2 not watch television at all; in the accompanying article the Kaiser study reported that 19 percent of children under 2 have a television in their bedrooms.

In the three graphs that follow, consider these elements in this order: First look at the three shaded boxes on the left side and note what

---

[6]For further instruction in interpreting graphs and charts, see Chapter 8.
[7]The home page of the Kaiser Family Foundation is www.kff.org/

they indicate (three different activities in the typical day of children under 6). Then look at the three bars that represent the average amount of time spent doing three different activities, followed by a final line graph showing the most common reasons parents cite for putting a television in their child's bedroom. After you study this information, answer the questions that follow.

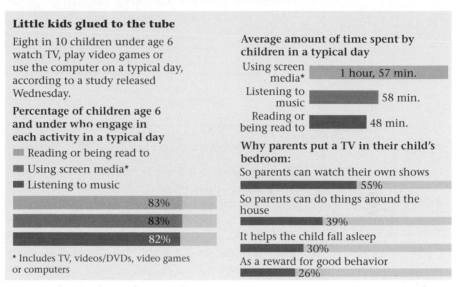

Little kids glued to the tube

Eight in 10 children under age 6 watch TV, play video games or use the computer on a typical day, according to a study released Wednesday.

Percentage of children age 6 and under who engage in each activity in a typical day

Reading or being read to
Using screen media*
Listening to music

83%
83%
82%

* Includes TV, videos/DVDs, video games or computers

Average amount of time spent by children in a typical day

Using screen media*   1 hour, 57 min.
Listening to music   58 min.
Reading or being read to   48 min.

Why parents put a TV in their child's bedroom:

So parents can watch their own shows
55%
So parents can do things around the house
39%
It helps the child fall asleep
30%
As a reward for good behavior
26%

Source: Kaiser Family Foundation   *Associated Press*

1. What difference is there in the percentages of children under 6 in a typical day who read or are read to, who use screen media (including TV, DVDs, and computers), and who listen to music?

    _____

2. What is the ratio between the amount of time children spend using screen media and reading or being read to on a typical day?

    _____

3. Consider the left-hand side of the chart again. What percentage of children under 6 do not use screen media in a typical day?

    _____

4. Study the line graph that summarizes parents' reasons for putting a TV in their children's bedrooms. Which is the most accurate conclusion that you can draw from these reasons?
    (a) Children demand a television for their rooms, and their parents give in.

(b) By putting a TV in their children's bedrooms, parents are encouraging their children to watch television.

(c) Parents have their children's best interests at heart in deciding to put a TV in their bedrooms.

(d) Young children can fall asleep more easily if they can watch television.

5. What information is missing from these graphs that a critical reader might want to know? _____

_____

_____

_____

Critical Thinking Exercise

Here are some headlines from various newspapers and websites that picked up Neergaard's Associated Press story. Put a check mark next to the headlines that seem accurate and objective and put a question mark next to those that seem questionable because they misrepresent the study's results. Consider only the information presented in the graph. Be prepared to defend your answers.

1. _____ "Many Parents Encourage Tots to Watch TV" (www.commonsensemedia.org)

2. _____ "Experts Debate Kids' Exposure to Television" (www.record-eagle.com)

3. _____ "Study: Parents Encourage Tots to Watch TV" (www.cbsnews.com)

4. _____ "Multimedia Babies: What's a Parent to Do?" (www.livescience.com)

5. _____ "Study Finds Tots Encouraged to Watch TV" (*Deseret News*, Salt Lake City)

6. _____ "83% of Little Kids Glued to Tube: Even Most Babies Watching TV" (*Chicago Sun-Times*)

7. _____ "TV, Video Big for 8 in 10 Tots" (*San Francisco Chronicle*)

■ CHAPTER EXERCISES

Selection 1   This excerpt comes from an article titled "Good Idea!"—a compendium of several offbeat suggestions to "fix the world" and to "spark your own creativity." This particular suggestion is called "Use Theater to Help Kids Settle Fights"; it was submitted by Michael Soth and posted on the Global Ideas Bank.

Michael Soth, an elementary school teacher in Oxford, England, was sick and tired of seeing his pupils get in fights. Trying a little socially inventive ingenuity, he drew on the writings of the Brazilian theatrical director Augusto Boal, whose work explores the boundaries between theater and social activism. Soth applied Boal's conflict-resolution tool called Forum Theater in his classroom.

When students fought, Soth assembled the entire class and had them reconstruct the fight stage by stage. When everyone agreed on what had happened, the kids involved re-enacted the fight from start to finish. Then they "performed" it again—but this time any student could yell "Stop!" at any point in the re-enactment and take the stage to show alternative responses and solutions. If the second re-enactment didn't lead to a peaceful conclusion, the fight was run again and again under the same rules, until a satisfactory solution emerged.

Soth discovered that the initial reconstruction of the fight was important— every student involved needed to be heard fully and fairly. But once the kids were sure that Forum Theater was a genuine forum for their fears, sense of justice, and creativity, they couldn't get enough of it. "My main work was to hold them back from all shouting 'Stop!' and wanting to suggest alternatives at once," said Soth.

"Good Idea!" *Utne*

A. Vocabulary

Here are five vocabulary words from the selection and their definitions. Study these definitions carefully. Then write the appropriate word in each space provided according to the context.

>*ingenuity*—originality, clever use of imagination
>*reconstruct*—to rebuild, assemble again
>*re-enactment*—going through a performance a second time
>*alternative*—describing a choice between various options
>*forum*—a place to voice ideas or to openly discuss something

When the children discovered that performing a _____ of a conflict was a legitimate _____ where they could express their fears and attain justice, they began to see the theater as a reasonable _____ to fighting. Asking students to _____ their conflicts was an example of using _____ to solve a seemingly unresolvable problem.

B. Inferences

On the basis of the evidence in the passage, mark these statements as follows: PA (probably accurate), PI (probably inaccurate), or NP (not in the passage).

1. _____ Michael Soth's idea for conflict resolution was adapted from a Brazilian theater director.
2. _____ The children were immediately convinced that acting out the conflict was a good idea.
3. _____ Oftentimes, Soth's students had to perform more than one re-enactment before the conflict could be resolved.
4. _____ The emphasis of Forum Theater is on finding alternatives to fighting rather than to deciding who actually was at fault in a dispute.
5. _____ Soth's Forum Theater has been effective but only in a limited way.
6. _____ On the basis of Soth's efforts, other elementary school teachers throughout England have adopted Forum Theaters of their own to stop their students from fighting.

Online Learning Center

As noted above, the conflict-resolution idea was submitted on the Global Ideas website, which offers ordinary people a forum for submitting ideas to solve environmental and social problems. Some ideas posted are wacky and improbable; others are ingenious and inspired. See what ideas have been submitted recently. The URL is www.globalideasbank.org/.

Answers for Selection 1

A. Vocabulary

re-enactment, forum, alternative, reconstruct, ingenuity

B. Inferences

1. PA   2. PI   3. PA   4. PA   5. PI   6. NP

Selection 2

The author, who lived in Belgium before World War II, had a childhood fascination with the Lowara band of Gypsies who camped every year near his village and who earned their livelihood by horsetrading. At the age of 12, in the 1930s, he asked his parents if he could leave home and live with the Gypsies, for at least part of each year, and incredibly, they agreed. This is the opening paragraph of his book recounting his experiences.

[1]As I approached the Gypsy camp for the first time, yellow, wild-looking stiff-haired dogs howled and barked. [2]Fifteen covered wagons were spread out in a

wide half circle, partly hiding the Gypsies from the road. ³Around the campfires sat women draped in deep-colored dresses, their big, expressive eyes and strong, white teeth standing out against their beautiful dark matte skin. ⁴The many gold pieces they wore as earrings, necklaces and bracelets sharpened their color even more. ⁵Their shiny blue-black hair was long and braided, the skirts of their dresses were ankle-length, very full and worn in many layers, and their bodices loose and low-cut. ⁶My first impression of them was one of health and vitality. ⁷Hordes of small barefoot children ran all over the campsite, a few dressed in rags but most nearly naked, rollicking like young animals. ⁸At the far end of the encampment a number of horses, tethered to long chains, were grazing; and of course there were the ever-present half-wild growling dogs. ⁹Several men lay in the shade of an oak tree. ¹⁰Thin corkscrews of bluish smoke rose skyward and the pungent, penetrating smell of burning wood permeated the air. ¹¹Even from a distance the loud, clear voices of these Gypsies resounded with an intensity I was not accustomed to. ¹²Mingling with them, farther away, were the dull thuds of an ax, the snorting and neighing of horses, the occasional snapping of a whip and the high-pitched wail of an infant, contrasting with the whisper of the immediate surroundings of the camp itself.

Jan Yoors, *The Gypsies*

A. Vocabulary

For each italicized word from the selection, write the dictionary definition most appropriate for the context.

1. health and *vitality* [sentence 6]: _____

2. *rollicking* like young animals [7]: _____

3. the *pungent*, penetrating smell [10]: _____

4. the smell *permeated* the air [10]: _____

B. Content and Structure

Complete the following questions.

1. What is the predominant mode of discourse in the paragraph?

   _____

2. Find the two nouns that Yoors uses to state his dominant impression

   of these Gypsies. _____

3. Yoors uses many words that appeal to our senses. Which of these four senses—sight, smell, sound, or touch—is *not* emphasized in the paragraph? _____

4. What adjective or descriptive word would you use to describe these gypsies? _____

5. A good title for this paragraph would be
   (a) "A Study of Gypsy Life."
   (b) "The Survival of the Gypsies."
   (c) "Why Gypsies Are Persecuted."
   (d) "First Impressions of a Gypsy Camp."

C. Inferences

On the basis of the evidence in the paragraph, mark these statements as follows: PA (probably accurate), PI (probably inaccurate), or NP (not in the passage).

1. _____ The Gypsy camp the author came across was in America.

2. _____ The writer had been to the Gypsy camp many times in the past.

3. _____ Gypsies have been persecuted over the years in many European countries.

4. _____ Gypsy culture, at least the culture represented by this particular group, is essentially nomadic.

5. _____ In Gypsy culture, the women do all the work while the men lie around, enjoying themselves.

6. _____ Despite the children's ragged appearance, they appeared to be happy.

Selection 3

[1]In Japan, specially licensed chefs prepare the rarest sashimi delicacy: the white flesh of the puffer fish, served raw and arranged in elaborate floral patterns on a platter. [2]Diners pay large sums of money for the carefully prepared dish, which has a light, faintly sweet taste, like raw pompano. [3]It had better be carefully prepared, because, unlike pompano, puffer fish is ferociously poisonous. [4]You wouldn't think a puffer fish would need such chemical armor, since its main form of defense is to swallow great gulps of water and become so bloated it is too large for most predators to swallow. [5]And yet its skin, ovaries, liver, and intestines contain tetrodotoxin, one of the most poisonous chemicals in the world, hundreds of times more lethal than strychnine or cyanide. [6]A shred small enough to fit under one's fingernail could kill an entire family. [7]Unless the poison is completely removed by a deft, experienced chef, the diner will die midmeal. [8]That's the appeal of the dish; eating the possibility of death, a fright your lips spell out as you dine. [9]Yet preparing it is a traditional art form in Japan, with widespread aficionados. [10]The most highly respected *fugu* chefs are the ones who manage to leave in the barest touch of the poison, just enough for the diner's lips to tingle from his

brush with mortality but not enough to actually kill him. **¹¹**Of course, a certain number of diners do die every year from eating *fugu*, but that doesn't stop intrepid *fugu*-fanciers. **¹²**The ultimate *fugu* connoisseur orders *chiri*, puffer flesh lightly cooked in a broth made of the poisonous livers and intestines. **¹³**It's not that diners don't understand the bizarre danger of puffer-fish toxin. **¹⁴**Ancient Egyptian, Chinese, Japanese, and other cultures all describe *fugu* poisoning in excruciating detail: It first produces dizziness, numbness of the mouth and lips, breathing trouble, cramps, blue lips, a desperate itchiness as of insects crawling all over one's body, vomiting, dilated pupils, and then a zombielike sleep, really a kind of neurological paralysis during which the victims are often aware of what's going on around them, and from which they die. **¹⁵**But sometimes they wake. **¹⁶**If a Japanese man or woman dies of *fugu* poison, the family waits a few days before burying them, just in case they wake up. **¹⁷**Every now and then someone poisoned by *fugu* is nearly buried alive, coming to at the last moment to describe in horrifying detail their own funeral and burial, during which, although they desperately tried to cry out or signal that they were still alive, they simply couldn't move.

Diane Ackerman, *A Natural History of the Senses*

A. Vocabulary

For each italicized word from the selection, write the dictionary definition most appropriate for the context.

1. a *deft*, experienced chef [sentence 7]: _____

2. with widespread *aficionados* [9]: _____

3. *intrepid* fugu-fanciers [11]: _____

4. the *ultimate* fugu connoisseur [12]: _____

5. the ultimate fugu *connoisseur* [12]: _____

   _____

6. in *excruciating* detail [14]: _____

B. Content and Meaning

Complete the following questions.

1. With regard to puffer fish, what is Ackerman's purpose in writing?

   _____

2. Which sentence in the paragraph represents the main idea?
Sentence _____

3. In sentence 3 what does Ackerman mean when she compares the puffer fish's poison to armor? _____

_____

4. This passage is quite long. If you were going to break it into two paragraphs, with which sentence would you end the first paragraph?
Sentence _____

C. Inferences

Answer these inference questions in your own words.

1. Without turning to the dictionary, what is the likely meaning of the word *fugu*?

_____

2. Under what circumstances (i.e., methods of preparation) is puffer fish poisonous?

_____

3. Why should a diner who wants to eat puffer fish have only an experienced chef prepare it?

_____

4. What is the primary motivation for people to eat puffer fish, especially when it's so dangerous?

_____

5. This passage comes from Ackerman's book, *A Natural History of the Senses*. Each section of the book takes up one of the five senses. From which section of the book does this excerpt most likely come?

_____

6. Do you think the author has sampled puffer fish? Is there any way to tell?

_____

PRACTICE ESSAY

"The Standing Babas," from *Shantaram*

Gregory David Roberts

This is not an essay in the traditional sense. It is taken from a long novel by Australian writer Gregory David Roberts, but because his book is based solely on his personal experience, it reads more like non-fiction. Originally from Melbourne, Roberts was sentenced to 19 years in prison for a series of armed robberies, but he escaped and fled. Using a fake New Zealand passport, he hid out in Bombay (now Mumbai), the sprawling city on the west coast of India. There he immersed himself in Indian culture, first by becoming friends with his guide, Prabaker, and later by establishing a medical clinic in one of the city's enormous slums. "Shantaram" means "man of peace," the name the residents of Prabaker's home village gave him. After many adventures in Mumbai, he returned to Australia and served out his sentence. He now lives in Mumbai and writes full time.

Three things you need to know: Karla, who accompanied him and Prabaker to the temple of the Standing Babas, is a Swiss woman with whom Roberts is infatuated. Charras (paragraphs 11 and 13) is another word for hemp or, in this case, hashish; a chillum *(paragraphs 6 and 13) is a short pipe, made of clay, used for smoking marijuana and other drugs.*

Preview Questions

1. What do you know about Bombay (now Mumbai)? If you are unfamiliar with this megacity in India, look up some basic information online before continuing.
2. If one never sat or lay down, and always stood up for years and years, even to sleep, what do you think the physical effects on the body would be?

1 The Standing Babas were men who'd taken a vow never to sit down, or lie down, ever again, for the rest of their lives. They stood, day and night, forever. They ate their meals standing up, and made their toilet standing up. They prayed and worked and sang standing up. They even slept while they were standing, suspended in harnesses that kept the weight of their bodies on their legs, but prevented them from falling when they were unconscious.

2 For the first five to ten years of that constant standing, their legs began to swell. Blood moved sluggishly in exhausted veins, and muscles thickened. Their legs became huge, bloated out of recognisable shape, and covered with purple varicose boils. Their toes squeezed out from thick, fleshy feet, like the toes of elephants. During the following years, their legs gradually became thinner, and thinner. Eventually, only bones

remained, with a paint-thin veneer of skin and the termite trails of withered veins.

3   The pain was unending and terrible. Spikes and spears of agony stabbed up through their feet with every downward pressure. Tormented, tortured, the Standing Babas were never still. They shifted constantly from foot to foot in a gentle, swaying dance that was as mesmerising, for everyone who saw it, as the sound-weaving hands of a flute player for his cobras.

4   Some of the Babas had made the vow when they were sixteen or seventeen years old. They were compelled by something like the vocation that calls others, in other cultures, to become priests, rabbis, or imams. A larger number of much older men had renounced the world as a preparation for death and the next level of incarnation. Not a few of the Standing Babas were businessmen who'd given themselves to ruthless pursuits of pleasure, power, and profit during their working lives. There were holy men who'd journeyed through many other devotions, mastering their punishing sacrifices before undertaking the ultimate vow of the Standing Baba. And there were criminals—thieves, murderers, major mafia figures, and even former warlords—who sought expiation, or propitiation, in the endless agonies of the vow.

5   The den was really a corridor between two brick buildings at the rear of their temple. Hidden from view forever, within the temple compound, were the secret gardens, cloisters, and dormitories that only those who made and kept the vow ever saw. An iron roof covered the den. The floor was paved with flat stones. The Standing Babas entered through a door at the rear of the corridor. Everyone else entered and left through an iron gate at the street end.

6   The customers, men from every part of the country and every level of society, stood along the walls of the corridor. They stood, of course: no-one ever sat in the presence of the Standing Babas. There was a tap fixed over an open drain near the entrance gate, where men drank water or leaned over to spit. The Babas moved from man to man and group to group, preparing hashish in funnel-shaped clay chillums for the customers, and smoking with them.

7   The faces of the Babas were radiant with their excruciation. Sooner or later, in the torment of endlessly ascending pain, every man of them assumed a luminous, transcendent beatitude. Light, made from the agonies they suffered, streamed from their eyes, and I've never known a human source more brilliant than their tortured smiles.

8   The Babas were also comprehensively, celestially, and magnificently stoned. They smoked nothing but Kashmiri—the best hashish in the world—grown and produced at the foothills of the Himalayas in Kashmir. And they smoked it all day, and all night, all their lives.

9   I stood with Karla and Prabaker at the back wall of the narrow den. Behind us was the sealed door through which the Standing Babas had entered. In front of us were two lines of men standing along the walls

all the way to the iron gate at the street end of the passage. Some of the men were dressed in suits. Some wore designer jeans. Workmen, wearing faded lungis, stood beside men in traditional dress from various regions of India. They were young and old, rich and poor. Their eyes were often drawn to Karla and me, pale-skinned foreigners, standing with our backs against the wall. It was clear that some of them were shocked to see a woman in the den. Despite their open curiosity, no-one approached us or acknowledged us directly, and for the most part they gave their attention to the Standing Babas and the hashish. Conversations, buzzing softly, blended with music and devotional chanting, coming from somewhere inside the compound.

10   'So, what do you think?'

11   'It's incredible!' she replied, her eyes gleaming in the soft light of the shaded lamps. She was exhilarated, and perhaps a little unnerved. Smoking the charras had relaxed the muscles of her face and shoulders, but there were tigers moving quickly in the eyes of her soft smile. 'It's amazing. It's horrible and holy at the same time. I can't make up my mind which is the holy part, and which is the horrible part. Horrible—that's not the right word, but it's something like that.'

12   'I know what you mean,' I agreed, thrilled that I'd succeeded in impressing her. She'd been in the city for five years, and she'd heard about the Babas many times, but that visit with me was her first. My tone implied that I knew the place well, but I couldn't fairly claim credit for the experience. Without Prabaker, who'd knocked on the gate for us and gained access with his golden smile, we wouldn't have been permitted to enter.

13   One of the Standing Babas approached us slowly with an acolyte who held a silver tray containing chillums, charras, and the paraphernalia of smoking. Other monks rocked and swayed along the length of the corridor, smoking and chanting prayers. The Baba standing before us was tall and lean, but his legs were so thickly swollen that dreadful ropes of distended veins throbbed on their surfaces. His face was thin. The bones of his skull, near the temples, were sharply defined. His cheekbones, majestic, presided over deep valleys that ran to a hard and hungry jaw. His eyes were huge, within the caverns ridged by his brows, and there was such madness and longing and love in them that he was at once fearsome and immensely pitiable.

14   He prepared the chillum, rocking from side to side and smiling absently. He never looked at us, but still it seemed to be the smile of a very close friend: indulgent, knowing, forgiving. He was standing and swaying so close to me that I could see each wiry strand in the forest of his brows. I heard the little gasps of his breathing. The rapid outward rushes of air sounded like wavelets on a steep shore. He finished preparing the chillum, and looked up at me. For a moment I was lost in the vision that swarmed and screeched in his eyes. For a tiny moment in the infinitude of his suffering I almost felt it, what the human will can drive the human

body to endure and achieve. I almost understood it, that smile of his, driven insane by the will that forced it to shine. I was sure that he was communicating it to me—that he wanted me to know. And I tried to tell him, with my eyes alone, that I could almost sense it, almost feel it. Then he held the chillum to his mouth, in the funnel of his hand, puffed it alight, and offered it to me. That terrible intimacy with his unending pain shrivelled, the vision shimmered, and the moment drifted away with the fading white shadows of the smoke. He turned, and tottered slowly back toward the street gate, muttering prayers in a soft drone.

A. *Structure and Meaning*

Choose the answer that best completes each statement. You may refer to the passage.

1. What is the main point Roberts makes about the Standing Babas? Who are they?

   _____

2. Explain the purpose of the harnesses mentioned in paragraph 1.

   _____

3. What is the predominant mode of discourse in paragraphs 2, 3, and 13?

   _____

4. What is the purpose of paragraph 4? _____

5. Write a one-sentence summary of paragraph 7. _____

   _____

6. In your own words, describe Karla's reaction to the Standing Babas quoted at the end of paragraph 11. _____

7. Read paragraph 14 carefully again. Write the phrase that best characterizes the communication between Roberts and the Baba who offers him the pipe. _____

B. *Vocabulary—Dictionary Definitions*

For each of these words from the selection, write the dictionary definition according to the context.

1. a paint-thin *veneer* of skin [paragraph 2]   _____

2. dance that was as *mesmerizing* [3]   _____

3. given themselves to *ruthless* pursuits [4]   _____

4. who sought *expiation* or *propitiation* [4]   _____

5. radiant with their *excruciation* [7]   _____

6. a luminous, transcendent *beatitude* [7]   _____

7. an *acolyte* who held a silver tray [13]   _____

8. the *paraphernalia* of smoking [13]   _____

C. Inferences

Write the answers to these inference questions in your own words. Paragraph numbers are provided to help you.

1. What does constant standing do to the human body? What primary bodily function does it disrupt? [paragraph 2]

   _____

2. What can you infer is the motivation to join the Standing Babas that these various members have in common? [paragraph 4]

   _____

3. What are the "customers," mentioned in paragraph 6, doing in the temple?

   _____

4. Why do you suppose the Standing Babas smoke hashish all day and all night long? [paragraph 8] _____

5. In paragraph 9, Roberts refers to "men"? Whom is he most likely refer-ring to? _____

6. Why were the bystanders shocked to see Roberts and Karla in the den?

   _____

7. How did the writer and Karla gain entrance to the Standing Babas' temple? [paragraph 12] _____

8. Why do the Standing Babas constantly sway? [paragraphs 3 and 14]

   _____

D. Questions for Discussion and Analysis

1. What was your initial impression of the Standing Babas after reading this excerpt? Is it similar to Karla's response, or different? Explain.

Online Learning Center

If you want to learn more about the Standing Babas, you can start by doing a search using Google or your favorite search engine. Type in "Standing Babas" and many submenus will come up. If you click on "Standing Babas, Mumbai," you will get several sites that refer to Roberts' book. "Standing Babas in India" gives you more general information about these mystics who deliberately inflict corporal punishment on themselves.

2. In paragraph 4, Roberts mentions vocations in other cultures that call people to become priests, rabbis, or imams. What other vocations can you think of that call on one to take such an extreme vow?

Discovering Meaning: The Importance of Form

OUTLINE

CHAPTER 4

Methods of Paragraph Development

In this chapter, you will learn eight methods of paragraph development, including:

- Facts and statistics
- Examples and illustration
- Process
- Comparison and contrast
- Cause and effect
- Classification and analysis
- Definition
- Analogy

■ MODES OF DISCOURSE AND METHODS OF DEVELOPMENT COMPARED

The eight methods of development you will study in this chapter are different from the modes of discourse that you studied in Chapter 2. *Mode of discourse* is a somewhat general term describing the principal types of nonfiction writing—narration, description, exposition, and persuasion. In an essay, one mode usually predominates, though you will remember that an essay may reflect mixed modes. In contrast, the methods of development[1] refer to the various ways a writer presents *evidence* to support the idea within an individual paragraph. A main idea cannot be left unexplored; it must be examined, supported, explained, illustrated, or defined as the subject dictates. These methods of development can be used in combination, so that a typical essay may reflect several methods. One paragraph might be developed with facts and statistics, another with the definition of an important term, a third with contrasting information. The writer chooses the method that best clarifies and supports the main assertion. Although some instructors call them *expository* methods, in fact, they are commonly found in persuasive writing as well. Because these methods reflect logical patterns of thinking, learning to identify them will help you think more analytically. An equally important skill is the ability to *predict* what method of development a writer is likely to use.

Online Learning Center

For a practice exercise in predicting methods of development by examining main-idea sentences, go to www.mhhe.com/spears. Click on Chapter 4 and scroll down to "Predicting Methods of Development."

■ METHODS OF PARAGRAPH DEVELOPMENT—THE FIRST GROUP

So that you can learn to identify them more readily, I have divided them into two groups, beginning with the relatively easy ones.

Facts and Statistics

As you recall from Chapter 3, a **fact** is a piece of verifiable objective information: One can prove its truth by scientific measurement, by personal observation, by duplication, and so on. **Statistics** are data in the form of numbers, derived from research studies, polls, census figures, or other similar sources. The use of statistics is the simplest method of development to recognize. This paragraph uses both facts and statistics to document the European and American taste for sweets.

> People will eat almost anything, it seems, as long as it's sweet. And, until fairly recently, this mental programming served them just fine. When Columbus introduced cane to the New World, the anthropologist Sidney Mintz has noted, sugar was an exotic luxury. Most Europeans had never eaten sugar, but they quickly developed a taste for it. By 1700, the Americas had become a vast sugar mill and the English were eating four pounds per person per year. By 1800, they were eating eighteen pounds; by 1900, ninety pounds.

[1]Although some teachers of reading use the term "organizational patterns," I have followed the terminology used in rhetorically arranged introductory-level composition readers to avoid confusion. Chapter 5 takes up patterns of organization.

But nowhere was the rise of sugar as dramatic as in the New World. Last year, the average American consumed about a hundred and forty pounds of cane sugar, corn syrup, and other natural sugars—fifty per cent more than the Germans or the French and nine times as much as the Chinese.

Burkhard Bilger, "The Search for Sweet," *The New Yorker*

Examples and Illustration

An **example** is a specific instance of a more general concept. Examples of exotic flavors of ice cream (the general concept) are passion fruit-mango, lavender-lemon verbena, and dulce de leche with sea salt. A writer who fails to supply examples (or illustrations) to support an idea that demands it risks not being taken seriously. A writer may support a general idea by citing two or three examples—specific instances—of the main idea or by using a single longer, extended example called an ***illustration***. Both methods function in the same way; both point to typical and concrete instances of a general idea. The difference between them is that examples are short and occur in clusters, whereas an illustration is extended, is more detailed, and stands by itself.

In the following passage, Marjorie Garber develops the main idea with three short examples. Study my annotations to see where each new example begins.

At a time when "universal" ideas and feelings are often compromised or undercut by group identities, the dog tale still has the power to move us. Paradoxically, the dog has become the repository of those model human properties which we have cynically ceased to find among human beings. On the evening news and in the morning paper, dog stories supply what used to be called "human interest." There was the story of <u>Lyric</u>, for instance—<u>the 911 dog</u>, who <u>dialled emergency services to save her mistress</u>, and wound up the toast of Disneyland. Or the saga of <u>Sheba</u>, the <u>mother dog in Florida who rescued her puppies</u> after they were buried alive by a cruel human owner. His crime and her heroic single-motherhood were reliable feature stories, edging out mass killings in Bosnia and political infighting at home. Here, after all, were the family values we'd been looking for as a society—right under our noses.

Indeed, at a time of increasing human ambivalence about human heroes and the human capacity for "unconditional love," dog heroes—and dog stories—are with us today more than ever. Near the entrance to Central Park at Fifth Avenue and Sixty-seventh Street stands the statue of <u>Balto</u>, the <u>heroic sled dog</u> who led a team <u>bringing medicine to diphtheria-stricken Nome, Alaska</u>, in <u>the winter of 1925</u>. Balto's story recently became an animated feature film, joining such other big-screen fictional heroes as Lassie, Rin Tin Tin, Benji, and Fluke.

Marginal annotations:
1—Lyric dialed 911

2—Sheba rescued puppies

3—Balto brought medicine in diphtheria outbreak

Marjorie Garber, "Dog Days," *The New Yorker*

Write a sentence stating the main idea of the passage. _____

_____

_____

These short examples of representative heroic dogs work well to explain Garber's point. One example of a single heroic dog would not constitute sufficient proof, since not all dogs are heroic. However, in this passage from the best-selling book *Freakonomics*, Steven D. Levitt and Stephen J. Dubner use a single extended **illustration**—that of a one-day-old car—to back up their assertion that information, even wrong information, is powerful.

> Information is a beacon, a cudgel, an olive branch, a deterrent, depending on who wields it and how. Information is so powerful that the *assumption* of information, even if the information does not actually exist, can have a sobering effect. Consider the case of a one-day-old car.
>
> The day that a car is driven off the lot is the worst day in its life, for it instantly loses as much as a quarter of its value. This might seem absurd, but we know it to be true. A new car that was bought for $20,000 cannot be resold for more than perhaps $15,000. Why? Because the only person who might logically want to resell a brand-new car is someone who found the car to be a lemon. So even if the car isn't a lemon, a potential buyer assumes that it is. He assumes that the seller has some information about the car that he, the buyer, does not have—and the seller is punished for this assumed information.
>
> And if the car *is* a lemon? The seller would do well to wait a year to sell it. By then, the suspicion of lemonness will have faded; by then, some people will be selling their perfectly good year-old cars, and the lemon can blend in with them, likely selling for more than it is truly worth.
>
> Steven D. Levitt and Stephen J. Dubner, *Freakonomics*

What do the writers mean when they refer to a new car as a "lemon"? What is the reason that the writers suggest that owners of a lemon car wait a year before selling it?_____

_____

The phenomenon the writers describe is common to all cars after they are driven off the lot, making further examples unnecessary. Notice that the writers use a transitional phrase ("Consider the case of a one-day-old car") to introduce their illustration. You will study these transitional elements in Chapter 5.

Illustration in Textbooks

At this point in the course, you should also be noting how these methods of development are manifest in your other textbooks. Textbook writers often use illustration to reinforce and add interest to their explanation of abstract concepts. For example, in a complicated discussion of long-term memory (LTM) and short-term memory (STM), the author of a leading psychology text augments the text with this passage titled "The Tip-of-the-Tongue Phenomenon":

The Tip-of-the-Tongue Phenomenon

We have all had the maddening experience of trying to recall a fact that we can *almost* remember—it's on the "tip of my tongue." Fortunately, there is a lesson in this on the nature of retrieval from LTM. The tip-of-the-tongue phenomenon was investigated by Harvard University psychologists Roger Brown and David NcNeil (1966) by giving definitions of uncommon words to college students and asking them to recall the words. For example, they might be read the definition of *sampan* ("a small boat used in shallow water in Asia that is rowed from behind using a single oar"). Often, the students could recall the word *sampan*. Sometimes, though, they could not quite recall the word, and the researchers were able to create the tip-of-the-tongue sensation in these students. When this happened, the students found that they were able to recall some information about the word ("It starts with *s*" or "It sounds like *Siam*") or recall something about the thing the word referred to ("It looks a little like a junk"), even when they could not retrieve the word. Then, moments later, the word would pop into memory for some students, proving that it was there all the time but just could not be retrieved for the moment. Studies suggest that about half of the things that we can't remember, but are on the tip of our tongues, are recalled within a minute or so (Schachter, 1999), but you can drive yourself nuts for hours trying to remember the other half!

Benjamin B. Lahey, *Psychology: An Introduction*

Process

Process is the next method of development. There are two kinds of process writing. The **directive** method, usually found in cookbooks or in laboratory or technical manuals, shows the reader how to perform a task, such as how to set up your wireless router, how to do an Internet search, or how to prepare a résumé. We are more interested in the **informative** process, in which the writer describes a phenomenon—how something works, how something developed, or how something came into existence. Unlike the directive process, the writer who uses the informative process does not expect us to duplicate the process, because it would be impossible or perhaps even dangerous to do so. Both types use chronological, or time, order to make the steps easy to identify.

The writer of this passage, Francisco Goldman, uses the informative process method to show how sleeper or rogue waves are formed. His wife, Aura, was killed by a giant wave as she bodysurfed in Mazunte, Mexico. As you read it, number the steps in the left margin.

Where, as we slept that night, was Aura's wave in its long journey to Mazunte? Having done some research on waves since then, I know that it already existed. Most surface waves of any decent size travel thousands of miles before they reach the shore. Wind blows ripples across a calm sea, and those ripples, providing the wind with something to get traction on, are blown into waves, and, as the waves grow in height, the wind pushes them along with more force, speeding them up, building them higher. It's not the water itself that travels, of course, but the wind's energy; in the turbulent medium between air and ocean, water particles move in circles like bicycle pedals, constantly transferring their energy forward, from swell to swell and back into the trough, then forward again. Aura's wave could easily have had its start a week or more before she encountered it, during a storm in the warm seas of the South Pacific. Where was it that night, as we slept in our bunks in Oaxaca?

Francisco Goldman, "The Wave," *The New Yorker*

In describing this process, what two common misconceptions about waves does Goldman overturn? _____

_____

The writer's purpose in the article from which this excerpt comes is to describe the circumstances surrounding his wife's death—essentially a narrative. Why do you think he includes this information, which is essentially expository? _____

_____

Comparison and Contrast

Writers use the **comparison and contrast** method to explain similarities and differences between two subjects. Comparison discusses *similarities*, often between two apparently dissimilar things, for example, how meeting a girlfriend's or boyfriend's parents is as stressful as a job interview. But comparison can also be used to examine two related things. If a writer in an automotive magazine is comparing two cars, two Japanese imported cars—say, Toyotas and Hondas—he or she would focus on insightful or significant similarities, rather than on obvious ones. That both models have steering wheels, engines, brakes, and other necessary equipment is hardly worth pointing out. In trying to recommend which make to buy, the writer would note the significant similarities in body styling, structural workmanship, and fuel efficiency. He or she might then assess the differences, the contrasting points.

Nearly everyone has either cooked or attended a Thanksgiving dinner. In this clever excerpt from one of America's leading cooking magazines, *Bon Appetit,* the writer uses *comparison* effectively to emphasize what it's like to cook in a restaurant.

Here's an exercise for you: Imagine that you're cooking Thanksgiving dinner. You're making a dozen dishes, including some that are pretty complicated. You're standing up all day. You're worried about pleasing your in-laws. You're rushing to get dinner served before your cousin's baby has a meltdown, or before your grandmother's bedtime, whichever comes first. And once it's all eaten, you've got to clean up the kitchen. Now, imagine that you're making Thanksgiving dinner every day. No matter how much you might love Thanksgiving, and how much you love to cook, that's a lot of work. That's what it's like to cook in a restaurant.

Molly Wizenberg, "If You Can't Stand the Heat...," *Bon Appetit*

Contrast properly refers to a discussion of the *differences* between two or more related or like things—for example, the presidential terms of George H. W. Bush and of his son, George W. Bush; the four *Pirates of the Caribbean* movies; or two hybrid automobiles—the Toyota Prius and the Honda Civic Hybrid. Comparison and contrast may be used together or singly, depending on the subject and the writer's purpose. Contrast is the dominant method of development in this next passage by Paco Underhill, an expert in shopping center design and shopping habits. In it, he examines the differences in shopping styles between men and women. Number the points of contrast in the left margin.

A recent study of how men and women differ when it comes to the mall turned up this fact: Men, once you get them in the door, are much more interested in the social aspect of malls than the shopping part, whereas women say the social aspect is important but shopping comes first. Men enjoy the mall as a form of recreation—they like watching people and browsing around in stores more than shopping. Maybe they'll spend fifteen minutes in a bookstore or a stereo store and leave without buying a thing. They treat it like an information-gathering trip. Men also like the nonretail parts—the rock-climbing walls, the food courts, anything that doesn't actually require them to enter stores and look at, try on, or buy merchandise. Women, of course, are there for *exactly* those things. The only females who truly love the nonshopping aspects of the mall are teenage girls. They love shopping, of course, but they also love the food courts and video arcades and all that stuff, too. And that's probably because the mall is the only nonhome, nonschool environment they have. But they outgrow that by the time they're in college. From then on, they're at malls to shop.

Paco Underhill, *Call of the Mall*

A paragraph developed by comparison or contrast does not have to give equal treatment to the two subjects under discussion. Read, for example, this excerpt by Luis Alberto Urrea.

One of the most beautiful views of San Diego is from the summit of a small hill in Tijuana's municipal garbage dump. People live on that hill, picking through the trash with long poles that end in hooks made of bent nails. They scavenge for bottles, tin, aluminum, cloth; for cast-out beds, wood, furniture. Sometimes they find meat that is not too rotten to be cooked.

This view-spot is where the city drops off its dead animals—dogs, cats, sometimes goats, horses. They are piled in heaps six feet high and torched. In that stinking blue haze, amid nightmarish sculptures of charred ribs and carbonized tails, the garbage-pickers can watch the buildings of San Diego gleam gold on the blue coastline. The city looks cool in the summer when heat cracks the ground and flies drill into their noses. And in the winter, when windchill drops night temperatures into the low thirties, when the cold makes their lips bleed, and rain turns the hill into a gray pudding of ash and mud, and babies are wrapped in plastic trash bags for warmth, San Diego glows like a big electric dream. And every night on that burnt hill, these people watch.

Luis Alberto Urrea, *Across the Wire: Life and Hard Times on the Mexican Border*

Why does Urrea focus more on the Tijuana side of the border than on the American side? _____

_____

_____

Critical Thinking Exercise

Let's say you are assigned to write an essay for your English class in which you discuss two majors side by side: the biotechnology program at Evergreen Community College (which is close to your home) and a similar program at Mapleton State College (which is 200 miles away from your home). Which method of development would you primarily use—*comparison* or *contrast*? Defend your choice.

Practice Exercise 1

Read the following paragraphs. First, decide which of the following methods of development predominates.

- Facts and statistics
- Examples or illustration
- Process
- Comparison and contrast

Then write a sentence stating the main idea in your own words.

A. This paragraph is excerpted from a review of Isabel Wilkerson's fine 2010 book about the African-American diaspora, *The Warmth of Other Suns*.

Between 1915 and 1918, five hundred thousand blacks left the South; 1.3 million between 1920 and 1930. They drove; they hitched rides; they saved till they could buy a train ticket. They went to cities, especially Chicago, Detroit, New York, Philadelphia, and Los Angeles. They fled Jim Crow, laws put on the books after Reconstruction. Georgia was the first state to demand separate seating for whites and blacks in streetcars, in 1891; five years later came Plessy v. Ferguson. By 1905, every Southern state had a streetcar law, and more: in courthouses, separate Bibles; in bars, separate sections; in post offices, separate windows; in libraries, separate branches. In Birmingham, it was a crime for blacks and whites to play checkers together in a public park. By the nineteen-seventies, after civil rights put an end to Jim Crow and the Great Migration stopped, six million people had left their homes. It was bigger than the Gold Rush. It was bigger than the Dust Bowl Okies. Before the Great Migration, ninety per cent of all blacks in the United States lived in the South; after it, forty-seven per cent lived someplace else. Today, more African-Americans live in the city of Chicago than in the state of Mississippi.

Jill Lepore, "The Uprooted," *The New Yorker*

Main idea: _____

Method of development: _____

What information in the paragraph suggests what Jim Crow laws were?

_____

_____

B. In this excerpt from an article on global warming, the writer is discussing the deaths of pine trees throughout British Columbia. As the climate has warmed, there has been an explosion in the number of mountain pine beetles, which have infested the province's forests.

In an attack played out millions of times over, a female beetle no bigger than a rice grain finds an older lodgepole pine, its favored host, and drills inside the bark. There, it eats a channel straight up the tree, laying eggs as it goes. The tree fights back. It pumps sap toward the bug and the new larvae, enveloping them in a mass of the sticky substance. The tree then tries to eject its captives through a small, crusty chute in the bark.

Countering, the beetle sends out a pheromone call for reinforcements. More beetles arrive, mounting a mass attack. A fungus on the beetle, called the blue stain fungus, works into the living wood, strangling its water flow. The larvae begin eating at right angles to the original up-and-down channel, sometimes girdling the tree, crossing channels made by other beetles.

The pine is doomed. As it slowly dies, the larvae remain protected over the winter. In spring, they burrow out of the bark and launch themselves into the wind to their next victims.

British Columbia is a buffet laid out before them. Years of successful battles against forest fires have allowed a thick concentration of old lodgepole pines to grow—a beetle feast that natural wildfire would have stopped.

Doug Struck, "Red Death in Canada's Forests,"
The Washington Post National Weekly Edition

Method of development:_____

Main idea:_____

C. Have you ever wondered how shopping malls got their names? Before you read this passage, be sure to look up the words *mimic* and *faux* if you are unsure of their meanings.

Corporate retailers have responded to the unease many Americans feel about our increasingly anemic community life by brashly asserting that their stores are the cure, not the culprit. The doublespeak begins with the names of their developments. In Memphis, one can visit The Commons, a standard big-box complex with Home Depot, Circuit City, Old Navy, and other chains. Walmart and Best Buy are part of New Hope Commons near Durham, North Carolina. "Village" is another popular corporate retail term, as in Erskine Village, a superstore development in South Bend, Indiana. Walmart has described itself as "the gathering place of the community." Some developers have gone so far as to adopt the term "town center" and arrange their stores to mimic the real thing. Just outside of Charleston, South Carolina, is Mount Pleasant Towne Centre, with chains like Barnes & Noble, Bed Bath & Beyond, and Chili's set along a faux Main Street, which is surrounded by parking lots with easy access to the highway. Corporate retailers have so eroded our sense of community that they have even managed to sell it back to us in the form of a superficial design concept.

Stacy Mitchell, *Big-Box Swindle*

Main idea: _____

Method of development: _____

Critical thinking question: What are the names of one or two shopping centers in your area? Do their names reflect the sentiment that Mitchell expresses here?

In your own words, explain what Mitchell accuses corporate retailers of doing to our communities. _____

D. The writer of this excerpt is an international economist who is originally from Zambia. Her subject is foreign aid to African countries, which she opposes.

To advance a country's economic prospects, governments need efficient civil service. But civil service is naturally prone to bureaucracy, and there is always the incipient danger of self-serving cronyism and the desire to bind citizens in endless, time-consuming red tape. What aid does is to make that danger a grim reality. This helps to explain why doing business across much of Africa is a nightmare. In Cameroon, it takes a potential investor around 426 days to perform 15 procedures to gain a business license. What entrepreneur wants to spend 119 days filling out forms to start a business in Angola? He's much more likely to consider the U.S. (40 days and 19 procedures) or South Korea (17 days and 10 procedures).

Even what may appear as a benign intervention on the surface can have damning consequences. Say there is a mosquito-net maker in small-town Africa. Say he employs 10 people who together manufacture 500 nets a week. Typically, these 10 employees support upward of 15 relatives each. A Western government-inspired program generously supplies the affected region with 100,000 free mosquito nets.

This promptly puts the mosquito net manufacturer out of business, and now his 10 employees can no longer support their 150 dependents. In a couple of years, most of the donated nets will be torn and useless, but now there is no mosquito net maker to go to. They'll have to get more aid. And African governments once again get to abdicate their responsibilities.

Dambisa Moyo, "Why Foreign Aid Is Hurting Africa," *The Wall Street Journal*

Main idea: _____

Method of development: _____

Is the mode of discourse in this passage primarily narrative, descriptive, expository, or persuasive? Explain your answer. _____

Explain the meaning of the term "benign intervention" at the beginning of the third paragraph. _____

E. This paragraph deals with the role of mules in the American military, both on the battlefield and in other settings.

The things they carry are Band-Aids, bullets, and cardboard cases of Meals Ready to Eat; also, sand for making concrete, Stinger missiles for making holes in airplane fuselages, rucksacks, machine guns, body armor, Kevlar helmets, blankets, boots. In another setting—not in Afghanistan, that is, and not on a battlefield—the load lashed to a mule's sawbuck saddle would be entirely different. It would be hunting supplies, perhaps, or tents, or cookstoves, strung together by a single long piece of rope, looped and knotted and then cinched tight into a sculpture of odd shapes and volumes. A mule is entirely nonpartisan about the contents of its load. It will carry as much as three hundred pounds, seven hours a day, twenty days straight, without complaint, strolling along under the huge, heavy cargo as if it were a bag of balloons.

Susan Orlean, "Riding High," *The New Yorker*

Main idea: _____

Method of development: _____

Explain the figure of speech (imaginative comparison) in the last sentence.

_____

F. The writer of this excerpt, Barbara Demick, is the bureau chief in Beijing for the *Los Angeles Times*. The DMZ mentioned in the first sentence stands for the Demilitarized Zone, the boundary line between the Republic of Korea (South Korea) and the Democratic People's Republic of Korea (North Korea).

A good deal of propaganda on both sides of the DMZ is devoted to how North and South Koreans are the same—*han nar,* one people, one nation—but after sixty years of separation the differences between the people are significant. South Korea is one of the world's most technologically advanced countries. While most North Koreans are unaware of the existence of the Internet, South Korea has a higher percentage of homes on broadband than do the United States, Japan, and most of Europe. North Korea has been frozen culturally and economically for the last half century. Their languages are no longer the same; the South Korean version is now peppered with words borrowed from English. Physically, too, the people have grown apart. The average South Korean seventeen-year-old male, fed on milk shakes and hamburgers, is five inches taller than his North Korean counterpart. North Koreans talk and eat like South Koreans did in the 1960s.

Barbara Demick, *Nothing to Envy*

Online Learning Center

Why has North Korea been so "frozen culturally and economically" for over 50 years? Go to Google or your favorite search engine and do some reading about this culture and its history of repressive leaders.

Main idea: _____

Method of development: _____

_____

G. This passage by surgeon-writer Richard Selzer is taken from the Practice Essay at the end of the chapter.

At first glance, it would appear that surgery and writing have little in common, but I think that is not so. For one thing, they are both sub-celestial arts; as far as I know, the angels disdain to perform either one. In each of them you hold a slender instrument that leaves a trail wherever it is applied. In one, there is the shedding of blood; in the other it is ink that is spilled upon a page. In one, the scalpel is restrained; in the other, the pen is given rein. The surgeon sutures together the tissues of the body to make whole what is sick or injured; the writer sews words into sentences to fashion a new version of human experience. A surgical operation is rather like a short story. You make the incision, rummage around inside for a bit, then stitch up. It has a beginning, a middle and an end. If I were to choose a medical specialist to write a novel, it would be a psychiatrist. They tend to go on and on. And on.

Richard Selzer, "The Pen and the Scalpel," *The New York Times*

Method of development: _____

Main idea: _____

■ METHODS OF PARAGRAPH DEVELOPMENT— THE SECOND GROUP

Like those in the first group, these methods of development—cause and effect, classification and analysis, definition, and analogy—are most commonly found in expository and persuasive writing.

Cause and Effect

In the **cause-and-effect method** of development, *cause* refers to reasons and *effect* refers to consequences or results. Writers use this method to explain complex events, problems, or issues. Like the comparison and contrast method, which can be used singly or in combination, a writer may discuss only causes of a problem or only its effects or both; further, they can be discussed in either order. In the opening sentence of this paragraph, the writer alerts the reader that she is using the cause-effect pattern.

Coral reefs are under threat for a host of reasons: bottom trawling, dynamite fishing, coastal erosion, agricultural runoff, and, nowadays, global warming. When water temperatures rise too high, corals lose—or perhaps expel, no one is quite sure—the algae that nourish them. (The process is called "bleaching," because without their zooxanthellae corals appear white.) For a particular reef, any one of these threats could potentially be fatal. Ocean acidification poses a different kind of threat, one that could preclude the very possibility of a reef.

Elizabeth Kolbert, "The Darkening Sea," *The New Yorker*

However, not all passages state the cause-and-effect relationship so obviously. Though short, the next paragraph is more complex. Here the cause-effect relationship forms a sort of chain—from the effect, to a list of three causes for that effect, ending with the ultimate effect. After you read the paragraph, identify these elements in the spaces provided.

> The average high-school student today is weaker academically than the average high-school student of 1950. This phenomenon is often ascribed to declining standards and the degradation of culture, but democratization has been a factor, too. We now expect public high schools to offer academics—the foundation of college work—to more, and more kinds of, children. In the past twenty years, the number of high-school students who say that they expect to finish college has doubled, to more than seventy-five per cent, with the largest gains shown by the urban poor. On the other hand, the increase in the number of students who actually finish college is less than ten per cent.
>
> Katherine Boo, "Expectations," *The New Yorker*

Effect: _____

_____

Three causes: _____

_____

Final effect: _____

_____

Cause and Effect Relationships in Visual Material

The following chart, "Don't Fence Me In," accompanied an article by Mark Derr titled "Big Beasts, Tight Space and a Call for Change" (*New York Times*, October 2, 2003).

1. What cause-and-effect relationship does the chart show? _____

    _____

2. Look again at the four species of animals listed. What conclusion can you draw about the relationship between animal species and the size of their natural home range? _____

    _____

3. Which species of animal has the highest infant mortality rate in captivity? _____

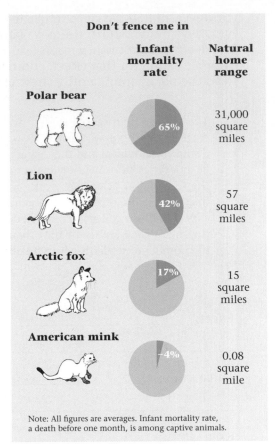

Note: All figures are averages. Infant mortality rate, a death before one month, is among captive animals.

Source: Used with permission of The Associated Press. Copyright © 2003. All rights reserved.

Analysis and Classification

Although they are actually separate methods, the underlying purpose of classification and analysis is the same: Both involve taking apart a larger subject and examining its separate parts to see how each relates to the whole. With the **classification** method, a writer puts *two or more* things into classes or categories, following a consistent system.[2] **Analysis** is different, because it involves only a *single* entity, the parts of which are examined one at a time.

We will discuss classification first. In the real world, we classify all the time. For example, if your CD collection is large, you need

[2]Some English rhetorics (composition textbooks) use the term *division* rather than classification when the subject is divided into only two categories.

to organize it in a way that makes sense. You might organize them by genre (rock, country, rap, and so on) or alphabetically by artist's name. Whatever system you use, it must be consistent so that you can locate a particular CD. You can identify classification passages because they often begin with a sentence like this one from an economic textbook: "There are three types of unemployment: frictional, structural, and cyclical."[3] The remainder of the passage goes on to examine each type.

Let us now look at some paragraphs using classification and analysis. Although the topic of this paragraph is a bit grisly, it illustrates the classification method clearly. In a chapter describing the horrors inflicted on residents of the Central African Republic by its former leader Bokassa, Alex Shoumatoff classifies cannibalism into four types.

> There are many kinds of cannibalism. Revenge cannibalism—the gloating, triumphant ingestion of a slain enemy's heart, liver, or other vital parts—is common at the warring-chiefdom stage of social evolution. Emergency cannibalism was resorted to by the Uruguayan soccer team whose plane crashed in the Andes. Ritual endocannibalism is practiced by certain tribes like the Yanonamo of northern Amazonia, whose women drink the pulverized ashes of slain kin mixed with banana gruel before their men go off on a raiding party. In the Kindu region of Zaire there are to this day leopard men who wear leopard skins, smear their bodies with leopard grease (which protects them even from lions), chip their teeth to points, and attack and eat people. Among their victims were some Italian soldiers who were part of the U.N. peace-keeping force during the turbulence after independence in 1960. The rarest kind of cannibals are gustatory cannibals—people who are actually partial to the taste of human flesh.

> Alex Shoumatoff, "The Emperor Who Ate His People," *African Madness*

What is the basis for the author's classification system? _____

_____

As stated earlier, analysis examines a *single* idea and looks at its separate parts to see how each contributes to the whole. Let's suppose a student has been assigned to analyze Richard Nixon's famous "Checkers" speech, one often studied in political science and communications courses. She would examine Nixon's purpose, the ideas expressed in the speech, his delivery, the logical fallacies, and manipulative or emotional appeals. In other words, she examines its important elements to see how they contribute to the whole.

[3]Campbell R. McConnell and Stanley L. Brue, *Economics: Principles, Problems, and Policies.*

Read this paragraph carefully and then answer the question at the end.

Alzheimer's can be divided into two categories. One is known as early-onset Alzheimer's, which is rare, and tends to strike between the ages of thirty and sixty. Almost half of early-onset Alzheimer's is straightforwardly genetic, and follows the simple laws of Mendelian inheritance: if you are born with the mutated gene, you get the disease. Much more common is the late-onset disease, which tends to afflict people who are sixty-five and older. Because the prevalence of late-onset Alzheimer's increases as the population ages, the number of cases is expected to double in the next twenty-five years. Late-onset Alzheimer's is thought to be genetically influenced, too, but in a much less predictable way: it appears to involve perhaps half a dozen genes that, individually or in combination, increase one's risk of dementia. Researchers all over the world have spent the past decade hunting for these risk-factor genes, spurred by the impending public-health crisis and the daunting insufficiency of available treatments. They believe that working out the genetics of late-onset Alzheimer's, and thus finding molecular pathways that influence the course of the disease, was the best—and possibly the only—hope for finding a cure. So far, only one of those risk-factor genes has been conclusively identified.

Sue Halpern, "The Gene Hunters," *The New Yorker*

Why is this passage an example of *analysis* rather than *classification*? Which key word helped you decide? _____

_____

Analysis in Textbooks

The analytical method is particularly useful in textbook material that must clarify how the parts of a whole work together. In explaining a plant's organs, Sylvia S. Mader classifies the subject into three parts: roots, stems, and leaves. As you read the excerpt on the root systems of plants, notice that analysis examines structure, size, significant characteristics, and function.

Roots

The root system in the majority of plants is located underground. As a rule of thumb, the root system is at least equivalent in size and extent to the shoot system. An apple tree has a much larger root system than a corn plant, for example. A single corn plant may have roots as deep as 2.5 m and spread out over 1.5 m, while a mesquite tree that lives in the desert may have roots that penetrate to a depth of over 20 m.

The extensive root system of a plant anchors it in the soil and gives it support. The root system absorbs water and minerals from the soil for the entire plant. The cylindrical shape of a root allows it to penetrate the soil as it grows and permits water to be absorbed from all sides. The absorptive capacity of a root is also increased by its many branches and root hairs located in a special zone near a root tip. Root hairs, which are projections from epidermal root-hair cells, are especially responsible for the absorption of water and minerals. Root hairs are so numerous that they increase the absorptive surface of a root tremendously. It has been estimated that a single rye plant has about 14 billion hair cells, and if placed end to end, the root hairs would stretch 10,626 km. Root-hair cells are constantly being replaced, so this same rye plant forms about 100 million new root-hair cells every day. A plant roughly pulled out of the soil will not fare well when transplanted; this is because small lateral roots and root hairs are torn off. Transplantation is more apt to be successful if you take a part of the surrounding soil along with the plant, leaving as much of the lateral roots and the root hairs intact as possible.

Sylvia S. Mader, Biology

Definition

Unlike the other methods, **definition** is usually associated with a secondary method of development, typically example or illustration, comparison and contrast, and analysis. Definition is used to clarify a term that may be open to varying interpretations (or to misinterpretation) or because the writer is using a word in a subjective or personal way. A writer uses definition to explain the meaning of a new concept. Finally, definition is useful for clarifying abstract terms like *machismo*, *feminism*, *hero*, *racism*, or *patriotism*. Even when we think we know what a word means, we may not share the writer's definition. In this passage, Michael Specter explains the origins of the computer term "spam."

The original Spam (a contraction of "spiced ham") is made by the Hormel Corporation, which sent enough cans of it overseas during the Second World War to feed every G.I. In a celebrated 1970 Monty Python skit, a diner tries repeatedly and in vain to order a dish, any dish, without Spam. She is drowned out by a group of Vikings in horned helmets, who chant the word dozens of times—"Spam! Spam! Spam! Spam! Spam! Spam! Spam! Spam!"—eliminating any possibility of rational thought. The word was rapidly adopted by computer programmers as a verb meaning to flood a chat room or a bulletin board with so much data that it crashes.

Michael Specter, "Damn Spam," The New Yorker

What is the connection between the Monty Python skit and computer programmers' adoption of the term? _____

_____

Definition in Textbooks

Textbooks typically print key terms in boldface or italic type so that they stand out from the rest of the text. In this excerpt from an introductory sociology textbook, the key term *deviance* is boldfaced and italicized, followed by an explanation of its sociological definitions.

What Is Deviance?

For sociologists, the term *deviance* does not mean perversion or depravity. *Deviance* is behavior that violates the standards of conduct or expectations of a group or society (Wickman 1991:85). In the United States, alcoholics, compulsive gamblers, and the mentally ill would all be classified as deviants. Being late for class is categorized as a deviant act; the same is true of wearing jeans to a formal wedding. On the basis of the sociological definition, we are all deviant from time to time. Each of us violates common social norms in certain situations.

Is being overweight an example of deviance? In the United States and many other cultures, unrealistic standards of appearance and body image place a huge strain on people—especially adult women and girls—based on how they look. Journalist Naomi Wolf (1992) has used the term *beauty myth* to refer to an exaggerated ideal of beauty, beyond the reach of all but a few females, which has unfortunate consequences. In order to shed their "deviant" image and conform to unrealistic societal norms many women and girls become consumed with adjusting their appearances. Yet what is deviant in one culture may be celebrated in another. In Nigeria, for example, being fat is considered a mark of beauty. Part of the coming-of-age ritual calls for young girls to spend a month in a "fattening room." Among Nigerians, being thin at this point in the life course is deviant (A. Simmons 1998).

Deviance involves the violation of group norms which may or may not be formalized into law. It is a comprehensive concept that includes not only criminal-behavior but also many actions that are not subject to prosecution. The public official who takes a bribe has defied social norms, but so has the high school student who refuses to sit in an assigned seat or cuts class. Of course, deviation from norms is not always negative, let alone criminal. A member of an exclusive social club who speaks out against a traditional policy of excluding women, Blacks, and Jews from admittance is deviating from the club's norms. So is a police officer who blows the whistle on corruption or brutality within the department.

Richard T. Schaefer, *Sociology: A Brief Introduction*

Analogy

The last method of development, **analogy**, is the most sophisticated and therefore the hardest to interpret. An analogy is an *extended metaphor*, in which the writer discusses the literal subject in terms of something else. In this imaginative linking of two unlike things, the writer emphasizes shared characteristics, resulting in a fresh insight. A writer, for instance, might explain the functioning of a human eye in terms of the way a camera works—in other words, to a more familiar object. The analogy starts with a metaphor:

A : B
A (the subject) is compared to B (the metaphor)
The human eye: A camera

Unlike a simple metaphor, however, the analogy is *sustained*, typically over a few sentences or—less commonly—even throughout an essay. Analogies explain concepts in new and inventive ways. The first example is from an article reviewing the new PlayBook by Research in Motion, maker of the BlackBerry. This new tablet—like dozens of others—is intended to compete with and catch up with Apple's wildly successful iPad 1 and 2. Notice that the writer, Casey Newton, chooses an analogy that we can all identify with to describe the PlayBook's defects:

> Research in Motion calls its new tablet computer the PlayBook, but it feels more like a first draft.
>
> Like the work of a promising young novelist, the BlackBerry PlayBook is well put together and shows flashes of inspiration.
>
> But it's so rough around the edges, and so badly in need of revision, that it wouldn't be surprising to see this book wind up in the remainder bin.

Casey Newton, "A Flawed PlayBook," San Francisco Chronicle,
April 20, 2011

What inference can you make about what a remainder bin is? What is Newton implying about the PlayBook's prospects for success in her analogy? _____

_____

Here is a more complicated analogy. The writer, the owner of peach orchards in California's Central Valley, imaginatively compares weeds to an advancing army. When a central metaphor is sustained, as this one is, it becomes an analogy.

> I used to have armies of weeds on my farm. They launch their annual assault with the first warm weather of spring, parachuting seeds behind enemy lines and poking up in scattered clumps around the fields.
>
> They work underground first, incognito to a passing farmer like me. By the end of winter, dulled by the holidays and cold fog, I have my guard down. The weeds take advantage of my carelessness.
>
> The timing of their assault is crucial. They anticipate the subtle lengthening of each day. With exact calculation they germinate and push upward toward the sunlight, silently rooting themselves and establishing a foothold. The unsuspecting farmer rarely notices any change for days.
>
> Then, with the first good spring rain, the invasion begins. With beachheads established, the first wave of sprouting creatures rises to boldly expose their green leaves. Some taunt the farmer and don't even try to camouflage themselves. Defiantly they thrust their new stalks as high as possible, leaves peeling open as the plant claims more vertical territory. Soon the concealed army of seeds explodes, and within a week what had been a secure, clear territory is claimed by weeds. They seem to be everywhere, no farm is spared the invasion.

Then I hear farmers launching their counterattack. Tractors roar from their winter hibernation, gunbarrel-gray exhaust smoke shoots into the air, and cold engines churn. Oil and diesel flow through dormant lines as the machines awaken. Hungry for work, they will do well when let loose in the fields. The disks and cultivators sitting stationary throughout winter rains await the tractor hitch. The blades are brown with rust stains, bearings and gears cold and still since last fall. But I sense they too may be anxious to cleanse themselves in the earth and regain their sleek steel shimmer.

David Mas Masumoto, *Epitaph for a Peach*

Good analogies like this one are effective and compelling: They are more than a mere attention-getting device, however, because they provide a novel way of looking at a subject. Analogies can also be fanciful and whimsical, as you will see in the question-and-answer exchange between *San Francisco Chronicle* movie critic Mick LaSalle and a reader inquiring about an earlier article LaSalle had written about Alfred Hitchcock's movies. The reader ends her letter like this: "I'm sure you've never married *Vertigo*, but have you ever dated her" to which LaSalle replies: "No. We did have a couple of one-night stands spaced 10 years apart, but neither of us wanted to take it any further" (Quoted in "Ask Mick LaSalle," *San Francisco Chronicle*, February 13–19, 2011).

Online Learning Center

For some exercises in verbal analogies, click on Chapter 4 in the Student Center at www .mhee.com/spears

Practice Exercise 2

Read the following paragraphs. Then decide which method of development predominates.

- Cause and effect
- Definition
- Classification and analysis
- Analogy

In the second space, write a sentence stating the main idea in your own words.

A.

"Aphasia" means, literally, a loss of speech, but it is not speech as such that is lost but language itself—its expression, or its comprehension, in whole or in part. (Thus congenitally deaf people who use sign language rather than speech may get a sign aphasia following a brain injury or stroke, an aphasia in every way analogous to the aphasia of speaking people.)

Oliver Sacks, "Recalled to Life," *The Best American Essays 2006*

Method of development: _____

Main idea: _____

B.

A quiet revolution is stirring in our food system. It is not happening so much on the distant farms that still provide us with the majority of our food: It is happening in urban neighborhoods, suburbs, and small towns. It has evolved out of a basic need to know our food and to have some sense of control over its safety and its security. It is a new agricultural revolution that provides poor people with a safety net, an opportunity to provide nourishment and income for their families. And it offers an oasis for the human spirit where urban people can gather, preserve something of their heritage through the native seeds and foods they've brought from other places, and teach their children about food and the earth.

Michael Ableman, "Agriculture's Next Frontier," *Utne*

Method of development: _____

Main idea: _____

_____

C.

The physical changes caused by methamphetamine are profound. The drug instantly increases the amount of at least three neurotransmitters in the brain: dopamine, serotonin, and norepinephrine. Those chemicals are released naturally by the body when we feel good, but crystal unlocks a constant flood of the substances, particularly dopamine. In contrast to cocaine, which is almost completely metabolized in the body, methamphetamine lasts much longer. As with all drugs, the bigger the rush the harder the crash. After long use, the effects diminish in intensity, and depression is common. Abusers forget to drink water, and can become dangerously dehydrated. The chemicals used to make the drug are so toxic that for those who smoke it there is the danger that their teeth can crumble and fall out. Severe anorexia and malnutrition are also risks. Methamphetamine can cause heart failure and stroke. All users, not just addicts, suffer some long-term damage to the brain; memory loss and paranoia are common.

Michael Specter, "Higher Risk," *The New Yorker*

Method of development: _____

Main idea: _____

_____

D.

Here's what I think now: At first, you fall in love. You wake in the morning woozy and your twilight is lit with astral violet light. You spelunk down into each other until you come to possess some inner vision of each other that becomes one thing, Us Together. And time passes. Like the forming of Earth itself, volcanoes rise and spew lava. Oceans appear. Rock plates shift. Sea turtles swim half the ocean to lay eggs on the mother island; songbirds migrate over continents for berries from a tree. You evolve—cosmically and geologically. You lose each other and find each other again. Every day. Until love gathers the turtles and the birds of your world and encompasses them, too.

Michael Paterniti, *Driving Mr. Albert: A Trip across America with Einstein's Brain*

Method of development: _____

Main idea: _____

_____

E.

To the Egyptians, a dead body was the vessel connecting earthly life to the after-life. Eternal life could be maintained by a sculpted image of the person or even by the repetition of the deceased's name, but the ideal circumstance was to have the body permanently preserved. At all stages of ancient Egyptian civilization a tomb had two parts: one, below ground, for housing the corpse, and a second area above for offerings. In simpler burial places, the upper part might be just the open area above ground.

The upper level makes clear the importance the ancient Egyptians attached to the preparation and eating of food. Elaborate funereal feasts were held in these spaces, and copious quantities of food were left as offerings. The feasts, and some-times the preparation of foods, were depicted on the walls. Every important pe-riod in ancient Egyptian history produced tombs containing detailed information about food. Though the intention was to leave this for the benefit of the deceased, it has given posterity a clear view of an elaborate and inventive ancient cuisine.

Mark Kurlansky, *Salt: A World History*

Method of development: _____ (Hint: Beginning with sentence 3)

Main idea: _____

Critical Thinking Exercise

Is bottled water left in the desert for border-crossers "garbage"? Daniel Millis of Tucson, a volunteer who left water bottles in a wildlife refuge near the Mexican border for thirsty illegal immi-grants was arrested for violating a law that forbids "littering of garbage." The Ninth Circuit Court of Appeals ruled that the law forbidding this activity did not apply in this case, since the water containers were intended for human consumption. What definition of "garbage" do you think the judges used to make their deci-sion? You can read the court's opinion in *United States vs. Millis* at this website: Scroll down to Section II [3] to see how the justices defined "garbage."

F.

One of the least examined but most important trends taking place in the United States today is the broad decline in the status and treatment of American workers—white-collar and blue-collar workers, middle-class and low-end workers—that began nearly three decades ago, gradually gathered momentum, and hit with full force soon after the turn of this century. A profound shift has left a broad swath of the American workforce on a lower plane than in decades past, with health coverage, pension benefits, job security, workloads, stress levels, and often wages growing worse for millions of workers.

That the American worker faces this squeeze in the early years of this century is particularly troubling because the squeeze has occurred while the economy, corporate profits, and worker productivity have all been growing robustly. In recent years, a disconcerting disconnect has emerged, with corporate profits soaring while workers' wages stagnated. . . .

The squeeze on the American worker has meant more poverty, more income inequality, more family tensions, more hours at work, more time away from the kids, more families without health insurance, more retirees with inadequate pensions, and more demands on government and taxpayers to provide housing assistance and health coverage. Twenty percent of families with children under six live below the poverty line, and 22 million full-time workers do not have health insurance. Largely as a result of the squeeze, the number of housing foreclosures and personal bankruptcies more than tripled in the quarter century after 1979. Economic studies show that income inequality in the United States is so great that it more closely resembles the inequality of a third world country than that of an advanced industrial nation.

Steven Greenhouse, *The Big Squeeze: Tough Times for the American Worker*

The method of development in this passage is cause and effect. Which does the writer emphasize, or is the discussion equally balanced between the two? Explain your answer. _____

Main idea: _____

Combination of Methods

Finally, you should recognize that not all paragraphs can be as neatly categorized as those you have examined here. Although some writers use an easily recognizable method of development, many do not. In particular, within an essay or article, a writer may use several different methods from paragraph to paragraph or within the same passage. In the following excerpt, adventure travel writer and photographer Derek Grzelewski uses two methods of development—*contrast* (briefly at the beginning to contrast the Sahara and the Australian deserts) and *examples* (the beautiful little things one sees while traveling in Australia and the moods and personalities of camels).

The deserts of Australia do not resemble the Sahara with its great expanses of sand. Part woodland and savanna, this land is flat and paved with soil that is as hard and red as crushed bricks. The beauty of the Australian desert lies in small things: an ant towing a dead grasshopper, many times its size; a frilled lizard, ingeniously camouflaged against the bone-dry branches of a mulga tree; the calligraphic squiggles of a passing sand python; the perfect geometry of a wildflower or a starfish-shaped seed the size of a nickel. The desert inspires both introspection and camaraderie—the first found in the meditative pace of walking, the second forged by living side by side and depending on one another. Invariably conversation turns toward the beasts that make all of this possible.

They are formidable animals, both in size and personality. A camel resting on its haunches is still tall enough to look a person in the eye. Each has distinct moods and dislikes. Traveling with more than a dozen of these immense animals is like taking a slow train. The creaking of the saddles, the swaying of loads, the shuffling pace of the caravan strung out into a graceful line soothe even the most nervous in our group.

Derek Grzelewski, "Camelot in the Dust," *Smithsonian*

Practice Exercise 3

Read the following passages. Then choose dominant methods of development from the choices provided. Then write a sentence stating the main idea in your own words.

A. This passage is by restaurant critic and food editor Ruth Reichl, in which she describes the challenges of working in a kitchen.

Every kitchen is filled with flames and shards, fire and glass, boiling liquids and sharp objects eager to attack you. Cooking is too dangerous to permit distraction. If you step into that arena without the proper respect, you will certainly get hurt.

"Blood!" screamed a sign over the stove in my first professional kitchen. Beneath, spelled out in large letters, were the appropriate steps to be taken in case of severed appendages, injured limbs, or major burns. Peril pounces on the careless cook, and for me this lurking menace is part of the attraction. I have found that meditation at the edge of the knife makes everything seem better.

But while cooking demands your entire attention, it also rewards you with endlessly sensual pleasures. The sound of water skittering across leaves of lettuce. The thump of the knife against watermelon, and the cool summer scent the fruit releases as it falls open to reveal its deep red heart. The seductive softness of chocolate beginning to melt from solid to liquid. The tug of sauce against the spoon when it thickens in the pan, and the lovely lightness of Parmesan drifting from the grater in gossamer flakes. Time slows down in the kitchen, offering up an entire universe of small satisfactions.

Ruth Reichl, *Garlic and Sapphires*

Choose the two predominant methods of development.

(a) contrast   (c) examples
(b) facts and statistics   (d) definition

Main Idea: _____

_____

B. The writer made five trips to Russia's Siberia starting in 2000. Here he describes Siberia's notorious mosquitoes.

With such astronomical numbers, Siberian mosquitoes have learned to diversify. There are the majority, of course, who just bite you anywhere. Those are your general practitioner mosquitoes, or GPs. Then you have your specialists—your eye, ear, nose, and throat mosquitoes. Eye mosquitoes fly directly at the eyeball and crash-land there. The reason for this tactic is a mystery. The ear mosquito goes into the ear canal and then slams itself deafeningly back and forth—part of a larger psyops strategy, maybe. Nose and throat mosquitoes wait for their moment, then surf into those passages as far as they can go on the indrawn breath of air. Even deep inside they keep flying as long as possible and emitting a desperate buzzing, as if radioing for backup.

Ian Frazier, from *Travels in Siberia*

Choose the two predominant methods of development.

(a) classification   (c) definition
(b) analogy   (d) analysis

Main idea: _____

What is the meaning of the word *psyops*? Why is it appropriate for the context? _____

C.

The word *censorship* refers to the deliberate removal of language, ideas, and books from the classroom or library because they are deemed offensive or controversial. The definition gets fussier, however, when making a distinction between censorship and selection. Selection is not censorship. Teachers have a responsibility to choose readings for their students, based on their professional judgment of what students are likely to understand and what they need to learn. Librarians, however, unlike teachers, are bound by a professional code that requires them to exclude no publication because of its content or point of view. It is also important to remember that people have a First Amendment right to complain about textbooks and library books that they don't like.

Censorship occurs when school officials or publishers (acting in anticipation of the legal requirements of certain states) delete words, ideas, and topics from textbooks and tests for no reason other than their fear of controversy. Censorship may take place before publication, as it does when publishers utilize guidelines that mandate the exclusion of certain language and topics, and it may happen

What do these books and authors have in common? Toni Morrison, *The Bluest Eye;* J. D. Salinger, *Catcher in the Rye;* Mark Twain, *Huckleberry Finn;* J. K. Rowling, the Harry Potter series; and Justin Richardson and Peter Parnell, *And Tango Makes Three.* All have been banned or challenged in recent years. Sponsored by the American Library Association, this site has a great deal of information on Banned Books Week and censorship in the United States. www.ala.org. Click on "Banned Books Week."

after publication, as when parents and community members pressure school officials to remove certain books from school libraries or classrooms. Some people believe that censorship occurs only when government officials impose it, but publishers censor their products in order to secure government contracts. So the result is the same.

Diane Ravitch, *The Language Police*

Choose the three predominant methods of development.

(a) example and illustration
(b) analysis and classification
(c) definition

(d) analogy
(e) contrast
(f) cause and effect

Main idea: _____

_____

_____

■ CHAPTER EXERCISES

Selection 1

¹We've all been there—that is, in the living room of friends who invited us to dinner without mentioning that this would include a full-evening performance by their four-year-old. He sings, he dances, he eats all the hors d'oeuvres. When you try to speak to his parents, he interrupts. Why should they talk to you, about things he's not interested in, when you could all be discussing how his hamster died? His parents seem to agree; they ask him to share his feelings about that event. You yawn. Who cares? Dinner is finally served, and the child is sent off to some unfortunate person in the kitchen. The house shakes with his screams. Dinner over, he returns, his sword point sharpened. His parents again ask him how he feels. It's ten o'clock. Is he tired? No! he says. You, on the other hand, find yourself exhausted, and you make for the door, swearing never to have kids or, if you already did, never to visit your grandchildren. You'll just send checks.

²This used to be known as "spoiling." Now it is called "overparenting"—or "helicopter parenting" or "hothouse parenting" or "death-grip parenting." The term has changed because the pattern has changed. It still includes spoiling—no rules, many toys—but two other, complicating factors have been added. One is anxiety. Will the child be permanently affected by the fate of the hamster? Did he touch the corpse, and get a germ? The other new element—at odds, it seems, with such solicitude—is achievement pressure. The heck with the child's feelings. He has a nursery-school interview tomorrow. Will he be accepted? If not, how

will he ever get into a good college? Overparenting is the subject of a number of recent books, and they all deplore it in the strongest possible terms.

Joan Acocella, "The Child Trap," *The New Yorker*

A. *Vocabulary in Context—Dictionary Definitions*

These two vocabulary words from the passage are followed by two dictionary definitions. Which one is better for the way the word is used in the context?

1. with such *solicitude* [paragraph 2]
   (a) showing care or concern
   (b) anxiety
2. they all *deplore* it [2]
   (a) express strong disapproval, condemn
   (b) express sorrow or grief over

B. *Content and Structure*

1. Write the main idea of the passage in your own words.

   _____

2. What method of development is most evident in paragraph 1?_____

   What two methods of development are most evident in paragraph 2?

   _____ and _____

3. How would you explain his tone when the child says "No!"?

   _____

4. What is the purpose of the writer's two references to the child's hamster?

   _____

5. Explain what the writer means in the first paragraph when she writes, "Dinner over, he returns, his sword point sharpened."

   _____

6. Using your own words, explain the meaning of these three kinds of parenting:

   "helicopter parenting" _____

   "hothouse parenting" _____

   "death-grip parenting" _____

C. Inferences

Answer these questions in your own words.

1. What might be the underlying reason that accounts for these hypothetical parents' overparenting?

   _____

2. From the writer's discussion, what can you infer about these hypothetical parents' social and economic class? What details suggest it?

   _____

3. What do you think the writer was expecting or hoping for at this dinner?

   _____

Critical Thinking Exercise

Some writers have used the term "snowplow parenting" to describe overparenting. What do you think this term means? What are the long-term effects on a child who has been raised by such over-protective parents?

Answers for Selection 1

A. Vocabulary

1. either a or b, as both definitions fit the way the word is used here
2. a

B. Content and Structure

1. The main idea is that many of today's parents indulge their children far beyond mere spoiling; by overparenting—overly solicitous or obsessive parenting—the child becomes the complete center of attention.
2. Method of development in paragraph 1—illustration
   Methods of development in paragraph 2—definition and examples
3. The tone is defiant and insolent; he knows he can get away with it.
4. In this child-centered house, the hamster represents everything wrong. First the child is encouraged to discuss his feelings about the pet's death in front of a guest who isn't interested, and then the parents express unwarranted anxiety over germs and the effects of the death on the child's psyche.
5. The boy has found another weapon to use to get his way—defiantly saying "No!"

6. "helicopter parenting" The parents hover over the child and make a lot of noise to get their way.

"hothouse parenting" The parents treat their child as a delicate little flower to be protected from the nasty elements in the outside world.

"death-grip parenting" The parents don't give the child any freedom to explore on his own, preferring to manage every aspect of his life.

C. Inferences

1. Perhaps the parents want to raise a perfect child, to allow him to express himself freely, to insulate him from the harsh realities of the outside world. Perhaps both parents work and feel guilty about that. One can only speculate here.

2. One detail in particular suggests that the parents are wealthy, or at least affluent: There's someone to help them in the kitchen.

3. The writer clearly expected to spend her evening socializing with other adults, not interrupted by a spoiled little boy.

Selection 2

[1]So many disturbing traits, once you look into them—with a somewhat morbid curiosity, I'd begun prowling around the University Science Library,[4] an airy new building with gestures toward native construction materials, a self-conscious sensitivity to the surrounding redwoods, and the rational and antiseptic calm of too many quantitative minds padding silently down well-carpeted corridors. [2]A few tidbits: sharks are the world's only known *intrauterine cannibals;* as eggs hatch within a uterus, the unborn young fight and devour each other until one well-adapted predator emerges. [3](If the womb is a battleground, what then the sea?) [4]Also, without the gas-filled bladders that float other fish, sharks, if they stop swimming, sink. [5]This explains their tendency to lurk along the bottom like twenty-one-foot, 4,600-pound benthic land mines with hundred-year life spans. [6]Hard skin bristling with tiny teeth sheathes their flexible cartilage skeletons—no bone at all. [7]Conical snouts, black eyes without visible pupils, black-tipped pectoral fins. [8]Tearing out and constantly being replaced, their serrated fangs have as many as twenty-eight stacked spares (a bite meter embedded in a slab of meat once measured a dusky shark's bite at eighteen tons per square inch). [9]And all of the following have been found in shark bellies: a goat, a tomcat, three birds, a raincoat, overcoats, a car license plate, grass, tin cans, a cow's head, shoes, leggings, buttons, belts, hens, roosters, a nearly whole reindeer, even a headless human in a full suit of armor. [10]Swimming with their mouths open, great whites are indiscriminate recyclers of the organic—my sensitive disposition, loving family and affection for life, my decent pickup, room full of books, preoccupation with chocolate in the afternoons, and tendency to take things too personally: all immaterial to my status as protein.

Daniel Duane, *Caught Inside: A Surfer's Year on the California Coast*

[4]The library Duane refers to is at the University of California, Santa Cruz.

A. Vocabulary

Here are five vocabulary words from the selection and their definitions. Study these definitions carefully. Then write the appropriate word in each space provided according to the context.

morbid—gruesome, preoccupied by unwholesome thoughts
lurk—to lie in wait
conical—shaped like a cone
serrated—sharply notched like the edge of a saw
indiscriminate—unselective, not making careful distinctions, random

Sharks are fascinating creatures: They _____ at the bottom of the ocean

and are completely _____ in what they eat. Their noses are an unusual

_____ shape, and their incredibly strong teeth are _____. Duane

studied the behavior of sharks with a _____ curiosity.

B. Content and Structure

Complete the following questions.

1. Locate the topic of the paragraph. _____

   Then write a phrase that represents the controlling idea. _____

   _____

2. Consider again the phrase you wrote for the question above. Which method of development in the remainder of the paragraph is most evident as support for that phrase? _____

3. Paraphrase Duane's parenthetical remark from sentence 3: "If the womb is a battleground, what then the sea?" _____

   _____

   _____

4. Why must sharks constantly swim? _____

5. Look again at sentence 5, in which Duane imaginatively compares the shark to "a benthic land mine." (Benthic is an adjective referring to benthos, or organisms that live on ocean or lake bottoms.) What does Duane intend to suggest in this comparison? _____

   _____

   _____

6. From the information given in sentences 9 and 10, we can conclude that sharks
   (a) can and will eat anything, whether it is food or not.
   (b) prefer humans to any other food.
   (c) are basically carnivorous.
   (d) are able to digest inorganic objects.
7. Consider again the list of items found in sharks' stomachs. Now read sentence 10 again and locate the phrase that best describes sharks' function in the ocean. _____

Selection 3

The writer of this passage, James E. Rosenbaum, is professor of sociology, education, and social policy at Northwestern University.[5]

New Dreams, New Misconceptions

[1]The past 40 years brought three radical social transformations that together have dramatically increased the percentage of students who want to attend college. [2]First, the earnings advantage of college graduates has grown (Grubb, 1996). [3]Second, college—especially community college (a minor factor in the prior generation)—has become much more accessible. [4]In the past four decades, while enrollments at four-year colleges doubled, enrollments increased five-fold at community colleges (NCES, 1999). [5]Third, and perhaps most remarkably, virtually all community colleges adopted a revolutionary policy of open admissions. [6]Unlike many four-year colleges, virtually all two-year colleges opened their doors to admit all interested high school graduates, regardless of students' prior academic achievements. [7]Even high school graduates with barely passing grades are routinely welcomed because almost all two-year colleges offer a wide array of remedial courses. [8]Indeed, in many cases, students do not even have to be high school graduates because most two-year colleges offer these students access to some non-credit courses, including GED courses.

[9]These three transformations have dramatically altered the rules of college attendance and given students remarkable new opportunities. [10]However, as with all revolutions, there are also unintended consequences. [11]The revolutions spawned a set of myths—we'll call them misconceptions—that combined to send a message to students: Don't worry about high school grades or effort; you can still go to college and do fine. [12]This message has not been sent to high achievers aiming for prestigious colleges, where grades and scores matter—and the students headed there know it. [13]But it is the message that students who know little about college have received—particularly those whose parents did not go to college. [14]These students (and their parents) are being misled with disastrous consequences. [15]Their motivation to work hard in high school is sapped; their time to prepare for college is wasted; their college savings are eaten up by remedial courses that they could have taken for free in high school; and their chances

[5]The entire article from which this excerpt comes is available online at www.aft.org. Click on "Publications/Reports," then on *American Educator*, and finally on "Previous Issues." Scroll down to the Spring 2004 issue.

of earning a college degree are greatly diminished. [16]Further, the effect on many colleges has been to alter their mission and lower their standards.

James E. Rosenbaum, "It's Time to Tell the Kids: If You Don't Do Well in High School, You Won't Do Well in College (or on the Job)," *American Educator*

A. *Vocabulary*

For each italicized word from the selection, write the dictionary definition most appropriate for the context.

1. a wide *array* of remedial courses [sentence 7]_____

   _____

2. the revolutions *spawned* a set of myths [11]:_____

   _____

3. their motivation to work hard . . . is *sapped* [15]:_____

   _____

B. *Content and Structure*

Complete the following questions.

1. Write a sentence stating the main idea of the passage. _____

   _____

   _____

2. Which best describes the logical relationship between the two paragraphs?
   (a) Paragraph 1 establishes causes and paragraph 2 examines their effects.
   (b) Paragraph 1 compares and paragraph 2 contrasts.
   (c) Paragraph 1 states a term to be defined and paragraph 2 explains it further.
   (d) Paragraph 1 classifies and paragraph 2 analyzes.

3. Whom does the writer primarily blame for sending the wrong message to high-school students that accounts for the "disastrous consequences" many students face in college? _____

   _____

   _____

4. Of these recommendations, which ones would the writer most likely support?
   (a) No student should be admitted to a community college without being a high-school graduate.
   (b) Community colleges should tighten up their admissions standards by revising their open-door policy.
   (c) High-school teachers and counselors should do a better job of educating students about the realities they will face in college.
   (d) High schools should establish trade and technical programs for students who are not college bound.
   (e) Colleges should stop looking at high-school grades and focus only on standardized test scores as a better predictor of college success.
   (f) Community colleges offer a helpful second chance for students if they are willing to work hard and show effort.

The article was accompanied by several charts, among them this one dated from 1982.

In the class of 1982, 86 percent of college-bound students with poor grades didn't graduate from college.

AVERAGE HIGH SCHOOL GRADES	As	Bs	Cs OR LOWER	ALL
Percentage attaining A.A. or higher	63.9	37.1	13.9	37.7
Percentage not attaining any degree	36.1	62.9	86.1	62.3

Seniors with college plans (A.A. or higher) who complete an A.A. degree or higher within 10 years of high school graduation.
Source: Beyond College for All; High School and Beyond data.

5. Write a sentence stating the relationship between high-school grades and the attainment of a college degree that these figures convey.

_____

_____

_____

6. The chart shows one anomaly—a rather surprising statistic concerning the figures for students who never attain a degree. What is it?

_____

_____

_____

7. These figures represent data from 1982. What is the justification for using such seemingly old data? _____

_____

_____

PRACTICE ESSAY

"The Pen and the Scalpel"
Richard Selzer

Richard Selzer (1928–) practiced surgery for many years in New Haven, Connecticut, where he was also on the faculty of the Yale School of Medicine. In 1986, as Selzer explains in this 1988 article from The New York Times, *he began writing in the middle of the night and practicing surgery during the day. Selzer has published several books and magazine articles, and he has received numerous awards for his writing. Among his many books are* Mortal Lessons *(1977),* Confessions of a Knife *(1979),* The Doctor Stories *(2004), and most recently a novel,* Knife Song Korea *(2009).*

Preview Questions

1. It may seem odd, but there are a relatively large number of physicians who have become writers. What might be some motivations for this seemingly odd combination of occupations?
2. What are some qualities or characteristics that writers and surgeons have in common? How many can you anticipate before you read Selzer's essay?

1 I had been a general surgeon for 15 years when, at the age of 40, the psychic energy for writing inexplicably appeared. It was an appearance that was to knock over my life. For 15 years I had studied, practiced and taught surgery at the Yale School of Medicine, all the while enjoying the usefulness and the *handsomeness* of the craft. For the next 16 years, until my recent retirement, I would practice both surgery and writing. But where to fit in the writing when all of my days and half of my nights were fully engaged? Certainly not evenings. In the evening, one visits with one's next-of-kin; in the evening one helps with homework; in the evening, if one is so inclined, one has a martini. Instead, I became the first adult in the state of Connecticut to go to bed in the evening. Having slept from 8:30 p.m. to 1 in the morning, I rose, went down to the kitchen, put on a pot of tea and wrote in longhand (a typewriter would disturb the household) until 3 o'clock. Then it was back upstairs and to sleep until

6 in the morning, when I began the day's doctoring. Plenty of sleep, only divided by two hours, when I was alone with my pen, and all the light in the world gathered upon a sheet of paper. In this way, I wrote three collections of stories, essays and memoirs.

2   Time was when in the professions—medicine and law—to patronize the arts was respectable; to practice them was not. For a surgeon it was even more questionable. Who wants to know, after all, what a surgeon does in his spare time? When it became known how I was spending my wild nights, my colleagues at the hospital were distressed. "Come, come" they coaxed in (more or less) the words of the poet Richard Wilbur, "Forsake those roses of the mind, and tend the true, the mortal flower." But because the subject of my writings was my work as a doctor, the two seemed inseparable. The one fertilized the other. Why, I wondered, doesn't every surgeon write? A doctor walks in and out of a dozen short stories a day. It is irresistible to write them down. When, at last, the time came to make a choice between my two passions, it had already been made for me. Listen:

3   In the operating room, the patient must be anesthetized in order that he feel no pain. The surgeon too must be "anesthetized" in order to remain at some distance from the event: when he cuts the patient, his own flesh must not bleed. It is this seeming lack of feeling that gives the surgeon the image of someone who is out of touch with his humanity, a person wanting only to cut, to perform. I assure you that it is the image only. A measure of insulation against the laying open of the bodies of his fellow human beings is necessary for the well-being of both patient and doctor. In surgery, if nowhere else, dispassion is an attribute. But the surgeon-writer is not anesthetized. He remains awake; sees everything; censors nothing. It is his dual role to open and repair the body of his patient and to report back to the waiting world in the keenest language he can find. By becoming a writer, I had stripped off the protective carapace. It was time to go. A surgeon can unmake himself; a writer cannot.

4   A Faustian bargain,[6] you say? Perhaps, but, truth to tell, New Haven had begun to seem rather like the Beast With a Thousand Gallbladders. And where is it graven in stone that, once having been ordained, a surgeon must remain at the operating table until the scalpel slips from his lifeless fingers? Nor had I any wish to become like the old lion whose claws are long since blunt but not the desire to use them. Still, one does not walk away from the workbench of one's life with a cheery wave of the hand. In the beginning, I felt a strange sense of dislocation. As though I were standing near a river whose banks were flowing while the stream itself stood still. Only now, after two years, have I ceased to have attacks of longing for the labor that so satisfied and uplifted my spirit. Then, too, there was the risk that by withdrawing from the hospital, with its rich cargo of patients and those who tend them, I would be

[6]In German legend, Dr. Faust, an alchemist, sold his soul to the devil in exchange for complete wisdom and knowledge. *Faustian* is the adjective derived from his name.

punished as a writer, suffer from impotence of the pen. A writer turns his back upon his native land at his own peril. Besides, to begin the life of a writer at the age of 56 is to toil under the very dart of death. As did another doctor-writer, John Keats, I too "have fears that I may cease to be before my pen has gleaned my teeming brain."

5   In medicine, there is a procedure called transillumination. If, in a darkened room, a doctor holds a bright light against a hollow part of the body, he will see through the outer tissues to the structures within that cavity— arteries, veins, projecting shelves of bone. In such a ruby gloom he can distinguish among a hernia, a hydrocele of the scrotum and a tumor of the testicle. Or he can light up a sinus behind the brow. Unlike surgery, which opens the body to direct examination, transillumination gives an indirect vision, calling into play the simplest perceptions of the doctor. To write about a patient is like transillumination. You hold the lamp of language against his body and gaze through the covering layers at the truths within.

6   At first glance, it would appear that surgery and writing have little in common, but I think that is not so. For one thing, they are both subcelestial arts; as far as I know, the angels disdain to perform either one. In each of them you hold a slender instrument that leaves a trail wherever it is applied. In one, there is the shedding of blood; in the other it is ink that is spilled upon a page. In one, the scalpel is restrained; in the other, the pen is given rein. The surgeon sutures together the tissues of the body to make whole what is sick or injured; the writer sews words into sentences to fashion a new version of human experience. A surgical operation is rather like a short story. You make the incision, rummage around inside for a bit, then stitch up. It has a beginning, a middle and an end. If I were to choose a medical specialist to write a novel, it would be a psychiatrist. They tend to go on and on. And on.

7   Despite that I did not begin to write until the middle of my life, I think I must always have been a writer. Like my father who was a general practitioner during the Depression in Troy, N.Y., and who wrote a novel. It was all about a prostitute with a heart of gold (her name was Goldie!) and the doctor who first saves her life, then falls in love with her. Mother read it and told him: "Keep it away from the children."

8   Father's office was on the ground floor of an old brownstone, and we lived upstairs. At night, after office hours, my brother Billy and I (we were 10 and 9 years old) would sneak downstairs to Father's darkened consultation room and there, shamefaced, by the light of a candle stub, we would take down from the shelves his medical textbooks. Our favorite was "The Textbook of Obstetrics and Gynecology."

9   It was there that I first became aware of the rich language of medicine. Some of the best words began with the letter C. *Carcinoma*, I read, and thought it was that aria from "Rigoletto" that mother used to sing while she washed and dried the dishes. *Cerebellum*. I said the word aloud, letting it drip off the end of my tongue like melted chocolate. And I read *choledochojejunostomy*, which later I was to learn as the name of an

operation. All those syllables marching off in my mind to that terminal *y*! If that was the way surgeons talked, I thought, I would be one of them, and live forever in a state of mellifluous rapture. I do not use these words in my writing, but I do try to use language that evokes the sounds of the body—the *lub-dup, lub-dup* of the garrulous heart, the gasp and wheeze of hard breathing, all the murmur and splash of anatomy and physiology. And I have tried to make use of the poetic potential in scientific language. Here, from my diary, this specimen:

> How gentle the countryside near Troy, with much farming everywhere. Farming gives a sense of health to the land. It is replenishing to watch at dusk as the herd of cattle flows like a giant amoeba toward the barn. First one cow advances. She pauses. Another pseudopodium is thrust ahead, pulling the others behind it until all of the cytoplasm, trailing milk, is inside the barn. All along the banks of the Hudson River, oak, elm and locust trees have grown very tall. The bark of the locust is thrown into deep folds coated with lichen and moss. So old are these trees that, without the least wind, one will drop off a quite large branch as if to shed a part of its burden. This letting-fall doesn't seem to do the tree any harm. It is more an anatomical relinquishment of a part so that the whole might remain healthy. Much as a diabetic will accept amputation of a gangrenous toe in order that he might once again walk on his foot. How clever of these locust trees to require no surgeon for their trimmage, only their own corporeal wisdom.

A. *Comprehension*

Choose the answer that best completes each statement. Do not refer to the selection while doing this exercise.

1. What was the reaction of Selzer's medical colleagues when they discovered that he was writing on the side?
   (a) They tried to talk him out of it.
   (b) They were envious.
   (c) They encouraged him to continue.
   (d) They warned him that writing on the side would interfere too much with surgery.
2. The chief advantage of being a surgeon-writer, as opposed to simply being a surgeon, is
   (a) the need to anesthetize himself from the less pleasant aspects of surgery.
   (b) the possibility of convincing readers to take up medicine, or at least to find the subject interesting.
   (c) the chance not only to observe the process of surgery and of healing but also to describe everything clearly to the reader.
   (d) the necessity of remaining dispassionate during both the process of surgery and the process of writing about it.

3. Selzer writes that nowhere is it "graven in stone" that one has to
   (a) perform the same job until he or she dies.
   (b) listen to the criticisms and warnings of his or her colleagues.
   (c) do a job that one has never been particularly suited for.
   (d) sacrifice one's own happiness just to please others.

4. For Selzer, the process of transillumination is similar to writing about a patient. Transillumination refers to
   (a) a special type of lighting used during surgery.
   (b) a bright light that reveals the body's internal structures.
   (c) a style of writing that is specific to medical topics.
   (d) a flashlight used to detect hernias and tumors.

5. When Selzer and his brother were growing up in Troy, New York, they particularly enjoyed
   (a) tagging along after their father, also a doctor, while he saw his patients.
   (b) playing with the equipment in their father's medical laboratory.
   (c) watching their father, a surgeon, perform operations.
   (d) sneaking into their father's office and reading his medical textbooks.

B. Vocabulary

For each italicized word from the selection, write the dictionary definition most appropriate for the context.

1. this psychic energy for writing *inexplicably* appeared [paragraph 1]

   _____

2. to *patronize* the arts [2] _____

3. dispassion is an *attribute* [3] _____

4. stripped off the protective *carapace* [3] _____

5. suffer from *impotence* of the pen [4] _____

6. the angels *disdain* to perform [6] _____

   _____

7. in a state of *mellifluous* rapture [9] _____

8. language that *evokes* the sounds [9] _____

9. the *garrulous* heart [9] _____

_____

10. their own *corporeal* wisdom [9] _____

C. Paraphrasing

Write the meaning of the following sentences from the essay in your own words.

1. "Still, one does not walk away from the workbench of one's life with a cheery wave of the hand." [paragraph 4] _____

_____

2. "As did another doctor-writer, John Keats, I too 'have fears that I may cease to be before my pen has gleaned my teeming brain.'" _____

_____

_____

3. ". . . they [surgery and writing] are both subcelestial arts; as far as I know, the angels disdain to perform either one." _____

_____

D. Structure and Meaning

Complete the following questions.

1. Apart from the obvious reason that he didn't want to wake his family, what might be another reason that Selzer wrote in the middle of the night? _____

_____

2. Look again at the beginning of paragraph 2. Why were Selzer's colleagues "distressed" when they found out he was writing on the side?

_____

_____

3. What method of paragraph development is most evident in paragraphs 3 and 6? _____

_____

4. Explain in your own words the main point of Selzer's journal entry at the end of the essay. _____

_____

_____

E. Questions for Discussion and Analysis

1. What exactly do the pen and the scalpel refer to? Why did he choose these objects to form the essay's title? Considering the essay's content, why is the title effective?

2. Look through the essay again and find sentences that show Selzer's interest in poetry. What does this interest reveal about Selzer?

3. Who is the audience for this essay? (Note its original publication in *The New York Times*.) Is this article directed toward general readers or to those well versed in medicine? Does Selzer make concessions for the general reader or not? Explain.

 IN THE LIBRARY

Besides Richard Selzer, there is a fairly large group of physician-writers. Here are a few of the best known. Anton Chekhov was a famous Russian writer of short stories and plays. Khaled Hosseini is a novelist, originally from Afghanistan. Verghese writes both fiction and nonfiction. All the rest are nonfiction writers.

Anton Chekhov, *The Stories of Anton Chekhov*. Translated by Richard Pevear and Larissa Volokhonsky (2000).

Atul Gawande, *Complications: A Surgeon's Notes on an Imperfect Science* (2003) and *Better: A Surgeon's Notes on Performance* (2007).

Jerome Groopman, *How Doctors Think* (2007) and *Second Opinions: Stories of Intuition and Choice in the Changing World of Medicine (2000).*

Khaled Hosseini, *The Kite Runner* (2003) and *A Thousand Splendid Suns* (2007).

Frank Huyler, *The Blood of Strangers: Stories from Emergency Medicine* (1999).

Perri Klass. *Baby Doctor* (1992).

John F. Murray, *Intensive Care: A Doctor's Journal* (2000).

Abraham Verghese, *The Tennis Partner* (1999) and *Cutting for Stone* (2009).

Siddharta Mukherjee, *The Emperor of All Maladies: A Biography of Cancer* (2010).

CHAPTER 5

Patterns of Paragraph Organization

CHAPTER OBJECTIVES

In Chapter 5 you will study the ways writers arrange ideas within paragraphs and transitional devices, specifically

- Patterns of paragraph organization
- Coherence in paragraphs

■ PATTERNS OF ORGANIZATION DEFINED

The **patterns of organization** refer to the various ways that a paragraph's sentences can be arranged. As you have seen, the paragraph is remarkably versatile; nevertheless, we can identify four standard patterns:

- Chronological
- Spatial
- Deductive
- Inductive

The first and second patterns are commonly found in narrative and descriptive writing; the other two are commonly found in expository or persuasive writing.

Chronological Order

Chronological (or time) order, the easiest pattern to recognize, refers to the order in which events happen. It is used to tell a story, to relate an incident, to recount a historical event, or to describe the steps in a process. Chronological order is evident in this paragraph from a psychology textbook, in which the writer describes babies' perceptual development.

> During infancy, children develop the ability to form cognitive representations of the world. For example, by 6 to 9 months of age, the child begins to understand that objects exist even when they are out of sight. This is called **object permanence**. Before that time, if an object at which the infant is looking is hidden from sight by a card, the infant will not push the card aside to look for it. It's as if the infant does not know that the object is still there—a variation of "out of sight, out of mind." After 6 to 9 months of age, however, the infant will search for the object behind the card, suggesting that the infant knows that it's back there somewhere. This is both a happy and a sad development for parents. Now that the 9-month-old knows that spoons still exist when thrown on the floor, the infant quickly masters the game of "dropsies" (McCall, 1979). Infants joyously fill their mealtimes with the game of throwing their spoons on the floor while Dad or Mom picks them up. By 14 months, infants even look for objects that were removed 24 hours earlier (Moore & Meltzoff, 2004), but although infants can represent parts of the world in mental images, they cannot yet use those images to reason.
>
> Benjamin B. Lahey, *Psychology: An Introduction*

Note that the transitional phrases referring to the baby's age ("by 6 to 9 months," "after 6 to 9 months," and "by 14 months") establish the chronological pattern.

Spatial Order

The term **spatial** is related to the word *space*. Spatial order refers to the arrangement of details observed in an environment. Most often used in descriptive writing, spatial order helps a writer organize his or her observations so that the reader can visualize the scene. In fiction and in nonfiction descriptive writing, spatial order helps us visualize the setting. Without it, the details would be a random assembly of impressions, making the scene difficult to re-create in our minds.

Some ways writers may arrange details are from left to right or right to left, near to far or far to near, top to bottom, or bottom to top. The transitions showing movement from one part of a scene to another are indicated by prepositional phrases. Here is a good example of spatial order from one of Alexander McCall Smith's charming detective novels set in Botswana, a country in the southern part of Africa. As Mma Ramotswe, the owner of the No. 1 Ladies' Detective Agency, drives her trademark tiny white van north out of the city, she observes the passing countryside. Spatial order is most evident in the last paragraph.

. . . Just past the Mochudi turnoff, the sun came up, rising over the wide plains that stretched away towards the course of the Limpopo. Suddenly it was there, smiling on Africa, a slither of golden red ball, inching up, floating effortlessly free of the horizon to dispel the last wisps of morning mist.

The thorn trees stood clear in the sharp light of morning, and there were birds upon them, and in flight—hoopoes, louries, and tiny birds which she could not name. Here and there cattle stood at the fence which followed the road for mile upon mile. They raised their heads and stared, or ambled slowly on, tugging at the tufts of dry grass that clung tenaciously to the hardened earth.

This was a dry land. Just a short distance to the west lay the Kalahari, a hinterland of ochre that stretched off, for unimaginable miles, to the singing emptinesses of the Namib. If she turned her tiny white van off on one of the tracks that struck off from the main road, she could drive for perhaps thirty or forty miles before her wheels would begin to sink into the sand and spin hopelessly. The vegetation would slowly become sparser, more desert-like. The thorn trees would thin out and there would be ridges of thin earth, through which the omnipresent sand would surface and crenellate. There would be patches of bareness, and scattered grey rocks, and there would be no sign of human activity. To live with this great dry interior, brown and hard, was the lot of the Batswana, and it was this that made them cautious, and careful in their husbandry.

Alexander McCall Smith, *The No. 1 Ladies' Detective Agency*

In this second example, Kenneth Boulding uses spatial order in an unusual way: to locate himself first in his narrow environment and then to locate Earth in the larger universe. By repeating the key preposition *beyond*, Boulding enables us to follow his mind's journey. (A basic knowledge of world geography also helps.)

As I sit at my desk, I know where I am. I see before me a window; beyond that some trees; beyond that the red roofs of the campus of Stanford University; beyond them the trees and the roof tops which mark the town of Palo Alto; beyond them the bare golden hills of the Hamilton Range. I know, however, more than I see. Behind me, although I am not looking in that direction, I know there is a window, and beyond that the little campus of the Center for the Advanced Study in the Behavioral Sciences; beyond that the Coast Range; beyond that the Pacific Ocean. Looking ahead of me again, I know that beyond the mountains that close my present horizon, there is a broad valley; beyond that a still higher range of mountains; beyond that other mountains, range upon range, until we come to the Rockies; beyond that the Great Plains and the Mississippi; beyond that the Alleghenies; beyond that the eastern seaboard; beyond that the Atlantic Ocean, beyond that is Europe; beyond that is Asia. I know, furthermore, that if I go far enough I will come back to where I am now. In other words, I have a picture of the earth as round. I visualize it as a globe. I am a little hazy on some of the details.

I am not quite sure, for instance, whether Tanganyika is north or south of Nyasaland.[1] I probably could not draw a very good map of Indonesia, but I have a fair idea where everything is located on the face of this globe. Looking further, I visualize the globe as a small speck circling around a bright star which is the sun, in the company of many other similar specks, the planets. Looking still further, I see our star the sun as a member of millions upon millions of others in the Galaxy. Looking still further, I visualize the Galaxy as one of millions upon millions of others in the universe.

Kenneth Boulding, *The Image*

Aside from his unusual geography tour, what is the central philosophical point Boulding makes?_____

_____

_____

Deductive Order

In Chapter 2, you learned that paragraphs often begin with a main idea, which is reinforced by specific supporting sentences. This pattern of organization, the most common in the English paragraph, is called **deductive** order. For this reason, deductive order is sometimes called **general-to-specific order.** This term actually refers to a pattern of thinking, which you will read about in more detail in Chapter 9. Deductive order and its opposite, inductive order, are determined by the placement of the main idea. You can easily visualize deductive order if you imagine an inverted triangle with the base at the top:

Deductive order is particularly useful in textbook and other expository material, whereby the main idea is stated directly at the beginning of a passage followed by explanatory material. The deductive pattern is evident in this passage from Elizabeth Gilbert's recent nonfiction bestseller, *Eat, Pray, Love*. Note that Gilbert restates the main idea from the first sentence in the third sentence.

Religious ceremonies are of paramount importance here in Bali (an island, don't forget, with seven unpredictable volcanoes on it—you would pray, too). It has been estimated that a typical Balinese woman spends one-third

[1]Since this passage was written, Tanganyika and Zanzibar joined together and are now called Tanzania; Nyasaland is now called Malawi.

of her waking hours either preparing for a ceremony, participating in a ceremony or cleaning up after a ceremony. Life here is a constant cycle of offerings and rituals. You must perform them all, in correct order and with the correct intention, or the entire universe will fall out of balance. Margaret Mead wrote about "the incredible busy-ness" of the Balinese, and it's true—there is rarely an idle moment in a Balinese compound. There are ceremonies here which must be performed five times a day and others that must be performed once a day, once a week, once a month, once a year, once every ten years, once every hundred years, once every thousand years. All these dates and rituals are kept organized by the priests and holy men, who consult a byzantine system of three separate calendars.

Elizabeth Gilbert, *Eat, Pray, Love*

Explain the parenthetical remark at the end of the first sentence.

Inductive Order

Inductive order, the opposite of deductive order, is sometimes called **specific-to-general order.** Inductive order derives from a kind of thinking called induction, which will be taken up in Chapter 9. For now, it is enough to know that inductive order involves a series of specific observations leading to a generalization (the main idea) that the reader can validly infer from those statements. Again, the placement of the main idea determines the pattern.

A diagram of an inductively arranged paragraph looks like this:

Malcolm Gladwell uses the inductive pattern in this paragraph about pit bulls. He begins with a series of observations about the breed, contrasting the behavior of pit bulls with that of another breed of guard dog, the German shepherd. He ends with a concise sentence that summarizes the main point of the paragraph—the main idea.

Pit bulls, descendants of the bulldogs used in the nineteenth century for bull baiting and dogfighting, have been bred for "gameness," and thus a lowered inhibition to aggression. Most dogs fight as a last resort, when staring and growling fail. A pit bull is willing to fight with little or no provocation. Pit bulls seem to have a high tolerance for pain, making it possible for them to fight to the point of exhaustion. Whereas guard dogs like German shepherds usually attempt to restrain those they perceive to be threats by biting and holding, pit bulls try to inflict the maximum amount of damage on an opponent. They bite, hold, shake, and tear. They don't growl or assume an aggressive facial expression as warning. They just attack. "They are often insensitive to behaviors that usually stop aggression," one scientific review of the breed states. "For example, dogs not bred for fighting usually display defeat in combat by rolling over and exposing a light underside. On several occasions, pit bulls have been reported to disembowel dogs offering this signal of submission." In epidemiological studies of dog bites, the pit bull is overrepresented among dogs known to have seriously injured or killed human beings, and, as a result, pit bulls have been banned or restricted in several Western European countries, China, and numerous cities and municipalities across North America. Pit bulls are dangerous.

Malcolm Gladwell, "Troublemakers," *The New Yorker*

Practice Exercise 1

Read the following paragraphs. First, decide which pattern of organization each represents.

- Chronological order
- Deductive order
- Spatial order
- Inductive order

Then write a sentence stating the main idea in your own words.

A.

Animals seem to have an instinct for performing death alone, hidden. Even the largest, most conspicuous ones find ways to conceal themselves in time. If an elephant missteps and dies in an open place, the herd will not leave him there; the others will pick him up and carry the body from place to place, finally putting it down in some inexplicably suitable location. When elephants encounter the skeleton of an elephant out in the open, they methodically take up each of the bones and distribute them, in a ponderous ceremony, over neighboring acres.

Lewis Thomas, *Lives of a Cell*

Pattern of organization:_____

Main idea:_____

B. This passage describing his Paris neighborhood is from George Orwell's classic semi-autobiographical book, *Down and Out in Paris and London.*

It was a very narrow street—a ravine of tall, leprous houses, lurching toward one another in queer attitudes, as though they had all been frozen in the act of collapse. All the houses were hotels and packed to the tiles with lodgers, mostly Poles, Arabs, and Italians. At the foot of the hotels were tiny *bistros,* where you could be drunk for the equivalent of a shilling. On Saturday nights about a third of the male population of the quarter was drunk. There was fighting over women, and the Arab navvies who lived in the cheapest hotels used to conduct mysterious feuds, and fight them out with chairs and occasionally revolvers. At night the policemen would only come through the street two together. It was a fairly rackety place. And yet amid the noise and dirt lived the usual respectable French shopkeepers, bakers and laundresses and the like, keeping themselves to themselves and quietly piling up small fortunes. It was quite a representative Paris slum.

George Orwell, *Down and Out in Paris and London*

Pattern of organization: _____

Main idea: _____

C. This passage is from the Egyptian Nobel Prize-winning writer, Naguib Mahfouz.

Except for the father, the family gathered shortly before sunset for what they called the coffee hour. The chosen site was the first-floor sitting room surrounded by the children's bedrooms, the parlor, and a fourth small room set aside for studying. Its floor was spread with colored mats. Divans with pillows and cushions stood in the corners. Hanging from the ceiling was a large lantern illuminated by an equally large kerosene lamp. The mother sat on a sofa in the center. In front of her was a large brazier where the coffeepot was half buried in the embers topped by ashes. To her right was a table holding a brass tray with cups lined up on it. The children were seated opposite her, including those permitted to drink coffee with her, like Yasin and Fahmy, and those barred from it by custom and etiquette, like the two sisters and Kamal, who contented themselves with the conversation.

Naguib Mahfouz, *Palace Walk*

Pattern of organization: _____

Main idea: _____

How does the pattern of organization help clarify the main idea? _____

_____

D.

Monday, August 6, 1945, began like any other wartime day in Japan. By 8 A.M. most Hiroshima office workers were at their desks, children were at school, soldiers were doing physical exercises, high-school students and civilian work gangs were busy pulling down wooden houses to clear more firebreaks. During the night, there had been two air-raid alerts—and then all-clears. At 7:09 A.M., there was another alert, as a B-29 on a last weather check approached the city, and, at 7:31 A.M., another all-clear as it turned away. Minutes after eight, watchers in the city saw two B-29s approaching from the northeast: these were an observation plane and the Enola Gay. (Colonel Paul Tibbets, the pilot, had only the day before named the bomber after his mother.) The Enola Gay, in the lead, held its course straight and level for ten miles; at eight-fifteen, it let fall its single bomb. Immediately, the other B-29 banked hard to the left, the Enola Gay to the right; both quit the scene. Released at thirty one thousand six hundred feet, or nearly six miles, the bomb fell for forty-three seconds and was triggered (by a barometric switch) by heavily symbolic chance nineteen hundred feet directly above a small hospital that was two hundred and sixty yards from the aiming point, the T-shaped Aoio Bridge.

Murray Sayle, "Letter from Hiroshima: Did the Bomb End the War?" *The New Yorker*

Pattern of organization: _____

Main idea: _____

_____

E.

As baths and their facilities grew more elaborate, Romans often spent most of their leisure hours there. With pools, exercise yards, gardens, libraries, meeting rooms and snack bars, the bath became a multi-purpose meeting point, a place to make connections, do business, flirt, talk politics, eat and drink. Prostitutes, healers and beauticians often had premises in the bath complex or in the shops around its perimeter, so it was possible to have sex, a medical treatment and a haircut as part of a regular visit. Although well-born men used their favourite bath as English aristocrats would later use their London club, the bathhouse was also the most democratic Roman institution. Unlike the Greek gymnasium, which was limited to middle-class and upper-class men, the Roman bath accommodated men and women, slaves and freedmen, rich and poor. A Roman, at least by the first century B.C., when there were 170 baths in the capital, had plentiful choice but usually settled on one as a regular haunt. It was common, when meeting a man, to ask where he bathed.

The purposes that cafés, town squares, clubs, gymnasiums, country clubs and spas served in other societies, including ours, were fulfilled here. Imagine a superbly equipped YMCA that covered some blocks, with gyms, pools, ball courts and meeting rooms. Then add onto it the massage and treatment rooms of a fancy spa and the public rooms and grounds of a resort. Finally, give it a fee structure that would allow the poorest people to use its facilities. That approximates, but does not equal, an Imperial bathhouse.

Katherine Ashenburg, *The Dirt on Clean: An Unsanitized History*

Pattern of organization (each paragraph): _____

Main idea: _____

Explain why Roman bathhouses were "the most democratic Roman institution."

_____

Critical Thinking Exercise

In our society, do we have a "multipurpose meeting point" comparable to the Roman baths where people can freely congregate, do business, talk politics, and enjoy themselves? The place you come up with it must, like the Roman baths, serve the same purposes and be open to all, no matter what their social status.

■ COHERENCE IN PARAGRAPHS

How do writers ensure that their readers stay on track, no matter which of the above patterns they use? As you learned in Chapter 2, careful writers try to help the reader follow the main idea by ensuring that the paragraph has *unity*, or singleness of purpose. In good writing, there should be no irrelevant or extraneous sentences to lead you astray. But in addition to unity, well-constructed paragraphs also have **coherence**, which literally means the quality of "sticking together," so that each sentence leads logically and smoothly to the next, the sentences in effect forming a chain of interconnected thoughts. (Not all writers accomplish this, of course, which is why some reading material is so tedious to read.) Good writers achieve coherence through three primary techniques: by using transitions, by repeating key words, and by using pronouns.

Achieving
Coherence:
Transitions

Transitions are signposts or markers that indicate a logical relationship or a shift in direction. Transitions can be single words or phrases; occasionally, an entire paragraph can serve as a bridge between the major sections of an essay. Although transitions may appear at the beginning of sentences, this is not a hard and fast rule; transitions can come in the middle or at the end of sentences as well. Paying attention to transitions will improve your concentration and comprehension and will help you see the logical connections between ideas. Sometimes a good understanding of a passage may depend on a seemingly unimportant little word like "but" or "for" or "as." To show you how crucial transitions are, this paragraph from a broadcasting textbook is printed without the transitions. The subject is virtual communities, in particular MySpace, where people congregate in cyberspace.

People congregate in many ways on MySpace. By posting a profile regarding one's musical interests, one may draw viewers to the page; it might be a poem or an unusual self-portrait that entices someone. Perhaps the thing that's so interesting about MySpace is its level of interactivity and the amorphous way it is possible to move from pictures, to words, to music, to people. If you'll accept a city street analogy, each click takes the viewer down a new street with new sights, sounds, and people to meet. Banner ads change as a new link is made. The website membership has skyrocketed, and it currently boasts some 50 million users. Not all is completely serene in the virtual world. There are concerns with MySpace and other virtual communities like it. Stories have surfaced about minors posting dangerously personal information like addresses and telephone numbers in their pages. Parents have complained about incidents of bullying from classmates, and there have been reports of sexual predators enticing minors into meeting for sexual encounters. A virtual community may pose the same risks as a real one.

Notice how difficult it is to follow the discussion. Reading this passage is like reading a novel with pages missing. Here is the actual version, this time printed with the transitions restored and italicized, making it much less tedious to read.

People congregate in many ways on MySpace. By posting a profile regarding one's musical interests, *for example*, one may draw viewers to the page, *but* it might also be a poem or an unusual self-portrait that entices someone. Perhaps the thing that's so interesting about MySpace is its level of interactivity and the amorphous way it is possible to move from pictures, to words, to music, to people. If you'll accept a city street analogy, each click takes the viewer down a new street with new sights, sounds, and people to meet. *Along the way*, banner ads change as a new link is made. *Over the last year*, the Web site's membership has skyrocketed, and it currently boasts some 50 million users. *However*, not all is completely serene in the virtual world. There are concerns with MySpace and other virtual communities like it. *Recently* stories have surfaced about minors posting dangerously personal information like addresses and telephone numbers on their pages. Parents have complained about incidents of bullying from classmates, and there have been reports of sexual predators enticing minors into meeting for sexual encounters. *Evidently* a virtual community may pose the same risks as a real one.

Joseph R. Dominick, Fritz Messere, and Barry L. Sherman,
Broadcasting. Cable, the Internet, and Beyond: An Introduction to Modern Electronic Media

The boxes in this section of the chapter present the various transitions according to their function, followed by a few examples of words or phrases indicating the logical relationship they bring to the sentences they join. An example is provided for each category of transition.

> ### Transitions Signaling an Additional Statement (usually of equal importance)
>
> and, in addition (to), additionally, as well as, besides, furthermore, moreover

Example: The house was badly neglected: the windows were broken, *and* the paint was blistered. *Moreover*, what had once been a well-tended lawn was now only an overgrown weed patch.

Transitions Signaling a Contrast

but, yet, however, nevertheless, nonetheless, while, whereas, on the other hand, in contrast (to), contrary to

---

Example: Basset hounds and St. Bernards are known for their placid and friendly natures; *in contrast*, terriers are often high-strung and highly excitable.

Transitions Signaling an Example or Illustration

for example, as an example, to illustrate, as an illustration, for instance, namely, specifically, a case in point, consider the following

---

Example: Many residents of urban neighborhoods believe that an influx of national franchise stores can ruin local businesses and destroy a neighborhood's unique quality, resulting in a homogenized, bland environment. *For instance*, neighbors of Larchmont Boulevard, a two-block street in Los Angeles lined with trees and small independent businesses, fought, unsuccessfully, to preserve its local character from intrusion by Payless Drugs, Koo Koo Roo, a fast-food enterprise, Starbucks, and a Rite Aid pharmacy.

Transitions Signaling Steps in a Process of Chronological Order

first, second, third, next, the next step, further, then, before, after that, finally, last, in July, last week, in a few days, in 2012

Example: To use the spelling-check function in Microsoft Word, *first* pull down under the "Tools" menu to "Spelling and Grammar." The computer will *then* scan through the document to identify any misspelled or questionable words. *After* each word is flagged, select the correct spelling. *Finally*, be sure to save the changes in your file.

Transitions Signaling Emphasis

indeed, in fact, certainly, without a doubt, undoubtedly, admittedly, unquestionably, truly

Example: The American public has grown increasingly frustrated over the Administration's current policies regarding the Middle East. *In fact*, the results of polls show that there is not much support for helping Middle East nations who are struggling to achieve democracy, if it involves sending military aid.

Transitions Signaling a Concession (an admission of truth)

although, even though, in spite of, despite, after all

Example: Although chimpanzee society is characterized by power displays, especially among males, the social hierarchy is usually quite stable. (In this sentence, the first clause *concedes* a truth. Another way to think of a concession is to substitute "regardless of the fact that" or "even though this is true, this is also true.")

Transitions Signaling a Summary or a Conclusion

therefore, thus, then, to conclude, in conclusion, in summary, to summarize, consequently, hence, in short

Example: There has been a movement growing in the United States toward eating more locally grown produce. *As a result*, farmers' markets have exploded in popularity in recent years, because they offer fresh produce at reasonable prices with better quality than one can find at the average supermarket.

Transitions Signaling Spatial Order

above, below, to the right, to the left, nearby, from afar, beyond, farther on, up the road, on top, underneath

Example: "Where the mountains meet the sea" is the official motto of Camden, Maine, a New England village known for its splendid harbor. No wonder. *Behind the harbor, not far from* where the schooners, sailboats, and cabin cruisers are anchored, Ragged Mountain rises precipitously. *Near the peak of the mountain* one can find Maiden Cliffs, where, according to legend, an Indian maiden leaped to her death because of an unhappy love affair. *At the base of the mountain* is Lake Megunticook, a local swimming hole for midcoast Maine residents.

Achieving Coherence: Repetition of Key Words and Phrases

Another way writers achieve coherence—thereby producing a chain of interconnected thoughts—is by repeating key words and phrases, which help keep the reader on track and maintain focus. Readers who want to improve their concentration, a fundamental goal of reading students, will gain mastery over their reading by learning to identify such repetitions. Read this paragraph taken from former South African president Nelson Mandela's autobiography. In it, he explains the significance of the circumcision tradition in Xhosa culture. Follow the links between the circled words to see how a good writer achieves coherence. Mandela's paragraph is easy to read because he repeats key words and uses synonyms to replace key words.

When I was sixteen, the regent decided that it was time that I became a man. In Xhosa tradition, this is achieved through one means only: circumcision. In my tradition, an uncircumcised male cannot be heir to his father's wealth, cannot marry or officiate in tribal rituals. An uncircumcised Xhosa man is a contradiction in terms, for he is not considered a man at all, but a boy. For the Xhosa people, circumcision represents the formal incorporation of males into society. It is not just a surgical procedure, but a lengthy and elaborate ritual in preparation for manhood. As a Xhosa, I count my years as a man from the date of my circumcision.

Nelson Mandela, *Long Walk to Freedom*

Achieving Coherence: Pronouns

A *pronoun* is a part of speech that refers to words that stand for nouns. For example, the pronouns *he* or *she* can be substituted for the noun *teacher*, depending on his or her gender. In the sentence that you just read, *his* and *her* are also pronouns, in this case, possessive pronouns describing gender and referring to *teacher*. Using pronouns like this allows the writer both to achieve coherence and to avoid unnecessary repetition.

To show you how pronouns help you keep on track in reading, look at these first sentences from an article about malaria. Following each italicized pronoun, in the spaces with parentheses, write the noun that the pronoun refers to.

Malaria starts suddenly, with violent chills, which are soon followed by an intense fever and, often, disabling headaches, convulsions, and delirium. As the parasites multiply, *they* (_____) take over the entire body. Anemia is common, because malaria parasites live by eating the red blood cells *they* (_____) infect; *they* (_____) can also attach themselves to blood vessels in the brain. If *it* (_____) doesn't kill you, malaria can recur for years.

Michael Specter, "What Money Can Buy," The New Yorker

You should have written in the noun "parasites" in the first three spaces and "malaria" in the last one.

Practice Exercise 2

A.   This paragraph describes Kabul, the capital of Afghanistan.

Kabul in winter is the color of the dust, though the dust is no color at all. It's a fine particulate lifted by winds from old stone mountains and sifted over the city like flour. It lies in the streets and drifts over the sidewalks where it compacts in hillocks and holes. Rain and snowmelt make it mud. Mountain suns bake it. Cart wheels break it down. Winds lift it and leave it on every surface—on the mud houses and the mud walls that surround them, on the dead grass and trees of the park, on shop windows and the broken sign of the cinema, on the brown shawls of men in the streets and the faces of children. Dust fills the air and thickens it, hiding from view the mountains that stand all around. Dust fills the lungs, tightens the chest, lies in the eyes like gravel, so that you look out on this obscure drab landscape always through something like tears.

Ann Jones, Life without Peace in Afghanistan

First, circle these words—"dust" and the pronoun "it" that refers to it. Next, consider the pronoun "it" in the second to the last sentence ("Dust fills the air and thickens it"). In this case, what noun does the pronoun "it" refer to?_____

B.

Historically, ballparks have been urban places, gardens in the middle of the city. The greatest of *them* (_____)—Wrigley, Ebbets, Fenway, Forbes Field, Shibe Park—emerged out of the form and shape of their cities. Fenway has the Green Monster, the thirty-seven-foot wall that compensates for the truncation of left field; at Griffith Stadium, in Washington, D.C., the center-field wall was notched inward because the owners of houses next to the stadium refused to sell. Ballparks weren't the same because the urban places *they* (_____) belonged to weren't the same. One football gridiron is identical to another, but a baseball field, once you get beyond the diamond, is not, which is part of the reason that even the ugliest *ones* (_____) are loved so fiercely by the fans and become such repositories of civic feeling.

Paul Goldberger, "Home," *The New Yorker*

In the three spaces with parentheses, insert the noun to which each italicized pronoun refers. Next, locate the single transitional word and indicate its function: _____

C.

There is much evidence that domestication physically changes the brains of animals. Darwin noticed that the brains of domestic rabbits are smaller than those of wild rabbits. A German scholar in the 1920s held that, on the average, domestic forms had brains 30 percent smaller than those of their wild ancestors. Brain-size reduction has been shown in rats, mice, rabbits, pigs, sheep, llamas, and domestic cats. German researchers found the brains of wolves to be as much as 29 percent bigger than the brains of dogs. Brain size, though, is not in itself a very reliable indicator of intelligence, and, at least in mammals, tends to correlate closely with body size. Some researchers believe that, if one scales the size of the brain to the size of the body, the shrinkage associated with domestication becomes insignificant. But there are structural differences between the brains of wild and domestic forms. In 1973, German researchers compared the brains of poodle dogs with those of wolves and found that the wolf brains were not just larger, but larger in particular regions. The wolf brains were 40 percent larger in the hippocampal region, which guides and regulates emotional reactions, aggression, and motivation, a finding that is consistent with the fact that domestication selects for gentleness and tractability. Some areas of the brain may also have a greater density of nerve cells—a difference that has been confirmed in comparisons of the brains of wild and domestic forms of cat.

Peter Steinhart, *Thinking Like a Wolf*

1. Write the main idea of the paragraph in your own words. _____

   _____

2. What are the *two* primary methods of paragraph development? _____

   _____

3. What pattern of organization is most evident? _____

4. What is the most important noun in the excerpt? _____ Circle this word every time it appears in any form throughout the passage. How many times does it appear? _____ Why do you suppose Steinhart didn't use a synonym for this word?_____

   _____

5. Next, underline the three instances of transitional expressions (individual words or phrases). In the spaces provided, write them again as well as their function.

_____   _____

_____   _____

_____   _____

6. _____ Which one of these inferences is accurate based on the evidence in the passage?
   (a) Brain size and intelligence are closely related in mammals, both large and small.
   (b) Wild animal brains are larger undoubtedly because they have to develop certain skills to survive not required of domesticated animals.
   (c) When domesticated animals are abandoned, they turn feral and develop larger brains as a result.
   (d) Domesticated cats can't survive in the wild because of their small brain size.

■ CHAPTER EXERCISES

Selection 1

[1]Consider perhaps the central dogma in the child-as-food-sage theology—that a child "knows" when he or she is full. [2]Such is the belief, repeated emphatically to this day, of many of the nation's leading nutritional authorities, both academic and popular. [3]This despite new research showing that children, just like adults, increasingly do not know when they are full. [4]In a recent study by the Penn State nutrition scholar Barbara Rolls, researchers examined the eating habits of two groups of children, one of three-year-olds, another of five-year-olds. [5]Both groups reported equal levels of energy expenditure and hunger. [6]The children were then presented with a series of plates of macaroni and cheese. [7]The first plate was a normal serving built around age-appropriate baseline nutritional needs; the second plate was slightly larger; the third was what we might now call "supersized." [8]The results were both revealing and worrisome. [9]The younger children consistently ate the same baseline amount, leaving more and more food on the plate as the servings grew in size. [10]The five-year-olds acted as if they were from another planet, devouring whatever was put on their plates. [11]Something had happened. [12]As was the case with their adult counterparts in another of Rolls's studies the mere presence of larger portions had induced increased eating. [13]Far from trusting their own (proverbial and literal) guts, children, the author concluded, should instead get "clear information on appropriate portion sizes."

Greg Critser, Fat Land: How Americans Became the Fattest People in the World

A. *Vocabulary*

For each italicized word from the selection, write the dictionary definition most appropriate for the context.

1. the central *dogma* [sentence 1]   _____

2. the child-as-food-*sage* theology [1]   _____

3. equal levels of energy *expenditure* [5] _____

4. their adult *counterparts* [12]   _____

5. *proverbial* and literal guts [13]   _____

B. *Structure and Meaning*

Complete the following questions.

1. The author's purpose is to
   (a) inform the reader about the results of one nutritional study.
   (b) urge parents not to supersize their children's meals.
   (c) warn parents about the dangers of fast food as a cause of childhood obesity.
   (d) explain exactly what the term "baseline" means in terms of food intake.

2. Which sentence *best* represents the main idea of the paragraph?

   _____

3. What pattern of organization is evident in the paragraph? _____

   _____

4. Which *two* methods of paragraph development are most evident in the paragraph? _____

5. One can conclude from the nutritional study cited that
   (a) most children are good judges of how much they should eat.
   (b) supersizing is the main cause of obesity in the United States.
   (c) parents should carefully monitor their children's meal portions.
   (d) by age 5, children will eat more than they need to if they have the opportunity.

6. So that we can understand the main point, the writer distinguishes between
   (a) the eating habits of children younger than 5 and 5-year-olds.
   (b) the results of two different nutritional studies, which came to different conclusions.
   (c) the various baseline amounts given for each group of children.
   (d) the nutritional needs of small children and adults.

7. Which one of the following can we logically infer from the paragraph?
   (a) More definitive studies need to be conducted on the subject of children's nutrition.
   (b) Children need to exercise more if they are to avoid gaining excessive weight.
   (c) If obesity is going to develop in a child, it is likely to begin around the age of 5.
   (d) Children should be allowed to choose their own foods and their own portion sizes.
8. Does the evidence in this paragraph primarily represent fact or opinion? Explain.

C. Paraphrasing

Write the meaning of these three excerpts from the passage in your own words.

1. "Consider perhaps the central dogma in the child-as-food-sage theology . . . " [sentence 1] _____

   _____

   _____

2. "The results were both revealing and worrisome." [8] _____

   _____

3. "Far from trusting their own (proverbial and literal) guts ..." [13]

   _____

Answers for Selection 1

A. Vocabulary

1. authoritative belief, principle, or doctrine

2. one who has wisdom and judgment

3. outlay, amount used

4. similar or corresponding people

5. referring to an widely accepted idea

B. Structure and Meaning

1. a

2. sentence 3

3. deductive order

4. cause and effect and process

5. c

6. a

7. c

8. facts (summary of a nutritional research study)

C. Paraphrasing

1. Let's look at an idea that is widely believed and accepted—that the child displays good judgment and wisdom about how much to eat.
2. The results of the study were informative but also troubling.
3. Rather than relying on their own stomachs and their own instincts.

Selection 2

[1]A key link between the obesity epidemic and economic hardship is chronic stress. Stress provokes the body to produce less growth hormone, a substance that reduces fat deposits and speeds up metabolism, and *more* of what are called stress hormones, which provoke cravings for soothing substances like glazed doughnuts and chocolate fudge ice cream.

[2]People don't invariably respond to stress by gobbling comfort foods, however. Many opt instead for cigarettes, and therein lies a luscious little irony. The obesity epidemic that government agencies and advocacy groups are battling to reverse resulted in part from the success of antismoking campaigns by these same organizations in the recent past. The number of smokers declined by about a third during the 1980s and 1990s, and when people give up smoking, they tend to gain weight.

[3]We social scientists call this the law of unintended consequences. Roughly the sociological equivalent of Newton's third law, it holds that any social intervention that produces beneficial outcomes will be likely to give rise to unintended negative effects as well. The obesity epidemic cannot be explained entirely, though, by way of the law of unintended consequences. Even a valid application of the law, such as the connection between antismoking campaigns and obesity, accounts for only a fraction of the nation's added tonnage. (The ranks of the obese include people who never smoked, and some people give up smoking without getting fat.)

Barry Glassner, from "What Made America Fat?" *The Gospel of Food*

A. Vocabulary

Here are four vocabulary words from the selection and their definitions. Study these definitions carefully. Then write the appropriate word in each space provided according to the context.

opted—chose

chronic—lasting, occurring over a period of time

irony—an occurrence that is the opposite of what is actually expected

provoke—cause, give rise to

There was a certain _____ that resulted from the government's anti-obesity campaign:

While obesity rates dropped, many _____ for another unhealthy activity—smoking cigarettes. Scientists know that stress can _____ cravings for unhealthy foods, which for some is a way of dealing with _____ stress.

B. Content and Structure

Complete the following questions.

1. The writer's purpose is specifically to
   (a) explain one interesting factor in the current obesity epidemic.
   (b) examine some common causes of stress in the contemporary lifestyle.
   (c) urge the reader to adopt a healthier lifestyle.
   (d) define the concept of the law of unintended consequences.
2. Which of the following accurately restates the "key link" described in paragraph 1?
   (a) Stress leads to obesity, which in turn leads to depression and economic hardship.
   (b) Stress is more common to economic hardship than it is to obesity.
   (c) Economic hardship leads to stress, which in turn can lead to obesity.
   (d) Obesity and economic hardship lead to stress, which in turn causes further stress.
3. Which of the following best explains the law of unintended consequences explained in paragraph 3? The government's campaign against obesity
   (a) has resulted in an increase in the number of people who have both lost weight and given up smoking.
   (b) has had better results than the government's campaign against smoking.
   (c) has resulted in people's stopping smoking, only to begin overeating, thus contributing to the obesity epidemic.
   (d) has resulted some people's eating less but taking up smoking, an equally unhealthy practice.
4. What method of development is most evident in both paragraphs 1 and 2? _____ In paragraph 3?_____
5. Using your own words, explain Glassner's conclusion about why Americans are so fat. _____

C. Inferences

Mark with an X any of the following statements that represent an accurate inference that one can make from the passage.

1. _____ The writer thinks that the government's anti-obesity campaign was a big mistake.

2. _____ In the law of unintended consequences, the consequences are sometimes positive.

3. _____ All people who stop smoking eventually gain weight.

4. _____ The fact that so many people have stopped smoking is the primary reason that the U.S. is experiencing an obesity epidemic today.

5. _____ Economic hardship is an important factor in the current obesity epidemic.

Critical Thinking Exercise

Can you think of another example of the "law of unintended consequences"—a "social intervention" that gave rise to "unintended negative consequences"?

Selection 3

Edward, O. Wilson is Pellegrino University Research Professor (emeritus) and the Honorary Curator in Entomology at the Museum of Comparative Zoology at Harvard University. He has won the Pulitzer Prize twice for nonfiction. This excerpt is from an article published in *American Educator* that was adapted from Wilson's introduction to *The Best American Science and Nature Writing, 2001.*

[1]Let me tell you a story. It is about two ants. In the early 1960s, when I was a young professor of zoology at Harvard University, one of the vexing mysteries of evolution was the origin of ants. Ants are the most abundant of insects, the most effective predators of other insects, and the busiest scavengers of small dead animals. They transport the seeds of thousands of plant species, and they turn and enrich more soil than earthworms. In totality (they number roughly in the million billions and weigh about as much as all of humanity), they are among the key players of Earth's terrestrial environment. Of equal general interest, they have attained their dominion by means of the most advanced social organization known among animals. I had chosen these insects for the focus of my research. It was the culmination of a fascination that dated back to childhood. Now, I spent a lot of time thinking about how they came to be.

[2]At first, the problem seemed insoluble because the oldest known ants, found in fossil deposits up to 57 million years old, were already advanced anatomically. In fact, they were quite similar to the modern forms all around us. And just as today, these ancient ants were among the most diverse and abundant of

insects. It was as though an opaque curtain had been lowered to block our view of everything that occurred before. All we had to work with was the tail end of evolution. I was afraid I would never see a real "Ur-species" (primitive ant) in my lifetime.

[3]Then, as so often happens in science, a chance event changed everything. One Sunday morning in 1967, a middle-aged couple, Mr. and Mrs. Edmund Frey, were strolling along the base of the seaside bluffs at Cliffwood Beach, N.J., collecting bits of amber. In one lump they rescued, clear as yellow glass, were two beautifully preserved ants.

[4]The Freys were willing to share their find, and soon the two specimens found their way to me for examination. There they came close to disaster. As I nervously fumbled the amber piece out of its mailing box, I dropped it to the floor, where it broke into two halves. Luck stayed with me, however. The break was as clean as though made by a jeweler, and each piece contained an undamaged specimen. Within minutes, I determined that the ants were the long-sought Holy Grail of ant paleontology, or at least very close to it. They were more primitive than all other known ants, living and fossil. Moreover, in a dramatic confirmation of evolution as a predictive theory, they possessed most of the intermediate traits that according to our earlier deductions should connect modern ants to the nonsocial wasps.

Edward O. Wilson, "The Power of Story," *American Educator*

A. Vocabulary

Look through the paragraphs listed below and find a word that matches each definition. Refer to a dictionary if necessary.

1. causing perplexity, puzzling [paragraph 1]   _____
2. the highest point reached, the end [1]   _____
3. pertaining to the earth or to land [1]   _____
4. neither transparent nor translucent, impenetrable by light [2]   _____
5. difficult to explain or to solve [2]   _____
6. conclusions drawn from observation [4]   _____

B. Structure and Meaning

1. Write a sentence stating the main idea of the passage. _____

_____

_____

2. Which *two* modes of discourse are most evident in the passage?

_____

3. Locate and write down three details that, according to Wilson, make ants worthwhile to study. _____

_____

_____

_____

4. What does Wilson mean when he writes in paragraph 1 "one of the vexing mysteries of evolution was the origin of ants"? Why, specifically, did this mystery exist? _____

_____

_____

_____

_____

5. An allusion[3] is a reference to something outside the selection that reinforces or sheds new light on the writer's ideas. Explain the meaning of this allusion from paragraph 4: "the ants were the long-sought Holy Grail of ant paleontology." Use either an unabridged dictionary or a Web-based information site like http://en.wikipedia.com, www.msn.com, or www.ask.com. _____

_____

_____

C. Inferences

On the basis of the evidence in the passage, mark these statements as follows: PA (probably accurate), PI (probably inaccurate), or NP (not in the passage).

1. _____ Primitive ants, also known as the Ur-species, are more than 57 million years old.
2. _____ Wilson had advertised that he was looking for primitive ants.
3. _____ Mr. and Mrs. Edmund Frey were colleagues of Wilson's in the entomology department at Harvard.
4. _____ Amber resembles yellow glass.
5. _____ The ants preserved in the amber looked more like wasps than like today's ants.
6. _____ Sometimes chance events change our lives in significant ways.

[3]You will study allusions in detail at the end of Chapter 7.

PRACTICE ESSAY

"Design Rising"
Henry Petroski

Henry Petroski is a professor of civil engineering and history at Duke University. He specializes in making the abstruse subject of industrial design clear to the lay reader. For example, he has examined the design of common everyday objects such as the pencil, the toothpaste tube, books, the paper clip, and silverware. He has published a dozen books, among them To Engineer Is Human: The Role of Failure in Successful Design *(1985) and* Small Things Considered: Why There Is No Perfect Design *(2003), from which this excerpt comes. In it, he discusses stairways.*

Preview Questions

1. If you were going to design a staircase, what are the important elements that you would need to take into consideration to ensure that it was safe?

2. What are some design elements that make some staircases unsafe? Consider particular staircases that you have encountered in the past that had dangerous features.

1   Among the tourist attractions in Edinburgh is a Writers' Museum dedicated to three of Scotland's most famous authors: Robert Burns, Sir Walter Scott, and Robert Louis Stevenson. The museum is located in a house that was built in 1622 and acquired in 1719 by a Lady Stair, whose name it bears today. Lady Stair's House is aptly named, for guides tend to focus not on the displays of memorabilia associated with the writers who lived and worked in the building but on the curious construction of its stairway.

2   For me, the description of the stairs leading to the second-floor bedroom was certainly the most unforgettable part of our introduction to the house and its historic significance. Before being allowed to climb upstairs, our small group of tourists was given a lecture on the stairway's idiosyncrasy. Our guide explained to us that the person who built the house, one William Grey, was concerned about intruders sneaking up to the bedroom in the middle of the night and stealing from or attacking him and his wife, Geida Smith. As a form of protection, Grey had the stairway designed and constructed so that "the height of each of the main steps is uneven, making them difficult to run up and down." Anyone unfamiliar with the house could not ascend the darkened stairway

without faltering on a step of an unexpectedly different height. The noise accompanying the misstep not only would awaken the owner but also would startle the intruder, thwarting his intentions and causing him to flee. The irregularity of the steps would also impede his flight back down them, if not actually cause him to fall, making it more likely that he would be caught.

3   Forewarned, we tourists were invited to climb the stairs and experience the irregularity ourselves. Since we weren't told exactly what the variation in the step height was, the man at the head of our expedition did trip on the way up, but, being on alert, he faltered but did not fall. Even though he had been warned of the irregularity of the steps, his strong predilection to find regularity in any stairs under his feet caused him to establish a rhythm of climbing that was soon thwarted. The rest of us, having observed how challenging the steps were, approached them with trepidation, experiencing the disruption of our own climbing rhythm but otherwise getting past the trap without incident, just as those residents who knew the secret of the stairway must have done even more quickly.

4   Even when they are not designed as booby traps, stairways can be tricky things. It seems that no two are exactly the same. Though they may have steps that are the same size, the number can vary from one or two to way too many. And even when the number is the same on two different stairways, the size of their (uniform) vertical and horizontal parts, known as the risers and treads, can vary according to the constraints of the space or the whims of the designer or builder. Indeed, it is a remarkable tribute to our ability to adapt to vastly different manifestations of technology that by paying close attention (which is possible in the daylight at least), we can negotiate even the most bizarrely designed and unfamiliar stairways with nary a fault.

5   Wouldn't it be nice if all stairways were not only regular but also had exactly the same proportions, the same dimensions for their risers and treads? While that would not make them effective burglar traps, it certainly could be expected to reduce missteps and accidents. In the United States alone each year, about a million people receive hospital treatment for falls on stairs, and about five thousand actually die. At least some of these accidents might be attributable to the oddities of stairways, if not to their downright faulty design.

A. *Structure and Meaning*

Choose the answer that best completes each statement. You may refer to the passage.

1. What is the writer's purpose in the passage? _____

_____

2. What *two* modes of discourse are represented in the passage?

_____

3. In the second paragraph where the writer discusses Lady Stair's House, what specifically does the "idiosyncrasy" refer to? _____

_____

4. Locate the transitional word in paragraph 4 and indicate its function.

_____

B. *Vocabulary in Context—Dictionary Definitions*

Each of these vocabulary words from the selection is followed by two or more dictionary definitions. Choose the best definition that fits the way the word is used in the context.

1. the displays of *memorabilia* associated with the writers [paragraph 1]
   (a) Objects valued for their connection with historical events, culture, or entertainment
   (b) Events or experiences worthy of remembrance
2. the *curious* construction of its stairway [1]
   (a) Eager to learn more
   (b) Unduly inquisitive, prying
   (c) Arousing interest because of novelty or strangeness
3. a lecture on the stairway's *idiosyncrasy* [2]
   (a) A structural or behavioral characteristic peculiar to an individual or a group
   (b) A physiological or temperamental peculiarity
   (c) An unusual individual reaction to food or a drug
4. *thwarting* his intentions [2]
   (a) To prevent the occurrence, realization, or attainment of
   (b) To oppose and defeat the efforts, plans, or ambitions of
5. he *faltered* but did not fall [3]
   (a) To be unsteady in purpose or action, as from loss of courage or confidence
   (b) To speak hesitatingly; stammer
   (c) To move ineptly or haltingly; stumble
6. approached them with *trepidation* [3]
   (a) A state of alarm or dread; apprehension
   (b) An involuntary trembling or quivering
7. Even when they are not designed as *booby traps* [4]
   (a) An explosive device designed to be triggered when an unsuspecting victim touches or disturbs a seemingly harmless object
   (b) A situation that catches one offguard; a pitfall

8. vastly different *manifestations* of technology [4]
   (a) An indication of the existence, reality, or presence of something
   (b) One of the forms in which someone or something, such as a person, a divine being, or an idea, is revealed
   (c) A public demonstration, usually of a political nature

C. Inferences

On the basis of the evidence in the paragraph, mark these statements as follows: PA (probably accurate), PI (probably inaccurate), or NP (not in the passage).

1. _____ Lady Stair's House was first occupied by a woman whose last name was Stair.
2. _____ An intruder—and anyone else for that matter—expects stairs in a stairway to be of a uniform and consistent height.
3. _____ William Grey and his wife Geida caught many intruders with their ingenious stairway.
4. _____ A burglar who encountered Grey's stairway would be more likely to be caught while trying to escape going down them than while going up them.
5. _____ The design of a stairway is dictated solely by the physical space that it will inhabit.
6. _____ The dangerous element about stairways that contributes to so many accidents is that no two are designed exactly alike.

D. Summary Writing

Write a summary of no more than 75 words of paragraphs 4 and 5.

E. Questions for Discussion and Analysis

1. What are some other ingenious devices or strategies that you have encountered or have used yourself to protect your home, apartment, or dorm room?

2. It seems as if one of Petroski's purposes in writing books on everyday objects like pencils, books, toothpaste tubes, and stairways is to get the reader to think about these objects not just as design elements but as objects worthy of being examined in a completely new way. How specifically does Petroski accomplish this purpose in the passage you have read?

Online Learning Center

For photographs of some unusual stairways, go to Google, click on "Images," and type in "unusual staircases" (not "stairways").

3

Discovering Meaning:
The Importance of Language

CHAPTER 6

Language and Its Effects on the Reader

CHAPTER OBJECTIVES

In this chapter, we will be concerned with language in prose writing—with words and the effect the writer intends them to have on you. Specifically, we will examine these elements of language:

- Denotation and connotation

- Figurative language (metaphors, similes, and personification)

- Connotation and our perception of the issues

- Language misused and abused

■ DENOTATION AND CONNOTATION

Good writers choose their words carefully. Most strive to re-create precisely the thoughts and emotions in their heads with words on the printed page. Gustave Flaubert, the nineteenth-century French writer, was the consummate craftsman. He agonized over his words, always searching for what he called "the right word" (*le mot juste*) and often spending an entire day working and reworking his sentences. On some days for his efforts he would produce only a single page. Much of our pleasure in reading derives from savoring the emotional associations such efforts afford us. An understanding of these associations will significantly improve your literal understanding, improve your ability to make inferences, and enhance your enjoyment of reading.

In the first section, we will study **word choice**, or **diction**. Some words are meant to be neutral or literal, some are meant to arouse positive feelings, while others are meant to convey a negative impression. The following chart shows the difference between **denotation** and **connotation**, the two basic elements characterizing word choice.

Denotation vs. Connotation

Denotation: The literal or explicit meaning of a word; often called the dictionary definition.

> Examples: *Home*—one's physical residence; the place where one lives
> *Lemon*—a sour yellow-skinned citrus fruit

Neither of these words implies any particular judgment or suggests an emotional attitude.

Connotation: The cluster of suggestions, ideas, or emotional associations a word carries:

> Examples: *Home*—a place of safety, privacy, comfort, nurturing
> *Lemon*—a piece of defective equipment, usually a car

These two examples show that connotative values refer to an emotional response, in this case, one positive, the other negative.

From this chart we can see that if we pay attention only to the denotative meaning of words, our understanding is limited to the surface meaning. Because connotation extends the meaning beyond the surface, we can see more in what we read—the implications and associations beyond the merely literal. Richard Altick, author of *Preface to Critical Reading*, has written: "Nothing is more essential to intelligent, profitable reading than sensitivity to connotation." However, no one can teach you this sensitivity. It comes from practice and experience, wide reading, and a willingness to consult the dictionary definitions and the accompanying usage notes. Further, this sensitivity may take years to develop. After all, the process of acquiring new words is a lifetime commitment, and learning the connotations of words is part of that commitment.

Connotation and Synonyms

The English language contains an irksome number of words that appear to be synonymous but that, upon closer examination, are not. It is this feature of the English language that makes its study so difficult and yet so gratifying. Consider, for example, these synonyms: *ask, inquire, interrogate,* and *grill.* But are these words really synonyms? *Ask* and *inquire* seem neutral, with *inquire* a bit more formal than *ask.* Because of its association with police or FBI interrogations, *interrogate* seems decidedly more negative, often carrying the unpleasant connotation of harshness or intimidation. *Grill* is less formal than *interrogate,* but it also suggests relentless questioning, and the dictionary definition bears this observation out.

How would you rank these near-synonyms for their connotative values? Which two have a positive connotation? Which two have a negative connotation?

stingy   frugal   cheap   thrifty

"Stingy" and "cheap" carry a negative connotation, while "frugal" and "thrifty" are positive.

Practice Exercise 1

1. The thesaurus feature on Microsoft Word lists these words as synonyms of the word *dislike:*

   hate   detest   abhor   loathe

   Without using a dictionary, which two of the above synonyms have the strongest *negative* connotative value?
2. Consider the word *poach* in these two sentences. Mark the denotative usage with D and the connotative usage with C. Below each sentence, write the meaning of the word according to the context.
   (a) _____ Mark often *poaches* eggs for Sunday morning breakfast.

   Meaning: _____
   (b) _____ Rob, an avid skin diver, *poached* ten abalone on the rocks near Shelter Cove.

   Meaning:_____

3. The following nouns all refer to a disagreement. Arrange them in order of severity, from least to most severe. Consider the change in meaning when each is inserted in this sentence:

Maria and her boyfriend had a _____ about his not taking out the garbage.

quarrel   *tiff*   *spat*   *fight*   *squabble*

Which two are the most neutral? _____

4. If someone says he has to travel to the *flyover* states, what does he mean? What is the denotative meaning?

_____

This word also has a connotative association. Is it positive or negative? Explain how a Chicagoan might react to this usage.

_____

5. Consider these phrases and the italicized word in each one. Three of them represent incorrect connotative values. Mark the incorrect ones with an X.
   (a) _____ a muscle *spasm*   (e) _____ *pangs* of regret
   (b) _____ the *sting* of defeat   (f) _____ a *pang* of nostalgia
   (c) _____ hunger *pinpricks*   (g) _____ *spasms* of hunger
   (d) _____ a *twinge* of regret   (h) _____ a *pinprick* of rejection

6. For the following pairs of words, mark the word that carries a positive connotation with a plus sign and the word that carries a negative connotation with a minus sign. If you aren't sure, use a question mark.

shopping binge	shopping spree
faux (as in jewelry)	fake
childish	childlike
wait	loiter
tattoo	body art
hide	lurk
conservative	reactionary
liberal	progressive
to be mired in a project	to be immersed in a project
personalization	tracking (websites or apps)

Practice Exercise 2

Study this cartoon by Steve Kelley, cartoonist for the New Orleans' daily newspaper, *The Times-Picayune*.

Explain in your own words the humor of the cartoon. Does the humor rely
on a problem with denotation or with connotation? _____

_____

_____

Connotative Restrictions and the Importance of Context

At the beginning of the chapter, the chart marking the difference between denotation and connotation showed that the word *home* suggests "safety, privacy, comfort, nurturing." But this interpretation assumes that one's experience living at home has been a positive one. A person who has had the misfortune to grow up in an abusive or loveless home will most likely have a different perspective, and therefore he or she may not interpret the word in the same way. If the writer suggests a positive connotation when he or she uses the word "home" and if the reader thinks of her unhappy experience, comprehension suffers.

Here are two quotations, each defining *home*. The first is by the American poet Robert Frost: "Home is the place where, when you have to go there, they have to take you in." Can you explain the connotative value of the way Frost used the word? And George Bernard Shaw, the British playwright (1856–1950), defined *home* like this: "Home is the girl's prison and the woman's workhouse." What larger picture of late-nineteenth-century British society and its treatment of women does this quotation suggest?

Personal interpretation is one problem with connotation. Here is another that has more to do with writing than reading, but is worthwhile to mention just the same. Often, students consult a thesaurus—a dictionary of word synonyms—when writing summaries or other college writing assignments. But thesauruses treat all synonyms as if they were interchangeable, with equal denotative and connotative values, when in fact nothing could be further from the truth. Often the connotative values of words are restricted to specific contexts.

For example, my version of Microsoft Word lists these synonyms for "home": *house, residence, dwelling, abode, habitat, quarters, domicile, address.* Consider this list carefully and the contexts you associate them with.

Which would be most suitable for describing a place where animals live?
_____

Which describes a place where military personnel live? _____

Which seems more like a legal word than a word used in everyday discourse? _____

Which two would a real estate agent be likely to use? _____ and _____

Which synonym might be most appropriate used to describe a house where the original inhabitants of an area lived, for example, Native Americans? _____

Finally, which two synonyms seem more decidedly formal than the others? _____ and _____

Finally, you will recall from Chapter 1 the admonition that memorizing new vocabulary words out of context is futile. Similarly, learning the connotative values of words is impossible out of context. Learning to appreciate the denotative and connotative values of words is best accomplished by wide and sustained reading. The exercises in the remainder of the chapter will give you practice in developing an appreciation for connotation, with the added benefit of deepening your enjoyment of reading.

Connotation and Levels of Language

The writer's subject and audience dictate the level of language, just as the occasion determines one's attire. You would not wear cut-off jeans and flip-flops to an important job interview; the occasion demands more formal attire, in the same way that a formal occasion in writing or speaking (for example a State of the Union Address or a serious opinion piece) requires an appropriate level of language. Levels of language also refer to the writer's style and to the connotations of the words chosen. A writer can employ an *informal* or casual style by using ordinary words that are part of everyone's spoken and reading vocabulary (called the *vernacular*); a writer can employ a *formal* style if the word choice is elevated, scholarly, perhaps even pretentious by using words derived from Latin and Greek. *Inquire*, for example, is a more formal word than *ask*. The adjective *everyday* is informal, *commonplace* is somewhat more formal, and the synonym *quotidian* is decidedly more formal and scholarly.

Practice Exercise 3

Study these pairs of synonyms. Label one *informal* (ordinary) and the other *formal* (elevated). If you are unsure of the meanings, check a dictionary.

osculate	kiss
quaff	drink
door	portal
particle	smidgeon
salty	saline
quotidian	daily
falsehood	lie

Online Learning Center

Go to www.mhhe.com/spears and click on Chapter 6 for further exercises in connotation.

Connotation in Reading

Let us turn to the matter of analyzing denotation and connotation in reading. Consider this short passage. As you read it, pay particular attention to the circled words and phrases.

> The persistent cloud cover, the almost constant patter of rain, are narcotic. They seem to seal Seattle inside a damp, cozy cocoon, muffling reality and beckoning residents to snuggle up with a good book and a cup of coffee or a glass of wine. (Mary Bruno, "Seattle Under Siege," *Lear's*)

Are these circled words and phrases most likely denotative or connotative? Are they primarily positive or negative in their associations?

_____

Taken together, do these words and phrases have a positive or a negative connotation? _____

Does the writer intend the word *narcotic* to have a positive or negative connotation? _____

Explain your thinking. How is the writer using the word here? _____

_____

How Denotation and Connotation Work Together

When examining a passage for denotative and connotative words, look first at the major words: nouns, verbs, adjectives, and adverbs. Obviously, nouns are necessary to identify the thing or person or idea being talked about. The connotative words are apt to be verbs, adjectives, and adverbs.

Read this passage from Sebastian Junger's best-selling nonfiction book, *The Perfect Storm*. Underline each word that is purely denotative and circle the connotative words. The first two sentences have been done for you.

> Swordfish are not (gentle) animals. They swim through schools of fish (slashing) (wildly) with their swords, trying to (eviscerate) as many as possible; then they (feast.) Swordfish have attacked boats, pulled fishermen to their deaths, slashed fishermen on deck. The scientific name for swordfish is *Xiphias gladius*; the first word means "sword" in Greek and the second word means "sword" in Latin. "The scientist who named it was evidently impressed by the fact that it had a sword," as one guidebook says.
>
> Sebastian Junger, *The Perfect Storm*

Studying the passage in this way reveals a pleasing and effective balance between denotative and connotative words. The verbs "slashing," "eviscerate," and "feast"—taken together—suggest an incredibly strong fish ("not gentle," as the first sentence so eloquently states), whereas the remainder of the excerpt is more denotative.

Denotation and Connotation in Nonfiction Prose

Junger's excerpt makes effective use of both denotative and connotative words. However, not all writers do this, and, depending on the writer, the balance between the two can vary widely. To show you the difference between highly denotative and highly connotative prose, consider these two passages. In the first the writer shows how capital and small letters developed in printing. Note that Wilkinson's word choice is strictly denotative, which suits his expository purpose perfectly.

> The alphabet was organized into capital and small letters around 800. The capital letters derived from inscriptions on Roman monuments, and the smaller letters from handwriting. Initially, all printing imitated handwriting. The first book that could be easily carried around was printed in Venice in 1501. It was called a pocket book. It was printed in italic, which was thinner than the other styles of type, and was said to be an imitation of Petrarch's handwriting. Printers kept their letters in cases arranged before them on a table. Each letter had a compartment. Capital letters were kept in the upper case, and small letters in the lower case. How many copies of each a printer kept on hand depended on the work he did.
>
> Alec Wilkinson, "Man of Letters," *The New Yorker*

The next passage by John Krakauer is very different. In it, he describes the ascendancy of Mormonism in the nineteenth century. The new religion, founded by Joseph Smith in 1830, had moved its headquarters to Nauvoo, Illinois, and was growing rapidly due to the charismatic force of Smith's personality. As you read the passage, circle the words with connotative value.

Life in Nauvoo, meanwhile, continued apace. The city of the Saints was booming. There on the banks of the great American river, the Mormons seemed to have at last found a secure foothold from which to spread Joseph's religion far and wide. He and his followers had come an impressively long way in the seventeen years since Moroni had entrusted Joseph with the gold plates. And new converts to the Mormon Church were arriving in Nauvoo in ever greater throngs, many now coming from as far afield as England and Scandinavia.

The Second Great Awakening had been crawling with impassioned, silver-tongued prophets who roamed the land hawking upstart creeds. Almost all of these novel faiths provided reassuring answers to the mysteries of life and death, and promised converts that they would be rewarded for their devotion by spending the hereafter on easy street. But almost none of the new churches managed to establish an enduring body of followers. Most are now long forgotten. So why did Joseph's new religion triumph when so many of his competitors vanished with scarcely a trace? To be sure, there were numerous reasons why so many people found Mormonism so appealing. Probably none, however, was more salient than the colossal force of Joseph's personality.

Jon Krakauer, *Under the Banner of Heaven*

Krakauer characterizes the era as rich in "silver-tongued prophets" of "novel faiths" all providing "reassuring answers to the mysteries of life and death." What was the primary reason that Mormonism succeeded when most of these other faiths failed? How does the connotative value of Krakauer's words enhance his discussion?

Connotation in Fiction

In fiction, a writer may use descriptive details that are designed to evoke in the reader a particular emotional response to the characters. These details help you both visualize and assess the character. In this paragraph from *David Copperfield*, Charles Dickens introduces the reader to a character named Miss Murdstone. As you read it, underline the descriptive words associated with metal and with unpleasantness.

It was Miss Murdstone who was arrived, and a gloomy-looking lady she was: dark, like her brother, whom she greatly resembled in face and voice, and with very heavy eyebrows, nearly meeting over her large nose, as if, being disabled by the wrongs of her sex from wearing whiskers, she had carried them to that account. She brought with her two uncompromising hard black boxes, with her initials on the lids in hard brass nails. When she paid the coachman she took her money out of a hard steel purse, and she kept the purse in a very jail of a bag which hung upon her arm by a heavy chain, and shut up like a bite. I had never, at that time, seen such a metallic lady altogether as Miss Murdstone was.

Charles Dickens, *David Copperfield*

Consider the words and phrases you underlined; then write a sentence explaining what these connotative words and phrases suggest about Miss Murdstone's character. _____

**Practice
Exercise 4**

The following passage is from Alexandra Fuller's memoir about growing up in Africa, specifically in Rhodesia, Zambia, and Malawi, on a series of farms her parents owned. Here, she describes a store owned by her Aunty Rena. As you read the passage, circle the words and phrases that refer to color, texture, and sounds.

Aunty Rena has a store on her farm. It is called the Pa Mazonwe store and it is sweet with treasures. There are bright nylon dresses hanging from the beams in the roof among the gleaming silver-black bicycle wheels. On the far right of the store, there are wads of thick gray and pink blankets which have a special itchy smell to them and the smell makes you think of the feeling of catching rough skin against polyester. And there are crates of Coca-Cola and bolts of cloth. Next are boxes of tea and coffee and Panadol and Enos Liver Salts and cigarettes, sold either by the box or by one stick, one stick.

And then comes the explosion of incandescent sweets: the butternut rocks wrapped in transparent paper with blue writing on it; bubble gum with gold foil inside a pink, bubbled wrapper; jars of yellow thumb-sized synthetic apricots and black, sweet gobstoppers which reveal layers of different colors when sucked. And next to the sweets, the bags of Willards chips and the rows of limp penny cools, which are cigar-shaped plastic packets of sugared water and which we drink by biting a corner of plastic off and squirting the warm nectar into the backs of our throats.

On the right, by the door which leads to Aunty Rena's clinic, are the stacks of Pronutro and baby food, powdered milk, sugar, salt, and hessian bags filled with dried kapenta—a tiny salted fish, complete with eyeballs and tail—which give the whole store its salty, sharp flavor. Under glass at the end of the counter are tinny gold earrings and spools of multicolored thread and cards of bright, shiny buttons. On the veranda, an old tailor sits whirring swaths of fabric through his fingers, his pedaling eating up the shapeless cloth and turning it magically into puff-sleeved dresses and button-down shirts. His treadle-treadle is a rhythmic, constant background noise along with the store's small black radio, its back hanging open to reveal batteries and wires, which plays the hip-swaying African music which I am supposed to despise but which is impossible for me not to listen to with guilty pleasure.

Alexandra Fuller, *Don't Let's Go to the Dogs Tonight: An African Childhood*

Critical Thinking Exercise

A week after the September 11, 2001, attacks, President George W. Bush warned Americans that "this crusade, this war on terrorism, is going to take awhile." After much criticism from both home and abroad, Bush stopped using the word *crusade*. Why? Begin with a good unabridged dictionary and then, using your favorite search engine, investigate the connotative values of the word *crusade*. What does the word connote to Muslims? What does it connote to Westerners?

■ FIGURATIVE LANGUAGE

Next, we come to the most difficult, but perhaps the most inventive and interesting use of language. **Figurative language** or **figures of speech** refers to language not in its literal sense, but in a metaphorical or imaginative way. Although you may associate figures of speech primarily with poetry, many prose writers also employ them to give immediacy or drama to their writing, to create a mental image, to establish a mood, or to clarify a difficult concept. Here is a summary of the kinds of figurative language we will take up in this section of the chapter:

Figures of Speech

- **Metaphor:** A direct and imaginative comparison
- **Simile:** An imaginative comparison using "like" or "as"
- **Personification:** A comparison in which something nonliving is described as if it were human

---

Metaphors
and Similes

Metaphors and **similes** are closely enough related that we should treat them together. Both represent imaginative comparisons between two *essentially unlike* things. This point is important. The sentence "My sisters and I look like our mother" is not figurative. Because people are in the same class and since children are likely to resemble a parent, there is no imaginative comparison. A good definition of metaphor can be found in the charming and poignant film, *Il Postino (The Postman)*. The main character, a semi-literate postman, wants to write a love poem to the barmaid Beatrice, the object of his affections. He asks the great Chilean poet, Pablo Neruda, who lives in his town, how to go about writing such a thing. Neruda says that love poems must have lots of metaphors, which he defines as "a way of describing something by comparing it to something else."

A **metaphor** refers to a *direct* comparison, in which a particular quality or characteristic of one thing (the figurative) is transferred to another (the literal). Although literally, such transfer of meaning does not make sense, the reader knows to interpret it as imaginative. Consider this sentence from a short story. The main character's boyfriend has died suddenly, and her life is falling apart. Using the third person, she describes herself like this: "She'd been unhappy at times, all the usual growing-up stuff: loneliness, self-hatred, the boys who hadn't loved her back, the drip drip drip of her mother's criticism." (Jean Thompson, "Do Not Deny Me")

To analyze this figure of speech (in this case, a metaphor), you first need to identify what the literal subject is and then what it is compared to. The subject is the way the character's mother used to criticize her; she metaphorically compares her criticism to a liquid constantly dripping. But the comparison suggests more than an annoying sound. The "drip

drip drip" is hurtful; it never ends. It implies that the daughter could do nothing right, nothing ever pleased her mother. It is like water torture. Added to her other adolescent woes, it's not surprising that she "had been unhappy at times." Jean Thompson could have expressed this same thought using denotative language instead of a metaphor. She might have written something like this: "Her mother constantly criticized her," but it just doesn't carry the same force.

A **simile**, in contrast, is an imaginative comparison stated *indirectly*, usually with the words "like," "as," "as though," "as if," and occasionally "seem." If Thompson had written this imaginative comparison as a *simile*, she might have expressed the same observation like this: "She'd been unhappy at times, all the usual growing-up stuff: loneliness, self-hatred, the boys who hadn't loved her back, her mother's criticism like water constantly dripping."

Notice that the metaphor is considered to be stronger than the simile, if only because the two things—the literal and the metaphorical—are joined without the reader's being *told* that they are similar, as occurs with similes. For this example, do you prefer the metaphor or the simile? Which is more effective?

Let us examine a few more figures of speech in detail before you analyze some on your own. Because they are easier to identify, we will begin with similes.

Good sportswriters often use figures of speech to enliven their style. As I write this in the spring of 2011, March Madness—the NCAA college basketball tournament—has just ended. (University of Connecticut was the final winner.) Sportswriter Vittorio Tafur wrote this the day after all four number one seeds were eliminated from the Final Four surprisingly early in the tournament:

> Not a single No. 1 seed survived the weekend, with Ohio State on Saturday and Kansas on Sunday joining Duke and Pittsburgh as chalk outlines on the hardcourt. (*San Francisco Chronicle*, March 28, 2011).

First, note that this sentence represents a *simile*, not a metaphor, because of the comparison word *as*. What is Tafur comparing these losing teams to? (Hint: It helps if you can visualize the chalk outlines TV crime shows use to mark the position of murder victims.) He compares these four favored teams to the outlines of dead people on a street or sidewalk; these four highly-rated teams are now just statistics.

Here is another simile from John Berendt's novel *Midnight in the Garden of Good and Evil*, describing the main character, Jim:

> He was tall, about fifty, with darkly handsome, almost sinister features: a neatly trimmed mustache, hair turning silver at the temples, and eyes so black they were like the tinted windows of a sleek limousine—he could see out, but you couldn't see in.

The word "sinister" at the beginning of the sentence is reinforced by the figure of speech, comparing his black eyes to a limousine's tinted windows. The simile also suggests a certain coldness, a deliberate attempt to separate himself from other people, which is why many celebrities travel in limousines with tinted glass. Here the familiar explains the unfamiliar.

Now let us examine a metaphor with the literal and figurative elements underlined. The selection below is from Gabriel García Marquez's novel *Love in the Time of Cholera:*

> The death of his mother left Florentino Ariza condemned once again to his maniacal pursuits: the office, his meetings in strict rotation with his regular mistresses, the domino games at the Commercial Club, the same books of love, the Sunday visits to the cemetery. It was the <u>rust of routine</u>, which he had despised and feared so much, but which had protected him from an awareness of age.

We see first the catalog of Ariza's humdrum weekly activities; then García Marquez ingeniously compares Ariza's routine to "rust." The pairing is brilliant. Metal rusts or corrodes from disuse, neglect, or exposure to the elements. But for Ariza, doing the same thing week after week has resulted in his figuratively rusting away. His life has become corroded by routine.

Figurative Language and the Imagination

Figures of speech serve to enhance the reading experience. Writers dream up appropriate metaphors and similes out of their artistic imagination, creating striking images in the reader's mind. To examine this concept further, here is a passage about the effects of the World Wide Web on us, in which the writer uses a series of metaphors to strengthen his point. As you read, underline the figures of speech.

> Overnight, the World Wide Web weaves tightly around you. A novelty at first, then invaluable, then life support, then heroin. It's a chance to recapture everything you've ever lost: college friends, out-of-print rarities, quotations that had vanished forever. Your online hours must come from somewhere, and it isn't from your TV viewing. You lose whole days on the roller coaster of real-time eBay auctions.
>
> Richard Powers, "To the Measures Fall"

What is the implied metaphor in the first sentence?

_____

What word suggests it? _____

The second sentence compares the Web metaphorically to two things. What are they?

_____ and _____

What is the relationship between these two things? _____

The final sentence adds a different dimension by comparing online auctions to _____.

Using your own words, write a sentence summarizing Powers's main point:

_____

Figurative Language and Inferences

In the examples you have examined thus far, the sentence includes both the literal and the figurative terms. Occasionally, however, you will be confronted with a metaphor or simile where the writer only suggests the comparison, in which case you have to infer both the metaphor and its significance. In a May 2006 article examining the threats from an expansion of offshore natural gas and oil drilling off the Gulf of Mexico, journalist Zachary Cole wrote this passage describing the fears of lawmakers who oppose drilling and who want to protect the environment. (This was written before the disastrous Deepwater Horizon spill of 2010.):

> Several lawmakers warned that allowing natural gas drilling would open the door to oil drilling. Some energy industry experts have said building expensive offshore rigs would only make economic sense if energy firms can drill for oil and gas. "Offshore gas drilling is nothing but the nose under the tent," said Rep. Alcee Hastings, D-Fla.
>
> Zachary Cole, "Offshore Drilling Bid Fails in House," *San Francisco Chronicle*

What does Representative Hastings mean by metaphorically comparing offshore drilling to "the nose under the tent"? Whose nose? The crucial word here is "tent." Readers with camping experience will recognize that the nose under the tent is a bear's nose and that a bear's presence in a campground is a sign of great danger. Thus, for Hastings, offshore drilling is a serious threat. The reader, however, must infer his meaning.

Here is another example of a figure of speech whose meaning you have to infer. In 2009 Palm introduced its new smart phone, the Pre, which was meant to compete with Apple's enormously popular iPhone. In reviewing Palm's new offering, technical analyst Jack Gold wrote this:

> This is a must-win for Palm. If the Pre isn't successful for them, they have no second chance. It's the fourth quarter, and they're down by a lot of points.

(Quoted in "Palm-Apple Showdown at Smart Phone Corral," *San Francisco Chronicle*, May 25, 2009.)

To what activity does the implied metaphor in Gold's quotation refer?

_____

Next, look at the title of the article from which this quotation comes. What does it metaphorically refer to? (Hint: It's the title of a movie.)

_____

Uses of Metaphors and Similes

Whether they occur in fiction or nonfiction, metaphors and similes have a wide range of uses. Study these purposes (in bold) and the accompanying examples.

- **To provide a visual image.** In this passage Noah Adams is describing a spider web.

  The land close by the river seems more comfortable when the weather's wet. At the corner of the fence line I saw a spiderweb's shimmer. The water drops looked like mercury, and the moisture edged the strands of the web. It was a tornado's funnel with steep sides leading down into a hole in the fence post. Inside, where the spider waited, it was dark and timeless. (*Far Appalachia*)

  Adams uses two visual figures of speech: The first, a simile, compares the drops of water glistening in the web to drops of mercury—shiny and silvery; the second, a metaphor, compares the appearance of the web to the funnel pattern a tornado cloud makes.

- **To establish a mood or situation.** During the 2008 presidential campaign, Hillary Clinton was the leading candidate against her primary challenger, Barack Obama. However, on the night that Clinton lost the Iowa caucuses to Obama, two veteran political writers, John Heilemann and Mark Halperin, described the shock of defeat Bill and Hillary Clinton experienced like this:

  . . . the Clintons were reeling like a pair of Vegas drunks the morning after struggling to come to grips with the scale of what they'd lost. (*Game Change: Obama and the Clintons, McCain and Palin, and the Race of a Lifetime*)

  The comparison is at once humorous and sad. Many Las Vegas gamblers (and politicians) can identify with the comparison these writers make: The high festivities and hopes of winning a big pile of money (or winning an important primary election) are dashed the morning after when they have to realize just how much they lost the night before.

- **To explain an emotional state.** In her novel, *The History of Love,* writer Nicole Krauss describes the main character's fear of death with an effective simile:

  > The fear of death haunted me for a year. I cried whenever anyone dropped a glass or broke a plate. But even when that passed, I was left with a sadness that couldn't be rubbed off. It wasn't that something new had happened. It was worse: I'd become aware of what had been with me all along without my notice. I dragged this new awareness around like a stone tied to my ankle. Wherever I went, it followed.

  The simile—comparing her sadness and fear to a stone that is always tied to her ankle and that she must drag everywhere with her—effectively clarifies and underscores these emotions.

- **To reinforce an observation.** This writer's observation, expressed in a simile, is especially helpful for the reader who has never visited Phoenix.

  > Phoenix is among the five fastest-growing metropolises in the country, and few places are as relentlessly suburban in character. It has a downtown so exiguous that a pedestrian outside its biggest office building at 9 on a weekday morning is a phenomenon as singular as a cow in Times Square. (Jerry Adler, "Paved Paradise," *Newsweek*)

  What is Adler saying about pedestrians in Phoenix? Understanding this simile depends wholly on an accurate understanding of what "exiguous" and "singular" mean in the last sentence. Write the definitions of both words in the space.

  exiguous   *singular*

- **To clarify a scientific concept or observation.** In this passage, the writer uses a series of metaphors to show the appearance of sea ice one particular summer in the Beaufort Sea (part of the Arctic Ocean):

  > Rumors that the pack ice was still thick near land had reached us when we were still far up the Mackenzie. Normally, the Beaufort Sea remains permanently frozen about fifty miles offshore, but in summer the sea ice closer in breaks up, shifting at the will of wind and current. This would prove to be one of the worst ice summers in decades; impassable ice would prevent supply boats from reaching some villages, and winter fuel would have to be airfreighted in at great expense. But we didn't know this yet.
  >
  > At first, we had no trouble crafting our way through the floes. Then the patches of open water became smaller, as if herding us from a six-lane highway to a four-lane road to a single country track. Trying to scout a route from our seats only a few inches above the waterline was like navigating a tricycle through a fleet of tractor-trailers. After a few days, when we found ourselves on the equivalent of a bike path, with open water becoming more of a concept

than a reality, we stopped to climb a rare hill for perspective. The view was so-bering. An unbroken sheet of ice stretched all the way to oblivion. It was not flat and smooth like a skating rink, but rather a jumble of blocks, most more than six feet thick, some the size of two-story houses, that leaned against one another at odd angles.

Jill Fredston, *Rowing to Latitude*

Fredston nicely shows the reader the size of the open water channels amid the ice floes by comparing them to something everyone is famil-iar with—a six-lane highway, a four-lane road, a single track, and finally a bike path. Further, because most readers might envision a sheet of ice, Fredston says that, in fact, it resembles "a jumble of blocks."

- **To persuade or convince.** This passage is from Martin Luther King's famous "Letter from Birmingham Jail," written in 1963 at the begin-ning of the nation's civil rights movement.

    We have waited for more than 340 years for our constitutional and God-given rights. The nations of Asia and Africa are moving with jetlike speed toward gaining political independence, but we still creep at horse-and-buggy pace toward gaining a cup of coffee at a lunch counter.

What contrast is at the heart of this passage? _____

_____

_____

Not all figures of speech can be classified in these ways, nor are figures of speech always used in the service of serious purposes. Do not worry about which of the foregoing classes a metaphor or simile belongs to. Some fig-ures of speech are simply inventive and playful, and some writers relish the chance to show off or to dazzle the reader with ingenious comparisons. Here are some examples of particularly inventive metaphors, adding force to what almost everyone has experienced in high school and beyond:

    I had been brutally, miserably unhappy in high school. But isn't almost every-one? And those who are not—high school's kings and queens and duchesses and dukes—often find all the rest of life a sad, outstretching desert, for rarely does their ascendancy last beyond graduation day.

Mark Edmundson, *Teacher: The One Who Made the Difference*

On separate paper, paraphrase Edmundson's passage and omit the figures of speech. Here is my paraphrase.

    The narrator was miserable in high school, but then almost ev-eryone is miserable in high school. The exception are the popular kids—those who run the school and win all the awards and are chosen to be prom king or prom queen, but their glory usually fades after high school. They often find that their adult lives are monotonous and dreary because it is impossible to maintain their superiority in the real world.

Although this paraphrase captures the essence of Edmundson's observation, when I omitted the metaphors (kings, queens, dukes, duchesses, the desert) it seemed drained of its energy and its laserlike judgment of high-school life.

Personification

The last figure of speech we will consider in this chapter is **personification,** in which something inanimate or nonhuman—for example, objects, animals, plants, or concepts—is given human attributes or feelings. Here are two examples. The places mentioned in this excerpt are cities in coastal Massachusetts.

> Fairhaven is a smaller version of New Bedford, which sits half a mile away across the Acushnet River. Both cities are tough, bankrupt little places that never managed to diversify during the century-long decline of the New England fishing industry. If Gloucester is the delinquent kid who's had a few scrapes with the law, New Bedford is the truly mean older brother who's going to kill someone one day.

Sebastian Junger, *The Perfect Storm*

What literal comparison is Junger making between Gloucester and New Bedford?_____

In her perceptive and humorous memoir about her life after an acrimonious divorce, writer Elizabeth Gilbert first goes to Italy, where she spends some months learning the language and dealing with her unhappiness. This excerpt uses personification effectively to show the power both depression and loneliness have on her psyche:

> Depression and Loneliness track me down after about ten days in Italy. I am walking through the Villa Borghese one evening after a happy day spent in school, and the sun is setting gold over St. Peter's Basilica, I am feeling contented in this romantic scene, even if I am all by myself, while everyone else in the park is either fondling a lover or playing with a laughing child. But I stop to lean against a balustrade and watch the sunset, and I get to thinking a little too much, and then my thinking turns to brooding, and that's when they catch up with me.
>
> They come upon me all silent and menacing like Pinkerton Detectives, and they flank me—Depression on my left, Loneliness on my right. They don't need to show me their badges. I know these guys very well. We've

been playing a cat-and-mouse game for years now. Though I admit that I am surprised to meet them in this elegant Italian garden at dusk. This is no place they belong.

I say to them, "How did you find me here? Who told you I had come to Rome?"

Depression, always the wise guy, says, "What—you're not happy to see us?"

"Go away," I tell him.

Loneliness, the more sensitive cop, says, "I'm sorry, ma'am. But I might have to tail you the whole time you're traveling. It's my assignment."

"I'd really rather you didn't," I tell him, and he shrugs almost apologetically, but only moves closer.

Elizabeth Gilbert, *Eat, Pray, Love*

Note that Depression and Loneliness make their appearance when she starts to brood; she extends the personification by comparing these two stalkers to Pinkerton Detectives.

Practice Exercise 5

Practice Exercises 5 through 7 offer several examples of figurative language to analyze. Use a separate sheet of paper for your answers. First, decide whether the excerpt represents a simile, a metaphor, or personification. Then decide what the literal subject is and what it is metaphorically being compared to. Finally, briefly explain the meaning. Start with these relatively easy ones.

1. [The writer is describing a taxi ride in Tripoli, the capital of the North African country of Libya. (This was written before the popular uprising against the long-time Libyan leader, Moammar Khadafy.)]

   The drive to the Prime Minister's office was terrifying, as most Libyan driving is. Tripolitans seem to think that traffic lights are just festive bits of colored glass strewn randomly along the roads. (Andrew Solomon, "Circle of Fire")

2. In 2009 USC and Boston College played in the Emerald Bowl. Both colleges have powerhouse football teams, though USC's reputation is undoubtedly stronger. The coach of Boston College, Frank Spaziani, was asked his thoughts when he found out that the Eagles were playing USC; he replied that it was a classic good news/bad news situation: "It's like your mother-in-law driving off a cliff in your Cadillac Escalade." (Quoted in Vittorio Tafur, "A Matchup That Sparkles," *San Francisco Chronicle*) Note: USC beat Boston College 24-13.

3. [Prudie is a high-school literature teacher. It's a hot day, and the students are having trouble staying awake.]

It was hard to keep the students' attention in May. It was always hard to keep the students' attention. The temperature made it impossible. Prudie looked around the room and saw several of them wilted over their desks, limp as old lettuce leaves. (Karen Joy Fowler, *The Jane Austen Book Club*)

4. Like a frog at the bottom of a well, she had seen nothing beyond the circle of blue sky that meant freedom. (Ruthanne Lum McCunn, *A Thousand Pieces of Gold*)

5. Regret grew only more insistent. She didn't just wait on his stoop any longer, she began to rap her icy knuckles against the door. (André Dubus III, *The House of Sand and Fog*)

6. In the mornings, before it was too hot, Ultima and I walked in the hills of the llano, gathering the wild herbs and roots for her medicines. We roamed the entire countryside and up and down the river. I carried a small shovel with which to dig, and she carried a gunny sack in which to gather our magic harvest. "¡Ay!" she would cry when she spotted a plant or root she needed, "what luck we are in today to find la yerbo del manso!" Then she would lead me to the plant her owl-eyes had found... (Rudolfo A. Anaya, *Bless Me, Ultima*)

7. [The narrator is describing a Mississippi River casino boat.]

   Wayne boarded the boat, found the guards' area, and drew his shirt, badge, and hat. Passing through a different door, he stepped out onto swirling orange, fuchsia, and teal carpet; the room was a dinging, chime-wracked labyrinth of worst colors and hooting, winking slot machines, each one with a customer attached like a tick. (Tim Gautreaux, "Something for Nothing," *Harper's*)

8. [The narrator is a media escort whose job it is to take visiting writers to Iowa City, home of the famous Iowa Writer's Workshop, to their lodgings, to bookstore signings, and generally, to keep them out of trouble while they are visiting. In this scene, he goes to a local bookstore and writes this description:]

   I headed into the bookstore, walked upstairs and into the café, and ordered a cinnamon roll and coffee. Before finding a table, I perused the wide selection of literary magazines—*The Rhode Island Review, North Carolina Quarterly, Kerouac's Eyes,* and *The Angry Scribbler.* There were hundreds of magazines out there where thousands of desperate writers sent their work, clamoring for enough pages for their precious short stories or poems, but even in Iowa City, as literate of a city as one is likely to find, the magazines sat gathering dust, slumped against one another like hobos in line at a soup kitchen. (John McNally, *After the Workshop*)

9. [J. M. Coetzee grew up in South Africa. This excerpt from his memoir describes a situation when he was about 13 and going through puberty.]

   To tide them over until his father's new law practice begins to bring in money, his mother returns to teaching. For the housework she hires a maid, a scrawny woman with hardly any teeth named Celia. Sometimes Celia brings along her younger sister for company. Coming home one afternoon, he finds the two of them sitting in the kitchen drinking tea. The younger sister, who is more attractive than Celia, gives him a smile. There is something in her smile that confuses him; he does not know where to look and retires to his room. He can hear them laughing and knows they are laughing at him.
       Something is changing. He seems to be embarrassed all the time. He does not know where to direct his eyes, what to do with his hands, how to hold his body, what expression to wear on his face. Everyone is staring at him, judging him, finding him wanting. He feels like a crab pulled out of its shell, pink and wounded and obscene. (J. M. Coetzee, *Boyhood: Scenes from Provincial Life*)

10. [The narrator is looking at a framed picture of her family.]

    It is not the photo Eliza was expecting. Her family doesn't look anything like the stuff of photography studios. Theirs is no pearl-finish portrait of interlocking hands and matching smiles. Instead, they more closely resemble odd puzzle pieces, mismatched slots and tabs jammed into each other to force a whole. (Myla Goldberg, *The Bee Season*)

Practice Exercise 6   The figures of speech in these passages are slightly more difficult, and they may contain more than one figure of speech. Follow the same directions as for Practice Exercise 5.

1. [In this fictional excerpt, the narrator is describing Miss Emily, the head guardian of a school called Hailsham.]

   Miss Emily didn't often say much; she'd just sit very straight on the stage, nodding at whatever was being said, occasionally turning a frosty eye toward any whispering in the crowd.... She'd rarely raise her voice, but there was something steely about her on these occasions and none of us, not even the Seniors, dared make a sound. (Kazuo Ishiguro, *Never Let Me Go*)

2. America is a large, friendly dog in a very small room. Every time it wags its tail, it knocks over a chair. (Arnold Toynbee)

3. It seems that Father had learned some painful lessons about prejudice while searching for an apartment in Paterson [New Jersey]. Not until years later did I hear how much resistance he had encountered with landlords who were panicking at the influx in Latinos into a neighborhood that had been Jewish for a couple of generations. But it was the American phenomenon of ethnic turnover that was changing the urban core of Paterson, and the human flood could not be held back with an accusing finger. (Judith Ortiz Cofer, *Silent Dancing*)

4. Parker's wife was sitting on the front porch floor, snapping beans. Parker was sitting on the step, some distance away, watching her sullenly. She was plain, plain. The skin on her face was thin and drawn as tight as the skin on an onion and her eyes were grey and sharp like the points of two toothpicks. (Flannery O'Connor, "Parker's Back")

5. The farm buildings huddled like little clinging aphids on the mountain skirts, crowded low to the ground as though the wind might blow them into the sea. (John Steinbeck, "Flight")

6. [In this passage the reader is introduced to Elisabeth Salander, the main character in the three-part Swedish detective novels by Stiegg Larsson. Lisbeth works for Milton Security; Armansky is her boss, and we see Salander from his point of view:]

   However, it was not Lisbeth Salander's astonishing lack of emotional involvement that most upset him. Milton's image was one of conservative stability. Salander fitted into this picture about as well as a buffalo at a boat show. Armansky's star researcher was a pale, anorexic young woman who had hair as short as a fuse, and a pierced nose and eyebrows. She had a wasp tattoo about an inch long on her neck, a tattooed loop around the biceps of her left arm and another around her left ankle. On those occasions when she had been wearing a tank top, Armansky also saw that she had a dragon tattoo on her left shoulder blade. She was a natural redhead, but she dyed her hair raven black. She looked as though she had just emerged from a week-long orgy with a gang of hard rockers. (Stiegg Larsson, *The Girl with the Dragon Tattoo*)

7. And his marriage, too, what was that if not shattered glass? Jesus Christ, he loved her, but they were as opposite as two people could get and still be considered part of the same species. Lauren was into

theater and books and films Sean couldn't understand whether they had subtitles or not. She was chatty and emotional and loved to string words together in dizzying tiers that climbed and climbed toward some tower of language that lost Sean somewhere on the third floor. (Dennis Lehane, *Mystic River*)

8. [In the best-selling novel from which this excerpt comes, Sarah Summers is married to Andrew O'Rourke, but she is also having an affair with Lawrence Osborn, which so far she has managed to hide from her husband. Sarah is the narrator:]

It became a source of sorry, hiding the affair. The actual assignations were simply concealed from Andrew, of course, and I made a point of never mentioning Andrew or his work when I was with Lawrence, in case he himself got too curious. I put up a high fence around the affair. In my mind I declared it to be another country and I policed its border ruthlessly. (Chris Cleave, *Little Bee*)

Practice Exercise 7	Complete your study of figurative language by analyzing these more difficult passages.

1. [The writer is describing the loss of wetlands in southern Louisiana.]

Five thousand years ago, much of southern Louisiana did not exist. A hundred years from now, it is unclear how much of it will remain. The region, it is often observed, is losing land at the rate of a football field every thirty-eight minutes. Alternatively, it is said, the area is shrinking by a large desktop's worth of ground every second, or a tennis court's worth every thirteen seconds, or twenty-five square miles a year. Between 1930 and 2000, some 1.2 million acres, an area roughly the size of Delaware, disappeared. Hurricanes Katrina and Rita stripped away an estimated seventy-five thousand acres—a loss as big as Manhattan and Brooklyn combined. (Elizabeth Kolbert, "Watermark")

2. [The narrator is describing an early morning reaction to her lover.]

And then, abruptly, she woke up beside him in her own bed one early spring morning and knew she loathed him and couldn't wait to get him out of the house. She felt guilty, but guilty in the way one feels guilty when about to discommode some clinging slug that has managed to attach itself to one's arm or leg. (Gail Godwin, "Amanuensis," *Mr. Bedford and the Muses*)

3. Hockey is a roughneck pastime from the Canadian prairie that was persuaded to leave the windswept town it was raised in, among miners and farmers and nuns who rapped its knuckles with rulers, and move to the city and try to hold down a job. Perhaps staring out a window at the lights of Moose Jaw, Hockey envisioned a place for itself among glamorous people and the stirring, chaotic exchanges of metropolitan life. . . . The city turned out to be only intermittently hospitable to the bumptious immigrant. Hockey now feels morose and forlorn, over-looked at the party. Late at night, Hockey walks down Broadway in the rain. Hockey has dined alone. Hockey has drunk too much. Passing before the window of a fashionable restaurant, Hockey stares balefully at a Major League Baseball, sharing champagne with models. (Alec Wilkinson, "First Period Slump")

4. The roots of the week lie deep, too deep to fully understand. An air of mystery surrounds the week; perhaps that, too, is part of its appeal. It is an observance that has been distilled over centuries of use, molded and fashioned through common belief and ordinary usage. Above all, it is a *popular* belief that took hold without magisterial sanction. This, more than anything, explains its durability. Less an intruder than an unof-ficial guest, the week was invited in through the kitchen door, and has become a friend of the family. A useful friend, for whatever else it did, the seven-day cycle provided a convenient structure for the repetitive rhythm of daily activities; not only a day for worship but also a day for baking bread, for washing, for cleaning house, for going to market— and for resting. (Witold Rybezynski, *Waiting for the Weekend*)

5. The man who has not the habit of reading is imprisoned in his im-mediate world, in respect to time and place. His life falls into a set routine; he is limited to contact and conversation with a few friends and acquaintances, and he sees only what happens in his immediate neighborhood. From this prison there is no escape. (Lin Yu-T'ang, "The Art of Reading")

6. [This excerpt describes Marco, a character who has left home to live in a hippie commune.]

There were times, hefting his pack, sticking out his thumb, waking in a strange bed or in some nameless place that was exactly like every other place, when it infected him with a dull ache, like a tooth starting to go bad, but mostly now his parents were compacted in his thoughts till they were little more than strangers. He'd skipped bail. There was a warrant out for his arrest, the puerile little brick of a misdemeanor compounded by interstate flight and the fugitive months and years till it had become a towering jurisdictional wall—with a charge of draft evasion cemented to the top of it. Home? This was his home now. (T. C. Boyle, *Drop City*).

7. [The province of Basilicata is in the southern portion of Italy. It forms the "arch" of the boot that Italy resembles. The writer and his wife spent a year living in Aliano, a small town in the mountainous area of this province. Southern Italy is generally more rural and poorer than the northern part.]

I think I was the happiest person in this compact little hill town on the edge of the verdant and mountainous oak forests of the Bosco Montepiano. Certainly I felt a lot happier than those sinister-looking village black widows appeared, wrapped defensively and identically in enormous black shawls and scurrying like beetles across the piazza in their black dresses, black stockings, and black shoes . . . black everything, in fact, including their perpetual shrouds of doom and gloom and the dark looks on their faces. When I or anybody else approached them, they would tighten their shawls around their mouths and chins, Islamic fashion, and glower through suspicious, coal-black eyes. I saw them as black volcanoes—little fiery Etnas—ready to blow at the slightest tectonic nudge of trouble. I had thought that this kind of thing had died out in Italy—this mourning for a spouse that can last for decades and all those deeply entrenched superstitions and *pagani* beliefs, including, around this part of Basilicata, the rumored shape-shifting and other mysterious protean abilities of elderly "sorcerer" women. But, as I was to learn later, ancient traditions had tentacles there, and strangenesses indeed remained. (David Yeadon, *Seasons in Basilicata*)

8. [This excerpt from Martin Luther King, Jr.'s Nobel Peace Prize Acceptance Speech was delivered in Oslo, Norway, on December 10, 1964.]

I refuse to accept the idea that man is mere flotsam and jetsam in the river of life unable to influence the unfolding events which surround him. I refuse to accept the view that mankind is so tragically bound to the starless midnight of racism and war that the bright daybreak of peace and brotherhood can never become a reality.

I refuse to accept the cynical notion that nation after nation must spiral down a militaristic stairway into the hell of thermonuclear destruction. I believe that unarmed truth and unconditional love will have the final word in reality. This is why right temporarily defeated is stronger than evil triumphant.

Critical Thinking Exercise

Just because a writer uses a metaphor or simile doesn't mean that the figure of speech is appropriate or useful in helping the reader understand the idea under discussion. Good figures of speech shed light on the subject, not distort it. The book *Nine Lives* by Dan Baum consists of interviews with nine residents of New Orleans about their lives during the period from the mid-sixties through the devastation of Hurricane Katrina. In this excerpt, Baum describes a white woman named Miss Duckie. She runs a playground, which in the 60s was segregated, meaning that blacks were not allowed to use the facilities. But Miss Duckie wasn't racist and often took Ronald Lewis, an African-American boy whom she had befriended, to the park while she worked. Here is the relevant passage. Ronald's best friend is Pete, also black. The figure of speech in question comes at the end.

> Miss Duckie ran the city park on Forstall Street, handing out bats and balls, managing the lifeguard at the pool. Colored kids were supposed to use the park back of town by Florida Avenue, and every now and then the white boys would think to run Ronald and Pete out, but Miss Duckie had none of that. At the first sign of trouble, she'd put her hands on her hips and stare at those white boys until they got their minds right. She didn't have to say a word; that park was hers. Sometimes she even let Ronald switch off the park lights at the end of the evening, throwing the big wall switch like sending a man to the electric chair.
>
> Dan Baum, *Nine Lives: Death and Life in New Orleans*

This is an example of an inappropriate figure of speech, in this case a simile. What's wrong with it?

Figurative Language and Politics

In the preceding discussion, you saw how figurative language in sports writing can enhance the writer's subject. Equally effective is the use of figures of speech in political writing. Consider this example, written by political writer Michael Gerson in 2010 during the contentious debate over health care reform:

> The final outcome of the health care reform debate is uncertain—who can predict where a writhing eel will land?

What is Gerson suggesting with this colorful metaphor? What does a writhing eel have to do with a political debate in Congress? You have to envision a squirming, thrashing eel that has just been caught and is flopping around on the deck of the boat. No one can predict where the eel will land, and this is Gerson's point: During the health care debate, no one could predict what would finally happen to the reform initiative.

Online Learning Center   Further exercises in analyzing figures of speech are available at www.mhhe.com/spears. Click on Chapter 6.

■ CONNOTATION AND OUR PERCEPTION OF THE ISSUES

From one edition of this book to the next, deceptive and manipulative uses of the language have proliferated and become even more entrenched. This portion of Chapter 6 begins with a discussion of how the media and politicians use connotative language to slant the truth and to shape our perceptions. The final part takes up the misuses and abuses of language.

In his Nobel Prize acceptance speech in 2005, British playwright Harold Pinter used the forum as an opportunity to offer his harsh criticisms of American foreign policy, in particular chastising the United States (and to some extent Great Britain) for waging an illegal and immoral war in Iraq. But more relevant for readers of this text is the way that Pinter's remarks relate to the subjects in this chapter, specifically how language can obscure reality. Pinter said that language can be used to "anesthetize the pubic":

> It's a scintillating stratagem. Language is actually employed to keep thought at bay. The words "the American people" provide a truly voluptuous cushion of reassurance. You don't need to think. Just lie back on the cushion. The cushion may be suffocating your intelligence and your critical faculties, but it's very comfortable.[1]

Government officials and politicians are especially guilty of providing us with what Pinter calls the "cushion of reassurance." They put the best spin on their proposals or on world events, using euphemisms to soften the impact of what might otherwise be more realistically interpreted, or using doublespeak and consciously vague or complicated language to confuse us and to hide the truth. Unscrupulous writers—whether in editorials or in blogs—may resort to language that incites and inflames passions. The result? We become immune to linguistic abuse. It's like elevator music. We no longer hear how awful—and how unlike good music—it is. There's a lot to learn about language in this section.

[1]Sarah Lyell, "Playwright Pinter Uses Prize Ceremony as Anti-War Pulpit," *The New York Times*, December 8, 2005. You can watch a video or read the text of Pinter's speech at this site: http://nobelprize.org/nobel_prizes/literature/laureates/2005/pinter-lecture.html.

How Word Choice Influences Our Perceptions— The Media

At the beginning of this chapter, you studied denotation and connotation. Most journalists are ethical and honest: they adhere to the principles of good journalism and strive to avoid injecting bias into news articles (as distinguished from opinion pieces, which by definition, are meant to express opinion). Still, problems with connotation can cause even the most professional and dedicated journalist to stumble. Let us briefly examine how word choice can affect our perception of a controversial issue or event.

Let's look at two examples. There is no question that the United States has a problem with people coming across the border to find work. The numbers of such people—I am deliberately using a vague term here—has leveled off to 11.2 million since its peak in 2009, when the number was estimated to be 12 million, probably due in part to the recent Great Recession.[2] Still, even this lower number represents about 5 percent of America's working population. There are two questions pertinent to this discussion: What should these people be called, and does the choice of words make a difference in our perception of the issue and of their status? Let's look at the most common characterizations, along with a comment about the connotation each carries, starting with the most negative and ending with the most positive.

- **Illegal aliens**—The word "aliens" is dehumanizing because it emphasizes their "otherness" and therefore carries a decidedly negative connotation. This term is sometimes used by social conservatives.

- **Illegals**—Using the adjective to stand for the noun (the group) suggests that they are not human beings—and it also confers a negative connotation. Further, some object to this usage because although actions can be illegal, human beings are not. This term is frequently used by social conservatives.

- **Illegal immigrants**—This is probably the most neutral term. Though one could argue that these immigrants did indeed break the law by entering the country illegally, they are not exactly criminals, which is what the term "illegal" usually implies.

- **Undocumented workers**—This term carries the most favorable connotation because it omits the pejorative "illegal." The word "undocumented" calls attention to the one thing these workers are missing—proper authority to be in the country. Changing "immigrants" to "workers" further distances them from the concept of coming across the border. This is also the term used by Justice Sonia Sotomayor (the first Latina judge on the Supreme Court) in a case brought before the court, *Mohawk Industries vs. Carpenter,* which involved a business accused of employing such workers. This phrase is most often used by progressives and liberals.

The next time you read a newspaper or magazine article or a blog that discusses the immigration issue, pay attention to the term the writer uses

[2]These figures are from early 2011. See www.nytimes.com/2011/02/02/us/02immig.html.

to describe these workers. As you have seen, each has a definite shade of meaning that influences our perception one way or another.

The second example: During the debate over health care reform, much was made of one of the bill's provisions, which would pay for medical personnel to counsel terminally ill patients about their treatment. Democrats called it "end-of-life counseling," but opponents of Barack Obama's health care legislation began referring to "death panels." This was a misinterpretation of the provision, which was not to establish panels of doctors who would decide who would receive care at the end of life and who wouldn't, but rather to offer a realistic appraisal of the efficacy of further treatment.

Critical Thinking Exercises

1. There is no doubt that the Iraq War was controversial. President George W. Bush, in defending his decision to invade Iraq in 2005, called the conflict between the Sunnis and the Shiites "sectarian violence" and the American intervention there "the central front in the war on terrorism." But critics of the war called the Sunni-Shiite conflict a "civil war." Why do you suppose that President Bush rejected this phrase to characterize the conflict in Iraq?

2. Because of California's budget crisis, the state proposed closing certain state parks in 2009, among them Pescadero State Beach.[3] PETA, People for the Ethical Treatment of Animals, lobbied the California legislature to change the name of the park, located about one hour south of San Francisco, to "Sea Kitten State Park." (The word "pescadero" is Spanish for "fishmonger" or "fishseller.") PETA offered to pay for the upkeep of the beach if the state changed the park's name and prohibited fishing there. The state declined the offer. In the same year, PETA began a campaign to encourage people to use the word "sea kitten" to replace "fish." Why? What does "sea kitten" connote that "fish" doesn't? What do you think is the likelihood that people will adopt the new term?

■ LANGUAGE MISUSED AND ABUSED

The remainder of the chapter will help you, the critical reader, understand what really lies beneath such language and to be vigilant about

---

[3]A poem by Mark Doty titled "Pescadero," set in a town of the same name, appears in Chapter 7.

attempts to influence your thinking through clever manipulative language, including:

- **Clichés:** Tired, overused expressions.
- **Code words:** Secret words or phrases that mean something special to insiders but something different to outsiders.
- **Jargon:** Specialized language used by a particular group.
- **Euphemisms:** Inoffensive language used as a substitute for possibly offensive terms.
- **Politically correct language:** Language that attempts to avoid insensitivity related to diversity, historical injustices, racism, and the like.
- **Sneer words:** Words with strong negative, derogatory connotations.
- **Doublespeak:** Language used to twist, to deceive, or to misrepresent the truth.

In this edition, to help students understand these concepts more readily, I have arranged them according to the harm they cause—from the relatively innocuous cliché, to euphemism, to sneer words, and finally to the most damaging of all, doublespeak, with its deliberate intention to mislead and deceive the unwary reader. All of the examples you will study are real. Do not worry if some of these terms appear to overlap because, in fact, they often do. Just as being aware of the connotative values of words develops over time, so experience and wide reading will increase your sensitivity to words and help you see through linguistic sludge.

Clichés

Clichés—tired, overused expressions—tell the careful reader that a lazy writer is at work. Good writers avoid clichés because these fossilized expressions long ago lost their power; many no longer make sense: for example, "That speech is like grist to the mill," "Let's get down to brass tacks," or "to fight someone tooth and nail." Some clichés probably sounded clever the first time, but now, in the twenty-first century, many sound quaint or ridiculous. In the first box are some standard clichés. See how many you recognize as clichés. (Note, of course, that if you have never heard a phrase labeled as clichéd, it is hard to identify it as such!)

> ### Common Clichés
>
> | | |
> |---|---|
> | as rich as Croesus | to be slower than molasses in January |
> | to come to a grinding halt | |
> | as smart as a whip | to be up in arms |
> | a labor of love | as cool as a cucumber |
> | as clear as mud | to leave no stone unturned |
> | bark up the wrong tree | a chip off the old block |

For fun, you might begin your own list of new clichés to add to this one that I have compiled.

Contemporary Clichés

to think outside the box	at the end of the day
to be (or not to be) a happy camper	outpouring of support
it's not rocket science	a level playing field
the third rail (of politics)	bells and whistles
to push the envelope	drink the Kool-Aid
warm and fuzzy	iconic

Code Words

Like secret handshakes or passwords shared by club members, **code words** are words or phrases that mean one thing to those in the know—to insiders—and something different to those on the outside. When negotiations take place between union and management or between diplomats, participants often describe the day's talks as "productive." Insiders know that "productive" is code meaning that "nothing significant happened." Another example is "inner city," which to the uninitiated might sound like the downtown area of a metropolis, but which is usually regarded as a code phrase for minority neighborhoods. Another example: During the economic crisis in the fall of 2008, representatives of the Treasury Department were trying to figure out what to do to prevent the banking system from collapsing. They often described their situation like this: "We're in uncharted territory," which political and economic experts interpreted as a code phrase for "We don't know what we're doing." And a final example: During what has been called the "Arab Spring" in 2011, a series of pro-democracy protests in the Middle East began in Tunisia and quickly spread to Egypt, Yemen, Bahrain, Libya, and Syria. These protests met with varying degrees of suppression by each government. The president of Syria, Bashar al-Assad, whose regime was particularly harsh, promised reforms to stave off further protests. One of the promised reforms was the legalization of "peaceful protests," which Middle East political observers widely understood as a code phrase meaning that only protests that were approved by the government would be allowed to take place.

Jargon

Jargon refers to the specialized language members of a particular trade, group, or profession use. Usually, jargon serves to make the writer or speaker sound more intelligent or learnèd than if he or she used ordinary language. In and of itself, jargon is not necessarily harmful. All *specialists*—whether they're plumbers, surgeons, or college reading teachers—have their own special terminology that nonspecialists or the ordinary lay audience might not readily understand. Here, for example, are three examples of jargon that became part of the American vocabulary during the Great Recession as homeowners increasingly became unable to pay their mortgages.

being underwater or *being upside down*	Both these phrases refer to a situation where a homeowner owes more on the mortgage than the house is worth, often leading to foreclosure.
jingle mail	Real estate jargon that refers to what happens when a homeowner stops paying the mortgage on his or her property. The owner walks away from the house and mails the keys to the bank.

These are inoffensive uses of jargon that readers could figure out by themselves or would be familiar with if they keep current with what's going on in the real estate market. But even if readers can't figure out a term's meaning, the intention is not to hoodwink. At its best, jargon is useful, providing a verbal shorthand between people who are fluent in the terminology and the subject. At its worst, however, jargon is pretentious, obscure, and impossible to read. Sociologist Gerald Rosen notes this about jargon: "The less secure a field of study is, the more intense is its use of jargon."

During the Congressional hearings into the banking crisis of 2009, one witness, a member of the banking community, offered this testimony:

> The leveraged capital arbitrage of the lowest CDOs were subject to the super-senior subprime exposure, as opposed to the triple A seniors, right? (Quoted in Peggy Noonan, "After the Crash, a Crashing Bore," *The Wall Street Journal*, April 10–11, 2010).

It's no wonder, with jargon like this, that the nation's banks were able to sell financial instruments that no one understood to an unsuspecting public.

One might expect that English departments in American colleges and universities would be sensitive to the use of mind-numbing, incomprehensible academic jargon. Though the following example of an English course offering is from a short story by Jean Thompson, and therefore fictional, the jargon rings true. Check your own college catalog for academic jargon in course descriptions.

New Course, Please Announce!

English 405, Indigenous Critical Theory: Oriented toward imagining far-reaching social change through knowledge production as sites of indigenous activism and political thought, the course develops analytical frames at intellectual crossroads where epistemologies that gather under the "indigenous" sign meet democratic inquiry (and its concerns with recognition) and a transhemispheric critical theory. (Jean Thompson, "Soldiers of Spiritos")

Euphemisms

A **euphemism** is an inoffensive word or phrase substituted for a more offensive one (or sometimes a more humdrum) one. Writers use euphemisms to soften our perception of unpleasant events, to change our beliefs, or perhaps even to cover up wrongdoing. Euphemisms pervade our culture, and you should learn to spot them readily. Here are a few examples:

The winner of the Miss America pageant no longer "reigns" (which sounds too royalist and elitist); now she does "a year of service." When Justin Timberlake accidentally or purposefully ripped off part of Janet Jackson's costume during the 2004 Super Bowl halftime entertainment, exposing her right breast on national television, he later termed the incident a "wardrobe malfunction." When former president Bill Clinton described his relationship with young White House intern Monica Lewinsky, he replied: "I had an "inappropriate encounter" and "I met with her alone." Euphemisms can enhance as well as soften. In the Arab world, for example, some militants describe suicide bombings as "sacred explosions."

Identify the euphemisms in each panel of this Dilbert cartoon.

While some may find these euphemisms more amusing than dangerous, what of the phrase "kinetic military action," which is how the White House referred to the U.S. air strikes against Moammar Khadafy's forces in Libya in spring 2011. The United States, along with its NATO allies, were combating Khadafy's forces, which were bombing the rebel forces. These rebels were trying to oust Khadafy and to prevent him from further attacks on his own people. But Americans were also war-weary. With military involvement still taking place in Iraq and Afghanistan, the Pentagon's decision to use the term "kinetic military action" rather than "war" seemed like a deliberate attempt to cover up the reality of America's getting involved militarily in yet another country and to make U.S. participation more palatable.

Another example: China has a strict policy of regulating Internet searches. For example, here are some of the taboo words that China routinely blocks as Internet search terms: "brainwash," "censorship," "demonstration," "dissident," "overthrow," "revolution," and "Tibet independence." However, China does not use the term *censorship*, instead using the preferred term, "guidance of public opinion." The careful and critical reader must be alert to such linguistic abuses. (Quoted in Barbara Demick, "China Has Its Own List of Dirty Words," *Los Angeles Times*, April 21, 2010)

Critical Thinking Exercise

Study the list of censored words and draw a conclusion about what they have in common. What kind of government does China apparently represent, based on this information?

This is not to say, however, that all euphemisms are bad and that they should be avoided at all costs. Sometimes euphemisms are necessary to soften the blow of harsh reality. To illustrate: During the recent Great Recession, unemployment reached 12 percent or more in some U.S. states. To keep people's spirits up, employment counselors who are charged with finding jobs for those out of work are advised to avoid the word "unemployed." Instead, they are encouraged to use the terms "job seekers," "separated employees," "affected people," or "people in transition." These are clearly euphemisms, but surely there is no reason to add to job seekers' anxiety and misery by reminding them that they are out of work.

Practice Exercise 8

Decide whether each of the following passages represents a cliché, code word or phrase, jargon, or euphemism.

1. People who are familiar with real estate terminology know that the term "gated community" refers to a wealthy white enclave. _____

2. The American Hair Loss Council prefers that toupees (men's hairpieces) now be called "hair systems." _____

3. In 2009 two Northwest pilots bound for Minneapolis got into a discussion and lost contact with air traffic control for over an hour. Later, the two pilots told the FBI that "they were in a heated discussion over airline policy and they lost situational awareness." (The two pilots were later fired.) _____

4. The American Farm Bureau recently urged its members to go on the offensive against "food activists," and a trade association representing

pesticide makers called CropLife America wrote to Michelle Obama suggesting that her organic garden had unfairly maligned chemical agriculture and encouraging her to use "crop protection technologies"—i.e. pesticides. (Quoted in Michael Pollan, "Food Fight," *Utne Reader,* September-October 2010) _____

5. Jack arrived at his own wedding just in the nick of time. Jill, his bride, was so mortified at the thought that she might be left standing at the altar that she was as red as a beet. But it was well worth the wait because Jack and Jill lived happily ever after. _____

6. During the summer of 2009, Governor Mark Sanford of South Carolina disappeared for several days. No one could find him or knew where he was, not even his aides or family. Finally, he emerged, saying that he had been "hiking the Appalachian Trail." But the truth eventually came out: Sanford, a married man, had actually flown to Argentina where he spent a few days having a tryst with his lover, Maria Belen Chaqur. From this time on, some people refer to a husband who is sneaking around behind his wife's back as "hiking the Appalachian Trail." _____

_____

7. Employees at Sea World in Orlando, Florida, are instructed to use a particular vocabulary, especially when answering park visitors' questions. Here are some examples: "enclosure" (not "cage"); "controlled environment" (not "captivity"); "natural environment" (not "wild"); and "acquired" (not "captured"). (Quoted in "Chickens of the Sea," *Harper's*) _____

8. In elementary schools today, multiple choice answers on a test are called "selected responses," an essay test is called "extended constructed responses," the day's lesson in subtracting is called "modeling efficient subtraction strategies," and the detention room for misbehaving students is called either the "alternative instruction room" or the "reflection room." (Quoted in Joel Kotkin, "GOP Wiped Out in Land of Reagan," *The Wall Street Journal*, November 6, 1998.) _____

_____

Politically Correct Language

During the 1980s, a movement called ***political correctness*** grew out of increased sensitivity to diversity in the country. Briefly, this movement was an attempt by liberals to purge the language of words and phrases that might be considered insensitive or racially charged or that called into question people's differences. Thus evolved a whole new vocabulary of **politically correct language.** The Officially Politically Correct Dictionary and Handbook suggests some semantic labels for dealing with race, gender, and people typically considered "disadvantaged." Here are a few examples. On the left is the conventional term; on the right is the new preferred PC term.

Members of minority groups: Use *people of color, emergent groups, traditionally underrepresented,* or *members of the world's majorities*

Mankind: Use *humanity* or *humankind*

Handicapped: Use *physically challenged* or *differently abled*

Prostitute: Use *sex worker*

Old person: Use *mature person, senior,* or *chronologically gifted*

Fat person: Use *person of size, differently sized person*

Fireman, policeman: Use *firefighter, police officer*

Critical Thinking Exercise

Is the word "squaw" offensive or not? In 2000 the Maine legislature voted to ban the word "Squaw" in the state's place names. What was the controversy about? Were Native Americans unanimous in their resentment of place names like Squaw Pond and Squaw Bay? Do an online search using your favorite search engine. (In Google, you can type in this string: "Maine, offensive word, squaw" and several sites will pop up.)

Sneer Words

As we learned in the previous section, a writer can shape our perception of events, making things seem less bad than they actually are, with euphemism. Conversely, a writer can intensify an already bad situation or cast doubt on an idea by using **sneer words**, words with strong negative connotations suggesting derision and contempt. Environmentalists often refer to farmers, ranchers, and corporate executives who are opposed to environmental protections as "toad stabbers." For their part, farmers, ranchers, and corporate executives often call environmentalists "tree huggers" or "wolf worshipers." Here are some other examples of sneer words:

Agenda: Term used to describe the thinking of a group one dislikes (i.e., the gay-rights agenda, the Christian agenda, the liberal agenda, and so on)

Flyover states: The states located between the East and West coasts; the term implies that they don't have much influence on American culture.

So-called: A term used to disparage whatever noun it precedes. Creationists often call scientists who support evolution "so-called scientists" to cast doubt on their authority.

Obamacare: Members of the Tea Party routinely use this
                            term when they refer to the health insurance
                            reform act passed in 2010. The term is meant
                            to call attention to their belief that Obama
                            shoved the measure down the throats of the
                            American people. This is a sneer word, though
                            a subtle one.

Doublespeak

As we move up the ladder from language that is relatively harmless to more dangerous forms, we come to **doublespeak.** George Orwell, in his novel *1984*, made up this word by combining parts of *double-think* and *newspeak*. The novel describes a future in which the government twists words to manipulate its citizens' thoughts. The totalitarian government indoctrinated its citizens with these three slogans: "War is peace, ignorance is strength, slavery is freedom." William D. Lutz, a member of Rutgers University's English department, for many years edited the *Quarterly Review of Doublespeak*, a periodical dedicated to publishing especially egregious examples of doublespeak. He has compared doublespeak to "an infection that sickens the language through the pollution of words carefully chosen." In the introduction to his recent book, *The New Doublespeak: Why No One Knows What Anyone's Saying Anymore*, Lutz writes:

> Doublespeak is language that pretends to communicate but really doesn't. It is language that makes the bad seem good, the negative appear positive, the unpleasant appear attractive or at least tolerable. Doublespeak is language that avoids or shifts responsibility, language that is at variance with its real or purported meaning.

He further describes doublespeak as language that is "grossly deceptive, evasive, euphemistic, confusing or self-contradictory" with the potential for "pernicious social or political consequences." Doublespeak may or may not involve *euphemism*, as we shall see later.

The war in Iraq and the war on terror have generated good examples of this linguistic abuse. During a 2007 debate among Republican presidential candidates, the subject of torture came up. Four candidates—Duncan Hunter, Tom Tancredo, Rudy Giuliani, and Mitt Romney—stated that they rejected torture but endorsed "enhanced interrogation." This phrase refers to a torture technique called waterboarding, which is outlawed under the Geneva Conventions. It involves binding, gagging, and blindfolding a prisoner, then holding him underwater, which creates the sensation of drowning. But does "enhanced interrogation" suggest this vicious practice?

Here are some more recent examples of doublespeak from a variety of fields:

Military Doublespeak (Pentagonese)

Frame-supported tension structure	Defense Department term for a tent
Manually powered fastener-driving impact device	Defense Department term for a hammer
Airborne sanitation	a bombing attack
Portable hand-held communications transcriber	pencil
Collateral damage	the killing of innocent civilians, used first in Kosovo and later in Iraq
Permanent pre-hostility	peace

Miscellaneous Examples of Doublespeak

Retrievable storage site	a nuclear fuel dump
Uncontrolled contact with the ground	a safety expert's term for an airplane crash
Runway incursion	the FAA's term for planes and airport vehicles that stray off course and cause a hazard or collision
Water landing	the term airlines use to describe a crash in the ocean
Therapeutic misadventure	the medical profession's term for a doctor's incompetence that results in a patient's death
Negative employee retention	corporate doublespeak for employee layoffs

As may be apparent, doublespeak may involve euphemism (though not all euphemisms involve doublespeak), and sometimes it's hard to distinguish between them clearly. If you examine the preceding examples, the primary difference seems to be that doublespeak is *deliberately* deceptive, whereas the motives for using euphemisms are less nefarious. One's interpretation of such phrases also may depend on one's political beliefs and one's worldview (see Chapter 8). For example, instead of using the term "body bags" to describe the aluminum boxes used to transport the bodies of dead soldiers back home, the Pentagon recently substituted the phrase "transfer cases." Is this an example of doublespeak—a deliberate attempt to make the idea of dead soldiers more palatable, or simply a harmless euphemism? These examples bear out the observation that the line between doublespeak and euphemism is often fuzzy.

Decide whether each of the following passages represents politically correct language, sneer words, or doublespeak.

1. Former President Richard Nixon: "Solutions are not the answer."

_____

2. Britain's Oxford University Press announced some changes in its *Junior Dictionary*. While adding words like "trapezium," "alliteration," "and "incisor," it eliminated the following words: "bishop," "chapel," "christen," "minister," "monk," "nun," and "saint." The publisher said that the changes reflect Britain's "multicultural, multifaith" society." (Quoted in thebeachsideresident.com/2009/03/news-of-the-weird-march-2009/) _____

3. In 2002 President George W. Bush publicized a plan called the Healthy Forests Initiative, which allowed the timber industry to do more clear-cutting of trees. _____

4. Recently, the student association at Carleton University in Ottawa, Canada, voted to deny student funding to a cystic fibrosis organization, one of several charities that the association supports. Their reason was that the disease almost exclusively affects white people, and therefore was not "inclusive" enough to warrant student funding. _____

_____

5. After the Deepwater Horizon Gulf of Mexico explosion and oil leak in 2010, Congress held hearings on the causes of the disaster. Tony Hayward, Chief Executive of British Petroleum, apologized for the accident. Then Republican Representative Joe Barton of Texas defended Mr. Hayward, saying that in effect, Congress was conducting a "shakedown" of BP and apologized to Hayward on behalf of his fellow representatives. Later in the day, Barton returned to the hearing room and revised his earlier remarks, saying this: "If anything I have said this morning has been misconstrued to the opposite effect, I want to apologize for that misconstrued misconstruction." (Quoted in Michael M. Phillips and Stephen Power, "BP Chief on Hot Seat," *The Wall Street Journal*, May 18, 2010) _____

6. Credit card companies refer to customers who pay off their credit card charges each month as "deadbeats" and customers who pay only the minimum balance as "preferred customers." _____

_____

7. The Puyallup School District in Washington state has banned all Halloween celebrations, including "decorations that include images of witches, pointed hats, black cats, or other similar decorations . . . intended to frighten or scare individuals." The school district cited this reason: "Use of derogatory stereotypes is prohibited, such as the traditional image of a witch, which is offensive to members of the Wiccan religion. The Wiccan (otherwise known as "witches") religion

is a bona fide religion under the law, and its followers are entitled to all the protections afforded more mainstream religions . . . ." (Quoted in "Warts and All," *Harper's*, March 2005.) _____

8. During the war on terror, a practice begun during the Reagan years called "rendition" (or "extraordinary rendition") intensified. American officials arrange for suspected terrorists to be kidnapped and taken to a foreign country, outside the boundaries of international law, where they are interrogated and tortured. Thus, the questioning is outside the American judicial system. _____

9. In its daily "News of the Weird" column (May 1, 2006), the *San Jose Mercury News* published this item about English preschools: "Teachers at several nursery schools in Oxfordshire, England, have been encouraging kids to learn the verse, ' *Baa, baa, black sheep/Have you any wool?*' without the word 'black,' but in its place a variety of emotions (e.g., 'Baa, baa, sad sheep') or colors (including 'Baa, baa, rainbow sheep') because they believe that kids with black skin might feel disrespected.

_____

10. A generation ago, calling someone a "pinko" implied that he or she had Communist sympathies. Today the word "liberal"—at least in some areas of the country—has become a similar derogatory term. San Francisco is a famously liberal city, but in recent years, members of the Board of Supervisors who used to call themselves "liberals" now refer to themselves as "progressives." That's because words like "pinko" and "liberal" are examples of _____.

■ CHAPTER EXERCISES

Selection 1

This excerpt is from Mark Spragg's excellent memoir, a collection of interlocking essays, about growing up on a Wyoming dude ranch, near Yellowstone National Park in the Shoshone National Forest. Spragg's jobs during the summer months were to care for the horses and to help the dudes (guests) on riding expeditions. In the fall and winter, the herd of horses was driven to the mountains, where they mingled with wild horses and foraged on their own. Late in the spring, Spragg and the other cowboys rounded them up and drove them back to the lodge, which necessitated maneuvering them through the town of Cody.[4]

1   We drove them the five miles into Cody, down Cody's main street, and out west of town, traveling upriver, toward the lodge, fifty miles in all. They shied, and snorted, and nipped at each other's withers, and kicked and bucked, and finally lined out in the borrow ditch for the long march back to a life of oats and work and new steel shoes.

2   When I was eleven and twelve I rode drag down the center of the highway, lagging a hundred yards behind the herd of horses. Ahead of me they frayed and grouped and swept back and forth over the macadam. The men kept them

[4]Another excerpt from Spragg's book, "A Boy's Work," appears in Part 5.

moving west. The sound of the hundreds of hooves on asphalt rolled back to me. I could feel the vibration of our passing. If I closed my eyes it was as though I rode in the wake of a hailstorm. I wagged a red kerchief tied to a stick at approaching cars. I reined my horse toward their grills. I shouted to the drivers. I asked them to drive slowly. I told them that in Wyoming horses have the right of way.

3   I remember a young man in a yellow Volkswagen Bug with Rhode Island plates, a young woman with him in the passenger's seat. He swerved around me honking his horn. My horse skittered on the pavement and nearly fell. The horses ahead of me were on the highway, the mob of them, and he slid into their ranks standing on his brakes. He drove at their heels, honking, his brake lights flashing on and off. I remember a leggy sorrel we owned. He was smooth mouthed, could be ridden or packed. If we put a child on him he sidestepped around the trunks of trees, careful not to rub their knees. His name was Sterling. The Rhode Island man pressed his yellow car hard on Sterling. His horn produced a constant wail. Sterling stopped, and turned. His ears were pricked. He stood for just a moment and then stepped onto the hood of the car. The metal winged up on either side of him to his knees. He was not panicked. He was simply getting out of the car's path. He stretched his head and neck to the river and snorted.

4   When he came over the Volkswagen's roof every window in the car splintered and fell onto the road. The honking stopped. He walked the back bumper off on his way down, and trotted to the side of the road, looped into the borrow pit, and continued west. The yellow car huffed and stalled. When I rode past I reminded the man that in Wyoming horses have the right of way. His girlfriend held up a hand in a jerky wave and nodded. She was laughing. She was trying not to let it show. Her other hand was held to her breast.

Mark Spragg, *Where Rivers Change Direction*

A. Content and Structure

1. Which two modes of discourse predominate in the passage?_____ and _____

2. In your own words, explain Spragg's purpose in this excerpt._____

   _____

3. Look again at paragraph 2. When Spragg writes that he "rode drag," what do you envision?_____

4. Why did Spragg carry a stick to which a red kerchief was tied?_____

   _____

5. Why does Spragg include the information that even children could ride Sterling?_____

6. Explain what Sterling, a sorrel horse, did when the visitor from Rhode Island drove close behind his heels, continuously honking his horn to get him to move._____

   _____

7. What is the main point that Spragg wants us to understand about the Rhode Island visitor?_____

8. Why did the girl in the car laugh at her companion?_____

B. Language Analysis

1. Comment on these verbs from paragraph 1: "shied," "snorted," "nipped," "kicked," "bucked." Taken together, what image are they meant to convey?_____

   _____

2. Consider again this sentence from paragraph 2: "If I closed my eyes it was as though I rode in the wake of a hailstorm." Analyze this figure of speech as follows:

   _____is compared to_____

   Is this figure of speech a metaphor, simile, or personification?_____
   How can you tell?_____

   _____

   Explain the meaning of the figure of speech._____

3. Anthropomorphism refers to giving something nonhuman, in this case, Sterling the sorrel horse, human characteristics. Look again at paragraph 3 and locate a phrase that suggests an example of anthropomorphism._____

4. Would you characterize Spragg's style as formal or informal? Explain.

   _____

Answers for Selection 1

A. Content and Structure

1. narration and description
2. Spragg's purpose is to relate a humorous story about one experience with an ignorant and arrogant visitor.
3. "Riding drag" means riding several yards behind the other cowboys and the herd of horses to keep any strays from wandering off.
4. The stick was like a baton—he could wave it at drivers to alert them to the procession.
5. Normally, Sterling was a gentle horse that one could trust even with children.
6. Sterling refused to move out of the way and simply walked on top of the hood of the car, over the top, and back down the rear end, thereby pretty much destroying it.
7. He was an arrogant jerk, who was in a hurry and refused to accept the fact that he didn't have right of way in this instance.
8. The scene must have been very funny, and the visitor behaved so badly that it served him right.

B. Language Analysis

1. These are all strong verbs that convey sound and movement.
2. The sound the horses make is compared to the sound hail makes.
   It's a simile because of "as though."
   The figure of speech is meant to clarify the sound of the hooves on the pavement.
3. "He stretched his head and neck to the river and snorted." (The horse wasn't going to let any honking deter him from the path he wanted to take.)
4. I would describe it as informal. The language is not difficult, and his sentences are simply constructed. That's why there isn't a vocabulary exercise to accompany the passage.

Selection 2

This excerpt is from the book *Friday Night Lights*, the basis of the 2004 film of the same name, starring Billy Bob Thornton, and the excellent former NBC drama series. In Texas high school football is almost a religion.

1   Logically they should have been united, not only by the common bond of oil that had kept them in clothes for sixty years, but by the bonds of loneliness. As your car fought its way across West Texas along Interstate 20 in the blistering heat and it felt as though you had been in the state for a week and had another week to go before you saw any sign of human life, they suddenly rose out of the emptiness like territorial forts.

2   There was Midland with its improbably tall buildings, glassy and shimmering in the sun like misplaced tanning reflectors. Fifteen miles to the west there was Odessa, sprawling and oozing, its most striking feature the fenced-off fields with row after row of oil field equipment that looked like rusting military weapons from a once-great war.

3   It seemed natural that they needed each other, as all good sister cities should, but instead they had spent most of their histories trying to prove just the opposite.

4   Midland was the fair-haired, goody-goody one, always doing the right thing, never a spot on that pleated dress, always staying up late to do her homework and prepare for the future. Odessa was the naughty one, the sassy one, the one who didn't stay at home but sat at a bar with a cigarette in one hand and the thin neck of a bottle of Coors in the other humming the tune of some country and western song about why it was silly to worry about tomorrow when you might get flattened by a pickup today, the one who dressed like an unmade bed and could care less about it, the one who liked nothing better than to drag her sanctimonious sister through the mud in a game of football and then kick her teeth in for good measure.

H. G. Bissinger, "Sisters," *Friday Night Lights*

A. Vocabulary

For each italicized word from the selection, write the dictionary definition most appropriate for the context.

1. sprawling and *oozing* [paragraph 2] _____
2. *goody-goody* one [4] _____
3. her *sanctimonious* sister [4] _____

B. Structure and Meaning

Complete the following questions.

1. What is the chief point that Bissinger makes in the passage?_____

   _____

   _____

2. What is the primary method of paragraph development in the passage as a whole? This method of development also suggests the writer's purpose._____

3. Paragraph 1 describes the part of Texas where Midland and Odessa are located. What is the primary dominant impression of the landscape?

   _____

   What phrase is key to identifying the dominant impression?_____

   _____

4. Look again at the last sentence of paragraph 1. What does the pronoun "they" refer to?_____

5. What inference can you make from paragraph 2 about the oil industry in Odessa, and what two clues provide support for it?_____

   _____

   _____

6. Paraphrase these two phrases from the passage:
   Paragraph 1: "the common bond of oil that had kept them in clothes for sixty years"_____

   _____

   Paragraph 4: "the one who liked nothing better than to drag her sanctimonious sister through the mud in a game of football and then kick her in the teeth for good measure."_____

   _____

C. Language Analysis

1. What particular kind of figure of speech lies at the heart of the passage? What is being compared to what, and what is the central meaning?

   _____

   _____

   _____

2. The writer also uses three figures of speech in paragraphs 1 and 2. Locate them and write them in the spaces provided. Then explain the meaning of each figure of speech.

(a) _____

_____

(b) _____

_____

_____

(c) _____

_____

_____

_____

Study the list of figures of speech in the question above. Are they examples of metaphor, simile, or personification? How can you tell?

_____

3. In paragraph 4, Bissinger uses the word "sassy" to describe Odessa. The dictionary shows two quite different meanings for this word: (a) rude and disrespectful, impudent; (b) lively and spirited, jaunty. Which of these two connotations do you think Bissinger has in mind? How can you tell? _____

_____

Selection 3

Margaret Atwood is a well-known Canadian novelist and essay writer.

1   The noses of a great many Canadians resemble Porky Pig's. This comes from spending so much time pressing them against the longest undefended one-way mirror in the world. The Canadians looking through this mirror behave the way people on the hidden side of such mirrors usually do: They observe, analyze, ponder, snoop and wonder what all the activity on the other side means in decipherable human terms.

2   The Americans, bless their innocent little hearts, are rarely aware that they are even being watched, much less by the Canadians. They just go on doing body language, playing in the sandbox of the world, bashing one another on the head and planning how to blow things up, same as always. If they think about Canada at all, it's only when things get a bit snowy, or the water goes off, or the Canadians start fussing over some piddly detail, such as fish. Then they regard them as unpatriotic; for Americans don't really see Canadians as foreigners, not like the Mexicans, unless they do something weird like speak French or beat the New York Yankees at baseball. Really, think the Americans, the Canadians are just like us, or would be if they could.

3   Or we could switch metaphors and call the border the longest undefended backyard fence in the world. The Canadians are the folks in the neat little bungalow with the tidy little garden and the duck pond. The Americans are the other folks, the ones in the sprawly mansion with the bad-taste statues on the lawn. There's a perpetual party, or something, going on there—loud music, raucous laughter, smoke billowing from the barbecue. Beer bottles and Coke cans land among the peonies. The Canadians have their own beer bottles and barbecue smoke, but they tend to overlook it. Your own mess is always more forgivable than the mess someone else makes on your patio.

4   The Canadians can't exactly call the police—they suspect that the Americans are the police—and part of their distress, which seems permanent, comes from their uncertainty as to whether or not they've been invited. Sometimes they do drop by next door, and find it exciting but scary. Sometimes the Americans drop by their house and find it clean. This worries the Canadians. They worry a lot. Maybe that Americans want to buy up their duck pond, with all the money they seem to have, and turn it into a cesspool or a water-skiing emporium.

Margaret Atwood, "Through the One-Way Mirror," *The Nation*

A. Structure and Meaning
Complete the following questions.

1. In your own words, write a sentence stating Atwood's main idea.

   _____

   _____

2. When Atwood writes at the beginning of paragraph 2, in referring to Americans, "bless their innocent little hearts," she is being
   (a) honest.
   (b) scornful.
   (c) sarcastic.
   (d) religious.
   (e) admiring.

3. From what Atwood implies in paragraph 2, explain what Americans think about Canadians._____

   _____

4. From the information in paragraph 4, why specifically do Canadians "worry a lot" about their southern neighbor? _____

   _____

5. What are the broader implications of Atwood's passage? What is the central inference you can make about the relationship between Canada and the United States?_____

   _____

B. Language Analysis

Complete the following questions.

1. Read paragraph 1 again. Why do Canadians' noses resemble Porky Pig's?_____

_____

_____

2. What does Atwood mean when she refers to the border between Canada and the United States as a "one-way mirror"? What does this metaphor say about Canadians?_____

_____

_____

3. How would you characterize the word "snoop" in the context it is used toward the end of paragraph 1? It suggests a
   (a) neutral, denotative meaning.
   (b) positive connotation.
   (c) negative connotation.
   (d) cliché.

4. Atwood says in paragraph 2 that Americans go on "playing in the sand-box of the world, bashing one another on the head and planning how to blow things up, same as always." What does the sandbox metaphor refer to? _____

   Explain what the metaphor means._____

   _____

5. In paragraph 3, Atwood switches metaphors, comparing the border between Canada and the United States to "the longest undefended backyard fence in the world." In your own words, explain Atwood's thinking about how these neighboring nations get along. Specifically, try to determine what she means when she refers to the Canadians' "neat little bungalow," the Americans' "sprawly mansion," and the "perpetual party" with the "raucous laughter" and the beer bottles and Coke cans thrown in the peonies._____

   _____

6. In paragraph 4, what is the literal meaning of these sentences? "Sometimes they do drop by next door, and find it exciting but scary. Sometimes the Americans drop by their house and find it clean."_____

   _____

   _____

   _____

   _____

PRACTICE ESSAY

"Joyas Voladoras"
Brian Doyle

Brian Doyle has won numerous awards for his writing, including the American Scholar Best Essay Award in 2000. As editor of Portland magazine, *a publication of the University of Portland, Doyle publishes material from some of America's most highly regarded writers. His own work has appeared in* The Atlantic Monthly, Georgia Review, Harpers, *and* The American Scholar. *This particular piece was first published in* The American Scholar *and was subsequently reprinted in both* The Best American Essays 2005 *and* The Best American Spiritual Writing 2004. *It is an adaptation from a piece in his book* The Wet Engine: Exploring the Mad Wild Miracle of the Heart (2005).

Preview Questions

1. What is it about hummingbirds that makes them so fascinating to watch?
2. In your mind, what image do you have of the heart relative to the size of the body in, say, a hummingbird, a blue whale, and a human being?
3. The heart is the conventional seat of emotions for Westerners. Is this a universal concept, or do other cultures view the locus of human emotions differently? If you are familiar with another culture, perhaps you can consider this question.

1   Consider the hummingbird for a long moment. A hummingbird's heart beats ten times a second. A hummingbird's heart is the size of a pencil eraser. A hummingbird's heart is a lot of the hummingbird. *Joyas voladoras*, flying jewels, the first white explorers in the Americas called them, and the white men had never seen such creatures, for hummingbirds came into the world only in the Americas, nowhere else in the universe, more than three hundred species of them whirring and zooming and nectaring in hummer time zones nine times removed from ours, their hearts hammering faster than we could clearly hear if we pressed our elephantine ears to their infinitesimal chests.

2   Each one visits a thousand flowers a day. They can dive at sixty miles an hour. They can fly backward. They can fly more than five hundred miles without pausing to rest. But when they rest they come close to death: on frigid nights, or when they are starving, they retreat into torpor, their metabolic rate slowing to a fifteenth of their normal sleep rate, their hearts sludging nearly to a halt, barely beating, and if they are not soon warmed, if they do not soon find that which is sweet, their hearts grow cold, and they cease to be. Consider for a moment those hummingbirds who did not

open their eyes again today, this very day, in the Americas: bearded helmet-crests and booted racket-tails, violet-tailed sylphs and violet-capped wood-nymphs, crimson topazes and purple-crowned fairies, red-tailed comets and amethyst woodstars, rainbow-bearded thornbills and glittering-bellied em-eralds, velvet-purple coronets and golden-bellied star-frontlets, fiery-tailed awlbills and Andean hillstars, spatuletails and pufflegs, each the most amaz-ing thing you have never seen, each thunderous wild heart the size of an infant's fingernail, each mad heart silent, a brilliant music stilled.

3   Hummingbirds, like all flying birds but more so, have incredible enor-mous immense ferocious metabolisms. To drive those metabolisms they have racecar hearts that eat oxygen at an eye-popping rate. Their hearts are built of thinner, leaner fibers than ours. Their arteries are stiffer and more taut. They have more mitochondria in their heart muscles—anything to gulp more oxygen. Their hearts are stripped to the skin for the war against gravity and inertia, the mad search for food, the insane idea of flight. The price of their ambition is a life closer to death; they suffer more heart attacks and aneurysms and ruptures than any other living creature. It's expensive to fly. You burn out. You fry the machine. You melt the engine. Every creature on earth has approximately two bil-lion heartbeats to spend in a lifetime. You can spend them slowly, like a tortoise, and live to be two hundred years old, or you can spend them fast, like a hummingbird, and live to be two years old.

4   The biggest heart in the world is inside the blue whale. It weighs more than seven tons. It's as big as a room. It *is* a room, with four chambers. A child could walk around in it, head high, bending only to step through the valves. The valves are as big as the swinging doors in a saloon. This house of a heart drives a creature a hundred feet long. When this creature is born it is twenty feet long and weighs four tons. It is waaaaay bigger than your car. It drinks a hundred gallons of milk from its mama every day and gains two hundred pounds a day, and when it is seven or eight years old it endures an unimaginable puberty and then it essentially dis-appears from human ken, for next to nothing is known of the mating habits, travel patterns, diet, social life, language, social structure, diseases, spirituality, wars, stories, despairs, and arts of the blue whale. There are perhaps ten thousand blue whales in the world, living in every ocean on earth, and of the largest mammal who ever lived we know nearly noth-ing. But we know this: the animals with the largest hearts in the world generally travel in pairs, and their penetrating moaning cries, their pierc-ing yearning tongue, can be heard underwater for miles and miles.

5   Mammals and birds have hearts with four chambers. Reptiles and tur-tles have hearts with three chambers. Fish have hearts with two cham-bers. Insects and mollusks have hearts with one chamber. Worms have hearts with one chamber, although they may have as many as eleven single-chambered hearts. Unicellular bacteria have no hearts at all; but even they have fluid eternally in motion, washing from one side of the cell to the other, swirling and whirling. No living being is without inte-rior liquid motion. We all churn inside.

6   So much held in a heart in a lifetime. So much held in a heart in a day, an hour, a moment. We are utterly open with no one, in the end—not mother and father, not wife or husband, not lover, not child, not friend. We open windows to each but we live alone in the house of the heart. Perhaps we must. Perhaps we could not bear to be so naked, for fear of a constantly harrowed heart. When young we think there will come one person who will savor and sustain us always; when we are older we know this is the dream of a child, that all hearts finally are bruised and scarred, scored and torn, repaired by time and will, patched by force of character, yet fragile and rickety forevermore, no matter how ferocious the defense and how many bricks you bring to the wall. You can brick up your heart as stout and tight and hard and cold and impregnable as you possibly can and down it comes in an instant, felled by a woman's second glance, a child's apple breath, the shatter of glass in the road, the words "I have something to tell you," a cat with a broken spine dragging itself into the forest to die, the brush of your mother's papery ancient hand in the thicket of your hair, the memory of your father's voice early in the morning echoing from the kitchen where he is making pancakes for his children.

A. Comprehension

Choose the answer that best completes each statement. Do not refer to the selection while doing this exercise.

1. The first white explorers called hummingbirds "Joyas Voladoras," a Spanish phrase meaning
   (a) tiny birds.
   (b) joyful treasures.
   (c) colorful bits of glass.
   (d) flying jewels.
2. At night when they rest, hummingbirds are apt to die because they are particularly susceptible to
   (a) frigid temperatures.
   (b) larger birds that prey on them.
   (c) heart attacks.
   (d) oxygen deprivation.
3. One characteristic of all flying birds, but in particular of hummingbirds, is their incredible
   (a) sense of direction.
   (b) speed.
   (c) metabolism.
   (d) seeming defiance of gravity.
4. Concerning the blue whale, the writer states that
   (a) scientists have developed a large body of knowledge about their habits and patterns.
   (b) we have accumulated very little knowledge about their habits.

(c) scientists use this species to determine the health of the world's oceans.

(d) their large size makes them impossible to study.

5. One mark of growing up, of gaining experience in the world is the realization that

(a) we must open our hearts to at least one person in this world.

(b) our hearts become bruised and scarred and then patched up.

(c) we are all in this life, with all its joys and tragedies, together.

(d) we must brick up our hearts if we are not to become permanently scarred.

B. Vocabulary

Below are definitions of key phrases from the passage. Look through the paragraph specified and locate the phrase that matches each definition. An example has been done for you.

Example: caused to fall down, struck down [6]_____felled_____

1. immeasurably minute, tiny [paragraph 1]_____

2. lethargy, a state of physical inactivity [2]_____

3. moving very slowly or sluggishly [2]_____

4. view, perception, understanding, knowledge [4]_____

5. inflicted with great distress or torment [6—used metaphorically]

_____

6. impossible to enter by force [6]_____

C. Inferences

On the basis of the evidence in the passage, mark these statements as follows: PA (probably accurate), PI (probably inaccurate), or NP (not in the passage).

1. _____ A hummingbird's heart is rather large in relation to the size of its body.

2. _____ Hummingbirds are native to the North American continent.

3. _____ Hummingbirds live on the nectar gathered from flowers.

4. _____ Tortoises live to be 200 years old even though their hearts beat just as fast as a hummingbird's.

5. _____ Oxygen is the single most important element that a hummingbird needs to survive.

6. _____ The necessity of flying at amazing speeds puts an incredible strain on a hummingbird's heart.

D. Structure and Meaning

Complete the following questions.

1. This essay has no stated thesis. Supply a thesis statement that accounts for all of Doyle's observations._____

_____

_____

2. In paragraph 1 the writer compares a hummingbird's heart to a pencil eraser and to an infant's fingernail to emphasize_____

_____

3. In paragraph 2, Doyle writes, "if they do not soon find that which is sweet." What is he specifically referring to?_____

4. Read paragraph 4 again. Locate and write three figures of speech Doyle uses to describe a blue whale._____

_____

_____

5. In paragraph 5 Doyle uses the classification method. What is the basis for classifying?_____

6. When Doyle writes at the end of paragraph 5, "No living being is without interior liquid motion," what specifically is he alluding to?

_____

7. Read paragraph 6 again, paying particular attention to details Doyle assembles in the second half. What point is he making about what is "held in a heart in a lifetime"?_____

_____

_____

8. Comment on the tone of the last example—of the father making pancakes for his children._____

_____

E. Questions for Discussion and Analysis

1. Why do you think this piece was included in an anthology titled *The Best American Spiritual Writing*?

2. Why does Doyle focus his attention in the first four paragraphs on the heart of a hummingbird and then on the blue whale before turning his attention to the human heart?

3. Read the last paragraph again very carefully. Explain the paradox that surrounds his observations that we must live alone "in the house of the heart" coupled with his metaphor about bricking up our heart as if it were a fortress. How does he reconcile this paradox?

Josephine was kneeling before the closed door with her lips to the keyhole, imploring for admission. "Louise, open the door! I beg; open the door—you will make yourself ill. What are you doing, Louise? For heaven's sake open the door,"

"Go away. I am not making myself ill." No; she was drinking in a very elixir of life through that open window.

Her fancy was running riot along those days ahead of her. Spring days, and summer days, and all sorts of days that would be her own. She breathed a quick prayer that life might be long. It was only yesterday she had thought with a shudder that life might be long.

She arose at length and opened the door to her sister's importunities. There was a feverish triumph in her eyes, and she carried herself unwittingly like a goddess of Victory. She clasped her sister's waist, and together they descended the stairs. Richards stood waiting for them at the bottom.

Some one was opening the front door with a latchkey. It was Brently Mallard who entered, a little travel-stained, composedly carrying his gripsack and umbrella. He had been far from the scene of accident, and did not even know there had been one. He stood amazed at Josephine's piercing cry; at Richards' quick motion to screen him from the view of his wife.

But Richards was too late.

When the doctors came they said she had died of heart disease—of joy that kills.

Questions for Discussion and Analysis

1. What is the situation at the beginning of the story? How does Louise Mallard react to the news of her husband's death?

2. Read again the description of how Louise cries upon hearing the news. What hints does Chopin provide that let the reader know that Louise's expression of grief is unusual?

3. What emotions does Louise experience as she sits alone in her room, contemplating her situation? Pay particular attention to the scene she observes through the open window.

4. How does Louise react emotionally to the realization of her new-found freedom? What consideration seems to be uppermost in her mind?

5. What do we learn about her marriage to Brently Mallard? What sort of husband was he? What were her prospects for the future?

6. Explain the twist that occurs at the end of the story.

7. What is significant about the story's title, "The Story of an Hour"?

8. Go through the story again and identify the words and phrases that pertain to convention and expectations of correct behavior and those that pertain to freedom, emotion, and self-fulfillment.

CHAPTER 7

Tone, Point of View, and Allusions

CHAPTER OBJECTIVES

In Chapter 7 several elements you have studied thus far come together. In this second chapter dealing with the importance of language, you will enhance your understanding of what you read by examining some rather sophisticated elements, including:

- Point of view

- Tone

- Allusions

■ POINT OF VIEW

The phrase ***point of view*** refers to the writer's attitude toward or position on a subject—his or her **stance**. One's point of view, especially with regard to controversial matters, can be favorable, unfavorable, neutral, or ambivalent. This point of view leads to certain choices the writer makes, to the other important elements in writing, for example, mode of discourse, word choice (diction) and the connotations of these words, and **tone** (the subject of this chapter).

245

Let us illustrate these connections with a passage by Harvard biologist Edward O. Wilson, in which he discusses the Incas' contributions to the world's food supply. (Wilson is the author of "The Power of Story," which was a practice exercise in Chapter 5.) As you read it, pay careful attention to the circled connotative words.

From the mostly unwritten archives of native peoples has come a wealth of information about wild and semicultivated crops. It is a remarkable fact that with a single exception, the macadamia nut of Australia, every one of the fruits and nuts used in western countries was grown first by indigenous peoples. The Incas were arguably the all-time champions in creating a reservoir of diverse crops. Without the benefit of wheels, money, iron, or written script, these Andean people evolved a sophisticated agriculture based on almost as many plant species as used by all the farmers of Europe and Asia combined. Their abounding crops, tilled on the cool upland slopes and plateaus, proved especially suited for temperate climates. From the Incas have come lima beans, peppers, potatoes, and tomatoes. But many other species and strains, including a hundred varieties of potatoes, are still confined to the Andes. The Spanish conquerors learned to use a few of the potatoes, but they missed many other representatives of a vast array of cultivated tuberous vegetables, including some that are more productive and savory than the favored crops. The names are likely to be unfamiliar: achira, ahipa, arracacha, maca, mashua, mauka, oca, ulloco, and yacon. One, maca, is on the verge of extinction, limited to 10 hectares in the highest plateau region of Peru and Bolivia. Its swollen roots, resembling brown radishes and rich in sugar and starch, have a sweet, tangy flavor and are considered a delicacy by the handful of people still privileged to consume them.

Edward O. Wilson, *The Diversity of Life*

Point of view
favorable

Purpose in writing
to inform, to explain

Mode of discourse
exposition

Tone
informative, also admiring

Diction
some words with favorable connotations

Now study this diagram. Begin at the top left with "point of view." Then follow the arrows clockwise from element to element to see how everything ties together.

Now write a one-sentence summary of the passage.

_____

_____

**Practice
Exercise 1**

Read this paragraph by philosopher and ethicist Sissela Bok, which comes from her classic study of lies and lying. As you read it, circle the connotative words. Then fill in the diagram that follows it.

Those who learn that they have been lied to in an important matter—say, the identity of their parents, the affection of their spouse, or the integrity of their government—are resentful, disappointed, and suspicious. They feel wronged; they are wary of new overtures. And they look back on their past beliefs and actions in the new light of the discovered lies. They see that they were manipulated, that the deceit made them unable to make choices for themselves according to the most adequate information available, unable to act as they would have wanted to act had they known all along.

Sissela Bok, *Lying: Moral Choices in Public and Private Life*

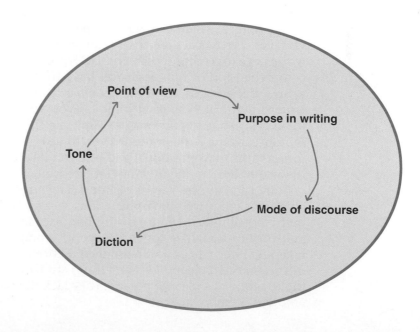

Critical Thinking Exercise

Look again at the paragraph by Sissela Bok. Explain the reason that she includes three examples (separated by dashes) in the first sentence. What implication is she making about lies and about types of lies? What would be another example of a lie that Bok would most likely find objectionable?

■ AN OVERVIEW OF TONE

As you see from these two examples, tone is the feeling or emotional quality a piece of writing conveys to the reader. In conversation, a speaker's tone is readily apparent from gestures, tone of voice, vocal pitch (the voice's rise and fall), facial expression, and body language, even without hearing the actual words spoken.

Imagine this encounter that takes place at a party. A young man introduces himself to an attractive woman. She replies, "I'm Charlotte Milan," which she pronounces MY - lun. He then asks, "What kind of name is Milan?," except that he pronounces it "mee - LAHN" like the Italian city. She corrects him: "It's Serbian, and it's pronounced MY - lun." The young man responds, *"Whatever."* Charlotte mutters to herself, "Jerk!" and moves away.

Can you hear the tone in the man's "whatever"? It's arrogant, rude, and dismissive. A recent survey of Americans revealed that the word "whatever," used this way, is considered the rudest word in the English language. But note: It's not the word that's rude; it's the <u>tone</u> in which it's uttered.

But tone in reading is hard to perceive because when we read, the visual and vocal cues are absent; all we have are the black words on the white page (or computer screen). Determining tone goes beyond a literal comprehension of the ideas. You have to infer it from the connotative values of the words, from the details included, and, of course, from the writer's point of view or attitude, as you saw in the preceding section. Identifying tone requires you to duplicate the "sound" or rhythm of the sentences as the writer intended you to hear them. Richard Altick defines tone as "the total emotional and intellectual effect of a piece of writing." It's a complicated undertaking but one well worth mastering.

Tone can run the gamut of human feelings or moods, reflecting the complex beings we humans are. This section will illustrate a few of the many possibilities. The following box lists some of the more common and easy-to-recognize tones. A second group of more difficult ones is taken up later. Check an unabridged dictionary if you are unsure of any of these words' meanings. Sometimes students have difficulty articulating the tone of a passage because they lack the vocabulary to express the emotion it embodies.

I have grouped them into clusters of similar tones that reflect grada-tions in meaning. Thus, the first one is typically mild; the second one, stronger; and so on. For example, in the second cluster below, "approv-ing" is more neutral than its more positive cousin "admiring," while "laudatory" is even more strongly admiring. Further, I have grouped them roughly according to whether they are neutral, positive, or nega-tive. Of course, context determines these characteristics. Note, for ex-ample, that one can be critical in a positive way but criticism can tip over into a negative tone if it's harsh or vindictive.

Common Varieties of Tone

Neutral

Informative, impartial, instructive

Generally Positive

Approving, admiring, laudatory
Sincere, honest, candid
Serious, somber, grave
Philosophical, reflective, pensive
Eager, fervent, passionate, zealous
Questioning, skeptical
Amusing, funny, humorous
Sorrowful, mournful, lamenting
Nostalgic, wistful, melancholy
Critical, analytical, judicious

Generally Negative

Critical, fault-finding, disparaging
Complaining, aggrieved, whining
Harsh, mean-spirited, nasty
Provocative, shrill, rabble-rousing, inflammatory
Sentimental, gushy, maudlin, mawkish

Space limitations make it impossible for us to examine each of these tones; for now it is sufficient just to know that they exist and that you will encounter them in all the reading you do. Many students often think that good nonfiction writing should be objective. This supposition is far from the truth. In fact, outside of textbooks and purely factual news articles, all writing has a tone or an emotional stance, and as you will see below, even textbook writers sometimes inject tone into their prose. If all writers strived for objectivity (assuming that it were both possible and desirable), what we read would be dry and lifeless and very boring. Thus, the advanced college reader must be alert to these subtle nuances. Recognizing and appreciating tone has a lot to do with enhancing our pleasure in reading.

Tone in Textbooks

The textbooks that you read in your academic courses illustrate academic discourse—writing that conveys factual information. Its tone corresponds to that purpose and is typically characterized by an unemotional, straightforward, and objective tone. In this light, reading academic discourse is different from reading newspapers, popular magazines, novels, or other leisure reading. Nor are textbooks forums for controversy or for stirring our emotions. However, textbook material, particularly the material in the explanatory sidebars, *may* convey an identifiable tone. Economics texts are known for being rather dry, but in this passage, the authors adopt a particular tone toward the subject—ticket scalping. Before you read the passage, ask yourself these questions:

- What does the term "scalping" mean? In what situations does scalping usually occur? Does the word have a positive or a negative connotation?
- Is scalping undesirable, unethical, perhaps even illegal?
- If you needed a ticket to, say, a sold-out concert to be performed by your favorite group, would you pay a scalper's price? Why or why not? How much above the ticket price would you be willing to pay?
- The title of this sidebar from a leading economics textbook is "Ticket Scalping: A Bum Rap!" What does the subtitle tell you about the writers' point of view?

Ticket Scalping: A Bum Rap!

Ticket prices for athletic events and musical concerts are usually set far in advance of the events. Sometimes the original ticket price is too low to be the equilibrium price. Lines form at the ticket window, and a severe shortage of tickets occurs at the printed price. What happens next? Buyers who are willing to pay more than the original price bid up the equilibrium price in resale ticket markets. The price rockets upward.

Tickets sometimes get resold for much greater amounts than the original price—market transactions known as "scalping." For example, an original buyer may resell a $75 ticket to a concert for $200, $250, or more. Reporters sometimes denounce scalpers for "ripping off" buyers by charging "exorbitant" prices.

But is scalping really a rip-off? We must first recognize that such ticket resales are voluntary transactions. If both buyer and seller did not expect to gain from the exchange, it would not occur! The seller must value the $200 more than seeing the event, and the buyer must value seeing the event at $200 or more. So there are no losers or victims here: Both buyer and seller benefit from the transaction. The scalping market simply redistributes assets (game or concert tickets) from those who would rather have the money (the other things money can buy) to those who would rather have the tickets.

Does scalping impose losses or injury on the sponsors of the event? If the sponsors are injured, it is because they initially priced tickets below the equilibrium level. Perhaps they did this to create a long waiting line and the attendant news media publicity. Alternatively, they may have had a genuine desire to keep tickets affordable for lower-income, ardent fans. In either case, the event sponsors suffer an opportunity cost in the form of less ticket revenue than they might have otherwise received. But such losses are self-inflicted and separate and distinct from the fact that some tickets are later resold at a higher price.

So is ticket scalping undesirable? Not on economic grounds! It is an entirely voluntary activity that benefits both sellers and buyers.

Campbell R. McConnell and Stanley L. Brue, "Ticket Scalping: A Bum Rap!"
Economics: Principles, Problems, and Policies

Now answer these questions:

1. What is the connotation of the word "scalping" and what is its origin? _____

   _____

2. What is McConnell and Brue's point of view toward scalping?

   _____

3. In the second paragraph, why do the authors put quotation marks around "ripping off" and "exorbitant"? _____

   _____

   _____

4. Locate and identify the *two* primary reasons that the writers think that scalping has been given a bum rap. _____

   _____

5. How would you describe the tone of the passage? _____

   _____

Tone in Nonfiction Prose

Because the majority of the readings in this text are from nonfiction prose, we will take up tone in that genre first. In this section, we will examine tone in five nonfiction passages, moving from straightforward prose to more complex examples. The first excerpt is from a magazine article about cloning written by a nonfiction writer. As you read it, be sure to look up any unfamiliar vocabulary, and after doing so, circle the connotative words. After you read it, fill in the diagram that follows.

> The notion that cloning might help conserve endangered species has been bandied around for years. Very little such bandying, though, is done by professional conservationists or conservation biologists. One lion biologist gave me a pointed response to the idea: "Bunkum." He and many others who study imperiled species and beleaguered ecosystems view cloning as irrelevant to their main concerns. Worse, it might be a costly distraction—diverting money, diverting energy, allowing the public to feel some bogus reassurance that all mistakes and choices are reversible and that any lost species can be re-created using biological engineering. The reality is that when a species becomes endangered its troubles are generally twofold: not enough habitat and, as the population drops, not enough diversity left in its shrunken gene pool. What can cloning contribute toward easing those troubles? As for habitat, nothing. As for genetic diversity, little or nothing—except under very particular circumstances. Cloning is copying, and you don't increase diversity by making copies.
>
> David Quammen, "Clone Your Troubles Away: Dreaming at the Frontiers of Animal Husbandry," *Harper's Magazine*

Now study the diagram below, beginning at the top again with "point of view" and going clockwise.

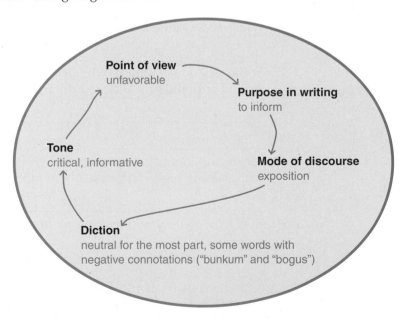

To determine the tone, study the elements in this analysis, remembering to read clockwise starting from the top.

In your own words, explain Quammen's objections to cloning. Why do conservationists and conservation biologists think that cloning is "bunkum"? _____

_____

_____

In this excerpt from her best-selling memoir, Elizabeth Gilbert recounts a new romantic entanglement with a man named David, the first man she dated after she and her husband had gone through a messy, acrimonious divorce.

> But, oh, we had such a great time together during those early months when he was still my romantic hero and I was still his living dream. It was excitement and compatibility like I'd never imagined. We invented our own language. We went on day trips and road trips. We hiked to the top of things, swam to the bottom of other things, planned the journeys across the world we would take together. We had more fun waiting in line together at the Department of Motor Vehicles than most couples have on their honeymoons. We gave each other the same nickname, so there would be no separation between us. We made goals, vows, promises and dinner together. He read books to me, and he *did my laundry.* (The first time that happened, I called Susan to report the marvel in astonishment, like I'd just seen a camel using a pay phone. I said, "A *man* just did *my* laundry! And he even hand-washed my delicates!" And she repeated: "Oh my God, baby, you are in so much trouble.")
>
> Elizabeth Gilbert, *Eat, Pray, Love*

How would you describe Gilbert's tone in this paragraph? When you examine the details and the romantic activities she and David engaged in, the tone is optimistic and passionate. There is a sense of wonder in what she feels.

A Special Case: Sentimentality

In the earlier list of tones at the beginning of the chapter, the final item is "sentimental," followed by its linguistic cousins—"gushy," "maudlin," and "mawkish." Because sentimentality is common in nonfiction prose (almost always badly written), each variation merits a little discussion. *Sentimentality* is an umbrella word describing a tone that appeals to one's tender emotions. My dictionary defines *gushy* as showing excessive displays of sentiment or enthusiasm. A maudlin tone is embarrassingly or tearfully sentimental, and mawkishness is even stronger—referring to sentimentality so overdone that it is objectionable, almost sickening.

Sentimentality can be genuine or fake, depending on the writer's motive and care in writing. And it can be both effective and affective, meaning that it can appeal to our tender and compassionate instincts and win us over. Many readers enjoy reading about those who have overcome serious obstacles, found true love, or conquered grave illnesses. Such stories ennoble us, give us hope, and inspire us to muddle through our daily lives and to cope with our fears and our shortcomings. The immense popularity of the *Chicken Soup for the Soul* books is a testimony to this observation.

What can go wrong with the sentimental point of view? It's the fake kind that we need to be alert to. If the writer deliberately plays to our heartstrings with counterfeit emotions and empty clichés, the effect is offensive or ludicrous. We see through the fakery. Richard D. Altick and Andrea A. Lunsford in their excellent textbook *Preface to Critical Reading* explain that writers may lapse into sentimentality because most of the important things in life—love, loss, the innocence of childhood, old age and death, for example—have already been written about, making it difficult to say anything new about them. Here is a passage that embodies the sentimental tone. It comes from the Online Writing Laboratory at Georgia Perimeter College.

> Jim and Mary Smith had looked forward to the trip for months. They were returning to a city they had fallen in love with during the five years it was their home over a decade ago. So many memories were rooted in those years when they lived near Washington D.C. They had bought their first house while they lived in a nearby suburb. Their two sons had begun school during those years, and Jim and Mary had established many close friendships. Above all, they had become caught up in the excitement of living in the nation's capital, with its continual political intrigue and constant awareness of international affairs. Indeed, they were more than eager to return, see friends, and visit the beautiful city they loved.

Writing like this is hollow; it sounds fake and affected. It is characterized by phony sentiment and meaningless clichés. Of course, there is nothing wrong with a couple looking forward to a trip to a city where they once lived. It's the sappy tone and the manner of expression that offends here. For fun, you might try rewriting this passage by eliminating the sentimental and empty clichés and adding concrete details in their place.

Practice Exercise 2

This is the first of two practice exercises in determining tone in nonfiction writing. In this one, you are given multiple-choice answers. Here are some passages for you to practice with. As before, pay careful attention to word choice (especially to connotation) and to the manner of expression. Underline key words and phrases. Determine how point of view, mode of discourse, and diction point to the writer's tone. Then decide which of the four choices best represents the writer's tone.

A.

I'm as sick of work as the next guy, but I'm still practical enough to recognize the need for it. Without work, where would all the new breed of millionaires that I read about in *Time* Magazine get their dry cleaning done? Who would fix their cars? Who would strip for them when they unload their trophy wives for the evening and go out for a night on the town? Us, the ununited workers of the world. I get the newspaper and dig through the classifieds.

It's the same old crap. "CAREER OPPORTUNITY!!!" screams an ad for a $6.25 an hour warehouse clerk. They mention that they drug test. Who are they kidding? They're discouraging their target market. Who but a crack head would want an opportunity like that? Opportunity, my ass. Why is it so difficult for the people who write these ads to present their jobs in a realistic and readable fashion? Why am I always looking at classifieds that say "FUN EXCITING PLACE TO WORK" and show up to see a bunch of desk jockeys a blink away from quitting, or suicide.

Iain Levison, *A Working Stiff's Manifesto: A Memoir*

Levison's tone is

1. arrogant, egotistical.
2. humorously scornful.
3. serious, stern.
4. critical, fault-finding.

B.   The author is a chef and restaurant owner in New York City.

People who order their meat well-done perform a valuable service for those of us in the business who are cost-conscious: they pay for the privilege of eating our garbage. In many kitchens, there's a time-honored practice called "save for well-done." When one of the cooks finds a particularly unlovely piece of steak—tough, riddled with nerve and connective tissue, off the hip end of the loin, and maybe a little stinky from age—he'll dangle it in the air and say, "Hey, Chef, whaddya want me to do with *this?*" Now, the chef has three options. He can tell the cook to throw the offending item into the trash, but that means a total loss, and in the restaurant business every item of cut, fabricated, or prepared food should earn at least three times the amount it originally cost if the chef is to make his correct food-cost percentage. Or he can decide to serve that steak to "the family"—that is, the floor staff—though that, economically, is the same as throwing it out. But no. What he's going to do is repeat the mantra of cost-conscious chefs everywhere: "Save for well-done." The way he figures it, the philistine who orders his food well-done is not likely to notice the difference between food and flotsam.

Anthony Bourdain, "Don't Eat before Reading This," *The New Yorker*

Bourdain's tone is

1. honest, candid, frank.
2. critical, fault-finding, disparaging.
3. philosophical, reflective.
4. approving, admiring, laudatory.

C. This poem was originally published on a website devoted to Mother's Day poems (www.poemsforfree.com/mothersdaypoems.html).

Happiness is like a sunny day:
All one's bitterness is drowned in light.
Praise be the light, though it must pass away,
Perhaps because compassion needs the night.
Yet when one feels like swallowing barbed wire,
More or less does nothing for the pain.
Old memories return as if on fire,
Tormenting one with unforgiving shame.
How can I, who love you, come inside,
Each wound to bind up with an ointment rare,
Restoring the once effervescent bride 'Neath misery no happiness can spare?
So shall I sing to you of all life's beauty,
Doing through the night my daytime duty.
A song of love may not bring back your noon,
Yet in your darkness, let me be your moon.

Nicholas Gordon, "Happiness Is like a Sunny Day"

The tone of the poem is

1. philosophical, reflective, pensive.
2. sincere, honest, candid.
3. nostalgic, melancholy.
4. sentimental, maudlin.

D. Abraham Lincoln's "Farewell at Springfield" was delivered to a vast audience of his fellow citizens on February 11, 1861, as he was leaving for Washington to assume the duties of president. Keep in mind as you read it that Lincoln's primary goal was to preserve the Union.

My friends—No one, not in my situation, can appreciate my feeling of sadness at this parting. To this place, and the kindness of these people, I owe everything. Here I have lived a quarter of a century, and have passed from a young man to an old man. Here my children have been born, and one is buried. I may return, with a task before me greater than that which rested upon Washington. Without that assistance, I cannot fail. Trusting in Him who can go with me, and remain with you, and be everywhere for good, let us confidently hope that all will be well. To His care commending you, as I hope in your prayers you will commend me, I bid you an affectionate farewell.

Apart from his obviously strong religious tone, which of the following best describes Lincoln's tone?

1. nostalgic, almost melancholy and dejected.
2. eloquent, yet modest and unassuming.
3. sorrowful, mournful, lamenting.
4. irritable, complaining, aggrieved.

Practice Exercise 3	In this second practice exercise, follow the directions from the first exercise. For these passages you will be asked to explain the tone in your own words.

A. This first excerpt is from an interview with Richard P. Feynmann, a renowned physicist.

Tyrannosaurus in the Window

We had the *Encyclopaedia Britannica* at home and even when I was a small boy [my father] used to sit me on his lap and read to me from the *Encyclopaedia Britannica,* and we would read, say, about dinosaurs and maybe it would be talking about the brontosaurus or something, or the tyrannosaurus rex, and it would say something like, "This thing is twenty-five feet high and the head is six feet across," you see, and so he'd stop all this and say, "Let's see what that means. That would mean that if he stood in our front yard he would be high enough to put his head through the window but not quite because the head is a little bit too wide and it would break the window as it came by."

Everything we'd read would be translated as best we could into some reality and so I learned to do that—everything that I read I try to figure out what it really means, what it's really saying by translating and so (LAUGHS) I used to read the *Encyclopaedia* when I was a boy but with translation, you see, so it was very exciting and interesting to think there were animals of such magnitude—I wasn't frightened that there would be one coming in my window as a consequence of this, I don't think, but I thought that it was very, very interesting, that they all died out and at that time nobody knew why.

Richard P. Feynmann, *The Pleasure of Finding Things Out*

How would you describe Feynmann's tone in this interview excerpt?

those stolen afternoons (and, on the up and up, sometimes on weekends) was a cross-section of early-thirties Hollywood, which was just then coming into high gear.

Roger Angell, "Movie Struck," *The New Yorker*

In describing his stolen afternoons at the movies, what is the dominant tone of the passage? _____

_____

Tone and Mood in Fiction

In literature, tone is conveyed not only by the writer's manner of expression but also by the thoughts and actions of the characters, by their relation to the other characters and to their environment, by figurative language, and by descriptions of the environment—both physical and psychological—of the characters. Further, unlike nonfiction, literature conveys **mood**—the atmosphere or emotional state that all these things evoke. Let us examine two examples. The first returns us to the example of flash fiction that you read in Chapter 3, "Town Life" by J. Robert Lennon (see page 99). How would you characterize the mood and tone of this selection? It is ordinary, unemotional, and conversational. The narrator reinforces these elements by showing how the townspeople tried hard to treat the actress as they would any other citizen. He accomplishes this by choosing a few homely details about shopping club memberships, coffee punch cards, home improvement loans, and property lines.

Let's look at one more example, this one set in a more contemporary fictional American high school. In Jeffrey Eugenides' three-generational novel about a hermaphrodite who grows up in a Greek-American family, the 12-year-old narrator, Callie, lives in Grosse Point, Michigan, a wealthy suburb near Detroit, where many executives in the automobile industry live. Callie has been sent to a girls' school called the Baker & Inglis School for Girls. In this excerpt, Callie is describing a group of girls—a clique—whom she refers to as the Charm Bracelets.

The Charm Bracelets: they were the rulers of my new school. They'd been going to Baker & Inglis since kindergarten. Since pre-kindergarten! They lived near the water and had grown up, like all Grosse Pointers, pretending that our shallow lake was no lake at all but actually the ocean. The Atlantic Ocean. Yes, that was the secret wish of the Charm Bracelets and their parents, to be not Midwesterners but Easterners, to affect their dress and lockjaw speech, to summer in Martha's Vineyard, to say "back East" instead of "out East," as though their time in Michigan represented only a brief sojourn away from home.

What can I say about my well-bred, small-nosed, trust-funded school-mates? Descended from hardworking, thrifty industrialists (there were two girls in my class who had the same last names as American car makers), did they show aptitudes for math or science? Did they display mechanical ingenuity? Or a commitment to the Protestant work ethic? In a word: no. There is no evidence against genetic determinism more persuasive than the children of the rich. The Charm Bracelets didn't study. They never raised their hands in class. They sat in the back, slumping, and went home each day carrying the prop of a notebook. (But maybe the Charm Bracelets understood more about life than I did. From an early age they knew what little value the world placed in books, and so didn't waste their time with them. Whereas I, even now, persist in believing that these black marks on white paper bear the greatest significance, that if I keep writing I might be able to catch the rainbow of consciousness in a jar. The only trust fund I have is this story, and unlike a prudent Wasp, I'm dipping into principal, spending it all . . .)

Jeffrey Eugenides, *Middlesex*

Probably all of us can identify with Callie's feelings about the Charm Bracelets. All high schools have such groups, the "rulers" of the school. How would you characterize Callie's tone in this passage? She is clearly scornful and resentful of their social standing, their shallowness, their arrogance, their refusal to study, the fact that they know that they don't need to study. Even at a young age, she is aware of her own role in life—her need to write, to accomplish something. So we might say that her tone toward the end of the passage is one of resignation to her fate. The tone is complicated and not easily reduced to a single feeling.

Practice Exercise 4

Here are four passages taken from contemporary fiction. Read them carefully and then answer the question or questions that follow.

A. The narrator in this novel, Amir, has returned to Afghanistan to search for his half-brother's son. This scene occurs just after his arrival in his home country.

I stepped outside. Stood in the silver tarnish of a half-moon and glanced up to a sky riddled with stars. Crickets chirped in the shuttered darkness and a wind wafted through the trees. The ground was cool under my bare feet and suddenly, for the first time since we had crossed the border, I felt like I was back. After all these years, I was home again, standing on the soil of my ancestors. This was the soil on which my great-grandfather had married his third wife a year before dying in the cholera epidemic that hit Kabul in 1915. She'd borne him what his first two wives had failed to, a son at last. It was on this soil that my grandfather had gone on a hunting trip with King Nadir Shah and shot a deer. My mother had died on this soil. And on this soil, I had fought for my father's love.

Khaled Hosseini, *The Kite Runner*

Online Learning Center

Hosseini is a master storyteller. If you are not acquainted with his books, go to www.amazon.com and read reviews of *The Kite Runner* and of his most recent book, also set in Afghanistan, *A Thousand Splendid Suns*.

Explain what Amir is feeling as he surveys the landscape of his native Afghanistan and ponders his family.

_____

_____

_____

_____

B.   In this passage from one of America's finest fiction writers, Wallace Stegner, the narrator focuses on Bruce Mason, one son of the main characters, who is driving home to Wyoming after finishing his first year studying law in Minnesota.

When Bruce drove west in June, after the frenzy of examinations and the rush to clear out his room, settle his bills, pack the Ford, have a last round of beers with the Law Commons boys, he drove directly from rainy spring into deep summer, from prison into freedom. That day was the first bright warm day in two weeks, and the year was over, he was loose. He watched the sun drink steam from the cornfields, heard the meadowlarks along the fences, the blackbirds in the spring sloughs. Even the smell of hot oil from the motor could not entirely blot out the lush smell of growth.

It was the end of his first year away from home, and he was going back. Ahead of him was the long road, the continental sprawling hugeness of America, the fields and farmhouses, the towns. Northfield, Faribault, Owatonna, Albert Lea, and then west on Highway 16—Blue Earth, Jackson, Luverne, and the junction of Big Sioux and Missouri. Then Sioux City, Yankton, Bridgewater, Mitchell, Chamberlain, Rapid City, the Badlands and the Black Hills breaking the monotonous loveliness of the Dakota plain. Then the ranges and the echoing names: Spearfish, Deadwood, Sundance, the Wyoming that was Ucross and Sheridan and Buffalo and Greybull and Cody, the Yellowstone of dudes and sagebrushers, the Idaho that was the Mormon towns along the Snake: St. Anthony, Rexburg, Sugar City, Blackfoot, Pocatello, and the Utah of Cache Valley and Sardine Canyon and the barricade of the Wasatch guarding the dead salt flats and the lake.

The names flowed in his head like a song, like the words of an old man telling a story, and his mind looked ahead over the long road, the great rivers and the interminable plains, over the Black Hills and the lovely loom of the Big Horns and the Absaroka Range white against the west from Cody.

It was a grand country, a country to lift the blood, and he was going home across its wind-kissed miles with the sun on him and the cornfields steaming under the first summer heat and the first bugs immolating themselves against his windshield.

But going home where? he said. Where do I belong in this? . . .

Wallace Stegner, *The Big Rock Candy Mountain*

1. What is the predominant mood of the passage? How does Bruce react to the "sprawling hugeness of America" that he muses about as he drives? Why does Stegner list so many place names? _____

_____

2. Consider again the last paragraph and explain the tone the narrator conveys. _____

C. This excerpt is from a novel by Irish writer William Trevor. The title character, Felicia, is a young Irish girl who has become pregnant by a man she barely knows after a one-night stand. She makes her way to England to search for him. Day after day, she wanders the streets of the town where she thinks he might work. In this passage, the narrator describes the various types of homeless who inhabit a particular part of town.

She wanders on eventually, resting sometimes on a pavement seat, moving again when it becomes too cold. At a stall beneath a bridge where taxi drivers stand about she buys a sausage roll that is reduced to fourpence because it's stale. The air is dank with mist.

Already, hours ago, the homeless of this town have found their night-time resting places—in doorways, and underground passages left open in error, in abandoned vehicles, in the derelict gardens of demolished houses. As maggots make their way into cracks in masonry, so the people of the streets have crept into one-night homes in graveyards and on building sites, in alleyways and court-yards, making walls of dustbins pulled close together, and roofs of whatever lies near by. Some have crawled up scaffolding to find a corner beneath the tarpaulin that protects an untiled expanse. Others have settled down in cardboard cartons that once contained dishwashers or refrigerators.

Hidden away, the people of the streets drift into sleep induced by alcohol or agitated by despair, into dreams that carry them back to the lives that once were theirs. They lie with their begging notices still beside them, with enough left of a bottle to ease the waking moment, with pavement cigarette butts to hand. *Homeless and hungry* is their pasteboard plea, scrawled without thought, one copying another: only money matters. All ages lie out in the places that have been found, men and women, children. The family rejects have ceased to weep into their make-do pillows; those brought low by their foolishness or by untimely greed plead silently for sleep. A one-time clergyman no longer dwells on his disgrace, but dreams instead that it never happened. Rejected husbands, abandoned wives, victims of chance, have passed beyond bitterness, and devote their energies to keeping warm. The deranged are lulled by voices that often in the night persuade them to rise and walk on, which obediently they do, knowing they must. Men who have failed lie on their own and dream of a reality they dare not contemplate by day: great hotels and deferential waiters, the power they once possessed, the limbs of secretaries. Women who were beautiful in their day are beautiful again. There is no arrogance among the people of the streets, no insistent pride in their sleeping features, no lingering telltale of a past's corruption. They have passed the stage of desperation, and on their downward path some among the women have sold themselves: faces chapped, fingernails ingrained, they are beyond that now. Men, in threes and fours, have offered the three-card trick on these same streets. Beards unkempt, hair matted, skin darkened with filth, they would not now attract the wagers of their passing trade. In their dreams there is occasionally the fantasy that they may be cured, that they may be loved, that all voices and visions will cease, that tomorrow they will discover the strength to resist oblivion. Others remain homeless by choice and for their own particular reasons would not return to a more settled life. The streets, they feel, are where they now belong.

William Trevor, *Felicia's Journey*

1. What is the dominant mood of the passage? _____

2. What is the narrator's apparent point of view with regard to the homeless?

_____

3. How do the dreams of the homeless contrast with the realities of daylight?

_____

Tone and Mood in Poetry

A thorough discussion of how to analyze and to appreciate poetry is outside the scope of this book. Still, your ability to identify figures of speech, connotative language, and emotional tone can be put into practice with poetry just as easily as it can with fiction or nonfiction prose. Consider this poem by Irish poet Seamus Heaney in which he describes the annual summertime ritual of blackberry picking. At least that's the subject of the first half of the poem; the second part, however, beginning with line 18, shifts mood and tone. Read the poem carefully—perhaps two or three times—and see if you can identify the contrasting tonal elements. Poetic language is compressed, carefully chosen, and evocative, as Heaney demonstrates well in this poem.

Late August, given heavy rain and sun
For a full week, the blackberries would ripen.

At first, just one, a glossy purple clot
Among others, red, green, hard as a knot.
5 You ate that first one and its flesh was sweet
Like thickened wine: summer's blood was in it
Leaving stains upon the tongue and lust for
Picking. Then red ones inked up and that hunger
Sent us out with milk cans, pea tins, jam-pots
10 Where briars scratched and wet grass bleached our boots.
Round hayfields, cornfields and potato-drills
We trekked and picked until the cans were full
Until the tinkling bottom had been covered
With green ones, and on top big dark blobs burned
15 Like a plate of eyes. Our hands were peppered
With thorn pricks, our palms sticky as Bluebeard's.
We hoarded the fresh berries in the byre.
But when the bath was filled we found a fur,
A rat-grey fungus, glutting on our cache.
20 The juice was stinking too. Once off the bush
The fruit fermented, the sweet flesh would turn sour.
I always felt like crying. It wasn't fair
That all the lovely canfuls smelt of rot.
Each year I hoped they'd keep, knew they would not.

Seamus Heaney, "Blackberry-Picking"

The first half of the poem celebrates the childhood pleasures of picking blackberries. Heaney compresses the experience in a series of well-chosen, highly connotative details: "a glossy purple clot," "red, green, hard as a knot," "thickened wine," "summer's blood." These phrases suggest the sensual, nearly intoxicating pleasure of picking both the unripe green berries as well as the ripe ones. The tone is one of eagerness and exhilaration—the coming again of a treasured childhood ritual. But in line 18 the tone changes. Anyone who has ever picked blackberries knows that they are highly perishable. Left for a day or so, they begin to rot. Heaney compresses the details of this eventuality with these phrases: "rat-grey fungus," "the juice was stinking," "the fruit fermented," and "smelt of rot." But Heaney isn't just talking about spoiled blackberries. The meaning of the poem is deeper than that: It suggests disappointment and loss, the first inkling that childhood pleasures don't last. It's a lovely poem, filled with the twin emotions of pleasure and heartache.

**Practice
Exercise 5**

Here is another poem for you to analyze. This one is by Mark Doty, winner of the 2008 National Book Award for poetry. A little over an hour south of San Francisco, Pescadero is a small rural town on the San Mateo County coast, and home to Harley Farms, whose owner makes goat cheese, the likely setting for this poem. Raised to be around humans, these goats are friendly and inquisitive little creatures. Goats also have an unusual way of apprehending the world around them: they use their upper lip to explore things, and you can get a sense of that characteristic in this poem.

> The little goats like my mouth and fingers,
> and one stands up against the wire fence, and taps on the fence board
> a hoof made blacker by the dirt of the field,
> pushes her mouth forward to my mouth,
> so that I can see the smallish squared seeds of her teeth,
> and the bristle-whiskers,
> and then she kisses me, though I know it doesn't mean "kiss,"
> then leans her head way back, arcing her spine, goat yoga,
> all pleasure and greeting and then good-natured indifference: she loves me,
> she likes me a lot, she takes interest in me, she doesn't know me at all
> or need to, having thus acknowledged me. Though I am all happiness,
> since I have been welcomed by the field's small envoy, and the splayed hoof,
> fragrant with soil, has rested on the fence board beside my hand.

Mark Doty, "Pescadero," *The New Yorker*

How would you describe the tone and mood Doty achieves in this poem?

_____

■ TONE CONTINUED: MORE DIFFICULT VARIETIES

In this section of the chapter you will be introduced to a group of more complex, sophisticated, and challenging tones. These are often, though not exclusively, associated with persuasive prose.

- wit
- irony
- sarcasm
- cynicism
- satire, ridicule, mockery

Do not worry if you find it hard to recognize and to distinguish among these more difficult varieties of tone. Many students are bewildered when they encounter this section of the book, because either they are unfamiliar with the vocabulary or because they are accustomed to thinking that print material is most always (or should be) serious and informative. Quite the contrary, as you will see! Study all of the examples carefully, and if you are uncertain, ask your instructor to explain in further detail.

Wit is amusing and playful; the others are more difficult to sort out and warrant detailed study. In the following section, we will examine and illustrate them one by one.

Wit

A **witty** tone reveals the writer's mental keenness and sense of playfulness and an ability to recognize the comic elements of a situation or condition. Unlike sarcasm, with its obvious mean streak, wit relies on a humorous, brief, and clever use of words and a pointed perception in describing human frailty and folly. Notice that some of these witticisms demonstrate a clever turn of phrase or a play on words. Here is a compendium of witty sayings by American writer and humorist Mark Twain (1835–1910):

- Get your facts first and then you can distort them as much as you wish.
- Don't go around saying the world owes you a living. The world owes you nothing. It was here first.
- Sometimes I wonder whether the world is run by smart people who are putting us on or by imbeciles who really mean it.
- I didn't attend the funeral, but I sent a nice letter saying I approved of it.
- In the first place, God made idiots. That was for practice. Then he made school boards.
- Man is the only animal that blushes—or needs to.

Here are more examples from other wits (A wit is a person who is known for clever, pithy, often humorous remarks.):

- American writer William Faulkner writing about fellow American writer Ernest Hemingway: "He has never been known to use a word that might send a reader to the dictionary."[1]
- Comedian Groucho Marx: "I've had a perfectly wonderful evening. But this wasn't it."
- Irish playwright Oscar Wilde: "Some cause happiness wherever they go; others whenever they go."

[1]One of Ernest Hemingway's best known short stories, "Hills Like White Elephants," appears in Part 6.

- Socrates: "By all means, marry. If you get a good wife, you'll become happy; if you get a bad one, you'll become a philosopher."
- Mae West, a famous American actress of the 1930s and 1940s, a "blonde bombshell" type known for her risqué remarks: "I was as pure as the driven snow—but I drifted."
- Movie director and actor Woody Allen: "It's not that I'm afraid to die—I just don't want to be there when it happens."
- Winston Churchill, describing Clement Attlee, who defeated him for Prime Minister of England in 1945: "A modest little person, with much to be modest about."
- Note that witticisms often involve a clever turn of phrase, as you can see in this observation by comedian Henny Youngman: What's the use of happiness? It can't buy you money."
- Ambrose Bierce, nineteenth-century American writer: "War is God's way of teaching Americans about geography."

Online Learning Center

A compendium of witticisms—widely circulated on the Internet—appears on the website accompanying the book. See www.mhhe.com/spears and scroll down to the material for Chapter 7.

Irony

Before we look at irony in reading material, let's first consider some examples of irony in the real world: Foreign visitors to the U.S. often marvel that a lot of Americans store junk in their garages but leave their cars in the driveway. Why is this practice ironic? Because *it's the opposite of what one would expect.* A garage is for storing cars, not junk. It's ironic to leave something worth a lot of money in the driveway and to store stuff that's most likely not worth as much in the garage.

Critical Thinking Exercise

Why do so many Americans do this? What characteristics does this common practice suggest about American culture?

A second example: In October 2010 President Obama received the Nobel Peace Prize. Under ordinary circumstances, this would be a cause for great joy and recognition. But critics pointed out the irony: Just nine days earlier Obama had announced that he was sending 30,000 more troops to fight the war in Afghanistan.

A final example of irony in the real world: There has been a great deal of controversy over fees paid to public speakers. Former senator and presidential candidate John Edwards was widely criticized for collecting $55,000 for giving a 2007 lecture at University of California, Davis. The topic? Ironically, the growing gap between rich and poor in the United States. Michael Moore, a firebrand outspoken liberal writer who often rails against the excesses of American capitalism and American corporations, was disinvited from giving a speech at George Mason University in 2004 after it was revealed that he would be paid $35,000. One might point to the hypocrisy in these two speakers' enormous fees, but irony is also strongly evident.

Irony serves many masters. An ironic tone occurs when a writer deliberately says the opposite of what he or she really means or points to the opposite of what one would typically expect to occur. This unexpected contrast results in a curious heightening of intensity about the real subject. Irony can be used to poke fun at human weaknesses and inconsistencies or, more seriously, to criticize, to encourage reform, or to cast doubt on someone's motives. The alert reader will see through the pretense and recognize that the words mean something different from their literal meaning.

Let's begin with some simple examples.

Irony is at the heart of many jokes. In this example, Page Smith uses irony to illustrate memory failure in older people. An old man and his wife are sitting on their front porch:

> Wife: "I certainly would appreciate a vanilla ice cream cone."
>
> Husband: "I'll hobble right down to the drugstore and get you one, dear."
>
> Wife: "Now, remember, I want vanilla. You always get chocolate. Write it down. Vanilla."
>
> Husband: "I can certainly remember vanilla. The store is only two blocks away."
>
> Husband comes back with a hamburger and hands it to his wife. She looks at it disgustedly. "I knew you'd forget the mustard," she says.
>
> Page Smith, "Coming of Age: Jokes about Old Age," *San Francisco Chronicle*

Although the Airport Hilton was long ago demolished when San Francisco International Airport expanded, this excerpt from a newspaper article is such a good example of irony that it's worth reprinting.

> It finally happened. The waiting is over. It's here now.
>
> The new off-ramp has opened at San Francisco International Airport.
>
> For years we drove into the airport from the Bayshore Freeway on the old off-ramp. The old off-ramp was a concrete cloverleaf that arched over the freeway and deposited the motorist just past the Airport Hilton Hotel.
>
> Ah, but the new off-ramp! The new off-ramp is a concrete cloverleaf that arches over the freeway and deposits the motorist just past the Airport Hilton Hotel.
>
> Steve Rubenstein, *San Francisco Chronicle*

Rubenstein uses irony to good advantage here. The short sentences at the beginning create an atmosphere of expectation and suspense. Further, he uses the same words to describe both the new and the old off-ramp. We would expect something as costly as a new off-ramp to be more efficient, more convenient, somehow different from the one it replaced. Rubenstein's use of irony allows him to leave his main point unstated: This project was a huge waste of taxpayer money. The irony leads the reader to recognize the ridiculousness of the situation.

Irony often is present in cartoons, as well. Study this *New Yorker* cartoon drawn by Harry Bliss. Then see if you can identify the irony underlying the situation depicted.

© Harry Bliss/The New Yorker Collection/
www.cartoonbank.com

Explain the irony. _____

_____

_____

Let us examine two examples of literary irony. The first is a fable by British writer W. Somerset Maugham. Its title is "Death Speaks."

Death speaks:

[1]There was a merchant in Bagdad who sent his servant to market to buy provisions and in a little while the servant came back, white and trembling, and said, Master, just now when I was in the market-place I was jostled by a woman in the crowd and when I turned I saw it was Death that jostled me. [2]She looked at me and made a threatening gesture; now, lend me your horse and I will ride away from this city and avoid my fate. [3]I will go to Samarra and there Death will not find me. [4]The merchant lent him his horse, and the servant mounted it, and he dug his spurs in its flanks and as fast as the horse could gallop he went. [5]Then the merchant went down to the market-place and he saw me standing in the crowd and he came to me and said, Why did you make a threatening gesture to my servant when you saw him this morning? [6]That was not a threatening gesture, I said, it was only a start of surprise. [7]I was astonished to see him in Bagdad, for I had an appointment with him tonight in Samarra.

W. Somerset Maugham, "Death Speaks," *Sheppey*

Online Learning Center   An inference exercise on Maugham's fable is available at www.mhhe.com/spears. See the material for Chapter 7. The exercise represents a good review of the inference-making process.

Explain the irony in the fable. ____

_____

_____

The second example is an excerpt from an article called "How to Write about Africa." The writer is Binyavanga Wainaina, a founding editor of the Kenyan literary magazine *Kwani?* Keep the title in mind as you read the passage.

Always use the word 'Africa' or 'Darkness' or 'Safari' in your title. Subtitles may include the words 'Zanzibar', 'Masai', 'Zulu', 'Zambezi', 'Congo', 'Nile', 'Big', 'Sky', 'Shadow', 'Drum', 'Sun', or 'Bygone'. Also useful are words such as 'Guerrillas', 'Timeless', 'Primordial', and 'Tribal'. Note that 'People' means Africans who are not black, while 'The People' means Africans.

Never have a picture of a well-adjusted African on the cover of your book, or in it, unless that African has won the Nobel Prize. An AK-47, prominent ribs, naked breasts: use these. If you must include an African, make sure you get one in Masai or Zulu or Dogon dress.

In your text, treat Africa as if it were one country. It is hot and dusty with rolling grasslands and huge herds of animals and tall, thin people who are starving. Or it is hot and steamy with very short people who eat primates. Don't get bogged down with precise descriptions. Africa is big: fifty-four countries, 900 million people who are too busy starving and dying and warring and emigrating to read your book. The continent is full of deserts, jungles, highlands, savannahs and many other things, but your reader doesn't care about all that, so keep your descriptions romantic and evocative and unparticular.

Make sure you show how Africans have music and rhythm deep in their souls, and eat things no other humans eat. Do not mention rice and beef and wheat; monkey-brain is an African's cuisine of choice, along with goat, snake, worms and grubs and all manner of game meat. Make sure you show that you are able to eat such food without flinching, and describe how you learn to enjoy it—because you care.

Taboo subjects: ordinary domestic scenes, love between Africans (unless a death is involved), references to African writers or intellectuals, mention of school-going children who are not suffering from yaws or Ebola fever or female genital mutilation.

Binyavanga Wainaina, "How to Write about Africa," *Granta 92, The View from Africa*

Critical Thinking Exercise

Binyavanga Wainaina presents a strong criticism of the way the media covers Africa. To what extent is his criticism fair? For the next few weeks, as you come across articles in the newspaper or in magazines, on television news or in online material, evaluate the coverage. To what extent, if any, does it bear out Wainaina's criticism, or does it seem unfair and unduly exaggerated?

Explain why this passage is an example of irony. How would you describe his tone concerning the way most writers treat the subject of Africa? _____

_____

Online Learning Center

Wikipedia, the online collaborative information website, offers a comprehensive discussion of irony and its various types (situational irony, verbal irony, cosmic irony, and so forth) with lots of examples. The address is http://en.wikipedia.org/wiki/Irony

_____

_____

_____

_____

A Note on Hyperbole

Before continuing, let us pause to look at a common element in writing whose tone is sarcastic, cynical, or satirical—hyperbole. Pronounced hī-pûr'-bə-lē, **hyperbole** is a figure of speech that uses deliberate exaggeration for effect. Here are two examples. In his memoir about growing up in Des Moines, Iowa, American writer and humorist Bill Bryson here describes the grandmother of his childhood friend, Jed:

> She was more than a thousand years old and weighed thirty-seven pounds, which included sixteen pounds of makeup. (*The Life and Times of the Thunderbolt Kid*)

The second example requires some background explanation: Bicyclist Lance Armstrong won the grueling Tour de France seven times in a row. After winning the race in 2005, he announced his retirement from racing, but he returned in 2009, this time finishing third. Writing in *The Wall Street Journal,* sportswriter Jason Gay said this about Armstrong:

> Moving over to Monaco, where tennis stars like to stash their moola: the Tour de France began Saturday, with a twisty time trial in the gilded streets of the famed tax haven and steroidal yacht capital.
>
> This year's Tour marks the return of Lance Armstrong, who began racing bikes in the late 17th century and is once again atop his carbon fiber steed after a failed attempt at retirement. ("Trials and Other Drama from the Tour de France," *The Wall Street Journal,* July 6, 2009)

Write the phrase from the excerpt that represents hyperbole. _____

_____

Sarcasm

Sarcasm derives from the Latin words for "flesh-cutting," and this etymology will help you remember its purpose. Sarcasm is a form of wit that taunts or ridicules the subject. Although we sometimes find it hard to discern the line between irony and sarcasm, I think the best way to separate the two is to consider the writer's intent. Sarcasm may involve irony, but it also is intended to sneer at and to mock the target. If a passage suggests a personal, heavy-handed insult, the tone is more likely sarcastic than ironic. Here are three examples of sarcasm.

- From a theater review by critic Terry Teachout: "The problem with Frank Wildhorn musicals is that they contain Frank Wildhorn songs." (Terry Teachout, "Turner, in Her Usual Role," *The Wall Street Journal,* April 20, 2011.)
- This excerpt is from a review of the 2011 movie, "The Green Hornet": "'The Green Hornet' was directed by Michel Gondry, and stars Seth Rogen, who also concocted the screenplay, with his writing partner, Evan Goldberg. Rogen says that he has been obsessed with comic books and superheroes for years. Well, I'm sorry to put it this way, but 'The Green Hornet' is what you get when someone who dropped out of high school to do standup comedy, then spent a decade in movies and television, conceives a Hollywood 'passion project.' Seth Rogen is talented and likable, but he's blinkered by pop culture. . . ." (David Denby, "Man Up," *The New Yorker*)

> **Critical Thinking Exercise**
>
> It wasn't just *The New Yorker* that panned "The Green Hornet." The movie received nearly universal negative reviews. (For example, the "Tomatometer" at www.rottentomatoes.com gave it only a 45 percent rating.) Yet in the first two weeks or so after its release, it was number one nationally at the box office. How do you account for this discrepancy?

- It was the habit of Winston Churchill, prime minister of England during World War II, to drink a quart of brandy every day. One evening a woman at a dinner party told Churchill that he was drunk. Churchill replied: "And you, madam, are ugly. But tomorrow I shall be sober."

Remember, too, that even experienced readers sometimes have difficulty distinguishing between irony and sarcasm; further, a passage might even blend the two together. The first example comes from a television critic, Tim Goodman, who is writing about network and cable coverage of the devastating earthquake and tsunami that hit northern Japan in March 2011. Goodman begins by accusing two media groups: the reporters and television anchors for "bungling the basics" and producers and executives in charge of reporters and anchors for having "fallen woefully short of leadership." Then Goodman writes this:

> How is it possible that on Monday evening (Tuesday in Japan), with the earthquake, tsunami and worries about radiation poisoning engulfing Japan, a CNN reporter can ask this question: "How scary has this been for you?"
>
> Let's see, my daughter was ripped from my arms in the tsunami, I almost died, I lost my home, my belongings, family, friends. There are constant aftershocks, new tsunami warnings and apparently we're about to have a nuclear meltdown. I don't know, dumbass, how scary does that sound to you?
>
> Tim Goodman, "Analysis: TV Cable Coverage of Japan Crisis Is Lacking,"
> www.hollywoodreporter.com. March 15, 2011.

Does Goodman's diatribe involve irony or sarcasm, or a combination of both? Explain. _____

_____

Cynicism

My generation, which came of age during the Watergate scandal and the Vietnam War, often identifies those two pivotal eras as the source of the **cynicism** that infects modern attitudes. But the younger generation has its own reasons to be cynical—with the recent corporate accounting scandals, a Congress that is often dysfunctional, and two unpopular wars—just to cite some examples. The *Random House College Dictionary* definitions of *cynical* are helpful:

- Distrusting or disparaging the motives or sincerity of others
- Sneeringly distrustful, contemptuous, or pessimistic

A cynic detects falseness in others and recognizes impure motives. Politicians are sometimes described as cynical because they underestimate the intelligence of the voting public. The cynical tone is sneering, just as sarcasm is, but it is on a deeper level and comes from a different motive: Cynicism suggests a questioning and distrusting of people's stated motives or virtues. It may or may not involve irony. Here are three examples, all of which have in common the twin elements of distrust and exposing foolishness:

- Voltaire, the eighteenth-century writer and philosopher said, "The first clergyman was the first rascal who met the first fool."
- L. Ron Hubbard, founder of the religion Scientology: "The best way to get rich in this country is to start a religion."

This example from Anthony Lane's *New Yorker* review of the 2006 movie *Pirates of the Caribbean: Dead Man's Chest,* starring Johnny Depp, mixes irony, sarcasm, and cynicism:

- This is the second part of a trilogy, Disney having decided that there were dense thematic issues, not to mention narrative niceties, that could not be constrained within a single *Pirates* film; any financial consideration is, of course, entirely secondary.

Satire

Satire refers to a type of writing (and to other artistic forms of expression, as well) that seeks to expose folly or wickedness, to hold human behavior up to ridicule, and to show the reader that certain actions or behavior would be more desirable. Satire typically relies on exaggeration and imitation of real literary forms. If you are a fan of "South Park," "The Daily Show," or "The Colbert Report" on Comedy Central, you are already familiar with the genre. Muriel Spark, twentieth-century British novelist was once quoted as saying: "Satire is far more important, it has a more lasting effect, than a straight portrayal of what is wrong. I think that a lot of the world's problems should be ridiculed, but ridiculed properly rather than, well, wailed over." (Quoted in Hal Hager, "About Muriel Spark," *The Prime of Miss Jean Brodie*)

Besides the above-mentioned television programs, The Onion, an online humor and satire site (www.theonion.com), is a good source of contemporary satire. Here, for example, is a recent article from the website that satirizes the state of affairs in the U.S. Congress. It was published in 2011, but given Congress's general ineffectiveness in the last ten years or so, it could have been published at any time:

WASHINGTON—Exhausted but satisfied leaders from both parties came together Tuesday night to announce that Congress had successfully completed

12 solid hours of nonstop gridlocking, once again going above and beyond to needlessly prevent the nation from moving forward.

In a marathon session that lawmakers proudly called "one of [their] least productive ever," each of the 535 members of the House and Senate gridlocked deep into the night to ensure that no bipartisan compromise could be reached, no laws intended to aid the American people could be passed, and no sense of national unity or progress could possibly be achieved.

"There is nothing more satisfying than knowing you've just put in a full day of bringing our nation's legislative branch to a complete standstill," said House Speaker John Boehner, who like the vast majority of his colleagues worked without break throughout the day and night fostering political disharmony and rejecting the passage of crucial legislation. "We got a lot of good, quality gridlocking done today. We gridlocked efficiently, we gridlocked passionately, and we gridlocked as best we could for the American people. Now we go home, rest up, and get ready for another full day of gridlocking tomorrow."

"It's a great feeling," Boehner added. "Today, everyone realized what it is we're here to do, and that's put a wrench right into the machinery of democracy."

According to Capitol sources, the impassioned gridlocking session was one of the most demanding in recent memory, requiring each and every member of Congress to work in total cooperation to frustrate one another's political agendas, and even requiring a number of dedicated lawmakers to stall as many as seven different bills at once.

Legislative leaders said they were enormously pleased with the sustained intensity of gridlocking Tuesday, especially considering the fact that, as early as last week, a number of laws under consideration were thought to have stood a decent chance of being passed.

"I wasn't sure at first if I would have the stamina to not advance a single item on my docket, but my constituents expect me to get in there, roll up my sleeves, and grind things to a halt, so that's exactly what I did," said Sen. Joe Manchin (D-WV), who claimed to have gridlocked straight through his lunch hour, despite protestations from concerned aides. "I think a lot of people out there may not realize just how much gridlocking we do here in Congress. They think we just sit around passing bills and turning the wheels of progress all day. Well, let me tell you, nothing could be further from the truth. We got some great gridlockers here, in both parties, many of whom have been thwarting our democracy for decades."

"This place is like a perfectly un-oiled machine," Manchin added. "We don't rest until absolutely nothing has been accomplished."

According to Boehner, Thursday's "spectacular display of inaction" was nearly derailed when Sens. John McCain (R-AZ) and Bill Nelson (D-FL) briefly attempted to pass crucial and long-delayed campaign finance reform, but key committee members acted quickly to weigh the bill down with needless riders before shuttling it off toward a certain death on the floor.

At another point, congressional sources reported, the rate of gridlocking was so intense that the passage of a resolution honoring Southern Sudan's recent independence as well as a bill mandating improved FAA safety regulations were blocked simultaneously in an astonishing 51-second period of time.

While pleased with their failure to do anything even close to what they were elected to do, the men and women of the United States Congress announced after Tuesday's session that it wasn't praise or recognition they sought, but merely the knowledge that they had done everything in their power to confirm every American's worst suspicions about the country's legislative system.

"My reward is the feeling I get when I arrive home at the end of the day, look my family in the eyes, and say, 'We didn't do it,'" a smiling Sen. Lindsey Graham (R-SC) said. "That's what really matters to me. Obviously we're not always going to agree on everything in Congress. But something that every single one of us, to a person, can agree on is that when there is important gridlocking to be done, then it's time to set aside the hopes and dreams of the American people and focus on what really matters: our own blind self-interest."

In response to the 112th Congress's solid showing of utter nothingness, President Obama issued a brief statement in recognition of the day's gridlocking.

"Congress truly lived up to its reputation today," read the president's statement. "This is exactly the kind of performance we have come to expect from our leaders in the House and Senate, and I for one am confident that we'll be seeing much, much more of it in the future."

Look again at the description of the characteristics of satire at the beginning of this section and then explain in your words how this spoof is an example of this literary genre. _____

_____

_____

Practice Exercise 6

Read the following passages. Then, keeping in mind the writer's purpose and intent, decide which of the following tones is most accurately reflected in each excerpt: witty, ironic, sarcastic, cynical, satirical. If hyperbole is present, indicate that as well.

A. Gloria Steinem, American feminist: "A woman without a man is like a fish without a bicycle."

The tone of this statement is _____. Explain. _____

_____

B.   Ilka Chase was a famous actress in the movies and on stage in the 1930s and 1940s. When she published her 1942 autobiography, *Past Imperfect,* she encountered an actor at a party. (Legend has it that the actor was Humphrey Bogart.) When the actor congratulated Chase, he said, "I thought your book was wonderful. I can't tell you how much I enjoyed it. By the way, who wrote it for you?" Chase responded, "I'm so glad you like it. By the way, who read it to you?"

The tone of this selection is _____. Explain the reason for

your answer. _____

C.   From a review of *Bolt of Fate* by Tom Tucker, a biography of Benjamin Franklin: ". . . a new book argues that the legend on which Franklin's reputation rests is dubious. There was no kite, no key, no bolt, no knuckle, no charge. He let people believe he had been places he never went, done things he never did, and seen things that never happened. No wonder he's been called the father of American journalism." (Adam Gopnik, "American Electric: Did Franklin Fly the Kite?" *The New Yorker*)

The tone of this excerpt is _____.

Explain your answer. _____

D.   Buster Posey, catcher for the San Francisco Giants, won the Rookie of the Year award for 2010, the year in which his team won the World Series. Scott Ostler, a San Francisco sportswriter, writing about Posey, begins like this: "Count your blessings." Then follows a list of things sports fans should be thankful for, including this item: "Most exciting young player. Buster Posey. Buster Ballgame's not perfect, though. As a kid he would sneak out behind the barn to chew gum."

The tone of this item is _____.

Explain why you chose your answer. _____

_____

E.   "The Kim Basinger movie *I Dreamed of Africa* bombed at the box-office last weekend. It wasn't supposed to be that way. It was originally expected to bomb way back in September." (Tom King, "Waiting for Their Closeups," *The Wall Street Journal,* May 12, 2000)

The tone of this selection is _____. Why did you choose

this answer? _____

F.   In 2011 Jack LaLanne died at the age of 97. LaLanne was probably the original fitness guru—he wrote books, sold nutritional products, and championed fitness way before it became a national activity. Here is one excerpt from his obituary, provided by LaLanne's nephew, Thomas, about his uncle's death: "It's kind of a shock. I didn't think

Jack was ever going to die. He would tell people, 'I can't die. It'll ruin my image.'"

The tone in this excerpt is _____.

Why did you choose your answer?_____

_____

G. This excerpt is by a British physician, Theodore Dalrymple, a pseudonym of Anthony Daniels. It is from a recent article on obesity.

The connection between the fragmentation of the family and obesity is easy to understand. Of course, there is no one-to-one correspondence between the two phenomena—in human affairs there never is such a close fit—but there is nevertheless a strong and comprehensible correspondence.

For much of the population, family meals are a ritual of the past: Thirty-six percent of British children never eat a meal at a table with another member of their family or household (we have now passed the milestone long desired by radical social reformers, more children being born illegitimate than legitimate). In the homes of the poor, the unemployed and the single parents that I used to visit as a doctor, I would find no evidence of cooking ever having been done there. Fatty take-away meals and ready-prepared foods heated in the microwave were the diet, together with almost constant snacks. There was not even a table to eat at: an absence that was not the consequence of raw poverty, since the flat-screen television would have been large enough, turned horizontal, to serve as a dining table.

Theodore Dalrymple, "Our Big Problem," *The Wall Street Journal,* May 1–2, 2010.

The tone of the passage is _____.

Explain your thinking. _____

H. This excerpt is by travel and fiction writer Paul Theroux from his book about returning to Africa after an absence of many years. (Theroux had served in the Peace Corps during the 1960s).

Traveling south of Egypt, I would be entering Sudan. I did not have a Sudanese visa, and for Americans such visas were hard to come by. The reason was understandable. On the pretext that Sudan was making anti-American bombs (and, some people felt, in order to correct the negative image created by his involvement in a sex scandal, to look decisive and presidential even if it meant risking lives and flattening foreign real estate), President Clinton ordered air strikes against Sudan. He succeeded in destroying a pharmaceutical plant outside Khartoum in August 1998. This bomb crater would be on my itinerary, for after the bombs were dropped no one in the United States took much interest.

Though we become hysterical at the thought that someone might bomb us, bombs that we explode elsewhere, in little countries far away, are just theater, of small consequence, another public performance of our White House, the event factory.

Paul Theroux, *Dark Star Safari*

Theroux's tone in this passage is _____.

Explain the reason for your answer. _____.

I.   This cartoon is by Roz Chast and was published in *The New Yorker*.

© Roz Chast/The New Yorker Collection/www.cartoonbank.com

The tone of the cartoon is _____.

Explain the thinking behind your answer. _____

_____

■ ALLUSION

An allusion is a pointed and meaningful reference to something outside the text that helps illuminate the subject. The allusion may be from any field, but these are the most common:

- The Bible or other religious texts
- History
- Literature
- Greek, Roman, or other mythology
- Popular culture, including movies, songs, works of art, fashion, the media, and so forth

Indeed, although allusions can come from any discipline, generally they come from works or events that educated readers would be familiar with. The reader who does not grasp the connection between the allusion and the subject misses out not only on the literal meaning but on the deeper connotative meaning as well. The ability to recognize allusions takes years to develop, but it is attainable through wide reading and exposure to our cultural traditions. In the meantime, ask your instructor to explain unfamiliar allusions or use reference books or websites. A good unabridged dictionary or websites like www.ask.com and www.wikipedia.com will most likely offer explanations of allusions you encounter in your reading.

Let's begin with this passage by mystery writer James Lee Burke. The lead character is Dave Robicheaux, homicide detective in New Iberia, Louisiana. Here he describes a local Alcoholics Anonymous (AA) meeting that he is attending:

> I attended the Friday noon meeting of an AA bunch known as the Insanity Group. The meeting was held in a dilapidated house in a poor section of town, and was supposedly a nonsmoking one. But people lit up in both the front and back doorways and flooded the house's interior with amounts of smoke that few bars contain. The people in the Insanity Group had paid hard dues—in jails, detox units, car wrecks, and the kind of beer-glass brawls that quickly turn homicidal. Few of the men shaved more than once every five or six days. Many of the women, most of whom were tattooed, considered themselves fortunate to have a job in a car wash. Anybody there whose life didn't trail clouds of chaos possessed the spiritual eminence of St. Francis of Assisi.
>
> James Lee Burke, *Crusader's Cross*

The allusion to St. Francis of Assisi in the last sentence refers to the thirteenth-century founder of the Franciscan order of monks and, for

Catholics, the patron saint of nature and ecology. St. Francis was revered for his life of simplicity and poverty (he is often depicted with birds sitting on his head and shoulders). The allusion means that these AA members led chaotic lives. If their lives weren't chaotic, they would be as saintly as St. Francis was. Here are some further questions pertaining to this passage:

First, identify the metaphor in the passage and explain its meaning.

_____

_____

Now identify the mood of the passage. _____

_____

Practice Exercise 7

Identify the allusion in these short selections. Then explain its meaning.

A. The narrator is a student working in the library at Indiana University in Bloomington:

So I was feeling blue, the weather going from bad to worse . . . and the books in the library cart growing progressively heavier (I felt like a bibliographic Sisyphus, the task unending, each shelved volume replaced by another, and yet another).

T. C. Boyle, *The Inner Circle*

_____

_____

_____

B. This excerpt, from a newspaper article by environmental writer Glen Martin, describes the Sacramento River in California's Glenn County.

The water is green and swift, and cottonwoods and willows crowd the shore. The sky is a piercing blue, and the air crisp as a winesap apple. Alarmed beavers slap their tails at the approach of the boat, and wood ducks and great blue herons rise from backside eddies.

It's easy to imagine you're in another time, when the trees were a lush, almost impenetrable forest that extended for miles beyond this river's banks.

But this is not the Sacramento River of 1870. Magnificent as they are, the trees are merely a thin buffer strip, a kind of Potemkin village, obscuring the huge agricultural complex that lies beyond. Just past the levees are thousands of acres of orchards and rice fields.

Glen Martin, "Wetlands, Birds and Salmon Returning to the Sacramento," *San Francisco Chronicle*

_____

_____

C.

Interstate driving is akin to driving in a dream, a dream where you get the feeling that you recognize everything but you don't really, a dream world full of sometimes magical scenery—like these classically wondrous mountains that support the vast blue sky we are driving beneath at this late-morning moment—that is punctuated with oddities, sometimes secretly dangerous, which makes our trip home across Montana, much less the entire country, a little like Ulysses' trip home to Ithaca. And just as Circe suggested Ulysses avoid the Wandering Rocks, those navigational hazards, so she might have frowned on stopping for toxic-waste-site golf. So as we enter the Deer Lodge Valley for interstate-side golf playing, let us look carefully at these hills that are alternately like sun-painted actors in scenic postcards and like a gigantic partially eaten sandwich.

Robert Sullivan, *Cross Country*

_____

_____

D. This excerpt is a persuasive piece that was published on the website of the American Civil Liberties Union (ACLU) of Pennsylvania. The focus is on the teaching of the doctrine called "intelligent design," which conservatives have promoted as a subject they want taught alongside evolution in American high school biology classes. Many conservatives consider evolution to be a theory, not scientific fact.

Harrisburg, PA—The American Civil Liberties Union of Pennsylvania, Americans United for Separation of Church and State and attorneys with Pepper Hamilton LLP filed a federal lawsuit today on behalf of 11 parents who say that presenting "intelligent design" in public school science classrooms violates their religious liberty by promoting particular religious beliefs to their children under the guise of science education.

"Teaching students about religion's role in world history and culture is proper, but disguising a particular religious belief as science is not," said ACLU of Pennsylvania Legal Director Witold Walczak, "Intelligent design is a Trojan Horse for bringing religious creationism back into public school science classes."

The Rev. Barry W. Lynn, Americans United Executive Director, added, "Public schools are not Sunday schools, and we must resist any efforts to make them so. There is an evolving attack under way on sound science education, and the school board's action in Dover is part of that misguided crusade. 'Intelligent design' has about as much to do with science as reality television has to do with reality."

"Pennsylvania Parents File First-Ever Challenge to 'Intelligent Design' Instruction in Public Schools," *ACLU of Pennsylvania Online* (www .aclupa.org/news/2004/intelligent-design.html).

E.

"My self-esteem was so low I just followed her
around everywhere she would go."

© Bruce Eric Kaplan/*The New Yorker* Collection/www.cartoonbank.com

■ CHAPTER EXERCISES

Selection 1

[1]Human beings find the most ingenious ways to protect their privacy, even under conditions of near-constant physical proximity to others. [2]In many cultures, even minimal control over physical access can be hard to come by in the midst of communal and family life. [3]Some villages have huts with walls so thin that sounds can easily be heard through them; others have no walls at all separating couples, or families. [4]Many ways are then devised to create privacy. [5]Villagers may set up private abodes outside the village to which they go for days or even months when they want to be alone or with just one or two others. [6]Many cultures have developed strict rules of etiquette, along with means of dissimulation and hypocrisy that allow certain private matters to remain unknown or go unobserved. [7]In such ways, it is possible to exercise some control over one's openness to others even in the midst of communal life or crowds.

[8]An arresting example of how such control can be maintained is provided by the Tuareg men of North Africa who wear blue veils and long robes of indigo cotton, so that little of them shows except their hands, their feet, and the area around their eyes. [9]The veil is worn at home as well as outside, even when eating or smoking. [10]Some wear it even when asleep. [11]It is raised to cover the face most completely in the presence of highly placed persons or family members granted special respect, such as in-laws. [12]One observer noted that the veil protects ceremonial reserve and allows a "symbolic withdrawal from a threatening situation."

[13]The veil, though providing neither isolation nor anonymity, bestows facelessness and the idiom of privacy upon its wearer and allows him to stand somewhat aloof from the perils of social interaction while remaining a part of it.

Sissela Bok, *Secrets: On the Ethics of Concealment and Revelation*

A. Vocabulary

For each italicized word from the selection, write the dictionary definition most appropriate for the context.

1. the most *ingenious* ways [sentence 1]: _____

2. near-constant physical *proximity* [1]: _____

3. means of *dissimulation* [6]:   _____

4. the veil *bestows* facelessness [13]:   _____

B. Structure and Meaning

1. The main idea of the paragraph is that
   (a) privacy is a universal concern.
   (b) loss of personal privacy may have serious emotional consequences.
   (c) clothing can sometimes establish one's privacy.
   (d) human beings have devised ingenious ways to protect their privacy.

2. The reader can infer that maintaining privacy is
    (a) more difficult in economically developed nations.
    (b) impossible to achieve or maintain in communal societies or in large families.
    (c) more important to cultures in North Africa than it is to Americans or Europeans.
    (d) a special problem in cultures where people live in close proximity.
3. Paraphrase sentence 13. _____

    _____

4. The author's tone can best be described as
    (a) philosophical, reflective.
    (b) admiring, laudatory.
    (c) informative, instructive.
    (d) ironic, amusing.
5. Write a summary of the passage. Try not to exceed 50 words.

    _____

    _____

    _____

Answers for Selection 1

A. Vocabulary

1. clever, imaginative
2. closeness
3. disguise, concealment
4. confers, presents

B. Content, Structure, and Tone

1. d   2. d
3. Though the veil does not allow its wearer to have either complete isolation or complete anonymity, it does provide a way to hide the face and allows some participation in social activities without being a wholly active participant.
4. c
5. In many cultures whose inhabitants live in close proximity, people must adopt ways to protect their privacy. For example, some people go to private houses outside the village or more ingeniously they wear long robes and veils, which provide some measure of isolation without cutting themselves off from social contact. (50 words)

Selection 2

The chimpanzee who is the subject of this passage, Cholmondeley—or Chumley as he was known to his friends—was being donated to the London Zoo. The author had promised the owner to take the chimp back to England on his way home from Africa.

[1]He arrived in the back of a small van, seated sedately in a huge crate. [2]When the doors of his crate were opened and Chumley stepped out with all the ease and self-confidence of a film star, I was considerably shaken; standing on his bow legs in a normal slouching chimp position, he came up to my waist, and if he had straightened up his head would have been on a level with my chest. [3]He had huge arms and must have measured at least twice my size round his hairy chest. [4]Owing to bad tooth growth, both sides of his face were swollen out of all proportion, and this gave him a weird pugilistic look. [5]His eyes were small, deep-set, and intelligent; the top of his head was nearly bald, owing, I discovered later, to his habit of sitting and rubbing the palms of his hands backward across his head, an exercise which seemed to afford him much pleasure and which he persisted in until the top of his skull was quite devoid of hair. [6]This was no young chimp such as I had expected, but a veteran about eight or nine years old, fully mature, strong as a powerful man, and, to judge by his expression, with considerable experience of life. [7]Although he was not exactly a nice chimp to look at (I had seen handsomer), he certainly had a terrific personality; it hit you as soon as you set eyes on him. [8]His little eyes looked at you with great intelligence, and there seemed to be a glitter of ironic laughter in their depths that made one feel uncomfortable.

[9]He stood on the ground and surveyed his surroundings with a shrewd glance, and then he turned to me and held out one of his soft, pink-palmed hands to be shaken, with exactly that bored expression that one sees on the faces of professional hand-shakers. [10]Round his neck was a thick chain, and its length drooped over the tailboard of the lorry and disappeared into the depths of his crate. [11]With an animal of less personality than Chumley, this would have been a sign of his subjugation, of his captivity. [12]But Chumley wore the chain with the superb air of a Lord Mayor; after shaking my hand so professionally, he turned and proceeded to pull the chain, which measured some fifteen feet, out of his crate. [13]He gathered it up carefully into loops, hung it over one hand, and proceeded to walk into the hut as if he owned it. [14]Thus, in the first few minutes of arrival, Chumley had made us feel inferior; he had moved in, not, we felt, because we wanted him to, but because he did. [15]I almost felt I ought to apologize for the mess on the table.

Gerald Durrell, *The Overloaded Ark*

A. *Vocabulary*

For each italicized word from the selection, write the dictionary definition most appropriate for the context.

1. *sedately* [sentence 1]:
   (a) calmly, in a dignified manner.
   (b) nervously, apprehensively.
   (c) arrogantly, haughtily.
   (d) uncomfortably, awkwardly.
2. *pugilistic* [4]: Having the appearance of a
   (a) military officer.
   (b) movie star.
   (c) fighter.
   (d) vicious animal.
3. *ironic* [8]: In this context,
   (a) cynical, distrustful.
   (b) satirical, ridiculing.
   (c) sarcastic, suggesting a superior attitude.
   (d) nasty, cruel.
4. *subjugation* [11]:
   (a) boredom, indifference.
   (b) defeat, enslavement.
   (c) cooperative spirit.
   (d) subjectivity, introspective nature.

B.   Content, Structure, and Tone

Complete the following questions.

1. The dominant impression of Chumley that Durrell wants to convey is his
   (a) weird appearance.
   (b) large size.
   (c) maturity.
   (d) superior attitude.
2. The passage contains three metaphors that describe Chumley's behavior. Identify each in the space provided.
   Sentence _____

   Sentence _____

   _____

   Sentence _____

   _____

3. These three figures of speech, taken together, suggest that Chumley was accustomed to _____

   _____.

4. Which of the following is an accurate inference?
   (a) Durrell had never seen a chimp before.

      (b) Chumley was embarrassed by the chains used to tether him to his crate.
      (c) Chumley insisted on having his surroundings be clean and orderly.
      (d) Durrell had expected Chumley to be an ordinary chimp.

5. The tone of the passage can best be described as
      (a) ironic, wry, and amused.
      (b) sarcastic, ridiculing.
      (c) serious, earnest.
      (d) sentimental, maudlin.

Selection 3

This passage comes from a chapter on the American government's mistreatment of various Indian tribes during the nineteenth century.

The most famous removal of Indians, of course, was the removal of the Cherokee from Georgia westward to Indian Territory in 1838 and 1839. There are many accounts of the forced march that came to be known as the Trail of Tears—of the Cherokee's previous peaceableness and prosperity on their lands in Georgia; of the Georgia settlers' hatred of Indians and desire for those lands; of the merci-lessness of President Andrew Jackson; of Supreme Court Justice John Marshall's ruling that the removal was illegal; of Jackson's response: "He has made his law. Now let him enforce it"; of the opposition of people as diverse as Ralph Waldo Emerson and Davy Crockett to the removal; of the U.S. soldiers' roundup of the Georgia Cherokee; of the Cherokee's suffering in the stockades and along the trail; of the death of more than four thousand Cherokee, about a third of the population of the tribe, before the removal was through. The Cherokee had their own written language, with an alphabet devised by the Cherokee leader Sequoyah during the 1820s. But their success at following the ways of the whites proved no defense. As would happen again elsewhere, building houses and farms only gave the Indians more to lose when government policy changed.

Ian Frazier, *On the Rez*

A. *Content and Structure*

1. A good title for this paragraph would be
      (a) "A Sad Day in American History"
      (b) "A History of the Cherokee Indians"
      (c) "Forced Removals in American History"
      (d) "The Cherokee and the Trail of Tears"

2. Which *two* of these reasons does Frazier offer to explain why the Chero-kee were forcibly removed from Georgia?
      (a) The Supreme Court refused to hear the Cherokees' case against removal.
      (b) The Cherokee had waged war against the Georgia settlers.
      (c) The Georgia settlers hated the Cherokee.
      (d) There was little public support for the Cherokee.

2   After the student gave his tale of woe and left, the phone rang. "I got a D in your class. Is there any way you can change it to 'Incomplete'?" Then the e-mail assault began: "I'm shy about coming in to talk to you, but I'm not shy about asking for a better grade. Anyway, it's worth a try." The next day I had three messages from students asking *me* to call *them*. I didn't.

3   Time was, when you received a grade, that was it. You might groan and moan, but you accepted it as the outcome of your efforts or lack thereof (and, yes, sometimes a tough grader). In the last few years, however, some students have developed a disgruntled-consumer approach. If they don't like their grade, they go to the "return" counter to trade it in for something better.

4   What alarms me is their indifference toward grades as an indication of personal effort and performance. Many, when pressed about why they think they deserve a better grade, admit they don't deserve one but would like one anyway. Having been raised on gold stars for effort and smiley faces for self-esteem, they've learned they can get by without hard work and real talent if they can talk the professor into giving them a break. This attitude is beyond cynicism. There's a weird innocence to the assumption that one expects (even deserves) a better grade simply by begging for it. With that outlook, I guess I shouldn't be as flabbergasted as I was that 12 students asked me to change their grades *after* the final grades were posted.

5   That's 10 percent of my class who let three months of midterms, quizzes and lab reports slide until long past remedy. My graduate student calls it hyperrational thinking: if effort and intelligence don't matter, why should deadlines? What matters is getting a better grade through an unearned bonus, the academic equivalent of a freebie T-shirt or toaster giveaway. Rewards are disconnected from the quality of one's work. An act and its consequences are unrelated, random events.

6   Their arguments for wheedling better grades often ignore academic performance. Perhaps they feel it's not relevant. "If my grade isn't raised to a D I'll lose my scholarship." "If you don't give me a C, I'll flunk out." One sincerely overwrought student pleaded, "If I don't pass, my life is over." This is tough stuff to deal with. Apparently, I'm responsible for someone's losing a scholarship, flunking out or deciding whether life has meaning. Perhaps these students see me as a commodities broker with something they want—a grade. Though intrinsically worthless, grades, if properly manipulated, can be traded for what has value: a degree, which means a job, which means money. The one thing college actually offers—a chance to learn—is considered irrelevant, even less than worthless, because of the long hours and hard work required.

7   In a society saturated with surface values, love of knowledge for its own sake does sound eccentric. The benefits of fame and wealth are more obvious. So is it right to blame students for reflecting the superficial values saturating our society?

8   Yes, of course it's right. These guys had better take themselves seriously now, because our country will be forced to take them seriously later, when the stakes are much higher. They must recognize that their

attitude is not only self-destructive, but socially destructive. The erosion of quality control—giving appropriate grades for actual accomplishments—is a major concern in my department. One colleague noted that a physics major could obtain a degree without ever answering a written exam question completely. How? By pulling in enough partial credit and extra credit. And by getting breaks on grades.

9   But what happens once she or he graduates and gets a job? That's when the misfortunes of eroding academic standards multiply. We lament that school children get "kicked upstairs" until they graduate from high school despite being illiterate and mathematically inept, but we seem unconcerned with college graduates whose less blatant deficiencies are far more harmful if their accreditation exceeds their qualifications.

10   Most of my students are science and engineering majors. If they're good at getting partial credit but not at getting the answer right, then the new bridge breaks or the new drug doesn't work. One finds examples here in Atlanta. Last year a light tower in the Olympic Stadium collapsed, killing a worker. It collapsed because an engineer miscalculated how much weight it could hold. A new 12-story dormitory could develop dangerous cracks due to a foundation that's uneven by more than six inches. The error resulted from incorrect information being fed into a computer. I drive past that dorm daily on my way to work, wondering if a foundation crushed under kilotons of weight is repairable or if this structure will have to be demolished. Two 10,000-pound steel beams at the new natatorium collapsed in March, crashing into the student athletic complex. (Should we give partial credit since no one was hurt?) Those are real-world consequences of errors and lack of expertise.

11   But the lesson is lost on the grade-grousing 10 percent. Say that you won't (not can't, but won't) change the grade they deserve to what they want, and they're frequently bewildered or angry. They don't think it's fair that they're judged according to their performance, not their desires or "potential." They don't think it's fair that they should jeopardize their scholarships or be in danger of flunking out simply because they could not or did not do their work. But it's more than fair; it's necessary to help preserve a minimum standard of quality that our society needs to maintain safety and integrity. I don't know if the 13th-hour students will learn that lesson, but I've learned mine. From now on, after final grades are posted, I'll lie low until the next quarter starts.

A. Comprehension

Choose the answer that best completes each statement. Do not refer to the selection while doing this exercise.

1. Wiesenfeld states that some college students do not consider grades a measure of their
   (a) mastery of the subject.
   (b) personal performance and effort.

4. How would you characterize the tone of paragraph 1, with regard to Wiesenfeld's attitude toward the student quoted? _____

Now characterize the tone of the entire article. _____

E. Questions for Discussion and Analysis

1. Do you see any contradiction in Wiesenfeld's explanation of what grades mean to many students today and what they should mean? (See paragraphs 3 and 4, in particular the writer's phrase "their indifference toward grades.")
2. Is Wiesenfeld accurate in his criticism of today's students and their attitude about grades? Do you detect any bias? Does he avoid generalizing about his students and, if so, how?
3. From your experience as a student and your observation of your fellow students' attitudes toward grades, comment on his most significant points.

⌐ ON THE WEB

According to recent reports, MGM Resorts International wants to destroy the brand-new Harmon Building, a condo and hotel complex that is part of the $9 billion CityCenter project on the Las Vegas Strip. Completed two years ago, the building has so many design and construction flaws that MGM wants to implode it. There is an ongoing controversy about exactly who is responsible for the building's problems, which are apparently so severe that engineers say it would collapse in a big earthquake. Do some research into the Harmon Building and find out more about why this building is doomed. Was it incompetence, shoddy materials, lack of oversight, cost-cutting measures, or perhaps a combination of all of them that caused this situation?

Critical Thinking Exercise

Study this chart on national GPA trends. The data was compiled from grading data from over 70 colleges and universities around the country by Stuart Rojstaczer, formerly a professor of geophysics at Duke University and now a writer on education issues. Study these figures. What conclusions can you draw from the three sets of figures? Which type of college shows the most obvious grade inflation? What are some reasons that might account for this phenomenon?

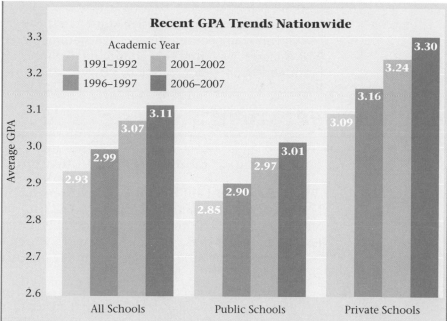

Source: "Grade Inflation at American Colleges and Universities." Reprinted by permission of Stuart Rojstaczer. http://GradeInflation.com

The figure above shows the average undergraduate GPAs for American colleges and universities from 1991–2006 based on data from: Alabama, Appalachian State, Auburn, Brown, Bucknell, Carleton, Central Florida, Central Michigan, Centre, Colorado, Colorado State, Columbia, Cornell, CSU-Fullerton, CSU-Sacramento, CSU-San Bernardino, Dartmouth, Duke, Elon, Florida, Furman, Georgia Tech, Georgetown, Georgia, Hampden-Sydney, Harvard, Harvey Mudd, Hope, Houston, Indiana, Kansas, Kent State, Kenyon, Knox, Messiah, Michigan, Middlebury, Nebraska-Kearney, North Carolina State, North Carolina-Asheville, North Carolina-Chapel Hill, North Carolina-Greensboro, Northern Iowa, Northern Michigan, Ohio State, Penn State, Pomona, Princeton, Purdue, Roanoke, Rutgers, Southern Illinois, Texas, Texas A&M, Texas State, UC-Berkeley, UC-Irvine, UCLA, UC-Santa Barbara, Utah, UW-Oshkosh, Virginia, Washington State, Washington-Seattle, Western Washington, Wheaton (IL), William & Mary, Winthrop, Wisconsin-La Crosse, and Wisconsin-Madison. Note that inclusion in the average does not imply that an institution has significant inflation. Institutions comprising this average were chosen strictly because they have either published their data or have made it otherwise available.

The entire report, including data on the GPAs for each institution, is available online at "National Trends in Grade Inflation,

American Colleges and Universities." In the report there is another chart showing community college grading patterns. Interestingly, Rojstaczer has found that community colleges have been largely immune from grade inflation. Why do you think this is?

PRACTICE SHORT STORY

Paul Theroux, "Eulogies for Mr. Concannon"

American writer Paul Theroux has written such well-received travel books as *The Great Railway Bazaar, The Old Patagonia Express,* and *Dark Star Safari,* as well as fictional works, notably *Mosquito Coast.* This story is an example of "flash fiction," a genre to which you were introduced in Chapter 3. This little story was originally published as one of "22 Stories" in *Harpers.*

I did not know Dennis Concannon. I was invited to his funeral by a friend of his son's who needed a ride. As it was a rainy day and I had nothing else to do, I stayed for the service, sitting in the back. The whole business was nondenominational, according to Mr. C's wishes. The turnout was very large—the church was filled. A reading of his favorite poem, by Robert Frost, with the memorable line, "That withered hag." Several sentimental songs. Then the eulogies.

One man got up and said, "I never met anyone else like Dennis. I worked for him for almost twenty-five years, and in all that time he didn't even buy me a cup of coffee." He went on—people laughed.

A woman: "I used to tremble whenever I was called to his office. I never knew whether he was going to make a pass at me or fire me."

Another man: "The salesmen put in their expense reports that they'd had their cars washed. 'Salesmen have to have clean cars.' But Dennis said, 'This was the fourteenth of last month. I compared the car washes to the weather report. It was raining that day. I'm not paying.'"

Someone else: "His partner, George Kelly, would be sitting next to him at some of the meetings. One would talk. Then the other, but saying the same thing. It was terrible. We called it 'Dennis in Stereo.'"

There were more speakers, with equally unpleasant stories of this man. At the end of the funeral I knew Dennis Concannon as a mean, unreasonable, bullying bastard who had gotten rich by exploiting and intimidating these people, the attendees at his funeral—not mourners but people who were having the last word.

Questions for Discussion and Analysis

1. Why did the narrator attend Dennis Concannon's funeral? Is his stated reason plausible?

2. What is the traditional function of a funeral? of funeral eulogies?

3. Explain the way Mr. Concannon's funeral proceeded. Before the eulogies, is there any hint that this funeral will be unusual?

4. Why did so many people attend Concannon's funeral if they disliked him so much?

5. What personality traits emerge from the various examples of eulogies that the narrator cites? Does the narrator's assessment at the end appear to be reliable and accurate?

6. The narrator states that attendees weren't mourners but rather people who wanted to have the last word. Why did they have to wait till Concannon's funeral to speak up?

7. In what way does this example of flash fiction represent a short story? What are its components?

PRACTICE POEM

Alexandra Teague, "Adjectives of Order"

Alexandra Teague is the author of *Mortal Geography,* a collection of poetry which was awarded the 2009 Lexi Rudnitsky Prize and the 2011 California Book Award. Formerly a Stegner Fellow in poetry at Stanford University, Teague has had her poetry published in *The Paris Review, Crazyhorse, Best American Poetry 2009,* among other journals. She taught English at City College of San Francisco and is now currently assistant professor of poetry at the University of Idaho. "Adjectives of Order" was first published in 2007 on *Slate's* website. You can hear Teague read the poem at this address: http://www.slate.com/id/2167799/

That summer, she had a student who was obsessed
with the order of adjectives. A soldier in the South
Vietnamese army, he had been taken prisoner when

Saigon fell. He wanted to know why the order
5 could not be altered. The sweltering city streets shook
with rockets and helicopters. The city sweltering

streets. On the dusty brown field of the chalkboard,
she wrote: *The mother took warm homemade bread
from the oven. City* is essential to *streets* as *homemade*

10 is essential to *bread.* He copied this down, but
he wanted to know if his brothers were *lost* before
older, if he worked security at a twenty-story modern

downtown bank or downtown twenty-story modern.
When he first arrived, he did not know enough English
15 to order a sandwich. He asked her to explain each part

of *Lovely big rectangular old red English Catholic*
leather Bible. Evaluation before size. Age before color.
Nationality before religion. Time before length. Adding

and, one could determine if two adjectives were equal.
20 After Saigon fell, he had survived nine long years
of torture. Nine *and* long. He knew no other way to say this.

Questions for Discussion and Analysis

1. Who is the subject of the poem? What facts are revealed about him?

2. Explain the significance of the title, "Adjectives of Order." What can you deduce about the rules for adjectives from the rules cited in lines 17–19?

3. Why do you suppose that the student is "obsessed" with these rules? Clearly, he is struggling to learn English, and the rules are important. But are they important in another way, apart from grammar?

4. What are the two themes in the poem? Explain how time functions in the poem.

5. What is the tone of the poem? the mood? How are they achieved?

6. If literature helps us make sense of the world, of our experience, in what way do the rules about placement of adjectives accomplish this for the Vietnamese student?

7. Comment on the last two lines. The rules of English suggest that "nine" and "long" aren't coordinate, meaning that they aren't equal nor can they be separated by "and." Yet Teague deliberately pairs them this way in line 21. Why?

Reading Critically

8

Elements of Critical Reading—Analyzing Arguments

CHAPTER OBJECTIVES

In this chapter, the first of three chapters dealing with reading critically, you will learn to identify and to analyze claims and evidence in arguments, building on the analytical skills developed in Parts 1, 2, and 3. The readings in Part 4 represent arguments concerning various issues and express a particular point of view; they come from newspaper and magazine editorials, letters to the editor, political speeches, cartoons, and websites.

- A definition of critical reading

- The reader's responsibilities

- Developing a worldview

- Analyzing the structure of arguments

- Analyzing visual images

■ A DEFINITION OF CRITICAL READING

In the term **critical reading,** *critical* does not mean tearing down or finding fault. Critical reading is the most deliberate and thorough kind of reading. It goes beyond literal and inferential comprehension. Critical reading means judging, evaluating, weighing the writer's words carefully, and applying your reasoning powers. It requires both keeping an open mind and developing a healthy skepticism, not accepting unquestioningly what you read just because it is in print, but also not rejecting ideas simply because they differ from your beliefs.

It means judging the legitimacy of the argument, as well as its accuracy, fairness, reliability, and larger significance. It involves detecting fallacious arguments, whether from deliberate manipulation, deceptive appeals to emotion, logical fallacies (errors in reasoning), or bias. These matters will be taken up in Chapters 9 and 10. And finally, critical reading extends to visual material and increasingly to material on the World Wide Web.

The terrorist attacks and the invasions of Afghanistan and Iraq changed our perceptions about ourselves and the world's perceptions of the United States. Globalization has produced more intertwined cultures; the world seems somehow more complicated, and our confidence has been undermined. Some issues—global warming, the increasing gulf between the rich and the poor, high unemployment, and immigration, four that first come to mind—seem intractable.

So much information is available today, from both traditional and electronic sources, that keeping up with the issues seems daunting. But despite these transformations, some things don't change: The foundation of a democratic society is the right to think freely for oneself. The way to accomplish that is to read widely on the issues confronting both the United States and the rest of the world, including unfamiliar points of view. A democratic society imposes responsibility on its citizens. Being informed and safeguarding our right to question seem to me the most crucial responsibilities.

■ THE READER'S RESPONSIBILITIES

When reading argumentative prose on controversial issues, our responsibility is to read carefully and thoughtfully—analyzing the writer's use of evidence and logic. If we misinterpret, laziness may be the culprit. We may not take the trouble to read carefully, being content to graze over the contents with no more concentration than if we were checking out the latest football scores. We may be too lazy to look up important words. Or we may skim through an article or editorial instead of reading it carefully because we already agree with the author's point of view. However, the author's position may be weak, supported by flimsy or flawed evidence. The evidence might not stand up to scrutiny. If we read haphazardly, we won't uncover these defects. Even worse, we may read material inattentively because we know in advance that we *don't* agree with the author, thus missing an important part of the intellectual experience, which is to examine opinions we do not share.

Another problem in critical reading is that we may let prejudice, bias, narrow personal experience, or parochial values interfere with a clear-headed appraisal. Critical readers try—insofar as it is humanly possible—to suspend their biases and personal prejudices so that they do not interfere with accurate comprehension. Admittedly, political polarization has become more intense in recent years, making it difficult to stand back and analyze things objectively. This polarization makes it even more difficult to examine a problem from other perspectives. Yet this exercise is an essential part of the intellectual experience, and it is best developed during the college years. It is done by exposing yourself to a range of political, social, and philosophical ideas. After college, you can refine your thinking and develop a worldview, one that makes sense to you, one based on careful thought and analysis, not on preformed ideas you have never questioned. Although it is impossible to be wholly free of bias and prejudice, uncovering our beliefs—and examining those we disagree with—helps us become better citizens, better people.

■ DEVELOPING A WORLDVIEW

One obstacle to critical thinking is **ethnocentrism**, the belief that our nation or social group is superior, that it is at the center of the universe, and that a different way of perceiving events is wrong or flawed, as if everyone else in the world should look at the world the same way we do. Sorting out the opinions that you are exposed to in your college experience is difficult. But as you grow intellectually and reflect on what you have read, learned, and experienced firsthand, you will develop a **worldview**—a perspective on events and issues. Too often, however, we are content to hang on to untested opinions because examining other viewpoints is too much trouble; then, too, our opinions are comfortable, like a pair of old slippers. Our opinions provide us with a ready-made set of beliefs that may be sufficient for day-to-day life experiences, but that may fall short with more serious matters.

Where does our worldview come from? Obviously, from the many influences during our formative years: parents, siblings, teachers, friends, acquaintances, the clergy, co-workers, to name a few. To these we add personal experience, observation of the world around us, and reading. Our worldview undergoes constant change as part of the educational process afforded by contact with the intellectual world but also with the everyday world. Education doesn't just take place in the classroom. The verb *educate* derives from Latin, meaning "a leading out" (from the prefix *e*, meaning "from," and the root *ducare*, meaning "leading"), but this process comes from many other sources besides education. Our worldview is also formed by intangibles like the value system we were raised with; our family's economic status, level of education, racial or ethnic background, and their expectations; and our religious and moral foundation.

All these influences leave their imprint on us and shape our view of the world. Sandra Day O'Connor was the first woman Supreme Court Justice in the United States (now retired). Although she graduated with honors from Stanford Law School in 1952, she couldn't get a job as a lawyer; in the 1950s the male-dominated legal profession did not readily accept women as equals. Eventually, she served as a trial judge in Maricopa County, Arizona, as a U.S. Court of Appeals judge, and finally as a Supreme Court justice.[1] On the Supreme Court, O'Connor was always sympathetic to plaintiffs in sex discrimination cases. The discrimination and rejection she suffered in her early career clearly shaped her worldview.

Here is a second example of how worldview might influence both policy and the future of the nation, again drawing from the U.S. Supreme Court. Associate Justice Sonia Sotomayor received a great deal of criticism during her 2009 confirmation hearings when it was revealed that she had made this statement during a lecture at Boalt Hall, UC Berkeley's law school, in 2001: "I would hope that a wise Latina woman with the richness of her experiences would more often than not reach a better conclusion than a white male who hasn't lived that life." The first Hispanic Supreme Court nominee (she is of Puerto Rican descent), Sotomayor was asserting the possibility of her worldview playing a role in her legal decisions. The degree to which this has occurred remains to be seen and is probably best left to legal scholars.

Critical Thinking Exercise

Why do you think Sotomayor's "wise Latina" comment engendered such a negative response by those who were challenging her nomination? Who do you think was offended by it? What particular point of view would be threatened by her worldview?

To determine your worldview, begin by questioning why you think the way you do. Consider your upbringing and the people who influenced you most. To what extent does your thinking conform to the way you were raised? To your formal education? To what you have read and experienced? Becoming an independent thinker involves developing one's *own* worldview, not uncritically adopting someone else's. Worldviews are personal and unique, and they should be respected, provided that

[1]phoenix.about.com/cs/famous/a/oconnor.htm

they derive from careful thought and conviction, rather than from an automatic, conditioned response. A television advertisement for Fujitsu expresses this idea well: "No two eyes see the same world."

Here is a final example of how worldviews can differ because of racial experience and identity. A 2005 NBC/Wall Street Journal poll found a big disparity between whites and African Americans about the federal government's response to Hurricane Katrina's victims in New Orleans. Seven out of 10 African Americans were of the opinion that the Bush administration would have done more to help the hurricane victims if the hurricane had struck white suburbs. Only 3 out of 10 white Americans expressed that opinion.[2]

Let us look at how worldviews differ between two cultures. For this edition of the text, I have chosen to focus on the Middle East, obviously a crucial element in world politics in recent years and a region that Americans are ambivalent about, assuming that they are familiar with its recent history. Beginning with the West's dependence on oil from the oil-rich countries of Saudi Arabia, Libya, and Kuwait, America's affairs have become increasingly entwined with the politics and economics of the Middle East. The 2001 terrorist attacks on New York's World Trade Center and other East Coast targets dramatically changed this uneasy relationship. To retaliate against Al Qaeda, America invaded Afghanistan in 2001 and drove out the Taliban; in 2005 the U.S. invaded Iraq.

A thorough discussion of these events, their origins, and the aftermath is beyond the scope of this text; however, it would seem logical that understanding differences in culture and in worldview between Arab nations and the West would be helpful, especially since many Americans are ignorant about this part of the world. In addition, there is a great deal of antipathy—some of it undoubtedly well-founded, some not—toward Islam, especially the brand of radical Islamic fundamentalism that has given rise to terrorist organizations like Al Qaeda and to repressive regimes like those in Syria and Saudi Arabia and the Taliban in Afghanistan.

To begin, do you know why Middle Eastern terrorists chose to bomb American and other Western targets like buildings, embassies, and ships? Is it the traditional Western support for Israel, the presence of American military bases in Saudi Arabia, or something deeper, as certain scholars have pointed out—the Arab sense of inferiority with regard to the West, the notion that the glories of the Crusades in the Middle Ages are long past and that the region has declined economically and technologically ever since? It's obviously a complicated issue, made even more complicated by what has come to be called the "Arab Spring" of 2011, when young people throughout the Middle East and North Africa (Tunisia, Egypt, Bahrain, Yemen, Libya, and Syria, as of this writing) began a series of protests to seek the basic freedoms of democracy and self-determination enjoyed by citizens of Western nations.

[2](www.eisenhowerfoundation.org/aboutus/media/sfchron.html)

With all of this in mind, here is information about the Middle East taken from three sources. The first presents some information from a website, Grapeshisha, which calls itself the "Insider's Guide to Dubai, Abu Dhabi, and the United Arab Emirates." The site is devoted to informing travelers about cultural differences in three Arab nations along the Gulf of Arabia. (The UAE is a group of seven sheikdoms on the Persian Gulf and the Gulf of Oman, the capital of which is Abu Dhabi.) Undoubtedly, the Middle East is not homogeneous, and these three entities do not represent the entire region. Still, this discussion will give you some insight into a different worldview from that of the West. Before continuing, you might want to consult a world map if you are unsure about the location of these Middle Eastern countries. Here is the pertinent information:

Key Concepts in understanding Arab Culture from a Western Perspective

Bridging the divide between cultures is based upon understanding the perspectives of each other. It is not a matter of who is right or wrong, but respecting each others' beliefs and way of life. Religion is an obvious difference, but religion aside, we have provided a simple table so that in understanding a new culture, you are able to understand the thought process relevant to the other.

Perspective	Arab	Western
Family	Considered the foremost, where the father is patriarchal	Important, but not as central to the life of the individual
Friends	Part of life, but considered more periphery	Core to a few, but mostly important in life
Honour	Very important—honour will be protected at all costs	Not as important, but can be in extreme circumstances
Shame	Avoided as much as possible, especially in relation to family, where gossip, insults and criticism taken to heart	Live by the sword, die by the sword
Time	Very relaxed	Very structured, deadlines are always of paramount importance
Religion	Central to life	Personal choice and not usually discussed or associated with individuals
Society	The Family, tribe or clan is important	The individual is important, especially with regard to rights
Government	Somewhat secular, with a focus on religion	The purpose is to protect rights, and is thus focused on adherence
Societal Focus	Age and Wisdom	Youth and Beauty
Wealth	Respected	Respected

In addition, the Arab world view is based on a number of concepts:

Atomism—whereby Arabs are considered to see events as isolated incidents rather than the bigger picture

Faith—all things are controlled by the will of Allah

Wish—conflict of need for modernity versus tradition

Justice—justice and equality is important amongst all Muslims

Family—Family pride is more important than individual honour

Paranoia—considered by the west, but the Arab is just suspicious of interest and intent to ensure the best possible outcome for their own people, country and land.

Source: www.grapeshisha.com/.../**arab-versus-western**-perspectives.html

To further your understanding, the second excerpt offers a slightly different perspective of the Middle East. The selection is part of the introduction to an article originally published by the American Philosophical Society by Gerhard Böwering, professor of Islamic Studies at Yale University. Titled "The Concept of Time in Islam," the article was published in 1997, four years before the 2001 terrorist attacks.

Today the world of Islam is estimated to count almost one billion people, one fifth of humanity. Islam occupies the center of the globe. It stretches like a broad belt across the map from the Atlantic to the Pacific, encircling both the "haves" of the consumer North and "have nots" of the disadvantaged South. It sits at the crossroads of America, Western Europe, and Russia on one side and black Africa, India, and East Asia on the other. Islam is not contained in any national culture; it is a universal force. Stretching from Morocco to Mindanao, it is built of five geographical blocks, the Muslims of black Africa, the Arab world, the Turco-Iranian lands, the Muslims of South Asia, and the inhabitants of the Indonesian archipelago.

Islam is also at a crossroads in history, destined to play an international role in politics and to become the most prominent world religion in the decades to come. In the seventh century of the Common Era, Islam entered the global scene with Muhammad at a turning point in time. With spectacular conquest and organic growth, it expanded through the centuries and became stretched taut in a bow of tension between striving for God and struggle for dominion. As we enter the third millennium of the Common Era, Islam looks back nostalgically at its medieval glory, when the Judaeo-Christian West studied at its feet, and sees fundamentalism as the fulcrum of its future in the struggle for preeminence with the secular and technologically superior West.

Proceedings of the American Philosophical Society, March 1997.
http://www.jstor.org/stable/987249

The final example is a short excerpt from Sandra Mackey's excellent study of Saudi Arabian society. Mackey, an American writer, lived in Saudi Arabia during the 1970s and 1980s, but she has updated her study in light of recent events in the Middle East. In this passage, Mackey examines the way that Saudis view themselves in relation to the rest of the world and, by extension, to other Arab nations.

> One must understand how Saudi Arabia views the world to appreciate the importance the Saudis attach to their standing among other Arabs. The Saudis see the world as a series of concentric circles, with Saudi Arabia in the center, surrounded by the Arab world, surrounded by the Islamic world. In this scheme, the world is largely bipolar—Moslem and non-Moslem. Central to this concept of bipolarization is an acute consciousness of being a member of the second ring, the Arab nation, a consciousness shared by all Arabs. Yet there exists an enormous gap between the ideal of Arab brotherhood and the national interests and ambitions of the individual countries. Consequently, all relations between Arab countries are conducted on the basis of unity and discord. Although profoundly confusing to Westerners, this is not contradictory to Arabs, who view Arab nations much like a family. Furthermore, the rules worked out for the survival of the Arab family are applied to the Arab nation: I against my brothers; I and my brothers against my cousins; I and my cousins against the world. Within this psychological context, all conflicts are viewed as temporary and any unity as permanent.
>
> Sandra Mackey, *The Saudis: Inside the Desert Kingdom*

Practice Exercise 1

Questions for Consideration and Discussion

1. Consider the three excerpts together. Summarize the Arab worldview.
2. Based on the information you have just read, what to you is the most significant difference between the Arab and Western worldview?
3. How might this difference account for the rise of Islamic fundamentalism in the region and for the terrorist attacks against the West?
4. Have the authors of the information on the website Grapeshisha accurately characterized Western values? Is there any characterization that you disagree with? If so, how would you revise it?
5. What connections do you see, if any, between the information in the chart and the discussion by Gerhard Böwering?
6. Is it possible that radical Islam and the terrorist attacks around the world have colored your perception of the Middle East? Does the information presented in this section change your perspective in any way? If so, how?

7. Though it is impossible to predict at the time of this writing (spring 2012), by the time you read this, the Arab Spring that started in 2011 may well be part of history. Yet it seems that the pro-democracy movements have already had profound changes. What future do you see for these nations in terms of granting more freedoms to citizens? Are there any possible dangers in demands for democracy in a region without this tradition?

8. What information would you like to obtain about the Middle East and how would you go about finding it?

■ TWO WORLD MAPS—TWO WORLDVIEWS

To what extent is our perception of our status in the world and our worldview influenced by its geography or by the image we have in our minds by its geographical position? Here are two maps of the world. The first map shows the world with North and South America toward the right, Africa in the center, and Eurasia and Australia toward the left; Antarctica (not shown) would be at the top. The second map shows North and South America in the center, with Eurasia split and Australia at the bottom left; Antarctica (again, not shown) would be at the bottom.

1. First locate North America (Canada, the United States, and Mexico) on both maps. Which map most closely reflects the image you have of the United States, either from your social studies classes or from your exposure to television news?

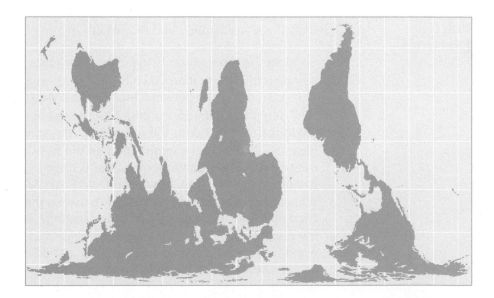

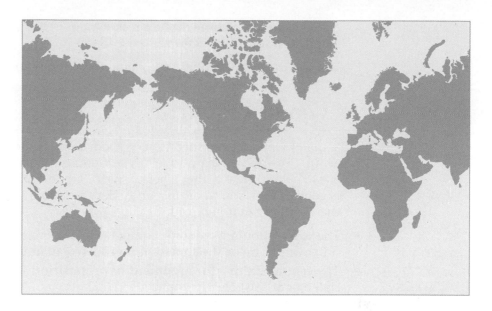

2. Comment on the difference in the two maps with regard to the position of the United States in the Western Hemisphere and in the world, particularly in relation to the continents of Asia and Africa.

3. How might the second map affect one's perception of America's size and influence in the world?

4. Does studying the first map in any way change your worldview with regard to America's role as the dominant superpower in world affairs?

■ ANALYZING THE STRUCTURE OF ARGUMENTS

According to rules established by rhetoricians in ancient Greece, a sound argument had to conform to a rigid format. Through the centuries, these rules have been relaxed so that the argumentative form today is as varied as any other kind of nonfiction writing. A conventional argument includes these elements, although they may not appear in the order presented here. Further, arguments also depend on unstated assumptions, which you will examine in this chapter and in Chapter 9.

- The claim (also called the thesis or proposition)—the writer's main idea or point.
- Evidence to support the claim.
- A refutation, sometimes called the concession—the writer's discussion of opposing viewpoints.

- A conclusion, which might be a restatement of the claim or a recommendation for future action.

You will examine each of these elements in the following sections.

■ THE TEST OF A GOOD ARGUMENT

Some of what is published is very good, some is mediocre, and some is awful. How do you learn to tell the difference? What criteria should you use to determine whether a persuasive or argumentative piece of writing is good or bad, sound or unsound? Here are some standards for judging the worth of what you read.

- The writer should have some competence or expertise in the area; in other words, he or she should be considered an **authority.**
- The central **claim**—the **argument** or **proposition**—should be clearly stated or at least clearly implied.
- **Key words** should be **defined** in clear and unambiguous language, especially abstract words open to subjective interpretation (like *amnesty, hero, torture, censorship, civil war*).
- The **supporting evidence** should be logically organized, relevant to the main idea, and sufficient to support the claim credibly. Moreover, the discussion should appeal to our intelligence and to our reason, not solely to our emotions.
- Ideally, the persuasive writer should include a **refutation**, also called the **counterargument**, in which he or she examines one or two of the opposition's strongest arguments and disproves them.

■ TAKING ARGUMENTS APART

The remainder of this chapter is concerned with how to break down an argument into its constituent elements. Since the process is complicated, we will take up these steps one at a time:

- Evaluating the writer as an authority
- Identifying the type of claim
- Stating the claim or argument in a sentence
- Ascertaining any unstated assumptions
- Evaluating the supporting evidence
- Locating the refutation, if one is present

The Question of Authority

An **authority** is defined in the dictionary as "an accepted source of expert information or advice." The writer of persuasive prose should have firsthand knowledge of and/or experience with the topic. The writer may be a college or university professor, a scientific researcher, or a person with practical experience in the field. However, these are not hard-and-fast requirements, since ordinary citizens may be experts on various issues by virtue of their experience, and they may express their opinions in the letters-to-the-editor section of newspapers, in chat rooms, and in other venues. To some extent, the popularity of blogs and collaborative websites like Wikipedia, to which ordinary people contribute information, has blurred the traditional definition of authority.

And although print journalists may not be experts in the strict sense of the word (as, for example, an academic is), they do often specialize in a subject, and they are experienced at delving into an issue and intelligently presenting their findings. When a writer establishes his or her credibility (or at least the reason for his or her interest in the subject), we can deem the information reliable. Knowing that the writer is an authority inspires our confidence. It does not mean, however, that we need to accept the argument, just that we can consider it.

Practice Exercise 2

Some of the people cited in the list below are authorities; some are not. Write "A" in the space if the person appears to be an authority on the particular subject. If the person appears *not* to be an authority, write "N." If you are unsure or if you think his or her authority is questionable, write a question mark. Try to justify each answer.

1. _____ Larry Sabato, professor of political science at the University of Virginia and director of UVA's Center for Politics, comments on the 2012 presidential race.

2. _____ Colby Buzzell, who served in the U.S. Army for several months in Iraq, wrote a well-known blog about his experiences there: http://cbftw.blogspot.com/. His blog postings were subsequently published in a book, *My War: Killing Time in Iraq.*

3. _____ Ernie Goldthorpe, a community college English teacher, criticized America's military presence in Iraq in a letter to the editor of the *New York Times.*

4. _____ George Abraham Thampy, a twelve-year-old boy who, along with his siblings, has been home-schooled all his life, writes on the virtues of home schooling.

5. _____ Tom Colicchio, chef-owner of three New York City restaurants—Gramercy Tavern, Craft, and 'Wichcraft—and Craftsteak in Las Vegas, winner of the James Beard Best New Restaurant award in 2002, serves as the head judge on Bravo's reality TV program *Top Chef.*

6. _____ Bjorn Lomborg is a Danish statistician who has written that concerns about global warming are exaggerated.

7. _____ Tom Cruise, actor and Scientology member, as a guest on *Oprah,* pronounced psychiatry to be a "pseudoscience" and

said that there is no such thing as a chemical imbalance in the brain that would require antidepressants.

8. _____ Louis Freeh, former director of the FBI, explained the mechanical failures that caused the crash of a TWA jet off Long Island in 1997.

9. _____ Robin McKnight, a 50-year-old resident of Detroit who has lived in the city all her life, writes a letter to the editor of the *Detroit Free Press* setting forth some suggestions for revitalizing the city's downtown.

10. _____ Roger Ebert, film critic at the *Chicago Sun-Times* since 1967, writes an editorial in *The Wall Street Journal* about why the Motion Picture Association of America should change its rating system for movies.

11. _____ Donald Trump, businessman, real estate magnate, and star of the TV reality show "Celebrity Apprentice," endorses Macy's men's clothing in various advertisements.

12. _____ Former rapper and manufacturer of a line of men's clothing, P. Diddy Combs, comments on fashion trends for black urban males.

13. _____ John R. Lott, Jr., a fellow at the University of Chicago Law School and author of *More Guns, Less Crime*, writes on common myths associated with gun-control laws.

14. _____ Deepak Chopra, author of many self-help books and consciousness-raising guru, discusses the child molestation scandals in the Catholic Church on CNN.

15. _____ Steven Tyler (formerly lead singer for Aerosmith), Jennifer Lopez (actress), and Randy Jackson (musician and record producer) serve as judges on TV's "American Idol."

16. _____ Brett Favre, former NFL quarterback who played for over 20 years for the Atlanta Falcons, the Green Bay Packers, the New York Jets, and the Minnesota Vikings touting the merits of Wranglers Jeans.

Identifying Claims

As stated above, the **claim** is the idea to be proved, the proposition. Claims can be divided into three types: **claims of fact**, **claims of value**, and **claims of policy**. Keep in mind that persuasive writing involves controversy, it is subject to speculation, and its essence is subjectivity. We begin with some simple examples:

Claims of Fact

- Blueberries contain antioxidants that help prevent cancer.
- Americans recycle only about 2 percent of plastic grocery bags.
- The sea ice cover in the Arctic Circle was the fifth-lowest since researchers began gathering data 30 years ago.

These claims can be proved by citing factual evidence and the results of scientific research.

Claims of Value

- Blueberry muffins taste better than bran muffins.
- Plastic shopping bags are an environmental and aesthetic nuisance.
- The melting of the polar ice caps in the Arctic Sea poses serious challenges to the world's future.

These claims are harder to prove because they involve matters of taste, morality, opinion, and ideas about right and wrong. The support would be in the form of reasons and examples from personal experience.

Claims of Policy

- All cities should follow the example of Oakdale and ban the use of plastic shopping bags.
- The federal school lunch program should offer children more fresh fruit and vegetables.
- Polar bear populations must continue to receive special protection as their habitat shrinks.

These claims indicate a course of action, a proposal for change, or a problem that requires a remedy. Note that claims of policy usually include a verb like *should*, *ought*, *need*, and *must*.

Practice Exercise 3	Label each of these arguments according to whether it represents a claim of fact, value, or policy. Note: One claim will have two answers.

1. _____ English 100 improved my writing skills.
2. _____ All college freshmen should be required to take English 100.
3. _____ English 100 is a more challenging and useful course than English 50.
4. _____ The incidence of bullying, both in schools and in the workplace, has been increasing in the United States in recent years.
5. _____ Cyberspace bullying can be even more dangerous and psychologically harmful than physical bullying.
6. _____ Schools must create a bullying-free environment by dealing swiftly and harshly with bullies.
7. _____ Texting while driving not only defies common sense, but it is also so dangerous that every state should have strict fines for drivers who engage in such activity.

8. _____ American schools must address the so-called "achievement gap" by providing quality education for all students, regardless of race, ethnicity, or economic background.

9. _____ The term "achievement gap" refers to differing test scores and grade point averages between Asians and whites, who generally score higher, and lower-scoring minorities.

10. _____ Solving the achievement gap in American education is a difficult proposition.

Identifying Claims in Editorials

The exercise you just completed consisted only of one-sentence claims. In reality, however, claims do not appear in isolation. Like any other kind of extended discourse, the claim (or thesis) may appear anywhere, yet here are the three most *likely* places where writers place the claim:

- At the very beginning—the direct-announcement approach. (This placement results in a **deductive argument**, because the claim or proposition, a general statement, is followed by the supporting evidence; for more on deductive reasoning, see Chapter 9, page 355)

- In a sentence immediately after the introductory "hook"—a telling anecdote, an attention-grabbing set of statistics, some relevant background. (This placement is sometimes referred to as the funnel pattern; see the introduction to Part 5 on page 444, for further explanation.)

- At the very end, following all of the supporting evidence. This placement is called an **inductive argument** because the claim or proposition derives from the specific evidence. (For more on inductive reasoning, see Chapter 9 on page 354)

Practice Exercise 4

In this next exercise you are asked to locate and isolate the claim. Reprinted here are the beginning portions of six representative opinion pieces one might encounter in newspapers or periodicals. First, identify the type of claim (fact, value, or policy). Next, write a sentence stating the writer's claim or argument in your own words. Do not include any evidence or support in your argument sentence. Finally, decide whether or not the writer or writers are authorities concerning the subject. Write Yes, No, or ? in the space provided.

A. Marla Rose is a freelance journalist with a creative arts background. She extensively researched the topic of plastics for this article.

We have a complicated relationship with plastic, despite its omnipresence in our consumer culture. Associated with the cheap and mass-produced, plastic is synonymous with disposability. The very qualities that have made it so perfect for mass production—its protean nature and ability to be reliably molded with heat and pressure into an astonishing variety of shapes and sizes—contribute to our perception of the material as utterly synthetic and machine-made. The word *plastic* is also used to describe someone who is inauthentic.

Plastic, in other words, is the perfect product for a throwaway, consumer-driven culture that values convenience and affordability over almost everything else.

Marla Rose, "Reduce, Reuse, Reform," *VegNews*

Type of claim: _____

Argument: _____

Authority: _____

B. Jerry Della Femina is chairman of a New York advertising agency.

It's a corny joke that goes back a million years. A man riding on the old Erie Railroad spots a bug crawling across his Pullman bed. Irate, he writes a letter complaining to the railroad.

He receives a letter from the president of the railroad apologizing and stating that this has never happened in the history of the railroad. Unfortunately, accidentally clipped to the letter is a note that the president had only intended for his secretary to see. It reads: "Send this guy the bug letter."

No one even gets the courtesy of "the bug letter" these days.

These days, what the consumer mostly gets is neglect. Firestone sells apparently defective tires but refuses to acknowledge responsibility. United Airlines cancels flights without notice; when weather grounds a flight, the airline holds you hostage on the runway with soft drinks and packets of peanuts to sustain you. Then, to make amends, it announces that it plans to cut down on the number of regular flights. Its new slogan, I guess, would be, "United Airlines . . . Fewer flights to fewer places, but it beats sitting on the runway for 12 hours."

Consumers feel as if they have no power. . . . In the shadow of these behemoths, the consumer is reduced to a tiny figure crying in the wilderness. More often than not, his protests go unheard—literally.

Jerry Della Femina, "They've Got Us Where They Want Us,"
The Washington Post National Weekly Edition, October 9, 2000

Type of claim: _____

Argument: _____

Authority: _____

C. Roger Ebert has been the film critic at the *Chicago Sun-Times* since 1967; he also was co-host of a long-running weekly TV program, *Siskel and Ebert*.

In the 42 years since Jack Valenti proudly unveiled his new Motion Picture Association of America ratings system, our national standards of taste have changed. Some might say they've become more vulgar, others might say more relaxed, but grade school students now talk like truck drivers did in 1970. I know, I know: not your kids.

The rise of cable TV, home video and the Internet also means that many American children have pragmatic knowledge of what the human body looks like unclothed and what it can do while in that state. This may be unfortunate, but it is a fact.

The MPAA has never revealed its guidelines for what qualifies a movie for a G, PG, PG-13, R or even the dreaded NC-17 rating, but Hollywood producers have a second sense for the tipping points between categories. Sometimes they're startled, as when the MPAA slapped the sad, thoughtful "Blue Valentine" with an NC-17, which meant it couldn't play in many theaters, be advertised in many newspapers or probably be nominated for Oscars. The Weinstein Co. loudly protested and won its appeal on Wednesday; the film was upgraded to an R despite its non-explicit depiction of oral sex, without nudity. Harvey Weinstein speculated that the board might be moving toward changes.

The MPAA should have changed its standards long ago, taking into account the context and tone of a movie instead of holding fast to rigid checklists.

Roger Ebert, "Getting Real About Movie Ratings," *The Wall Street Journal*

Type of claim: _____

Argument: _____

Authority: _____

D. Philip K. Howard is a lawyer and chair of Common Good; he also has published a book, *Life Without Lawyers* (2009).

Calling for a "new era of responsibility" in his inaugural address, President Barack Obama reminded us that there are no limits to "what free men and women can achieve." Indeed, America achieved greatness as the can-do society. This is, after all, the country of Thomas Paine and barn raisings, of Grange halls and Google. Other countries shared, at least in part, our political freedoms, but America's had something different—a belief in the power of each individual. President Obama's clarion call of self-determination—"Yes We Can"—hearkens back to the core of our culture.

But there's a threshold problem for our new president. Americans don't feel free to reach inside themselves and make a difference. The growth of litigation and regulation has injected a paralyzing uncertainty into everyday choices. All around us are warnings and legal risks. The modern credo is not "Yes We Can" but "No You Can't." Our sense of powerlessness is pervasive.

Philip K. Howard, "How Modern Law Makes Us Powerless," *The Wall Street Journal*

Type of claim: _____

Argument: _____

Authority: _____

E. Richard Wilkinson is professor emeritus of social epidemiology at the University of Washington Medical School; Kate Pickett is a professor at the University of York and a career scientist with the United Kingdom's National Institute for Health Research.

Let's consider the health of two babies born into two different societies. Baby A is born in one of the richest countries in the world, the United States, home to more than half of the world's billionaires. It is a country that spends somewhere between 40 and 50 percent of the world's total spending on health care, although it contains less than 5 percent of the world's population. Spending on drug treatments and high-tech scanning equipment is particularly high. Doctors in this country earn almost twice as much as doctors elsewhere and medical care is often described as the best in the world.

Baby B is born in one of the poorer of the western democracies, Greece, where average income is not much more than half that of the United States. Whereas America spends about $6,000 per person per year on health care, Greece spends less than $3,000. This is in real terms, after taking into account the different costs of medical care. And Greece has six times fewer high-tech scanners per person than the United States.

Surely Baby B's chances of a long and healthy life are worse than Baby A's?

In fact, Baby A, born in the United States, has a life expectancy of 1.2 years less than Baby B, born in Greece. And Baby A has a 40 percent higher risk of dying in the first year after birth than Baby B. Had Baby B been born in Japan, the contrast would be even bigger: babies born in the United States are twice as likely to die in their first year as babies born in Japan. As in Greece, in Japan average income and average spending on health care are much lower than in the United States.

Richard Wilkinson and Kate Pickett, "Greater Equality," *American Educator*

Type of claim: _____

Argument: _____

Authority: _____

F.   Eamonn Fingleton is the author of *In the Jaws of the Dragon: America's Fate in the Coming Era of Chinese Hegemony* (2008).

Almost everything the Apple computer company sells these days comes with the following statement of origin: "Designed by Apple in California, Assembled in China."

The implication is obvious: A few brilliant, creative Americans did the real work, while low-skilled Chinese assembly workers, laboring in serflike conditions, did the rest. Citing Apple's iPod at a Virginia trade conference last year, former U.S. Treasury secretary John Snow commented, "China gets to do what they do well: low-value manufacturing. America gets to do what we do well: return on intellectual capital. It's good for both of us, but I would rather be on our end of that."

Such talk panders to one of the most consequential illusions of contemporary American economic thought: that by dint of its unique creativity alone, the United States can count on remaining the world economy's top dog. This assumption, shared by intellectuals on both sides of the U.S. political divide, goes a long way toward explaining the electorate's relative apathy about the collapse of America's manufacturing sector. As the Harvard-educated Japan historian Ivan P. Hall points out, it is just "smug ethnocentric American complacency—little more than whistling in the dark."

Eammon Fingleton, "The Creativity Conceit," *American Conservative*

Type of claim: _____

Argument: _____

Authority: _____

G. This cartoon by David Horsey was published during graduation
season, 2011.

David Horsey/Seattlepi.com © 2011 Hearst Newspapers, LLC.

Type of claim: _____

Argument: _____

Authority: _____

Unstated Assumptions

Just as important as evaluating a writer's authority and identifying the claim is the need to uncover the **unstated assumptions** underlying arguments. In our daily lives, we operate from assumptions all the time, most of which we never bother to articulate. For example, if you tell your friend that you will meet him at Gino's Pizzeria at 6 p.m. after your last final exam, your statement implies several obvious assumptions:

- You will both be alive tomorrow.
- The bus you rely on to get you to Gino's Pizzeria by 6 p.m. will arrive on time.
- You will finish your final exam in time for you to get to Gino's by 6.
- Gino's will be open for business.

An *assumption* is a seemingly self-evident belief underlying the argument. Sometimes the assumptions are stated explicitly, as you can see in this introduction to a *New York Times* editorial:

> New York City has decided to offer cash rewards to some students based on their attendance records and exam performance. Diligent, high-achieving seventh graders will be able to earn up to $500 a year. The plan is the brainchild of Roland G. Fryer, an economist who has been appointed as "chief equality officer" of the city's Department of Education.
>
> The assumption that underlies the project is simple: people respond to incentives. If you want people to do something, you have to make it worth their while. This assumption drives virtually all of economic theory.

> Barry Schwartz, "Money for Nothing," *The New York Times*, July 2, 2007

When the assumptions are not explicitly stated and the writer assumes that we share them, critical reading requires us to separate them from the argument. This is more difficult than it sounds, and it takes some practice. Further, we must decide if we accept the assumption on which the argument rests. Let us look at an example of an argument concerning the ethical questions surrounding the use of embryonic stem cells, which has been much in the news. In 2005 President George W. Bush vetoed legislation that would have extended the number of cell lines available for research. He defended his intention to veto this legislation, saying this:

> I've made my position very clear on embryonic stem cells. I'm a strong supporter of adult stem cell research, of course, but I have made it very clear to the Congress that the use of federal money, taxpayers' money, to promote science which destroys life in order to save life is—I'm against that.[3]

The Republican Senator from Kansas, Sam Brownback, expressed a similar opinion:

> These so-called guidelines for destructive human embryonic stem cell research try to put a good face on an unethical line of research. We should not be destroying young human lives for the benefit of others.[4]

[3]Quoted in Edward Epstein, "Bush Vows to Veto Stem Cell Bill," *San Francisco Chronicle*, May 21, 2005.
[4]Quoted in Rick Weiss, "Stem Cell Guidelines Issued," *The Washington Post*, April 27, 2005.

Unstated assumption: _____

_____

10. In 2006, President George W. Bush addressed the problem of Fidel Castro, President of Cuba, who at the time was seriously ill. (In fact, Castro later relinquished power to his younger brother, Raul.) Bush said this: "The United States and the American people will do everything that we can to stand by the Cuban people in their aspirations for a democracy."

Unstated assumption: _____

_____

After you complete this exercise, go back through these arguments and test each against your own experience and worldview. Next study your responses. Do you question the validity of any of the original arguments because the underlying assumption is false or flawed in some way?

The Importance of Definitions in Arguments

Is a burrito a sandwich? The Panera Bread Company bakery chain wanted to prevent Qdoba Mexican Grill from operating a restaurant in the White City Shopping Center in Shrewsbury, Massachusetts. Panera's lawyers argued that a clause in its lease prevented another sandwich shop from opening in the center and that the burritos on Qdoba's menu would actually be "sandwiches." Superior Court judge Jeffrey Locke ruled against Panera, citing Webster's Dictionary definition and the testimony of a chef and a federal agricultural official. Panera claimed that a tortilla was a piece of bread and that the food product that fills the bread makes it a sandwich. But the judge said that the argument came down to the difference between two slices of bread and one tortilla. Since a burrito is a single tortilla stuffed with meat, rice, and beans, it does not fit the definition of sandwich. Panera lost the suit. ("Burrito Outlet Wins Food Fight at Mall," Associated Press, November 11, 2006)

Though we can see that competing definitions were at the heart of the case, the argument over burritos and sandwiches is not a crucial ethical issue. However, other arguments are not so easily dispensed with. Are frozen human embryos "human beings"? Is the conflict in Iraq between the Shiites, Sunni, and the Kurds a "civil war"? Agreeing on the definitions of "human being" and "civil war" is essential for determining guidelines for stem cell research and military policy, for example, the question of whether the United States should get entangled in another country's civil war. When examining arguments, check to see if the writer has defined key terms that might be open to misinterpretation or to multiple definitions.

Evaluating Evidence

The term *evidence* refers to information or support used to back up a claim. (Before continuing with this section, it might help to review the methods of paragraph development in Chapter 4.) Each type of evidence can be used alone or in combination. Here are the common ones:

- Facts, statistics, including survey or poll results
- Examples and illustrations from observation, personal experience, or reading
- Good reasons (part of the cause-effect pattern)
- Historical analysis or citing of precedents from history
- Testimony of experts and authorities in the field
- Analogy

In judging the worth of an argument, first annotate the main supporting points in the margin. Then ask if the evidence is relevant to the claim and if it is sufficient to persuade you to accept the claim. If the writer uses statistics, are they current? Is the source of the statistics provided?

An opinion writer most often combines various types of evidence. Return for a moment to Practice Exercise 4, E., Richard Wilkinson and Kate Pickett, "Greater Equality," in which the writers argue that babies born in the U.S. are less well off than those born in poorer countries. Notice that they rely on facts and statistics as well as the two illustrations of babies born in different countries.

Practice Exercise 6	Examine these excerpts from editorials and opinion pieces. First, write a sentence stating the writer's argument. Then identify the type(s) of evidence used to support the claim.

A.   Marc Ambinder is politics editor at *The Atlantic*.

In 1960, when President-elect John F. Kennedy fretted about fitness in an essay for *Sports Illustrated* titled "The Soft American," roughly 45 percent of adults were considered overweight, including 13 percent who were counted as obese; for younger Americans, ages 6 to 17, the rate was 4 percent. Obesity rates remained relatively stable for the next 20 years, but then, from 1980 to 2000, they doubled. In 2001, the U.S. surgeon general announced that obesity had reached "epidemic" proportions. Seven years later, as the obesity rate continued to rise, 68 percent of American adults were overweight, and 34 percent were obese; roughly one in three children and adolescents was overweight, and nearly one in five was obese. Americans now consume 2,700 calories a day, about 500 calories more than 40 years ago. In 2010, we still rank as the world's fattest developed nation, with an obesity rate more than double that of many European nations.

For that dubious distinction, we pay a high price. . . .

I'm intimately acquainted with the struggle against fat. I may have been skinny as a child—my family used to joke about putting meat on my bones—and I played sports in school, but by the time I was bar mitzvahed, I was overweight. In my 20s, I spent hundreds of hours with personal trainers and diet doctors, and tried virtually every popular diet at least once. Lots of money in the pockets of the gurus; no joy for me. Approaching the age of 30, I passed the nebulous but generally accepted clinical threshold separating the merely overweight from the obese: a ratio of weight (in kilograms) to the square of height (in meters) of 30 or more. (A body-mass index, or BMI, of 18.5 to 24.9 is considered "normal";

so brutal that it ends up backfiring by creating sympathy for the terrorists' cause. Their targets are often ordinary civilians, and, even when terrorists are trying to kill soldiers, their attacks often don't take place on the field of battle. The modern age of suicide terrorism can be said to have begun with Hezbollah's attack, in October of 1983, on U.S. marines who were sleeping in their barracks in Beirut.

Once you take terrorists to be rational actors, you need a theory about their rationale. Robert Pape, a political scientist at the University of Chicago, built a database of three hundred and fifteen suicide attacks between 1980 and 2003, and drew a resoundingly clear conclusion: "What nearly all suicide terrorist attacks have in common is a specific secular and strategic goal: to compel modern democracies to withdraw military forces from territory that the terrorists consider to be their homeland." As he wrote in "Dying to Win: The Strategic Logic of Suicide Terrorism" (2005), what terrorists want is "to change policy," often the policy of a faraway major power. Pape asserts that "offensive military action rarely works" against terrorism, so, in his view, the solution to the problem of terrorism couldn't be simpler: withdraw. Pape's "nationalist theory of suicide terrorism" applies not just to Hamas and Hezbollah but also to Al Qaeda; its real goal, he says, is the removal of the U.S. military from the Arabian Peninsula and other Muslim countries. Pape says that "American military policy in the Persian Gulf was most likely the pivotal factor leading to September 11"; the only effective way to prevent future Al Qaeda attacks would be for the United States to take all its forces out of the Middle East.

Nicholas Lemann, "Terrorism Studies," *The New Yorker*

Argument: _____

_____

Type(s) of evidence: _____

F.   Obama's Speech to the American People about His Decision to Engage in Air Strikes in Libya, delivered March 28, 2011.

For generations, the United States of America has played a unique role as an anchor of global security and advocate for human freedom. Mindful of the risks and costs of military action, we are naturally reluctant to use force to solve the world's many challenges. But when our interests and values are at stake, we have a responsibility to act. That is what happened in Libya over the course of these last six weeks.

. . .

Last month, Gaddafi's grip of fear appeared to give way to the promise of freedom. In cities and towns across the country, Libyans took to the streets to claim their basic human rights. As one Libyan said, "For the first time we finally have hope that our nightmare of 40 years will soon be over."

In the face of the world's condemnation, Gaddafi chose to escalate his attacks, launching a military campaign against the Libyan people. Innocent people were targeted for killing. Hospitals and ambulances were attacked. Journalists were arrested, sexually assaulted, and killed. Supplies of food and fuel were choked off.

> The water for hundreds of thousands of people in Misratah was shut off. Cities and towns were shelled, mosques destroyed, and apartment buildings reduced to rubble. Military jets and helicopter gunships were unleashed upon people who had no means to defend themselves against assault from the air.
>
> Confronted by this brutal repression and a looming humanitarian crisis, I ordered warships into the Mediterranean. . . .

Argument: _____

_____

Type(s) of evidence: _____

The Refutation

The final element in analyzing arguments is to look for a **refutation**—a section in the editorial or opinion piece that anticipates the opposition and offers a counterargument. Sometimes called a **concession**, the refutation forces the writer to consider differing viewpoints and to explain where the opposition falls short. Even though many editorial writers—for whatever reason (ignorance, space considerations, laziness)—do not include a refutation section, a sound persuasive or argumentative piece should include one, even if it is just a sentence or a short paragraph.

To see what a refutation looks like, first read excerpts from an editorial about gay rights. The writer is David Boies, an attorney who brought suit in federal court to overturn California's controversial Proposition 8, which sought to ban gay marriage. Reprinted first are the two introductory paragraphs:

> When I got married in California in 1959 there were almost 20 states where marriage was limited to two people of different sexes and the same race. Eight years later the Supreme Court unanimously declared state bans on interracial marriage unconstitutional.
>
> Recently, Ted Olson [U.S. Solicitor General] and I brought a lawsuit asking the courts to now declare unconstitutional California's Proposition 8 limitation of marriage to people of the opposite sex. We acted together because of our mutual commitment to the importance of this cause, and to emphasize that this is not a Republican or Democratic issue, not a liberal or conservative issue, but an issue of enforcing our Constitution's guarantee of equal protection and due process of all citizens.

Since the editorial is quite lengthy, I have summarized the major points Boies makes in support of his position:

- The argument that marriage between people of the same sex threatens traditional marriage is not even worthy of discussion. Two heterosexuals would hardly decide not to marry just because gays also have that right.
- Depriving gays of the right to marry will not make them change their sexual orientation, which in any event, is just as much a personal characteristic as the color of their skin.

- Other countries—notably Spain, Sweden, South Africa, and Canada— have legalized gay marriage with no discernible effect. Several states in the U.S. also allow gays to marry (Iowa, Connecticut, Maine, Massachusetts, New Hampshire, and Vermont).
- Proposition 8, which won by only 52 percent, is a holdover of centuries of gay-bashing. Gays are asking only to be treated like heterosexual citizens and end this form of discrimination.

Now comes Boies's refutation. Notice that the refutation anticipates criticisms that opponents will make:

> There are those who sincerely believe that homosexuality is inconsistent with their religion—and the First Amendment, as well as the Due Process and Equal Protection clauses, preclude the enshrinement of their religious-based disapproval in state law.
>
> Gays and lesbians are our brothers and sisters, our teachers and doctors, our friends and neighbors, our parents and children. It is time, indeed past time, that we accord them the basic human right to marry the person they love. It is time, indeed past time, that our Constitution fulfill its promise of equal protection and due process for all citizens by now eliminating the last remnant of centuries of misguided state discrimination against gays and lesbians.
>
> The argument in favor of Proposition 8 ultimately comes down to no more than the tautological assertion that a marriage is between a man and a woman. But a slogan is not a substitute for constitutional analysis. Law is about justice, not bumper stickers.

David Boies, "Gay Marriage and the Constitution," *The Wall Street Journal*

Underline the two sentences that represent Boies's refutation in these concluding paragraphs.

Critical Thinking Exercise

Consider these questions concerning Boies's editorial:

- What is Boies's interest in this controversy? Why did he bring suit?
- Study the summarized supporting ideas. Which is the strongest? the weakest?
- In the refutation, Boies uses the term "tautological." What is a "tautology"? Consult a dictionary if you are unsure. Once you understand the term, do you agree with his statement, "a marriage between a man and a woman" is a "tautological assertion"?
- Has Boies's editorial affected your thinking about this controversy in any way?

■ ANALYZING VISUAL IMAGES

In this portion of Chapter 8, we will examine two types of visual images—charts and graphs and photographs. Public service announcements, advertisements, and political cartoons are taken up in Chapter 10.

Graphic material—specifically illustrations and photographs—complements, enhances, and supports the ideas expressed in print. Charts and graphs reinforce the ideas, but they also serve in another capacity: They help us absorb complex data and statistical information.

Charts and Graphs

One can "read" graphic material just as one reads print. The same skills that you have been practicing with persuasive material can be used to understand, interpret, and evaluate graphs and charts, which typically accompany newspaper and magazine articles, as well as textbook material. Graphs and charts compress data into manageable, comprehensible visual form; they allow us to see trends, statistics, and connections between pieces of information. Graphic material may present an argument, it may make unstated assumptions, and it may try to persuade a reader to accept a conclusion. Therefore, it is just as important to subject a graphic to careful scrutiny as it is to evaluate the accompanying article.

The most common kinds of graphic images are pie charts, bar graphs, and line graphs. When evaluating any of these visual aids, start by considering these elements:

- What is the title or subject of the graph or chart?
- What relationships or trends does the graph or chart show?
- Is the chart or graph accompanied by an illustration?

Then consider the data provided in the graph:

- What years does the data cover? Is it recent enough to be reliable?
- Does the data seem complete? Are there any obvious gaps? For example, are any years or relevant groups missing?
- Is the source of the data identified? Does the source have an agenda to promote or is it impartial?
- Does the graph or chart support the point the text is trying to make?

We begin with the simplest kind of graph—the pie chart. The following chart accompanied an article titled "White House Obesity Plan Mixes Carrots with Sticks" by Janet Adamy (*The Wall Street Journal,* May 12, 2010). You may recall that Michele Obama made the obesity epidemic her project as First Lady. The article summarizes the White House's campaign to limit marketing unhealthy food to children, to encourage schools to replace French fries with salads and fruits, and to encourage physical activity. Study these two pie charts and then answer the questions that follow:

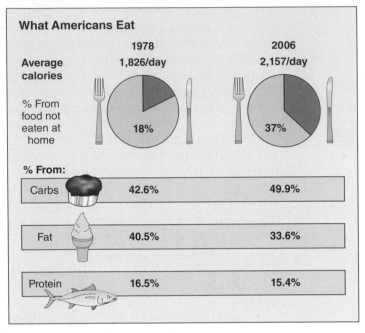

What Americans Eat

	1978	2006
Average calories	1,826/day	2,157/day
% From food not eaten at home	18%	37%

% From:

	1978	2006
Carbs	42.6%	49.9%
Fat	40.5%	33.6%
Protein	16.5%	15.4%

1. Consider the title of the article. What is the meaning of the phrase "carrots with sticks"? (The more common phrase is "to use a carrot rather than a stick.")_____

2. What is the title of the chart? _____

3. What is the chart intended to show?_____

4. Consider the two pie charts. What do they depict?_____

   _____

   What does "not eaten at home" mean?_____

5. How many more calories per day did the average American eat in 2006 as compared to 1978, in other words, in about one generation?

   _____

6. What specifically does the lower part of the chart depict?_____
   Study the figures in this section. Which is the only type of food to show a gain? _____

   _____

7. What do these charts have to do with the obesity epidemic? What inferences can you draw? _____

8. Is the source of the data provided? _____

Next, we will look at a typical bar graph. This graph accompanied a 2006 Associated Press article by medical writer Marilynn Marchione titled "College Weight Gain Not Limited to Freshmen, Studies Find."[5] The article summarizes two comprehensive studies of weight gain: The first, undertaken by Brown University Medical School, studied freshmen; the second, sponsored by the Robert Wood Johnson Foundation, included both freshman and sophomore college students.

Like the two pie charts in the preceding section, you will see that this bar graph is rather rudimentary. For example, the chart does not indicate how many students were studied or who conducted the studies. That information is contained in the article: The first study by Brown University Medical School tracked the weight gain of 382 freshmen at an unnamed private northeastern university; the second study by the Robert Wood Johnson Foundation tracked the weight gain of 907 students at an unidentified public university in the Midwest after their freshman and sophomore years.

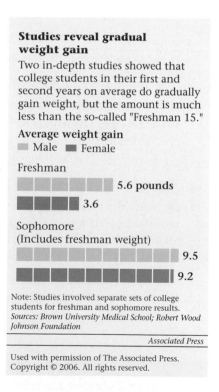

Studies reveal gradual weight gain

Two in-depth studies showed that college students in their first and second years on average do gradually gain weight, but the amount is much less than the so-called "Freshman 15."

Average weight gain
■ Male ■ Female

Freshman

5.6 pounds

3.6

Sophomore
(Includes freshman weight)

9.5

9.2

Note: Studies involved separate sets of college students for freshman and sophomore results.
Sources: Brown University Medical School; Robert Wood Johnson Foundation

Associated Press

[5]Marchione's article, though not the bar graph, is readily available on the Web. In the search box, type in "marilynn marchione, college weight gain."

Study the bar graph on college students' weight gain and then answer these questions.

1. What was the purpose of the two studies? _____

_____

2. What do you think the term "Freshman 15" refers to? _____

_____

3. Summarize in your own words the results of the two studies. _____

_____

4. What do the light and dark green blocks in each chart represent? ___

_____

5. How much weight did men and women gain in their freshman
   year? Who gained more weight? _____

_____

6. What does the second bar graph show? _____

7. How much weight did men gain in their sophomore year? _____
   How much weight did women gain in their sophomore year? _____
   What piece of information accompanying the second bar graph is
   crucial for answering these questions? _____

_____

8. Are the source and dates of these studies included?_____

9. Do you consider the numbers of students who participated in these
   two studies sufficient (382 at a private northeastern university
   and 907 at a public midwestern university) sufficient to allow the
   researchers to draw conclusions? _____

_____

10. What other data might have led to a more accurate or convincing
    conclusion? _____

_____

Critical Thinking Exercise

What might be some reasons that college students gain weight during
their first two years? Why might freshman males gain more weight
than females? What is the long-term significance of these studies?

**Practice
Exercise 7**

It might seem logical that Facebook users, especially college students, spend so much time on the popular social media site that they neglect other matters, like their studies. Is this true? Do college students who use Facebook have lower GPAs than non-using students? In 2008 a survey was taken of 219 Ohio State University undergraduates and graduate students; the results were presented at the American Educational Research Association meeting. As the article accompanying the chart below says, the study generated frightening headlines, like these: "Study Finds Facebook Goofing Hurts Grades," "Study Says Facebook Can Impact Studies," and "Research Finds the Website is Damaging Students' Academic Performance." Were these headlines alarmist or not? Study the data presented in this bar chart and then answer the questions that follow.

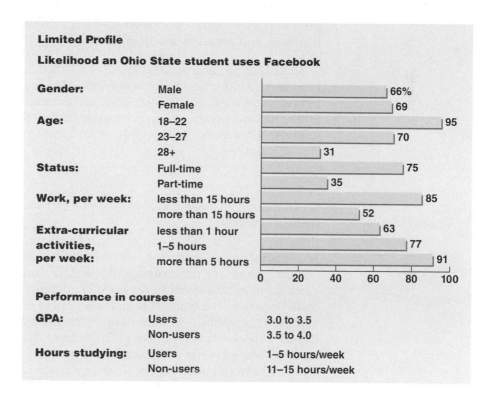

Carl Bialik, "Facebook Users—and Research—Need Further Study," *The Wall Street Journal,* April 22, 2009.

1. What two subjects are dealt with in the chart? Explain the meaning of the word "likelihood" in the top category. _____

_____

2. According to the bar graph, who uses Facebook more, men or women?

_____

3. In terms of the age of college Facebook users, what information does the graph show? _____

4. What inference can you make about why part-time students might use Facebook less than full-time students? _____

5. Concerning the number of hours worked, what is the likelihood, in percentage terms, that a student who works less than 15 hours a week uses Facebook? _____ And for students who work more than 15 hours a week? _____

6. Summarize the data concerning the number of hours per week spent on extracurricular activities. _____

7. Most important, what conclusion does the study draw about users of Facebook and nonusers and their GPAs? _____

_____

8. Examine the information on the numbers of hours spent studying between users and nonusers of Facebook. Evaluate this data in relation to the information about Facebook usage and GPA. Is this conclusion justified? What questions does this information raise? _____

_____

_____

9. Is information included about who conducted the survey as well as when and where? _____

10. Consider the following information that that was included in the article accompanying the chart: The two researchers[6] found that Facebook was used more as a procrastination device by students and did not cause users to have lower GPAs. The 219 students were all from Ohio State University, the majority from the school of education. The participants were students who showed up in the professors' classes on the day the survey was administered.[7] Grades and study hours were self-reported and were not controlled by the students' field of study. Now that you have this information, what conclusion can you draw about the survey, its findings, and its validity? The title of the article reveals its skeptical stance. Is this stance justified, judging from the study's findings? Explain your thinking. _____

_____

[6] Aryn Parpinski, a doctoral student in education at Ohio State University, and Adam Duberstein, an academic adviser at Ohio Dominican University.
[7] In Chapter 9 you will learn about the importance of sampling in opinion polls and surveys.

Critical Thinking Exercise

Devise a better survey than the one cited here, including both sampling methods and questions, to determine the degree to which usage of Facebook (or other social media websites) affects college students' GPAs.

Practice Exercise 8

There is no question that marriage as an institution has undergone enormous changes since the end of World War II, when the Baby Boomer generation of children was born. The following charts accompanied a study summarizing American attitudes toward marriage conducted by the highly respected nonpartisan think tank, the Pew Research Center. If you are interested, the entire report can be accessed at the following address:

www.pewsocialtrends.org/.../barely-half-of-u-s-adults-are-married-a-record-low/

Reprinted here are four sets of data—a line graph, two bar graphs, and a pie chart. Study the data and then answer the questions that follow. The questions are divided into two categories—questions on the data itself, following each graph, and then more general discussion questions.

A.   Questions on Marital Status

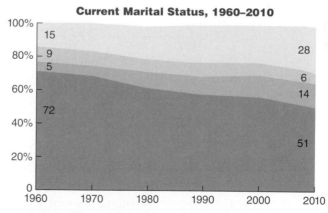

Current Marital Status, 1960–2010

☐ Never married ☐ Widowed ☐ Divorced or separated ■ Married

Note: Based on adults ages 18 and older. Percents may not total 100% due to rounding.
Source: Pew Research Center analysis of Decennial Census (1960–2000) and American Community Survey data (2008, 2010), IPUMS.

Questions

1. What do the numbers printed vertically on the right and left sides of the graph represent?

   _____

2. How many years are covered in this survey?

   _____

3. Summarize the data shown in this graph in your own words.

   _____

   _____

B.   Questions on Marriage Age

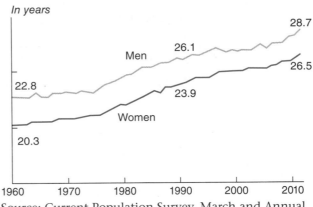

Median Age at First Marriage, 1960–2011

Source: Current Population Survey, March and Annual Social and Economic Supplements.

Questions

1. What does the term "median age" mean?

   _____

2. What were the median ages when men and women married in 1960? What were the median ages when men and women married in 2010?

   _____

3. Summarize the data represented in this graph in your own words.

   _____

   _____

C.   Marriage Share by Age

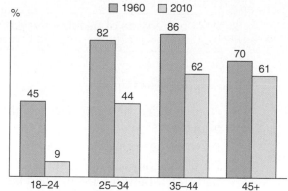

Share Currently Married by Age, 1960 and 2010

Source: Pew Research Center analysis of Census
1960 and ACS 2010, IPUMS.

Questions

1. What do the light green and dark green bars in this graph represent?

    _____

2. What percentage of people aged 18–24 were married in 1960? in 2010?

    _____

3. Summarize the data represented in this graph in your own words.

    _____

D.   Marriage and Future Plans

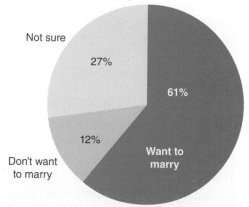

Do You Want to Get Married?

% of never married saying...

Note: Based on adults who have never been
married (n=759). "Don't know/Refused"
responses are shown but not labeled.
Source: Pew Research Center survey of
2,691 adults, Oct 1–21, 2010.

Questions

1. What group of people were surveyed for this data?

_____

2. What percentage of people surveyed said they want to marry?

_____

Discussion Questions

1. Now consider the four charts together. What conclusions can you draw from them?
2. For which age group has the recent trend in marriage been most dramatic?
3. Do you see any disconnect or discrepancy among the charts, particularly between the first and last ones?
4. What are some possible reasons that attitudes toward marriage have changed, specifically in the fact that the median age of men and women marrying is so much higher now than it was in 1960?
5. What might be some consequences of delayed marriage for the larger society and for the individuals themselves?
6. Of your circle of friends and acquaintances, what percentage are married? What age group do they represent?
7. One of the questions the Pew Research Center addressed was "Is Marriage Obsolete"? How would you answer this question? And if you think marriage is indeed obsolete, why is it?

Photographs

Like graphs and charts, photographs present information—the content of the image—but they also convey a sense of character or place and often evoke an emotional response in the viewer. Because photographs can be so powerful, it's crucial to analyze them carefully to avoid a purely emotional response. When analyzing photographs, consider these following elements:[8]

- When was the photograph taken? Under what circumstances was it taken? What is the historical context?
- What is the subject of the photograph? What or who is being depicted?
- How are the figures or objects arranged? Does one particular figure or object dominate the photograph? Are there background elements that are of interest?
- What activity is being depicted? Of what significance is this activity?
- Examine the faces of the person or people depicted. What emotions or feelings do their faces reveal? What do they seem to be thinking?

[8]I am indebted to Robert Keith Miller whose "Establishing a Framework for Analysis" in _Motives for Writing_, fourth edition, clearly lays out an extensive system for analyzing visual material. I have adapted and simplified some of his criteria.

- What are the people in the photograph wearing? Does their clothing reveal anything about them—their position, status, occupation, or any other relevant information?
- Does the photograph appeal to the emotions or to reason?
- How do you think the photographer intended you to respond to the image?
- What is the larger significance of the photograph? What is it meant to represent?

Some photographs become icons, capturing a particular time and place in history. Consider, for example, this iconic photograph taken during the Vietnam War. In late April 1975, Saigon was surrounded by the North Vietnamese forces, and it was only a matter of time before the city fell. Thousands of people were being evacuated on April 29—American civilians, Vietnamese citizens, and other foreigners—most airlifted onto transport planes to be flown to American bases out of the country. As Hubert Van Es, a Dutch citizen who was present at the evacuation explained, in a *New York Times* article published on the 30th anniversary of the Fall of Saigon,[9] most people thought that the helicopter depicted as evacuating people had landed on the roof of the American Embassy; in fact, it had actually landed on the roof of an apartment building where CIA employees lived.

The photo is dramatic, fixing in our minds an era that continues to haunt America today.

What do you imagine those people lined up waiting to ascend the rope ladder were thinking?

© Bettman/Corbis

[9]A *New York Times* article titled "Thirty Years at 300 Millimeters" (April 29, 2005) is available online and includes many photos by Hubert Van Es, a Dutch photographer who worked for United Press International (UPI) during the Vietnam War. Besides Van Es's photographs, the article is worth reading to get a sense of what Saigon, now Ho Chi Minh City, was like before it fell.

**Practice
Exercise 9**

This exercise asks you to examine three photographs that capture a particular moment in history. They are arranged in chronological order.

A. In its landmark 1954 decision in *Brown v. the Board of Education*, the Supreme Court ruled that segregation in public schools was illegal. This photograph from the *Arkansas Democrat Gazette* archives shows a student shouting at Elizabeth Eckford, one of nine students who attempted to attend the all-white Central High School in Little Rock, Arkansas, in 1957. Eckford and a group of black students had sought admission to the high school, but were turned away from the school by the Arkansas National Guard.

How effective is this photograph at showing the racial division that existed 50 years ago in the United States? What was the photographer's intent? What emotions does this photograph arouse in the viewer? _____

**Online
Learning
Center**

In August 2007 the Little Rock Nine held their 50th reunion. Several sites published stories and photographs about the event; the group also appeared on "Oprah." Using Google or your favorite search engine, type in "Little Rock Nine 50th Reunion."

_____

_____

_____

_____

B. In June 1989, pro-democracy protestors staged an uprising in Beijing's Tiananmen Square. Chinese troops sent in tanks to quell the disturbance and restore order. This photograph shows a solitary man carrying only two shopping bags who confronted a convoy of approaching tanks and refused to move. To this day, the man's identity and fate remain a mystery. This showdown lasted for several minutes until he was finally pulled from danger by some onlookers.

Comment on the effectiveness of this photograph. What is its particular larger significance? What emotions does this photograph arouse in the viewer?

_____

_____

_____

C. During the so-called "Arab Spring" of 2011, pro-democracy protests erupted all over the Middle East, starting first in Tunisia, and then quickly spreading to Egypt, Bahrain, Yemen, Syria, and Libya. This photograph was taken by Peter Macdiarmid in Cairo in early February 2011. The photo caption says this: "A young man waves Egyptian flags in Cairo's Tahrir Square, where hundreds of thousands of protesters had gathered."

What emotion is conveyed in the photograph? What emotion is aroused in the viewer?

_____

Contrast this photo with the preceding one of the single protester taken in Beijing's Tiananmen Square. Which is more effective at depicting the power of a single individual fighting oppression and tyranny?_____

_____

_____

Photo by Peter Macdiarmid. An Egyptian protestor waving two flags during the Arab Spring in Cairo. Published in San Francisco Chronicle, Feb. 2, 2011, p A.1.

■ CHAPTER EXERCISES: EVALUATING EDITORIALS

The following editorials will give you practice in putting everything together that you have learned in this chapter. For this edition of the book these four editorials take up a single theme—contemporary education. Consider these questions as you read them:

- Who is the writer? Look at the information provided in the head-note. Does he or she represent an authority? On what basis? (If you need more background than the headnote provides for a particular writer, go to your favorite search engine, type in the writer's name + "information" or "biography.")
- What is the writer's main argument or claim? State the claim in your own words.
- What type of claim does the argument represent?
- If possible, list one or two unstated assumptions underlying the argument.
- Is the evidence relevant to the argument? Is it sufficient to support the claim adequately? List two or three of the main supporting points.
- What types of evidence are represented?
- Is the argument, as the author presents it, convincing or at least worth considering?
- Do you accept the argument? Why or why not? What other information would you need before you could accept it?

To guide you as you learn to analyze opinion pieces, the first editorial is followed by suggested answers. To analyze subsequent editorials in this chapter and in Chapter 9, refer to the above list. Finally, you might want to look ahead to the example in Chapter 9 on how to analyze an opinion piece (see page 361).

Selection 1

Arthur Levine is currently President of The Woodrow Wilson National Fellowship Foundation. At the time of this editorial's publication, he was President and Professor of Education at Teachers College, Columbia University. Prior to this, he served in various capacities at the Harvard Graduate School of Education.

1   The merits of reducing the college degree to three years from four are being broadly discussed in academic circles. The debate was started by Fred Starr, the president of Oberlin, and is being fueled by a Stanford University curriculum reexamination that considers whether the time it takes to earn a baccalaureate degree should be reduced to three years.

2   The idea is appealing on the surface. At a time when college tuitions are soaring, cutting a year from undergraduate study would appear to reduce costs 25%. But like many other academic exercises, it is out of touch with reality.

3   The idea is not new. Harvard had a three-year degree in the 1640s. Its second president got into a battle royal with his board of trustees when he turned it into a four-year degree. Periodically in the years since, both the debate and "new" three-year degree have reappeared. Most recently, in the early 1970s, the Carnegie Corporation supported the creation of three-year programs at colleges and universities across the country. Nearly all of those programs are now gone. There was too little student interest to justify their continuation.

4   If anything, three-year degree programs probably would be even less successful now than they were then. There are several reasons:

5   First, student academic skills have declined since the late 1960s. More than a third of undergraduates report that they are in need of remedial courses. In short, students appear to need more education today, not less.

6   Second, the average time required to earn a college degree is actually increasing. A growing proportion of students are taking five years of classes, particularly at large public universities, which the majority of students now attend.

7   Third, a majority of college students work today while attending college. Most work 20 hours or more a week to be able to pay their tuition. The promise of not paying a fourth year of tuition would not eliminate their need to work. As a consequence, the notion of extending the college year or even the college day is impractical.

8   Fourth, eliminating the final year of college would be a financial disaster for most institutions, which are heavily dependent on tuition or enrollments to fund their operations. Schools would lose a quarter of their student bodies. Outside the West and the South, the demographics of the nation are such that the loss of students simply could not be made up. Colleges might have to raise tuition substantially to compensate.

9   However, there is a much larger problem for the three-year degree than any mentioned so far: It does not make educational sense. The four-year degree is entirely arbitrary. And so is the three-year degree. Degree time measures how long students sit in class. It is not a measure of how much they learn.

10   Imagine taking your clothes to a laundry and having the proprietor ask, "How long do you want me to wash them: three hours or four?" The question would be absurd. We don't care how long the clothes are washed. We want them clean. We want the launderer to focus on the outcome of his washing, not the process.

11   Education should operate similarily. Colleges and universities should define the skills and knowledge a student needs to possess in order to earn a baccalaureate degree, rather than the number of hours of lectures and classes a student should attend to earn a degree.

12   Students enrolled in college now are more heterogeneous than ever before. More than half of all high-school graduates are going on to some form of post-secondary education, and the fastest-growing group attending college is older adults.

13   As a result there is a greater range of knowledge, skills and experience among college students than in the past. Many will require more than four years of instruction to earn a degree. Others will come to college with such rich backgrounds that they will be able to complete a degree in less than four years and perhaps less than three. For these reasons, it is a mistake for colleges to tie in their degrees to time served.

Arthur Levine, "College—More Than Serving Time,"
The Wall Street Journal, December 21, 1993

- Who is the writer? Look at the information provided in the head-note. Does he or she represent an authority? On what basis?

  _____

  _____

- What is the writer's main argument or claim? Be sure to state it in your own words. _____

  _____

- What type of claim does the argument represent? _____
- If possible, list one or two unstated assumptions underlying the argument. _____

  _____

  _____

  _____

- Is the evidence relevant to the argument? Is it sufficient to support the claim adequately? List two or three of the main supporting points. _____

  _____

- What types of evidence are represented? _____

  _____

  _____

- Is the argument, as the author presents it, convincing or at least worth considering? _____

  _____

- Do you accept the argument? Why or why not? What other information would you need before you could accept it? _____

Critical Thinking Exercise

At the same time that Levine argues against proposals to shorten the length of time college students spend pursuing a degree, several American colleges and universities—among them Manchester College, the University of North Carolina at Greensboro, and Florida State University— have begun to offer accelerated three-year degree programs.

A recent article discusses these programs—their advantages and disadvantages—in depth. Using Google or your favorite search engine, locate the article online by typing in this information: "Sue Shellenbarger, Speeding College to Save $10,000." Read the article in light of Levine's comments. Then come to a conclusion of your own about the merits of such programs.

Consider these questions: What kind of students benefit the most from an accelerated program? Is it worth the money saved on tuition to undertake such an arduous path to a degree? Why is it that the average college student today needs five years to graduate rather than the traditional four? Would you be a candidate for a three-year program?

Selection 2

The next three opinion pieces are followed by a few discussion questions specifically designed for each reading.

Alvaro Huerta, Ph.D. is currently a Visiting Scholar at UCLA in the Chicano Studies Research Center. He wrote this editorial as part of the *San Francisco Chronicle*'s Open Forum on Education.

It takes more than a village for youths from America's barrios and ghettos to attend elite universities. It also takes great teachers and government-funded, college-prep programs catered specifically to historically disadvantaged students. I know, because I benefited from both.

Growing up on welfare in a poor village—East Los Angeles' Ramona Gardens housing project—I am well aware of the obstacles young people from the inner city confront on a daily basis. In addition to attending overcrowded public schools, these youths must cope with living in blighted environments plagued with abject poverty, institutional racism, low educational attainment levels, high gang activity and drug addiction, along with rampant police abuse.

Despite these tremendous obstacles, my Mexican immigrant parents managed to send four of their eight children to elite universities. In my case, if not for the support of my late parents, key teachers, college-prep programs and, today, my wife Antonia, I would not have received my bachelor's and master's degrees from UCLA, nor been accepted into a UC Berkeley Ph.D. program.

From Day One, I had to maneuver a broken public school system that put up roadblocks throughout my academic journey. Despite excelling in mathematics, for instance, when it came to reading and writing at the university level, the public school system—Los Angeles Unified School District—failed me.

While Ms. Cher at Murchison Elementary School motivated me in school, Upward Bound—a summer residential, college-prep program for historically disadvantaged students—provided me with a college-oriented path that escaped most of my childhood friends.

Always cheery, Ms. Cher, who had hair like actress Lucille Ball, helped foster my mathematical skills. Once I had exhausted the assigned sixth-grade math books, she took the extra time to teach me algebra using an old middle-school text. She also took me, along with other class members, on a field trip to her Big Bear cabin, providing us with a rare opportunity to see a world beyond the railroad tracks, freeways and polluting factories surrounding our neighborhood.

Attending Oxy[10] during the summers of my high school years allowed me to take college-prep courses not offered at my public high school. The college teachers and staff created a rigorous and supportive academic environment for us all to excel.

While by no means a scientific study, my story is an example of how it takes more than a village for someone from the inner city to attend elite universities like UCLA and UC Berkeley.

How in the world can a kid from the projects, who was only assigned one book, John Steinbeck's "the Pearl," and one two-page essay in high school, compete with privileged kids from the suburbs? To compensate, as a math major at UCLA, I literally taught myself how to read and write at the university level to compete on equal terms with America's brightest students.

I've been very successful in my academic career, and I owe much of my scholarly accomplishments to key teachers and my participation in Upward Bound.

Alvaro Huerta, "It Takes More Than a Village,"
San Francisco Chronicle, April 25, 2011

Discussion Questions

First, work through the general questions on page 344. Then consider these:

1. In the first paragraph, Huerta opens with the phrase "It takes more than a village." What is the origin and meaning of this phrase?
2. What factors contributed to Huerta and his siblings' gaining admission to good universities? Which one do you consider the most important?
3. Comment on the examples of Huerta's high school English assignments that he provides.

[10] Oxy is the nickname of Occidental College, a four-year liberal arts college in Los Angeles. Coincidentally, it is also the college where President Barack Obama began his academic work.

4. What is the wider implication of Huerta's claim and thesis? What changes in our educational system are necessary to help students like him?

Selection 3

Ruben Navarrette, Jr., a member of the Washington Post Writers Group, writes a twice-weekly syndicated column on matters of ethnicity and national origin from a conservative point of view. He has written for *The Arizona Republic* and the *Dallas Morning News,* among other newspapers. Currently, he writes for the *San Diego Union-Tribune.*

In a recent column on outsourcing, I wrote about a college student who told CNN that he was giving up on his chosen career—that of a computer programmer—because there were people in India and other countries who would do the job for a lot less than he would accept.

I blasted the lad, saying that his willingness to surrender his dream was inconsistent with good ol' American values such as determination, ingenuity and courage.

Soon I was buried under an avalanche of angry e-mails. Readers defended the college student, insisting that he had done the right and rational thing.

One woman wrote that she wasn't surprised the young man would lose interest in becoming a computer programmer because of concerns about money. After all, she said, the money—that is, the potential for earning a good salary—was probably why he chose that career in the first place.

I can't speak to the young man's motives. But if this correspondent is right, then that's a big part of the problem. If many of the white-collar workers who now feel vulnerable because of the outsourcing of American jobs are in those jobs mainly because of the size of their paychecks, then it stands to reason that they'd be ready to give up when they find out that someone in a foreign country can do those jobs for less. But if many of them are in those jobs because they enjoy the work, or because they feel that this is precisely what they were put on Earth to do, or because they can't imagine doing anything else, then the possibility that they might not earn as much as they would prefer won't be enough to get them to give up on careers they love.

When I speak to college audiences, I tell them: When choosing a career, be open to the possibility that the career will choose you.

A speaker at a banquet I attended recently referred to it as "answering the call." He said it was his experience that the happiest people are those who figure out what they were called to do, and then just go out and do it.

I know the economic realities. I know that many young people graduate from college today already thousands of dollars in debt, thanks to school loans and credit cards. And so naturally, most can't wait to go out into the world and make what they hope will be lots of money.

And that's where many go astray: They start with the money. They go into a given line of work precisely because they think they can make a good living at it, and not for the reason they should—because pursuing that path will allow them to spend their days doing something they really enjoy, something they would, in fact, do for free.

That's why I tell college students that they only have one task at hand—to find their passion.

If you do that, I tell them, the rest will take care of itself. Because once you determine your calling, you'll find that you love doing it enough to put in the hours that are usually required to become really good at something. And when someone is really good at something, they tend to be better compensated for it.

Listen to what Earl Woods said about his famous son, Tiger. A few years ago, Woods told an interviewer that his son would rather play golf than eat or sleep. Consequently, Tiger Woods has become really good at golf. And for that, he is incredibly well-compensated.

People make choosing a career much more complicated than it has to be. I did. It's been almost 10 years since I decided, with some difficulty, that I'd rather be a poor writer than a wealthy lawyer—something that had once been my chosen career path. And true to my word, in my first year as a freelance writer, I made $12,000.

But you keep pushing and you hone your skills and you never give up. And one day, your paycheck catches up with your passion. It's only when one surpasses the other—and you have more paycheck than passion—that you should call it a career and move on to something else.

Ruben Navarrette, Jr., "Don't Surrender Your Dream,"
Dallas Morning News, April 25, 2004

Discussion Questions

First, work through the general questions on page 344. Then consider these:

1. Why did Navarrette receive angry e-mails after writing his column about the student who changed his mind and decided not to follow his dream of studying computer programming?
2. Explain what Navarrette means when he writes that students go astray when they "start with the money." What is he advocating instead?
3. This column was published in 2004, before the Great Recession. Does Navarrette sufficiently anticipate the harsh economic realities of poor job markets for college graduates? for students who must repay burdensome college loans? Are his ideas realistic?
4. What is Navarrette's advice about choosing a career? Is Tiger Woods a good example to prove his point?

Selection 4

Journalist Naomi Schaefer Riley was formerly deputy Taste editor for *The Wall Street Journal,* where this editorial was originally published. Her articles have been published in *The New York Times,* the *Los Angeles Times,* and the *Chronicle of Higher Education.* She is also author of the book *God on the Quad: How Religious Colleges and the Missionary Generation are Changing America* (2004).

There are two sheets of lined paper, covered in illegible red scrawl, that have been sitting on my kitchen table for four months now. They make my blood boil every time I glance at them, but I can't bear to throw them out. I've come to think of them as evidence. And now that college application season is over—most schools want to know by May 1 whether admitted students plan to attend—I'd like to offer them as Exhibit A in what's wrong with American education.

At the end of December, my niece Jazmine came to visit. Her college process had stalled, and her parents and teachers seemed disinclined or unable to help. So I offered a weekend visit with her uncle and me as a sort of application bootcamp. We'd plow through all the forms and essays in 48 hours. It was an ambitious plan, but she had done some of the work in advance. She had asked her teachers for recommendations.

I should pause here to say that my niece goes to one of the worst schools in Buffalo, N.Y. There are security guards at the door and, as far as I can tell, Jazmine has learned very little in the past four years. Still, she is a smart, respectful young lady who has steered clear of trouble. Which makes her one of her school's very few candidates for matriculation to a four-year college.

Back to the papers on my kitchen table. Last fall, Jazmine twice asked her AP English teacher to complete a letter of recommendation for her, a crucial part of applying to any college. The letter was to be sent to the school's guidance counselor, not directly to Jazmine. But nothing happened. Rather than ask the teacher herself, the guidance counselor told Jazmine to go back and make the request a third time. She did, and this time the teacher instructed her to wait while she wrote out a recommendation, by hand, right then and there. She told Jazmine to "type it up" herself.

I don't know whether the teacher also expected Jazmine to correct the grammar and spelling, but here is a sample of the letter's prose: "Jazmine is enlightened by the journey of academia the twist, turns and heights elevated to farthest stretch imagined. Jazmine will bring a willingness to work, thought provoking, openess and challenges of the worlds positive attributes. . . . Jazmine has shared with her peers & cohorts her beliefs of academia and the wherewithal to never give up to keep trying, to keep learning and to always keep growing."

At least Jazmine had the letter. She had another one, too, from another teacher, but it was barely a paragraph. Then the guidance counselor failed to send Jazmine's midyear grades to two of the schools she applied to.

Is this any way to get into college? Of course not, but it is far too typical of the way the process goes at too many urban schools. Last week the Chronicle of Higher Education released a study showing that the proportion of low-income students (whose families, like Jazmine's, had incomes of less than $40,000) at the nation's top colleges actually declined in the past couple of years. The drop has been seen by educators as particularly disappointing in light of the fact that many colleges have recently started using endowment income to offer free tuition to poor families.

But what stands between disadvantaged kids and college is not mere money. It is orderliness, attentive mentoring and simple organizational guidance. Public schools used to be the great equalizer in America—the institutions that allowed the children of immigrants and the descendants of slaves to become fluent in the English language and prepare them for careers. In too many urban areas, they don't perform such basic educational functions. But they don't offer structured environments, either, for the few students who are trying to lift themselves up and get a better educational experience at college.

Before they can even apply for college, kids need a real high-school education, complete with literate, motivated teachers. University administrators might want to give some more consideration to their own admissions procedures, bearing in mind the incompetence and laziness that kids like my niece encounter from their high schools.

Once she was back in Buffalo and all the applications had been sent in, Jazmine began receiving letters from the colleges she had applied to. Several each week. Letters saying that, though her application had been received, some piece was missing, that a scholarship was available but only if she filled out three more forms and sent in another essay, letters informing her about interviews and school visits and financial aid. Sometimes multiple letters would arrive from different offices at the same school saying seemingly contradictory things. Or just baffling things: One admissions staffer told me that Jazmine's family income qualified her for a scholarship from New York State but, alas, that her grades were too *high.*

It is all too much to sort out, even for an upper-class "organization kid." Of late, college administrators have taken to complaining about the excessive involvement of parents in the admissions process, but let's face it: In order to deal with the bureaucratic nightmare of college applications you need constant adult supervision. Simplifying the admissions process won't guarantee more low-income students attend. But it couldn't hurt.

Naomi Schaefer Riley, "Not By Tuition Breaks Alone,"
The Wall Street Journal, May 2, 2008

Discussion Questions

First, work through the general questions on page 344. Then consider these:

1. Comment on the experience the writer's niece went through to get teacher recommendations for college. If you have gone through the same process before attending college, was your experience similar or different? Explain.
2. Evaluate the sample reprinted from the letter of recommendation Jazmine's AP English teacher wrote for her. What's wrong with it?
3. Explain the meaning of the title and show how it relates to the writer's claim.
4. What is the implication of this editorial? How can urban high schools do a better job of helping qualified students apply and get admitted to college? What can colleges do? And how did the situation get to be so bad in the first place?

Problems in Critical Reading—Evaluating Arguments

CHAPTER OBJECTIVES

Building on the skills you learned in Chapter 8, this chapter examines more complex elements of argumentation, specifically how to use a more sophisticated system for analyzing arguments and detecting flaws and weaknesses in persuasive writing. Learning to recognize deceptive techniques—whether they are intentional or unintentional—will sharpen your critical reading skills and safeguard your ability to think independently. The chapter ends with four more opinion pieces to analyze. In this chapter you will study:

- Inductive and deductive reasoning

- Analyzing the component parts of arguments

- Problems with arguments

- Emotional appeals in arguments

- Common logical fallacies

■ ANALYZING THE COMPONENT PARTS OF ARGUMENTS

In the next two sections you will learn to identify the components of arguments. We begin by isolating the various elements of a controversial environmental issue, followed by instruction in analyzing an opinion piece.

Analyzing a Current Issue—The Problem with Plastic Shopping Bags

Plastic shopping bags have been in the news in the past few years. In fact, some cities in the U.S. have voted to ban large chain supermarkets and drugstores from giving them to customers. First, study this *deductive syllogism* again:

> **Premise 1:**   Things that harm the environment should be banned.
> **Premise 2:**   Nonbiodegradable plastic shopping bags are harmful to the environment.
> **Conclusion:** Therefore, plastic bags should be banned.

Premise 1 is the assumption underlying the argument and also a claim of policy. Premise 2 is an example that derives from the claim; because it is a claim of fact, it proves the first premise true. The adjective "nonbiodegradable" qualifies the premise; not all shopping bags are harmful, only this kind. These two premises indisputably lead to the conclusion—in this case, a claim of policy—what "should" be done. Thus, we have a deductive argument; if the terms of the two premises are true, then the conclusion also must be true.

Now, to support the claim the writer adds *evidence,* something that confirms the truth of the conclusion. The writer might come up with these pieces of confirming evidence—examples and good reasons to prove the gravity of the problem:

- Nonbiodegradable plastic bags clog landfills, and landfill space is dwindling.
- Plastic shopping bags are made from petroleum, a nonrenewable natural resource.
- It's estimated that plastic bags take 1,000 years to break down (degrade).
- If seagulls and other sea creatures ingest plastic bags, they can suffocate and die.
- A huge floating mass of plastic in the Pacific Ocean has been variously estimated to be the size of Texas or the size of the U.S. Plastic bags account for some of this garbage patch.[1]

[1] You can find information online as well as images of this huge mass of floating plastic by typing in "Great Pacific Garbage Patch" or "Pacific Plastic Sea" into the search box of your favorite search engine.

Further, as you learned in Chapter 8, an argument may rest on *unstated assumptions*. Consider these three implicit assumptions that this argument rests on. Perhaps you can think of others.

- We have damaged the environment in the past. (a claim of fact)
- Many people want to restore and protect the environment. (an ethical concern)
- We must adopt serious measures to undo this damage. (a claim of policy)

Finally, there is the *refutation*. Remember that an argument with a refutation, however brief, is more convincing than one without. If the reader raises objections that the writer doesn't address, the argument loses effectiveness and cogency. For the plastic shopping bag issue, these three possibilities occurred to me as counterarguments that a good opinion writer might include:

- There are more pressing environmental problems to worry about than plastic shopping bags—for example, our dependence on fossil fuels, the melting of the polar ice caps, and given the severity of recent hurricanes and tornadoes, global warming.
- Science can find ways to recycle plastic bags to keep them out of landfills and the ocean.
- We need to educate people to use cloth bags when they go shopping and to recycle plastic bags rather than setting up costly mechanisms to prohibit them.

Putting It All Together: Analyzing an Opinion Piece

Now you are ready to apply the same skills you studied above to an opinion piece, following this analytical model. Printed below is an editorial titled "Educated, Unemployed and Frustrated" written by Matthew C. Klein, a 24-year old research associate at the Council on Foreign Relations. It was published on the opinion page of *The New York Times* on March 20, 2011, during the uprising in Egypt, which eventually became known as the Arab Spring.

The protests started in early 2011 in Tunisia, when a disgruntled young fruit seller, Muhammad Al Bouazizi, set himself on fire on a busy street. Al Bouazizi, a college graduate, was upset over not being able to find a job. To support himself, he had become a street fruit vendor, but he was hassled by government officials for not having a permit, among other perceived insults.[2] After this horrific incident, Tunisians began a series of street protests, and the revolution soon spread across the Middle East, fueled in great part by educated young people with bleak job prospects

---

[2] You can read about Muhammad Al Bouazizi's place in Arab history by typing in "Tunisian fruit seller" + "revolution" in the search box of any search engine.

E. **Refutation.** Klein does not include a refutation. Pretend that you are the writer. List one or two counterarguments that he might have used to refute the editorial's assessment of sufficient opportunities for the educated population.

_____

_____

F. **Summary Writing.** Klein's editorial is about 600 words. Write a summary of the piece that not does exceed 150 words, or roughly 25 percent of the original.

_____

_____

_____

_____

■ PROBLEMS WITH ARGUMENTS

With this background in mind, we can now turn to errors in reasoning that writers of argument sometimes make. The critical reader must be alert to weaknesses in arguments, because of either insufficient evidence, lack of sufficient grounds or backing, an unacceptable unstated assumption, various emotional appeals and logical fallacies, or any other of the myriad problems that arise in persuasive writing—whether out of the writer's laziness or ignorance, or the deliberate intent to mislead. To make identifying these problems easier, I have simplified the illustrative arguments.

Hasty or Unqualified Generalizations and Stereotyping

A common error in inductive reasoning results from conclusions derived from insufficient or unrepresentative evidence. **A hasty generalization** is an all-inclusive statement and is made "in haste," without allowing for exceptions and qualifiers. For example,

> One often reads or hears this generalization in the media: "It's time that we solve the federal deficit problem by enacting tax reform. The rich should pay their share of taxes."

What's wrong with this assertion? "The rich" are an easy target, since it is assumed that they are evading taxes and finding legal loopholes that are not available to the less wealthy or to the poor. The problem is that "the rich" is a generalized category with no qualifiers. The writer of this generalization offers no specific data about who constitutes the rich and why they don't pay their share of taxes.

Stereotyping is similar to the hasty generalization because it involves a sweeping characterization that admits no exceptions. Stereotyping typically refers to unfair and usually prejudicial generalizations about groups of people, based on their gender, age, ethnic background, race, attire, or other characteristics. For example, it's easy to recognize the stereotyping in a statement like this: "Asians must be really good in math. There are more Asians in my math classes than any other group, and that makes it hard for the rest of us who have to struggle just to pass."

But stereotyping doesn't just apply to groups of people; it can be used with places, as well. In California, where I live, for example, two universities have a reputation of being party schools—UC Santa Barbara and California State University, Chico. (Despite their best efforts to combat this reputation, these two campuses continue to appear on various lists of Best Party Colleges.) One might hear this, for example: "My cousin Bryan is going to Chico State next fall. I guess he's more interested in partying than in studying." Whether deserved or not, this is a stereotype—a single student is assumed to share the stereotyped characteristic. Obviously, there are serious, non-party-happy students at any college so identified.

Critical Thinking Exercise—Is Faber College a Party School?

Let's assume you are thinking of transferring to Faber College, which is not only affordable but which also offers an unusual program that you want to pursue. The college, however, also has a reputation for being a party school, and you are a serious student who wants to make the most of academic life. You know that stereotypes can be unfair, so you decide to verify this characterization by assembling objective data. Rather than merely soliciting opinions on websites like www.collegeconfidential.com, you visit the campus to do first-hand research. Who would be most likely to tell you the truth? What questions would you ask?

Incorrect Sampling

Inductive arguments often include a **sampling** of a larger group, which, if done incorrectly, can produce a flawed conclusion. Consider the results of this study based on a sample: In 2000 a team of scientists at the University of California at Berkeley published a study in the science journal *Nature* saying that differences in finger lengths might yield clues to sexual orientation. In brief, the researchers found that lesbians had more "masculine" hands than heterosexual women. Supposedly, the index fingers of lesbians—unlike those of heterosexual women—are significantly shorter than their ring fingers. The researchers concluded that "homosexual women were exposed to greater levels of fetal andro-gen than heterosexual women." (Quoted in Carl T. Hall, "Finger Length Points to Sexual Orientation," *San Francisco Chronicle,* March 30, 2000.) This article was picked up by the national media and had women all over the country measuring their index fingers.

However, the method of sampling was problematic: The scientists had set up booths at gay pride events in Berkeley and San Francisco. Then they offered willing participants a free $1 lottery ticket if they agreed to have their hands measured and to answer a detailed questionnaire. The team examined the hands of 720 adults.

Why is this an example of faulty inductive reasoning? Wouldn't 720 pairs of hands be enough evidence to lead to a valid conclusion?

A similar problem can arise from faulty deductive reasoning, if the argument is based on an untrue premise or if the premise is an unaccept-able generalization. Consider this syllogism.

Premise 1:   All Frenchmen are good lovers.

Premise 2:   Raoul is French.

Conclusion: Therefore Raoul is a good lover.

Because Raoul has been placed in a class in which all the members are said to share the same characteristic, the statement is valid. Therefore, we can deduce (arrive at the conclusion) that he shares that character-istic. Yet the argument is unacceptable and therefore unsound because the major premise—that all Frenchmen are good lovers—is obviously untrue, representing a generalization that could be easily invalidated by only one unromantic Frenchman. Many sloppy or weak arguments de-rive from such errors.

Notice that this argument rests on a faulty inductive argument, which might be diagrammed like this:

Evidence: Claude is a romantic lover who has left behind a string of broken hearts.

Evidence: André is such a good lover that he has all the women swooning.

Evidence: Jules is a connoisseur of romance and is an excellent lover.

Conclusion: Therefore all Frenchman are good lovers.

What is wrong with this conclusion?

Faulty deductive reasoning can also proceed from an unsound or unacceptable assumption (or warrant). For example, consider this argument:

Premise 1:   Only English speakers should be allowed to vote.

Premise 2:   This group of people cannot speak English.

Conclusion: These people should not be allowed to vote.

Here, Premise 1 rests upon a restrictive assumption that not everyone would accept. While there are other ways in which syllogisms can be invalid or unsound, they lie outside the scope of this text. Suffice it to say that the careful reader should be alert to arguments proceeding from faulty inductive arguments and faulty deductive syllogism.

Practice Exercise 1

Each of the following arguments is faulty, containing one of these errors in reasoning: generalization, stereotyping, incorrect (small) sampling, questionable premise.

1. A salesman who travels for a living is looking for a new car and says this: "Over the years I've bought several South Korean and Japanese models, but they never last more than 100,000 miles, and they seem always to need expensive repairs. From now on I'm buying German cars. Everyone knows that Germans are the best automotive engineers in the world." _____

   _____

2. It's no wonder the security personnel at Denver International Airport took a passenger aside for a more thorough search before allowing him to board my flight. He looked distinctly Middle Eastern.

   _____

3. I don't see why people get so upset about small children seeing violent movies. Before the new codes went into effect, I took my seven-year-old nephew to see horror movies all the time, and he turned out all right. You don't see him committing violent crimes!

   _____

4. A college instructor with five years of experience observes that students who sit in the front rows of a classroom get A's and B's, and those who sit in the back of the room get C's or lower. He concludes that all college students should sit closer to the front of the room.

   _____

5. A study of 219 students enrolled in education classes at Ohio State University revealed that students who use Facebook had lower overall GPAs and studied ten hours less a week than students who did not use

the social website. The students surveyed were those attending class on the day the two researchers conducted the study. So I guess college students who use Facebook are jeopardizing their studies. (See Practice Exercise 7 in Chapter 8 for a fuller explanation of the study and its results.) _____

Armed with this foundation in examining the structure of arguments, we can now turn to some manipulative techniques writers use to get readers to accept conclusions they might otherwise reject. In this section, we will look at appeals and at logical fallacies.

■ APPEALS IN ARGUMENTS

Writers of argumentative and persuasive prose often use emotional and manipulative appeals. An **appeal** is something that makes an argument attractive, worth considering, or plausible. Appeals are not necessarily bad, unless there is no other evidence to support the argument. But an argument that relies *solely* on an emotional appeal is actually a type of fallacy, in other words, false reasoning. As you will see later, advertisers commonly appeal to various needs—the need to be loved, to be attractive, to be popular or cool, and so forth.

When you examine a persuasive piece of writing, ask yourself this question: How good is this argument or product *without the appeal*? Is there any evidence? Strip away the fluff from the argument and examine the claim *for itself*, unobscured by emotion or sentiment. Be aware that the more emotional the appeal, the weaker the argument. This section examines several types of appeals, which I have divided into two sections—emotional appeals and other manipulative appeals. A practice exercise follows each section.

■ EMOTIONAL APPEALS

Appeal to Authority

An argument that uses the **appeal to authority** allows the claim to rest solely on the fact that a supposed authority is behind it. There are various types of false appeals to authority. The authority may not be identified ("Doctors say. . ." or "Nine out of ten dentists recommend"). An authority may be biased because he or she has something to gain financially from our accepting their position. For example, when Nina and Tim Zagat write that the restaurant industry will survive economic downturns, they are authorities by virtue their occupation as publishers of the annual Zagat Survey and the popular Zagat.com restaurant review website. But because their livelihoods depend on people eating at restaurants, they are not completely unbiased authorities.

An authority may be irrelevant. Here is one example: Linus Pauling, a two-time Nobel Prize winner and professor of chemistry at Stanford University, believed that massive doses of Vitamin C could prevent cancer. The fact that a famous scientist believes something doesn't make it so, and in this case, the scientific and medical community rejected this theory. Pauling was a chemist, not a cancer specialist.

Finally, we have the vague appeal to some past authority: "The Bible tells us" or "Kennedy believed" or "Martin Luther King, Jr. was often quoted as saying," or "Shakespeare observed. . . ." One can find quotations to fit any position, but they are not evidence or proof—just an appeal to a supposed authority.

Appeal to Fear

The **appeal to fear** arouses fear about what will happen if we adopt (or fail to adopt) a certain course. Probably the most relevant and recent example was the War on Terror, a term deliberately chosen to keep the public in a high state of fear and anxiety. The Bush administration used the War on Terror to justify governmental intrusions that the public might otherwise find unacceptable (some provisions of the Patriot Act, like warrantless wiretapping and investigating the books certain people borrow from the library, are only two examples).

During the long and acrimonious debate over health care reform, one provision caused a great deal of controversy. The provision was to allow payment for "end-of-life counseling," meaning that doctors would consult with terminally ill patients and their families about living wills, health care proxy, hospice options, and pain medications. (The proposal was that Medicare would reimburse doctors for such counseling.) Former Alaska Governor, Sarah Palin, began calling this a proposal to institute "death panels," preying on people's fears that terminally ill patients would be forced to accept minimal end-of-life care to reduce the cost of caring for them. This blatant appeal to fear was so successful that the provision was dropped from the final bill.

In 2009, Swiss voters were asked to vote on a referendum banning minarets, structures built next to mosques to call Muslims to prayer. The Muslim population in Switzerland is small, estimated at around 400,000, or about 6 percent, of a population of 7.5 million. There has been a great deal of anti-Muslim sentiment in Europe recently (particularly in France), and sentiments have been running high. This photo was distributed by the Swiss People's Party, one of the backers of the referendum. Notice that the minarets look like missile weapons. The slogan in French means "Yes to the ban on minarets!"

The ad campaign—which appealed to Swiss voters' fears about Muslim immigrants—was successful. The vote was 57.5 to 42.5 to ban minarets. (Alexander G. Higgins, "Minaret Ban Approved by Wide Margin." Associated Press, November 30, 2009.)

Photo of Swiss People's Party poster—anti-minaret campaign. Reprinted in the *San Francisco Chronicle*, November 28, 2009, pA4.

Appeal to Patriotism	The British writer and dictionary maker Samuel Johnson once observed: "Patriotism is the last refuge of scoundrels." The **appeal to patriotism** (also called "jingoism") suggests that an argument is worth holding out of loyalty to one's country or to one's political party or to some other group to which we belong. The appeal implies the accusation that going against the country's or group's policies is wrong or even treasonous. The naming of the measures used to counter terrorism after 9/11—the Patriot Act— was undoubtedly chosen just for this reason, as an appeal to patriotism.

- If you were a true American patriot, you would support American foreign policy.
- Common bumper sticker during the Vietnam War: "America: Love it or leave it."
- If my union tells its members to vote for Joe Santini for mayor, it must be right.

Appeal to Pity or Sympathy	Should we accept an argument simply because we feel sorry for someone? An **appeal to sympathy** or **pity** asks us to suspend our critical judgment because we pity a victim of sad circumstances or because we can identify with someone else's troubles.

- The fact that Emma Jones hasn't paid her rent for six months is no reason for her landlord to evict her. Her husband died, she recently found out that she suffers from high blood pressure, and she has three children to support on her salary as a Walmart sales clerk. (How might one argue for the landlord's right to evict a nonpaying tenant without sounding so hard-hearted and without resorting to blatant appeals to sympathy?)

- When President Barack Obama nominated Sonia Sotomayor to be the nation's first Latino Supreme Court Justice, much was made of these facts: She was of Puerto Rican descent, she was raised by a single mother in the Bronx, and she was the first member of her family to attend college (Princeton University and Yale University Law School). Was her background a legitimate reason to support her candidacy, or does it seem more like an appeal to sympathy?

- After South Carolina governor Mark Sanford was caught having an affair with his Argentine mistress after disappearing ("walking the Appalachian Trail"), he said this: "This was a whole lot more than a simple affair, this was a love story. A forbidden one, a tragic one, but a love story at the end of the day." (Quoted in an Associated Press story, July 1, 2009.)

Appeal to Prejudice

Like the appeal to fear, the **appeal to prejudice** uses popular prejudices to convince others of the correctness of one's position. The intention is to inflame negative feelings, beliefs, or stereotypes about racial, ethnic, or religious groups or about gender or sexual orientations. Emotion replaces reasoned discourse.

- Of course the federal government should build a fence along the Mexican border. Illegal immigrants sneak across the border now and take jobs away from Americans who are out of work, and then once they're here their children automatically become American citizens.

- I don't see what's wrong with TSA singling out airline passengers who look Middle Eastern and subjecting them to further patdowns and searches. You don't see little old ladies or small children trying to bring down airplanes.

- All right-thinking people know that people on welfare are just a bunch of lazy freeloaders who are nothing more than social parasites.

- Why would a man ever want to become a nurse? After all, women are the traditional caregivers in our culture.

Appeal to Tradition

An **appeal to tradition** asks us to accept a practice because it has always been done that way or because it represents some long-standing venerable tradition. During the financial crisis of 2008, Americans heard a lot about why the government should bail out General Motors—because it was a respected corporation and an important component of the Dow Jones Industrial Average and had employed generations of auto workers.

GM was often described as being "too big to fail," which also implied that it was too old to fail. Here are two more examples of the appeal to tradition:

- The Roman Catholic Church has forbidden women to become priests for nearly 2,000 years. Why should the Church abandon this practice now?
- The Democratic party has always stood up for the working class. That's why I'm a Democrat.

Practice Exercise 2

Using the information in the preceding section, study these examples and identify the emotional appeal each represents. For easier reference, the appeals are listed here:

- Appeal to authority
- Appeal to patriotism
- Appeal to prejudice
- Appeal to fear
- Appeal to pity or sympathy
- Appeal to tradition

1. If God wanted gays to marry, he would have created Adam and Steve instead of Adam and Eve.

   Appeal:_____

2. The San Francisco Board of Supervisors recently enacted a law requiring residents to separate their compostable trash from regular garbage and recycling. One Supervisor, Sean Elsbernd, voted against the measure, saying that the new law "takes Big Brother to an extreme I'm not comfortable with. I don't want the government going through my garbage."

   Appeal: _____

3. Governor Rod Blagojevich of Illinois was forced out of office in 2009 after allegations of corruption and abuse of power. The charges were so serious that Blagojevich has been barred from public office in Illinois for the rest of his life. When he talked to reporters after the vote to oust him, Blagojevich called the verdict "un-American," and added: "There are tens of thousands of people across America just like me who are losing their jobs, or who have lost their jobs." (Quoted in Karl Lydersen and Peter Slevin, *The Washington Post,* January 30, 2009)

   Appeal: _____

4. Michael Crichton, a writer of popular science-based novels, was trained as a medical doctor at Harvard. Before his death, he questioned the problem of global warming, claiming that it was merely a fad and rejecting the conclusions reached by the National Academy of Sciences. He argued that rising temperatures have not resulted from human

activities, like burning fossil fuels. One of his last novels, *State of Fear,* used this perspective as the basis for the plot.

Appeal: _____

5. In the last days of the 2008 presidential campaign, Pennsylvania's Republican Party sent an e-mail to 75,000 Jewish voters across the state addressed to "Fellow Jewish Voters." The e-mail included these statements: "In the 5,769 years of our people, there has never been a more important time for us to take pro-active measures in order to stop a second Holocaust. . . . Many of our ancestors ignored the warning signs in the 1930s and 1940s and made a tragic mistake. Let's not make a similar one this year." (Quoted in Bonnie Goldstein, "How the GOP Scares Jews," www.slate.com. Posted October 28, 2008)

Appeal: _____

6. The government should not have forced the Citadel, a military college in South Carolina, to admit women. The Citadel has always been a men's college, and it should have been allowed to stay that way.

Appeal: _____

7. During the impeachment trial of President Bill Clinton, Democratic Senator Dale Bumpers from Arkansas urged his Senate colleagues to drop the impeachment hearings, arguing that the Clintons "have been about as decimated as a family can get." Bumpers continued: "The relationship between husband and wife, father and child, has been incredibly strained, if not destroyed. There's been nothing but sleep-less nights, mental agony for this family for almost five years." (Quoted in "Ex-Senator Pleads with His Old Friends to Acquit," *San Francisco Chronicle,* January 22, 1999)

Appeal: _____

8. Letter to the editor (paraphrased): Those so-called homeless people who hold up signs at intersections saying "Will Work for Food" are just scam artists and slackers. What they really mean is "Will Gladly Take Your Money." Work is the last thing on their minds!

Appeal: _____

Other Manipulative Appeals

Appeals to the emotion are not the only way writers of opinion pieces can influence our thinking. Like appeals to the emotions, these appeals manipulate and trick the unwary reader into accepting the argument or entice the unwary consumer to buy a product, based not on its quality but on something associated with it, as you will see in this next section.

Alaska. . . We have trade missions back and forth." This prompted CNN political analyst Paul Begala to remark, "I can see the moon from my backyard, so I'm an astronaut"—a clear instance of ridicule.

- Palin herself used the manipulative appeal of ridicule during her acceptance speech as McCain's running mate. Noting that Barack Obama had been a community organizer in Chicago, Palin, who was formerly mayor of Wasilla, Alaska, said this: "Being a mayor is kind of like a community organizer, except that you have actual responsibilities."

Testimonial

The **testimonial** appeal is a staple of television and magazine advertisements, in which a person is paid to endorse a product. One technique is to use celebrities (called "celebrity endorsements"). Actor William Shatner, of "Star Trek" fame, has endorsed both lasik eye treatments and Priceline.com. Russian-born tennis star Maria Sharapova signed a contract with Nike in 2010 worth $70 million over eight years. One might argue that Sharapova is an authority on athletic footwear (presumably as long as she wears Nikes on the court). However, such endorsements carry risk if the celebrity becomes ensnared in scandals that by extension taint the product he or she has endorsed. This has happened in recent years with three sports figures—football players Michael Vick and Brett Favre and championship golfer Tiger Woods. Still, there is a subliminal process at work here: if a prominent figure—a singer, an athlete, an actor or actress—endorses a product, the implication is that it must be good. Testimonial is similar to transfer, as you will see in the next section.

The trend today in advertising is toward using real people—often people who aren't particularly attractive or who are overweight or who wear glasses (in other words, people who look "just like the rest of us") rather than celebrities, to serve as testimonials. Using real people—housewives, office workers, computer users, teachers—lends a certain verisimilitude to the advertisement. You can flip through the pages of any magazine or watch television for just a few minutes to see examples of both types of testimonial.

Transfer

Like testimonial, the manipulative appeal known as **transfer** is most commonly associated with advertising. By using transfer, the advertiser suggests that favorable associations about a product will transfer or carry over to the consumer. In this case the image is almost more important than the product itself. Advertisers identify this phenomenon as "selling the sizzle, not the steak." A glance through *Cosmopolitan, GQ, Marie Claire, Self,* and similar glossy magazines will yield many examples of transfer. (Note that transfer operates with the appeals of both flattery and just plain folks.) Liquor, automobile, and cigarette ads make liberal use of transfer, with beautiful people laughing as they drink scotch, gorgeous models standing next to the car being advertised, or the Marlboro man riding off into the range.

A classic example of transfer can be seen in the old TV commercial from the 1980s for Vick's Cough Syrup starring Peter Bergman, who played a doctor on the soap opera *The Young and the Restless*. Bergman, who wore a white physician's coat for this ad, uttered this famous line: "I'm not a doctor, but I play one on TV." Not only is this an appeal to a false authority, but the white physician's coat "transferred" the aura of a real doctor to the actor.

Transfer can be used to ascribe more than a fake authority; it can also be used to ascribe greater knowledge or intelligence to a person by using a carefully chosen backdrop. In December 2006, President Bush gave an address to the nation about his new strategy for the Iraq war, which, by all accounts, was going badly. At the time only 25 percent of the American public approved of Bush's handling of the war. The address was filmed in the White House library, and as Bush spoke, behind him a bookcase was clearly visible filled with leatherbound books, thus giving Bush, who was not known for his intellectualism, a scholarly, bookish demeanor.

Practice Exercise 3

Using the information in the preceding section, study these examples and identify the emotional appeal each represents. For easier reference, the appeals are listed again.

- Bandwagon appeal
- Just plain folks
- Ridicule
- Transfer

- Flattery
- Name calling
- Testimonial

1. Let's face it. More than 75 percent of the American people in a recent poll voiced concern that the war in Afghanistan isn't going well and that we should leave. All those people can't be wrong.
   Appeal: _____

2. In spring 2001 President George W. Bush gave two speeches on national parks. In one, Bush stood before a magnificent giant sequoia in Sequoia National Park; the other occurred in the Florida Everglades, where the backdrop was a grove of sawgrass and mangrove. (Note: Bush was not known during his two administrations for being a supporter of the green or environmental movement.)
   Appeal: _____

3. Republican Fred Thompson became wealthy as a Washington lobbyist and later as an actor on *Law and Order*. In 1994, Thompson decided to run for the Senate in his home state of Tennessee. He bought a used red truck, "not too flashy or macho," and drove it around the state campaigning for votes.
   Appeal: _____

4. Paint store clerk to author: "Why did you choose Benjamin Moore paint to use on your bookcases?"

   Author: "I heard it's the best paint on the market."

   Clerk: "You made the right decision. Benjamin Moore paint is definitely the best paint available. You can't go wrong choosing it."

   Appeal(s): _____

5. Commentator Frank Gaffrey said this about the terrorists who bombed London's subways in 2005: "In the wake of July's London transport bombings by home-grown British Islamists, the dangers of mistaking one type of Muslim community for another have become obvious. Prime Minister Tony Blair's government has gone from ignoring Islamofascists in its midst—if not actually accommodating their efforts to proselytize and recruit in Britain—to cracking down forcefully on their activities and presence in the United Kingdom." (Quoted in *Jewish World Review,* August 30, 2005.) Notice that the word "Islamists" in the first sentence becomes "Islamofascists" in the second sentence. Consider the latter word.

   Appeal: _____

6. In February 2010 Former Republican VP candidate Sarah Palin addressed the Tea Party's convention in Nashville. Part of her speech was devoted to the government's stimulus plan of 2009, which had injected billions of dollars into the economy to stimulate jobs and to get people spending money again. Referring to President Barack Obama's stimulus plan, Palin said this: "Now, this was all part of that hope and change and transparency. And now a year later I've got to ask those supporters of all that: How's that hopey-changey stuff working out for you?"

   Appeal: _____

7. Pop singer Rhianna, Drew Barrymore, Ellen DeGeneres, and Queen Latifah have all appeared in recent magazine advertisements touting CoverGirl products, promoting sales of foundation, mascara, and moisturizers.

   Appeal: _____

8. After Sonia Sotomayor caused a ruckus with her "wise Latina" comment (see the worldview section in Chapter 8), she appeared at her confirmation hearing on Capitol Hill wearing a cast and walking on crutches, the result of a broken ankle. Conservative radio host Rush Limbaugh had this to say: "I hope she can find a wise Latina doctor to set that ankle as opposed to an average white doctor, because the wise Latina doctor has much richer experience with broken ankles, and would probably do a much better job of setting that ankle than an average white doctor who has not lived the rich experiences of a Latina med student." (Quoted in an Associated Press article by Julia Hirschfeld Davis, June 9, 2009)

   Appeal: _____

Online Learning Center—The Appeal to "Cool"

There is one more emotional and manipulative appeal that is generally not included in discussions of this topic, but it has become so prevalent in our consumer society that it is worth mentioning. Apple is the master at the appeal to "cool"—the wow or I-have-to-have-it factor that a release of one of Apple's new products elicits—iPhones, iPods, the iPad, in particular. To see an ad using this technique, go to YouTube, type in "iPhone4 vs HTC Evo" and scroll down to the one made by "tinywatchproductions." (There are lots of imitators). The purchaser wants an Apple iPhone so badly that she refuses to listen to all the arguments promoting the other brand. An alternative is to watch the latest television ad for the latest model of iPad or iPhone.

9. The liberal antiwar activist group, MoveOn, accused General Petraeus, former war commander in Iraq, of putting a positive spin on the war's progress. The group sponsored an ad in *The New York Times* that also appeared on their website that said, "General Petraeus or General Betray Us."

   Appeal: _____

10. During the presidential campaign of 2007–2008, Michele Obama gave speeches to supporters. During the course of several speeches, she complained about Barack Obama's habit of leaving dirty socks lying around and not putting the butter away after breakfast.

    Appeal: _____

Legitimate Appeals in Argument

You are probably wondering if there is such a thing as an acceptable appeal. Indeed, an argument can legitimately appeal to our nobler instincts. This excerpt from an editorial printed in the *International Herald Tribune* describes the situation an Iraqi Christian woman named Rita faced. Rita had helped the Americans by sharing information about impending terrorist attacks on U.S. military forces. Seeking revenge, insurgents kidnapped her 16-year-old son and demanded a ransom. After paying the ransom, her husband divorced her because he blamed her cooperation with the Americans for their son's kidnapping. The husband then took the son and their daughter to Syria, where they disappeared. Rita asked for asylum in the United States, but she will not be admitted to the United States without a waiver from the homeland security office. Here is the relevant excerpt:

> Does this woman, who lost everything because she worked for the Americans, who had a security clearance from our government to work in its embassy, pose a threat to the United States? If she does, then who doesn't?
>
> After all this time, we see hearts and minds as bombs and guns. If we cannot recover such basic distinctions, then we have surely lost more than the war.
>
> Five years before we invaded Iraq, one senator had the remarkable foresight to speak about our responsibility to any Iraqis who might help the United States: "If we would have people in Iraq, or elsewhere in the world, trust us and work with us, then we need to take care that the United States maintains a reputation for trustworthiness and for taking care of its friends." He was even more direct about what was at stake: "The world will

be watching and judging how America treats people who are seen to be on our side. We cannot afford to foster a perception of unfairness that will make it more difficult for the United States to recruit supporters in the future." So spoke Senator Kyl in 1998.[3]

Kirk W. Johnson, "Abandoned by America,"
The International Herald Tribune, April 19, 2007

■ LOGICAL FALLACIES: PART 1

Logical fallacies are errors in reasoning or defects present in an argument, thereby either weakening or invalidating it. If logical supporting evidence is present, then the fallacy only weakens the argument. But if the argument rests entirely on the fallacy, meaning that the only evidence is the error in reasoning, then the argument can be deemed invalid and therefore not worth considering. The difficulty with logical fallacies is that they are so common that they sound right; also, as you will see in the following examples, they can seem very persuasive, unless you take the trouble to analyze them objectively based on the characteristics of each type. Because these fallacies are somewhat difficult, I have divided the thirteen most basic fallacies into two sections arranged alphabetically; a practice exercise follows each section. It should be noted that, like emotional appeals, not all fallacies are purposely intended to manipulate or to deceive the unwary reader. Many writers lapse into them as a result of ignorance or sloppy thinking.

Ad Hominem
Argument

Ad hominem in Latin literally means "to the man." This fallacy can take two forms: The first is to attack the person's personality traits or events in his or her life rather than his or her position on an issue. For example, calling George W. Bush "stupid" and a "lightweight" or Barack Obama "arrogant" and "cerebral" or Hillary Clinton "cold" and "cerebral" is unfair if these characterizations are irrelevant to their positions on the issues. Here is a typical argument using the ad hominem fallacy:

- New York Democratic Representative Anthony Weiner made headlines and became the butt of jokes in 2011 when it was revealed that he had "sexted" (sent provocative photos of himself) several women he was corresponding with online via Twitter and Facebook. It didn't help his case that Weiner is married, that his wife is pregnant with their first child, and that he lied for two weeks before finally confessing the truth. Many Republicans and some Democrats called for his resignation, saying that he was unfit for office. (He eventually did resign.) The question is: Should a politician's personal life (extramarital affairs, sending provocative photos of oneself to women, one's sexual preferences) be

[3] Jon Kyl is the junior Republican U.S. senator from Arizona. He has announced that he will not seek another term.

grounds for criticism? In the case of Weiner (and President Clinton before him), it appeared that the problem was not the bad behavior, but the lying and stonewalling that followed it, which might indeed suggest a serious character flaw. It's a difficult question, but if the argument rests solely on the personal attack, the fallacy remains.

The second form attacks the character and reputation of the person because of individuals he or she associates with (guilt by association), rather than on the basis of his or her actions. Here are some examples:

- During the Vietnam War, Vice President Spiro Agnew characterized intellectuals (who were generally opposed to President Nixon's war policies) with this famous alliterative phrase—"nattering nabobs of negativism"—thereby attacking their collective character rather than the principles they stood for.
- Letter to the editor (paraphrased): Republican Senator Bill Frist of Tennessee should never have been nominated to take over as Senate Majority Leader. His father and brother founded HCA, the hospital corporation that got itself into a lot of legal trouble for various wrongdoings.
- Barack Obama was accused of being friends with terrorists when it was revealed that he had crossed paths in Chicago with William Ayers at various meetings of nonprofit agencies in the years prior to the presidential campaign. A retired professor of education at the University of Illinois at Chicago, Ayers was a co-founder of the Weather Underground, a revolutionary group that was engaged in bombing public buildings in the 1960s and 1970s as a form of protest against the Vietnam War. Fallacy _____

Begging the Question

The term **begging the question** is often misunderstood and misused. The phrase is commonly used to mean "to raise the question." In this sense, the phrase is not a fallacy. As a logical fallacy, *begging the question* means that a writer asserts to be true an idea that has not yet been proved to be true. In other words, the person making the argument is saying, "This is true because this is true." This unproved "truth" then becomes the basis of the discussion. A simpler way of understanding this fallacy is to think of it as a circular argument: The writer assumes to be true that which it is his duty to prove. The classic example of this fallacy is this question: When did you stop beating your wife? Either a yes or a no answer confirms that the person either has beaten his wife or still beats her, when in fact that charge itself needs to be established. Here are two more examples:

- Teenager to parent: "What's so bad about drinking alcohol?" Parent: "It's not good for you."
- Who is the best person to censor controversial articles in the campus newspaper? In phrasing the question like this, the writer begs the question, assuming without proof that censorship of the campus newspaper is desirable in the first place.

Cause-Effect Fallacies

Fallacies involving cause-effect relationships can be divided into two types:

False Cause

This first type results either from citing a false or a remote cause to explain a situation or from oversimplifying the cause of a complicated issue.

- Letter to the editor (paraphrased): Has anyone else noticed that all of these schoolyard killings have occurred in suburban areas and that minorities are never responsible for such acts? This tells me that the suburbs breed violence more than inner cities.

- Signs along I-5, the major north-south Interstate Highway in California: "Congress Created Dust Bowl," next to which are dusty, unplanted fields. The Dust Bowl that affected the Great Plains states in the 1930s was caused by a combination of factors: poor farming techniques, a severe drought, and winds that blew away rich top soil. Although the highway signs point to Congress as the culprit, in fact it was a federal judge who restricted water shipments to California's Central Valley farmers to protect the state's fisheries. Many Central Valley farmers had to let their fields go fallow—hence the signs up and down Interstate 5. But this argument is fallacious in another way, because it rests on a false cause. The 1930s Dust Bowl was created by a combination of human and environmental factors, not because of government restrictions on the water supply.

Post Hoc, Ergo Propter Hoc

This second kind of cause-effect fallacy comes from Latin and means "after this, therefore because of this." The fallacy suggests that because event B occurred after event A, event A caused event B; in other words, the writer makes a connection based on chronology. This fallacy accounts for many silly superstitions, for example, when someone breaks a mirror and then blames that action for seven years of bad luck.

- Yesterday I forgot to wear my special Hawkeye hat during the annual Michigan-Iowa football game. No wonder Iowa lost.

- Every time a Democrat gets into the White House, the U.S. experiences a budget crisis. That's why I didn't vote Democratic in the last presidential primary.

- One problem with cause-and-effect arguments is that it may be difficult to determine which is the cause and which is the effect. For example, a recent study showed that pregnancy rates are higher among teens who watch TV programs with a lot of sexy dialog and plot lines. Teenage girls who watched programs like this were twice as likely, according to the researchers, to become pregnant over the next three years, as opposed to girls who didn't watch such programs.[4] But does one really cause the other? Is it possible that teenage girls who are experimenting with unprotected sex

[4]Lindsey Tanner, "Teen Pregnancy Linked to Sexy TV," Associated Press, November 3, 2008.

are more attracted to programs of this nature? So rather than the programs causing the increased pregnancy rate, there really might not be any definitive cause-effect relationship at all. Or perhaps it's just a coincidence.

Either-Or Fallacy

Sometimes called **false dilemma**, the either-or fallacy discusses an issue as if there are only two alternatives available, thereby ignoring other possibilities. Rejecting one choice requires one to accept the other. Here are some examples:

- A conservative writes this about the new TSA rules authorizing body scans or patdowns at U.S. airports: "These searches are intrusive, but they're better than crossing the country in a covered wagon."
- In the summer of 2011, Secretary of State Hillary Clinton appealed to Congressional Democrats to continue to support U.S. military involvement in Libya by asking this blunt question: "Whose side are you on— Moammar Khadafy or the Libyan people?"
- Letter to editor (paraphrased): In our emphasis on safety, pools with diving boards are no longer allowed. Having dived competitively in high school and college, I had planned to teach my sons to dive, but our world is now so sanitized that there's nothing left for a boy to do but stay indoors and play violent video games.

Evasion

Evasion is a fallacy that occurs when a speaker or writer evades or ignores the question by talking around it.

- In August 1997 the Democratic National Committee was under investigation for questionable fund-raising practices. When asked for his reaction to recent revelations about the alleged laundering of foreign money into the DNC coffers, President Clinton responded, "I was sick at heart" and "disappointed."
- Pastor Rick Warren asked Barack Obama, during the Presidential campaign in 2008, what his thoughts were about when life begins, undoubtedly hoping to elicit his views on abortion. Obama replied, rather snippily some critics said, that the question of when life begins was "beyond my pay grade."

Practice Exercise 4

Study the following arguments carefully and decide which of these fallacies each represents.

- *Ad hominem* argument
- Begging the question
- Either-or fallacy (false dilemma)
- Evasion
- False cause
- *Post hoc, ergo propter hoc*

1. The Lytton band of Pomo Indians has proposed building a gigantic casino in San Pablo with 2,500 slot machines. Because more and more people are becoming addicted to gambling, I am opposed to this project.
   Fallacy: _____

2. Jack read a recent newspaper article summarizing a study that found Danes to be the happiest people on earth. Jack tells his roommate about this finding, and adds: "You know, even though the citizens of Denmark pay 65 percent of their income in taxes, they are still happy. Denmark has full health care for everyone. No wonder they're so happy."

Fallacy: _____

3. When it was learned that none of Republican Presidential candidate Mitt Romney's five sons were enlisted in the military during the Iraq war, Romney had this to say: "One of the ways my sons are showing support for our nation is helping me get elected because they think I'd be a great president." (Quoted in Glen Johnson, "Romney Defends Sons' Lack of Military Service," Associated Press, August 9, 2007.)

Fallacy: _____

4. The President of XYZ Widget Company reports, "The recent settlement between management and the labor union was a huge mistake: Giving in to the union's demands for a wage increase has resulted in low production figures."

Fallacy: _____

5. A speechwriter for President George W. Bush, David Frum, wrote in 2001 that North Korea, Iran, and Iraq constituted the "Axis of Evil" because their leaders are vicious and evil.

Fallacy: _____

6. Before the terrorist attacks on the World Trade Center, a tenant in one of the complex's office buildings bought a large insurance policy that specifically referred to terrorist attacks. He must have had advance knowledge that the buildings would be destroyed.

Fallacy: _____

7. Charlie Gibson, news anchor at ABC, asked President George W. Bush in an interview at Camp David whether he would still have waged war against Iraq in 2005 if he had known that Saddam Hussein, in fact, did not possess Weapons of Mass Destruction. Bush replied, "You know, that's an interesting question. That is a do-over that I can't do. It's hard for me to speculate."

Fallacy: _____

8. During the 2008 presidential campaign, Republican nominee John McCain released a television ad in which his Democratic opponent, Barack Obama, was referred to as a "celebrity." The ad intercut photos of Obama with images of Britney Spears and Paris Hilton.

Fallacy: _____

9. During a murder trial, the prosecuting attorney asks the jury, "Does it make sense to release this murderer so he can commit the same atrocities again and again? We need to lock this person up for a very long time so that he can never kill someone again."

Fallacy: _____

10. In 2002 Oregon's Measure 23 asked voters to approve a single payer or universal health care system. Supporters of the measure, which was defeated in the election, had argued that the big medical and health insurance companies were pouring a lot of money into the campaign to defeat the measure. They concluded that if big corporations opposed it, it must have been a good bill.
    Fallacy: _____

11. Letter to the editor (paraphrased): I listen to my iPod in class all the time, and I still have an A average. I don't think that my school has any right to ban students from listening to iPods in class. They should put their energy into helping students pass the state high school exit exam, not acting like the iPod police.
    Fallacy: _____

12. All those terrorists being held at Guantanamo Bay deserve to be there. If they weren't terrorists, then they wouldn't have been arrested or been detained.
    Fallacy: _____

13. Sidney has read a great deal about the increase in the number of children diagnosed with autism in recent years. He notices that this increase coincided with the wide adoption of cell phones and Wi-Fi. Sidney says, "I wager that autism must have something to do with these new forms of technology."
    Fallacy: _____

14. In France, where face-covering veils worn by Muslim women are now prohibited, Roman Catholic Monsignor Andre Vingt-Trois said that he does not oppose the anti-veil rules; however, he doesn't want to see the government intrude in the way people dress. He was quoted as saying, "Shall we choose between the full-body veil and nude women in ads on top of four-wheel drive [cars]?" (Associated Press, January 26, 2010)
    Fallacy: _____

Critical Thinking Exercise—False Cause or Post Hoc, Ergo Propter Hoc

After a series of earthquakes around the world in 2010 (Haiti, China, Puerto Rico, and Chile), Iranian president Mahmoud Ahmadinejad said that the recent number of devastating earthquakes is caused by women dressing immodestly. Iranian women traditionally wear either the chador (a full length cloak) or the hijab (a head covering), but many young women have adopted Western dress.

This is clearly a cause-effect fallacy, but which one?

■ LOGICAL FALLACIES: PART 2

False Analogy   As you will recall from Chapter 4, an analogy discusses one subject in terms of another, completely different subject. Although it does not carry the same force as factual evidence or good reasons, arguing by analogy can be effective and persuasive in supporting an argument. An analogy can break down, however, and become a **false analogy** if there are fewer similarities than differences, if the resemblance is remote or ambiguous, or if there is no connection between the two subjects at all. For example, consider this argument:

- A few years ago, I bought a pedigreed German shepherd puppy from a reputable dog breeder. After the dog was found to have a serious defect requiring expensive corrective surgery, I asked the breeder to compensate me for half of the surgery's cost. The breeder argued: "You wouldn't expect your obstetrician to reimburse you if she delivered your baby and found that the baby needed surgery."

This argument rests on the dubious comparison of a dog breeder and a pediatrician. Let's examine these two occupations to see why the analogy (actually an extended false comparison) breaks down:

- The dog breeder is in the business of breeding dogs. The parents create the baby, not the obstetrician.
- The dog breeder sells dogs for a fee; the obstetrician collects no fee for the baby itself, only for the delivery.
- This dog breeder offered papers showing that the dog was free from physical defects. An obstetrician makes no such guarantee.
- The breeder sells dogs to prospective owners; the obstetrician does not sell babies.
- According to my veterinarian, some dog breeders pay some or all of the surgery costs in cases like this; an obstetrician would never do this.

When you examine this argument in light of these discrepancies, the argument completely breaks down. The only thing a dog breeder and a physician have in common is that both offer a service.

- In 2010 the NCAA sanctioned the University of Southern California for violations by two former high-profile athletes, football star Reggie Bush and basketball star O. J. Mayo. Both players had reportedly received cash and gifts from sports marketers (Bush) and a sports agent (Mayo), which NCAA rules forbid. In addition, Bush's family lived in a rent-free house paid for by a marketer. USC football coach Lane Kiffin addressed a group of boosters and used this analogy: He compared the coach's attempts to make sure that all team members followed the NCAA rules to a father watching over 120 kids. "It's a difficult situation." (Quoted in David Wharton, "Heads in the Sand' at USC," *The Los Angeles Times,* June 6, 2010) Explain why Kiffin's argument rests on a false analogy.

An argument that relies on an analogy for evidence may be sound and valid if the analogy is sustainable and if there are enough points of similarity between the two things compared. Consider, for example, this portion of an argument by two U.C. Berkeley professors opposed to a plan to offer bachelor's degrees for online study:

> **Online teaching cannot replace the classroom experience.** Internet use is most effective if it supplements the face-to-face dialogue that is the hallmark of university education. Knowledge moves too fast in the contemporary world to justify any teaching medium that is not extremely flexible, and the most flexible medium of all is conversation. It is no coincidence that the main technology firms—Apple, Cisco, Google and Microsoft—all have central campuses, where innovators consult and work together. (Timothy Hampton and Garrison Sposito, "UC Must Put Emphasis on Education, Not Brand," *San Francisco Chronicle,* July 13, 2010)

Comparing a university campus to a corporate campus—to emphasize the collaboration that goes on in both institutions—seems a legitimate analogy, which therefore gives the argument credibility.

Over-simplification

The fallacy of **oversimplification** can involve either reducing a complicated issue to overly simple terms or suppressing information that would strengthen the argument.

- Strikes should be illegal because they inconvenience innocent people.
- The Roman Catholic Church faced a crisis as more stories of sexual abuse, usually of boys, by Catholic priests going back decades came to light. After months of investigation, the results of a study conducted by the John Jay College of Criminal Justice, with the Church's cooperation, found this: The seminarians had been poorly trained and the culture of the 1960s and 1970s saw an increase in divorce and in marijuana use.
- Human DNA has 23 chromosomes, while dogs have 39. Therefore, dogs are more complex than humans. (This argument oversimplifies the differences between humans and dogs and rests on a simplistic definition of the word *complex.*)

The last example is both an example of oversimplification and false analogy. Where is the analogy, and why is it false?

14. New York City recently passed a law banning trans fats in restaurant food. Many New Yorkers shared the sentiments of this resident: "Mayor Bloomberg and his 'food nannies' won't be satisfied with this prohibition, though. Pretty soon, they'll have officials going through people's garbage cans, looking for empty Ho Ho wrappers and Oreo cookie packages, and levying fines against people who eat junk food."

Fallacy: _____

15. French scientists inserted jellyfish genes into a rabbit embryo to create a bunny that emitted a green glow in the dark. Supporters of this sort of tinkering with nature by manipulating an organism's genes defended it, saying that dog breeders manipulate mating all the time to produce dogs with desirable qualities, so why can't biotech breeders create glowing bunnies?

Fallacy: _____

Online Learning Center

Here are two websites with additional information about appeals and logical fallacies, along with examples:

- The Nizkor Project Fallacies: www.nizkor .org/features/fallacies
- The University of North Carolina: www .unc.edu. In the search box, type in "logical fallacies" or try this link: www.unc.edu/ depts/wcweb/handouts/fallacies.html. At the bottom of the handout page, click on the link under "Can I Get Some Practice with This?" for a sample argument full of various fallacies and an explanation of each one, along with an argument based on sound reasoning on the same subject.

Summary of Emotional Appeals and Logical Fallacies

The fallacies and appeals discussed in this chapter are tricks to get us to accept the argument, but they work only for the unwary reader. Critical awareness is the best defense against fallacious reasoning and deceptive manipulative techniques. Also keep in mind that not all writers who engage in these techniques have evil motives. Many writers are such fervent crusaders for their cause that they stray from the rules, and many are simply ignorant of legitimate forms of argumentation.

Online Learning Center

For more practice in identifying logical fallacies, go to www.mhhe.com/spears. Click on Chapter 9 and then on "Logical Fallacies."

■ DETECTING BIAS

The media is often accused of bias. Critics who adhere to the right say that the *New York Times,* the *Washington Post,* the *San Francisco Chronicle,* the *Los Angeles Times,* and the cable TV stations CNN and MSNBC are biased toward liberalism, while media critics who adhere to the left say that the *Washington Times, The Wall Street Journal,* and Fox News are biased toward conservatism, to cite a few examples. There may be a certain amount of truth in these observations. but what do they really mean? Is the charge of bias based on a rational appraisal, or is it that the critics don't agree with the opinions these media outlets express? This section of the book will help you decide for yourself whether or not these charges are true.

Bias is such a loaded word, often hurled at those whose opinions we find objectionable. However, the word's connotations have changed meaning in recent decades. In the past, the word referred to a one-sided tendency or direction. But today the word *bias* has come to mean—at least when used to describe the media—an attempt to influence or to affect, *often using unfair tactics*. In other words, the word is commonly used as a pejorative.

Bias or Point of View—What's Acceptable and What's Not

Let's look at an illustration of these two senses of the word *bias,* apart from the media. A human resources manager might say, "I have a bias against people who submit résumés and job applications with grammar and spelling errors. If they are that sloppy when they're applying for a job, why would they do a good job after they're hired?" This is a bias widely shared by other personnel managers, but it's not unfair bias, even though the unlucky job applicant who failed to proofread carefully might think otherwise.

But what if this same personnel manager rejects a job applicant because of the person's race or gender or religion or any number of other personal characteristics? That is bias based on prejudice. It's injurious, and it's obviously unfair (not to mention illegal). It's the same thing in writing: bias—in the sense of a tendency or a point of view—in and of itself isn't bad. It's *unfair bias* that poses the problem and that makes an argument questionable.

Another point must be made on this subject: Students often assume that it's wrong for a writer to demonstrate a point of view or a bias, that all writing in the media must strive for objectivity. In newspaper reporting—news articles reporting on the events of the day—we should in fact expect the writer to keep personal opinions from intruding, as much as is humanly possible. But in persuasive writing—for example, editorials, opinion pieces, and blog entries—we expect the writer to present a particular point of view. That's the whole point. As long as the writer presents valid, logical support for the claim and adheres to the rules of sound argumentation, it's fair. When opinion writing is done well, it's probably better to use the term ***point of view,*** because it lacks the negative emotional connotation that the word *bias* carries.

To sum up, when evaluating opinion pieces and editorials, look for evidence of bias in the pejorative sense. Inappropriate or unfair bias in writing—or in television newscasts, for that matter—manifests itself by demonstrating certain characteristics:

- The discussion is distorted by the writer's intolerant, prejudicial, and often extreme views about race, religion, politics, culture, and so forth. We may say that he or she has an ax to grind.

The fact that nobody in power is talking about jobs does not mean, however, that nothing could be done.

Bear in mind that the unemployed aren't jobless because they don't want to work, or because they lack the necessary skills. There's nothing wrong with our workers—remember, just four years ago the unemployment rate was below 5 percent.

The core of our economic problem is, instead, the debt—mainly mortgage debt—that households ran up during the bubble years of the last decade. Now that the bubble has burst, that debt is acting as a persistent drag on the economy, preventing any real recovery in employment. And once you realize that the overhang of private debt is the problem, you realize that there are a number of things that could be done about it.

For example, we could have W.P.A.-type programs putting the unemployed to work doing useful things like repairing roads—which would also, by raising incomes, make it easier for households to pay down debt. We could have a serious program of mortgage modification, reducing the debts of troubled homeowners. We could try to get inflation back up to the 4 percent rate that prevailed during Ronald Reagan's second term, which would help to reduce the real burden of debt.

So there are policies we could be pursuing to bring unemployment down. These policies would be unorthodox—but so are the economic problems we face. And those who warn about the risks of action must explain why these risks should worry us more than the certainty of continued mass suffering if we do nothing.

In pointing out that we could be doing much more about unemployment, I recognize, of course, the political obstacles to actually pursuing any of the policies that might work. In the United States, in particular, any effort to tackle unemployment will run into a stone wall of Republican opposition. Yet that's not a reason to stop talking about the issue. In fact, looking back at my own writings over the past year or so, it's clear that I too have sinned: political realism is all very well, but I have said far too little about what we really should be doing to deal with our most important problem.

As I see it, policy makers are sinking into a condition of learned helplessness on the jobs issue: the more they fail to do anything about the problem, the more they convince themselves that there's nothing they could do. And those of us who know better should be doing all we can to break that vicious circle.

Questions for Analysis

1. According to Krugman, what is the fundamental problem that the United States and other Western countries are facing right now?
2. Who is responsible for this problem? What has been done about it?
3. Identify Krugman's two "unorthodox" proposals for resolving the situation. Why do you suppose he describes them in this way? To whom would they be "unorthodox"?

4. What unstated assumption underlies Krugman's argument about who should fix the problem he describes? Would you say that his position reflects a conservative or a liberal point of view? What evidence can you cite in support of your determination?
5. Is the opinion piece biased? If so, is the bias fair or unfair? appropriate or inappropriate? Are there examples of deliberate manipulation, of any logical fallacies, of slanted language, or of misrepresentation and prejudice?

Kathleen Parker, "Eat, Drink and Watch Out," *Orlando Sentinel,* **May 23, 2011.**

Once upon a time, Ma would say: "Sit up and eat your vegetables." Pa said: "Don't talk with your mouth full."

Other common utterances included: "Go outside and play." And, "After you finish your chores."

Families may not have been happier—and family dinners may have been daily rituals of tiny tortures (the ennui that passeth all understanding)—but neither were the words "childhood obesity" part of the vernacular.

Fat kids (can we say that?) have always been among us, but obesity was not the plague it is today. Nor was it necessary for the federal government to instruct families about how and what to eat. We all knew the pyramid scheme of nutrition. I seem to remember it tacked to school bulletin boards, just beneath the portrait of George Washington.

This isn't nostalgia speaking. And though I tried to provide family dinners most nights when the kids were small, I told my son when he left for college: "You're gonna miss my takeout."

Then again, it's no mystery why kids are fatter these days or what is required to fix the problem. Eat less; move more; listen to your parents—if you can find them.

Hold the Nobel. Really.

Bless Michelle Obama for trying to get the word out that eating vegetables and playing ball are, as Martha Stewart would put it, "good things." I'm as willing as anyone to be cynical about such insights—and hated nanny statism before it was cool. Yet the message is important and someone has to say it. Who better than the mother in chief?

But maternal advice is one thing and a government-enforced nutritional mandate is another. Trans fats are now outlawed in places; spuds in school lunches are the latest target.

Personally, I wouldn't touch a trans fat if you wrapped it in gold and sprinkled it with diamonds, but this is because I can read, comprehend, digest, recall and act on the free will allotted to all sentient adults. In the absence of willpower among some, should trans fats be forbidden to all? Where exactly does one stop drawing that little line?

The questions of when and whether the government should intervene in matters of personal taste are not harmless. As government becomes more involved in health decisions, as inevitably will be the case under the Affordable

Health Care Act, government necessarily will become more involved in personal nutrition issues.

The same strategy that created pariahs out of smokers now is being aimed at people who eat unattractively. It isn't only that you're hurting yourself by eating too much of the wrong foods; you're hurting the rest of us by willfully contributing to your own poor health and therefore to the cost of public health. Fat is the new nicotine.

Once the numbers crunchers start quantifying the cost to society incurred by people who eat too much ($100 billion a year, according to one estimate), you can be sure that not-such-good-things are coming your way soon. Think Nurse Ratched in an apron.

The stats *are* alarming, to be sure, especially regarding children. The rate of childhood obesity has doubled for preschool children in the past three decades. About 9 million children over age 6 are considered obese.

The issue isn't only about spuds in the school lunches, though overconsumption of high glycemic carbohydrates has to be factored into any calculation about obesity. At least as significant, if not utterly crucial, are poverty and shattered families, which often go hand-in-hand. Also significant are the high cost of healthy food (rent "Food Inc." for an overview) versus cheap, fast food. Our drive-through culture, which applies to relationships as well as mealtimes, is the real enemy of fitness and health.

Thus, it seems clear that the real solution to obesity isn't more government regulation but more personal responsibility. I know, sheer genius. This now-dusty notion is the impetus behind the recently launched "Together Counts" campaign, created by The Healthy Weight Commitment Foundation, a coalition of 160 organizations. Essentially, it's a private effort to encourage families to become healthier by spending more time exercising and eating together.

Once upon a time we called this "life," but we post-modernists apparently need a little help with the basics. At minimum, we need a website: *http://www.togethercounts.com*

Whatever works, I reckon, but, fuddy-duddily speaking, more chores and fewer gadgets—and married parents who torture their kids with rules—probably would do the trick as well. As with most problems, the solution is family.

Questions for Analysis

1. Identify the problem that Parker addresses in the editorial.
2. Who is responsible for this problem? How did it develop and become so serious in the first place?
3. Explain the reference to Michele Obama, as the "mom in chief." What is her role in this situation?
4. What solution to the problem does Parker propose? What solution does she *not* advocate?
5. What unstated assumption underlies Parker's argument about who should fix the problem she describes? Would you say that her position reflects a conservative or a liberal point of view (or bias)? What evidence can you cite in support of your determination?

6. Is the opinion piece biased? If so, is the bias fair or unfair? appropriate or inappropriate? Are there examples of deliberate manipulation, of any logical fallacies, of slanted language, or of misrepresentation and prejudice?

Critical Thinking Exercise—Bias

This text represents a portion of 72 changes made to middle-school and high-school health education textbooks that were proposed by Terri Leo, a member of the Texas State Board of Education. Study the deletions and comment on the contrast between the original sentences and the edited versions. What biases does each version represent?

> Later in adolescence, or in early adulthood, most ~~people~~ **males and females** begin to form romantic relationships based on love.
>
> The sex hormones your body produces may make you interested in romantic relationships with ~~others~~ **the opposite sex.** Friendships and dating relationships help you prepare for ~~adult relationships~~ **stable marital commitment.**
>
> If you discuss the issue of homosexuality in class, ~~discuss it respectfully. Be~~ be aware that ~~someone in your class may be homosexual or related to someone who is homosexual, or have a friend who is homosexual.~~ **Texas law rejects homosexual "marriage." Students can therefore maintain that homosexuality and heterosexuality are not moral equivalents, without being charged with "hate speech."**
>
> ~~Surveys indicate that 3 to 10 percent of the population is gay.~~ **Opinions vary on** ~~No one knows for sure why some people are straight, some are bisexual, and others~~ **homosexuals, lesbians, and bisexuals as a group** are ~~gay~~ **more prone to self-destructive behaviors like depression, illegal drug use, and suicide.**

"Sex Edit," *Harpers*

■ CONSTRUCTING A WORLDVIEW OF YOUR OWN

College students are exposed to a wide variety of opinions, representing every political and social stripe. That's the whole purpose of a liberal education. But the welter of ideas also makes it hard to sort everything out, especially with the constant noise from the media— 24-hour cable television; political pundits and their guests, sometimes yelling at each other; the barrage of advertising, pamphleteering, and polling during election years. What if you have never taken the time to codify your beliefs? What if you're not sure if you're a liberal or a conservative, a libertarian, a centrist, or a contrarian, a social progressive or a traditionalist?

These three websites offer a summary of liberal and conservative positions on a variety of current issues.

- Personal Philosophy Quiz www .politicalquiz.net/
- Pew Research Center for the People and the Press: Beyond Red vs. Blue 2011 Pew Research Political Typology www.people-press.org/typology/
- www.studentnewsdaily.com. Choose "Conservative vs. Liberal Beliefs"

You can learn to evaluate opinion writers using the criteria discussed in Part 4, and reading widely among columnists will help you refine your own thinking. But what if you aren't sure where you stand on the issues? It's easy to be manipulated into believing one thing or another if you don't have a starting point. If you haven't thought much about the big picture—how you stand on social and political issues—in the box above are some suggestions for putting everything together. You can find lots of quizzes online to determine if you are a liberal or a conservative. Some of them are better than others.[5]

CHAPTER EXERCISES: EVALUATING EDITORIALS

Here are four opinion pieces on a variety of topics to analyze. Three are from major newspapers, and one is from a political website. Before you analyze them, you should review the questions at the end of Chapter 8 on page 344. Each opinion piece is followed by questions for discussion.

Selection 1

Bob Herbert, "How Many Deaths Are Enough?" *The New York Times*

Formerly a columnist for *The New York Times* where this editorial was published in January 2011, Bob Herbert is a syndicated columnist who writes on contemporary issues, in particular, the Iraq war, race, and poverty.

On April 22, 2008, almost exactly one year after 32 students and faculty members were slain in the massacre at Virginia Tech, the dealer who had sold one of the weapons used by the gunman delivered a public lecture on the school's campus. His point: that people at Virginia Tech should be allowed to carry concealed weapons on campus.

Eric Thompson, owner of the online firearms store that sold a .22-caliber semiautomatic handgun to the shooter, Seung-Hui Cho, did not think that his appearance at Virginia Tech was disrespectful or that his position was extreme. He felt so strongly that college students should be allowed to be armed while engaged in their campus activities that he offered discounts to any students who wanted to buy guns from him.

---

[5] I've investigated several of these sites. Many of them are overly simplistic and contain grammar or spelling errors. Perhaps I'm biased myself, but I eliminated any with these errors.

Thompson spun the discounts as altruistic. He told ABCNews.com, "This offers students and people who might not have otherwise been able to afford a weapon to purchase one at a hefty discount and at a significant expense to myself."

The sale to Cho was not Thompson's only unfortunate link to a mass killer. His firm sold a pair of 9-millimeter Glock magazines and a holster to Steven Kazmierczak, a 27-year-old graduate student in DeKalb, Ill., who, on the afternoon of Feb. 14, 2008, went heavily armed into an auditorium-type lecture hall at Northern Illinois University. Kazmierczak walked onto the stage in front of a crowd of students and opened fire. He killed five people and wounded 18 others before killing himself.

We've allowed the extremists to carry the day when it comes to guns in the United States, and it's the dead and the wounded and their families who have had to pay the awful price. The idea of having large numbers of college students packing heat in their classrooms and at their parties and sporting events, or at the local pub or frat house or gymnasium, or wherever, is too stupid for words.

Thompson did not get a warm welcome at Virginia Tech. A spokesman for the school, Larry Hincker, said the fact that he "would set foot on this campus" was "terribly offensive" and "incredibly insensitive to the families of the victims."

Just last week, a sophomore at Florida State University, Ashley Cowie, was shot to death accidentally by a 20-year-old student who, according to authorities, was showing off his rifle to a group of friends in an off-campus apartment complex favored by fraternity members. A second student was shot in the wrist. This occurred as state legislators in Florida are considering a proposal to allow people with permits to carry concealed weapons on campuses. The National Rifle Association thinks that's a dandy idea.

The slaughter of college students—or anyone else—has never served as a deterrent to the gun fetishists. They want guns on campuses, in bars and taverns and churches, in parks and in the workplace, in cars and in the home. Ammunition everywhere—the deadlier, the better. A couple of years ago, a state legislator in Arizona, Karen Johnson, argued that adults needed to be able to carry guns in all schools, from elementary on up. "I feel like our kindergartners are sitting there like sitting ducks," she said.

Can we get a grip?

The contention of those who would like college kids and just about everybody else to be armed to the teeth is that the good guys can shoot back whenever the bad guys show up to do harm. An important study published in 2009 by researchers at the University of Pennsylvania School of Medicine estimated that people in possession of a gun at the time of an assault were 4.5 times more likely to be shot during the assault than someone in a comparable situation without a gun.

"On average," the researchers said, "guns did not seem to protect those who possessed them from being shot in an assault. Although successful defensive gun uses can and do occur, the findings of this study do not support the perception that such successes are likely."

Approximately 100,000 shootings occur in the United States every year. The number of people killed by guns should be enough to make our knees go weak. Monday was a national holiday celebrating the life of the Rev. Dr. Martin Luther King Jr. While the gun crazies are telling us that ever more Americans need to be walking around armed, we should keep in mind that more than a million people have died from gun violence—in murders, accidents and suicides—since Dr. King was shot to death in 1968.

We need fewer homicides, fewer accidental deaths and fewer suicides. That means fewer guns. That means stricter licensing and registration, more vigorous background checks and a ban on assault weapons. Start with that. Don't tell me it's too hard to achieve. Just get started.

Questions for Analysis

1. Why do Eric Thompson, the firearms dealer, and the NRA want students to be able to carry guns on college campuses? What do you think of Thompson's giving a lecture at Virginia Tech a year after the massacre on campus?
2. Consider the evidence Herbert provides—the mass killings by Seung-Hui Cho and Steven Kazmierczak—at two different campuses. Explain the unstated assumption that governs Herbert's choice of these two examples that support his argument.
3. Herbert does not offer a refutation. Is this a weakness in the argument or not?
4. Is there any evidence of charged language in the editorial? For example, consider the phrases "gun fetishists" and "gun crazies" that Herbert uses to describe those who want students to be able to carry guns. Is this a loaded term or not? Throughout the editorial, is there any evidence of unfair bias?
5. Which support do you consider the strongest in defending Herbert's claim? Which is the weakest?

Selection 2

Michelle Malkin, "'Undocumented' Folly: A Liberal Reporter's Illegal Alien Sob Story" www.michellemalkin.com (Posted June 24, 2011).

Michelle Malkin is a syndicated columnist and political blogger. She currently writes for the *St. Louis Globe-Democrat*. Her opinion pieces can be found at the website listed above. She is also the author of *Culture of Corruption: Obama and His Team of Tax Cheats, Crooks and Cronies* (2010). This is Malkin's introduction to the piece, which provides the background. The actual editorial begins after the three asterisks below:

The DREAM Act mob is on the march again—and this time they have a prominent left-wing journalist leading the charge. My syndicated column below spotlights the serial law-breaking of former Washington Post reporter Jose Antonio Vargas, who is now an illegal alien activist clamoring for amnesty with the backing of the radical Tides Center, a project of George Soros and the former chief organizer of ACORN, Drummond Pike. (Hey, maybe they'll hire Obama's grousing illegal alien aunt Zeituni Onyango as a senior fellow.)

Vargas's splashy revelations in The New York Times come—no coincidence, of course—amid a renewed push for the DREAM Act illegal alien student bailout.

Remember: This is a brazen "down payment" on a larger shamnesty.

Remember: This is nothing more than a 2.1 million future Democrat voter recruitment drive and a massive open-borders entitlement program for untold numbers of multi-culti ethnic tribalists who pretend to embrace assimilation for show.

And remember: The CBO score estimated that the last, failed DREAM Act bill would increase projected deficits by more than $5 billion in at least one of the four consecutive 10-year periods starting in 2021.

Citizenship is a privilege, not an entitlement.

What part of "no" doesn't the open-borders lobby understand?

***

With great fanfare and elite media sympathy, Jose Antonio Vargas publicly declared himself an "undocumented immigrant" this week. "Undocumented" my you-know-what. In the felony-friendly pages of The New York Crimes—er, Times—the Pulitzer Prize-winning journalist turned illegal-alien activist spilled the beans on all the illegal IDs he amassed over the years. He had documents coming out of his ears.

The Times featured full-color photos of Vargas' fake document trove—including a fake passport with a fake name, a fake green card and a Social Security card his grandfather doctored for him at a Kinko's. He committed perjury repeatedly on federal I-9 employment eligibility forms. In 2002, while pursuing his journalism career goals, an immigration lawyer told him he needed to accept the consequences of his law-breaking and return to his native Philippines.

Following the rules would have meant a 10-year bar to reentry into America. Making false claims of citizenship is a felony offense. Document fraud is a felony offense.

Vargas, who frames himself as a helpless victim, freely chose instead to secure yet more dummy documents. He used a friend's address to obtain an Oregon driver's license under false pretenses. It gave him an eight-year golden ticket to travel by car, board trains and airplanes, work at prestigious newspapers, and even gain access to the White House—where crack Secret Service agents allowed him to attend a state dinner using his bogus Social Security number. (Reminder: Illegal aliens were able to get through White House security under the Bush administration, too.)

At least Vargas tells the truth when he says he's not alone. Go visit a 7-11 in the D.C. suburbs. Or the countless vendors in MacArthur Park. Or any of the 19 cities in 11 states from Massachusetts to Ohio to Kentucky where a massive, Mexico-based "highly sophisticated and violent" fraudulent-document trafficking ring operated until February 2011. "Undocumented workers" and "undocumented immigrants" have plenty of documents.

The persistent use of these open-borders euphemisms to describe Vargas and countless millions like him is a perfect illumination of the agenda-driven, dominant progressive media.

They're as activist inside their newsrooms as Vargas is out in the open now. Bleeding-heart editors were hoaxed by a prominent colleague, exposed to liability, and yet still champion his serial subversion of the law. San Francisco Chronicle editor Phil Bronstein bragged that he was "duped" by Vargas, but endorses his "subterfuge" because Vargas' lobbying campaign for the illegal-alien student bailout known as the DREAM Act "just might lubricate the politically tarred-up wheels of government and help craft sane immigration policy."

Who's insane? The Vargas deceit is not an object lesson about America's failure to show compassion. It's another stark reminder of America's dangerous failure to learn from 9/11.

Time and again, security experts have warned about how jihadists have exploited lax immigration and ID enforcement. Driver's licenses are gateways into the American mainstream. They allow residents to establish an identity and gain a foothold into their communities. They help you open bank accounts, enter secure facilities, board planes, and do things like drive tractor-trailers carrying hazardous materials.

It's been nearly 10 years since several of the 19 9/11 hijackers operated in the country using hundreds of illicitly obtained fake driver's licenses and IDs. Most states tightened licensing rules, yet Vargas easily obtained a driver's license not only in Oregon, but more recently in Washington State. He again used a friend's residence to pass muster. Washington State's licensing bureaucracy still does not check citizenship. The man sitting in the White House campaigned to keep driver's license laws as loose as possible for the open-borders lobby. He appointed illegal-alien lobbyists to top federal immigration positions. His head of Immigration and Customs Enforcement just signed a memo pushing the DREAM Act through by administrative fiat. And the privacy of illegal aliens still trumps national security.

I ask again: Who's insane?

Vargas believes his sob story is an argument for giving up on immigration enforcement and passing a mass amnesty. It's a sob story, all right. Homeland security officials across the country should be weeping at the open mockery Vargas and his enablers have made of the law.

Questions for Analysis

1. Comment on the title of the editorial. What does the phrase "sob story" mean? Why does Malkin use the phrase?
2. The DREAM Act is a proposal that would allow a path to citizenship for children of illegal immigrants who were brought to this country by their parents before the age of 15 and who have been in this country five years or longer. (As of spring 2012, the bill remains stalled in Congress.) What does the DREAM Act have to do with Malkin's opinion piece? What does she think about this proposal?

3. What is the central concern that Malkin expresses in her editorial? Is that concern clearly expressed? What does Jose Antonio Vargas's admission that he worked as a journalist for several years while remaining an undocumented immigrant have to do with her claim?
4. Comment on Malkin's choice of language throughout the editorial. How would you characterize it? Locate examples of charged language and comment on its effectiveness.
5. What is Malkin's opinion of the progressive, or liberal, media?
6. Malkin's piece is clearly biased. Why do you think she writes in this fashion? What are some instances of bias that you can point to throughout the piece? For fun, choose a paragraph and rewrite it, removing the biased elements.

Critical Thinking Exercise

Malkin's editorial is clearly biased on the right. For two completely different perspectives regarding the case of Jose Antonio Vargas, here are two more editorials on his situation. In the search box of your favorite search engine, type in

1. Dick Rogers, A Reporter's Secret
2. Ruben Navarrette, One Reporters's Lies Make Life Harder for the Rest of Us

Which writer does a better job of evaluating the ramifications of Vargas's illegal status? Another task is to investigate Vargas's case more thoroughly to determine how exactly he came to be in the U.S. illegally.

Selection 3

Bill McKibben, "A Link between Climate Change and Joplin Tornadoes? Never!" *The Washington Post.*

Bill McKibben is an environmental writer who has published more than a dozen books on the subject of environmental change, beginning with his first book, *The End of Nature* (1989). His articles have also appeared in the *Washington Post, Atlantic, Harper's,* and *The New York Times.* He is also the founder of the global climate campaign 350.org and a distinguished scholar at Middlebury College in Vermont. This editorial was published during tornado season in the spring of 2011, one of the worst on record. Tornadoes swept through a wide swath of the Midwest and South, devastating towns and killing dozens of people in Iowa, Oklahoma, Missouri, Alabama, and elsewhere.

Caution: It is vitally important not to make connections. When you see pictures of rubble like this week's shots from Joplin, Mo., you should not wonder: Is this

Notice to my friends: I love you all dearly.

But I don't give a hoot that you are "having a busy Monday," your child "took 30 minutes to brush his teeth," your dog "just ate an ant trap" or you want to "save the piglets." And I really, really don't care which Addams Family member you most resemble. (I could have told you the answer before you took the quiz on Facebook.)

Here's where you and I went wrong: We took our friendship online. First we began communicating more by e-mail than by phone. Then we switched to "instant messaging" or "texting." We "friended" each other on Facebook, and began communicating by "tweeting" our thoughts—in 140 characters or less—via Twitter.

All this online social networking was supposed to make us closer. And in some ways it has. Thanks to the Internet, many of us have gotten back in touch with friends from high school and college, shared old and new photos, and become better acquainted with some people we might never have grown close to offline.

Last year, when a friend of mine was hit by a car and went into a coma, his friends and family were able to easily and instantly share news of his medical progress—and send well wishes and support—thanks to a Web page his mom created for him.

But there's a danger here, too. If we're not careful, our online interactions can hurt our real-life relationships.

Like many people, I'm experiencing Facebook Fatigue. I'm tired of loved ones—you know who you are—who claim they are too busy to pick up the phone, or even write a decent e-mail, yet spend hours on social-media sites, uploading photos of their children or parties, forwarding inane quizzes, posting quirky, sometimes nonsensical one-liners or tweeting their latest whereabouts. ("Anyone know a good restaurant in Berlin?")

One of the big problems is how we converse. Typing still leaves something to be desired as a communication tool; it lacks the nuances that can be expressed by body language and voice inflection. "Online, people can't see the yawn," says Patricia Wallace, a psychologist at Johns Hopkins University's Center for Talented Youth and author of "The Psychology of the Internet."

But let's face it, the problem is much greater than which tools we use to communicate. It's what we are actually saying that's really mucking up our relationships. "Oh my God, a college friend just updated her Facebook status to say that her 'teeth are itching for a flossing!'" shrieked a friend of mine recently. "That's gross. I don't want to hear about what's going on inside her mouth."

That prompted me to check my own Facebook page, only to find that three of my pals—none of whom know each other—had the exact same status update: "Zzzzzzz." They promptly put me to "zzzzzzz."

This brings us to our first dilemma: Amidst all this heightened chatter, we're not saying much that's interesting, folks. Rather, we're breaking a cardinal rule of companionship: Thou Shalt Not Bore Thy Friends.

"It's called narcissism," says Matt Brown, a 36-year-old business-development manager for a chain of hair salons and spas in Seattle. He's particularly annoyed by a friend who works at an auto dealership who tweets every time he sells a car, a married couple who bicker on Facebook's public walls and another couple so "mooshy-gooshy" they sit in the same room of their house posting love messages to each other for all to see. "Why is your life so frickin' important and entertaining that we need to know?" Mr. Brown says.

'I Just Ate a Frito Pie'

Gwen Jewett, for her part, is sick of meal status updates. "A few of my friends like to post several times a day about what they are eating: 'I just ate a Frito pie.' 'I am enjoying a double hot-fudge sundae at home tonight.' 'Just ate a whole pizza with sausage, peppers and double cheese,'" says the 49-year-old career coach in suburban Dallas. "My question is this: If we didn't call each other on the phone every time we ate before, why do we need the alerts now?"

For others, boredom isn't the biggest challenge of managing Internet relationships. Consider, for example, how people you know often seem different online—not just gussied up or more polished, but bolder, too, displaying sides of their personalities you have never seen before.

Alex Gilbert, 27, who works for a nonprofit in Houston that teaches creative writing to kids, is still puzzling over an old friend—"a particularly masculine-type dude"—who plays in a heavy-metal band and heads a motorcycle club yet posts videos on Facebook of "uber cute" kittens. "It's not fodder for your real-life conversation," Mr. Gilbert says. "We're not going to get together and talk about how cute kittens are."

James Hills discovered that a colleague is gay via Facebook, but he says that didn't bother him. It was after his friend joined groups that cater to hairy men, such as "Furball NYC," that he was left feeling awkward. "This is something I just didn't need to know," says Mr. Hills, who is 32 and president of a marketing firm in Elgin, Ill. "I'd feel the same way if it was a straight friend joining a leather-and-lace group."

And then there's jealousy. In all that information you're posting about your life—your vacation, your kids, your promotions at work, even that margarita you just drank—someone is bound to find something to envy. When it comes to relationships, such online revelations can make breaking up even harder to do.

"Facebook prolongs the period it takes to get over someone, because you have an open window into their life, whether you want to or not," says Yianni Garcia of New York, a consultant who helps companies use social media. "You see their updates, their pictures and their relationship status."

Mr. Garcia, 24, felt the sting of Facebook jealousy personally last spring, after he split up with his boyfriend. For a few weeks, he continued to visit his ex's Facebook page, scrutinizing his new friends. Then one day he discovered that his former boyfriend had blocked him from accessing his profile.

Why? "He said he'd only 'unfriended' me to protect himself, because if someone flirted with me he would feel jealous," Mr. Garcia says.

Facebook can also be a mecca for passive-aggressive behavior. "Suddenly, things you wouldn't say out loud in conversation are OK to say because you're sitting behind a computer screen," says Kimberly Kaye, 26, an arts writer in New York. She was surprised when friends who had politely discussed health-care reform over dinner later grew much more antagonistic when they continued the argument online.

Just ask Heather White. She says her college roommate at the University of Georgia started an argument over text about who should clean their apartment. Ms. White, 22, who was home visiting her parents at the time, asked her friend to call her so they could discuss the issue. Her friend never did.

A few days later, Ms. White, who graduated in May, updated her Facebook status, commenting that her favorite country duo, Brooks & Dunn, just broke up. Almost immediately, her roommate responded, writing publicly on her wall: "Just like us." The two women have barely spoken since then.

Band-Aid Tactics

So what's the solution, short of "unfriending" or "unfollowing" everyone who annoys you? You can use the "hide" button on Facebook to stop getting your friends' status updates—they'll never know—or use TwitterSnooze, a Web site that allows you to temporarily suspend tweets from someone you follow. (Warning: They'll get a notice from Twitter when you begin reading their tweets again.)

But these are really just Band-Aid tactics. To improve our interactions, we need to change our conduct, not just cover it up. First, watch your own behavior, asking yourself before you post anything: "Is this something I'd want someone to tell me?" "Run it by that focus group of one," says Johns Hopkins's Dr. Wallace.

And positively reward others, responding only when they write something interesting, ignoring them when they are boring or obnoxious. (Commenting negatively will only start a very public war.)

If all that fails, you can always start a new group: "Get Facebook to Create an Eye-Roll Button Now!"

Questions for Analysis

1. Bernstein cites several objections to Facebook with its apparently pernicious influence on friendships. What is it exactly, according to her, about Facebook that has created this negative effect?
2. Bernstein provides a refutation fairly early on in the article. Identify it. Can you think of other arguments in favor of Facebook that Bernstein might have included?
3. Who is Bernstein's audience? How can you tell?
4. Comment on the concept of narcissism that is part of this discussion. What is narcissism, and how has Facebook contributed to this increasingly common phenomenon?
5. What does it say about Americans when they prefer to discuss problems, for example, with who should clean the house, via Facebook rather than on the telephone or in person?
6. Why are actions like "unfriending," "unfollowing," or using the "hide" button merely "Band-Aid Tactics"? What is Bernstein's recommendation for salvaging friendships in the Age of Facebook?

H A P T E R

10

Practical Applications in Evaluating Arguments

Chapter 10 completes the discussion of critical reading by providing arguments from a variety of sources to analyze and evaluate, including these activities:

- Analyzing advertisements
- Analyzing public service announcements
- Analyzing editorial cartoons
- Evaluating speeches
- Evaluating websites
- Reading blogs

■ ANALYZING ADVERTISEMENTS

Advertisements have become ubiquitous in our society. They are on billboards, on television, on the radio, on the Web, at bus stops, at sports stadiums, even in movie theaters. These ads, for the most part, are designed to get us to consume—to buy this brand of soft drink, cereal, or potato chips, to shop at Walmart, Family Dollar, or Macy's, to eat at Joe's Café, Olive Garden, or Gino's Pizzeria. In effect, advertisements are mini-arguments that use both words and images to persuade us to spend our money or, in the case of public-service announcements, to change our thinking or to adopt a course of action.

When examining advertisements critically, start with many of the same criteria that you use when analyzing a photograph. Consider:

- The subject—who (or what) is being depicted?
- The action—what is happening and what is the significance of what's happening?
- The arrangement—what is in the foreground? What is in the background? Does one figure or object dominate? Are the background elements of interest?
- The people—what are they wearing? Does their clothing reveal anything about their status or occupation? What emotions or feelings do they display?

Next, consider the copy (or text) in the ad:

- The words—what does the text in the ad say?
- What tone is suggested in the ad?
- What emotional or symbolic overtones does the copy convey? Is there a more neutral word that could have been used to convey the same idea?

Because an advertisement combines text, called ad copy, with images, it's important to understand how they work together to create an argument. You should look for the various manipulative and emotional appeals that you studied in Chapter 9.

- What does the advertiser want me to do, think, or buy?
- How is the image in the advertisement designed to further this end?
- How is the text in the advertisement (the ad copy) written to further this end?
- What emotional appeals does the advertisement use—authority? fear? patriotism? pity or sympathy? tradition? transfer?
- Are any logical fallacies evident, such as *post hoc, ergo propter hoc* (suggesting a cause-effect relationship where there really isn't one), false analogy (making an invalid comparison), oversimplification (reducing a complicated issue to a single term or omitting inconvenient information)?

Most readers are familiar with advertisements for cosmetics and beauty products, which often feature models chosen for their sex appeal and in various stages of undress. The advertiser uses flattery and transfer and a questionable cause-effect relationship to entice the consumer to accept an implied claim: If you use this product, you will miraculously be endowed with the same appeal that the model enjoys. Advertisements for other items, from liquor and cigarettes to consumer goods and clothing, may also use these implied claims and emotional appeals.

Paris Hilton is famous for being famous. The celebrity is also the face of a recent advertising campaign for Rich Prosecco. Rich Prosecco is a sparkling wine that, unlike other similar beverages, comes in a can. Hilton has appeared in a variety of racy ads for Rich Prosecco. You can view two or three of them on YouTube if you type in "Rich Prosecco Paris Hilton" in the search box of your favorite search engine. Here is a tamer ad showing Hilton touting the beverage.

Paris Hilton, advertisement for Rich Prosecco. Appeared in *San Francisco Chronicle,* February 13, 2011, pF7.

1. State the claim of this ad in your own words. _____

   _____

2. What is the emotional appeal of the ad? _____

   _____

3. Why do you think Paris Hilton was chosen as the face of this particular ad campaign? Describe the expression on her face, her demeanor. _____

   _____

<table>
<tr><td>

**Practice
Exercise 1**

</td><td>

Here are three advertisements for you to consider—two are from print sources, and the third is from television, but for the purposes of this exercise, you will access all of them online. Study each ad carefully and then answer the questions that follow.

</td></tr>
</table>

Advertisement 1

A full-page advertisement for Ford's Edge appeared in several national magazines in 2010. The Edge is a crossover vehicle, one that combines the features of a traditional station wagon and an SUV. Here are two websites where Ford's print ad is displayed. In the search box of your favorite search engine, type in "Ford Edge advertisement, woman's lips."

1. What does the advertisement depict? _____

    _____

2. Comment on the name *Edge*. What is the connotation of this brand name? _____

    _____

3. Consider the advertising copy. What does the photo have to do with the New Edge's ability to understand voice commands?

    _____

4. The advertisement is intended to sell a Ford automobile, but no model is depicted. Why not? _____

    _____

Advertisement 2

Now consider the ad for Pom$_x$ Pills, a nutritional supplement made from pomegranates. You can access the ad at the company's website, www.pompills.com. Both display the same image of a bottle of Pom$_x$ Pills.

1. Examine the design of the bottle for Pom$_x$ Pills. Comment on the shape of the "O" in the word "Pom."_____

    _____

2. Explain what the little "x" is doing at the end of the word "Pom."

    _____

3. Who is the audience for this ad? How can you tell? _____

    _____

4. What evidence is provided to support the contention that this POM product is superior to other nutritional supplements tested?

_____

Advertisement 3

Go to google.com or to your favorite search engine. In the search box, type in "Apple IPad TV Ad—iPad is Delicious." There you will find Apple's TV ad campaign for the first iPad (the iPad 1.) Below the ad is this advertising copy:

> The iPad isn't just one thing. It's thousands of things. Go to www.apple.com/ipad and learn exactly what makes iPad so magical and revolutionary.

1. After viewing the ad two or three times, explain the structure of the ad. How does this structure reinforce the ad copy quoted above? _____

_____

Online Learning Center

Do pomegranates really contain more healthy antioxidants than other fruits, as the makers of Pom juice and Pom$_x$ Pills say? Investigate this claim by locating information about the amount of antioxidants in pomegranates as compared to other fruits like strawberries, mangoes, and blueberries. You might start by locating articles on this subject by Marion Nestle, professor in the nutrition, food studies, and public health department at New York University and author of _Food Politics_ and _What to Eat._

2. What is the audience for Apple's iPad? How does the advertisement emphasize this? _____

_____

_____

3. What emotional appeal is evident in this ad? _____

_____

_____

■ ANALYZING PUBLIC SERVICE ANNOUNCEMENTS

Public service announcements are intended to persuade the reader or listener just as advertisements are. But whereas ads aim to sell us a product that we may or may not need, public service announcements serve the greater good. The Federal Communications Commission (FCC) requires television stations to air a certain amount of material "in the public interest." One way television broadcasters meet this requirement is to broadcast PSAs. The American Ad Council is an umbrella group that sponsors ad campaigns for ways to improve our lives, addressing the critical issues of the day and raising public awareness. Some of the Ad Council's slogans have become part of the national psyche, for example "Friends Don't Let Friends Drive Drunk" and "A Mind Is a Terrible Thing to Waste." Public service announcements differ from ads in a number of ways. PSAs have three main purposes, which I list here along with some examples:

- To get people to change their behavior (for example, to stop smoking, to conserve water, to get their blood pressure checked regularly, to take reusable shopping bags to the supermarket, not to drink and drive)
- To donate money to a particular cause or charity (for example, the United Negro College Fund, the American Red Cross, the National Leukemia and Lymphoma Society, Doctors Without Borders, the National Disaster Search Dog Foundation)[1]
- To make people aware of a social problem to be solved (improving literacy rates, preventing high school dropouts, helping adolescents resist the lure of gangs, decreasing our dependence on foreign oil, eliminating discrimination in housing by landlords)

Below is reprinted a full-page magazine ad, "The $10,000 Dog," which is intended to solicit donations for the National Disaster Search Dog Foundation. In 2010 and 2011, search dogs were much in the news, rescuing victims of various natural disasters—buried in avalanches, earthquake rubble, and the like.

This is an extremely effective advertisement. The photo of the sleeping puppy dominates the page and is irresistible. Only a hard-hearted reader could ignore this image and turn the page without reading the ad copy. Now consider why the ad agency used a photo of a puppy rather than of an adult dog. Puppies not only appeal to our best instincts, but the implication is that it takes a lot of money to train a dog to be a search-and-rescue dog—$10,000, to be exact. Next examine the ad copy, which is both intriguing and unusual: Each of the dog's physical features is described, and while they are described in familiar terms, there is a big difference. Look at the description, for example, beneath "Tail" and "Nose." It's not just that these dogs wag their tails—all dogs do that when they're happy—or that they have a keen sense of smell. A search dog is a working dog—and his tail wags when he finds a survivor. And unlike the family pet, who sniffs bushes and trees when out for a walk, these dogs are trained to ignore all other scents but those of live human beings. This attribute is remarkable. That training, the ad implies, takes both time and money. The appeal is not manipulative in the pejorative sense that we saw in Chapter 9. In sum, the ad both captivates and impresses us.

---

[1]Some might call PSAs that solicit for money ads. I am distinguishing here between ads by corporations for consumer products and for charities and organizations whose mission is to benefit society. They are ads, of course, but their intent is to improve society rather than to fatten corporate coffers.

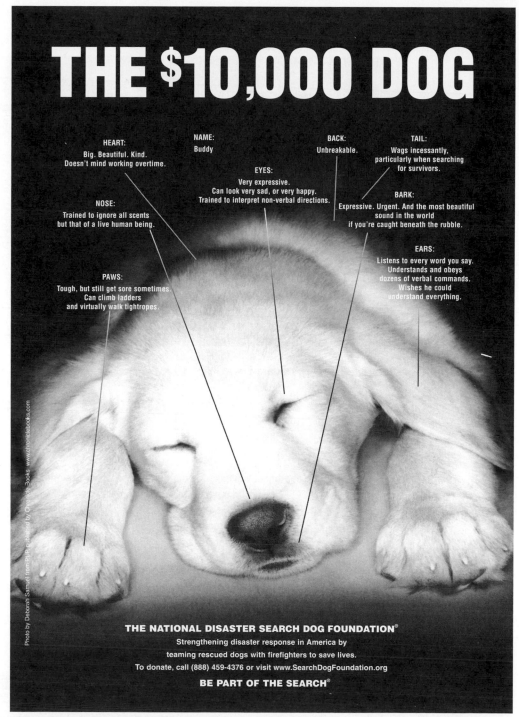

Public service announcement. The National Disaster Search Dog Foundation. "The $10,000 Dog," *The New Yorker,* May 2, 2011.

**Practice
Exercise 2**

A. Study this PSA sponsored by the National Fair Housing
Alliance. Then answer the questions that follow.

DISCRIMINATION IS RARELY THIS OBVIOUS,
BUT IT'S JUST AS REAL. AND JUST AS ILLEGAL.

If the landlord gives you the runaround or says:

"We don't take kids."
"The apartment you asked about on the phone has been rented."
"We only take people who speak English clearly."
"We don't take teenagers."
"The ad was wrong – the rent is really $50 more."
"I can't assign you a handicap parking space."

THAT COULD BE HOUSING DISCRIMINATION.
The only way to stop housing discrimination is to report it, so we can investigate it.

Visit **www.hud.gov/fairhousing** or call HUD's Housing Discrimination Hotline
1-800-669-9777 (voice) **1-800-927-9275** (TTY)

The federal Fair Housing Act prohibits discrimination because of race,
color, religion, national origin, sex, family status or disability.

Public service announcement. The National Fair Housing Alliance. "Now
Renting—No Kids, No Blacks, No Latinos," *The New Yorker,* March 15, 2010.

1. Examine the structure and layout of the ad. Is it effective, and if so why? _____

   _____

   _____

2. What is the audience for this PSA? How can you tell? _____

   _____

   _____

3. Why does the NFHA provide so many examples of ways in which a landlord might discriminate (beneath the photo)?_____

   _____

   _____

4. Does the PSA appeal to the emotions or to our reason or to something else altogether? Explain._____

   _____

   _____

B. The American Ad Council sponsors dozens of PSAs every year. Go to their website at www.adcouncil.org. At the bottom of the home page, click on "Current Work" and then on "Education." You can examine "High School Dropout Prevention," "Supporting Minority Education," or any of the other topics that appeal to you. Do an analysis as you did before, examining the photo or art work and the ad copy. Be sure to indicate what particular appeal the PSA is making.

■ ANALYZING EDITORIAL CARTOONS

Cartoons are powerful weapons. In 2006, protests erupted throughout the Middle East after a Danish newspaper published a series of cartoons that offended Muslims. The most provocative cartoon in the series showed the Prophet Mohammed wearing a turban with a lit bomb. And in August 2011, during the violent uprising against Syrian President Bashar Assad, thugs kidnapped Ali Ferzat, a famous Syrian cartoonist. Ferzat was known for his caricatures of Arab autocrats like Saddam Hussein, Moammar Khadafy, and Assad. The thugs beat him, broke his hands, and dumped him on a road, telling him, "This is just a warning. We will break your hands so that you'll drop drawing." Autocrats know well the power of cartoons. Long a staple of newspaper editorial pages, cartoons are powerful weapons against folly and corruption. Using exaggeration in the form of caricature, irony, and parody, editorial cartoons also comment succinctly and humorously on the issues of the day, presenting a stark version of an argument or issue stripped down to its essential elements. Here is an example that comments on the controversy about cartoons by Walt Handelsman, political cartoonist for Long Island's *Newsday*.

In this cartoon, a policeman guard is protecting a frightened public from a political cartoonist. Notice that the cartoonist's dress and demeanor make him appear harmless, but the caption suggests that he is capable of inflicting great damage. In other words, cartoons are like weapons, but of the pen and ink variety.

Practice Exercise 3

This exercise reprints three cartoons from various American publications on these topics: global warming, education, and immigration. The first one deals with gender issues; the second and third pertain to the Iraq War. Study them and then answer the questions that follow.

A. This cartoon by Tom Toles was published in *The Washington Post.*

5·31·10

1. What does the cartoon depict? _____

_____

2. What argument is the cartoonist making? _____

_____

3. Explain the reference to cockroaches. _____

_____

4. Explain the meaning of the little sentence at the very bottom of the cartoon. _____

_____

now available on YouTube or other video websites, we can judge not only the persuasive and manipulative devices embodied in the words, but also the speaker's delivery, gesture, facial expression, pitch and tone of voice, and nonverbal cues (body language). Two speeches are reprinted here. The first is one of Barack Obama's stump speeches that he often delivered during his first run for the American presidency in 2008. The speech is accompanied by an analysis of Obama's rhetoric by Larry Nista and Patterson Clark of *The Washington Post*. The second one in Practice Exercise 4 is Martin Luther King's classic civil rights speech, "I Have a Dream."

Barack Obama's Stump Speech

Anatomy of a Stump Speech

Sen. Barack Obama's stump speech is a 45-minute, ever-evolving set piece that he has given as often as three or four times a day for months and months, from tiny county fairgrounds in Iowa last summer to packed basketball arenas in big cities around the country in recent weeks.

The speech, delivered without notes, includes some building blocks that have girded it for a year and sections that have been dropped or added in over time. Many of the additions are riffs that he's created in response to criticisms made against him, lines of attack that he absorbs and tries to turn against the opposition. Following is a partial transcript of a representative speech given in Boise, Idaho, on Feb. 2 to a crowd of about 14,000 in the Boise State basketball arena.

OBAMA'S COMMENTS	ANALYSIS OF COMMENTS
It has now been almost a year, just a week short of a year, since I stood on the steps of the old state Capitol in Springfield, Illinois, the place where Abraham Lincoln served for many years before he went to Washington, the city where I served for many years before I went to the United States Senate, and announced that I was embarking on this unlikely journey to change America.	◄ He establishes his credibility and his rationale for his candidacy and defuses the critics of his inexperience—critical if his following main points are to be believed. What Obama's accomplished here is the major objective of the intro—motivate the audience to listen.
I know that people have been looking through my kindergarten papers, but that's not why I decided to run. . . .	◄ Added after the Clinton campaign produced a kindergarten essay by Obama saying he wanted to be president.
. . . I decided to run because of what Dr. King called the "fierce urgency of now."	◄ Introduced this line at an Iowa fundraising dinner in early November that many viewed as a key turning point for campaign.

What I've learned, when I decided to run, what I was betting on, was that change in America does not happen from the top down, it happens from the bottom up.

◀ Important to emphasize the argument for separation; he's not one of "them"—the established Beltway groups. He is soliciting help from the audience not just with votes. Makes audience feel a direct relationship with him.

For the first time in anybody's memory we had folks 30 and younger voting at the same rate as folks 60 and over. It has not happened in a generation, but it has happened in this election.

◀ Obama here appeals to the 18-to-29 voting bloc. No one knows better than that group how they've been taken for granted by the old-line pols—but not by Obama. He's their banner carrier.

If you are ready for change, we can go and tell the lobbyists that their days of setting the agenda in Washington are over. They have not funded my campaign, they will not run my White House, and they will not drown out the voices of the American people when I'm president of the United States of America.

◀ Obama amplified language such as this leading up to the Iowa caucuses to try to fend off the populist challenge of John Edwards.

But I don't just want to end the war, I want to end the mind-set that got us into the war.

◀ Added to the stump speech in the past month, after using the line at a Los Angeles debate.

There was a time where folks were saying, "Well, maybe he's too nice. I'm not sure he can take on the Republicans the way we need to, because he's always reaching out to them." I try to explain to people, if you know who you are, if you know what you're fighting for and you know what your principles are, then you can afford to reach out across the aisle and start bringing people together.

◀ Added this line in response to charges from Edwards shortly before the Iowa caucuses that Obama was too conciliatory.

Now, it's true that I do talk about hope a lot. Out of necessity. Think about what the odds are of me standing here before you in Boise. I wasn't born into wealth, I wasn't born into fame, my father left when I was 2, I was raised by a single mother and my grandparents, and they gave me love, they gave me an education, and they gave me hope.

◀ Added this riff after New Hampshire, both to rebut charges of naivete and make clear that he comes from modest roots, to appeal better to working-class voters.

in America until the Negro is granted his citizenship rights. The whirlwinds of revolt will continue to shake the foundations of our nation until the bright day of justice emerges.

But there is something that I must say to my people, who stand on the warm threshold which leads into the palace of justice: In the process of gaining our rightful place, we must not be guilty of wrongful deeds. Let us not seek to satisfy our thirst for freedom by drinking from the cup of bitterness and hatred. We must forever conduct our struggle on the high plane of dignity and discipline. We must not allow our creative protest to degenerate into physical violence. Again and again, we must rise to the majestic heights of meeting physical force with soul force.

The marvelous new militancy which has engulfed the Negro community must not lead us to a distrust of all white people, for many of our white brothers, as evidenced by their presence here today, have come to realize that their destiny is tied up with our destiny. And they have come to realize that their freedom is inextricably bound to our freedom.

We cannot walk alone.

And as we walk, we must make the pledge that we shall always march ahead. We cannot turn back.

There are those who are asking the devotees of civil rights, "When will you be satisfied?" We can never be satisfied as long as the Negro is the victim of the unspeakable horrors of police brutality. We can never be satisfied as long as our bodies, heavy with the fatigue of travel, cannot gain lodging in the motels of the highways and the hotels of the cities. We cannot be satisfied as long as the negro's basic mobility is from a smaller ghetto to a larger one. We can never be satisfied as long as our children are stripped of their self-hood and robbed of their dignity by signs stating: "For Whites Only." We cannot be satisfied as long as a Negro in Mississippi cannot vote and a Negro in New York believes he has nothing for which to vote. No, no, we are not satisfied, and we will not be satisfied until "justice rolls down like waters, and righteousness like a mighty stream."

I am not unmindful that some of you have come here out of great trials and tribulations. Some of you have come fresh from narrow jail cells. And some of you have come from areas where your quest—quest for freedom left you battered by the storms of persecution and staggered by the winds of police brutality. You have been the veterans of creative suffering. Continue to work with the faith that unearned suffering is redemptive. Go back to Mississippi, go back to Alabama, go back to South Carolina, go back to Georgia, go back to Louisiana, go back to the slums and ghettos of our northern cities, knowing that somehow this situation can and will be changed.

Let us not wallow in the valley of despair, I say to you today, my friends.

And so even though we face the difficulties of today and tomorrow, I still have a dream. It is a dream deeply rooted in the American dream.

I have a dream that one day this nation will rise up and live out the true meaning of its creed: "We hold these truths to be self-evident, that all men are created equal."

I have a dream that one day on the red hills of Georgia, the sons of former slaves and the sons of former slave owners will be able to sit down together at the table of brotherhood.

I have a dream that one day even the state of Mississippi, a state sweltering with the heat of injustice, sweltering with the heat of oppression, will be transformed into an oasis of freedom and justice.

I have a dream that my four little children will one day live in a nation where they will not be judged by the color of their skin but by the content of their character.

I have a *dream* today!

I have a dream that one day, down in Alabama, with its vicious racists, with its governor having his lips dripping with the words of "interposition" and "nullification"—one day right there in Alabama little black boys and black girls will be able to join hands with little white boys and white girls as sisters and brothers.

I have a *dream* today!

I have a dream that one day every valley shall be exalted, and every hill and mountain shall be made low, the rough places will be made plain, and the crooked places will be made straight; "and the glory of the Lord shall be revealed and all flesh shall see it together."

This is our hope, and this is the faith that I go back to the South with.

With this faith, we will be able to hew out of the mountain of despair a stone of hope. With this faith, we will be able to transform the jangling discords of our nation into a beautiful symphony of brotherhood. With this faith, we will be able to work together, to pray together, to struggle together, to go to jail together, to stand up for freedom together, knowing that we will be free one day.

And this will be the day—this will be the day when all of God's children will be able to sing with new meaning:

My country 'tis of thee, sweet land of liberty, of thee I sing.
Land where my fathers died, land of the Pilgrim's pride,
From every mountainside, let freedom ring!

And if America is to be a great nation, this must become true.

And so let freedom ring from the prodigious hilltops of New Hampshire.

Let freedom ring from the mighty mountains of New York.

Let freedom ring from the heightening Alleghenies of Pennsylvania.

Let freedom ring from the snow-capped Rockies of Colorado.

Let freedom ring from the curvaceous slopes of California.

But not only that:

Let freedom ring from Stone Mountain of Georgia.

Let freedom ring from Lookout Mountain of Tennessee.

Let freedom ring from every hill and molehill of Mississippi.

From every mountainside, let freedom ring.

And when this happens, when we allow freedom to ring, when we let it ring from every village and every hamlet, from every state and every city, we will be able to speed up that day when *all* of God's children, black men and white men,

Jews and Gentiles, Protestants and Catholics, will be able to join hands and sing in the words of the old Negro spiritual:

Free at last! Free at last!
Thank God Almighty, we are free at last!

Questions for Analysis

1. King's rhetoric is famous not just for its soaring quality but also for the quality of his figurative language. Go through the speech carefully and identify the figures of speech. Then study them to see the thematic patterns or clusters that they represent.

2. Next, identify the use of appeal throughout the speech. Would you characterize the appeal as emotional or rational or perhaps a combination of both? Point to examples to support your thinking.

3. Comment on some of King's most stirring rhetorical flourishes—for example, his use of repetition.

Critical Thinking Exercise

Barack Obama's speech on race, delivered in March 2008, is widely regarded as one of the most important speeches of the era. You can access the speech, titled "A More Perfect Union," online at YouTube. Watch both this speech by Obama and King's "I Have a Dream," also accessible on YouTube. Then compare the two. What elements do they have in common? Which is more effective? Have the intervening 50 years affected our perception of King's ideas, or do they remain as stirring as they did when he first delivered his words in 1963? Based on the fact that Obama was elected the first African-American president of the United States, is it possible that we have entered what is sometimes called a "post-racial" era?

■ EVALUATING WEBSITES

A thorough guide to the World Wide Web is outside the scope of this book. But as high-speed Internet access has become increasingly available and affordable and as we spend more and more time each year online, it seems worthwhile to offer a few observations about critical reading skills as they pertain to accessing information online. First, a warning: Some of the information that you read in this section by, say, 2014, may sound as antiquated as doilies on tables or telephones with cords. The Internet is changing so rapidly that even the most innovative technology can quickly become obsolete. A decade ago, no one had ever heard of 'zines, blogs, social network sites like LinkedIn or Facebook, gaming services like Zynga, or the iPad.

Reading Online versus Reading Print

There is no question that the World Wide Web has revolutionized the way information is disseminated and retrieved; ironically, that advantage is also its main drawback. The Web has exacerbated the problem of information overload, and we may feel overwhelmed by the glut of information available to us. In addition, turning to the Web first, as many people now do, rather than to traditional research tools in the library as a source of information, requires new warnings and new criteria for judging what we read. Despite the convenience of information available with a single mouse click at any time of the day or night, there are crucial differences between reading material on the printed page and reading material on a computer screen. Here is a summary of these differences as I see them:

- *Reading print on the Web is more difficult than reading a printed text.* Researchers at Ohio State University found that college students who read essays on a computer screen "found the text harder to understand, less interesting and less persuasive than students who read the same essay on paper."[2] These results were the same no matter how much computer experience students had.

- *Concentrating is more difficult.* There are two reasons for this problem: The colorful waving, blinking, flashing, or pulsating banner ads or other elements distract us, as they are meant to. More important, hyperlinks that allow the Web surfer to move from one link to another to another and so on are *antithetical to the act of sustained reading* and, by extension, to concentration. When we surf, we tend to zip from one site to the next, skimming and scanning, sampling here, clicking there. This is a different sort of reading! Only the most dedicated, focused reader can withstand the temptation not to move quickly from link to link.

- *Technology is seductive.* The novelty of finding what we are looking for on a website with blazing speed may cause us to suspend our critical judgment. That, coupled with the sheer quantity of material available on a subject, makes sorting out the good from the bad even more difficult. It takes concentration to ignore the dazzle and the glitz; it takes concentration to work through a series of sites until you find exactly what you want.

These factors suggest that the critical reader must be even more vigilant when reading and gathering information on the Web than when reading in traditional print sources. Trying to sort out the fair from the unfair, the true from the false takes time, skill, and a healthy skepticism. The important point is this: Use the critical reading skills from Chapters 8 and 9 to help you appraise Web material. Because by nature

---

[2]"Reading Comprehension: Cellulose Over Silicon," sponsored by the National Center for Policy Analysis, available online.

Web material is so different from conventional print material, these additional observations may help you make good use of your online time.

- ***Websites are not commercial free, so you must be alert to sales pitches.*** Health-care sites are particularly prone to disguises for what turns out to be pure marketing hype. The site may appear to provide unbiased information until you look further and discover that you are meant to subscribe to a newsletter or to buy a product.

- ***Editorial scrutiny is not a given.*** Undoubtedly, the Internet has democratized and expanded access to information. However, the typical magazine or newspaper article, for example, is pored over by editors and copy editors before it arrives in your mailbox or at the newsstand. But with the Web (except for those sites sponsored by media outlets, news organizations, and nonprofit or research organizations), editorial scrutiny and fact checking are not a requirement. The exception to this is Wikipedia, because the information on that site has been vetted by multitudes of people who serve as quasi-authorities on the topic under discussion. Still, errors have crept into Wikipedia entries, sometimes deliberately, so most computer experts suggest that you verify the information gleaned there with another source.

- ***The Web is a paradox, at once egalitarian and anarchistic.*** Thousands of new websites are added each week. If you are experienced in navigating websites, you are aware that anyone with an opinion or interest—no matter how trustworthy, no matter how crackpot—can create a site, resulting in an abundance of terrifically useful material—and an abundance of junk. In essence, the Web represents an anarchic nation, with few rules or strictures as to what can be published. These twin characteristics—egalitarianism and anarchy—are at once the Web's greatest virtues (no censorship) and its greatest handicap (no external objective analysis for fairness, bias, evidence, and the like).

Here are some questions to consider when you are doing research and getting information from the Web:

- Who sponsors the site? Is the sponsor clearly identified?
- What does the organization stand for? Is there a button to click on for "Who We Are" or "Mission Statement"? Is there a "Contact Us" button?

Online Learning Center

Whether you are a seasoned Internet user or a complete novice, City College of San Francisco's Rosenberg Library offers a wealth of helpful information about how to conduct online searches.

- First, go to the college's website: www. ccsf.edu.
- On the home page menu, click on "Library."
- Under "Finding Information," click on "On the Web," where you will find a discussion of Subject Directories, Search Engines, and Image, Audio, and Video Search Engines.
- Finally, under "Related Links" there are two more relevant handouts: "Web Search Techniques" and "Evaluating Information."

- Is the website dated? Where does the date appear? Does the site indicate how often information is updated?
- Is the website trying to sell you something?

Practice Exercise 5	Choose one or two of these websites to evaluate according to the criteria listed above, as well as the tasks listed after each site.

- www.focusonthefamily.com   Focus on the Family

  Click on "Parenting" at the main menu and locate information on Schooling and Discipline. What authority governs the information presented on this site? Would you consider this site as liberal or conservative? How do you know?

- www.talkingpointsmemo.com   Talking Points Memo, a blog by Joshua Micah Marshall

  Read through several stories on this site. Is its political slant liberal or conservative? How do you know?

- www.worldwildlife.org/   World Wildlife Fund

  What is this organization doing to save the tiger? What species are currently listed as being "Under Threat"?

- www.plannedparenthood.org   Planned Parenthood Federation of America, Inc.

  What kinds of counseling does this organization offer? If you or someone you know was seeking an abortion in South Dakota, Iowa, or Kansas, where would they find that information?

- www.foodsafetynetwork.ca   Food Safety Network

  Skim through some of the articles intended for the general public on this site sponsored by Canada's University of Guelph.

- www.foodsafety.gov   The American counterpart, sponsored by the U.S. Department of Health and Human Services

  Which site provides more information? On each site, search for and locate the safe internal temperature for cooking your Thanksgiving turkey.

- www.ifcnr.com/   International Foundation for the Conservation of Natural Resources

  Click on "Wildlife Ecology" or go to www.wildecology.ifcnr.com/

  How does this organization define "conservation"? What does the name of the organization imply? Does it appear to be as protective of wild animal populations as its name suggests?

- www.cis.org/   Center for Immigration Studies

  Click on "About Us." Does the position of this site regarding immigration appear to be liberal or conservative? How do you know? What is the organization's position on the Dream Act?

**Practice
Exercise 6**

Here are four more subjects to explore online.

1. www.babyfirsttv.com   Baby First TV

   At the home page, click on "Parents," "Baby U," and any other links that look interesting. What is available on this site? How much do their services cost? What claims are made? What evidence is presented in support of the products? Are any obvious emotional appeals evident?

   www.babyeinstein.com   Baby Einstein

   What products are available? How much do they cost? Click on "Ask the Expert." Who is the expert, and what are her qualifications? What claims does she make about Baby Einstein products? What fears does she attempt to dispel? What evidence is presented in support of the products? Are any obvious emotional appeals evident?

2. At www.google.com, type in "Stress reduction, college students."

   Open each of the first six or seven sites that appear and peruse the information offered. Which ones do you consider most authoritative? Which ones are trying to sell you something?

3. At www.google.com, type in "Obesity help."

   Read through the information on the first six or seven sites that appear. How many of them are commercial sites intending to sell you something? Which ones do you consider to be most objective and informative? How can you tell?

4. Finally, for something fun, investigate this unusual Christmas tradition in Sweden. On Christmas Eve, December 24, most of the nation's residents stop whatever they are doing and watch a Donald Duck cartoon (in Swedish "Calle Anka"). How did this tradition start?

**Practice
Exercise 7**

Can a site concerned with politics and current events ever be completely free of bias? Below are some political and policy websites. Look through these sites and try to ascertain how upfront each is about its political leanings. Can you tell anything about the organization's leanings from the name alone? Which would you feel comfortable about using as a source if you were writing an essay on, say, global warming or immigration? You may want to consider some of the following:

- The explanation of the organization's mission
- Coverage of news of the day
- Evidence of slanted language and bias
- Frequency of updates
- Appeals for donations

The Heritage Foundation	www.heritage.org/
People for the American Way	www.pfaw.org/
Accuracy in Media	www.aim.org/
The Brookings Institution	www.brookings.edu/
Progressive Policy Institute	www.ppionline.org/
Pew Internet and American Life Project	www.pewinternet.org/
Heartland Institute	www.heartland.org/issues/environment
The Center for American Progress	www.americanprogress.org
MoveOn.org	www.moveon.org
The American Enterprise Online	www.aei.org/
Real Clear Politics	www.realclearpolitics.com
Andrew Breitbart's Big Government	www.breitbart.com

■ READING BLOGS

Anything written here about blogs and the blogosphere will very likely be outdated by the time you read this book. Blogs are proliferating at a phenomenal rate every week. Whatever your interests—cooking, motorcycles, child raising, politics, massage therapy—there are dozens of blogs available for your perusal. For readers of this book, I want to focus on political blogs because they present a special problem.

Authority is the biggest one. Who is the blogger? What are his or her credentials? Why should we believe the blogger's opinion? Lack of both editorial oversight and simple fact-checking is the other big problem. When anyone can become a writer, when everyone has a forum where he or she can express opinions, the reader has to be even more vigilant than usual. Sorting out the truth from distortion and detecting bias and manipulative appeals become even more crucial. One way to do this is to read widely enough that you can get a sense of what's right, what's fair, what's commonly accepted—not that the crowd is always right, of course.

As noted before, you should faithfully subject anything you read—and especially what you read in blogs—to the sort of critical scrutiny explained throughout Chapters 8 and 9. If it's a truism that you can't believe everything in print, it's even truer with blogs!

If you are interested in politics, there are a number of blogs that you can investigate further on your own. Rather than list individual blogs, I provide here some resources for locating political blogs representing various points of view.

- www.etalkinghead.com   On the home page, click on "Political Blog Directory," where you will find an extensive list of blogs representing various points of view—conservative, independent, liberal, libertarian, humor, moderate, religious, and so forth.

- www.blogs.com   Lists "Ten Popular Conservative Blogs" and "Ten Popular Liberal Blogs"
- www.uspolitics.about.com   Lists the best libertarian blogs

■ CHAPTER EXERCISE: FOUR EDITORIALS FOR ANALYSIS

Chapter 10 concludes with four editorials for practice in reading and evaluating opinion pieces. The first two take opposite positions on the question of whether national service should be compulsory for young Americans. The second two editorials both make a case for the same argument: Because the prison system in the U.S. is broken, we should reinstate corporal punishment. Questions for analysis follow each editorial, and questions on each pair of editorials appear after them.

Should American Youth Be Required to Perform National Service?

Selection 1   YES

William A. Galston, Compulsory National Service Would Strengthen American Citizenship

William A. Galston is a former advisor to President Bill Clinton and the Ezra K. Zilkha chair in governance studies at the Brookings Institution. This article was posted on the website of *U.S. News & World Report* (www.usnews.com) on October 19, 2010.

There are different kinds of rights. Some we enjoy simply because we are human beings—the rights enumerated in the Declaration of Independence, for example. Others are linked to a particular status: American citizens possess some rights that noncitizens do not. We do not have to earn human rights, and no one can take them away from us. By contrast, we may have to perform specified acts to obtain citizenship rights (that's what naturalization laws are about), and we may act in ways that lead to forfeiture of some of those rights, at least temporarily, as in the case of convicted criminals not being allowed to vote.

Citizenship, then, is a package of rights and responsibilities. But there is no theory that tells us exactly what is or should be in that package. It's up to us to decide.

In recent decades, we've expanded old rights and created new ones. While often controversial, that process has in many respects made us a fairer and more inclusive society. We've spent less time on the other half of the equation—the responsibilities that citizens share for the well-being of others and for the country as a whole. It's time to redress the balance.

Citizens' due. Some responsibilities are not controversial, such as obeying duly enacted laws. Another example: Most people recognize that the right to trial by a jury of our peers exists only on paper unless we appear for jury duty when summoned. No doubt the summons can arrive at an inconvenient moment, but we can't take the position that mandatory jury duty is an illegitimate limitation on individual liberty without threatening the basis of our justice system.

In the past, we have regarded military service as a responsibility of citizenship. After Vietnam, in which the fairness of the draft emerged as a major issue, we turned toward all-volunteer armed forces. In many respects the shift has been a success. The military has attracted a steady stream of highly qualified recruits, and the skills and discipline of our armed forces have never been higher.

But we have paid a price: A small percentage of Americans do the fighting for the rest of us, creating a wedge between military professionals and average citizens. Many elected officials lack military experience, and few have children in uniform. For most of us, defending our country is something we watch on television. Little in the lives of young Americans helps them understand that citizenship is more than a list of rights to which they are entitled.

There's something we can do about this. Suppose that upon high school graduation or reaching the age of 18, every American were given a randomly selected lottery number based on their birthday and that a certain portion were selected for civic service. They would be offered a choice—two years of either military or civilian service. Those doing civilian service would receive stipends large enough to pay living expenses, as members of AmeriCorps do today.

This system would produce a number of desirable results for the country, as it would benefit from such service, but also for those who perform it. By the time they entered high school, young people would know that they might be asked to serve, and they would begin to talk to their older siblings or relatives about their options. They would begin to understand that there's more to citizenship than simply asserting their rights.

Those called to serve would spend time helping their country in their communities, in hard-hit areas far from home, or overseas. They would meet people unlike themselves, members of other classes and ethnic groups, with different aspirations. Some would begin to reshape their conceptions of how to spend their lives, opting for military, nonprofit, or public service careers. Most would form enduring friendships; all would have formative experiences they would never forget.

Some will object to this proposal as an unwarranted limitation on liberty, and surveys probably would show a majority of high school students opposed. But we have to ask ourselves whether we're satisfied with the condition of American citizenship today and, if not, how we're prepared to strengthen it. This is a national debate we should all welcome.

Questions for Analysis—Galston's Editorial

1. According to Galston, what is the relationship between our rights as citizens of the United States and our responsibilities? Why is there an imbalance between the two today?

2. What role did the Vietnam War in general and the switch to an all-volunteer armed forces in particular play in this situation?

3. What is Galston's specific proposal regarding compulsory national service? How would it work? Who would be affected?

4. In what ways would Galston's proposal help young people understand the true meaning of citizenship?

5. What kind of evidence does Galston use in support of his claim? Is it fair and sufficient, according to the rules of good argumentation?

6. Does Galston appear to be a liberal or a conservative, at least in this one area? How can you tell?

Selection 2   **NO**

Matthew Spalding, "Compulsory National Service Would Undermine the American Character"

Matthew Spalding is the director of the B. Kenneth Simon Center for American Studies at the Heritage Foundation. This editorial was posted on the website of *U.S. News & World Report* (www.usnews.com), on October 19, 2010.

Americans have always exhibited a strong sense of compassion toward their neighbors and those less fortunate. Volunteerism, what Alexis de Tocqueville called our "spirit of association," is in the national DNA. Policymakers have long recognized the importance of citizen engagement and philanthropic volunteerism to a thriving civil society.

But government should not attempt to compel its citizens to engage in these worthwhile endeavors. Its proper role is merely to energize a culture of personal commitment to those in need as a way of strengthening the natural grounds of citizenship and community.

The goal of citizen service should be to protect and strengthen civil society. Tocqueville observed that one of American society's great virtues is its tendency to create local voluntary associations to meet the most important needs of the people. Other nations handled these needs through and by government; but in the United States, private individuals of all ages, conditions, and dispositions formed associations.

"I have often admired the extreme skill with which the inhabitants of the United States succeed in proposing a common object to the exertions of a great many men, and in getting them voluntarily to pursue it," Tocqueville wrote in Democracy in America. "What political power could ever carry on the vast multitude of lesser undertakings which American citizens perform every day, with the assistance of the principle of association?" He added, "The more [government] stands in the place of associations, the more will individuals, losing the notion of combining together, require its assistance."

The traditional associations of civil society—families, schools, churches, and voluntary organizations—sustain social order and public morality, moderate individualism and materialism, and cultivate personal character.

The concept of national service is altogether different.

Government programs, like AmeriCorps, do not encourage sacrificial giving of time and resources, which has the character-forming effect of teaching compassionate responsibility. Instead, they suggest that "volunteerism" could just as well mean a paid job with benefits—or worse, a mandatory obligation. Such government-directed "volunteerism," by encouraging individuals and associations to look to the state as the provider of assistance, belittles authentic volunteerism, the process by which individuals choose without economic benefit to help their neighbor. It also threatens the independence of the private associations that have always been the engine of moral and social reform in America.

The American way. The call to service is best answered not by government, but by the citizens in voluntary associations, local communities, and private organizations that are at the heart of American charity. Last year alone, 63.4 million Americans volunteered, well exceeding the 500,000 involved in national service. Total private giving is estimated to exceed $300 billion a year, with individuals accounting for 75 percent of that, overwhelming the Corporation for National and Community Service's budget of just under $1 billion. One organization, the Knights of Columbus, made charitable contributions of over $150 million and generated some 70 million volunteer service hours. The depth of private American charity and the vast potential to expand these great activities ought to be highlighted and strongly encouraged.

These private voluntary organizations thrive today precisely because their work is privately organized, highly decentralized, and directly focused on community needs and local conditions.

At a time when Americans are volunteering in unprecedented numbers (and ways), policymakers should reject the model of government-centered national service, which undermines the American character and threatens to weaken private associations.

The better course is to bolster the call to service by encouraging a true and voluntary citizen service that is consistent with principles of self-government, is harmonious with a vibrant civil society, and promotes a service agenda based on personal responsibility, independent citizenship, and civic volunteerism.

Questions for Analysis—Spalding's Editorial

1. State the main claim in the editorial. What is Spalding's underlying premise?
2. Who was Alexis de Tocqueville, and what do his comments about America's "spirit of association" have to do with Spalding's claim? Is he citing de Toqueville as an authority, or as something else?
3. According to Spalding, what is the chief role of government? Why shouldn't the American government demand compulsory service of its citizens?
4. What is the role of traditional associations in American society? Do you agree with his assessment that "families, schools, churches, and

voluntary associations . . . sustain social order and public morality?" Can you think of any other institutions that serve these functions?

5. Spalding states that a government-mandated program would "undermine American character." What would be another disadvantage of a government program that administers public service? What solution does he propose to take the place of a government program?

6. What kind of evidence does Spalding use in support of his claim? Is it fair and sufficient, according to the rules of good argumentation?

7. Does Spalding appear to be a liberal or a conservative, at least in this one area? How can you tell?

Questions for Analysis—Both Editorials

1. If you have thought about the possibility of compulsory national service before reading these editorials, what is your position? Which of these editorials more closely mirrors your thinking? Did either of them change your thinking, and if so, how?

2. What is one apparent weakness in Galston's editorial? in Spalding's?

3. One weakness that I observed is that neither writer offers any specific examples of what kinds of service might be performed as part of a mandatory government program. Do you agree that this is a weakness? What other information would have strengthened these editorials and made them more convincing?

4. Which writer, Galston or Spalding, does a better job of supporting his claim? (Note: This does *not* mean which one you agree with. Consider only the argument made and the writer's evidence.)

5. Does either writer appear to have a hidden agenda? If so, what is it?

How to Fix Our Broken Prison System—Corporal Punishment

Selection 3

Jeff Jacoby, "Bring Back Flogging"

Since 1994 Jeff Jacoby has brought a conservative perspective to the *Boston Globe,* where this much-reprinted opinion piece was published in 1997. As before, questions for analysis follow each editorial, and at the end are questions concerning both opinion pieces.

Boston Globe
Newspaper Columnist
Jeff Jacoby.

1 Boston's Puritan forefathers did not indulge miscreants lightly.

2 For selling arms and gunpowder to Indians in 1632, Richard Hopkins was sentenced to be "whipt, & branded with a hott iron on one of

his cheekes." Joseph Gatchell, convicted of blasphemy in 1684, was ordered "to stand in pillory, have his head and hand put in & have his toung drawne forth out of his mouth, & peirct through with a hott iron." When Hannah Newell pleaded guilty to adultery in 1694, the court ordered "fifteen stripes Severally to be laid on upon her naked back at the Common Whipping post." Her consort, the aptly named Lambert Despair, fared worse: He was sentenced to 25 lashes "and that on the next Thursday Immediately after Lecture he stand upon the Pillory for . . . a full hower with Adultery in Capitall letters written upon his brest.

3   Corporal punishment for criminals did not vanish with the Puritans—Delaware didn't get around to repealing it until 1972—but for all relevant purposes, it has been out of fashion for at least 150 years. The day is long past when the stocks had an honored place on the Boston Common, or when offenders were publicly flogged. Now we practice a more enlightened, more humane way of disciplining wrongdoers: We lock them up in cages.

4   Imprisonment has become our penalty of choice for almost every offense in the criminal code. Commit murder; go to prison. Sell cocaine; go to prison. Kite checks; go to prison. It is an all-purpose punishment, suitable—or so it would seem—for crimes violent and nonviolent, motivated by hate or by greed, plotted coldly or committed in a fit of passion. If anything, our preference for incarceration is deepening—behold the slew of mandatory minimum sentences for drug crimes and "three-strikes-you're-out" life terms for recidivists. Some 1.6 million Americans are behind bars today. That represents a 250 percent increase since 1980, and the number is climbing.

5   We cage criminals at a rate unsurpassed in the free world, yet few of us believe that the criminal justice system is a success. Crime is out of control, despite the deluded happy talk by some politicians about how "safe" cities have become. For most wrongdoers, the odds of being arrested, prosecuted, convicted, and incarcerated are reassuringly long. Fifty-eight percent of all murders do not result in a prison term. Likewise 98 percent of all burglaries.

6   Many states have gone on prison-building sprees, yet the penal system is choked to bursting. To ease the pressure, nearly all convicted felons are released early—or not locked up at all. "About three of every four convicted criminals," says John Dilulio, a noted Princeton criminologist, "are on the streets without meaningful probation or parole supervision." And while everyone knows that amateur thugs should be deterred before they become career criminals, it is almost unheard-of for judges to send first- or second-time offenders to prison.

7   Meanwhile, the price of keeping criminals in cages is appalling—a common estimate is $30,000 per inmate per year. (To be sure, the cost to society of turning many inmates loose would be even higher.) For tens of thousands of convicts, prison is a graduate school of criminal studies:

They emerge more ruthless and savvy than when they entered. And for many offenders, there is even a certain cachet to doing time - a stint in prison becomes a a sign of manhood, a status symbol.

8   But there would be no cachet in chaining a criminal to an outdoor post and flogging him. If young punks were horsewhipped in public after their first conviction, fewer of them would harden into lifelong felons. A humiliating and painful paddling can be applied to the rear end of a crook for a lot less than $30,000—and prove a lot more educational than 10 years' worth of prison meals and lockdowns.

9   Are we quite certain the Puritans have nothing to teach us about dealing with criminals?

10   Of course, their crimes are not our crimes: We do not arrest blasphemers or adulterers, and only gun control fanatics would criminalize the sale of weapons to Indians. (They would criminalize the sale of weapons to anybody.) Nor would the ordeal suffered by poor Joseph Gatchell— the tongue "peirct through" with a hot poker—be regarded today as anything less than torture.

11   But what is the objection to corporal punishment that doesn't maim or mutilate? Instead of a prison term, why not sentence at least some criminals—say, thieves and drunk drivers—to a public whipping?

12   "Too degrading," some will say. "Too brutal." But where is it written that being whipped is more degrading than being caged? Why is it more brutal to flog a wrongdoer than to throw him in prison—where the risk of being beaten, raped, or murdered is terrifyingly high?

13   The Globe reported in 1994 that more than 200,000 prison inmates are raped each year, usually to the indifference of the guards. "The horrors experienced by many young inmates, particularly those who . . . are convicted of nonviolent offenses," former Supreme Court Justice Harry Blackmun has written, "border on the unimaginable." Are those horrors preferable to the short, sharp shame of corporal punishment?

14   Perhaps the Puritans were more enlightened than we think, at least on the subject of punishment. Their sanctions were humiliating and painful, but quick and cheap. Maybe we should readopt a few.

Questions for Analysis—Jeff Jacoby

1. Before analyzing the editorial and its claim, be sure that you know what these words refer to (see paragraphs 2–3): *flogging, pillory, whipping post, the stocks.*

2. Why does Jacoby begin with a recitation of various corporal punishments beginning in the days of the Puritans? Comment on the tone in the last part of paragraph 3 and on the connotation in Jacoby's word choice in this sentence: "We lock them [wrongdoers] up in cages." Why doesn't he use the more common term "cells"? What point is he making here?

3. What evidence does Jacoby present to show that our criminal justice system has failed? What are his objections to prisons as they function now?

4. Explain the meaning of the word *cachet* in the sense of receiving a prison sentence at the end of paragraph 7. Jacoby does not say what segment of society feels this way. Do you know? Why would flogging end the cachet of doing time?

5. Read paragraph 10 again. What point is Jacoby making? Why does he include it?

6. Does Jacoby provide a refutation? If so, where does it appear? How does he anticipate objections to his proposal to restore flogging for certain crimes?

7. Which of the following underlies Jacoby's proposal to copy the Puritans' preferred punishment of flogging—the rehabilitation of criminals, prevention of further crimes, saving money, reforming our judicial system, or something else altogether? Explain.

8. What would a liberal say about Jacoby's proposal? What do you think?

Selection 4

Peter Moskos, "In Lieu of Prison, Bring Back the Lash," *The Washington Post*

The author of *In Defense of Flogging* (2011), Peter Moskos is also an assistant professor of law and police science at John Jay College of Criminal Justice as well as a faculty member in the doctoral program in sociology at the City University of New York.

Author Peter Moskos.

1   Suggest adding the whipping post to America's system of criminal justice and most people recoil in horror. But offer a choice between five years in prison or 10 lashes and almost everybody picks the lash. What does that say about prison?

2   America has a prison problem. Never in the history of the world has a country locked up so many of its people. We have more prisons than China, and it has a billion more people than we do. Forty years ago America had 338,000 people behind bars. Today 2.3 million are incarcerated. We have more prisoners than soldiers. Something has gone terribly wrong.

3   The problem—mostly due to longer and mandatory sentences combined with an idiotic war on drugs—is so abysmal that the Supreme Court recently ordered 33,000 prisoners in California to be housed elsewhere or released. If California could simply return to its 1970 level of incarceration, the savings from its $9 billion prison budget would cut the state's budget deficit in half. But doing so would require the release

of 125,000 inmates, and not even the most progressive reformer has a plan to reduce the prison population by 85 percent.

4   I do: Bring back the lash. Give convicts the choice of flogging in lieu of incarceration.

5   Ironically, when the penitentiary was invented in post-revolutionary Philadelphia, it was designed to replace the very punishment I propose. Corporal punishment, said one early advocate of prisons, was a relic of "barbarous" British imperialism ill-suited to "a new country, simple manners, and a popular form of government." State by state, starting with Pennsylvania in 1790 and ending with Delaware in 1972 (20 years after the last flogging), corporal punishment was struck from the criminal code.

6   The idea was that penitentiaries would heal the criminally ill just as hospitals cured the physically sick. It didn't work. Yet despite—or perhaps because of—the failures of the first prisons, states authorized more and larger prisons. With flogging banned and crime not cured, there was simply no alternative. We tried rehabilitation and ended up with supermax. We tried to be humane and ended up with more prisoners than Stalin had at the height of the Soviet Gulag. Somewhere in the process, we lost the concept of justice and punishment in a free society.

7   Today, the prison-industrial complex has become little more than a massive government-run make-work program that profits from human bondage. To oversimplify—just a bit—we pay poor, unemployed rural whites to guard poor, unemployed urban blacks.

8   Of course some people are simply too dangerous to release—pedophiles, terrorists and the truly psychopathic, for instance. But they're relatively few in number. And we keep these people behind bars because we're afraid of them.

9   As to the other 2 million common criminals, the 2 million more than we had in 1970, we can't and won't keep them locked up forever. Ninety-five percent of prisoners are eventually released. The question is not if but when and how.

10   Incarceration not only fails to deter crime but in many ways can increase it. For crime driven by economic demand, such as drug dealing, arresting one seller creates a job opening for others, who might fight over the vacant position.

11   Incarceration destroys families and jobs, exactly what people need to have in order to stay away from crime. Incarcerated criminals are more likely to reoffend than similar people given alternative sentences. To break the cycle of crime, people need help. And they would need less help if they were never incarcerated in the first place.

12   Flogging, as practiced in Singapore or Malaysia, is honest, cheap and, compared to prison, humane. Caning succeeds in part simply because it is not incarceration. Along with saving tens of billions of dollars a year, corporal punishment avoids all the hogwash about prisons somehow being good for the soul.

13   Some would argue that flogging isn't harsh enough. While this moves beyond the facile belief that flogging is too cruel to consider, if flogging shouldn't be offered because it's too soft—if we need to keep people locked up precisely because overcrowded jails and prisons are so unbelievably horrific—then perhaps we need to question our humanity.

14   Is there a third way, something better than both flogging and prison? I hope so. But until we figure out what that is and have the political fortitude to adopt it, we should not let the perfect be the enemy of the good. Flogging may be distasteful, but surely there's little harm in offering the choice. If it takes a defense of flogging to make us face the truth about prison and punishment, I say bring on the lash.

Questions for Analysis—Peter Moskos

1. Before analyzing the editorial and its claim, be sure that you know what these words refer to: *whipping post, the lash, corporal punishment, caning.*

2. What, according to Moskos, is the reason for America's "prison problem"? How does this problem manifest itself? Is it merely that we appear to lock up more people in prisons than any other country, or is there a bigger concern? And why does America lock up so many people in the first place?

3. What are Moskos's specific objections to the way penitentiaries work? Why have they failed? Why aren't today's prisons "good for the soul"? What does he propose as an alternative to incarceration?

4. What kinds of criminals would not be appropriate candidates for flogging? Why not?

5. What are the particular advantages of flogging? Why does he endorse it as a more humane alternative to prison? In what ways is prison not only inhumane but ineffective?

6. Does Moskos provide a refutation? If so, where does it appear? How does he anticipate objections to his proposal to restore flogging for certain crimes?

7. Does Moskos appear to be a liberal or a conservative? How can you tell?

Questions for Analysis—Both Editorials

1. In terms of the criteria for good argumentation, which editorial does a better job of arguing that restoring flogging—or corporal punishment—for certain criminals would be a good idea? Defend your choice.

2. Both editorial writers endorse the same claim. Which one does a better job of presenting evidence in support of it?

5

Reading Essays and Articles

■ INTRODUCTION TO READING ESSAYS

Why Read Essays in the First Place?

The essay is the staple of college English courses where the assigned textbook is an anthology. The essay form has several advantages: It is short, it can be read in one sitting, and it can be discussed in one or two class meetings. Further, students acquire analytical skills more easily by studying short pieces of nonfiction prose, which they can then transfer to book-length works. By the time you reach Part 5, you will have undoubtedly already been assigned a few essays from the earlier portions of the book. It might be a good idea to review the discussion in Part 1 about annotating, paraphrasing, and summarizing, since your instructor may very well assign you to complete similar assignments when you read essays in this part.

Often students are unsure of their instructors' expectations with essay assignments. Part 5 will give you ample practice in various essay-reading skills. The truism that practice makes perfect surely applies here. The more experience you get reading your assignments attentively and the more you actively read by annotating the text, the more competent you will become and the more you will enjoy preparing your assignments. Besides learning more about the day's current issues and gathering interesting information, an added bonus might be higher grades. There is no advantage in *not* reading. Students who seldom read on their own, who skim through their assignments, or who sit in the back of the classroom or look down, pretending to be engrossed in the text and hoping to avoid being called on, miss a significant part of the college intellectual experience.

The Characteristics of an Essay

If the paragraph is an essay in miniature, as it has often been described, then the essay exemplifies the techniques and characteristics that you studied in Chapters 2 through 5 in Parts 1 and 2. The essay form derives from the seventeenth-century French writer Michele de Montaigne. His short pieces were an *attempt* to explain his observations of human behavior and customs. (In French, the verb *essayer* means "to attempt," and an essay—*un essai*—pertains to the work itself.) Today an **essay** describes a sustained piece of nonfiction prose with a myriad of purposes and characteristics.

Like the paragraph, an essay must contain or suggest a main idea, which is called the ***thesis;*** the essay has a direction; and it has development, unity, and coherence. Unlike the paragraph, however, whose short length limits its scope, the essay is more varied in length, organization, and methods of development. Typically, essays published by professional writers run between 500 and 5,000 words, but length is not an important criterion for defining the form.

Essays may be personal narrative, a description or a scene or an emotion, a presentation of scientific information, a personal confession, an emotional plea to resolve a controversy, a satire on a practice or custom that the writer wants to mock, an explanation of a social or political issue, or an examination of a problem and its repercussions. In short, the essay is infinitely adaptable. An essay may represent any of the four modes of discourse—narration, description, exposition, or persuasion—singly or in combination, though one mode usually predominates. In short, the form is a diverse instrument for communicating a writer's ideas.

This remark from a professional writer sheds further light on the essay form. In *A Writer's Companion,* Richard Marius says that the essay "inevitably has about it the scent of an argument," by which he means that even in narrative and descriptive essays, there is an underlying persuasive intent.

The Parts of an Essay

The essay is traditionally divided into three parts: the beginning (the introduction), the middle (the body or supporting paragraphs), and the end (the conclusion). We will look at these structural parts one by one. When you read each new essay, try to separate it into these three parts by asking at what point the introduction ends and the body paragraphs begin and at what point the body paragraphs give way to the conclusion. The importance of this skill cannot be emphasized enough. Rather than drowning in a sea of words, seeing the logical progression of ideas will help you distinguish the main points from the support. Often, making a brief outline of the component parts will help you see the overall structure, just as an aerial view of a city reveals its layout better than a ground-level view does. And annotating while you read, as noted before, will help you to master the content. In free form essays, of course, it may not be possible to identify this tripartite structure.

The Introduction

Writing teachers often tell their students that the opening paragraph of their essays should grab the reader's attention by using a hook to entice the reader to continue reading. Beginning college readers should be aware of this device as well. There are no particular rules governing the hook—only the writer's estimation of how best to get into the subject. Someone once described the opening of an essay as a way to "invite us into the world of the essay," as good a description as any. The introductory portion, which may actually comprise two or more paragraphs, may contain the essay's **thesis**—the main idea—or it may suggest it, in which case the thesis is **implied**. Few professional writers use the obvious direct-announcement approach for the thesis.

Given the diverse form of the essay, finding the thesis poses a difficulty because writers are under no obligation to adhere to a formula. Where should you look for the thesis? A writer may provide a thesis somewhere near the beginning of the essay, often following an opening paragraph or two (which provides the hook), introducing the general subject, setting the scene, establishing a problem to be solved—in other words, orienting us to the topic. The writer might begin with a personal anecdote or a short narrative, he or she may provide historical background or present the background of a problematic issue. Then comes the thesis. (Some textbooks refer to this type of opening as the funnel pattern.)

To illustrate this pattern, study these three opening paragraphs from a newspaper article about Barack Obama's childhood in Hawaii:

> On weekday mornings as a teenager, Barry Obama left his grandparents' apartment on the 10th floor of the 12-story high-rise at 1617 S. Beretania, a mile and a half above Waikiki Beach, and walked up Punahou Street in the shadows of capacious banyan trees and date palms. Before crossing the overpass above the H1 freeway, where traffic zoomed east to body-surfing beaches or west to the airport and Pearl Harbor, he passed Kapiolani Medical Center, walking below the hospital room where he was born on Aug. 4, 1961. Two blocks farther along, at the intersection with Wilder, he could look left toward the small apartment on Poki where he had spent a few years with his little sister, Maya, and his mother, Ann, back when she was getting her master's degree at the University of Hawaii before she left again for Indonesia. Soon enough he was at the lower edge of Punahou School, the gracefully sloping private campus where he studied some and played basketball more.
>
> An adolescent life told in five Honolulu blocks, confined and compact, but far, far away. Apart from other unprecedented aspects of his rise, it is a geographical truth that no politician in American history has traveled farther than Barack Obama to be within reach of the White House. He was born and spent most of his formative years on Oahu, in distance the most removed population center on the planet, about 2,390 miles from California, farther from a major landmass than anywhere but Easter Island. In the westward impulse of American settlement, his birthplace was the last frontier, an outpost with its own time zone, the 50th of the United States, admitted to the union only two years before Obama came along.
>
> Those who come from islands are inevitably shaped by the experience. For Obama, the experience was all contradiction and contrast.
>
> David Marannis, "Son of Hawaii: How an Island Childhood Shaped Obama,"
> *The Washington Post National Weekly Edition*

Write the sentence that represents the thesis in the space. Then, as you did for main-idea sentences in Chapter 2, underline the topic once and the controlling idea twice.

_____

_____

Did you see how the article's subtitle reinforces the thesis statement?

Do not expect every essay you read, however, to use the funnel pattern, and in adult prose you won't hear a bell ring when you come to the thesis.

Practice Exercise 1	To test your reading acumen and your ability to identity the thesis, I selected six introductory sections for essays from several books on my bookshelves. Read each carefully and then follow these instructions: First, write the mode of discourse (narration, description, exposition, or persuasion) that you *predict* will occur in the essay as a whole, not the mode of discourse represented in the excerpt. If you are unsure, write a question mark. Second, write the thesis statement or main idea, if one is represented, in your own words. If there is no thesis stated or implied, write another question mark.

A.   Amy Tan is the writer of many best-selling novels, including *The Joy Luck Club* and *The Kitchen God's Wife*. "Mother Tongue" is a modern classic essay, reprinted in many college anthologies.

I am not a scholar of English or literature. I cannot give you much more than personal opinions on the English language and its variations in this country or others.

I am a writer. And by that definition, I am someone who has always loved language. I am fascinated by language in daily life. I spend a great deal of my time thinking about the power of language—the way it can evoke an emotion, a visual image, a complex idea, or a simple truth. Language is the tool of my trade. And I use them all—all the Englishes I grew up with.

Amy Tan, "Mother Tongue"

Mode of discourse: _____

Thesis statement: _____

_____

B.   Judith Ortiz Cofer, a professor of English and creative writing at the University of Georgia, is best known for *Silent Dancing,* a collection of nonfiction pieces examining her life as a Puerto Rican in her newly adopted country.

We lived in Puerto Rico until my brother was born in 1954. Soon after, because of economic pressures on our growing family, my father joined the United States Navy. He was assigned to duty on a ship in Brooklyn Yard—a place of cement and steel that was to be his home base in the States until his retirement more than twenty years later. He left the Island first, alone, going to New York City and tracking down his uncle who lived with his family across the Hudson River in Paterson, New Jersey. There my father found a tiny apartment in a huge tenement that had once housed Jewish families but was just being taken over and transformed by Puerto Ricans, overflowing from New York City. In 1955 he sent for us. My mother was only twenty years old, I was not quite three, and my brother was a toddler when we arrived at *El Building,* as the place had been christened by its newest residents. . . . given strict orders by my father to keep the doors locked, the noise down, ourselves to ourselves.

It seems that Father had learned some painful lessons about prejudice while searching for an apartment in Paterson. Not until years later did I hear how much resistance he had encountered with landlords who were panicking at the influx of Latinos into a neighborhood that had been Jewish for a couple of generations. It made no difference that it was the American phenomenon of ethnic turnover which was changing the urban core of Paterson, and that the human flood could not be held back with an accusing finger.

Judith Ortiz Cofer, "Silent Dancing"

Mode of discourse: _____

Thesis statement: _____

_____

_____

C. Barry Lopez is one of the country's most distinguished non-fiction writers. He is best known for *Arctic Dreams* and *Of Wolves and Men.*

The deserts of southern California, the high, relatively cooler and wetter Mojave and the hotter, dryer Sonoran to the south of it, carry the signatures of many cultures. Prehistoric rock drawings in the Mojave's Coso Range, probably the greatest concentration of petroglyphs in North America, are at least three thousand years old. Big-game-hunting cultures that flourished six or seven thousand years before that are known from broken spear tips, choppers, and burins left scattered along the shores of great Pleistocene lakes, long since evaporated. Weapons and tools discovered at China Lake may be thirty thousand years old; and worked stone from a quarry in the Calico Mountains is, some argue, evidence that human beings were here more than 200,000 years ago.

Because of the long-term stability of such arid environments, much of this prehistoric stone evidence still lies exposed on the ground, accessible to anyone who passes by—the studious, the acquisitive, the indifferent, the merely curious. Archaeologists do not agree on the sequence of cultural history beyond about twelve thousand years ago, but it is clear that these broken bits of chalcedony, chert, and obsidian, like the animal drawings and geometric designs etched on walls of basalt throughout the desert, anchor the earliest threads of human history, the first record of human endeavor here.

Barry Lopez, "The Stone Horse," *Antaeus*

Mode of discourse _____

Thesis statement _____

_____

D. Meredith Broussard is an independent writer living in Philadel-
    phia. She teaches writing at the University of Pennsylvania.

Of little concern to most parents or educators only a generation ago, food allergies are now seen as a childhood epidemic. The American Academy of Pediatrics recently began recommending that peanuts be withheld until a child
turns three; hundreds of food-allergy nonprofits and local parents groups have
formed; and six states have passed laws requiring food-allergy safety measures
in their schools, with similar legislation currently being considered in Congress.
Children are even being recruited to help battle this supposed threat, as in this
Food Allergy & Anaphylaxis Network (FAAN) brochure, which enjoins young
students to "Be a PAL" and protect the lives of their classmates. But the rash of
fatal food allergies is mostly myth, a cultural hysteria cooked up with a few key
ingredients: fearful parents in an age of increased anxiety, sensationalist news
coverage, and a coterie of well-placed advocates whose dubious science has fed
the frenzy.

Meredith Broussard, "Everyone's Gone Nuts," Harper's Magazine

Mode of discourse: _____

Thesis statement: _____

_____

_____

E. Bill Bryson has written numerous books of nonfiction. This
    excerpt is from his travel narrative of Great Britain.

Nothing gives the English more pleasure, in a quiet but determined sort of way,
than to do things oddly. They put milk in their tea, drive on the wrong side of the
road, pronounce Cholmondeley as "Chumley" and Belvoir as "Beaver," celebrate
the Queen's birthday in June even though she was born in April, and dress their
palace guards in bearskin helmets that make them look as if, for some private and
unfathomable reason, they are wearing fur-lined wastebaskets on their heads.
    Almost every realm of British life you could care to name, from the rules of
cricket to the running of Parliament, is predicated on a system guaranteed to
confound foreigners (that is, of course, the whole purpose of it), but in one area

■ ANALYZING ESSAYS: QUESTIONS TO ASK

1. Who is the author? Most anthologies provide a brief biographical headnote, along with information about where the material was originally published, which may help you determine the writer's authority, the audience, purpose, and point of view or possible bias.

2. This question follows from the first. Who is the audience? Are the writer's ideas intended for the general reading public, or do the vocabulary and subject matter suggest that the writer is appealing to a narrower group with specialized knowledge? What clues does the author provide that identify whom he or she is writing for? If the piece comes from a magazine or periodical, is it a mainstream vehicle like *Time, Newsweek, The New Yorker,* or *Vanity Fair,* or is it a source apt to appeal to a more specialized audience, for example, *Scientific American, Mother Jones, Yankee Magazine,* or *Foreign Affairs*?

3. What is the writer's purpose? Remember that purpose is closely related to mode of discourse. Is there a secondary purpose, as well?

4. What is the thesis? Where is it located? Is its placement appropriate for the writer's purpose and subject? Try to restate the thesis in your own words.

5. What are the main parts of the essay? Note the divisions between introduction, body, and conclusion. How do these parts fit together?

6. Because we read to learn new information, what did you learn? What are the essay's main ideas? What are the major supporting points for the thesis?

7. What inferences did you draw? What conclusions? What has the essay done to educate you about the world? How do the essay's ideas accord with what you already know? What further information do you need?

8. Aside from unfamiliar words—which you should add to your vocabulary notebook as suggested in Part 1—are any words used in unusual ways? Any metaphors or similes? Any strongly connotative words? Is the writer's word choice appropriate for the purpose, audience, and content?

■ PRACTICE ESSAY: ANNOTATION, ANALYSIS, AND SUMMARY

In Chapter 1 you were introduced to the interrelated skills of annotating, paraphrasing, and summarizing. In this section we briefly review these three skills with a more sophisticated and complex reading passage. Reprinted below is a short essay by the renowned scientist Stephen Jay Gould on the fate of the rhinoceros, surely one of nature's more preposterous-looking creatures. First, read the essay and study the annotations in the left margin. Then read the answers to the eight questions for analysis posed above. This section ends with a short review of paraphrasing skills and a sample summary of Gould's selection. Note: Each selection in Part 5 contains an exercise in one or more of these crucial academic skills.

"Preposterous: What Has Happened to the Rhinoceros Is as Hard to Fathom as the Beast Itself"

Stephen Jay Gould

Stephen Jay Gould was the consummate scientific writer on the topic of evolution. After receiving his Ph.D. from Columbia University in 1967, he was Agassiz professor of zoology at Harvard University until his recent death. In addition, he served as curator of invertebrate paleontology for Harvard's Museum of Comparative Zoology. Nine collections of his essays on scientific subjects have been published. His 1989 essay, "The Creation Myths of Cooperstown," was selected for inclusion in The Best American Essays of the Century. *The essay reprinted here, which has been annotated for you, is from a column Gould published in* The Sciences.

Though preposterous in appearance, rhinos' numbers are declining & survival is threatened

1 From numerous versifications in books for children, rhinoceroses have acquired a one-word definition in a near rhyme: preposterous. The five living species of rhinoceroses, viewed as tanklike vestiges of a pre-historic past, and barely hanging on as threatened populations in their African and Asian homes, do convey an image of superannuated heavy-weights from a lost world where brawn could overcome stupidity and ensure survival.

Fossil records— rhinos adapted well to environment w/ varied species. Now only 3 groups remain

2 Modern rhinoceroses do represent a remnant of past glory: they were once maximally prosperous, rather than preposterous. Their enormously successful fossil forebears included Paraceratherium, the largest land mammal of all time—eighteen feet high at the shoulder and a browser of treetops. Their extensive ecological range included small and lithe running forms no bigger than a goat (the hyracodontines), and rotund river dwellers that looked like hippopotamuses (the teleoceratines). Moreover, modern rhinoceroses are a vestige within a vestige. The formerly dominant order of odd-toed hoofed mammals has now dwindled to three groups: the rhinoceroses and the tapirs, each barely hanging on, and the horses, given an artificial boost and a new lease on life by human needs for transport and human foibles for warfare and wagering.

Dilemma they pose: Horn defines species but also has caused their demise. Horns believed to have curative powers, esp to cure impotence

3 A dilemma, in technical terms, is a problem with two logical solutions, each untenable or unpleasant. We speak of being caught on the "horns of a dilemma," in reference, I suppose, to the crescent moon with its two points, or horns (or perhaps to the devil himself). The dilemma of the rhinoceroses also rests upon two aspects of their distinctive and defining horns. On one point, horns mark the rhinoceros's fascination as

7. *What inferences and conclusions can you draw?* The rhinoceros may be a preposterous-looking animal, as Gould suggests from the references to children's books, but the threatened existence of this animal is only one example of human exploitation of nature for our own frivolous ends. Nor does Gould exempt earlier generations of natural scientists from his accusations, and he implies in paragraph 5 that museum collections, in this case of rhinoceros horns, are the result of their habit of "wanton" collecting of specimens.

8. *Is the language unusual?* Although Gould is a scientist, his style is measured, nuanced, and occasionally poetic. Look again, for example, at his writing in paragraph 3, where he connects the horns of the dilemma the rhinoceros presents to the rhinoceros's actual horns and to the symbolic horns of the devil, thereby suggesting that the practice of killing rhinos for their horns is evil. In paragraph 5, Gould concludes with three sentence fragments expressing the sadness with which he views the collection of horns at the Museum of Comparative Zoology at Harvard: "Detached horns, often severed with pieces of surrounding skin. The part that dooms the whole. A strangely beautiful picture of elegance separated from a symbol of ungainliness."

■ WRITING PARAPHRASES AND SUMMARIES—A REVIEW

You will recall that to paraphrase means to restate a writer's ideas in your own words and that accurate paraphrasing is the first step in writing a good summary. Here are the five suggestions for writing paraphrases, repeated from Chapter 1, along with illustrating sentences from Gould's essay.

1. **Use synonyms for key words without changing the meaning.**
   Original sentence:

   Modern rhinoceroses do represent a remnant of past glory.

   Paraphrase:

   The rhinoceros today signifies a vestige of its former magnificence.

2. **Change the order of ideas within the original sentence.**
   Original sentence:

   Their extensive ecological range included small and lithe running forms no bigger than a goat (the hyracodontines), and rotund river dwellers that looked like hippopotamuses (the teleoceratines).

   Paraphrase:

   The forebears of the modern rhinoceros covered a wide territory, ranging from large river dwellers, somewhat like the modern hippopotamus, to smaller forms the size of goats, which were nimble runners.

3. **Omit unimportant details or excess verbiage.**

In the preceding example, the terms "hyracodontines" and "teleoceratines" have been dropped.

4. **Combine ideas and sentences.**

Original sentences:

I wish I could portray naturalists as perennial opponents of such exploitation. We certainly function in this manner today, but our past does not always measure up to current practices.

Paraphrase:

Although natural scientists today are careful not to exploit the animal populations they study, unfortunately in the past naturalists were not so careful.

5. **Maintain the same tone and style as the original passage.**

Original sentence:

We all have a personal breaking point, where moral indignation swamps dispassionate analysis.

Paraphrase:

Everyone has a threshold where our sense of moral outrage overwhelms our ability to analyze a problem without prejudice.

Your instructor may require you to paraphrase short passages as a test of your comprehension and to write summaries. In addition, paraphrasing is required in writing research papers for other college classes. Whatever the assignment, paraphrasing is a most useful skill to work on.

■ SAMPLE SUMMARY

Gould's essay is about 550 words in length. A good summary should be 10 to 25 percent of the original. This one is 102 words long, or just under 20 percent.

Stephen Jay Gould's essay, "Preposterous," examines the plight of today's rhinoceros population. Though often characterized in children's books as preposterous in appearance, in prehistoric times these magnificent creatures thrived in a variety of environments. Today, however, the survival of the five remaining species is threatened. Poachers kill them because their horns are reputed to cure sexual impotence or they are collected as trophies. Gould finds this practice morally repugnant; he abandons his scientific objectivity when he encounters stories of animals slaughtered for a single part, especially for frivolous or fallacious reasons. What is truly preposterous is our wanton killing of these creatures.

■ TEN ESSAYS AND ARTICLES FOR FURTHER PRACTICE

The ten essays in this anthology portion of the text represent an eclectic mix of nonfiction writing, which will both enhance your analytical reading skills and expand your knowledge. Half of the selections are followed by questions for discussion and analysis; the other half are accompanied by a variety of exercises for further practice in comprehension, analysis of structure, vocabulary, and, occasionally, paraphrasing and summarizing.

Selection 1

"Uno: They," from "Borderland Blues: Six Impressions"

Luis Alberto Urrea

Luis Alberto Urrea is the son of an American mother and a Mexican father. Born in Tijuana, Mexico, a border city next to San Diego, California, Urrea has also done relief work with immigrants and has taught expository writing at Harvard. His two best-known books are Across the Wire: Life and Hard Times on the Mexican Border *and* The Devil's Highway. *This passage reprints the first of six impressions called "Borderland Blues" from his 1996 book* By the Lake of Sleeping Children.

Preview Questions

1. What do you imagine life is like for illegal immigrants who make it across the border from Mexico to San Diego? What do you think day-to-day existence is like for them?

2. What particular jobs do recent immigrants—whether legal or illegal—perform in twenty-first-century America? Does the U.S. economy need illegal immigrants? If yes, why?

3. Does your particular community have a sizable immigrant population? If so, how has that population changed the area?

1   They come across the wires in the dark. We walk through their gates on the same night. They dream of our beds, our cars, our clothing. We eat the fruits they pick for us—our salads are washed in their sweat, our strawberries and tomatoes and cotton are passed to us by their fingers. They stare at us through the fence and wonder what our problem is. We keep our doors locked to them, and we let them feed us, and when we're through with them, we pay men in Jeeps to throw them out. We send our losers to their town to entertain themselves. We pass each other on the way, and we never look into each other's eyes.

2   Early evening, as daylight turned violet-gray and the sea horizon torched copper, I stood at the end of E Street in Chula Vista. Chula Vista (the Precious View) is one of the little scraps of town between San Diego and Tijuana—a buffer zone consisting of National City, Nestor, Imperial Beach, Chula Vista, and San Isidro, the whole region oddly flattened by the pressure of the twins above and below it.

3   Cutting through it all is the massive flow of Interstate 5 in the west and 805 in the east. There are many ways across the line for "wetbacks" (an odd name for people who don't have to swim across the Rio Grande to get here—maybe they're wet only with blood). Those who don't get out of Tijuana through Colonia Libertad or by being smuggled by car often get trapped by 5's concrete river. It flows dead west along the Mexican border, then veers north and heads all the way up the West Coast. The Border Patrol has come to count on the freeway to siphon the wetbacks along the coast, in a thin strip easily patrolled by helicopter. They get trapped in the saltbogs, the brackish swamps, the navy yards and slag heaps that run from the border to San Diego. Often at night they try to run across the lanes of traffic, and they are run down.

4   I was in front of Anthony's Fish Grotto restaurant, poking around for no obvious reason. A helicopter cut in a bit closer on its fly-by, checking to see what this gringo-looking fool with a notebook was doing down here. I can imagine one of the agents saying, Some sort of reporter. Looking to get shot, I guess. I wonder if they thought of me as a drive-by poet.

5   E Street dead-ends at the edge of Anthony's parking lot. Across the street from the restaurant is a weed-choked lot with the foundation of a house in it. Beyond the dead end is a farm, and this property spills into the Deep South swamps of San Diego Bay. Near here, a colony of sea turtles has immigrated into the hot-water ponds off the electric company's big turbines. Apparently the steaming effluent mimics the tropical tides of the Caribbean. Sea World officials, zookeepers, and animal control officers regularly stop them and check them for papers; the bright-hued plastic tags punched into their fins pass for turtle green cards. The Mark of the Aquatic Beast. Another road runs at right angles to E, and the two form a dusty T. The arm of this T that runs north, toward San Diego, ends abruptly at the edge of a briny area of tide marshes and bogs. It is barricaded. Parallel to this road is a set of rusted train tracks. It was here, along this road, that I found myself among the remnants of what seemed a lost race, the spoor of courage and desperation.

6   I walked north along the closed road, veering around a barricade that kept cars from the area. Grass had worked its way through the blacktop, cracking and lifting triangular pieces of it. There was a ditch on the left, and every few yards there were clumps of tired pine trees. I could see the abandoned rail line through the trees. There were peeling PRIVATE PROPERTY signs posted all along the edge of the farm. A crumpled pair of blue jeans in the road. The silence. A cottontail broke from cover in the crumbling

foundation and ran in panicked jags. The river-hiss of 5 to my right underlined the quiet. A blue-and-yellow CAT baseball cap was dangling from a twig.

7   It was so lonely out there. Not restive, not solitary; *lonely.* I began to feel sad, then furtive. I was convinced somebody was watching me. I imagined a rifle scope trained on my back. I wanted to hide.

8   It was like a smell. I looked around for its source and suddenly got a hunch. I cautiously stepped down one of the little banks into the ditch between the road and the tracks. I crawled under a pine.

9   They'd been there.

10   There were cardboard sleeping mats, small white roses of crumpled paper, flat liquor bottles, dry scat. All along the ditch there were hidey-holes burrowed out among the roots and pine needles, dens scraped out between a flood of cars and a dead railway.

11   I moved into the hole. There was dust all over the cardboard mats. It had clearly been a while since anyone hid here. Had the people been arrested? Had this spot been compromised, discovered by la migra, and rendered permanently unsafe? Perhaps they made it north. Maybe locals found them and made sport of them. (The Ku Klux Klan had been patrolling the region, "assisting" the U.S. government in the roundup of unwanted humans.)

12   A broken bottle of Mexican beer. Magazine pages smashed into petrified stools. I could feel the pulse of these men, lying here, hiding night after night. Who, I wondered, who? I might have known them. I might have fed them the week before they came here.

13   One stained mattress. A shattered TV set on the tracks. There was nothing left here. Not a voice. I felt watched by shadows as I climbed out, hurried away from the traces of sorrow downwind of the city.

A. *Comprehension*

Choose the answer that best completes each statement. Do not refer to the selection while doing this exercise.

1. What term does Urrea use to describe Chula Vista, National City, Imperial Beach, and San Isidro—communities located between Tijuana, Mexico, and San Diego?
   (a) a no-man's land
   (b) a hellhole
   (c) a buffer zone
   (d) a haven

2. Interstate 5 poses several problems for illegal immigrants trying to cross into the United States. Which one was *not* mentioned?
   (a) They get trapped by it and are forced to flee to the beach area.
   (b) It is dangerous to cross; one can get run over by the speeding cars.
   (c) The area is easy for the Border Patrol to survey by helicopter.
   (d) They get easily lost after smugglers drop them off.

3. Illegal immigrants apparently congregate along the tide marshes and bogs, specifically
   (a) next to an abandoned railway line.
   (b) in a restaurant parking lot.
   (c) at Sea World.
   (d) under a freeway overpass.

4. The predominant feeling or atmosphere of the area as Urrea describes it is one of
   (a) great danger.
   (b) impending death.
   (c) loneliness.
   (d) restlessness.

5. Urrea expresses his fear about the fate of a particular group of immigrants at the encampment, especially since the Border Patrol in the area was being "assisted" by
   (a) the FBI.
   (b) La Migra.
   (c) the local police.
   (d) the Ku Klux Klan.

B. Vocabulary

For each italicized word from the selection, write the dictionary definition most appropriate for the context.

1. It flows dead west along the Mexican border and then *veers* north [paragraph 3—also *veering* in paragraph 6] _____

   _____

2. the *brackish* swamps [3]: _____

3. the steaming *effluent* [5] _____

4. the *spoor* of courage and desperation [5] _____

   _____

5. not *restive,* not solitary [7] _____

6. I began to feel sad, then *furtive* [7] _____

   _____

7. *rendered* permanently unsafe [11] _____

C. Structure and Meaning

Complete the following questions.

1. Which of the following quotations from the essay represents Urrea's thesis?
   (a) "I felt watched by shadows as I climbed out, hurried away from the traces of sorrow downwind of the city." (paragraph 13)

      (b) "We pass each other on the way, and we never look into their eyes." (paragraph 1)

      (c) "Those who don't get out of Tijuana through Colonia Libertad or by being smuggled by car often get trapped by 5's concrete river." (paragraph 3)

      (d) "It was here, along this road, that I found myself among the remnants of what seemed a lost race, the spoor of courage and desperation." (paragraph 5)

2. Look again at the details in paragraph 1. What is the central point Urrea is making about the presence of illegal immigrants in our culture? _____

_____

_____

3. In the last sentence of paragraph 2, Urrea writes "the whole region oddly flattened by the presence of the twins above and below it." What specifically does the word "twins" refer to? _____

4. What is ironic about the Sea World officials, zookeepers, and animal control officers who tag the sea turtles who live in the warm lagoon waters near the electric plant? (See paragraph 5.) _____

_____

_____

_____

5. In addition to the loneliness Urrea describes in the area between the railway line and Interstate 5, what are some other dominant impressions he conveys of this area? _____

_____

D. Summarizing Exercise

Although paragraph 1 of Urrea's essay is quite impressionistic, he nonetheless makes an argument. Write a summary of this paragraph, which is 121 words long. Try to keep your summary to between 25 and 35 words._____

_____

_____

_____

E. Questions for Discussion and Analysis

1. Why do you think that Urrea included this vignette in his "Six Impressions"? Aside from describing this area, what do you think he hopes to impart to the reader?

2. When Urrea concludes the essay with "I felt watched by shadows," how does this conclusion serve his larger purpose? Why do we never see any illegal immigrants in this piece?

Selection 2   ## "A Boy's Work"
Mark Spragg

American essayist and novelist Mark Spragg writes about the West, spe-
cifically about Wyoming and the Yellowstone Plateau. He is the author of
four books, among them his memoir of growing up on a Wyoming dude
ranch in the 1960s, Where Rivers Change Direction, *from which this*
selection comes, and a novel, An Unfinished Life *(2004). Spragg's writ-*
ings have won awards from the Wyoming's Arts Council and from the
Mountains & Plains Booksellers.

Preview Questions

1. What is a dude ranch? What motivates city dwellers to go to a dude
   ranch for a vacation? What do you think it would be like to grow
   up on a ranch in Wyoming?
2. The title of the book from which this excerpt comes is *Where Rivers
   Change Direction.* What do you think this refers to?
3. How do most American parents help their male children become men?

"Your horse is wire-cut." My father has pulled up to the corrals with a
four-horse trailer. This is his second and last load. The rest of the horses
have been left on winter pasture. The snow still lies in dirty, humped drifts
around the buildings and in the timber. The grass has just started to work
up through the smear of gray, gauzelike mold that has spread under the
winter's snowcover. Our Forest Service grazing lease won't begin for several
weeks. Any horses we have on the place will have to be fed hay. Hay is
expensive.

"My horse?"

"You have so many you can't remember which one?"

"They all belong to you."

He steps to the back of the trailer. He turns with one hand on the
trailer's gate. He looks tired, hungry. "The horse you rode last summer
and fall," he says.

"Socks?"

"I think riding a single animal every day of your life allows you some
privileges."

He swings the trailer's gate open and backs out a big sorrel gelding and
hands me its halterrope, stepping into the trailer again and turning out
a black we call Bird.

"Don't let Bird get by you," he shouts from inside the trailer.

"Wire-cut a little, or a lot?" Bird trails his leadrope, holding his head to
the side, careful not to step on the thing. I catch up the leadrope.

My father steps the third horse out of the trailer. We have spring bear
hunters coming in on the weekend and need just enough transportation
to get us all back and forth to the bait-ground.

"I mean he tried to cut a hoof off." I'm following the horse he leads, bringing the other two with me.

"With what?" I know it doesn't really matter.

"With a wire gate. Some asshole left it open on the ground and Socks got in it. I found him when I was gathering these. He worked himself loose of the gate but the damage had been done."

"He's at the vet's?"

"His leg's gangrenous." He pauses just inside the corrals. He turns his horse into the corrals and looks back over a shoulder at me. He's looping the leadrope over the halter's headstall. "I hope you've just gotten hard of hearing. You were a good deal brighter when I left this morning."

"You killed him?"

He takes the two other horses from me. His hat is pulled down. I don't get a good look at his eyes. He speaks softly. "He's in the trailer," he says.

When I step in the trailer I can smell him. It is the smell of something that has died in the sun. A hopeless odor that brings memories of road-killed deer and elk—flies, gums drawn back over yellowing teeth. He nickers softly and I move to his head. He's gaunt. His winter coat is shedding in large, uneven gouts. I run a hand along his side, my fingers tracing the cage of his ribs. There are sprigs of dried weed tangled in his tail and mane. I untie his leadrope and lead him from the trailer. Every time he steps with his right front foot his shoulder sinks as though he's stepping into a hole. Outside the trailer my father lights a cigarette.

"Put him in with the others and spill some grain for them."

"Why?"

"Because I told you to."

"He's not going to get any better."

The cigarette smoke rises and holds against the brim of my father's hat. "No," he says, "he's not going to get any better."

There is more light out of the trailer. I can see that Socks's leg is swollen badly. From his hoof to his shoulder the skin has split in several weeping slices. His pastern is as thick as his forearm should be and blackened, crusted with dried blood. When he takes a step the heel of his foot flops loose and snaps back up against the pastern. It makes a sucking sound, and then a click.

My father speaks with the cigarette in the corner of his mouth. He's latching the trailer. "I'd give a lot to get my hands on the son of a bitch who was in such a hurry he couldn't close a gate."

"I don't feel very well."

"You're going to feel worse."

He drops his cigarette at the toe of his boot and methodically grinds it out. He doesn't look up when he speaks. "I've got to be in town tomorrow or I wouldn't ask you."

"I've got school."

"If you think you need to go to school your mother can run you down the valley after lunch."

My father is looking up at me now. He's pulling on a pair of yellow cloth gloves.

"You could have killed him in town," I tell him. "If you didn't have a gun you could have borrowed one." A knot of panic rises in my chest like some small, waking animal clawing its way out of hibernation.

"I want him baited."

"Bear-baited?"

"We don't exactly have the kind of money to kill a usable horse. Everything else'll make it until this fall. Kind of looks like Socks volunteered, don't you think?"

I do not, but I'm part of the family and this is part of our work. I'm fifteen. Old enough to be asked. We bait horses for bear, allowing their corpses to ripen, hoping they will attract an otherwise elusive grizzly. Our hunters fire from a blind at the bear that feeds on the dead horse.

I stand staring at my father's boots. They are worn down to the same color as the soil. Socks lips the collar of my denim jacket. His breath feels warm and moist against my neck. This is the first time I've been prompted to draw any conclusions about sport. The horses we have baited in the past were derelict, their teeth gone, ready to die. I have never before connected sorrow with our family's business.

"Where?" I don't look up.

"That little meadow up Kitty Creek. Where we killed the big boar two springs ago. It's close; there's no creeks to cross. If he's alive in the morning you might get him up there."

I nod. I'm not sure there is enough light left for my father to see the movement of my head.

"I'm sorry about this," he says. "You have your supper?"

"Elk roast."

"Your mother make a dessert?"

"Just canned pears."

"Ask your brother for a hand if you think you need it."

"I'll be fine."

"This won't be the hardest thing you'll ever do. You believe me?"

"Not yet."

"I'll see you tomorrow."

I listen to his footfalls grow fainter as he walks away from me. It is dark enough now that I can't distinguish his outline. But I feel the heat of him leave. The night seems to drop ten degrees. I get Socks in the round corral, away from the other horses, heap a coffee can with oats and pour them in his trough, make sure he has clean water. For a while I stand in the dark and listen to him chew—a blunted, rhythmic rasp; the sound of pack rats at work in a hay loft. And a single owl hooting periodically, well rested, watching us with its wide night eyes.

When I pass my parents' cabin I can see my father at the supper table. He still wears his neckerchief. His hair is so short it hasn't needed to be combed, his sleeves are rolled above his elbows, the brown hair on his

snorts, and starts to buck. He's never been very fancy in his tantrums, and I manage to keep his head pulled up and out of the rhythm of his clumsy plunges. The crow-hopping stops as abruptly as it has begun, and he steps out stiffly, as though only now come fully awake. I spur him into a trot for the quarter mile down to the mailbox and back and step off. He stands like a gentleman, his ears up and alert. I slide the rifle into the saddle scabbard. The horizon has just started to lighten. Bird and I can still see our breaths in the morning air, but our blood is hot. I return quickly to the corrals and halter Socks.

Socks has never offered to buck. He's fourteen and has given me nothing but work. He's a rangy bay whose legs run white from his knees down. Without being bred for it he's naturally gaited and one of the smartest horses about terrain I've ever ridden. He studies the ground like some horses study cows. He moves with the same sure ease over loose scree, through downed timber, in fast water, over open ground. If I give him his head after dark he invariably brings me home, stepping in the same prints he's made on the ride out. As one of our hands has said about him, he's the kind of horse that comes early and stays late. I can hardly look back at him as he haltingly follows Bird and me. A step, a pause to gather his weight in his hindquarters, a step. At times he groans so mournfully that I turn in the saddle, prepared to watch him die. The waking knot of panic comes alive again in my gut, rises in my throat. I swallow. My throat burns, my mouth tastes of copper.

I've expected Bird to be impatient and fight the bit for the whole trip, but perhaps there is a communion between animals that I do not understand. I wonder if they find a community in one another's miseries. Bird walks as though he is picking his way through a field littered with cactus and broken stone. He looks back so often that I have to continually rein him back onto the trail. When Socks's breaths come in rasps Bird stops completely, refuses to move, stands with his head hanging low, as though listening.

Traveling the three miles to the bait-ground takes us four hours. By the time we get to the little meadow where I intend to kill him, Socks is almost dead. His eyes appear glazed, as though grown over with bluish cataracts. He sways as he stands. The swelling has spread to his shoulder and chest, and he wheezes without the effort of moving. I pray he is so deeply in shock that he has forgotten he is a horse, forgotten the taste of clear water. I think that a lesser horse could not have made this trip to be killed. A lesser horse would have died tangled in the wire. I feel he has made the effort for me.

I tie Bird in the trees and walk quickly back to Socks and unsnap his halter and let it drop. I'm in a hurry. There is a chance that he can endure more. I know that I cannot. I chamber a shell, sight quickly, and stop his struggle before he can respond to the sound of metal slipping against metal. He falls, kicks once, and is still. The gunshot's report echoes against the opposite side of the valley. A magpie starts up and will not stop his squawking.

The shot and the immediate presence of death spikes through Bird like a lightning strike. He circles the tree where I have tied him, snorting, glaring into the middle distance of every direction, sawing against his leadrope. I drop the empty halter by him as I pass and keep walking through the spare timber. When I get into the creek it is over my knees and my boots fill with the icy water. And then I am out and struggling up a sharp embankment and into a nest of pine boughs heaped around and over the crude pole frame that acts as our blind.

A thick downfall keeps the whole affair held against the hillside, and there is the noise of Kitty Creek to further separate it from the meadow. If there is a breeze it reliably sweeps down this tight drainage and holds the hunter's scent away from the bait. It is a fine place to sit and raise a rifle and kill a bear.

I stare at the reddish brown mound seventy-five yards in front of me. I have killed Socks in a good place. Close to the timber that borders the meadow. A bear will feel safe in his approach. Far enough into the meadow that a hunter will have a good shot. And then I remember that I should have cut a window in his gut. Sawed through his hair and opened him to decay. A sore that coyotes and ravens can worry. A place that will help him rot. My father will be disappointed. I think of my father's disappointment and remember the ruined leg. The smell of the leg will attract a bear. Socks has gotten a head start at decay. I have an excuse. I wonder suddenly why I am not crying. I think a boy would cry. I think maybe I have begun to be a man. I feel only quietly blunt, and desperate. I feel as though I want to stand and run, but do not have the strength. I tighten my chest to exhale, and suck at the air to reinflate. Again, and then again. My eyes water, but the breathing helps. It is my only weapon against the release of the thing that struggles inside me. A small fight. I fear that if I allow myself to empty I will be filled only with the regret of what I have just done.

I look down at the rifle that lies across my knees and think of the bear hunters that pay us for this. They come every spring and fall. Usually from the East. More recently from the Midwest and South. Professional men. Lawyers, executives, doctors. Not bad men. But men who believe in trophy. They are hard men to respect. In hunting camp they drink every night. They stagger out of the dining tent and fall to their knees and vomit and wipe their mouths on the tails of the new shirts they have bought for hunting bear. In the mornings they suffer the shits. When they are drunk they tell us about fucking their wives. They tell us about fucking women who are not their wives. They tell us about fucking the men they are in business with. Not all of them. But the drunks and the braggarts are the ones I remember. Every fall

I sit behind the woodstove in the tent and watch them. They only look my way to ask for a dipper of water, or to send me to their sleeping tents for cigarettes. I do not think of them as men. I think of them as big, loud Scouts—overweight and balding children. I imagine that they come to us to earn a bear badge. Not to kill something ordinary that can be eaten, but to kill something extraordinary that is capable of eating them.

I slump against the hillside and look up into the scatter of sunlight through the pines. I think of our hunters' nervousness in this and other blinds where I've sat with them. When it rains they smell of excitement and they smell of fear. They ask what it is like to kill a bear. They ask how others have done the thing. To the sounds that magnify with the dusk they ask in a tight whisper, "What is that? Is there something out there?" There is no whiskey in the blind. And I am not just a boy sitting behind a stove. Now I am a boy who's watched bears die, and they have not.

I tell them that seeing a bear for the first time is like hearing a rattlesnake for the first time. I tell them that there will be no mistake. Sometimes a man moans. Most men just sit and stare. A few smile a terrible smile. They are the ones we do not accept back. There are limits to any profession.

My father tells our hunters to take out the ball of the shoulder with the first shot so that the bear cannot charge. Simple instructions to ruin bone and flesh. He tells them to never shoot at the head, that a grizzly's skull will deflect their bullet. I have no way of knowing if they remember. Some make good shots. Others fire wildly. Some bear are wounded, and we track them and kill them up close where they have curled to die. Some fall where they feed, across the body of the horse. A few have healed themselves, tracked us, become wilder and more dangerous.

My immediate future looms suddenly and vividly real. Within a week a bear can be killed here. That bear might die atop the body of the horse I have just shot. Socks. The skinning of the bear will fall to me. I think that perhaps I might then cry. I promise myself to try. Cry while I twist and lever one dead thing away from the other. Cry while I strip the furred skin away from its flesh. I think of the rank smell, the maggots, the blood gone dark and thick. If it is a boar and the hunter knows the peculiar anatomies of animals, there will be the matter of the bone around which the bear's penis grows. Bear bone. Dick bone. Joke bone. The hunter will want that solid bone. I will knife the muscle away and scrape the thing clean. And then I will take the rolled hide up in my arms. The horses will shy in apprehension as I approach them. The hide will be heavier than it appears, and it will stink. A packhorse might snap its lead-rope and run wildly into the timber.

The hide will be made into a rug. The rug will be mounted against a wall. I have just killed a horse so that a man can display the hair of an animal in his den. We often receive pictures of a bear hide nailed to a wall. The hunter stands in front of the thing holding a drink, his legs wide, smiling, looking as though he will be called to dinner shortly. Sometimes his wife poses with him. I have often wondered what ultimately happens to those trophies. I imagine them older, dusty, lackluster, insect ridden, making their way to garage sales, or into trunks littered with mothballs. I imagine them as a gift to a favorite son. I imagine them as proof that a man came West and had an adventure.

In the years that my family has guided hunters we've killed two or three bears each spring, and again in the fall. No one has been mauled. The deck seems stacked. I flex my feet against the insteps of my wet boots. I have just killed a horse and my only punishment is cold feet.

My father has loaned me his copy of the Lewis and Clark journals. I have read that when they traveled through parts of Montana they flanked their party on both sides with several men who did nothing but kill bear who posed some threat. I look up again at Socks's brown body. I do not think that a bear will come here to harm me. I think that a bear will come to eat a dead horse. Because he is hungry. I do not think that he will brag about the thing to his sow. If he knows he is in jeopardy it will not excite him, make the meal more tantalizing. He will run. Or he will not show himself at all. I wonder about the bears who come and are killed. I think that their souls must be disappointed to be killed by a thing who does not even have a solid bone in its penis.

I run my thumb along the length of the rifle's barrel and think that there are boys who play baseball. Boys who ride bicycles, not horses. Boys who complain about having to mow a yard. I have a friend in town who watches a television show titled *Zorro*. He practices snapping a small whip and longs to own a sword.

In the magazines my father gets each month I've read that there are boys who do not go to school because they have none. Hundreds of thousands of boys who starve. Boys who beg. Boys who spend their days in prayer. I have traced the outlines of their countries with a finger, holding the atlas open on my lap. And I know that someday I will no longer be a boy. Someday I will be a man, perhaps with a son of my own.

I rewade the creek and sit on the bank and empty the water from my boots. Bird has settled and nickers as I approach. The day has warmed. Squirrels chatter. Raven-shadow occasionally blots the trail before us as we move home. It feels good to have something alive and warm beneath me. Bird's ears are pricked, his gait loose, he seems alert to every movement. He stops unexpectedly on the bridge over the Shoshone and stares down into the water. I strain to see if there is a moose, or otter, or fisherman. There is nothing. Only sunlight on water. I smile and feel ashamed that light makes me happy. I tap Bird's sides with my spurs, and he moves ahead. It takes us less than an hour to return to the corrals.

There is a note from my mother tacked to their cabin door telling me that she has had to help a friend who lives farther up the valley. That I will find enough in the refrigerator for a sandwich. That she loves me. I eat and then strip and soak in their tub, half napping. I dream that I run wild in a forest. It is a common dream. My feet grip the earth with certainty. The earth yearns for my touch, arches against me. I lie down upon the soil to feel its care for me, and imagine that I am recognized, that I am held dear. I think that I will fall in love with a girl who is raised on this same wilderness. I do not think I will fall in love with a girl from a city. And then I come fully awake and sit up in a tub of tepid water. I stare at a clock on the shelf by the sink. It is almost four. The yellows and golds in the pine walls catch and hold the afternoon light. It will be summer in six weeks and there will be water in all the cabins, and I will move into the bunkhouse with the older cowboys.

I'm in the tackshed oiling saddles when my father comes home. He has picked up my brother from school, and my brother runs ahead of him and stands shuffling in the doorway of the building. He carries his books and when he can think of nothing to say opens one and stares at the page as though he needs to find out what next to do. He is worried. He wonders if we have grown apart in a day. If I am less a boy, and he more alone.

"How was your report?" I ask him.

"It was great." He snaps the book shut and smiles. "Thompson's Labrador had pups."

"Did you see them?"

"No. Dad says we can go down this weekend. Pete says he's saving us the one that came out with the cord wrapped around its neck." Relief shows on his face. I am still his brother.

My father joins him in the doorway. They lean into its separate jambs and watch me work the neat's-foot into the leather.

"He tell you about the dog you're going to get?"

"This weekend."

We all nod.

"You got an early start this morning," my father says.

I look up from my work. "I'm not good at waiting," I say.

"I can understand that," he tells me. "I'm no good at it myself." He lights a cigarette, and we watch the smoke mute and slide in the last slanting light of the day.

Questions for Discussion and Analysis

1. From his words and actions in the first part of the story, how would you describe the narrator's father?

2. What exactly happened to Socks that he has to be put down, or in this case, used for bear bait?

3. Spragg's father says that he would kill Socks himself except that he has to go to town the next day. Do you believe this statement? Are there other reasons that the father might give his son, who is 15 years old, this terrible task?

4. How does the narrator react to his father's command? What emotions do you think he is experiencing? In what way is this situation—having to destroy an otherwise healthy horse—novel to him?

5. When the narrator's father tells Mark, "This won't be the hardest thing you'll ever do," what do you think he means?

6. Comment on the lives of this family—their schooling, their recreation, their work. What devices does Spragg use to reveal the intimate details of their lives? How do you judge Spragg's family, who makes a living out of men who come there solely for the thrill of killing a bear?

7. Identify the emotions you felt as you read the scenes describing the preparation for putting down Socks and the aftermath.

8. There is an evident communion between the boy and the two horses, Socks and Bird. Is this the same communion one might have with, say, a dog or a cat, or does it somehow seem different?

9. Read again the passage where Spragg describes the men who come to the dude ranch to hunt bears. What does he find especially despicable about them?

10. Toward the end, Spragg thinks, "I wonder suddenly why I'm not crying. I think a boy would cry. I think maybe I have begun to be a man," Aside from the literal meaning, what exactly does he mean? How would you describe the emotional trajectory he experiences? that you experience reading this excerpt?

Annotating Exercise

Assume for the purpose of this exercise that you have been assigned to write an essay on Spragg' memoir. Here is the topic:

> Mark's father's order for his son to kill Socks stirs up a potent mix of emotions in the boy as he goes through the process—first from receiving the request, to the preparation, to the task itself, and to its aftermath. Analyze these emotions as they unfold and explain how they reinforce the change that this experience brings about in the narrator.

Annotate the essay, making comments in the margin as if you were preparing to write this paper.

Selection 3

The Iguana
Isak Dinesen

Isak Dinesen is the pseudonym of Karen Blixen (1885–1962), un-doubtedly the best-known Danish writer of the twentieth century. She is best known for Seven Gothic Tales *(1934),* Winter's Tales *(1942), and* Out of Africa *(1938), which describes her life on a coffee planta-tion in Kenya, from which this little classic essay is taken.*

Preview Questions

1. When you were younger, did you ever collect wet rocks and shells at the beach? What did they look like after they dried?
2. Apart from those who need to kill game to survive, what is the impulse that makes people kill a wild animal?
3. What is another example of something that looks beautiful in its natural environment but that loses its beauty when seen in a different environment?

1   In the Reserve I have sometimes come upon the Iguana, the big lizards, as they were sunning themselves upon a flat stone in a river-bed. They are not pretty in shape, but nothing can be imagined more beautiful than their colouring. They shine like a heap of precious stones or like a pane cut out of an old church window. When, as you approach, they swish away, there is a flash of azure, green and purple over the stones, the colour seems to be standing behind them in the air, like a comet's luminous tail.

2   Once I shot an Iguana. I thought that I should be able to make some pretty things from his skin. A strange thing happened then, that I have never afterwards forgotten. As I went up to him, where he was lying dead upon his stone, and actually while I was walking the few steps, he faded and grew pale, all colour died out of him as in one long sigh, and by the time that I touched him he was grey and dull like a lump of concrete. It was the live impetuous blood pulsating within the animal, which had ra-diated out all that glow and splendour. Now that the flame was put out, and the soul had flown, the Iguana was as dead as a sandbag.

3   Often since I have, in some sort, shot an Iguana, and I have remem-bered the one of the Reserve. Up at Meru I saw a young Native girl with a bracelet on, a leather strap two inches wide, and embroidered all over with very small turquoise-coloured beads which varied a little in colour and played in green, light blue and ultramarine. It was an extraordi-narily live thing; it seemed to draw breath on her arm, so that I wanted it for myself, and made Farah buy it from her. No sooner had it come upon my own arm than it gave up the ghost. It was nothing now, a small, cheap, purchased article of finery. It had been the play of colours, the

duet between the turquoise and the "nègre",—that quick, sweet, brownish black, like peat and black pottery, of the Native's skin,—that had created the life of the bracelet.

4   In the Zoological Museum of Pietermaritzburg, I have seen, in a stuffed deep-water fish in a showcase, the same combination of colouring, which there had survived death; it made me wonder what life can well be like, on the bottom of the sea, to send up something so live and airy. I stood in Meru and looked at my pale hand and at the dead bracelet. It was as if an injustice had been done to a noble thing, as if truth had been suppressed. So sad did it seem that I remembered the saying of the hero in a book that I had read as a child; "I have conquered them all, but I am standing amongst graves."

5   In a foreign country and with foreign species of life one should take measures to find out whether things will be keeping their value when dead. To the settlers of East Africa I give the advice: "For the sake of your own eyes and heart, shoot not the Iguana."

Questions for Discussion and Analysis

1. Dinesen's essay has three distinct parts. What do these three parts have in common?

2. Why did Dinesen shoot the iguana? What observation did she make after it died?

3. From the scene with the Native girl and the bracelet, what can we infer about Dinesen's character? Why did the bracelet look so "small" and "cheap" on her own arm?

4. At the Zoological Museum at Pietermaritzburg, Dinesen observed a stuffed fish in a showcase. What connection does she make between the fish and the bracelet?

5. Are Dinesen's remarks at the end of the essay, "For the sake of your own eyes and heart, shoot not the Iguana," directed only to the settlers of East Africa, or could her advice apply to contemporary readers, as well? What is the larger significance of this "advice"?

Selection 4

"Connectivity and Its Discontents," from *Alone Together: Why We Expect More from Technology and Less from Each Other*
Sherry Turkle

Sherry Turkle is a professor of the social studies of science and technology at MIT and also a clinical psychologist. These complementary roles make her well versed to explore the subject of technology and its effects on social interaction. The excerpt reprinted here is from her 2010 book,

Alone Together: Why We Expect More from Technology and Less from Each Other. The title of the selection, "Connectivity and Its Discontents," is a play on the title of Sigmund Freud's book, Civilization and Its Discontents, *as she explains at the end of paragraph 5.*

Preview Questions

1. How many times a day do you check your e-mail? How many text messages do you receive each month? (It has been estimated that some American teenagers send and receive as many as 8,000 text messages a month. College students might well send fewer.)
2. Do you sleep with your cell phone next to you? Do you feel untethered if you don't have your cell phone with you?
3. Which of these is the preferable way to communicate with your friends—a telephone call or a text message?

1   Online connections were first conceived as a substitute for face-to-face contact, when the latter was for some reason impractical: Don't have time to make a phone call? Shoot off a text message. But very quickly, the text message became the connection of choice. We discovered the network—the world of connectivity—to be uniquely suited to the over-worked and overscheduled life it makes possible. And now we look to the network to defend us against loneliness even as we use it to control the intensity of our connections. Technology makes it easy to communicate when we wish and to disengage at will.

2   A few years ago at a dinner party in Paris, I met Ellen, an ambitious, elegant young woman in her early thirties, thrilled to be working at her dream job in advertising. Once a week, she would call her grandmother in Philadelphia using Skype, an Internet service that functions as a telephone with a Web camera. Before Skype, Ellen's calls to her grandmother were costly and brief. With Skype, the calls are free and give the compelling sense that the other person is present—Skype is an almost real-time video link. Ellen could now call more frequently: "Twice a week and I stay on the call for an hour," she told me. It should have been rewarding; instead, when I met her, Ellen was unhappy. She knew that her grandmother was unaware that Skype allows surreptitious multitasking. Her grandmother could see Ellen's face on the screen but not her hands. Ellen admitted to me, "I do my e-mail during the calls. I'm not really paying attention to our conversation."

3   Ellen's multitasking removed her to another place. She felt her grandmother was talking to someone who was not really there. During their Skype conversations, Ellen and her grandmother were more connected than they had ever been before, but at the same time, each was alone. Ellen felt guilty and confused: she knew that her grandmother was happy, even if their intimacy was now, for Ellen, another task among multitasks.

4   I have often observed this distinctive confusion: these days, whether you are online or not, it is easy for people to end up unsure if they are closer together or further apart. I remember my own sense of disorientation the first time I realized that I was "alone together." I had traveled an exhausting thirty-six hours to attend a conference on advanced robotic technology held in central Japan. The packed grand ballroom was Wi-Fi enabled: the speaker was using the Web for his presentation, laptops were open throughout the audience, fingers were flying, and there was a sense of great concentration and intensity. But not many in the audience were attending to the speaker. Most people seemed to be doing their e-mail, downloading files, and surfing the Net. The man next to me was searching for a *New Yorker* cartoon to illustrate his upcoming presentation. Every once in a while, audience members gave the speaker some attention, lowering their laptop screens in a kind of curtsy, a gesture of courtesy.

5   Outside, in the hallways, the people milling around me were looking past me to virtual others. They were on their laptops and their phones, connecting to colleagues at the conference going on around them and to others around the globe. There but not there. Of course, clusters of people chatted with each other, making dinner plans, "networking" in that old sense of the word, the one that implies having a coffee or sharing a meal. But at this conference, it was clear that what people mostly want from public space is to be alone with their personal networks. It is good to come together physically, but it is more important to stay tethered to our devices. I thought of how Sigmund Freud considered the power of communities both to shape and to subvert us, and a psychoanalytic pun came to mind: "connectivity and its discontents."

6   The phrase comes back to me months later as I interview management consultants who seem to have lost touch with their best instincts for what makes them competitive. They complain about the BlackBerry revolution, yet accept it as inevitable while decrying it as corrosive. They say they used to talk to each other as they waited to give presentations or took taxis to the airport; now they spend that time doing e-mail. Some tell me they are making better use of their "downtime," but they argue without conviction. The time that they once used to talk as they waited for appointments or drove to the airport was never downtime. It was the time when far-flung global teams solidified relationships and refined ideas.

7   In corporations, among friends, and within academic departments, people readily admit that they would rather leave a voicemail or send an e-mail than talk face-to-face. Some who say "I live my life on my Black-Berry" are forthright about avoiding the "real-time" commitment of a phone call. The new technologies allow us to "dial down" human contact, to titrate its nature and extent. I recently overheard a conversation in a restaurant between two women. "No one answers the phone in our house anymore," the first woman proclaimed with some consternation. "It used to be that the kids would race to pick up the phone. Now they are up in their rooms, knowing no one is going to call them, and texting

and going on Facebook or whatever instead." Parents with teenage children will be nodding at this very familiar story in recognition and perhaps a sense of wonderment that this has happened, and so quickly. And teenagers will simply be saying, "Well, what's your point?"

8   A thirteen-year-old tells me she "hates the phone and never listens to voice-mail." Texting offers just the right amount of access, just the right amount of control. She is a modern Goldilocks: for her, texting puts people not too close, not too far, but at just the right distance. The world is now full of modern Goldilockses, people who take comfort in being in touch with a lot of people whom they also keep at bay. A twenty-one-year-old college student reflects on the new balance: "I don't use my phone for calls any more. I don't have the time to just go on and on. I like texting, Twitter, looking at someone's Facebook wall. I learn what I need to know."

9   Randy, twenty-seven, has a younger sister—a Goldilocks who got her distances wrong. Randy is an American lawyer now working in California. His family lives in New York, and he flies to the East Coast to see them three or four times a year. When I meet Randy, his sister Nora, twenty-four, had just announced her engagement and wedding date via e-mail to a list of friends and family. "That," Randy says to me bitterly, "is how I got the news." He doesn't know if he is more angry or hurt. "It doesn't feel right that she didn't call," he says. "I was getting ready for a trip home. Couldn't she have told me then? She's my sister, but didn't have a private moment when she told me in person. Or at least a call, just the two of us. When I told her I was upset, she sort of understood, but laughed and said that she and her fiance just wanted to do things simply, as simply as possible. I feel very far away from her."

10   Nora did not mean to offend her brother. She saw e-mail as efficient and did not see beyond. We have long turned to technology to make us more efficient in work; now Nora illustrates how we want it to make us more efficient in our private lives. But when technology engineers intimacy, relationships can be reduced to mere connections. And then, easy connection becomes redefined as intimacy. Put otherwise, cyber-intimacies slide into cybersolitudes.

11   And with constant connection comes new anxieties of disconnection, a kind of panic. Even Randy, who longs for a phone call from Nora on such an important matter as her wedding, is never without his Black-Berry. He holds it in his hands during our entire conversation. Once, he puts it in his pocket. A few moments later, it comes out, fingered like a talisman. In interviews with young and old, I find people genuinely terrified of being cut off from the "grid." People say that the loss of a cell phone can "feel like a death." One television producer in her mid-forties tells me that without her smartphone, "I felt like I had lost my mind." Whether or not our devices are in use, without them we feel disconnected, adrift. A danger even to ourselves, we insist on our right to send text messages while driving our cars and object to rules that would limit the practice.

12   Only a decade ago, I would have been mystified that fifteen-year-olds in my urban neighborhood, a neighborhood of parks and shopping malls, of front stoops and coffee shops, would feel the need to send and receive close to six thousand messages a month via portable digital devices or that best friends would assume that when they visited, it would usually be on the virtual real estate of Facebook. It might have seemed intrusive, if not illegal, that my mobile phone would tell me the location of all my acquaintances within a ten-mile radius. But these days we are accustomed to all this. Life in a media bubble has come to seem natural. So has the end of a certain public etiquette: on the street, we speak into the invisible microphones on our mobile phones and appear to be talking to ourselves. We share intimacies with the air as though unconcerned about who can hear us or the details of our physical surroundings.

13   I once described the computer as a second self, a mirror of mind. Now the metaphor no longer goes far enough. Our new devices provide space for the emergence of a new state of the self, itself, split between the screen and the physical real, wired into existence through technology.

14   Teenagers tell me they sleep with their cell phone, and even when it isn't on their person, when it has been banished to the school locker, for instance, they know when their phone is vibrating. The technology has become like a phantom limb, it is so much a part of them. These young people are among the first to grow up with an expectation of continuous connection: always on, and always on them. And they are among the first to grow up not necessarily thinking of simulation as second best. All of this makes them fluent with technology but brings a set of new insecurities. They nurture friendships on social-networking sites and then wonder if they are among friends. They are connected all day but are not sure if they have communicated. They become confused about companionship. Can they find it in their lives on the screen? Could they find it with a robot? Their digitized friendships—played out with emoticon emotions, so often predicated on rapid response rather than reflection—may prepare them, at times through nothing more than their superficiality, for relationships that could bring superficiality to a higher power, that is, for relationships with the inanimate. They come to accept lower expectations for connection and, finally, the idea that robot friendships could be sufficient unto the day.

15   Overwhelmed by the volume and velocity of our lives, we turn to technology to help us find time. But technology makes us busier than ever and ever more in search of retreat. Gradually, we come to see our online life as life itself. We come to see what robots offer as relationship. The simplification of relationship is no longer a source of complaint. It becomes what we want. These seem the gathering clouds of a perfect storm.

16   Technology reshapes the landscape of our emotional lives, but is it offering us the lives we want to lead? Many roboticists are enthusiastic about having robots tend to our children and our aging parents, for instance. Are these psychologically, socially, and ethically acceptable propositions? What are our responsibilities here? And are we comfortable

with virtual environments that propose themselves not as places for recreation but as new worlds to live in? What do we have, now that we
have what we say we want—now that we have what technology makes
easy? This is the time to begin these conversations, together. It is too late
to leave the future to the futurists.

A. *Comprehension*

Choose the answer that best completes each statement. Do not refer to the
selection while doing this exercise.

1. According to Turkle, the new connection of choice is
   (a) the telephone, specifically cell phones.
   (b) text messaging.
   (c) Facebook and other social media websites.
   (d) direct communication, face-to-face conversation.

2. Which of the following observations about technology and relationships
   best exemplifies the title of Turkle's book, *Alone Together?*
   (a) We no longer have time to converse with people in real time.
   (b) We multitask all the time and have difficulty concentrating on one
       task at a time.
   (c) We feel alone even though we are constantly connected with
       others via technology.
   (d) We have forgotten how to talk face-to-face with our friends.

3. Turkle says that the problem with the "Blackberry revolution" is that it
   allows us to
   (a) avoid the commitment of a phone call in real time.
   (b) avoid confronting difficult topics of conversation.
   (c) waste time looking at photos of other people's children and pets.
   (d) have access to instant communication at all hours of the day and
       night.

4. It's one thing to use technology to become more efficient at work, but
   Turkle apparently believes that using technology to gain efficiency in
   relationships
   (a) makes for insincere friendships, based on unimportant things.
   (b) is dangerous, since if the devices fail or are lost, we too are lost.
   (c) makes our friendships less important than our work, when it should
       be the other way around.
   (d) reduces our friendships to mere connections, not to meaningful
       relationships.

5. Turkle expresses several worries for this generation of teenagers who
   have been raised their whole lives in a world of "continuous connection."
   Which one was <u>not</u> mentioned?
   (a) They wonder if they are communicating despite the constant
       connection.

(b) Their friendships are based on quick responses and superficiality, not on reflection.

(c) Despite the constant connection, they are confused, uncertain, and insecure.

(d) Their relationships may not stand the test of time, the way friendships used to.

B. Vocabulary

Here are 10 vocabulary words from the selection and their definitions. Study these definitions carefully. Then write the appropriate word in each space provided according to the context.

1. *corrosive*—gradually destructive, steadily harmful
   disengage—withdraw, detach
   decry—condemn or denounce openly
   subverts—undermines the character of
   superficiality—shallowness, focus only on the surface

Turkle examines the way our being tethered to technology _____ true friendships, even though many of us _____ its _____ influence in our lives. Technology makes our friendships be based on _____ , and we _____ ourselves from the intensity of personal connections.

2. *talisman*—an object that is thought to have magical powers
   adrift—being without direction, lost
   intrusive—forcing into one's life in an unwelcome manner
   via—by way of
   virtual—existing in the world of computers, rather than in the real world

Teenagers in particular feel _____ if they don't have their cell phone with them at all times, almost as if is a _____ . Our dependency on the _____ world separates us from the real world. Two other dangers are the sheer numbers of text messages that many teenagers receive each month _____ their cell phone and the fact that smart phones are capable of showing one's whereabouts, a technological development that Turkle finds _____ if not illegal.

C. Structure and Meaning

Where appropriate, answer these questions in your own words.

1. Explain the central point Turkle makes in this selection. _____

   _____

   _____

Preview Questions

1. Do you watch network television news? Cable television news? What channel or channels do you prefer? Why?
2. Can you tell if a particular television news program is liberal or conservative? Is there a news channel that you consider politically objective and neutral?
3. Why have young people turned away from television news programs? What other sources are they using to get news?
4. What are some essential differences between getting news by means of television broadcasts and by means of newspapers? Which is the better form? Why?

1 The anchor changes at NBC and CBS News, combined with the emergence of Fox News, have brought up, again, apocalyptic thoughts about traditional television news. Network news will never be the same. Viewers are turning away from the evening programs. Cable can cover the big events. The Internet is quicker and livelier. All three networks are going the way of the dinosaur.

2 It will surprise no one that, despite such doomsayers, I see a bright future ahead for network news, a future that can be even brighter than our past. There is a real and present danger, but it's not the changing technology and the increase in news outlets that everyone likes to talk about. To the contrary, I believe the new world offers us exciting opportunities to reach our audiences, as we find ways to deliver news that is available to people when and where they want it. For me, the real danger we face lies not in how we provide the news, but in what we are providing.

3 As we've watched an explosion in news outlets, we've seen a simultaneous explosion in the opinions being expressed every minute of every day over these "news" outlets. This rush to present opinion is beginning to drown out our reporting of facts. The clash of ideas is moving to center stage, while the search for truth is being pushed into the wings.

4 There are powerful business reasons for the embrace we're seeing of opinion journalism on TV. It's vivid, it's entertaining, and—let's face it— it's less expensive than reporting out a difficult story. Opinion offers a quick, efficient, and effective way to attract an audience in a cluttered world.

5 Seeking to report the factual truth of a matter, on the other hand, can be hard work, expensive, and inefficient. It requires developing or hiring reporters who truly know what they're reporting about. It requires following leads that may go nowhere. The emphasis on opinion is therefore understandable. But I have two concerns about where we are headed.

6 First, and perhaps most obvious, the more we fill up our reports with opinion, the less time we have for reporting facts. It's all well

and good, for example, to have people who know what they're talking about give their views, for example, about whether we're doing what we should be doing to make our ports safer. But before we get to that discussion, shouldn't we spend some time finding out what security and risks already exist at U.S. ports? It may be interesting to hear a heated debate about health care in the United States, but shouldn't we know where we stand now, what the future is likely to hold, and what the options might be? Emphasizing opinion to the exclusion of factual reporting undermines the very value of the opinions being expressed. Opinion is interesting—and valuable—only if it is based on facts.

7   There's a second, far more disturbing, problem with the expansion of opinion in television news. It can create the impression among the audience that everything they're seeing is an expression of someone's opinion. Many outlets fail to do a good job of distinguishing between opinion and fact. As a result, audiences see people who look like one another on sets that look alike with similar graphics either expressing strong opinions or reporting the facts. Is it any wonder that the audience starts to believe that it's all the same?

8   Unless we're careful, we who are charged with reporting the news could lose sight of truth as our ultimate goal. We could end up in a world where, implicitly, none of us—not the audience and not the reporters—even believe any longer in the truth.

9   This may seem a radical—even a ridiculous—suggestion. How could it be that we would give up our belief in the truth? But look at some of the reporting we see on television today. Increasingly, some reporters don't even ask whether something is true or false. They jump over this basic question and go straight to an analysis of who's doing the talking and why. What is their affiliation? What hidden motive may they have for saying what they're saying? It's all about strategy and the political game rather than the facts underlying a debate.

10   Take, for example, the much-publicized Swift Boat Veterans for Truth. When their advertisements hit the airwaves last August, there was enormous media coverage of what they said, followed quickly by a thorough examination of who these people were and what motives they had, and then by comments from the Kerry campaign. But whether or not one agreed with the group's ultimate conclusions about Senator John Kerry, here was someone asserting claims of fact—claims that are susceptible to being proven right or wrong. Yet how much of the media attention was directed to the basic question: Were the accounts of what happened in Vietnam thirty-five years ago true or false?

11   The question of whether anyone can discern the "truth" about what happened thirty-five years ago—or even what is happening today—is one that has occupied philosophers for years. But as interesting as that academic question may be, those of us in network news don't have the luxury of giving up on our goal of truth-telling.

seeking truth? What do you think is Westin's opinion about the group's observations concerning what happened in Vietnam almost 40 years ago?

8. When the producers of *Nightline* approved the reading of the names of all the American service personnel who died in Iraq during one broadcast, they were accused of antiwar bias. Was this charge justified or not? What are the two counterarguments that Westin presents against the charge of bias? If Fox News had broadcast these names, would Westin have approved?

9. Ultimately, what is Westin arguing for and why is it important? Why is our "survival at risk"?

10. Who is the audience for this article, which was published both online and in print? Is he writing for the general public who reads newspapers and watches television news, or is it perhaps more specialized?

Summarizing Exercise

Write a summary of Westin's article. The length of the original is about 1700 words; try to keep your summary to no more than 200 words.

_____

_____

_____

_____

_____

_____

Critical Thinking Exercise

On September 9, 2010, Emily Miller published an online story titled "How David Westin Ruined ABC News." Locate this article at the home page of Human Events, a conservative news website. Read it carefully. What are Miller's specific criticisms of Westin's tenure at ABC News? Evaluate her criticisms in light of Westin's *CJR* article. What are the economic realities that Miller brings up that Westin does not anticipate in his article? To what extent do these realities make it difficult to fulfill what Westin says is the role of news—to find "the underlying truth of our situation in the world"?

Selection 6   ## "Is Google Making Us Stupid?"
                   ### Nicholas Carr

Nicholas Carr, a 2011 Pulitzer Prize finalist, specializes in writing about technology, culture, and economics and how they intersect. Carr has written for The Guardian *in London, the* New York Times, The Wall Street Journal, The New Republic, *and* The Atlantic. *In addition, he has published three noteworthy books,* Does IT Matter? *(2004),* The Big Switch: Rewiring the World, from Edison to Google *(2008), and* The Shallows: What the Internet Is Doing to Our Brains. *This selection is taken from the last book, though it was first published in* The Atlantic. *It has also been included in* The Best American Science and Nature Writing 2009 *and* The Best Technology Writing 2009.

Preview Questions

1. Have you had the Internet—e-mail, hyperlinks, web browsers—all your life or not? If you haven't, are you aware that it has caused changes in your thinking, your reading habits, or your concentration?

2. The next time you turn on the television, notice how elements from the Internet have made their way into TV programming. Do the same with the daily newspaper and your favorite magazines.

3. Can you anticipate what Carr might argue from his title about why Google might be making us stupid?

1   "Dave, stop. Stop, will you? Stop, Dave. Will you stop, Dave?" So the supercomputer HAL pleads with the implacable astronaut Dave Bowman in a famous and weirdly poignant scene toward the end of Stanley Kubrick's *2001: A Space Odyssey.* Bowman, having nearly been sent to a deep-space death by the malfunctioning machine, is calmly, coldly disconnecting the memory circuits that control its artificial brain. "Dave, my mind is going," HAL says, forlornly. "I can feel it. I can feel it."

2   I can feel it, too. Over the past few years I've had an uncomfortable sense that someone, or something, has been tinkering with my brain, remapping the neural circuitry, reprogramming the memory. My mind isn't going—so far as I can tell—but it's changing. I'm not thinking the way I used to think. I can feel it most strongly when I'm reading. Immersing myself in a book or a lengthy article used to be easy. My mind would get caught up in the narrative or the turns of the argument, and I'd spend hours strolling through long stretches of prose. That's rarely the case anymore. Now my concentration often starts to drift after two or three pages. I get fidgety, lose the thread, begin looking for something else to do. I feel as if I'm always dragging my wayward brain back to the text. The deep reading that used to come naturally has become a struggle.

3   I think I know what's going on. For more than a decade now, I've been spending a lot of time online, searching and surfing and sometimes adding to the great databases of the Internet. The Web has been a godsend to me as a writer. Research that once required days in the stacks or periodical rooms of libraries can now be done in minutes. A few Google searches, some quick clicks on hyperlinks and I've got the telltale fact or pithy quote I was after. Even when I'm not working, I'm as likely as not to be foraging in the Web's info-thickets—reading and writing e-mails, scanning headlines and blog posts, watching videos and listening to podcasts, or just tripping from link to link to link. (Unlike footnotes, to which they're sometimes likened, hyperlinks don't merely point to related works; they propel you toward them.)

4   For me, as for others, the Net is becoming a universal medium, the conduit for most of the information that flows through my eyes and ears and into my mind. The advantages of having immediate access to such an incredibly rich store of information are many, and they've been widely described and duly applauded. "The perfect recall of silicon memory," *Wired*'s Clive Thompson has written, "can be an enormous boon to thinking." But that boon comes at a price. As the media theorist Marshall McLuhan pointed out in the 1960s, media are not just passive channels of information. They supply the stuff of thought, but they also shape the process of thought. And what the Net seems to be doing is chipping away my capacity for concentration and contemplation. My mind now expects to take in information the way the Net distributes it: in a swiftly moving stream of particles. Once I was a scuba diver in the sea of words. Now I zip along the surface like a guy on a Jet Ski.

5   I'm not the only one. When I mention my troubles with reading to friends and acquaintances—literary types, most of them—many say they're having similar experiences. The more they use the Web, the more they have to fight to stay focused on long pieces of writing. Some of the bloggers I follow have also begun mentioning the phenomenon. Scott Karp, who writes a blog about online media, recently confessed that he has stopped reading books altogether. "I was a lit major in college, and used to be [a] voracious book reader," he wrote. "What happened?" He speculates on the answer: "What if I do all my reading on the web not so much because the way I read has changed, i.e. I'm just seeking'convenience, but because the way I THINK has changed?"

6   Bruce Friedman, who blogs regularly about the use of computers in medicine, also has described how the Internet has altered his mental habits. "I now have almost totally lost the ability to read and absorb a longish article on the web or in print," he wrote earlier this year. A pathologist who has long been on the faculty of the University of Michigan Medical School, Friedman elaborated on his comment in a telephone conversation with me. His thinking, he said, has taken on a "staccato" quality, reflecting the way he quickly scans short passages of text from many sources online. "I can't read *War and Peace* anymore," he admitted.

"I've lost the ability to do that. Even a blog post of more than three or four paragraphs is too much to absorb. I skim it."

7   Anecdotes alone don't prove much. And we still await the long-term neurological and psychological experiments that will provide a definitive picture of how Internet use affects cognition. But a recently published study of online research habits, conducted by scholars from University College London, suggests that we may well be in the midst of a sea change in the way we read and think. As part of the five-year research program, the scholars examined computer logs documenting the behavior of visitors to two popular research sites, one operated by the British Library and one by a U.K. educational consortium, that provide access to journal articles, e-books, and other sources of written information. They found that people using the sites exhibited "a form of skimming activity," hopping from one source to another and rarely returning to any source they'd already visited. They typically read no more than one or two pages of an article or book before they would "bounce" out to another site. Sometimes they'd save a long article, but there's no evidence that they ever went back and actually read it. The authors of the study report:

> It is clear that users are not reading online in the traditional sense; indeed there are signs that new forms of "reading" are emerging as users "power browse" horizontally through titles, contents pages and abstracts going for quick wins. It almost seems that they go online to avoid reading in the traditional sense.

8   Thanks to the ubiquity of text on the Internet, not to mention the popularity of text-messaging on cell phones, we may well be reading more today than we did in the 1970s or 1980s, when television was our medium of choice. But it's a different kind of reading, and behind it lies a different kind of thinking—perhaps even a new sense of the self. "We are not only *what* we read," says Maryanne Wolf, a developmental psychologist at Tufts University and the author of *Proust and the Squid: The Story and Science of the Reading Brain*. "We are *how* we read." Wolf worries that the style of reading promoted by the Net, a style that puts "efficiency" and "immediacy" above all else, may be weakening our capacity for the kind of deep reading that emerged when an earlier technology, the printing press, made long and complex works of prose commonplace. When we read online, she says, we tend to become "mere decoders of information." Our ability to interpret text, to make the rich mental connections that form when we read deeply and without distraction, remains largely disengaged.

9   Reading, explains Wolf, is not an instinctive skill for human beings. It's not etched into our genes the way speech is. We have to teach our minds how to translate the symbolic characters we see into the language we understand. And the media or other technologies we use in learning and practicing the craft of reading play an important part in shaping the

neural circuits inside our brains. Experiments demonstrate that readers of ideograms, such as the Chinese, develop a mental circuitry for reading that is very different from the circuitry found in those of us whose written language employs an alphabet. The variations extend across many regions of the brain, including those that govern such essential cognitive functions as memory and the interpretation of visual and auditory stimuli. We can expect as well that the circuits woven by our use of the Net will be different from those woven by our readine of books and other printed works.

10   Sometime in 1882, Friedrich Nietzsche bought a typewriter—a Malling-Hansen Writing Ball, to be precise. His vision was failing, and keeping his eyes focused on a page had become exhausting and painful, often bringing on crushing headaches. He had been forced to curtail his writing, and he feared that he would soon have to give it up. The typewriter rescued him, at least for a time. Once he had mastered touch-typing, he was able to write with his eyes closed, using only the tips of his fingers. Words could once again flow from his mind to the page.

11   But the machine had a subtler effect on his work. One of Nietzsche's friends, a composer, noticed a change in the style of his writing. His already terse prose had become even tighter, more telegraphic. "Perhaps you will through this instrument even take to a new idiom," the friend wrote in a letter, noting that, in his own work, his "'thoughts' in music and language often depend on the quality of pen and paper."

12   "You are right," Nietzsche replied, "our writing equipment takes part in the forming of our thoughts." Under the sway of the machine, writes the German media scholar Friedrich A. Kittler, Nietzsche's prose "changed from arguments to aphorisms, from thoughts to puns, from rhetoric to telegram style."

13   The human brain is almost infinitely malleable. People used to think that our mental meshwork, the dense connections formed among the 100 billion or so neurons inside our skulls, was largely fixed by the time we reached adulthood. But brain researchers have discovered that that's not the case. James Olds, a professor of neuro-science who directs the Krasnow Institute for Advanced Study at George Mason University, says that even the adult mind "is very plastic." Nerve cells routinely break old connections and form new ones. "The brain," according to Olds, "has the ability to reprogram itself on the fly, altering the way it functions."

14   As we use what the sociologist Daniel Bell has called our "intellectual technologies"—the tools that extend our mental rather than our physical capacities—we inevitably begin to take on the qualities of those technologies. The mechanical clock, which came into common use in the fourteenth century, provides a compelling example. In *Technics and Civilization,* the historian and cultural critic Lewis Mumford described how the clock "disassociated time from human events and helped create the belief in an independent world of mathematically measurable sequences." The "abstract framework of divided time" became "the point of reference for both action and thought."

15   The clock's methodical ticking helped bring into being the scientific mind and the scientific man. But it also took something away. As the late MIT computer scientist Joseph Weizenbaum observed in his 1976 book, *Computer Power and Human Reason: From Judgment to Calculation*, the conception of the world that emerged from the widespread use of timekeeping instruments "remains an impoverished version of the older one, for it rests on a rejection of those direct experiences that formed the basis for, and indeed constituted, the old reality." In deciding when to eat, to work, to sleep, to rise, we stopped listening to our senses and started obeying the clock.

16   The process of adapting to new intellectual technologies is reflected in the changing metaphors we use to explain ourselves to ourselves. When the mechanical clock arrived, people began thinking of their brains as operating "like clockwork." Today, in the age of software, we have come to think of them as operating "like computers." But the changes, neuroscience tells us, go much deeper than metaphor. Thanks to our brain's plasticity, the adaptation occurs also at a biological level.

17   The Internet promises to have particularly far-reaching effects on cognition. In a paper published in 1936, the British mathematician Alan Turing proved that a digital computer, which at the time existed only as a theoretical machine, could be programmed to perform the function of any other information-processing device. And that's what we're seeing today. The Internet, an immeasurably powerful computing system, is subsuming most of our other intellectual technologies. It's becoming our map and our clock, our printing press and our typewriter, our calculator and our telephone, and our radio and TV.

18   When the Net absorbs a medium, that medium is recreated in the Net's image. It injects the medium's content with hyperlinks, blinking ads, and other digital gewgaws, and it surrounds the content with the content of all the other media it has absorbed. A new e-mail message, for instance, may announce its arrival as we're glancing over the latest headlines at a newspaper's site. The result is to scatter our attention and diffuse our concentration.

19   The Net's influence doesn't end at the edges of a computer screen, either. As people's minds become attuned to the crazy quilt of Internet media, traditional media have to adapt to the audience's new expectations. Television programs add text crawls and pop-up ads, and magazines and newspapers shorten their articles, introduce capsule summaries, and crowd their pages with easy-to-browse info-snippets. When, in March of this year, *The New York Times* decided to devote the second and third pages of every edition to article abstracts, its design director, Tom Bodkin, explained that the "shortcuts" would give harried readers a quick "taste" of the day's news, sparing them the "less efficient" method of actually turning the pages and reading the articles. Old media have little choice but to play by the new-media rules.

feed us advertisements. Most of the proprietors of the commercial Internet have a financial stake in collecting the crumbs of data we leave behind as we flit from link to link—the more crumbs, the better. The last thing these companies want is to encourage leisurely reading or slow, concentrated thought. It's in their economic interest to drive us to distraction.

30   Maybe I'm just a worrywart. Just as there's a tendency to glorify technological progress, there's a countertendency to expect the worst of every new tool or machine. In Plato's *Phaedrus,* Socrates bemoaned the development of writing. He feared that, as people came to rely on the written word as a substitute for the knowledge they used to carry inside their heads, they would, in the words of one of the dialogue's characters, "cease to exercise their memory and become forgetful." And because they would be able to "receive a quantity of information without proper instruction," they would "be thought very knowledgeable when they are for the most part quite ignorant." They would be "filled with the conceit of wisdom instead of real wisdom." Socrates wasn't wrong—the new technology did often have the effects he feared—but he was shortsighted. He couldn't foresee the many ways that writing and reading would serve to spread information, spur fresh ideas, and expand human knowledge (if not wisdom).

31   The arrival of Gutenberg's printing press, in the fifteenth century, set off another round of teeth gnashing. The Italian humanist Hieronimo Squarciafico worried that the easy availability of books would lead to intellectual laziness, making men "less studious" and weakening their minds. Others argued that cheaply printed books and broadsheets would undermine religious authority, demean the work of scholars and scribes, and spread sedition and debauchery. As New York University professor Clay Shirky notes, "Most of the arguments made against the printing press were correct, even prescient." But, again, the doomsayers were unable to imagine the myriad blessings that the printed word would deliver.

32   So, yes, you should be skeptical of my skepticism. Perhaps those who dismiss critics of the Internet as Luddites or nostalgists will be proved correct, and from our hyperactive, data-stoked minds will spring a golden age of intellectual discovery and universal wisdom. Then again, the Net isn't the alphabet, and although it may replace the printing press, it produces something altogether different. The kind of deep reading that a sequence of printed pages promotes is valuable not just for the knowledge we acquire from the author's words but for the intellectual vibrations those words set off within our own minds. In the quiet spaces opened up by the sustained, undistracted reading of a book, or by any other act of contemplation, for that matter, we make our own associations, draw our own inferences and analogies, foster our own ideas. Deep reading, as Maryanne Wolf argues, is indistinguishable from deep thinking.

33   If we lose those quiet spaces, or fill them up with "content," we will sacrifice something important not only in our selves but in our culture. In a recent essay, the playwright Richard Foreman eloquently described what's at stake:

I come from a tradition of Western culture, in which the ideal (my ideal) was the complex, dense and "cathedral-like" structure of the highly educated and articulate personality—a man or woman who carried inside themselves a personally constructed and unique version of the entire heritage of the West. [But now] I see within us all (myself included) the replacement of complex inner density with a new kind of self—evolving under the pressure of information overload and the technology of the "instantly available."

As we are drained of our "inner repertory of dense cultural inheritance," Foreman concluded, we risk turning into "'pancake people'—spread wide and thin as we connect with that vast network of information accessed by the mere touch of a button."

34   I'm haunted by that scene in *2001*. What makes it **so** poignant, and so weird, is the computer's emotional response to the disassembly of its mind: its despair as one circuit after another goes dark, its childlike pleading with the astronaut—"I can feel it. I can feel it. I'm afraid"—and its final reversion to what can only be called a state of innocence. HAL's outpouring of feeling contrasts with the emotionlessness that characterizes the human figures in the film, who go about their business with an almost robotic efficiency. Their thoughts and actions feel scripted, as if they're following the steps of an algorithm. In the world of *2001*, people have become so machinelike that the most human character turns out to be a machine. That's the essence of Kubrick's dark prophecy: as we come to rely on computers to mediate our understanding of the world, it is our own intelligence that flattens into artificial intelligence.

Questions for Discussion and Analysis

1. In what specific ways has Carr's thinking and reading changed? How does he account for this change?

2. Explain what Carr means in paragraph 4 when he writes that the "boon to thinking" that the Internet provides comes at a price. What is the primary difference between the way information is delivered via the printed page as opposed to the Internet?

3. Who are the authorities that Carr cites in paragraphs 5 and 6 to confirm his observations? Why does he choose these particular people as illustrations? Are they meant to be representative of the general public, or not? Why are these observations necessarily of limited use?

4. According to the study conducted at University College London, how has reading online changed the way we read? If "new forms of reading are emerging," is this a bad thing? What is "deep reading" and how does it differ from the way we read online? Do you ever do deep reading? Where else do you engage in deep reading, aside from the reading you do in this textbook?!

5. In the past, how have new forms of technology altered the human brain and our mental capacities? Like the typewriter for Nietzsche and the mechanical clock, the Internet promises also to change cognition. What is cognition?

6. Read paragraph 18 again. How, specifically, does the Internet "scatter our attention and diffuse our concentration"? How has the Internet affected the look of television programs, magazines, and newspapers?

7. Explain the revolutionary change to industry brought about by research done by Frederick Winslow Taylor. How have Taylor's discoveries been transferred to the world of computers?

8. What is the vision for human intelligence as propounded by Google's founders, Sergey Brin and Larry Page? What does Carr think of this vision? Why don't corporate Internet sites want viewers to linger on their sites or to do deep reading of their "content"?

9. What does Carr mean when he advises us in paragraph 32 to "be skeptical of my skepticism"? What does Foreman mean in paragraph 33 by "pancake people"?

10. Carr begins and ends the article with an allusion to HAL, the computer in the movie "2001: A Space Odyssey." What is the point of this allusion? Ultimately, what is Carr's answer to the question his title poses, "Is Google making us stupid"?

Annotating Exercise

Assume for the purpose of this exercise that you have been assigned to write an essay on the negative effects of the Internet on the human mind and on our society. Annotate Carr's essay, making comments in the margin to prepare a paper on this subject.

Selection 7   # "In Defense of Literacy"
Wendell Berry

Wendell Berry (1934–) combines two unusual livelihoods—writing and farming. He and his family actively farm 125 acres in Henry County, located in northwestern Kentucky on the banks of the Kentucky River. Berry, a poet, novelist, and essayist, has published more than thirty books. Some of his novels are set in the fictional community of Port William, Kentucky, among them Nathan Coulter *(1960) and* Hannah Coulter *(2004). Probably his best known collection of essays is* A Continuous Harmony *(1972), from which this essay is taken.*

Preview Questions

1. Consider the title of the essay, "In Defense of Literacy." Why do you think literacy needs defending? What forces might operate against literacy in our culture?

2. What is your definition of literacy? After you read Berry's essay, how might you refine and/or revise your definition?

3. In the age of the Internet, is literacy obsolete, or in danger of becoming obsolete?

1   In a country in which everybody goes to school, it may seem absurd to offer a defense of literacy, and yet I believe that such a defense is in order, and that the absurdity lies not in the defense, but in the necessity for it. The published illiteracies of the certified educated are on the increase. And the universities seem bent upon ratifying this state of things by declaring the acceptability, in their graduates, of adequate—that is to say, of mediocre—writing skills.

2   The schools, then, are following the general subservience to the "practical," as that term has been defined for us according to the benefit of corporations. By "practicality" most users of the term now mean whatever will most predictably and most quickly make a profit. Teachers of English and literature have either submitted, or are expected to submit, along with teachers of the more "practical" disciplines, to the doctrine that the purpose of education is the mass production of producers and consumers. This has forced our profession into a predicament that we will finally have to recognize as a perversion. As if awed by the ascendency of the "practical" in our society, many of us secretly fear, and some of us are apparently ready to say, that if a student is not going to become a teacher of his language, he has no need to master it.

3   In other words, to keep pace with the specialization—and the dignity according to specialization—in other disciplines, we have begun to look upon and to teach our language and literature as specialties. But whereas specialization is of the nature of the applied sciences, it is a perversion of the disciplines of language and literature. When we understand and teach these as specialties, we submit willy-nilly to the assumption of the "practical men" of business, and also apparently of education, that literacy is no more than an ornament: when one has become an efficient integer of the economy, *then* it is permissible, even desirable, to be able to talk about the latest novels. After all, the disciples of "practicality" may someday find themselves stuck in conversation with an English teacher.

4   I may have oversimplified that line of thinking, but not much. There are two flaws in it. One is that, among the self-styled "practical men," the practical is synonymous with the immediate. The long-term effects of their values and their acts lie outside the boundaries of their interest. For such people a strip mine ceases to exist as soon as the coal has been extracted. Short-term practicality is long-term idiocy.

5   The other flaw is that language and literature are always *about* something else, and we have no way to predict or control what they may be about. They are about the world. We will understand the world, and preserve ourselves and our values in it, only insofar as we have a language that is alert and responsive to it, and careful of it. I mean that literally. When we give our plows such brand names as "Sod Blaster," we are imposing on their use conceptual limits which raise the likelihood that they will be used destructively. When we speak of man's "war against nature," or of a "peace offensive," we are accepting the limitations of a metaphor that suggests and even proposes violent solutions. When students ask for the right of "participatory input" at the meetings of a faculty organization, they are thinking of democratic process, but they are *speaking* of a convocation of robots, and are thus devaluing the very traditions that they invoke.

6   Ignorance of books and the lack of a critical consciousness of language were safe enough in primitive societies with coherent oral traditions. In our society, which exists in an atmosphere of prepared, public language—language that is either written or being read—illiteracy is both a personal and a public danger. Think how constantly "the average American" is surrounded by premeditated language, in newspapers, and magazines, on signs and billboards, on TV and radio. He is forever being asked to buy or believe somebody else's line of goods. The line of goods is being sold, moreover, by men who are trained to make him buy it or believe it, whether or not he needs it or understands it or knows its value or wants it. This sort of selling is an honored profession among us. Parents who grow hysterical at the thought that their son might not cut his hair are *glad* to have him taught, and later employed, to lie about the quality of an automobile or the ability of a candidate.

7   What is our defense against this sort of language—this language-as-weapon? There is only one. We must know a better language. We must speak, and teach our children to speak, a language precise and articulate and lively enough to tell the truth about the world as we know it. And to do this we must know something of the roots and resources of our language, we must know its literature. The only defense against the worst is a knowledge of the best. By their ignorance people enfranchise their exploiters.

8   But to appreciate fully the necessity for the best sort of literacy we must consider not just the environment of prepared language in which most of us now pass most of our lives, but also the utter transience of most of this language, which is meant to be merely glanced at, or heard only once, or read once and thrown away. Such language is by definition, and often by calculation, not memorable; it is language meant to be replaced by what will immediately follow it, like that of shallow conversation between strangers. It cannot be pondered or effectively criticized. For those reasons, an unmixed diet of it is destructive of the informed, resilient, critical intelligence that the best of our traditions have sought to create

and to maintain—an intelligence that Jefferson held to be indispensable to the health and longevity of freedom. Such intelligence does not grow by bloating upon the ephemeral information and misinformation of the public media. It grows by returning again and again to the landmarks of its cultural birthright, the works that have proved worthy of devoted attention.

9   "Read not the Times. Read the Eternities," Thoreau said. Ezra Pound wrote that "literature is news that STAYS news." In his lovely poem, "The Island," Edwin Muir spoke of man's inescapable cultural boundaries and of his consequent responsibility for his own sources and renewals:

> Men are made of what is made,
> The meat, the drink, the life, the corn,
> Laid up by them, in them reborn.
> And self-begotten cycles close
> About our way; indigenous art
> And simple spells make unafraid
> The haunted labyrinths of the heart. . . .

10   These men spoke of a truth that no society can afford to shirk for long: we are dependent, for understanding, and for consolation and hope, upon what we learn of ourselves from songs and stories. This has always been so, and it will not change.

11   I am saying, then, that literacy—the mastery of language and the knowledge of books—is not an ornament, but a necessity. It is impractical only by the standards of quick profit and easy power. Longer perspective will show that it alone can preserve in us the possibility of an accurate judgment of ourselves, and the possibilities of correction and renewal. Without it, we are adrift in the present, in the wreckage of yesterday, in the nightmare of tomorrow.

A. Comprehension

Choose the answer that best completes each statement. Do not refer to the selection while doing this exercise.

1. Berry begins his essay by criticizing universities for turning out graduates with mediocre language skills. Which *two* are criticisms he makes about universities?
   (a) They favor the "practical" disciplines rather than literature.
   (b) They hire instructors who themselves do not write very well, who are therefore unable themselves to teach students to write well.
   (c) They are more interested in high graduation rates rather than in whether or not students are actually educated.
   (d) They are producing students to be producers and consumers.
   (e) They place undue emphasis on their money-making athletic programs at the expense of humanities.

5. Berry quotes Thoreau at the beginning of paragraph 9: "Read not the Times. Read the Eternities." What does this quotation mean?

_____

_____

_____

6. Read paragraph 11 again, in which Berry uses the pronoun "it" three times. What group of words does "it" specifically refer to?

_____

_____

D. Paraphrasing

Write the meaning of the following sentences from the essay in your own words.

1. As if awed by the ascendancy of the "practical" in our society, many of us secretly fear, and some of us are apparently ready to say, that if a student is not going to become a teacher of his language, he has no need to master it. (paragraph 2)

_____

_____

_____

_____

2. Short-term practicality is long-term idiocy. (paragraph 4)

_____

_____

3. The only defense against the worst is a knowledge of the best. By their ignorance people enfranchise their exploiters. (paragraph 7)

_____

_____

_____

4. I am saying, then, that literacy—the mastery of language and the knowledge of books—is not an ornament, but a necessity. . . . Without it, we are adrift in the present, in the wreckage of yesterday, in the nightmare of tomorrow. (paragraph 11)

_____

_____

_____

_____

E. Questions for Discussion and Analysis

1. What exactly does Berry mean when he uses the word "literacy"? Is it the ability to read and write, or does the word seem to have a more expansive meaning for him?

2. Berry's essay was published in 1972, many years before computers and the Internet were in wide use. How might Berry view Internet usage in light of the remarks he makes about "practical" and "immediate" things? How do you think he would view reading material online rather than in the traditional print form?

3. Berry does not mention or include any examples of literature that he would find appropriate. Why not? Is this a flaw in the essay, or does it matter?

4. Comment on Berry's distinction between the "best language" and the "language-as-weapon." What are some examples, apart from advertising copy, that would fit the latter description?

ON THE WEB

M. A. Grubbs of the University of Kentucky offers an essay called "Wendell Berry: People, Land and Fidelity," which, among other things, offers some advice Berry gave at a 1989 graduation at College of the Atlantic in Maine. You can locate the article by doing a search.

Selection 8

"Discomfort Food: When Veterinarians Make Dinner and Other Tales of Woe from Aerospace Test Kitchens"

Mary Roach

Mary Roach is a popular science writer who specializes in writing about off-beat scientific subjects. After the success of Bonk: The Curious Coupling of Science and Sex _(2008), she published her best-selling 2010 book,_ Packing for Mars: The Curious Science of Life in the Void, _from which this selection comes. Of this book, which takes up space exploration and the difficulties astronauts endure in outer space, the_ Portland Oregonian _said this: "Roach's inimitable style is on display in_ Packing for Mars, _as it has been in her previous books. She is part serious science journalist, part human guinea pig, part_ long. They needed to know: What happens to the digestive health of a man who consumes regular servings of lard flakes and pregelatinized waxy maize starch? How long could a human being survive on the kinds of foods being dreamed up by military test kitchens? More direly, how long would he *want* to? What does this sort of food do to morale?

9   Throughout the 1960s, NASA paid lots of people lots and lots of money to answer these questions. Space food R&D contracts were handed out to the Aerospace Medical Research Laboratories (AMRL) at Wright-Patterson Air Force Base and, later, the School of Aerospace Medicine (SAM) at Brooks Air Force Base. The U.S. Army Natick Laboratories drafted the manufacturing requirements, commercial vendors did the cooking, and AMRL and SAM inflicted them on Earth-bound test subjects. Both these bases constructed elaborate space cabin simulators where teams of volunteers were confined for mock spaceflights, some for as long as seventy-two days. Food was often tested at the same time as spacesuits, hygiene regimens, and different cabin atmospheres—including, delightfully, 70 percent helium.

10   Three times a day, experimental meals would be left by dieticians inside a pretend airlock. Over the years, recruits survived on all manner of processed and regimented aerospace foods: cubes, rods, slurries, bars, powders, and "rehydratables." Dieticians weighed, measured, and analyzed what went in, and they did the same with what came back out. "Stool samples were . . . homogenized, freeze-dried, and analyzed in duplicate," wrote First Lieutenant Keith Smith in a nutritional evaluation of an aerospace diet that included beef stew and chocolate pudding. You had to hope Lieutenant Smith kept his containers straight.

11   A photograph from this era depicts a pair of men in impossibly cramped conditions, wearing hospital scrubs and belts with some variety of vital-signs monitor. One young man sits hunched on the lower tier of a bunk bed so narrow and thin as to resemble a double-decker ironing board. He holds what appears to be a petit-four in his left hand, and a plastic bag containing four more layered cubes in his lap: dinner. A piece of tubing is taped to his nose. His roommate wears black Clark Kent glasses and a communications headset and sits at the kind of console that looked futuristic in 1965 and now looks Star Trek campy. The caption unhelpfully reads: "Space food personnel, 1965 to 1969." Perhaps the writer had tried something more informative—"Testing the effects of miniature sandwiches on heart and breathing rates"—but could find no way to phrase it without compromising Air Force dignity.

12   Many of the shots are Before photos, luckless smiling airmen posed on the threshold of the SAM test chamber alongside dietitian May O'Hara before they step inside and she closes the hatch. O'Hara looks exactly as you imagine an Air Force dietician to look—neither over- nor underweight, well coiffed and nice-looking, though unlikely to have a profound effect on the heart rate and oxygen uptake of young Air Force recruits. O'Hara was a good Egg Bite. In a military news service article,

she voices concern over the acceptability of the various space foods "day after day for 30 days or more."

13   She seemed to be the lone voice of reason. Though cube foods were getting tepid ratings, their developers pressed on enthusiastically, relentlessly, hydraulically. They could not see that foods that require you to rehydrate them with your own saliva—by holding them "in the mouth for 10 seconds"—might be a spirit dampener on a week-long flight. And they were. On mission after mission, sandwich cubes were, says retired NASA food scientist Charles Bourland, "some of the things that routinely came back." (He means they were still on board after landing, not that they were regurgitated. I think.)

14   I telephoned O'Hara at her home in Texas, just after lunch on a weekday afternoon. She is in her seventies now. I asked her what she'd eaten. It was a dietician's lunch, and a dietician's answer, laid out like a cafeteria menu: "Grilled beef and cheese sandwich, grapes, and fruit punch." I asked May whether the SAM simulator subjects often quit the studies early or busted out of the airlock to make a midnight run for Whataburger. They did not. "They were all just as cooperative as they could be," said May. For one thing, she explained, they'd just come out of basic training. The prospect of a month with no physical demands more strenuous than chewing had a certain appeal. Plus, in exchange for volunteering, they were given their choice of Air Force assignment, rather than simply being sent someplace.

15   Over at the AMRL simulator, the volunteers were paid undergrads from nearby Dayton University. Perhaps because they were paid, or because Dayton was a Catholic school, these men too were compliant and generally well behaved. Though missing Communion[2] occasionally became an issue. One volunteer became so agitated that the scientists broke protocol and summoned a priest, who gave Holy Communion over closed-circuit TV and microphone. Into the pass-through port was placed a small portion of wine and a single Communion wafer, whose palatability probably scored on a par with more typical chamber fare.

16   One test diet scored even lower than the cubed foods. "It was milk shakes in the morning, lunch, and supper. And the next day, it was milk

---

[2]Religious observations are even tougher in a real spacecraft. Launch weight limitations forced Buzz Aldrin to pack a "tiny Host" and thimble-sized wine chalice for his DIY Communion on the moon. Zero gravity and a ninety-minute orbital day created so many questions for Muslim astronauts that a "Guideline of Performing Ibadah at the International Space Station" was drafted. Rather than require Muslim astronauts to pray five times during each ninety-minute orbit of Earth, the guidelines allowed them to go by the twenty-four-hour cycle of the launch location. Wipes ("not less than 3 pieces") could be used for preprayer cleansing. And since the orbiting Muslim who began his prayer while facing Mecca was likely, by prayer's end, to be mooning Mecca, provisions were made allowing him to simply face the Earth or "wherever." Lastly, instead of lowering the face to the ground, a trying maneuver in zero gravity, prostrating oneself could be approximated by "bringing down the chin closer to the knee," "using the eye lid as an indicator of the changing of posture" or—in the vein of "wherever"—simply "imagining" the sequence of movements.

shakes in the morning, lunch, and supper," says John Brown, the officer who had been in charge of the AMRL space cabin simulator. On a scale of 1 to 9, volunteers who lived on them for thirty days gave the food an average score of 3 (dislike moderately). Brown told me 3 probably meant 1: "The subjects filled out their forms telling you what you wanted to hear." One subject confided to Brown that he and his fellow volunteers had been regularly dumping portions of their formula under the cabin flooring. Despite the diet's unpopularity, the researchers evaluated no less than twenty-four different commercial and experimental liquid diet formulas. I once read an Air Force technical report that lists the desired attributes of edible paper: "Tasteless, flexible, and tenacious." It's how I imagine some of these space food guys.

17   Meanwhile, over at SAM, Norman Heidelbaugh was testing a liquid diet of his own devising. An Air Force press release called it the "eggnog diet." May O'Hara described it as "sort of a powdered Ensure." "That was really not acceptable," she said with uncharacteristic bite to her words. Heidelbaugh himself seemed to leave a bad taste in people's mouths.

18   Though it appeared that the science of nutrition was attracting a unique breed of gustatory sadist, other forces were at work here. It was the mid-sixties. Americans were enraptured by convenience and the space-age technologies that bestowed it. Women were going back to work, and they had less time to cook and keep house. A meal in a stick or a pouch was both a novelty and a welcomed time-saver.

19   That was the mindset that propelled one of the AMRL's least popular liquid diets into a long and lucrative career as Carnation Instant Breakfast. The Space Food Stick also began life as a military washout. What the Air Force called "rod-shaped food for high-altitude feeding" was originally intended as food that could be poked through the port of a pressure suit helmet. "We couldn't get them stiff enough," O'Hara told me. So Pillsbury took back its rods and went commercial with them. Bourland says they occasionally went up with the astronauts simply as an onboard snack—sometimes under the name Nutrient-Defined Food Sticks and other times as Caramel Sticks, fooling no one.

20   Even the companies who made food sticks and breakfast drinks didn't expect the American family to eat nothing else. I have reason to believe that a cabal of extreme nutritionists was influencing thought at NASA. These were men who referred to a cocktail as a "two-carbon compound." Who wrote entire textbook chapters on "topping strategies." Here is MIT nutritionist Nevin S. Scrimshaw defending the liquid formula diet at the Conference on Nutrition in Space and Related Waste Problems in 1964: "Persons with other worthwhile and challenging things to fill their time do not necessarily require bits to hold in their mouth and chew or a variety of foods in order to be productive and to have high morale." Scrimshaw boasted of having fed his MIT subjects liquid formula dinners for two months with no complaint. The Gemini astronauts narrowly escaped a fate worse than cubes. "We are hoping, in the Gemini program,"

said NASA man Edward Michel at that same conference, "to go to some type of formula diet. . . .We will use it during preflight, during the flight, and for a 2-week period post-flight."

21 Scrimshaw was wrong. People *do* "necessarily require bits to hold in their mouth and chew." Put them on liquid diets and they crave solid food. I spent just one morning on the Mercury-era tube diet, and I did. The astronauts no longer eat tubed food, but military pilots do, when they're in the middle of a mission and can't stop to unwrap a sandwich. Vicki Loveridge, a helpful and congenial food technologist with the Combat Feeding Directorate at U.S. Army Natick, said the formulation and technology have changed little since the Mercury era. Loveridge invited me to Natick. ("Dan Nattress will be making Apple Pie in the tubes on the morning of the 21st.") I couldn't go, but she was kind enough to send me a sampler box. They look like my stepdaughter Lily's tubes of oil paint.

22 Tube eating is a uniquely disquieting experience. It requires bypassing the two quality control systems available to the human organism: looking and sniffing. Bourland told me the astronauts hated the tubes for precisely this reason: "Because they could not see or smell what they were eating." Also unnerving is the texture, or "mouthfeel," to use a food technology coinage. When a label says Sloppy Joe, you expect some Joe. The Natick version has no discernible ground-beef qualities. It's puréed. All tubed food is, because, as Charles Bourland put it, "the texture is limited to the orifice of the tube." The very first space food was essentially baby food. But even babies get to eat off spoons. Mercury astronauts had to suckle theirs from an aluminum orifice. It wasn't heroic at all. Or, as it turned out, necessary. A spoon and an open container will work fine in zero gravity as long as the food possesses, to quote the adorable May O'Hara, "stick-to-it-ive-ness or whatever." If it's thick and moist enough, surface tension will keep it from drifting off.

23 The Sloppy Joe tasted like frozen enchilada sauce. The Natick vegetarian entrée—which someone, obviously at a loss, had simply labeled "Vegetarian"—was another vaguely spicy tomatoey purée. Being a Mercury astronaut must have been like being trapped in the sauces aisle of a very small grocery store. But the Natick applesauce—identical in formulation to John Glenn's history-making applesauce tube[3]—was A-okay.

24 Partly, I imagine, because it's familiar. You expect applesauce to be puréed. One of the problems with the early space foods was their strangeness. When you're hurtling through space in a cramped, sterile can, you want something comforting and familiar. Space cuisine appealed to the

---

[3]The first food consumed by a NASA astronaut, but not the first food in space. The Soviets won this space race, too. Glenn's applesauce lost out to Laika's powdered meat and breadcrumb gelatin and the unnamed snack of Yuri Gagarin (in the words of Elena, the Gagarin Museum archivist, "Some say soup, some say purée. For sure there was something in the tube!").

American public as a novelty, but astronauts had had enough novelty for several lifetimes.

25   From time to time, there was talk among the astronauts that it might be nice to have a drink with dinner. Beer is a no-fly, because without gravity, carbonation bubbles don't rise to the surface. "You just get a foamy froth," says Bourland. He says Coke spent $450,000 developing a zero-gravity dispenser, only to be undone by biology. Since bubbles also don't rise to the top of a stomach, the astronauts had trouble burping. "Often a burp is accompanied by a liquid spray," Bourland adds.

26   Bourland was in charge of a short-lived effort to serve wine with meals on board Skylab. University of California oenologists steered him toward sherry, because it's heated during production, and thus keeps better. It's the pasteurized orange juice of the wine kingdom. Bottles aren't allowed in space, for safety reasons, so it was decided that the sherry, a Paul Masson cream sherry, would be packaged in plastic pouches inside pudding cans. Further limiting the already limited appeal of cream sherry.

27   The sherry cans, like any other new technology bound for space, were taken up on a parabolic flight for zero-gravity testing. Though the packaging worked fine, no one on board that day left with much enthusiasm for the product. A heavy sherry smell quickly saturated the cabin, compounding the more standard nauseating attributes of a parabolic flight. "As soon as you opened it," recalls Bourland, "you'd see people grabbing for their barf bags."

28   Nonetheless, Bourland filled out a government purchase order for several cases of Paul Masson. Just before the sherry went into the packaging, someone mentioned it in an interview and letters from teetotaling taxpayers began arriving at NASA. And so, after having spent God knows how much money on the packaging, requisitioning, and testing of canned cream sherry, NASA scrapped the whole endeavor.

29   Had it flown, the Skylab sherry would not have been the first alcoholic drink requisitioned by a government as rations for a mission of national service. British Navy rations included rum until 1970. From 1802 to 1832, U.S. military rations included one gill—a little over two shots—of rum, brandy, or whisky with the daily allotment of beef and bread. Every hundred rations, the soldiers were also given soap and a pound and a half of candles. The latter could be used for lighting, barter, or, were you the tidy sort, melted down and used to coat your beef sandwiches.

30   Nutritionists were not entirely to blame for the inhumanity of early space food. Charles Bourland alerted me to something I'd overlooked: the abbreviation "USAF VC" after liquid diet promulgator Norman Heidelbaugh's name. Heidelbaugh was a member of the Air Force Veterinary Corps. So was Robert Flentge, one of the editors of *Manufacturing Requirements of Food for Aerospace Feeding,* a 229-page handbook for preparers of astronaut foods. "A lot of the food science guys were military veterinarians," Bourland told me. Dating back to the Aerobee monkey launches and Colonel Stapp's work with the deceleration sleds, the Air

Force has had colonies of test animals and, by necessity, veterinarians (or, for those who felt six syllables weren't enough, "bioastronautics support veterinarians.") According to the 1962 article "The Sky's the Limit for USAF Veterinarians!" their responsibilities came to include "testing and formulating foodstuffs"—first animal and eventually astronautical. Bad news for space crews.

31   Veterinarians in charge of feeding research animals or livestock were concerned with three things: cost, ease of use, and avoiding health problems. Whether the monkeys or cows liked the food didn't much enter into it. This goes a long way toward explaining butterscotch formula diets and Compressed Corn Flake and Peanut Cream Cubes. It's what happens when veterinarians make dinner. Recalls Bourland, "The vets would say, 'When I feed animals, I just mix up a bag of feed and take it out there and they get everything they need. Why can't we do that with astronauts?'"

32   Sometimes they did. Witness Norman Heidelbaugh's 1967 technical report, "A Method to Manufacture Pelletized Formula Foods in Small Quantities." Heidelbaugh made Astronaut Chow! The top two ingredients, by weight, were Coffee-mate "coffee whitener" and dextrose/maltose, casting doubt on the vet's claim that the human pellets were "highly palatable." Again, deliciousness was not among this man's overriding concerns. Weight and volume were. By those criteria, Heidelbaugh had a winner: "Caloric density would be sufficient to provide 2600 kcal [2.6 million calories] from approximately 37 cubic inches of food."

33   Heidelbaugh's space-saving methods sound extreme, but only until you read the solution proposed in 1964 by Samuel Lepkovsky, professor of poultry husbandry at the University of California, Berkeley. "If it were possible to find suitable astronauts who are obese," Lepkovsky begins, seemingly unaware that he is nuts.[4] "An obese person with 20 kilograms of fat. . . carries reserves of 184,000 calories. This would provide over 2900 calories daily for 90 days." In other words: Think of the rocket fuel that could be saved by not launching *any food at alll*!

34   Starving your astronauts for the duration of the mission would resolve another early NASA concern: waste management. Not only was the act of using a fecal bag powerfully objectionable, but the end product stank and took up precious cabin space. "What the astronauts wanted to do is to just be able to take a pill and not eat," says Bourland. "They talked about it all the time." The food scientists tried but failed to make it happen. The astronauts' fallback solution was to skip meals, a deprivation made bearable by the knowledge of what awaited them inside the meal pouches.

[4]Sorry, I mean innovative. That is the adjective used by the author of Lepkovsky's 1985 UC Berkeley obituary. Here we learn that Lepkovsky coauthored the first atlas of the chicken brain and isolated riboflavin from "several hundred thousand gallons of milk." In what little spare time remained, he enjoyed dancing and amateur stock-market analysis, no doubt reaping great gains in dairy futures.

43   What would Fahey have fed the early astronauts? As a starch, he recommended rice, because it's the lowest-residue of all the carbohydrates. (This is why Purina makes Lamb & Rice, not Lamb & Fingerling Potatoes.) Fresh fruits and vegetables he'd skip, as they create a high-volume, high-frequency stool situation. On the other hand, if you feed someone highly processed foods with no residue, no fiber at all, they'll be constipated. Which, depending on the length of the flight, could be ideal: "Under current conditions," wrote Franz Ingelfinger, "with the emphasts on short-term flights, I am sure that the most practical solution to the waste-disposal problem has been a constipated astronaut."

44   Twelve years after the corned-beef-sandwich incident, astronaut John Young yet again embarrassed his employer in the national news media. Young, along with Apollo 16 crewmate Charlie Duke, was sitting in the Lunar Module Orion after a day out and about collecting rocks. During a radio debriefing with Mission Control, out of the blue, Young declares, "I got the farts again. I got 'em again, Charlie. I don't know what the hell gives them to me. . . . I think it's acid in the stomach." Following Apollo 15, in which low potassium levels were blamed for the heart arrhythmias of the crew, NASA had put potassium-laced orange grapefruit, and other citrus drinks on the menu.

45   Young kept going. It's all there in the mission transcript "I mean, I haven't eaten this much citrus fruit in 20 years. And I'll tell you one thing, in another 12 fucking days, I ain't never eating any more. And if they offer to serve me potassium with my breakfast I'm going to throw up. I like an occasional orange, I really do. But I'll be damned if I'm going to be buried in oranges." Moments later, Mission Control comes on the line and provides Young with yet more fodder for indigestion.

CAP COM [capsule communicator]: *Orion, Houston*
YOUNG: *Yes, sir.*
CAP COM: *Okay, you [have] a hot mike.*
YOUNG: *Oh. How long have we had that?*
CAP COM: *It's been on through the debriefing.*

46   This time, it wasn't Congress that got riled. The day after Young's comments hit the press, the governor of Florida issued a statement in defense of his state's key crop, which Charlie Duke paraphrases in his memoir: "It is not our orange juice that is causing the trouble. It's an artificial substitute that doesn't come from Florida."

47   In fact, it was the potassium, not the orange juice. The "coefficient of flatulence" for orange juice—to use the terminology of USDA flatus researcher Edwin Murphy, another panelist at the 1964 Conference on Nutrition in Space and Related Waste Problems—is low.

48   Murphy reported on research he had done using an "experimental bean meal" fed to volunteers who had been rigged, via a rectal catheter, to outgas into a measurement device. He was interested in individual differences—

not just in the overall volume of flatus but in the differing percentages of constituent gases. Owing to differences in intestinal bacteria, half the population produces no methane. This makes them attractive as astronauts, not because methane stinks (it's odorless), but because it's highly flammable. (Methane is what utility companies sell, under the rubric "natural gas.")[8]

49   Murphy had a unique suggestion for the NASA astronaut selection committee: "The astronaut may be selected from that part of our population producing little or no methane or hydrogen"—hydrogen is also explosive—"and a very low level of hydrogen sulfide or other malodorous trace flatus constituents not yet identified. . . . Further, since some individual astronauts may vary in the degree of flatulent reaction to a given weight of food, individuals can be chosen who demonstrate a high resistance to intestinal upset and flatus formation."

50   In his work, Murphy had encountered one such ideal astronaut candidate. "Of special interest for further research was the subject who produced essentially no flatus on 100 grams dry weight of beans." As opposed to the average gut, which will, during the peak flatulence period (five to six hours post–bean consumption) pass anywhere from one to almost three cups of flatus per hour. At the high end of the range, that's about two Coke cans full of fart. In a small space where you can't open the window.

51   As an alternative to recruiting the constitutionally nonflatulent, NASA could create non-"producers" by sterilizing their digestive tract. Murphy had fed the notorious bean meal to a subject who was taking an antibacterial drug and found that the man expelled 50 percent less gas. The saner approach, and the one NASA actually took, was to simply avoid your high coefficient-of-flatus foods. Up through Apollo, beans, cabbage,[9] Brussels sprouts, and broccoli were blacklisted. "Beans were not used until Shuttle," states Charles Bourland.

52   There are those who welcomed their arrival, and not just because they're tasty. The zero-gravity fart has been a popular orbital pursuit, particularly on all-male flights. One hears tell of astronauts using intestinal gas like rocket propellant to "launch themselves across the middeck," as astronaut Roger Crouch put it. He had heard the claims and was dubious. "The mass and velocity of the expelled gas," he told me in an e-mail that has forever-more endeared him to me, "is very small compared to the mass of the human body." Thus it was unlikely that it could accelerate a 180-pound astronaut. Crouch pointed out that an exhaled breath doesn't propel an astronaut in any direction, and the lungs hold about

[8]If you're among the 50 percent of the population who produce methane, you can play human pilot light. Your friends can hold a match to your gas and watch it ignite and burn blue.

[9]Cabbage resurfaced in the form of kimchi—fermented spiced cabbage—on board the International Space Station when Korea's first astronaut visited. Space kimchi developer Lee Ju-woon works at the Korean Atomic Energy Research Institute, where scientists are developing ways to harness energy from intestinal kimchi fission. No, they aren't. But they should be.

shedding its skin several times, it acquires its missing organs, mates, and is then prepared to attack warm-blooded animals.

2   The eyeless female is directed to the tip of a twig on a bush by her photosensitive skin, and there she stays through darkness and light, through fair weather and foul, waiting for the moment that will fulfill her existence. In the Zoological Institute, at Rostock, prior to World War I ticks were kept on the ends of twigs, waiting for this moment for a period of eighteen years. The metabolism of the insect is sluggish to the point of being suspended entirely. The sperm she received in the act of mating remains bundled into capsules where it, too, waits in suspension until mammalian blood reaches the stomach of the tick, at which time the capsules break, the sperm are released and they fertilize the eggs which have been reposing in the ovary, also waiting in a kind of time suspension.

3   The signal for which the tick waits is the scent of butyric acid, a substance present in the sweat of all mammals. This is the only experience that will trigger time into existence for the tick.

4   The tick represents, in the conduct of its life, a kind of apotheosis of subjective time perception. For a period as long as eighteen years nothing happens. The period passes as a single moment; but at any moment within this span of literally senseless existence, when the animal becomes aware of the scent of butyric acid it is thrust into a perception of time, and other signals are suddenly perceived.

5   The animal then hurls itself in the direction of the scent. The object on which the tick lands at the end of this leap must be warm; a delicate sense of temperature is suddenly mobilized and so informs the insect. If the object is not warm, the tick will drop off and reclimb its perch. If it is warm, the tick burrows its head deeply into the skin and slowly pumps itself full of blood. Experiments made at Rostock with membranes filled with fluids other than blood proved that the tick lacks all sense of taste, and once the membrane is perforated the animal will drink any fluid, provided it is of the right temperature.

6   The extraordinary preparedness of this creature for that moment of time during which it will re-enact the purpose of its life contrasts strikingly with the probability that this moment will ever occur. There are doubtless many bushes on which ticks perch, which are never by-passed by a mammal within range of the tick's leap. As do most animals, the tick lives in an absurdly unfavorable world—at least so it would appear to the compassionate human observer. But this world is merely the environment of the animal. The world it perceives—which experimenters at Rostock called its *umwelt,* its perceptual world—is not at all unfavorable. A period of eighteen years, as measured objectively by the circuit of the earth around the sun, is meaningless to the tick. During this period, it is apparently unaware of temperature changes. Being blind, it does not see the leaves shrivel and fall and then renew themselves on the bush where it is affixed. Unaware of time it is also unaware of space, and the multitudes of forms and colors which appear in space. It waits, suspended in

duration for its particular moment of time, a moment distinguished by being filled with a single, unique experience; the scent of butyric acid.

7   Though we consider ourselves far removed as humans from such a lowly insect form as this, we too are both aware and unaware of elements which comprise our environment. We are more aware than the tick of the passage of time. We are subjectively aware of the aging process; we know that we grow older, that time is shortened by each passing moment. For the tick, however, this moment that precedes its burst of volitional activity, the moment when it scents butyric acid and is thrust into purposeful movement, is close to the end of time for the tick. When it fills itself with blood, it drops from its host, lays its eggs, and dies.

8   For us humans, death seems to come in a more random fashion. Civilized as we pretend to be, we know very little about time and the transformations of living things that occur within it. We know little about growth and aging, which, it would seem, are stimulated by the passage of time which streams around us carrying us with it; and about death, or the termination of biological time.

A. Comprehension

Choose the answer that best completes each statement. Do not refer to the selection while doing this exercise.

1. The subject of this selection is
   (a) experiments with insects at the Rostock Institute.
   (b) the life history of the cattle tick.
   (c) the difference between animal and human perceptions of time.
   (d) the difference in the manner of death for animals and humans.

2. The adult cattle tick's metabolism cannot be activated until it becomes aware of the scent of butyric acid, a substance present
   (a) only in cattle.
   (b) in the blood of all mammals.
   (c) in the sweat of all mammals.
   (d) in tree sap.

3. Ironically, the adult cattle tick has
   (a) no sense of taste.
   (b) no sense of smell.
   (c) no sense of direction.
   (d) no sex organs.

4. According to Bleibtreu, the suspended existence of the cattle tick, perhaps for as long as 18 years, illustrates
   (a) a long period of waiting.
   (b) a hostile environment.
   (c) objective time perception.
   (d) subjective time perception.

5. Bleibtreu emphasizes that, like the cattle tick, humans
   (a) are completely unaware of the environment around us.
   (b) know little about growth, aging, and death.
   (c) are keenly aware of the passage of time.
   (d) undergo the same reproductive cycle.

B. Inferences

On the basis of the evidence in the passage, mark these statements as follows: PA (probably accurate), PI (probably inaccurate), or NP (not in the passage).

1. _____ The cattle tick is unable to detect light.

2. _____ For the cattle tick, reproduction, which occurs when the tick lays its eggs, signifies that death is near.

3. _____ A cattle tick who never comes into contact with a mammal eventually dies.

4. _____ The cattle tick can detect temperature changes both in the environment and on an animal's skin.

5. _____ It is probable that many cattle ticks never complete their life cycle.

6. _____ The Zoological Institute at Rostock is the only scientific institution where the cattle tick has been studied.

C. Structure and Meaning

1. Which sentence from the essay best represents both the thesis statement and the writer's underlying purpose?
   (a) "The cattle tick is a small, flat-bodied, blood-sucking insect with a curious life history."
   (b) "This [the scent of butyric acid] is the only experience that will trigger time into existence for the tick."
   (c) "The tick represents, in the conduct of its life, a kind of apotheosis of subjective time perception."
   (d) "We know little about growth and aging, which, it would seem are stimulated by the passage of time which streams around us carrying us with it; and about death, or the termination of biological time."

2. The mode of discourse in the selection is predominantly
   (a) narration.
   (b) description.
   (c) exposition.
   (d) persuasion.

3. When Bleibtreu states that the cattle tick's existence depends solely on the presence of butyric acid, from the human point of view this emphasizes the tick's
   (a) uselessness.
   (b) slim chances for fulfillment.

    (c) impossibility of fulfillment.

    (d) meaningless, senseless existence.

4. Look again at paragraph 4. When Bleibtreu writes, "this span of literally senseless existence," what does he mean by the word *senseless?*

    (a) meaningless, empty

    (b) having no capability of physical sensation, insensate

    (c) foolish

5. What is the purpose of paragraphs 7 and 8?

    (a) to summarize the tick's biological cycle.

    (b) to show the similarities between the cattle tick and humans in terms of life processes and the perception of time passing.

    (c) to warn the reader that life is short and too easily taken up with trivial matters.

    (d) to contrast the lowly cattle tick with human ideals and lofty aspirations.

6. The writer's tone can best be described as

    (a) objective, informative.

    (b) arrogant, superior.

    (c) critical, judgmental.

    (d) reflective, philosophical.

D. *Vocabulary*

For each italicized word from the selection, choose the best definition according to the context in which it appears.

1. her *photosensitive* skin [paragraph 2]—sensitive to

    (a) heat.

    (b) sight.

    (c) scent.

    (d) light.

2. the eggs have been *reposing* in the ovary [2]

    (a) waiting in storage.

    (b) lying at rest.

    (c) developing, maturing.

    (d) multiplying.

3. an *apotheosis* of subjective time perception [4]

    (a) legend passed from one generation to the next.

    (b) rule to be followed.

    (c) ideal, primary example.

    (d) apocalypse.

4. a *lowly* insect form [7]

    (a) simple, humble.

    (b) unaware.

    (c) complicated.

    (d) pitiable.

5. its burst of *volitional* activity [7]—describing an act of
   (a) coming into being.
   (b) will.
   (c) maturing.
   (d) dying.

E. Summarizing Exercise

Write a summary of paragraphs 7 and 8. Try to keep the length to 25–30 words. _____

_____

_____

F. Questions for Discussion and Analysis

1. Surely other animals or insects possess the same characteristics that Bleibtreu assigns to the cattle tick, namely the lack of awareness of time and space. Why, then, has he chosen this lowly insect as the subject of his essay?

2. What is ironic about the cattle tick's life cycle after it has been activated by the scent of butyric acid? What point is Bleibtreu making in describing in such detail the suspension of time in the tick's life?

3. The title of the book from which this selection comes is *The Parable of the Beast.* What is a parable? In what way does this essay represent one?

Selection 10   An Earth without People

An Interview with Alan Weisman

A new book by Alan Weisman, professor of journalism at the University of Arizona, begins with a premise that sounds as if it comes from a science fiction movie: What would happen if human beings were suddenly to vanish from the earth? In his new book, The World without Us *(2007), Weisman looks at such a world. This selection represents an interview that Steven Mirsky, an editor at* Scientific American, *conducted with Weisman about his book—why he wrote it and what we can learn from it. In addition to his current book, Weisman has published many articles in such diverse publications as* Harpers, The New York Times Magazine, Mother Jones, *and* Condé Nast Traveler.

Preview Questions

1. Imagine cities like New York City, Chicago, or Los Angeles without people. What would you guess would happen to the infrastructure without human intervention or maintenance?

2. Would the world be a better place without humans? Have we irrevocably ruined the environment, or have our contributions to culture (monuments, museums, churches, and the like) compensated for our failures?

3. Imagine your own community without human residents. What do you think it would look like in, say, 50 years?

1   *If human beings were to disappear tomorrow, the magnificent skyline of Manhattan would not long survive them. Weisman describes how the concrete jungle of New York City would revert to a real forest.*

2   "What would happen to all of our stuff if we weren't here anymore? Could nature wipe out all of our traces? Are there some things that we've made that are indestructible or indelible? Could nature, for example, take New York City back to the forest that was there when Henry Hudson first saw it in 1609?

3   "I had a fascinating time talking to engineers and maintenance people in New York City about what it takes to hold off nature. I discovered that our huge, imposing, overwhelming infrastructures that seem so monumental and indestructible are actually these fairly fragile concepts that continue to function and exist thanks to a few human beings on whom all of us really depend. The name 'Manhattan' comes from an Indian term referring to hills. It used to be a very hilly island. Of course, the region was eventually flattened to have a grid of streets imposed on it. Around those hills there used to flow about 40 different streams, and there were numerous springs all over Manhattan island. What happened to all that water? There's still just as much rainfall as ever on Manhattan, but the water has now been suppressed. It's underground. Some of it runs through the sewage system, but a sewage system is never as efficient as nature in wicking away water. So there is a lot of groundwater rushing around underneath, trying to get out. Even on a clear, sunny day, the people who keep the subway going have to pump 13 million gallons of water away. Otherwise the tunnels will start to flood.

4   "There are places in Manhattan where they're constantly fighting rising underground rivers that are corroding the tracks. You stand in these pump rooms, and you see an enormous amount of water gushing in. And down there in a little box are these pumps, pumping it away. So, say human beings disappeared tomorrow. One of the first things that would happen is that the power would go off. A lot of our power comes out of nuclear or coal-fired plants that have automatic fail-safe switches to make sure that they don't go out of control if no humans are monitoring their systems. Once the power goes off, the pumps stop working. Once the pumps stop working, the subways start filling with water. Within 48 hours you're going to have a lot of flooding in New York City. Some of this would be visible on the surface. You might have some sewers overflowing. Those sewers would very quickly

become clogged with debris—in the beginning the innumerable plastic bags that are blowing around the city and later, if nobody is trimming the hedges in the parks, you're going to have leaf litter clogging up the sewers.

5   "But what would be happening underground? Corrosion. Just think of the subway lines below Lexington Avenue. You stand there waiting for the train, and there are all these steel columns that are holding up the roof, which is really the street. These things would start to corrode and, eventually, to collapse. After a while the streets would begin cratering, which could happen within just a couple of decades. And pretty soon, some of the streets would revert to the surface rivers that we used to have in Manhattan before we built all of this stuff.

6   "Many of the buildings in Manhattan are anchored to bedrock. But even if they have steel beam foundations, these structures were not designed to be waterlogged all the time. So eventually buildings would start to topple and fall. And we're bound to have some more hurricanes hitting the East Coast as climate change gives us more extreme weather. When a building would fall, it would take down a couple of others as it went, creating a clearing. Into those clearings would blow seeds from plants, and those seeds would establish themselves in the cracks in the pavement. They would already be rooting in leaf litter anyhow, but the addition of lime from powdered concrete would create a less acidic environment for various species. A city would start to develop its own little ecosystem. Every spring when the temperature would be hovering on one side or the other of freezing, new cracks would appear. Water would go down into the cracks and freeze. The cracks would widen, and seeds would blow in there. It would happen very quickly."

7   *How would the earth's ecosystems change if human beings were out of the picture? Weisman says we can get a glimpse of this hypothetical world by looking at primeval pockets where humanity's footprint has been lightest.*

8   "To see how the world would look if humans were gone, I began going to abandoned places, places that people had left for different reasons. One of them is the last fragment of primeval forest in Europe. It's like what you see in your mind's eye when you're a kid and someone is reading Grimm's fairy tales to you: a dark, brooding forest with wolves howling and tons of moss hanging off the trees. And there *is* such a place. It still exists on the border between Poland and Belarus. It was a game reserve that was set aside in the 1300s by a Lithuanian duke who later became king of Poland. A series of Polish kings and then Russian czars kept it as their own private hunting ground. There was very little human impact. After World War II it became a national park. You go in there and you see these enormous trees. It doesn't feel strange. It almost feels right. Like something feels complete in there. You see oaks and ashes nearly 150 feet tall and 10 feet in diameter, with bark furrows so deep that woodpeckers stuff pinecones in them. Besides wolves and elk, the

forest is home to the last remaining wild herd of *Bison bonasus,* the native European buffalo.

9   "I also went to the Korean DMZ, the demilitarized zone. Here you have this little stretch of land—it's about 150 miles long and 2.5 miles wide—that has two of the world's biggest armies facing off against each other. And in between the armies is an inadvertent wildlife preserve. You see species that might be extinct if it weren't for this one little piece of land. Sometimes you'll hear the soldiers screaming at one another through loudspeakers or flashing their propaganda back and forth, and in the middle of all this tension you'll see the flocks of cranes that winter there.

10   "But to really understand a world without humans, I realized I would have to learn what the world was like before humans evolved. So I went to Africa, the place where humans arose and the only continent where there are still huge animals roaming around. We used to have huge animals on all the other continents and on many of the islands. We had enormous creatures in North and South America—giant sloths that were even bigger than the mammoths; beavers the size of bears. It's controversial as to what actually wiped them out, but a lot of indications point the finger at us. The extinctions on each landmass seemed to coincide with the arrival of humans. But Africa is the place where human beings and animals evolved together, and the animals there learned strategies to avoid our predation. Without humans, North America would probably become a giant deer habitat in the near term. As forests would become reestablished across the continent, eventually—in evolutionary time—larger herbivores would evolve to take advantage of all the nutrients locked up in woody species. Larger predators would evolve accordingly."

11   *Thinking about an earth without humans can have practical benefits. Weisman explains that his approach can shed new light on environmental problems.*

12   "I'm not suggesting that we have to worry about human beings suddenly disappearing tomorrow, some alien death ray taking us all away. On the contrary, what I'm finding is that this way of looking at our planet—by theoretically just removing us—turns out to be so fascinating that it kind of disarms people's fears or the terrible wave of depression that can engulf us when we read about the environmental problems that we have created and the possible disasters we may be facing in the future. Because frankly, whenever we read about those things, our concern is: Oh, my God, are we going to die? Is this going to be the end? My book eliminates that concern right at the beginning by saying the end has already taken place. For whatever reason, human beings are gone, and now we get to sit back and see what happens in our absence. It's a delicious little way of reducing all the fear and anxiety. And looking at what would happen in our absence is another way of looking at, well, what goes on in our presence.

13   "For example, think about how long it would take to wipe out some of the things we have created. Some of our more formidable inventions have a longevity that we can't even predict yet, like some of the persistent organic pollutants that began as pesticides or industrial chemicals. Or some of our plastics, which have an enormous role in our lives and an enormous presence in the environment. And nearly all of these things weren't even here until after World War II. You begin to think there's probably no way that we are going to have any kind of positive outcome, that we are looking at an overwhelming tide of geologic proportions that the human race has loosed on the earth. I raise one possibility toward the end of the book that humans can continue to be part of the ecosystem in a way that is much more in balance with the rest of the planet.

14   "It's something that I approach by first looking at not just the horrible things that we have created that are so frightening—such as our radioactivity and pollutants, some of which may be around until the end of the planet—but also some of the beautiful things that we have done. I raise the question, Wouldn't it be a sad loss if humanity was extirpated from the planet? What about our greatest acts of art and expression? Our most beautiful sculpture? Our finest architecture? Will there be any signs of us at all that would indicate that we were here at one point? This is the second reaction that I always get from people. At first they think, This world would be beautiful without us. But then they think, Wouldn't it be sad not to have us here? And I don't think it's necessary for us to all disappear for the earth to come back to a healthier state."

The Winners . . .

Our demise would be good news for many species. Below is a small sample of the animals and plants that would benefit from the disappearance of humans.

BIRDS:

Without skyscrapers and power lines to fly into, at least a billion birds would avoid breaking their necks every year.

TREES:

In New York, oaks and maples, along with the invasive Chinese ailanthus, would claim the city.

MOSQUITOES:

As extermination efforts cease and wetlands rebound, great clouds of the insects would feed on other wildlife.

FERAL HOUSE CATS:

They would probably do well dining on small mammals and birds in the posthuman world.

. . . And the Losers

No doubt about it: our parasites and livestock would miss us. Below is a list of species that would probably suffer as a result of our disappearance.

DOMESTICATED CATTLE:

They would become a delicious steak dinner for mountain lions, coyotes and other predators.

RATS:

Bereft of our garbage, they would either starve or be eaten by raptors nesting in fallen buildings.

COCKROACHES:

Without heated buildings to help them survive the winter, they would disappear from temperate regions.

HEAD LICE:

Because these insects are so specifically adapted to humans, our demise would lead to their extinction.

Questions for Discussion and Analysis

1. Describe the first changes that would occur in New York City if there were no electrical power. To what extent would Manhattan revert to its original form?
2. When Weisman says in paragraph 6 that New York City "would start to develop its own little ecosystem," what does he mean? What specific changes would occur?
3. Why is Weisman interested in the forest that lies on the border of Poland and Belarus and in the Korean DMZ (Demilitarized Zone)? What do these two places have in common?
4. What lessons does Africa hold for animal and human populations' coexisting?
5. In what ways is Weisman's book intended to allay our fears about environmental disaster? Do you agree with his premise that "the end has already taken place"? What do you think he means?
6. In what specific ways does Weisman suggest hope for the future? What lessons can be drawn from his interview?

7. Look again at the rhetorical questions that Weisman poses in his concluding paragraph. How would you, based on your worldview, answer them? For example, "Wouldn't it be sad not to have us here?"

8. In what concrete ways might we as individuals help to create a healthier environment? What suggestions does Weisman make that we could adopt in our daily lives?

ON THE WEB

A podcast of the interview with Alan Weisman is available at www.SciAm .com/ontheweb. Type "Alan Weisman interview" into your web browser's search box.

PART 6

Reading Short Stories

Literature, Aristotle wrote, serves to delight and to instruct. The stories in Part 6 provide you with an opportunity to round out your reading experience, to give you pleasure, and to enhance your understanding of the human experience. The questions for discussion and analysis accompanying each story can be supplemented by these more general questions on plot, character, and theme. Both sets of questions will guide your interpretation and add to your enjoyment of each story.

■ QUESTIONS ABOUT PLOT

1. How does the story begin? How much exposition does the writer provide, or does the story start *in medias res,* Latin for "in the middle of things"?
2. How do the incidents that make up the plot relate to each other? Is there a cause-effect relationship implied?
3. What is the conflict in the story? Who or what is responsible for it?
4. Is the conflict resolved, and if it is, is it resolved satisfactorily?

■ QUESTIONS ABOUT CHARACTER

1. Define each character in terms of his or her "essence," behavior, and motivation.
2. How are the characters revealed to us (through direct comment, through contact with others, through their own words, or through their behavior)?
3. Why do the characters act as they do? Are their actions consistent with what has been revealed about them?
4. What is your response to each character?
5. Does any character stand for something greater than the individual?

■ QUESTIONS ABOUT THEME

1. What is the theme, and how is it embodied in the story?
2. What do we learn about human existence, human behavior, and human nature from the story?
3. Ultimately, after we finish the story, what are we meant to come away with?

■ FIVE STORIES FOR PRACTICE

Selection 1   ## "The Cement Mailbox"
J. Robert Lennon

You have already read an example of flash fiction, "Town Life," a sub-genre of the short story, in Chapter 3. (See page 98.) Here is another. Like all of the 100 pieces in Lennon's collection, Pieces for the Left Hand *(2005), the story is set in an unnamed American location, and the characters are identified only by their occupations or by an initial. The story reveals something about both the American character in particular and about human nature in general.*

A farmer who lives on our road had lost three mailboxes in as many weeks to the drunken antics of some local youths, who had taken to driving past late at night and smashing the mailboxes with a baseball bat. Because the police had been uncooperative in apprehending the youths, the farmer devised a solution to the problem: he bought two mailboxes—a gigantic, industrial-strength one and a small aluminum one—and arranged the boxes one inside the other, with a layer of cement between the two. He mounted this monstrous megabox on a length of eight-inch steel pipe, which was set into a four-foot post hole and stabilized there with thirty additional gallons of cement.

The following weekend the youths sped past in their convertible, and T., the captain of the high school baseball team and a local slugger of some renown, swung at the box from a standing position in the back seat. With the bat moving at more than seventy-five miles per hour relative to the car, and the car itself traveling nearly as fast, the combined velocity of the impact was approximately 150 miles per hour. It was at this speed that the bat ricocheted and struck the head of J., a seventeen-year-old girl who had been sitting in the car, killing her instantly.

A series of criminal charges and civil suits followed. T. was tried as an adult and convicted of involuntary manslaughter. The driver of the car was sentenced to community service on charges of vandalism and reckless endangerment. The farmer was also convicted of reckless endangerment and fined; in response he sued the police department for failing to address the problem beforehand. The parents of the dead girl lobbied to have all the car's living occupants, five in all, expelled from school; they also sued T., the driver and the farmer for several million dollars. They even tried, and failed, to sue the hardware store where the farmer had bought his cement-mailbox supplies, arguing that the store's employees ought to have figured out what the farmer was doing, and stopped him. In a peripheral case, T.'s parents sued the hospital where he was treated for a broken arm; apparently the doctors there had set the break improperly, resulting in a painful re-setting that was likely to ruin T.'s chances to play baseball in the major leagues. Their lawyers demanded a percentage of T.'s projected future salary.

In the end, all judgments were reversed on appeal. It seemed that everyone involved was to blame, which the courts determined was no different from no one being to blame. All that remains, apart from the many legal debts incurred by the litigants and the accused, is the cement mailbox, which has proven too costly and cumbersome to remove.

Questions for Discussion and Analysis

1. What inference can you make about the community where the story is set? How can you tell? Describe the "local youths" who are the subject of the story. How old are they? Why do you think they commit acts of vandalism?

2. Why does the farmer decide to take matters into his own hands regarding his damaged mailboxes? What exactly does the farmer do?

3. How do the principal characters in the story respond to the tragedy? What point do you think Lennon is trying to make in assessing the aftermath?

4. Do you agree that T., the perpetrator of the deed and surely a major contributor to J.'s death, should have been tried as an adult and convicted of involuntary manslaughter? Were T.'s parents right to sue the hospital for damages, the result of the doctor's setting his broken arm incorrectly?

5. Why did the court throw out all the judgments on appeal? What was the court's thinking? Do you agree with the court's thinking? If not, who do you think should have received the major share of the blame in this situation? In the final analysis, what is this story about?

Selection 2   ## "White Sands," from *Granta*
Geoff Dyer

Geoff Dyer is a British author who lives in London. His best known work is But Beautiful: A Book about Jazz *(1991), which Keith Jarrett called the best book ever written about jazz. Dyer has contributed articles and stories to several publications, including* The Guardian, The New Statesman, Esquire, *and the literary quarterly* Granta, *where this story first appeared. His most recent publication is a novel,* Jeff in Venice, Death in Varanasi *(2009).* White Sands National Monument, near Alamogordo, New Mexico, is the setting for the beginning of the story.

My wife and I were driving south on Highway 54 from Alamogordo to El Paso. We'd spent the afternoon at White Sands and my brain was still scorched from the glare. I worried that I might even have done some permanent damage to my eyes. The sand is made of gypsum—whatever that is—and is as bright as new-fallen snow. Brighter, actually. It's quite unbelievable that anything can be so bright. Looking at that sand is like staring at the sun. The underside of my chin was burned from the sun bouncing up off the white sand. It's a good name for the National Park, White Sands, though we thought the place a bit disappointing at first. The sand was a little discoloured, not quite white. Then, as we drove further, the sand started to creep on to the road and it became whiter and soon everything was white, even the road, and then there was no road, just this bright whiteness. We parked the car and walked into it, into the whiteness. It was hard to believe that such a place existed. The sky was pristine blue but the thing that must, that really must be emphasized, is the whiteness of the sand which could not have been any whiter. There was no shade to speak of but we sat and sheltered as best we could, huddled together under a sarong.

I said, 'Life like a dome of many-coloured glass stains the white radiance of eternity.'

'It's like being dead here, isn't it?' said Jessica.

'Yes,' I said. 'There's no life. Hence the white radiance. Unstained.'

We would like to have stayed longer in that unstained wilderness but we had to get to El Paso that night. We walked back to the car and drove out of the park. Ideally one would spend at least a day at the aptly named White Sands but there was nothing we could do about it. Not that that made leaving any easier. It's no good just having a glimpse of a desert, but if it's a choice between a glimpse and nothing at all I would always settle for a glimpse. Frustrating though that is.

Jessica was driving. It was early evening. We were about sixty miles south of Alamogordo and the light was fading. A freight train was running parallel to the road, also heading south.

'Hitch-hiker!' I said, pointing. 'Shall we pick him up?'

'Shall we?' My wife was slowing down. We could see him more clearly now, a black guy, in his late twenties, clean and not looking like a maniac or someone who smelled bad. We slowed to a crawl and took a good look at him. He looked fine. I lowered my window, the passenger window. He had a nice smile.

'Where ya going?' he said.

'El Paso,' I said.

'That'd be great for me.'

'Sure. Get in.'

He opened the door and climbed into the back seat. Our eyes met in the mirror. Jessica said, 'Hi.'

'Preciate it,' he said.

'You're welcome.' Jessica accelerated and soon we were back up to seventy and drawing level once again with the long freight train to our left.

'Where've you come from?' I asked, twisting round in my seat. I could see now that he was perhaps older than I had initially thought. He had deep lines in his face but his eyes were kind and his smile was still nice.

'Albuquerque,' he said. I was slightly surprised. The logical way to have got to El Paso from Albuquerque would have been to go straight down I-25. 'Where you from?' he asked.

'London,' I said. 'England.'

'The Kingdom,' he said.

'Right.' I was facing straight ahead again because I worried that twisting around in my seat would give me a cricked neck, to which I am prone.

'I thought so,' he said. 'I love your accent.'

'What about you?'

'Arkansas originally.'

'That's where my mother's from,' said Jessica. 'El Dorado.'

'I'm from Little Rock,' he said.

'Like Pharoah Sanders,' I said. It was a pointless thing to have said but I have this need to show off, to show that I know things; in this instance to show that I knew about jazz, about black jazz musicians. The guy, evidently, was not a jazz fan. He nodded but said nothing and we prepared to settle into the occasionally interrupted silence that tends to work best in these situations. We had established where we were all from and a pleasant atmosphere filled the car.

Less than a minute later, this pleasant atmosphere was changed absolutely by a sign:

NOTICE

DO NOT PICK UP HITCH-HIKERS

DETENTION FACILITIES IN AREA

I had seen the sign. Jessica had seen the sign. Our hitch-hiker had seen the sign. We had all seen the sign and the sign had changed our relationship totally. What struck me was the plural: not a detention facility but detention facilities. Several of them. The notice—and I took some heart from the fact that the sign described itself as a 'notice' rather than a 'warning'—did not specify *how* many, but there were, evidently, more than one. I did not glance at Jessica. She did not glance at me. There was no need because at some level everyone was glancing at everyone else. As well as not glancing, no one said a word. I have always believed in the notion of the vibe: good vibes, bad vibes. After we saw the sign the vibe in the car—which had been a good vibe—changed completely and became a very bad vibe. This was a physical fact. Somehow the actual molecules in the car underwent a chemical change. The car was not the same place it had been just a minute earlier. And the sky had grown darker—that was another factor.

We soon came to the facilities which had unmistakably been designed with detention in mind. Both places—there were two of them, one on the right and one on the left—were set back from the road, surrounded by high walls of razor wire, and brightly lit by arc lights. There were no windows. In the intensity and single-mindedness of their desire to contain menace they exuded it. At the same time, both places had something of the quality of Ikea outlets. I wished they were Ikea outlets. It would have been so nice if our hitch-hiker had said that he had come to buy a sofa or some kitchen units and that his car had broken down. We could have sympathized with that. As it was, no one said anything. No one said anything but I know what I was thinking: I was thinking that I had never been in a position where I so wished I could wind back the clock just one or two minutes. I would love to have wound back the clock, would love to have said to Jessica 'Shall we pick him up' and heard her reply 'No, let's not' and just sped past, leaving him where he was. But you cannot wind the clock back in this life, not even by two seconds. Everything that has happened stays happened. Everything has consequences. As a consequence we couldn't have not picked him up but I could have asked him to get out. I could have said, 'Look man, I'm sorry, but in the circumstances would you mind getting the fuck out of our car?'. I could have done this but I didn't, for several reasons. First I was worried that if I did suggest he get out he might go berserk, might kill us. Second, I was worried that by asking—by telling him, really—to get out I would be being rude.

So instead of asking him to get out we drove on in tense silence. The car sped along. There seemed no point in slowing down. In any situation there is always something positive to emphasize. In this one it was the fact that there were no traffic hold-ups at all. Jessica was gripping the wheel. No one was speaking. The silence was unendurable but impossible to break. Unsure what to do, I turned on the radio. We were still tuned to a classic-rock station that we had been listening to earlier in the day, before we got to White Sands, and as soon as the radio came on, in the fading light of New Mexico, I recognized the piano tinkle and swish of 'Riders on the Storm'. I am a big fan of the Doors but I did not want to hear this song now. It was just unbelievable. A few moments later we heard Jim Morrison crooning:

> There's a killer on the road
> His brain is squirming like a toad . . .

Having turned on the radio with such disastrously appropriate results it seemed impossible, now, to turn it off. The three of us sat there, listening:

> If you give this man a ride
> Sweet memory will die . . .

Jessica followed the advice offered by Jim Morrison elsewhere in his oeuvre. She was keeping her eyes on the road and her hands upon the wheel. I kept my eyes on the road and my hands in my lap. Day was still turning to night. The lights of oncoming cars were dazzling and

guy's brother worked in the supermarket and one day, when he was meant to be at work but had bunked off because he had flu . . .

I was looking at the cars coming, the hypnotic blur of lights, the inky sky, wondering what time we might get to El Paso . . .

And then when he came back to the supermarket . . . I realized I had drifted off, lost track of the story. In truth it wasn't a very good story, or at least he wasn't a very good storyteller. He kept bringing in all this irrelevant detail. I was very interested in his story but not in the way he told it. A few minutes earlier I was worried that he might be a murderer; now I was worried that he might be a bore but it was possible, of course, that he was a murderer and a bore. I had been feeling for several years now that I was losing the ability to concentrate, to listen to what people said, but I had never before reached such a pitch of inattentiveness at a time when it was important—so obviously in my best interests—to concentrate. It was so important to listen, to follow his story carefully, to pay attention, but I couldn't. I wanted to, I should have, but I couldn't. I just couldn't. It is because there are people like me doing jury service, people who can't follow what other people are saying, that there are so many wrongful convictions, so many miscarriages of justice. Whatever I was meant to be thinking about and concentrating on, I thought to myself, I was always thinking about something else, and that something else was always myself and my problems. As I was thinking this I realized that his voice had fallen silent. He had come to the end of his story. The defence had rested its case.

'We need petrol,' said Jessica.

'She means gas,' I said. A few miles later we pulled into a gas station and stopped. I hate putting gas in a car, especially in America where you have to pay first and it's all quite complicated and potentially oily. On this occasion, though, both Jessica and I wanted to put the gas in so that we would not be left alone in the car with this guy but we could not both get out because then he might have clambered over the seats and driven off without us. Except he could not drive off because we needed the key to unlock the fuel cap. I was not thinking straight because of the hitch-hiker and everything pertaining to the hitch-hiker situation. Both Jessica and I got out of the car. I did the filling up. It was quite easy. I watched the numbers—dollars, gallons and gallons of gas—spinning round the gauge on the gas pump. Although it was not my main concern it was impossible not to be struck by how much cheaper petrol was in America than in England.

Then our new friend got out of the car too. He was wearing black jeans and trainers.[1] The trainers were not black but they were quite old. Jessica got back in the car. I was pumping gas. He looked at me. We were about the same height except he was a bit shorter. Our eyes met. When they had met before it was in the rear-view mirror of the car but now

---

[1] British for tennis shoes.

they were really meeting. In the neon of the gas station his eyes had a look that was subject to any number of interpretations. We looked at each other man to man. Black man and white man, English man and American man.

'I need to take a leak,' he said.

'Right,' I said. 'Go right ahead.' I said this in as neutral a tone as possible. I made sure my facial expression gave nothing away and then, worried that this non-expression manifested itself as a rigidity of expression which in fact gave everything away, I relaxed and smiled a bit.

'You ain't gonna up and leave me here are you?' he said.

'Leave you here?' I said. 'No, of course not.'

'You sure about that, brother?'

'I swear,' I said. He nodded and began walking slowly to the restrooms. He was dragging his left leg slightly. He took his time and did not look back. I watched his retreating form. As soon as he disappeared inside I released the trigger of the fuel line, clattered it out of the side of the car and banged it back into the metal holster of the pump. It fell noisily to the ground.

'You need to push the lever back up,' said Jessica. I did that. I pushed the lever back up and settled the awkward nozzle of the fuel hose back into it.

'Quickly!' said Jessica. I twisted the cap back on to the fuel tank but I did it too quickly and it would not go on properly and then, when I had got it on properly, I had problems with the key which I could neither turn nor extricate. There is much truth in the old adage 'more haste, less speed'. Eventually the lock turned and after much wiggling the key came out. I tossed it to Jessica who dropped it.

'Butterfingers!' I said.

'Why didn't you just *hand* it to me?' she said.

'Why can't you catch?' I said. I picked up the key, handed it to her and ran round the front of the car while she turned the key in the ignition. The engine roared into life.

'Go! Go! Go!' I shouted as I climbed into the passenger door. Jessica pulled away calmly and quickly, without squealing the tyres, and I shut the door.

We exited the gas station safely and smoothly and in seconds were out on the road. At first we were elated to have made our getaway like this. We high-fived each other. Ha ha!

'Did you like the way I said "I swear"?' I said.

'Genius!' said Jessica. We went on like this for a bit but we soon ran out of steam because although we still felt a bit elated we were starting to feel a bit ashamed too, and then, bit by bit, the elation ebbed away.

'Your door's not shut,' Jessica said after a while.

'Yes it is,' I said.

'No it's not,' said Jessica. I opened the door a crack and slammed it shut, shutter than it had been shut before.

'Sorry,' I said. 'You were right.'

'Doesn't matter,' said Jessica. Then, 'Was that a really terrible thing we just did?'

'I think it might have been.'

'Do you think it was racist?'

'I think it was just kind of rude. Judgemental. Rash.'

'Think how he's going to feel when he comes out of the toilet. He'll be so let down. He'll feel we treated him so shabbily.'

We drove on. The scene was the same—cars, lights, almost darkness. We were safe but perhaps we had always been safe. Now that we were out of danger it seemed possible that there had never been any danger.

'It's as if he were testing us,' said Jessica.

'I know. It's never a good feeling, failing a test,' I said. 'I still remember how I felt when I was seventeen and failed my driving test.'

'How did you feel?'

'I don't remember exactly,' I said. 'Not great. What about you? You probably passed first time.'

'I did,' she said, but there was no avoiding the real subject of the moment. After a pause Jessica said, 'Should we go back?'

'Perhaps we should.'

'But we won't, right?'

'Absolutely not,' I said and we both laughed. We drove in silence for several minutes. We were no longer elated but the vibe in the car was good again even though we were still ashamed, innocent of nothing and guilty of nothing, relieved at what we had done and full of regret about what we had done.

'You know those urban legends?' said Jessica.

'The vanishing hitch-hiker?'

'Yes. There's probably an axe in the back seat.'

I twisted around to look—a bit awkward with the seat belt. There was nothing on the back seat and nothing on the floor either, except two Coke cans and a bottle of water; all empty, and a torn map of White Sands.

'Nothing,' I said, rubbing my neck. We drove on. It was quite dark now. Night had fallen on New Mexico.

The dashboard lights glowed faintly. The fuel gauge was pointing almost to full.

'Well,' I said. 'We performed one useful service. At least we got him away from that area where it told you not to pick up hitch-hikers. He should be really grateful for that.' I said this but as I imagined him back there, coming out of the restroom and looking round the gas-station forecourt, I knew that gratitude would not be uppermost in his mind. There would have been plenty of other cars coming and going but he must have known, deep down, that the car he wanted to see, the car whose make he would have known—it was a Ford but beyond that I had not taken any notice—and which he hoped would still be there would be long gone. I could imagine how he felt and I was glad that I was not him feeling these things and I was glad, also, that it was just the two of us again, safe and in our car, married, and speeding towards El Paso.

Questions for Discussion and Analysis

1. Comment on the setting at the beginning of the story. What dominant impression of White Sands and the desert does the narrator provide for this setting?

2. Why do the narrator and Jessica pick up the hitch-hiker? What is the first indication that the hitch-hiker might not be a trustworthy citizen?

3. What effect does the sign about not picking up hitch-hikers in the area have on the car's occupants? How does the "vibe" in the car change?

4. The fact that the narrator doesn't ask the hitch-hiker to get out of the car reveals something about his character. What is it? Does the fact that the hitch-hiker is black confirm this character trait, or would the narrator have reacted the same if he had been white?

5. Comment on the lyrics of the Doors' song that Jim Morrison sings. Why does Dyer insert this seemingly minute detail at this point in the story?

6. Explain the significance of the narrator's thoughts about men and women, usually black, who have been convicted of terrible crimes. Why does he indulge in these thoughts?

7. Where is the turning point in the story—the point at which Jessica and the narrator decide to take action?

8. Why does the narrator have trouble following the hitch-hiker's story? Does it matter that we as readers never learn exactly what the hitch-hiker's story was or why he was in prison?

9. A dilemma is defined as a situation with two alternatives, usually bad. In what way does this story embody a dilemma?

10. After they make their getaway, how would you describe the various moods Jessica and her husband experience? Can you identify with their emotions?

11. In justifying their action—by leaving the hitch-hiker in a place where it would be easy for him to find another ride—do we find these characters admirable, rational, self-serving, or perhaps something else altogether?

12. In the same circumstances, what would you have done?

Selection 3

"Hills Like White Elephants"

Ernest Hemingway

Ernest Hemingway (1899–1961) had an immense influence on American literature, in particular serving as a model for young writers who hoped to imitate his minimalist style. Initially a journalist, Hemingway worked as a

volunteer ambulance driver in World War I in Italy. After the war, he con-
tinued to work as a journalist, but he soon returned to Europe in the 1920s,
where he became a member of the group of American expatriates floating
around France and Spain. Fascinated by bullfighting, big game hunting, and
fishing, Hemingway incorporated these activities into many of his works.
Known for writing both short fiction and novels, his most famous works are
The Sun Also Rises *(1926),* A Farewell to Arms *(1929),* For Whom the
Bell Tolls *(1940), and* The Old Man and the Sea *(1952). "Hills Like White*
Elephants," published in 1927, is a good introduction to Hemingway's short
fiction, noted for its directness, objectivity, concise dialog, and use of under-
statement to reveal character and theme.

The hills across the valley of the Ebro were long and white. On this side
there was no shade and no trees and the station was between two lines of
rails in the sun. Close against the side of the station there was the warm
shadow of the building and a curtain, made of strings of bamboo beads,
hung across the open door into the bar, to keep out flies. The American
and the girl with him sat at a table in the shade, outside the building. It
was very hot and the express from Barcelona would come in forty minutes. It stopped at this junction for two minutes and went on to Madrid.

"What should we drink?" the girl asked. She had taken off her hat and
put it on the table.

"It's pretty hot," the man said.

"Let's drink beer."

"*Dos cervezas*," the man said into the curtain.

"Big ones?" a woman asked from the doorway.

"Yes. Two big ones."

The woman brought two glasses of beer and two felt pads. She put the
felt pads and the beer glasses on the table and looked at the man and the
girl. The girl was looking off at the line of hills. They were white in the sun
and the country was brown and dry.

"They look like white elephants," she said.

"I've never seen one," the man drank his beer.

"No, you wouldn't have."

"I might have," the man said. "Just because you say I wouldn't have
doesn't prove anything."

The girl looked at the bead curtain. "They've painted something on
it," she said. "What does it say?"

"Anis del Toro. It's a drink."

"Could we try it?"

The man called "Listen" through the curtain. The woman came out
from the bar.

"Four reales."

"We want two Anis del Toro."

"With water?"

"Do you want it with water?"

"I don't know," the girl said. "Is it good with water?"

"It's all right."

"You want them with water?" asked the woman.

"Yes, with water."

"It tastes like licorice," the girl said and put the glass down.

"That's the way with everything."

"Yes," said the girl. "Everything tastes of licorice. Especially all the things you've waited so long for, like absinthe."

"Oh, cut it out."

"You started it," the girl said. "I was being amused. I was having a fine time."

"Well, let's try and have a fine time."

"All right I was trying. I said the mountains looked like white elephants. Wasn't that bright?"

"That was bright."

"I wanted to try this new drink: That's all we do, isn't it—look at things and try new drinks?"

"I guess so."

The girl looked across at the hills.

"They're lovely hills," she said. "They don't really look like white elephants. I just meant the coloring of their skin through the trees."

"Should we have another drink?"

"All right."

The warm wind blew the bead curtain against the table.

"The beer's nice and cool," the man said.

"It's lovely," the girl said.

"It's really an awfully simple operation, Jig," the man said. "It's not really an operation at all."

The girl looked at the ground the table legs rested on.

"I know you wouldn't mind it, Jig. It's really not anything. It's just to let the air in."

The girl did not say anything.

"I'll go with you and I'll stay with you all the time. They just let the air in and then it's all perfectly natural."

"Then what will we do afterward?"

"We'll be fine afterward. Just like we were before."

"What makes you think so?"

"That's the only thing that bothers us. It's the only thing that's made us unhappy."

The girl looked at the bead curtain, put her hand out and took hold of two of the strings of beads.

"And you think then we'll be all right and be happy."

"I know we will. You don't have to be afraid. I've known lots of people that have done it."

"So have I," said the girl. "And afterward they were all so happy."

3. What can you infer about the past relationship between the American and the girl? What has been holding them together?

4. The reference to "hills like white elephants" is obviously important, not only because it's the title and because of their physical proximity to the town, but also because it's an observation that the girl makes and that the man responds to. Explain this exchange. What do the hills represent to the girl? To the man? What is the mood in this exchange of dialog? What is another meaning of the term "white elephant"? In the story how does a white elephant symbolize something larger than its literal meaning?

5. What topic does the man suddenly introduce? What sort of "operation" is he talking about? Why doesn't he use a more precise term? How does he justify the surgery to the girl, Jig? What is his prognosis for their relationship if she goes ahead with the operation? Does she seem to agree, or not?

6. Assess the credibility of both characters. Should we believe the man when he says that he doesn't want the girl to do it (i.e., have the operation) if she doesn't want to? What are his motives and thinking in this exchange? What are hers? Why does she say, "Would you please please please please please please please stop talking"? What is the effect of this repetition?

7. Ultimately, what do we learn about these characters from the dialog? What do you think will happen to their relationship? Who wins the discussion? Who is morally and emotionally more grounded? Justify your evaluation.

8. Comment on the structure and style of the story, which is composed almost entirely of dialog between the two characters and very little description. What are the advantages of this structure? What are the disadvantages?

Selection 4   ## "The Open Window"
Saki (H. H. Munro)

Saki (1870–1916) was the pseudonym of Hector Hugh Munro. Born in Burma and educated in England, Munro joined the military police in Burma (as did his compatriot, George Orwell). After recuperating from malaria in England, he became a political sketch writer for the Westminster Gazette, *and later served as a foreign correspondent for the* Morning Post *in the Balkans, Russia, and France. Saki died in the trenches of France during World War I. His pseudonym apparently derives from the name of the cupbearer in the* Rubaiyat of Omar Khayyam, *which his sister described as one of Munro's favorite books. Under this pen name, Munro published several collections of short stories, which are marked by their careful observation of society, their*

polish and brevity, and, most characteristic, the surprise twist used to resolve the story, as you will see in this work, which appeared in The Short Stories of Saki *(1930).*

"My aunt will be down presently, Mr. Nuttel," said a very self-possessed young lady of fifteen; "in the meantime you must try and put up with me."

Framton Nuttel endeavoured to say the correct something which should duly flatter the niece of the moment without unduly discounting the aunt that was to come. Privately he doubted more than ever whether these formal visits on a succession of total strangers would do much towards helping the nerve cure which he was supposed to be undergoing.

"I know how it will be," his sister had said when he was preparing to migrate to this rural retreat; "you will bury yourself down there and not speak to a living soul, and your nerves will be worse than ever from moping. I shall just give you letters of introduction to all the people I know there. Some of them, as far as I can remember, were quite nice."

Framton wondered whether Mrs. Sappleton, the lady to whom he was presenting one of the letters of introduction came into the nice division.

"Do you know many of the people round here?" asked the niece, when she judged that they had had sufficient silent communion.

"Hardly a soul," said Framton. "My sister was staying here, at the rectory, you know, some four years ago, and she gave me letters of introduction to some of the people here."

He made the last statement in a tone of distinct regret.

"Then you know practically nothing about my aunt?" pursued the self-possessed young lady.

"Only her name and address," admitted the caller. He was wondering whether Mrs. Sappleton was in the married or widowed state. An undefinable something about the room seemed to suggest masculine habitation.

"Her great tragedy happened just three years ago," said the child; "that would be since your sister's time."

"Her tragedy?" asked Framton; somehow in this restful country spot tragedies seemed out of place.

"You may wonder why we keep that window wide open on an October afternoon," said the niece, indicating a large French window that opened on to a lawn.

"It is quite warm for the time of the year," said Framton; "but has that window got anything to do with the tragedy?"

"Out through that window, three years ago to a day, her husband and her two young brothers went off for their day's shooting. They never came back. In crossing the moor to their favourite snipe-shooting ground they were all three engulfed in a treacherous piece of bog. It had been that dreadful wet summer, you know, and places that were safe in other years gave way suddenly without warning. Their bodies were never recovered. That was the dreadful part of it." Here the child's voice lost its self-possessed note and became falteringly human. "Poor aunt always thinks that they will come back someday, they and the little brown spaniel that was lost with them, and walk in at that window just as they used to do. That is why the window is kept open every evening till it is quite dusk. Poor dear aunt, she has often told me how they went out, her husband with his white waterproof coat over his arm, and Ronnie, her youngest brother, singing 'Bertie, why do you bound?' as he always did to tease her, because she said it got on her nerves. Do you know, sometimes on still, quiet evenings like this, I almost get a creepy feeling that they will all walk in through that window - "

She broke off with a little shudder. It was a relief to Framton when the aunt bustled into the room with a whirl of apologies for being late in making her appearance.

"I hope Vera has been amusing you?" she said.

"She has been very interesting," said Framton.

"I hope you don't mind the open window," said Mrs. Sappleton briskly; "my husband and brothers will be home directly from shooting, and they always come in this way. They've been out for snipe in the marshes today, so they'll make a fine mess over my poor carpets. So like you menfolk, isn't it?"

She rattled on cheerfully about the shooting and the scarcity of birds, and the prospects for duck in the winter. To Framton it was all purely horrible. He made a desperate but only partially successful effort to turn the talk on to a less ghastly topic, he was conscious that his hostess was giving him only a fragment of her attention, and her eyes were constantly straying past him to the open window and the lawn beyond. It was certainly an unfortunate coincidence that he should have paid his visit on this tragic anniversary.

"The doctors agree in ordering me complete rest, an absence of mental excitement, and avoidance of anything in the nature of violent physical exercise," announced Framton, who laboured under the tolerably widespread delusion that total strangers and chance acquaintances are hungry for the least detail of one's ailments and infirmities, their cause and cure. "On the matter of diet they are not so much in agreement," he continued.

"No?" said Mrs. Sappleton, in a voice which only replaced a yawn at the last moment. Then she suddenly brightened into alert attention - but not to what Framton was saying.

"Here they are at last!" she cried. "Just in time for tea, and don't they look as if they were muddy up to the eyes!"

Framton shivered slightly and turned towards the niece with a look intended to convey sympathetic comprehension. The child was staring out through the open window with a dazed horror in her eyes. In a chill shock of nameless fear Framton swung round in his seat and looked in the same direction.

In the deepening twilight three figures were walking across the lawn towards the window, they all carried guns under their arms, and one of them was additionally burdened with a white coat hung over his shoulders. A tired brown spaniel kept close at their heels. Noiselessly they neared the house, and then a hoarse young voice chanted out of the dusk: "I said, Bertie, why do you bound?"

Framton grabbed wildly at his stick and hat; the hall door, the gravel drive, and the front gate were dimly noted stages in his headlong retreat. A cyclist coming along the road had to run into the hedge to avoid imminent collision.

"Here we are, my dear," said the bearer of the white mackintosh, coming in through the window, "fairly muddy, but most of it's dry. Who was that who bolted out as we came up?"

"A most extraordinary man, a Mr. Nuttel," said Mrs. Sappleton; "could only talk about his illnesses, and dashed off without a word of goodby or apology when you arrived. One would think he had seen a ghost."

"I expect it was the spaniel," said the niece calmly; "he told me he had a horror of dogs. He was once hunted into a cemetery somewhere on the banks of the Ganges by a pack of pariah dogs, and had to spend the night in a newly dug grave with the creatures snarling and grinning and foaming just above him. Enough to make anyone lose their nerve."

Romance at short notice was her speciality.

Questions for Discussion and Analysis

1. Comment on the opening paragraphs of the story, the expository section that establishes the setting, the time, and the characters and that sets the plot in motion. Who is Framton Nuttel, and why has he come to the rectory?

2. What is the first indication in the story that Vera, the niece, might not be a reliable character? How old is she?

3. Describe the mood and feeling surrounding the story that Vera tells Framton.

4. Why does Framton bolt from the house? What are the other characters' reactions to his departure?

5. Now that you have finished the story, reread the first paragraph. How does Vera's introduction of herself complement the story's subsequent events? Comment on this foreshadowing device.

6. Why does Vera tell the story about Framton's "horror of dogs"? What might be her motives?

7. Comment on the surprise twist at the end of the story. What does the narrator mean by the phrase "romance at short notice"?

8. Is this story meant to be a comedy, a tragedy, a horror story, a satire—or perhaps something else entirely different?

Selection 5   ## "Miss Brill"
                     Katherine Mansfield

Born in Wellington, New Zealand, Katherine Mansfield (1888–1923) published her first book of stories, In a German Pension, *in 1911. Two more collections followed:* Bliss and Other Stories *(1920) and* The Garden Party *(1922). She died in France of tuberculosis, at the peak of her success, at the age of thirty-four.*

Although it was so brilliantly fine—the blue sky powdered with gold and great spots of light like white wine splashed over the Jardins Publiques—Miss Brill was glad that she had decided on her fur. The air was motionless, but when you opened your mouth there was just a faint chill, like a chill from a glass of iced water before you sip, and now and again a leaf came drifting—from nowhere, from the sky. Miss Brill put up her hand and touched her fur. Dear little thing! It was nice to feel it again. She had taken it out of its box that afternoon, shaken out the moth powder, given it a good brush, and rubbed the life back into the dim little eyes. "What has been happening to me?" said the sad little eyes. Oh, how sweet it was to see them snap at her again from the red eiderdown! . . . But the nose, which was of some black composition, wasn't at all firm. It must have had a knock, somehow. Never mind—a little dab of black sealing-wax when the time came—when it was absolutely necessary . . . Little rogue! Yes, she really felt like that about it. Little rogue biting its tail just by her left ear. She could have taken it off and laid it on her lap and stroked it. She felt a tingling in her hands and arms, but that came from walking, she supposed. And when she breathed, something light and sad—no, not sad, exactly—something gentle seemed to move in her bosom.

There were a number of people out this afternoon, far more than last Sunday. And the band sounded louder and gayer. That was because the Season had begun. For although the band played all the year round on Sundays, out of season it was never the same. It was like some one playing with only the family to listen; it didn't care how it played if there weren't any strangers present. Wasn't the conductor wearing a new coat, too? She was sure it was new. He scraped with his foot and flapped his arms like a rooster about to crow, and the bandsmen sitting in the green rotunda blew out their cheeks and glared at the music. Now there came a little "flutey" bit—very pretty!—a little chain of bright drops. She was sure it would be repeated. It was; she lifted her head and smiled.

Only two people shared her "special" seat: a fine old man in a velvet coat, his hands clasped over a huge carved walking-stick, and a big old woman, sitting upright, with a roll of knitting on her embroidered apron. They did not speak. This was disappointing, for Miss Brill always looked forward to the conversation. She had become really quite expert, she thought, at listening as though she didn't listen, at sitting in other people's lives just for a minute while they talked round her.

She glanced, sideways, at the old couple. Perhaps they would go soon. Last Sunday, too, hadn't been as interesting as usual. An Englishman and his wife, he wearing a dreadful Panama hat and she button boots. And she'd gone on the whole time about how she ought to wear spectacles; she knew she needed them; but that it was no good getting any; they'd be sure to break and they'd never keep on. And he'd been so patient. He'd suggested everything—gold rims, the kind that curve round your ears, little pads inside the bridge. No, nothing would please her. "They'll always be sliding down my nose!" Miss Brill had wanted to shake her.

The old people sat on the bench, still as statues. Never mind, there was always the crowd to watch. To and fro, in front of the flower beds and the band rotunda, the couples and groups paraded, stopped to talk, to greet, to buy a handful of flowers from the old beggar who had his tray fixed to the railings. Little children ran among them, swooping and laughing; little boys with big white silk bows under their chins, little girls, little French dolls, dressed up in velvet and lace. And sometimes a tiny staggerer came suddenly rocking into the open from under the trees, stopped, stared, as suddenly sat down "flop," until its small high-stepping mother, like a young hen, rushed scolding to its rescue. Other people sat on the benches and green chairs, but they were nearly always the same, Sunday after Sunday, and—Miss Brill had often noticed—there was something funny about nearly all of them. They were odd, silent, nearly all old, and from the way they stared they looked as though they'd just come from dark little rooms or even—even cupboards!

Behind the rotunda the slender trees with yellow leaves down drooping, and through them just a line of sea, and beyond the blue sky with gold-veined clouds.

Tum-tum-tum tiddle-um! tiddle-um! tum tiddley-um tum ta! blew the band.

Two young girls in red came by and two young soldiers in blue met them, and they laughed and paired and went off arm-in-arm. Two peasant women with funny straw hats passed, gravely, leading beautiful smoke-colored donkeys. A cold, pale nun hurried by. A beautiful woman came along and dropped her bunch of violets, and a little boy ran after to hand them to her, and she took them and threw them away as if they'd been poisoned. Dear me! Miss Brill didn't know whether to admire that or not! And now an ermine toque and a gentleman in gray met just in front of her. He was tall, stiff, dignified, and she was wearing the ermine toque she'd bought when her hair was yellow. Now everything, her hair, her face, even her eyes, was the same color as the shabby ermine, and her hand, in its cleaned glove, lifted to dab her lips, was a tiny yellowish paw. Oh, she was so pleased to see him—delighted! She rather thought they were going to meet that afternoon. She described where she'd been—everywhere, here, there, along by the sea. The day was so charming—didn't he agree? And wouldn't he, perhaps? . . . But he shook his head, lighted a cigarette, slowly breathed a great deep puff into her face, and, even while she was still talking and laughing, flicked the match away and walked on. The ermine toque was alone; she smiled more brightly than ever. But even the band seemed to know what she was feeling and played more softly, played tenderly, and the drum beat, "The Brute! The Brute!" over and over. What would she do? What was going to happen now? But as Miss Brill wondered, the ermine toque turned, raised her hand as though she'd seen some one else, much nicer, just over there, and pattered away. And the band changed again and played more quickly, more gayly than ever, and the old couple on Miss Brill's seat got up and marched away, and such a funny old man with long whiskers hobbled along in time to the music and was nearly knocked over by four girls walking abreast.

Oh, how fascinating it was! How she enjoyed it! How she loved sitting here, watching it all! It was like a play. It was exactly like a play. Who could believe the sky at the back wasn't painted? But it wasn't till a little brown dog trotted on solemn and then slowly trotted off, like a little "theater" dog, a little dog that had been drugged, that Miss Brill discovered what it was that made it so exciting. They were all on stage. They weren't only the audience, not only looking on; they were acting. Even she had a part and came every Sunday. No doubt somebody would have noticed if she hadn't been there; she was part of the performance after all. How strange she'd never thought of it like that before! And yet it explained why she made such a point of starting from home at just the same time each week—so as not to be late for the performance— and it also explained why she had quite a queer, shy feeling at telling her English pupils how she spent her Sunday afternoons. No wonder! Miss Brill nearly laughed out loud. She was on the stage. She thought of the old invalid gentleman to whom she read the newspaper four afternoons a week while he slept in the garden. She had got quite used to the frail head on the cotton pillow, the hollowed eyes, the open mouth and the high pinched nose. If he'd been dead she mightn't have noticed for weeks; she wouldn't have minded. But suddenly he knew he was having the paper read to him by an actress! "An actress!" The old head lifted; two points of light quivered in the old eyes. "An actress—are ye?" And Miss Brill smoothed the newspaper as though it were the manuscript of her part and said gently: "Yes, I have been an actress for a long time."

The band had been having a rest. Now they started again. And what they played was warm, sunny, yet there was just a faint chill—a something, what was it?—not sadness—no, not sadness—a something that made you want to sing. The tune lifted, lifted, the light shone; and it seemed to Miss Brill that in another moment all of them, all the whole company, would begin singing. The young ones, the laughing ones who were moving together, they would begin, and the men's voices, very resolute and brave, would join them. And then she too, she too, and the others on the benches—they would come in with a kind of accompaniment—something low, that scarcely rose or fell, something so beautiful—moving . . . And Miss Brill's eyes filled with tears and she looked smiling at all the other members of the company. Yes, we understand, we understand, she thought—though what they understood she didn't know.

Just at that moment a boy and girl came and sat down where the old couple had been. They were beautifully dressed; they were in love. The hero and heroine, of course, just arrived from his father's yacht. And still soundlessly singing, still with that trembling smile, Miss Brill prepared to listen.

"No, not now," said the girl. "Not here, I can't."

"But why? Because of that stupid old thing at the end there?" asked the boy. "Why does she come here at all—who wants her? Why doesn't she keep her silly old mug at home?"

"It's her fu-fur which is so funny," giggled the girl. "It's exactly like a fried whiting."

"Ah, be off with you!" said the boy in an angry whisper. Then: "Tell me, ma petite chère—"

"No, not here," said the girl. "Not *yet*".

On her way home she usually bought a slice of honeycake at the baker's. It was her Sunday treat. Sometimes there was an almond in her slice, sometimes not. It made a great difference. If there was an almond it was like carrying home a tiny present—a surprise—something that might very well not have been there. She hurried on the almond Sundays and struck the match for the kettle in quite a dashing way.

But today she passed the baker's by, climbed the stairs, went into the little dark room—her room like a cupboard—and sat down on the red eiderdown. She sat there for a long time. The box that the fur came out of was on the bed. She unclasped the necklet quickly; quickly, without looking, laid it inside. But when she put the lid on she thought she heard something crying.

Questions for Discussion and Analysis

1. Who is Miss Brill? What kind of life does she lead, from the details Mansfield provides? Why doesn't Mansfield provide her with a first name?

2. How does Miss Brill perceive herself? How does she perceive the people around her?

3. What do the Jardins Publiques (Public Gardens) represent to Miss Brill? Who are the gardens' usual occupants? In what way does Miss Brill see herself as different from them?

4. How does Miss Brill like to occupy herself on Sundays during the Season? How are we to interpret her observations about the people she watches and the conversations she overhears?

5. Look again at the exchange between the "ermine toque" and the "gentleman in grey." Through whose eyes are we seeing them? Who

is the woman with the toque, in actuality? What has really taken place between these two?

6. Read again the paragraph where Miss Brill describes the scene as like being in a play. What is ironic about her interpretation of this scene in this way?

7. In what way does Miss Brill change during the course of the story? What is the impetus for that change? How are we to interpret her actions in the last paragraph? When she puts her fur back into the box, what is crying?

8. Is Miss Brill a tragic figure or a silly woman? How do you think Mansfield intends us to see her? Point to details that might suggest how Mansfield intends us to respond.

Permissions Acknowledgments

Photo Credits

Text Credits

INDEX